Blackstone's Statutes on

Criminal Justice & Sentencing

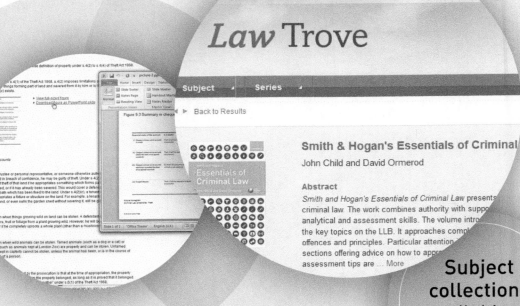

Blackstone's Statutes on
Criminal Justice & Sentencing

6th edition

edited by

Nicola Padfield

Master, Fitzwilliam College, Cambridge
Reader in Criminal and Penal Justice, University of Cambridge

OXFORD
UNIVERSITY PRESS

OXFORD

UNIVERSITY PRESS

Great Clarendon Street, Oxford, OX2 6DP,
United Kingdom

Oxford University Press is a department of the University of Oxford.
It furthers the University's objective of excellence in research, scholarship,
and education by publishing worldwide. Oxford is a registered trade mark of
Oxford University Press in the UK and in certain other countries

Third edition 2007
Fourth edition 2008
Fifth edition 2014
Sixth edition 2016

Impression:2

Published in the United States of America by Oxford University Press
198 Madison Avenue, New York, NY 10016, United States of America

British Library Cataloguing in Publication Data

Data available

ISBN 978–0–19–876836–4

Printed in Great Britain by
Ashford Colour Press Ltd.

Editor's preface to the sixth edition

We have left the preface to the first edition of this book in place—this edition remains a testament to the energy and creativity of the first editors. We at the University of Cambridge were happy for several years to recommend the use of Mitchell and Farrar's *Statutes on Criminal Justice & Sentencing* for students taking our examination in 'Criminology, Sentencing and the Penal System'. But sadly the years passed since the fourth edition (2008) and, in 2014, I successfully convinced the publishers to produce a fifth edition. Those teaching sentencing law in particular were no longer able to recommend to students a book produced in June 2008: it missed not only the vital changes of the Criminal Justice and Immigration Act 2008, but also the myriad changes of the Legal Aid, Sentencing and Punishment of Offenders Act 2012. Within two years, we have had reason to produce a sixth edition: change is still happening far too fast. There's been the Anti-social Behaviour, Crime and Policing Act 2014, the Offender Rehabilitation Act 2014, the Serious Crime Act 2015, and the Criminal Justice and Courts Act 2015—and others. They make endless small and large amendments to earlier Acts of Parliament—what a nightmare it is to keep up to date! Those statutes don't themselves appear—they have largely amended earlier statutes and OUP persuaded me that we did not need to include the sources of all amendments.

So I am delighted that OUP have decided to produce a sixth edition of this book. I feel somewhat churlish that only my name appears on the cover. We are of course indebted to Barry Mitchell and Salim Farrar, for their work over four editions. I am particularly grateful to Catherine Ideson, an efficient member of the administrative staff in the Law Faculty of the University of Cambridge who worked on the production of the fifth edition, under a very tight timetable. She moved on, and for the sixth edition I am hugely grateful to Antonia Gray, who picked up the challenge of updating this edition with enthusiasm and absolutely no complaint. My name is on the cover—all errors are my responsibility. All complaints and (constructive!) comments should be directed to me (at nmp21@cam.ac.uk). But it is to Catherine Ideson and Antonia Gray that users of this book owe significant thanks. I record my own thanks to them both loudly here.

Given the frequency of legislative change in this area, it is difficult to ensure that our statute book is truly up to date or accurate. I apologise for any errors or omissions. I have not tried to include 'everything': this is a book for exam purposes only! I hope that OUP will encourage us to produce a new edition biannually. So your comments really will be appreciated and carefully considered. Thanks are also due to the team at OUP who have turned this book around swiftly and efficiently: Natasha Ellis-Knight, Sarah Stephenson, and Joy Ruskin-Tompkins.

Nicola Padfield
Master, Fitzwilliam College, Cambridge
Reader in Criminal and Penal Justice, University of Cambridge
March 2016

Editors' preface to the first edition

There are numerous undergraduate and postgraduate courses in law and other disciplines such as criminology which include various aspects of criminal justice and sentencing. In the general sense at least, sentencing is an integral part of the criminal justice process, and it is arguable therefore that there is no need to identify sentencing separately. We have done so however simply because not all courses include it—some do not go beyond the point of conviction—and we obviously want to make it clear that this book encompasses important statutory provisions which apply across the whole gamut of the criminal justice system.

As most of us appreciate (if only through the media), there has been a constant stream of legislation, especially during the last fifteen years or so, which has affected all dimensions of criminal justice. Although this has precipitated a considerable number of statutory instruments, working guidelines and practice directions, this book confines itself to relevant statutory provisions (including the Codes of Practice under the Police and Criminal Evidence Act 1984). In an attempt to consolidate what had become an increasingly unmanageable mass of provisions on sentencing contained in several statutes, Parliament enacted the Powers of Criminal Courts (Sentencing) Act 2000. As is evident from the Contents pages at the start of this book, this has simplified the situation, but amendments have already been made to it (which we have incorporated) by, for example, the Criminal Justice and Court Services Act 2000. Furthermore, there are some sections of the Powers of Criminal Courts (Sentencing) Act 2000 which contain important changes to the law but which have not yet been brought into force. For example, sections 87 and 88 will replace section 67 of the Criminal Justice Act 1967 on time spent in custody on remand, and section 61 of the PCC(S)A 2000 will abolish detention in a young offender institution and thereby lower the eligibility for imprisonment from 21 to 18 years of age. At the time of writing, no dates have been fixed for implementing these changes but they have been included in italic type. Other amendments to the PCC(S)A 2000 include the introduction of exclusion orders, a new type of community order, but it is unknown when this amendment will be brought into effect and the relevant provisions have been omitted from this book.

One area in which Parliament has recently been active is surveillance and electronic searches. The statutes relating to these issues are the Police Act 1997 and the Regulation of Investigatory Powers Act 2000, but the subject is very complex and one which we feel merits separate consideration elsewhere.

There were various formats available to us for structuring the book. We suspect that most people will want to use it by reference to a particular topic—arrest and detention, bail, disclosure, etc.—and we have set the book out on that basis.

We should like to record our thanks to colleagues at Oxford University Press, especially to Barbara Laing and John Grandidge, for their support, assistance and patience. As ever, though, any errors remain our responsibility.

Barry Mitchell and Salim Farrar
August 2002

New to this edition

The sixth edition of *Blackstone's Statutes on Criminal Justice & Sentencing* has been fully updated to include amendments introduced by the Anti-social Behaviour, Crime and Policing Act 2014, the Offender Rehabilitation Act 2014, the Serious Crime Act 2015, and the Criminal Justice and Courts Act 2015.

Contents

Alphabetical contents

Chronological contents

Part I

Criminal Justice

European Convention on Human Rights

Article 5   Right to liberty and security

1. Everyone has the right to liberty and security of person. No one shall be deprived of his liberty save in the following cases and in accordance with a procedure prescribed by law:

    (a) the lawful detention of a person after conviction by a competent court;

    (b) the lawful arrest or detention of a person for non-compliance with the lawful order of a court or in order to secure the fulfilment of any obligation prescribed by law;

    (c) the lawful arrest or detention of a person effected for the purpose of bringing him before the competent legal authority on reasonable suspicion of having committed an offence or when it is reasonably considered necessary to prevent his committing an offence or fleeing after having done so;

    (d) the detention of a minor by lawful order for the purpose of educational supervision or his lawful detention for the purpose of bringing him before the competent legal authority;

    (e) the lawful detention of persons for the prevention of the spreading of infectious diseases, of persons of unsound mind, alcoholics or drug addicts or vagrants;

    (f) the lawful arrest or detention of a person to prevent his effecting an unauthorised entry into the country or of a person against whom action is being taken with a view to deportation or extradition.

2. Everyone who is arrested shall be informed promptly, in a language which he understands, of the reasons for his arrest and of any charge against him.

3. Everyone arrested or detained in accordance with the provisions of paragraph 1.c of this article shall be brought promptly before a judge or other officer authorised by law to exercise judicial power and shall be entitled to trial within a reasonable time or to release pending trial. Release may be conditioned by guarantees to appear for trial.

4. Everyone who is deprived of his liberty by arrest or detention shall be entitled to take proceedings by which the lawfulness of his detention shall be decided speedily by a court and his release ordered if the detention is not lawful.

5. Everyone who has been the victim of arrest or detention in contravention of the provisions of this article shall have an enforceable right to compensation.

Article 6   Right to a fair trial

1. In the determination of his civil rights and obligations or of any criminal charge against him, everyone is entitled to a fair and public hearing within a reasonable time by an independent and impartial tribunal established by law. Judgment shall be pronounced publicly but the press and public

may be excluded from all or part of the trial in the interests of morals, public order or national security in a democratic society, where the interests of juveniles or the protection of the private life of the parties so require, or to the extent strictly necessary in the opinion of the court in special circumstances where publicity would prejudice the interests of justice.

2. Everyone charged with a criminal offence shall be presumed innocent until proved guilty according to law.

3. Everyone charged with a criminal offence has the following minimum rights:

(a) to be informed promptly, in a language which he understands and in detail, of the nature and cause of the accusation against him;

(b) to have adequate time and facilities for the preparation of his defence;

(c) to defend himself in person or through legal assistance of his own choosing or, if he has not sufficient means to pay for legal assistance, to be given it free when the interests of justice so require;

(d) to examine or have examined witnesses against him and to obtain the attendance and examination of witnesses on his behalf under the same conditions as witnesses against him;

(e) to have the free assistance of an interpreter if he cannot understand or speak the language used in court.

Article 8 Right to respect for private and family life

1. Everyone has the right to respect for his private and family life, his home and his correspondence.

2. There shall be no interference by a public authority with the exercise of this right except such as is in accordance with the law and is necessary in a democratic society in the interests of national security, public safety or the economic well-being of the country, for the prevention of disorder or crime, for the protection of health or morals, or for the protection of the rights and freedoms of others.

Criminal Appeal Act 1968

2 Grounds for allowing an appeal under s. 1

(1) Subject to the provisions of this Act, the Court of Appeal—

(a) shall allow an appeal against conviction if they think that the conviction is unsafe; and

(b) shall dismiss such an appeal in any other case.

(2) In the case of an appeal against conviction the Court shall, if they allow the appeal, quash the conviction.

(3) An order of the Court of Appeal quashing a conviction shall, except when under section 7 below the appellant is ordered to be retired, operate as a direction to the court of trial to enter, instead of the record of conviction, a judgment and verdict of acquittal.

7 Power to order retrial

(1) Where the Court of Appeal allow an appeal against conviction and it appears to the Court that the interests of justice so require, they may order the appellant to be retried.

(2) A person shall not under this section be ordered to be retried for any offence other than—

(a) the offence of which he was convicted at the original trial and in respect of which his appeal is allowed as mentioned in subsection (1) above;

(b) an offence of which he could have been convicted at the original trial on an indictment for the first-mentioned offence; or

(c) an offence charged in an alternative count of the indictment in respect of which no verdict was given in consequence of his being convicted of the first-mentioned offence.

23 Evidence

(1) For the purposes of an appeal, or an application for leave to appeal, under this Part of this Act the Court of Appeal may, if they think it necessary or expedient in the interests of justice—

(a) order the production of any document, exhibit or other thing connected with the proceedings, the production of which appears to them necessary for the determination of the case;

(b) order any witness to attend for examination and be examined before the Court (whether or not he was called in the proceedings from which the appeal lies); and

(c) receive any evidence which was not adduced in the proceedings from which the appeal lies.

(1A) The power conferred by subsection (1)(a) may be exercised so as to require the production of any document, exhibit or other thing mentioned in that subsection to—

(a) the Court;

(b) the appellant;

(c) the respondent.

(2) The Court of Appeal shall, in considering whether to receive any evidence, have regard in particular to—

(a) whether the evidence appears to the Court to be capable of belief;

(b) whether it appears to the Court that the evidence may afford any ground for allowing the appeal;

(c) whether the evidence would have been admissible in the proceedings from which the appeal lies on an issue which is the subject of the appeal; and

(d) whether there is a reasonable explanation for the failure to adduce the evidence in those proceedings.

(3) Subsection (1)(c) above applies to any evidence of a witness (including the appellant) who is competent but not compellable . . .

(4) For the purposes of an appeal, or an application for leave to appeal, under this Part of this Act, the Court of Appeal may, if they think it necessary or expedient in the interests of justice, order the examination of any witness whose attendance might be required under subsection (1)(b) above to be conducted, in manner provided by rules of court, before any judge or officer of the Court or other person appointed by the Court for the purpose, and allow the admission of any depositions so taken as evidence before the Court.

(5) A live link direction under *section 22(4)* does not apply to the giving of oral evidence by the appellant at any hearing unless that direction, or any subsequent direction of the court, provides expressly for the giving of such evidence through a live link.

(6) In this section, 'respondent' includes a person who will be a respondent if leave to appeal is granted.

23A   Power to order investigations

(1) On an appeal against conviction or an application for leave to appeal against conviction the Court of Appeal may direct the Criminal Cases Review Commission to investigate and report to the Court on any matter if it appears to the Court that—

(a)   in the case of an appeal the matter is relevant to the determination of the appeal and ought, if possible, to be resolved before the appeal is determined;

(aa)   in the case of an application for leave to appeal, the matter is relevant to the determination of the application and ought, if possible, to be resolved before the application is determined;

(b)   an investigation of the matter by the Commission is likely to result in the Court being able to resolve it; and

(c)   the matter cannot be resolved by the Court without an investigation by the Commission.

(1A) A direction under subsection (1) above may not be given by a single judge, notwithstanding that, in the case of an application for leave to appeal, the application may be determined by a single judge as provided for by section 31 of this Act.

(2) A direction by the Court of Appeal under subsection (1) above shall be given in writing and shall specify the matter to be investigated.

(3) Copies of such a direction shall be made available to the appellant and the respondent.

(4) Where the Commission have reported to the Court of Appeal on any matter which they have been directed under subsection (1) above to investigate, the Court—

    (a) shall notify the appellant and the respondent that the Commission have reported; and

    (b) may make available to the appellant and the respondent the report of the Commission and any statements, opinions and reports which accompanied it.

(5) In this section 'respondent' includes a person who will be a respondent if leave to appeal is granted.

33   Right of appeal to Supreme Court

(1) An appeal lies to the Supreme Court, at the instance of the defendant or the prosecutor, from any decision of the Court of Appeal on an appeal to that court under Part I of this Act or Part 9 of the Criminal Justice Act 2003 or section 9 (preparatory hearings) of the Criminal Justice Act 1987 or section 35 of the Criminal Procedure and Investigations Act 1996 or section 47 of the Criminal Justice Act 2003.

(1B) An appeal lies to the Supreme Court, at the instance of the acquitted person or the prosecutor, from any decision of the Court of Appeal on an application under section 76(1) or (2) of the Criminal Justice Act 2003 (retrial for serious offences).

(2) The appeal lies only with the leave of the Court of Appeal or the Supreme Court ; and leave shall not be granted unless it is certified by the Court of Appeal that a point of law of general public importance is involved in the decision and it appears to the Court of Appeal or the Supreme Court (as the case may be) that the point is one which ought to be considered by that House.

(3) Except as provided by this Part of this Act and section 13 of the Administration of Justice Act 1960 (appeal in cases of contempt of court), no appeal shall lie from any decision of the criminal division of the Court of Appeal.

(4) In relation to an appeal under subsection (1B), references in this Part to a defendant are references to the acquitted person.

Theft Act 1968

27   Evidence and procedure on charge of theft or handling stolen goods

(1) Any number of persons may be charged in one indictment, with reference to the same theft, with having at different times or at the same time handled all or any of the stolen goods, and the persons so charged may be tried together.

(2) On the trial of two or more persons indicted for jointly handling any stolen goods the jury may find any of the accused guilty if the jury are satisfied that he handled all or any of the stolen goods, whether or not he did so jointly with the other accused or any of them.

(3) Where a person is being proceeded against for handling stolen goods (but not for any offence other than handling stolen goods), then at any stage of the proceedings, if evidence has been given of his having or arranging to have in his possession the goods the subject of the charge, or of his undertaking or assisting in, or arranging to undertake or assist in, their retention, removal, disposal or realisation, the following evidence shall be admissible for the purpose of proving that he knew or believed the goods to be stolen goods—

    (a) evidence that he has had in his possession, or has undertaken or assisted in the retention, removal, disposal or realisation of, stolen goods from any theft taking place not earlier than twelve months before the offence charged; and

    (b) (provided that seven days' notice in writing has been given to him of the intention to prove the conviction) evidence that he has within the five years preceding the date of the offence charged been convicted of theft or of handling stolen goods.

(4) In any proceedings for the theft of anything in the course of transmission (whether by post or otherwise), or for handling stolen goods from such a theft, a statutory declaration made by any person that he despatched or received or failed to receive any goods or postal packet, or that any goods

or postal packet when despatched or received by him were in a particular state or condition, shall be admissible as evidence of the facts stated in the declaration, subject to the following conditions:—

    (a) a statutory declaration shall only be admissible where and to the extent to which oral evidence to the like effect would have been admissible in the proceedings; and

    (b) a statutory declaration shall only be admissible if at least seven days before the hearing or trial a copy of it has been given to the person charged, and he has not, at least three days before the hearing or trial or within such further time as the court may in special circumstances allow, given the prosecutor written notice requiring the attendance at the hearing or trial of the person making the declaration.

    (5) This section is to be construed in accordance with section 24 of this Act; and in subsection (3)(b) above the reference to handling stolen goods shall include any corresponding offence committed before the commencement of this Act.

Juries Act 1974

1 Qualification for jury service

    (1) Subject to the provisions of this Act, every person shall be qualified to serve as a juror in the Crown Court, the High Court and county courts and be liable accordingly to attend for jury service when summoned under this Act if—

    (a) he is for the time being registered as a parliamentary or local government elector and is not less than eighteen nor more than seventy years of age;

    (b) he has been ordinarily resident in the United Kingdom, the Channel Islands or the Isle of Man for any period of at least five years since attaining the age of thirteen;

    (d) he is not disqualified for jury service.

    (3) The persons who are disqualified for jury service are those listed in Part 2 of that Schedule 1.

3 Electoral register as basis of jury selection

    (1) Every electoral registration officer under the Representation of the People Act 1983 shall as soon as practicable after the publication of any register of electors for his area deliver to such officer as the Lord Chancellor may designate such number of copies of the register as the designated officer may require for the purpose of summoning jurors, and on each copy there shall be indicated those persons on the register whom the registration officer has ascertained to be, or to have been on a date also indicated on the copy, less than eighteen or more than seventy years of age.

    (1A) If a register to be delivered under subsection (1) above includes any anonymous entries (within the meaning of that Act of 1983) the registration officer must, at the same time as he delivers the register, also deliver to the designated officer any record prepared in pursuance of provision made as mentioned in paragraph 8A of Schedule 2 to that Act which relates to such anonymous entries.

    (2) The reference in subsection (1) above to a register of electors does not include a ward list within the meaning of section 4(1) of the City of London (Various Powers) Act 1957.

8 Excusal for previous jury service

    (1) If a person summoned under this Act shows to the satisfaction of the appropriate officer, or of the court (or any of the courts) to which he is summoned—

    (a) that he has served on a jury, or duly attended to serve on a jury, in the prescribed period ending with the service of the summons on him, or

    (b) that the Crown Court or any other court has excused him from jury service for a period which has not terminated,

the officer or court shall excuse him from attending, or further attending, in pursuance of the summons.

(2) In subsection (1) above 'the prescribed period' means two years or such longer period as the Lord Chancellor may prescribe by order made by statutory instrument subject to annulment in pursuance of a resolution of either House of Parliament, and any such order may be varied or revoked by a subsequent order under this subsection.

(3) Records of persons summoned under this Act, and of persons included in panels, shall be kept in such manner as the Lord Chancellor may direct, and the Lord Chancellor may, if he thinks fit, make arrangements for allowing inspection of the records so kept by members of the public in such circumstances and subject to such conditions as he may prescribe.

(4) A person duly attending in compliance with a summons under this Act shall be entitled on application to the appropriate officer to a certificate recording that he has so attended.

(5) In subsection (1) above the words 'served on a jury' refer to service on a jury in any court, including any court of assize or other court abolished by the Courts Act 1971, but excluding service on a jury in a coroner's court.

9   Excusal for certain persons and discretionary excusal

(2) If any person summoned under this Act shows to the satisfaction of the appropriate officer that there is good reason why he should be excused from attending in pursuance of the summons, the appropriate officer may, subject to section 9A(1A) of this Act, excuse him from so attending.

(2A) Without prejudice to subsection (2) above, the appropriate officer shall excuse a full-time serving member of Her Majesty's naval, military or air forces from attending in pursuance of a summons if—

    (a) that member's commanding officer certifies to the appropriate officer that it would be prejudicial to the efficiency of the service if that member were to be required to be absent from duty, and

    (b) subsection (2A) or (2B) of section 9A of this Act applies.

(2B) Subsection (2A) above does not affect the application of subsection (2) above to a full-time serving member of Her Majesty's naval, military or air forces in a case where he is not entitled to be excused under subsection (2A).

(3) Criminal Procedure Rules shall provide a right of appeal to the court (or one of the courts) before or any failure by the appropriate officer to excuse him as required by subsection (2A) above which the person is summoned to attend against any refusal of the appropriate officer to excuse him under subsection (2) above.

(4) Without prejudice to the preceding provisions of this section, the court (or any of the courts) before which a person is summoned to attend under this Act may excuse that person from so attending.

9A   Discretionary deferral

(1) If any person summoned under this Act shows to the satisfaction of the appropriate officer that there is good reason why his attendance in pursuance of the summons should be deferred, the appropriate officer may, subject to subsection (2) below, defer his attendance, and, if he does so, he shall vary the days on which that person is summoned to attend and the summons shall have effect accordingly.

(1A) Without prejudice to subsection (1) above and subject to subsection (2) below, the appropriate officer—

    (a) shall defer the attendance of a full-time serving member of Her Majesty's naval, military or air forces in pursuance of a summons if subsection (1B) below applies, and

    (b) for this purpose, shall vary the dates upon which that member is summoned to attend and the summons shall have effect accordingly.

(1B) This subsection applies if that member's commanding officer certifies to the appropriate officer that it would be prejudicial to the efficiency of the service if that member were to be required to be absent from duty.

(1C) Nothing in subsection (1A) or (1B) above shall affect the application of subsection (1) above to a full-time serving member of Her Majesty's naval, military or air forces in a case where subsection (1B) does not apply.

(2) The attendance of a person in pursuance of a summons shall not be deferred under subsection (1) or (1A) above if subsection (2A) or (2B) below applies.

(2A) This subsection applies where a deferral of the attendance of the person in pursuance of the summons has previously been made or refused under subsection (1) above or has previously been made under subsection (1A) above.

(2B) This subsection applies where—

    (a) the person is a full-time serving member of Her Majesty's naval, military or air forces, and

    (b) in addition to certifying to the appropriate officer that it would be prejudicial to the efficiency of the service if that member were to be required to be absent from duty, that member's commanding officer certifies that this position is likely to remain for any period specified for the purpose of this subsection in guidance issued under section 9AA of this Act.

(3) Criminal Procedure Rules shall provide a right of appeal to the court (or one of the courts) before which the person is summoned to attend against any refusal of the appropriate officer to defer his attendance under subsection (1) above or any failure by the appropriate officer to defer his attendance as required by subsection (1A) above.

(4) Without prejudice to the preceding provisions of this section, the court (or any of the courts) before which a person is summoned to attend under this Act may defer his attendance.

17   Majority verdicts

(1) Subject to subsections (3) and (4) below, the verdict of a jury in proceedings in the Crown Court or the High Court need not be unanimous if—

    (a) in a case where there are not less than eleven jurors, ten of them agree on the verdict; and

    (b) in a case where there are ten jurors, nine of them agree on the verdict.

(2) Subject to subsection (4) below, the verdict of a jury (that is to say a complete jury of eight) in proceedings in a county court need not be unanimous if seven of them agree on the verdict.

(3) The Crown Court shall not accept a verdict of guilty by virtue of subsection (1) above unless the foreman of the jury has stated in open court the number of jurors who respectively agreed to and dissented from the verdict.

(4) No court shall accept a verdict by virtue of subsection (1) or (2) above unless it appears to the court that the jury have had such period of time for deliberation as the court thinks reasonable having regard to the nature and complexity of the case; and the Crown Court shall in any event not accept such a verdict unless it appears to the court that the jury have had at least two hours for deliberation.

(5) This section is without prejudice to any practice in civil proceedings by which a court may accept a majority verdict with the consent of the parties, or by which the parties may agree to proceed in any case with an incomplete jury.

20A   Offence: research by jurors

(1) It is an offence for a member of a jury that tries an issue in a case before a court to research the case during the trial period, subject to the exceptions in subsections (6) and (7).

(2) A person researches a case if (and only if) the person—

    (a) intentionally seeks information, and

    (b) when doing so, knows or ought reasonably to know that the information is or may be relevant to the case.

(3) The ways in which a person may seek information include—

    (a) asking a question,

    (b) searching an electronic database, including by means of the internet,

    (c) visiting or inspecting a place or object,

    (d) conducting an experiment, and

    (e) asking another person to seek the information.

(4) Information relevant to the case includes information about—

    (a) a person involved in events relevant to the case,

    (b) the judge dealing with the issue,

    (c) any other person involved in the trial, whether as a lawyer, a witness or otherwise,

(d) the law relating to the case,

(e) the law of evidence, and

(f) court procedure.

20C   Offence: jurors engaging in other prohibited conduct

(1) It is an offence for a member of a jury that tries an issue in a case before a court intentionally to engage in prohibited conduct during the trial period, subject to the exceptions in subsections (4) and (5).

(2) 'Prohibited conduct' means conduct from which it may reasonably be concluded that the person intends to try the issue otherwise than on the basis of the evidence presented in the proceedings on the issue.

(3) An offence under this section is committed whether or not the person knows that the conduct is prohibited conduct.

20D   Offence: disclosing jury's deliberations

(1) It is an offence for a person intentionally—

(a) to disclose information about statements made, opinions expressed, arguments advanced or votes cast by members of a jury in the course of their deliberations in proceedings before a court, or

(b) to solicit or obtain such information,

subject to the exceptions in sections 20E to 20G.

(2) A person guilty of an offence under this section is liable, on conviction on indictment, to imprisonment for a term not exceeding 2 years or a fine (or both).

SCHEDULE 1   PERSONS DISQUALIFIED FOR JURY SERVICE

PART 1   PERSONS SUBJECT TO MENTAL HEALTH ACT 1983 OR MENTAL CAPACITY ACT 2005

1 A person for the time being liable to be detained under the Mental Health Act 1983.

1A A person for the time being resident in a hospital on account of mental disorder as defined by the Mental Health Act 1983.

2 A person for the time being under guardianship under section 7 of the Mental Health Act 1983 or subject to a community treatment order under section 17A of that Act.

3 A person who lacks capacity, within the meaning of the Mental Capacity Act 2005, to serve as a juror.

PART 2   PERSONS DISQUALIFIED

5 A person who is on bail in criminal proceedings (within the meaning of the Bail Act 1976).

6 A person who has at any time been sentenced in the United Kingdom, the Channel Islands or the Isle of Man—

(a) to imprisonment for life, detention for life or custody for life,

(b) to detention during her Majesty's pleasure or during the pleasure of the Secretary of State,

(c) to imprisonment for public protection or detention for public protection,

(d) to an extended sentence under section 226A, 226B, 227 or 228 of the Criminal Justice Act 2003 (including such a sentence imposed as a result of section 219A, 220, 221A or 222 of the Armed Forces Act 2006) or section 210A of the Criminal Procedure (Scotland) Act 1995, or

(e) to a term of imprisonment of five years or more or a term of detention of five years or more.

7 A person who at any time in the last ten years has—

(a) in the United Kingdom, the Channel Islands or the Isle of Man—

(i) served any part of a sentence of imprisonment or a sentence of detention, or

(ii) had passed on him a suspended sentence of imprisonment or had made in respect of him a suspended order for detention,

(b) in England and Wales, had made in respect of him a community order under section 177 of the Criminal Justice Act 2003, a community rehabilitation order, a community punishment order, a community punishment and rehabilitation order, a drug treatment and testing order or a drug abstinence order, or

(c) had made in respect of him any corresponding order under the law of Scotland, Northern Ireland, the Isle of Man or any of the Channel Islands or service community order or overseas community order under the Armed Forces Act 2006..

8 For the purposes of this Part of this Schedule—

(a) a sentence passed (anywhere) in respect of a service offence within the meaning of the Armed Forces Act 2006 is to be treated as having been passed in the United Kingdom, and

(b) a person is sentenced to a term of detention if, but only if—

(i) a court passes on him, or makes in respect of him on conviction, any sentence or order which requires him to be detained in custody for any period, and

(ii) the sentence or order is available only in respect of offenders below a certain age, and any reference to serving a sentence of detention is to be construed accordingly.

Bail Act 1976

Incidents of bail in criminal proceedings

3 General provisions

(1) A person granted bail in criminal proceedings shall be under a duty to surrender to custody, and that duty is enforceable in accordance with section 6 of this Act.

(2) No recognizance for his surrender to custody shall be taken from him.

(3) Except as provided by this section—

(a) no security for his surrender to custody shall be taken from him.

(b) he shall not be required to provide a surety or sureties for his surrender to custody, and

(c) no other requirement shall be imposed on him as a condition of bail.

(4) He may be required, before release on bail, to provide a surety or sureties to secure his surrender to custody.

(5) He may be required, before release on bail, to give security for his surrender to custody.
The security may be given by him or on his behalf.

(6) He may be required to comply, before release on bail or later, with such requirements as appear to the court to be necessary—

(a) to secure that he surrenders to custody.

(b) to secure that he does not commit an offence while on bail,

(c) to secure that he does not interfere with witnesses or otherwise obstruct the course of justice whether in relation to himself or any other person,

(ca) for his own protection or, if he is a child or young person, for his own welfare, or in his own interests,

(d) to secure that he makes himself available for the purpose of enabling inquiries or a report to be made to assist the court in dealing with him for the offence.

(e) to secure that before the time appointed for him to surrender to custody, he attends an interview with an authorised advocate or authorised litigator, as defined by section 119(1) of the Courts and Legal Services Act 1990;

and, in any Act, 'the normal powers to impose conditions of bail' means the powers to impose conditions under paragraph (a), (b), (c) or (ca) above.

(6ZAA) The requirements which may be imposed under subsection (6) include electronic monitoring requirements.

The imposition of electronic monitoring requirements is subject to section 3AA (in the case of a child or young person granted bail in criminal proceedings of the kind mentioned in section 1(1)(a) or (b)), section 3AAA (in the case of a child or young person granted bail in connection with extradition proceedings), section 3AB (in the case of other persons) and section 3AC (in all cases).

(6ZAB) In this section and sections 3AA to 3AC 'electronic monitoring requirements' means requirements imposed for the purpose of securing the electronic monitoring of a person's compliance with any other requirement imposed on him as a condition of bail.

(6ZA) Where he is required under subsection (6) above to reside in a bail hostel or probation hostel, he may also be required to comply with the rules of the hostel.

(6A) In the case of a person accused of murder the court granting bail shall, unless it considers that satisfactory reports on his mental condition have already been obtained, impose as conditions of bail—

    (a) a requirement that the accused shall undergo examination by two medical practitioners, for the purpose of enabling such reports to be prepared; and

    (b) a requirement that he shall for that purpose attend such an institution or place as the court directs and comply with any other directions which may be given to him for that purpose by either of those practitioners.

(6B) Of the medical practitioners referred to in subsection (6A) above at least one shall be practitioner approved for the purposes of section 12 of the Mental Health Act 1983.

(6C) Subsection (6D) below applies where—

    (a) the court has been notified by the Secretary of State that arrangements for conducting a relevant assessment or, as the case may be, providing relevant follow-up have been made for the local justice area in which it appears to the court that the person referred to in subsection (6D) would reside if granted bail; and

    (b) the notice has not been withdrawn.

(6D) In the case of a person ('P')—

    (a) in relation to whom paragraphs (a) to (c) of paragraph 6B(1) of Part 1 of Schedule 1 to this Act apply;

    (b) who, after analysis of the sample referred to in paragraph (b) of that paragraph, has been offered a relevant assessment or, if a relevant assessment has been carried out, has had relevant follow-up proposed to him; and

    (c) who has agreed to undergo the relevant assessment or, as the case may be, to participate in the relevant follow-up,

the court, if it grants bail, shall impose as a condition of bail that P both undergo the relevant assessment and participate in any relevant follow-up proposed to him or, if a relevant assessment has been carried out, that P participate in the relevant follow-up.

(6E) In subsections (6C) and (6D) above—

    (a) 'relevant assessment' means an assessment conducted by a suitably qualified person of whether P is dependent upon or has a propensity to misuse any specified Class A drugs;

    (b) 'relevant follow-up' means, in a case where the person who conducted the relevant assessment believes P to have such a dependency or propensity, such further assessment, and such assistance or treatment (or both) in connection with the dependency or propensity, as the person who conducted the relevant assessment (or conducts any later assessment) considers to be appropriate in P's case,

and in paragraph (a) above 'Class A drug' and 'misuse' have the same meaning as in the Misuse of Drugs Act 1971, and 'specified' (in relation to a Class A drug) has the same meaning as in Part 3 of the Criminal Justice and Court Services Act 2000.

(6F) In subsection (6E)(a) above, 'suitably qualified person' means a person who has such qualifications or experience as are from time to time specified by the Secretary of State for the purposes of this subsection.

(7) If a parent or guardian of a child or young person consents to be surety for the person for the purposes of this subsection, the parent or guardian may be required to secure that the person complies with any requirement imposed on him by virtue of subsection (6), (6ZAA) or (6A) above, but—

> (a) no requirement shall be imposed on the parent or the guardian by virtue of this subsection where it appears that the person will attain the age of seventeen before the time to be appointed for him to surrender to custody; and
>
> (b) the parent or guardian shall not be required to secure compliance with any requirement to which his consent does not extend and shall not, in respect of those requirements to which his consent does extend, be bound in a sum greater than £50.

(8) Where a court has granted bail in criminal proceedings that court or, where that court has sent a person on bail to the Crown Court for trial or committed him on bail to the Crown Court to be sentenced or otherwise dealt with, that court or the Crown Court may on application—

> (a) by or on behalf of the person to whom bail was granted, or
>
> (b) by the prosecutor or a constable,

vary the conditions of bail or impose conditions in respect of bail which has been granted unconditionally.

(9) This section is subject to subsection (3) of section 11 of the Powers of Criminal Courts (Sentencing) Act 2000 (conditions of bail on remand for medical examination).

(10) This section is subject, in its application to bail granted by a constable, to section 3A of this Act.

3A   Conditions of bail in case of police bail

(1) Section 3 of this Act applies, in relation to bail granted by a custody officer under Part IV of the Police and Criminal Evidence Act 1984 or Part 3 of the Criminal Justice Act 2003 in cases where the normal powers to impose conditions of bail are available to him, subject to the following modifications.

(2) Subsection (6) does not authorise the imposition of a requirement to reside in a bail hostel or any requirement under paragraph (d) or (e).

(3) Subsections (6ZAA), (6ZA) and (6A) to (6F) shall be omitted.

(4) For subsection (8), substitute the following—

'(8) Where a custody officer has granted bail in criminal proceedings he or another custody officer serving at the same police station may, at the request of the person to whom it was granted, vary the conditions of bail; and in doing so he may impose conditions or more onerous conditions.'.

(5) Where a constable grants bail to a person no conditions shall be imposed under subsections (4), (5), (6) or (7) of section 3 of this Act unless it appears to the constable that it is necessary to do so—

> (a) for the purpose of preventing that person from failing to surrender to custody, or
>
> (b) for the purpose of preventing that person from committing an offence while on bail, or
>
> (c) for the purpose of preventing that person from interfering with witnesses or otherwise obstructing the course of justice, whether in relation to himself or any other person, or
>
> (d) for that person's own protection or, if he is a child or young person, for his own welfare or in his own interests.

(6) Subsection (5) above also applies on any request to a custody officer under subsection (8) of section 3 of this Act to vary the conditions of bail.

3AA   Conditions for the imposition of electronic monitoring requirements: children and young persons released on bail other than in extradition proceedings

(1) A court shall not impose on a child or young person a requirements on a child or young person released on bail in criminal proceedings of the kind mentioned in section 1(1)(a) or (b) unless each of the following conditions is met.

(2) The first condition is that the child or young person has attained the age of twelve years.

(3) The second condition is that—

> (a) the child or young person is charged with or has been convicted of a violent or sexual offence, or an offence punishable in the case of an adult with imprisonment for a term of fourteen years or more; or

(b) he is charged with or has been convicted of one or more imprisonable offences which, together with any other imprisonable offences of which he has been convicted in any proceedings—

(i) amount, or

(ii) would, if he were convicted of the offences with which he is charged, amount, to a recent history of repeatedly committing imprisonable offences while remanded on bail or subject to custodial remand.

(4) The third condition is that the court is satisfied that the necessary provision for dealing with the person concerned can be made under arrangements for the electronic monitoring of persons released on bail that are currently available in each local justice area which is a relevant area.

(5) The fourth condition is that a youth offending team has informed the court that in its opinion the imposition of electronic monitoring requirements will be suitable in the case of the child or young person.

(11) The references in subsection (3)(b) to an imprisonable offence include a reference to an offence—

(a) of which the child or young person has been convicted outside England and Wales, and

(b) which is equivalent to an offence that is punishable with imprisonment in England and Wales.

(12) The reference in subsection (3)(b) to a child or young person being subject to a custodial remand is to the child or young person being—

(a) remanded to local authority accommodation or youth detention accommodation under section 91 of the Legal Aid, Sentencing and Punishment of Offenders Act 2012,

(b) remanded to local authority accommodation under section 23 of the Children and Young Persons Act 1969 or to prison under that section as modified by section 98 of the Crime and Disorder Act 1998 or under section 27 of the Criminal Justice Act 1948, or

(c) subject to a form of custodial detention in a country or territory outside England and Wales while awaiting trial or sentence in that country or territory or during a trial in that country or territory.

Bail for accused persons and others

4 General right to bail of accused persons and others

(1) A person to whom this section applies shall be granted bail except as provided in Schedule 1 to this Act.

(2) This section applies to a person who is accused of an offence when—

(a) he appears or is brought before a magistrates' court or the Crown Court in the course of or in connection with proceedings for the offence, or

(b) he applies to a court for bail or for a variation of the conditions of bail in connection with the proceedings.

This subsection does not apply as respects proceedings on or against a person's conviction of the offence.

(2A) This section also applies to a person whose extradition is sought in respect of an offence, when—

(a) he appears or is brought before a court in the course of or in connection with extradition proceedings in respect of the offence, or

(b) he applies to a court for bail or for a variation of the conditions of bail in connection with the proceedings.

(2B) But subsection (2A) above does not apply if the person is alleged to have been convicted of the offence.

(3) This section also applies to a person who, having been convicted of an offence, appears or is brought before a magistrates' court or the Crown Court to be dealt with under—

(za) Schedule 1 to the Powers of Criminal Courts (Sentencing) Act 2000 (referral orders: referral back to appropriate court), (zb) Schedule 8 to that Act (breach of reparation order),

(a)   Schedule 2 to the Criminal Justice and Immigration Act 2008 (breach of certain youth community orders),

(b)   Part 2 of Schedule 8 to the Criminal Justice Act 2003 (breach of requirement of community order), or

(c)   the Schedule to the Street Offences Act 1959 (breach of orders under section 1(2A) of that Act).

(4) This section also applies to a person who has been convicted of an offence of enabling inquiries or a report to be made for the purpose of enabling inquiries or a report to be made to assist the court in dealing with him for the offence.

(5) Schedule 1 to this Act also has effect as respects conditions of bail for a person to whom this section applies.

(6) In Schedule 1 to this Act 'the defendant' means a person to whom this section applies and any reference to a defendant whose case is adjourned for inquiries or a report is a reference to a person to whom this section applies by virtue of subsection (4) above.

(7) This section is subject to section 41 of the Magistrates' Courts Act 1980 (restriction of bail by magistrates' court in cases of treason).

(8) This section is subject to section 25 of the Criminal Justice and Public Order Act 1994 (exclusion of bail in cases of homicide and rape).

(9) In taking any decisions required by Part I or II of Schedule 1 to this Act, the considerations to which the court is to have regard include, so far as relevant, any misuse of controlled drugs by the defendant ('controlled drugs' and 'misuse' having the same meanings as in the Misuse of Drugs Act 1971).

5   Supplementary provisions about decisions on bail

(1) Subject to subsection (2) below, where—

(a)   a court or constable grants bail in criminal proceedings, or

(b)   a court withholds bail in criminal proceedings from a person to whom section 4 of this Act applies, or

(c)   a court, officer of a court or constable appoints a time or place or a different time or place for a person granted bail in criminal proceedings to surrender to custody, or

(d)   a court or constable varies any conditions of bail or imposes conditions in respect of bail in criminal proceedings,

that court, officer or constable shall make a record of the decision in the prescribed manner and containing the prescribed particulars and, if requested to do so by the person in relation to whom the decision was taken, shall cause him to be given a copy of the record of the decision as soon as practicable after the record is made.

(2) Where bail in criminal proceedings is granted by endorsing a warrant of arrest for bail the constable who releases on bail the person arrested shall make the record required by subsection (1) above instead of the judge or justice who issued the warrant.

(2A) Where a magistrates' court or the Crown Court grants bail in criminal proceedings to a person to whom section 4 of this Act applies after hearing representations from the prosecutor in favour of withholding bail, then the court shall give reasons for granting bail.

(2B) A court which is by virtue of subsection (2A) above required to give reasons for its decision shall include a note of those reasons in the record of its decision and, if requested to do so by the prosecutor, shall cause the prosecutor to be given a copy of the record of the decision as soon as practicable after the record is made.

(3) Where a magistrates' court or the Crown Court—

(a)   withholds bail in criminal proceedings, or

(b)   imposes conditions in granting bail in criminal proceedings, or

(c)   varies any conditions of bail or imposes conditions in respect of bail in criminal proceedings, and does so in relation to a person to whom section 4 of this Act applies, then the court shall give reasons for withholding bail or for imposing or varying the conditions.

(4) A court which is by virtue of subsection (3) above required to give reasons for its decision shall include a note of those reasons in the record of its decision and shall (except in a case where, by virtue of subsection (5) below, this need not be done) give a copy of that note to the person in relation to whom the decision was taken.

(5) The Crown Court need not give a copy of the note of the reasons for its decision to the person in relation to whom the decision was taken where that person has legal representation unless his legal representative requests the court to do so.

(6) Where a magistrates' court withholds bail in criminal proceedings from a person who does not have legal representation is not represented by counsel or a solicitor, the court shall—

(a) if it is sending him for trial to the Crown Court, or if it issues a certificate under subsection (6A) below, inform him that he may apply to the Crown Court to be granted bail.

(6A) Where in criminal proceedings—

(a) a magistrates' court remands a person in custody under section 52(5) of the Crime and Disorder Act 1998, section 11 of the Powers of Criminal Courts (Sentencing) Act 2000 (remand for medical examination) or any of the following provisions of the Magistrates' Courts Act 1980—

(ii) section 10 (adjournment of trial);

(iia) section 17C (intention as to plea: adjournment);

(iii) section 18 (initial procedure on information against adult for offence triable either way); or

(iv) section 24C (intention as to plea by child or young person: adjournment),

after hearing full argument on an application for bail from him; and

(b) either—

(i) it has not previously heard such argument on an application for bail from him in those proceedings; or

(ii) it has previously heard full argument from him on such an application but it is satisfied that there has been a change in his circumstances or that new considerations have been placed before it,

it shall be the duty of the court to issue a certificate in the prescribed form that they heard full argument on his application for bail before they refused the application.

(6B) Where the court issues a certificate under subsection (6A) above in a case to which paragraph (b)(ii) of that subsection applies, it shall state in the certificate the nature of the change of circumstances or the new considerations which caused it to hear a further fully argued bail application.

(6C) Where a court issues a certificate under subsection (6A) above it shall cause the person to whom it refuses bail to be given a copy of the certificate.

(7) Where a person has given security in pursuance of section 3(5) above and a court is satisfied that he failed to surrender to custody then, unless it appears that he had reasonable cause for his failure, the court may order the forfeiture of the security.

(8) If a court orders the forfeiture of a security under subsection (7) above, the court may declare that the forfeiture extends to such amount less than the full value of the security as it thinks fit to order.

(8A) An order under subsection (7) above shall, unless previously revoked, have effect at the end of twenty-one days beginning with the day on which it is made.

(8B) A court which has ordered the forfeiture of a security under subsection (7) above may, if satisfied on an application made by or on behalf of the person who gave it that he did after all have reasonable cause for his failure to surrender to custody, by order remit the forfeiture or declare that it extends to such amount less than the full value of the security as it thinks fit to order.

(8C) An application under subsection (8B) above may be made before or after the order for forfeiture has taken effect, but shall not be entertained unless the court is satisfied that the prosecution was given reasonable notice of the applicant's intention to make it.

(9) A security which has been ordered to be forfeited by a court under subsection (7) above shall, to the extent of the forfeiture—

    (a) if it consists of money, be accounted for and paid in the same manner as a fine imposed by that court would be;

    (b) if it does not consist of money, be enforced by such magistrates' court as may be specified in the order.

(9A) Where an order is made under subsection (8B) above after the order for forfeiture of the security in question has taken effect, any money which would have fallen to be repaid or paid over to the person who gave the security if the order under subsection (8B) had been made before the order for forfeiture took effect shall be repaid or paid over to him.

(10) In this section 'prescribed' means, in relation to the decision of a court or an officer of a court, prescribed by Civil Procedure Rules, Court Martial Appeal Rules, or Criminal Procedure Riles, as the case requires or, in relation to a decision of a constable, prescribed by direction of the Secretary of State.

(11) This section is subject, in its application to bail granted by a constable, to section 5A of this Act.

5A   Supplementary provisions in cases of police bail

(1) Section 5 of this Act applies, in relation to bail granted by a custody officer under Part IV of the Police and Criminal Evidence Act 1984 or Part 3 of the Criminal Justice Act 2003 in cases where the normal powers to impose conditions of bail are available to him, subject to the following modifications.

(1A) Subsections (2A) and (2B) shall be omitted.

(2) For subsection (3) substitute the following—

(3) Where a custody officer, in relation to any person,—

    (a) imposes conditions in granting bail in criminal proceedings, or

    (b) varies any conditions of bail or imposes conditions in respect of bail in criminal proceedings,

the custody officer shall, give reasons for imposing or varying the conditions.

(3) For subsection (4) substitute the following—

(4) A custody officer who is by virtue of subsection (3) above required to give reasons for his decision shall include a note of those reasons in the custody record and shall give a copy of that note to the person in relation to whom the decision was taken.

(4) Subsections (5) and (6) shall be omitted.

5B   Reconsideration of decisions granting bail

(A1) This section applies in any of these cases—

    (a) a magistrates' court has granted bail in criminal proceedings in connection with an offence to which this section applies or proceedings for such an offence;

    (b) a constable has granted bail in criminal proceedings in connection with proceedings for such an offence;

    (c) a magistrates' court or a constable has granted bail in connection with extradition proceedings.

(1) The court of the appropriate court in relation to the constable may, on application by the prosecutor for the decision to be reconsidered—

    (a) vary the conditions of bail,

    (b) impose conditions in respect of bail which has been granted unconditionally, or

    (c) withhold bail.

(2) The offences to which this section applies are offences triable on indictment and offences triable either way.

(3) No application for the reconsideration of a decision under this section shall be made unless it is based on information which was not available to the court or constable when the decision was taken.

(4) Whether or not the person to whom the application relates appears before it, the magistrates' court shall take the decision in accordance with section 4(1) (and Schedule 1) of this Act.

(5) Where the decision of the court on a reconsideration under this section is to withhold bail from the person to whom it was originally granted the court shall—

(a) if that person is before the court, remand him in custody, and

(b) if that person is not before the court, order him to surrender himself forthwith into the custody of the court.

(6) Where a person surrenders himself into the custody of the court in compliance with an order under subsection (5) above, the court shall remand him in custody.

(7) A person who has been ordered to surrender to custody under subsection (5) above may be arrested without warrant by a constable if he fails without reasonable cause to surrender to custody in accordance with the order.

(8) A person arrested in pursuance of subsection (7) above shall be brought as soon as practicable, and in any event within 24 hours after his arrest, before a justice of the peace and the justice shall remand him in custody.

In reckoning for the purposes of this subsection any period of 24 hours, no account shall be taken of Christmas Day, Good Friday or any Sunday.

(8A) Where the court, on a reconsideration under this section, refuses to withhold bail from a relevant person after hearing representations from the prosecutor in favour of withholding bail, then the court shall give reasons for refusing to withhold bail.

(8B) In subsection (8A) above, 'relevant person' means a person to whom section 4(1) (and Schedule 1) of this Act is applicable in accordance with subsection (4) above.

(8C) A court which is by virtue of subsection (8A) above required to give reasons for its decision shall include a note of those reasons in any record of its decision and, if requested to do so by the prosecutor, shall cause the prosecutor to be given a copy of any such record as soon as practicable after the record is made.

(9) Criminal Procedure Rules Magistrates' court rules shall include provision—

(a) requiring notice of an application under this section and of the grounds for it to be given to the person affected, including notice of the powers available to the court under it;

(b) for securing that any representations made by the person affected (whether in writing or orally) are considered by the court before making its decision; and

(c) designating the court which is the appropriate court in relation to the decision of any constable to grant bail.

6 Offence of absconding by person released on bail

(1) If a person who has been released on bail in criminal proceedings fails without reasonable cause to surrender to custody he shall be guilty of an offence.

(2) If a person who—

(a) has been released on bail in criminal proceedings, and

(b) having reasonable cause therefor, has failed to surrender to custody,

fails to surrender to custody at the appointed place as soon after the appointed time as is reasonably practicable he shall be guilty of an offence.

(3) It shall be for the accused to prove that he had reasonable cause for his failure to surrender to custody.

(4) A failure to give to a person granted bail in criminal proceedings a copy of the record of the decision shall not constitute a reasonable cause for that person's failure to surrender to custody.

(5) An offence under subsection (1) or (2) above shall be punishable either on summary conviction or as if it were a criminal contempt of court.

(6) Where a magistrates' court convicts a person of an offence under subsection (1) or (2) above the court may, if it thinks—

(a) that the circumstances of the offence are such that greater punishment should be inflicted for that offence than the court has power to inflict, or

(b) in a case where it sends that person for trial to the Crown Court for another offence, that it would be appropriate for him to be dealt with for the offence under subsection (1) or (2) above by the court before which he is tried for the other offence,

commit him in custody or on bail to the Crown Court for sentence.

(7) A person who is convicted summarily of an offence under subsection (1) or (2) above and is committed to the Crown Court for sentence shall be liable to imprisonment for a term not exceeding 3 months or to a fine not exceeding level 5 on the standard scale or to both and a person who is so committed for sentence or is dealt with as for such a contempt shall be liable to imprisonment for a term not exceeding 12 months or to a fine or to both.

(8) In any proceedings for an offence under subsection (1) or (2) above a document purporting to be a copy of the part of the prescribed record which relates to the time and place appointed for the person specified in the record to surrender to custody and to be duly certified to be a true copy of that part of the record shall be evidence of the time and place appointed for that person to surrender to custody.

(9) For the purposes of subsection (8) above—

(a) 'the prescribed record' means the record of the decision of the court, officer or constable made in pursuance of section 5(1) of this Act:

(b) the copy of the prescribed record is duly certified if it is certified by the appropriate officer of the court or, as the case may be, by the constable who took the decision or a constable designated for the purpose by the officer in charge of the police station from which the person to whom the record relates was released;

(c) 'the appropriate officer' of the court is—

  (i) in the case of a magistrates' court, the designated officer for the court;

  (ii) in the case of the Crown Court, such officer as may be designated for the purpose in accordance with arrangements made by the Lord Chancellor;

  (iii) in the case of the High Court, such officer as may be designated for the purpose in accordance with arrangements made by the Lord Chancellor;

  (iv) in the case of the Court of Appeal, the registrar of criminal appeals or such other officer as may be authorised by him to act for the purpose;

  (v) in the case of the Courts-Martial Appeal Court, the registrar or such other officer as may be authorised by him to act for the purpose.

(10) Section 127 of the Magistrates' Courts Act 1980 shall not apply in relation to an offence under subsection (1) or (2) above.

(11) Where a person has been released on bail in criminal proceedings and that bail was granted by a constable, a magistrates' court shall not try that person for an offence under subsection (1) or (2) above in relation to that bail (the 'relevant offence') unless either or both of subsections (12) and (13) below applies.

(12) This subsection applies if an information is laid for the relevant offence within 6 months from the time of the commission of the relevant offence.

(13) This subsection applies if an information is laid for the relevant offence no later than 3 months from the time of the occurrence of the first of the events mentioned in subsection (14) below to occur after the commission of the relevant offence.

(14) Those events are—

(a) the person surrenders to custody at the appointed place;

(b) the person is arrested, or attends at a police station, in connection with the relevant offence or the offence for which he was granted bail;

(c) the person appears or is brought before a court in connection with the relevant offence or the offence for which he was granted bail.

7   Liability to arrest for absconding or breaking conditions of bail

(1) If a person who has been released on bail in criminal proceedings and is under a duty to surrender into the custody of a court fails to surrender to custody at the time appointed for him to do so the court may issue a warrant for his arrest.

(1A) Subsection (1B) applies if—

    (a) a person has been released on bail in connection with extradition proceedings,

    (b) the person is under a duty to surrender into the custody of a constable, and

    (c) the person fails to surrender to custody at the time appointed for him to do so.

(1B) A magistrates' court may issue a warrant for the person's arrest.

(2) If a person who has been released on bail in criminal proceedings absents himself from the court at any time after he has surrendered into the custody of the court and before the court is ready to begin or to resume the hearing of the proceedings, the court may issue a warrant for his arrest; but no warrant shall be issued under this subsection where that person is absent in accordance with leave given to him by or on behalf of the court.

(3) A person who has been released on bail in criminal proceedings and is under a duty to surrender into the custody of a court may be arrested without warrant by a constable—

    (a) if the constable has reasonable grounds for believing that that person is not likely to surrender to custody;

    (b) if the constable has reasonable grounds for believing that that person is likely to break any of the conditions of his bail or has reasonable grounds for suspecting that that person has broken any of those conditions; or

    (c) in a case where that person was released on bail with one or more surety or sureties, if a surety notifies a constable in writing that that person is unlikely to surrender to custody and that for that reason the surety wishes to be relieved of his obligations as a surety.

(4) A person arrested in pursuance of subsection (3) above—

    (a) shall, except where he was arrested within 24 hours of the time appointed for him to surrender to custody, be brought as soon as practicable and in any event within 24 hours after his arrest before a justice of the peace; and

    (b) in the said excepted case shall be brought before the court at which he was to have surrendered to custody.

(4A) A person who has been released on bail in connection with extradition proceedings and is under a duty to surrender into the custody of a constable may be arrested without warrant on any of the grounds set out in paragraphs (a) to (c) of subsection (3).

(4B) A person arrested in pursuance of subsection (4A) above shall be brought as soon as practicable and in any event within 24 hours after his arrest before a justice of the peace for the petty sessions area in which he was arrested.

(5) A justice of the peace before whom a person is brought under subsection (4) or (4B) above may, subject to subsections (5A) and (6) below, if of the opinion that that person—

    (a) is not likely to surrender to custody, or

    (b) has broken or is likely to break any condition of his bail,

remand him in custody or commit him to custody, as the case may require, or alternatively, grant him bail subject to the same or to different conditions, but if not of that opinion shall grant him bail subject to the same conditions (if any) as were originally imposed.

(5A) A justice of the peace may not remand a person in, or commit a person to, custody under subsection (5) if—

    (a) the person has attained the age of eighteen,

    (b) the person was released on bail in non-extradition proceedings,

    (c) the person has not been convicted of an offence in those proceedings, and

    (d) it appears to the justice of the peace that there is no real prospect that the person will be sentenced to a custodial sentence in the proceedings.

(6) Where a person brought before a justice under subsection (4) or (4B) is a child or young person and the justice does not grant him bail, subsection (5) above shall have effect subject to the provisions of section 91 of the Legal Aid, Sentencing and Punishment of Offenders Act 2012 (remands of children otherwise than on bail).

(7) In reckoning for the purposes of this section any period of 24 hours, no account shall be taken of Christmas Day, Good Friday or any Sunday.

(8) In the case of a person charged with murder or with murder and one or more other offences—

(a) subsections (4) and (5) have effect as if for 'justice of the peace' there were substituted 'judge of the Crown Court',

(b) subsection (6) has effect as if for 'justice' (in both places) there were substituted 'judge', and

(c) subsection (7) has effect, for the purposes of subsection (4), as if at the end there were added ', Saturday or bank holiday.'

SCHEDULE 1 PERSONS ENTITLED TO BAIL: SUPPLEMENTARY PROVISIONS

PART I DEFENDANTS ACCUSED OR CONVICTED OF IMPRISONABLE OFFENCES

Exceptions to right to bail

2 (1) The defendant need not be granted bail if the court is satisfied that there are substantial grounds for believing that the defendant, if released on bail (whether subject to conditions or not) would—

(a) fail to surrender to custody, or

(b) commit an offence while on bail, or

(c) interfere with witnesses or otherwise obstruct the course of justice, whether in relation to himself or any other person.

(2) Where the defendant falls within paragraph 6B, this paragraph does not apply unless—

(a) the court is of the opinion mentioned in paragraph 6A, or

(b) paragraph 6A does not apply by virtue of paragraph 6C.

2ZA (1) The defendant need not be granted bail if the court is satisfied that there are substantial grounds for believing that the defendant, if released on bail (whether subject to conditions or not), would commit an offence while on bail by engaging in conduct that would, or would be likely to, cause—

(a) physical or mental injury to an associated person; or

(b) an associated person to fear physical or mental injury.

(2) In sub-paragraph (1) 'associated person' means a person who is associated with the defendant within the meaning of section 62 of the Family Law Act 1996.

2A The defendant need not be granted bail if—

(a) the offence is an indictable offence or an offence triable either way, and

(b) it appears to the court that the defendant was on bail in criminal proceedings on the date of the offence.

2B The defendant need not to be granted bail in connection with extradition proceedings if—

(a) the conduct constituting the offence would, if carried out by the defendant in England or Wales, constitute an indictable offence or an offence triable either way; and

(b) it appears to the court that the defendant was on bail on the date of the offence.

3 The defendant need not be granted bail if the court is satisfied that the defendant should be kept in custody for his own protection or, if he is a child or young person, for his own welfare.

4 The defendant need not be granted bail if he is in custody in pursuance of a sentence of a court or a sentence imposed by an officer under the Armed Forces Act 2006.

5 The defendant need not be granted bail where the court is satisfied that it has not been practicable to obtain sufficient information for the purpose of taking the decisions required by this Part of this Schedule for want of time since the institution of the proceedings against him.

6 The defendant need not be granted bail if, having previously been released on bail in, or in connection with, the proceedings, the defendant has been arrested in pursuance of section 7.

6ZA If the defendant is charged with murder, the defendant may not be granted bail unless the court is of the opinion that there is no significant risk of the defendant committing, while on bail, an offence that would, or would be likely to, cause physical or mental injury to any person other than the defendant.

Paragraphs 6A and 6B (exception applicable to certain drug-users) apply only where courts separately notified by Secretary of State.

Restrictions of conditions of bail

8 (1) Subject to sub-paragraph (3) below, where the defendant is granted bail, no conditions shall be imposed under subsections (4) to (6B) or (7) (except subsection (6)(d) or (e)) of section 3 of this Act unless it appears to the court that it is necessary to do so—

>(a) for the purpose of preventing the occurrence of any of the events mentioned in paragraph 2(1) of this Part of the Schedule, or (b) for the defendant's own protection or, if he is a child or young person, for his own welfare or in his own interests.

(1A) No condition shall be imposed under section 3(6)(d) of this Act unless it appears to be necessary to do so for the purpose of enabling inquiries or a report to be made.

(2) Sub-paragraphs (1) and (1A) above also apply on any application to the court to vary the conditions of bail or to impose conditions in respect of bail which has been granted unconditionally.

(3) The restriction imposed by sub-paragraph (1A) above shall not apply to the conditions required to be imposed under section 3(6A) of this Act or operate to override the direction in section 11(3) of the Powers of Criminal Courts (Sentencing) Act 2000 to a magistrates' court to impose conditions of bail under section 3(6)(d) of this Act of the description specified in the said section 11(3) in the circumstances so specified.

9 In taking the decisions required by paragraph 2(1) or in deciding whether it is satisfied as mentioned in paragraph 2ZA(1), or of the opinion mentioned in paragraph 6ZA or 6A of this Part of this Schedule, the court shall have regard to such of the following considerations as appear to it to be relevant, that is to say—

>(a) the nature and seriousness of the offence or default (and the probable method of dealing with the defendant for it),
>
>(b) the character, antecedents, associations and community ties of the defendant,
>
>(c) the defendant's record as respects the fulfilment of his obligations under previous grants of bail in criminal proceedings,
>
>(d) except in the case of a defendant whose case is adjourned for inquiries or a report, the strength of the evidence of his having committed the offence or having defaulted,
>
>(e) if the court is satisfied that there are substantial grounds for believing that the defendant, if released on bail (whether subject to conditions or not), would commit an offence while on bail, the risk that the defendant may do so by engaging in conduct that would, or would be likely to, cause physical or mental injury to any person other than the defendant,

as well as to any others which appear to be relevant.

Magistrates' Courts Act 1980

17   Certain offences triable either way

(1) The offences listed in Schedule 1 to this Act shall be triable either way.

(2) Subsection (1) above is without prejudice to any other enactment by virtue of which any offence is triable either way.

17A   Initial procedure: accused to indicate intention as to plea

(1) This section shall have effect where a person who has attained the age of 18 years appears or is brought before a magistrates' court on an information charging him with an offence triable either way.

(2) Everything that the court is required to do under the following provisions of this section must be done with the accused present in court.

(3) The court shall cause the charge to be written down, if this has not already been done, and to be read to the accused.

(4) The court shall then explain to the accused in ordinary language that he may indicate whether (if the offence were to proceed to trial) he would plead guilty or not guilty, and that if he indicates that he would plead guilty—

    (a) the court must proceed as mentioned in subsection (6) below; and

    (b) he may (unless section 17D(2 below were to apply) be committed for sentence to the Crown Court under section 3 of the Powers of Criminal Courts (Sentencing) Act 2000 below if the court is of such opinion as is mentioned in subsection (2) of that section.

(5) The court shall then ask the accused whether (if the offence were to proceed to trial) he would plead guilty or not guilty.

(6) If the accused indicates that he would plead guilty the court shall proceed as if—

    (a) the proceedings constituted from the beginning the summary trial of the information; and

    (b) section 9(1) above was complied with and he pleaded guilty under it.

(7) If the accused indicates that he would plead not guilty section 18(1) below shall apply.

(8) If the accused in fact fails to indicate how he would plead, for the purposes of this section and section 18(1) below he shall be taken to indicate that he would plead not guilty.

(9) Subject to subsection (6) above, the following shall not for any purpose be taken to constitute the taking of a plea—

    (a) asking the accused under this section whether (if the offence were to proceed to trial) he would plead guilty or not guilty;

    (b) an indication by the accused under this section of how he would plead.

(10) If in respect of the offence the court receives a notice under section 51B or 51C of the Crime and Disorder Act 1998 (which relate to serious or complex fraud cases and to certain cases involving children respectively), the preceding provisions of this section and the provisions of section 17B below shall not apply, and the court shall proceed in relation to the offence in accordance with section 51 or, as the case may be, section 51A of that Act.

17B   Intention as to plea: absence of accused

(1) This section shall have effect where—

    (a) a person who has attained the age of 18 years appears or is brought before a magistrates' court on an information charging him with an offence triable either way.

    (b) the accused is represented by a legal representative,

    (c) the court considers that by reason of the accused's disorderly conduct before the court it is not practicable for proceedings under section 17A above to be conducted in his presence, and

    (d) the court considers that it should proceed in the absence of the accused.

(2) In such a case—

    (a) the court shall cause the charge to be written down, if this has not already been done, and to be read to the representative;

    (b) the court shall ask the representative whether (if the offence were to proceed to trial) the accused would plead guilty or not guilty;

    (c) if the representative indicates that the accused would plead guilty the court shall proceed as if the proceedings constituted from the beginning the summary trial of the information, and as if section 9(1) above was complied with and the accused pleaded guilty under it;

(d) if the representative indicates that the accused would plead not guilty section 18(1) below shall apply.

(3) If the representative in fact fails to indicate how the accused would plead, for the purposes of this section and section 18(1) below he shall be taken to indicate that the accused would plead not guilty.

(4) Subject to subsection (2)(c) above, the following shall not for any purpose be taken to constitute the taking of a plea—

   (a) asking the representative under this section whether (if the offence were to proceed to trial) the accused would plead guilty or not guilty;

   (b) an indication by the representative under this section of how the accused would plead.

17C   Intention as to plea adjournment

A magistrates' court proceeding under section 17A or 17B above may adjourn the proceedings at any time, and on doing so on any occasion when the accused is present may remand the accused, and shall remand him if—

   (a) on the occasion on which he first appeared, or was brought, before the court to answer to the information he was in custody or, having been released on bail, surrendered to the custody of the court; or

   (b) he has been remanded at any time in the course of proceedings on the information;

and where the court remands the accused, the time fixed for the resumption of proceedings shall be that at which he is required to appear or be brought before the court in pursuance of the remand or would be required to be brought before the court but for section 128(3A) below.

18   Initial procedure on information against adult for offence triable either way

(1) Sections 19 to 23 below shall have effect where a person who has attained the age of 18 years appears or is brought before a magistrates' court on an information charging him with an offence triable either way and—

   (a) he indicates under section 17A above that (if the offence were to proceed to trial) he would plead not guilty, or

   (b) his representative indicates under section 17B above that (if the offence were to proceed to trial) he would plead not guilty.

(2) Without prejudice to section 11(1) above, everything that the court is required to do under sections 19 to 22 below must be done before any evidence is called and, subject to subsection (3) below and section 23 below, with the accused present in court.

(3) The court may proceed in the absence of the accused in accordance with such of the provisions of sections 19 to 22 below as are applicable in the circumstances if the court considers that by reason of his disorderly conduct before the court it is not practicable for the proceedings to be conducted in his presence; and subsections (3) to (5) of section 23 below, so far as applicable, shall have effect in relation to proceedings conducted in the absence of the accused by virtue of this subsection (references in those subsections to the person representing the accused being for this purpose read as references to the person, if any, representing him).

(4) A magistrates' court proceeding under sections 19 to 23 below may adjourn the proceedings at any time, and on doing so on any occasion when the accused is present may remand the accused, and shall remand him if—

   (a) on the occasion on which he first appeared, or was brought, before the court to answer to the information he was in custody or, having been released on bail, surrendered to the custody of the court; or

   (b) he has been remanded at any time in the course of proceedings on the information;

and where the court remands the accused, the time fixed for the resumption of the proceedings shall be that at which he is required to appear or be brought before the court in pursuance of the remand or would be required to be brought before the court but for section 128(3A) below.

(5) The functions of a magistrates' court under sections 19 to 23 below may be discharged by a single justice, but this subsection shall not be taken as authorising—

    (a) the summary trial of an information (otherwise than in accordance with section 20(7) below); or

    (b) the imposition of a sentence,

by a magistrates' court composed of fewer than two justices.

19 Decision as to allocation

(1) The court shall decide whether the offence appears to it more suitable for summary trial or for trial on indictment.

(2) Before making a decision under this section, the court—

    (a) shall give the prosecution an opportunity to inform the court of the accused's previous convictions (if any); and

    (b) shall give the prosecution and the accused an opportunity to make representations as to whether summary trial or trial on indictment would be more suitable.

(3) In making a decision under this section, the court shall consider—

    (a) whether the sentence which a magistrates' court would have power to impose for the offence would be adequate; and

    (b) any representations made by the prosecution or the accused under subsection (2)(b) above,

and shall have regard to any allocation guidelines (or revised allocation guidelines) issued as definitive guidelines under section 122 of the Coroners and Justice Act 2009.

(4) Where—

    (a) the accused is charged with two or more offences; and

    (b) it appears to the court that the charges for the offences could be joined in the same indictment or that the offences arise out of the same or connected circumstances,

subsection (3)(a) above shall have effect as if references to the sentence which a magistrates' court would have power to impose for the offence were a reference to the maximum aggregate sentence which a magistrates' court would have power to impose for all of the offences taken together.

(5) In this section any reference to a previous conviction is a reference to—

    (a) a previous conviction by a court in the United Kingdom;

    (aa) a previous conviction by a court in another member State of a relevant offence under the law of that State; or

    (b) a previous finding of guilt in—

        (i) any proceedings under the Army Act 1955, the Air Force Act 1955 or the Naval Discipline Act 1957 (whether before a court-martial or any other court or person authorised under any of those Acts to award a punishment in respect of any offence); or

        (ii) any proceedings before a Standing Civilian Court.

(5A) For the purposes of subsection (5)(aa) an offence is 'relevant' if the offence would constitute an offence under the law of any part of the United Kingdom if it were done in that part at the time when the allocation decision is made.

(6) If, in respect of the offence, the court receives a notice under section 51B or 51C of the Crime and Disorder Act 1998 (which relate to serious or complex fraud cases and to certain cases involving children respectively), the preceding provisions of this section and sections 20, 20A and 21 below shall not apply, and the court shall proceed in relation to the offence in accordance with section 51(1) of that Act.

20 Procedure where summary trial appears more suitable

(1) If the court decides under section 19 above that the offence appears to it more suitable for summary trial, the following provisions of this section shall apply (unless they are excluded by section 23 below).

(2) The court shall explain to the accused in ordinary language—

(a) that it appears to the court more suitable for him to be tried summarily for the offence,

(b) that he can consent to be so tried or, if he wishes, be tried on indictment; and

(c) that if he is tried summarily and is convicted by the court, he may be committed for sentence to the Crown Court under section 3 or (if applicable) section 3A of the Powers of Criminal Courts (Sentencing) Act 2000 if the court is of such opinion as is mentioned in subsection (2) of the applicable section.

(3) The accused may then request an indication ('an indication of sentence') of whether a custodial sentence or non-custodial sentence would be more likely to be imposed if he were to be tried summarily for the offence and to plead guilty.

(4) If the accused requests an indication of sentence, the court may, but need not, give such an indication.

(5) If the accused requests and the court gives an indication of sentence, the court shall ask the accused whether he wishes, on the basis of the indication, to reconsider the indication of plea which was given, or is taken to have been given, under section 17A or 17B above.

(6) If the accused indicates that he wishes to reconsider the indication under section 17A or 17B above, the court shall ask the accused whether (if the offence were to proceed to trial) he would plead guilty or not guilty.

(7) If the accused indicates that he would plead guilty the court shall proceed as if—

(a) the proceedings constituted from that time the summary trial of the information; and

(b) section 9(1) above were complied with and he pleaded guilty under it.

(8) Subsection (9) below applies where—

(a) the court does not give an indication of sentence (whether because the accused does not request one or because the court does not agree to give one);

(b) the accused either—

(i) does not indicate, in accordance with subsection (5) above, that he wishes; or

(ii) indicates, in accordance with subsection (5) above, that he does not wish,

to reconsider the indication of plea under section 17A or 17B above; or

(c) the accused does not indicate, in accordance with subsection (6) above, that he would plead guilty.

(9) The court shall ask the accused whether he consents to be tried summarily or wishes to be tried on indictment and—

(a) if he consents to be tried summarily, shall proceed to the summary trial of the information; and

(b) if he does not so consent, shall proceed in relation to the offence in accordance with section 51(1) of the Crime and Disorder Act 1998.

20A   Procedure where summary trial appears more suitable: supplementary

(1) Where the case is dealt with in accordance with section 20(7) above, no court (whether a magistrates' court or not) may impose a custodial sentence for the offence unless such a sentence was indicated in the indication of sentence referred to in section 20 above.

(2) Subsection (1) above is subject to sections 3A(4), 4(8) and 5(3) of the Powers of Criminal Courts (Sentencing) Act 2000.

(3) Except as provided in subsection (1) above—

(a) an indication of sentence shall not be binding on any court (whether a magistrates' court or not); and

(b) no sentence may be challenged or be the subject of appeal in any court on the ground that it is not consistent with an indication of sentence.

(4) Subject to section 20(7) above, the following shall not for any purpose be taken to constitute the taking of a plea—

(a) asking the accused under section 20 above whether (if the offence were to proceed to trial) he would plead guilty or not guilty; or

(b) an indication by the accused under that section of how he would plead.

(5) Where the court gives an indication of sentence under section 20 above, it shall cause each such indication to be entered in the register.

(6) In this section and in section 20 above, references to a custodial sentence are to a custodial sentence within the meaning of section 76 of the Powers of Criminal Courts (Sentencing) Act 2000, and references to a non-custodial sentence shall be construed accordingly.

21 Procedure where trial on indictment appears more suitable

If the court decides under section 19 above that the offence appears to it more suitable for trial on indictment, the court shall tell the accused that the court has decided that it is more suitable for him to be tried on indictment, and shall proceed in relation to the offence in accordance with section 51(1) of the Crime and Disorder Act 1998.

22 Certain offences triable either way to be tried summarily if value involved is small

(1) If the offence charged by the information is one of those mentioned in the first column of Schedule 2 to this Act (in this section referred to as 'scheduled offences') then, the court shall, before proceeding in accordance with section 19 above, consider whether, having regard to any representations made by the prosecutor or the accused, the value involved (as defined in subsection (10) below) appears to the court to exceed the relevant sum.

For the purposes of this section the relevant sum is £5,000.

(2) If, where subsection (1) above applies, it appears to the court clear that, for the offence charged, the value involved does not exceed the relevant sum, the court shall proceed as if the offence were triable only summarily, and sections 19 to 21 above shall not apply.

(3) If, where subsection (1) above applies, it appears to the court clear that, for the offence charged, the value involved exceeds the relevant sum, the court shall thereupon proceed in accordance with section 19 above in the ordinary way without further regard to the provisions of this section.

(4) If, where subsection (1) above applies, it appears to the court for any reason not clear whether, for the offence charged, the value involved does or does not exceed the relevant sum, the provisions of subsections (5) and (6) below shall apply.

(5) The court shall cause the charge to be written down, if this has not already been done, and read to the accused, and shall explain to him in ordinary language—

> (a) that he can, if he wishes, consent to be tried summarily for the offence and that if he consents to be so tried, he will definitely be tried in that way; and
>
> (b) that if he is tried summarily and is convicted by the court, his liability to imprisonment or a fine will be limited as provided in section 33 below.

(6) After explaining to the accused as provided by subsection (5) above the court shall ask him whether he consents to be tried summarily and—

> (a) if he so consents, shall proceed in accordance with subsection (2) above as if that subsection applied;
>
> (b) if he does not so consent, shall proceed in accordance with subsection (3) above as if that subsection applied.

(8) Where a person is convicted by a magistrates' court of a scheduled offence, it shall not be open to him to appeal to the Crown Court against the conviction on the ground that the convicting court's decision as to the value involved was mistaken.

(9) If, where subsection (1) above applies, the offence charged is one with which the accused is charged jointly with a person who has not attained the age of 18 years, the reference in that subsection to any representations made by the accused shall be read as including any representations made by the person under 18.

(10) In this section 'the value involved', in relation to any scheduled offence, means the value indicated in the second column of Schedule 2 to this Act, measured as indicated in the third column of that Schedule; and in that Schedule 'the material time' means the time of the alleged offence.

(11) Where—

    (a) the accused is charged on the same occasion with two or more scheduled offences and it appears to the court that they constitute or form part of a series of two or more offences of the same or a similar character; or

    (b) the offence charged consists in incitement to commit two or more scheduled offences,

this section shall have effect as if any reference in it to the value involved were a reference to the aggregate of the values involved.

(12) Subsection (8) of section 12A of the Theft Act 1968 (which determines when a vehicle is recovered) shall apply for the purposes of paragraph 3 of Schedule 2 to this Act as it applies for the purposes of that section.

22A   Low-value shoplifting to be a summary offence

(1) Low-value shoplifting is triable only summarily.

(2) But where a person accused of low-value shoplifting is aged 18 or over, and appears or is brought before the court before the summary trial of the offence begins, the court must give the person the opportunity of electing to be tried by the Crown Court for the offence and, if the person elects to be so tried—

    (a) subsection (1) does not apply, and

    (b) the court must proceed in relation to the offence in accordance with section 51(1) of the Crime and Disorder Act 1998.

(3) 'Low-value shoplifting' means an offence under section 1 of the Theft Act 1968 in circumstances where—

    (a) the value of the stolen goods does not exceed £200,

    (b) the goods were being offered for sale in a shop or any other premises, stall, vehicle or place from which there is carried on a trade or business, and

    (c) at the time of the offence, the person accused of low-value shoplifting was, or was purporting to be, a customer or potential customer of the person offering the goods for sale.

(4) For the purposes of subsection (3)(a)—

    (a) the value of the stolen goods is the price at which they were being offered for sale at the time of the offence, and

    (b) where the accused is charged on the same occasion with two or more offences of low-value shoplifting, the reference to the value involved has effect as if it were a reference to the aggregate of the values involved.

(5) A person guilty of low-value shoplifting is liable on summary conviction to—

    (a) imprisonment for a period not exceeding 51 weeks (or 6 months, if the offence was committed before the commencement of section 281(4) and (5) of the Criminal Justice Act 2003),

    (b) a fine, or

    (c) both.

(6) A person convicted of low-value shoplifting by a magistrates' court may not appeal to the Crown Court against the conviction on the ground that the convicting court was mistaken as to whether the offence was one of low-value shoplifting.

(7) For the purposes of this section, any reference to low-value shoplifting includes aiding, abetting, counselling or procuring the commission of low-value shoplifting.

23   Power of court, with consent of legally represented accused, to proceed in his absence

(1) Where—

    (a) the accused is represented by a legal representative who in his absence signifies to the court the accused's consent to the proceedings for determining how he is to be tried for the offence being conducted in his absence; and

(b) the court is satisfied that there is good reason for proceeding in the absence of the accused,

the following provisions of this section shall apply.

(2) Subject to the following provisions of this section, the court may proceed in the absence of the accused in accordance with such of the provisions of sections 19 to 22 above as are applicable in the circumstances.

(3) If, in a case where subsection (1) of section 22 above applies, it appears to the court as mentioned in subsection (4) of that section, subsections (5) and (6) of that section shall not apply and the court—

(a) if the accused's consent to be tried summarily has been or is signified by the person representing him, shall proceed in accordance with subsection (2) of that section as if that subsection applied; or

(b) if that consent has not been and is not so signified, shall proceed in accordance with subsection (3) of that section as if that subsection applied.

(4) If the court decides under section 19 above that the offence appears to it more suitable for summary trial then—

(a) if the accused's consent to be tried summarily has been or is signified by the person representing him, section 20 above shall not apply, and the court shall proceed to the summary trial of the information; or

(b) if that consent has not been and is not so signified, section 20 above shall not apply and the court shall proceed to inquire into the information as examining justices and may adjourn the hearing without remanding the accused.

(5) If the court decides under section 19 above that the offence appears to it more suitable for trial on indictment, section 21 above shall not apply and the court shall proceed in relation to the offence in accordance with section 51(1) of the Crime and Disorder Act 1998.

25 Power to change from summary trial to committal proceedings, and vice versa

(1) Subsections (2) to (2D) below shall have effect where a person who has attained the age of 18 years appears or is brought before a magistrates' court on an information charging him with an offence triable either way.

(2) Where the court is required under section 20(9) above to proceed to the summary trial of the information, the prosecution may apply to the court for the offence to be tried on indictment instead.

(2A) An application under subsection (2) above—

(a) must be made before the summary trial begins; and

(b) must be dealt with by the court before any other application or issue in relation to the summary trial is dealt with.

(2B) The court may grant an application under subsection (2) above but only if it is satisfied that the sentence which a magistrates' court would have power to impose for the offence would be inadequate.

(2C) Where—

(a) the accused is charged on the same occasion with two or more offences; and

(b) it appears to the court that they constitute or form part of a series of two or more offences of the same or a similar character,

subsection (2B) above shall have effect as if references to the sentence which a magistrates' court would have power to impose for the offence were a reference to the maximum aggregate sentence which a magistrates' court would have power to impose for all of the offences taken together.

(2D) Where the court grants an application under subsection (2) above, it shall proceed in relation to the offence in accordance with section 51(1) of the Crime and Disorder Act 1998.

26 Power to issue summons to accused in certain circumstances

(1) Where, in the circumstances mentioned in section 23(1)(a) above, the court is not satisfied that there is good reason for proceeding in the absence of the accused, the justice or any of the justices

of which the court is composed may issue a summons directed to the accused requiring his presence before the court.

(2) In a case within subsection (1) above, if the accused is not present at the time and place appointed for the proceedings under section 19 or section 22(1) above, the court may issue a warrant for his arrest.

108   Right of appeal to the Crown Court

(1) A person convicted by a magistrates' court may appeal to the Crown Court—

    (a) if he pleaded guilty, against his sentence;

    (b) if he did not, against the conviction or sentence.

(1A) Section 14 of the Powers of Criminal Courts (Sentencing) Act 2000 (under which a conviction of an offence for which an order for conditional or absolute discharge is made is deemed not to be a conviction except for certain purposes) shall not prevent an appeal under this Act, whether against conviction or otherwise.

(2) A person sentenced by a magistrates' court for an offence in respect of which a probation order or an order for conditional discharge has been previously made may appeal to the Crown Court against the sentence.

(3) In this section 'sentence' includes any order made on conviction by a magistrates' court, not being—

    (b) an order for the payment of costs;

    (c) an order under section 37(1) of the Animal Welfare Act 2006 (which enables a court to order the destruction of an animal); or

    (d) an order made in pursuance of any enactment under which the court has no discretion as to the making of the order or its terms, and also includes a declaration of relevance, within the meaning of section 23 of the Football Spectators Act 1989.

(4) Subsection (3)(d) above does not prevent an appeal against a surcharge imposed under section 161A of the Criminal Justice Act 2003.

(5) Subsection (3) does not prevent an appeal against an order under section 21A of the Prosecution of Offences Act 1985 (criminal courts charge).

111   Statement of case by magistrates' court

(1) Any person who was a party to any proceeding before a magistrates' court or is aggrieved by the conviction, order, determination or other proceeding of the court may question the proceeding on the ground that it is wrong in law or is in excess of jurisdiction by applying to the justices composing the court to state a case for the opinion of the High Court on the question of law or jurisdiction involved; but a person shall not make an application under this section in respect of a decision against which he has a right of appeal to the High Court or which by virtue of any enactment passed after 31st December 1879 is final.

(2) An application under subsection (1) above shall be made within 21 days after the day on which the decision of the magistrates' court was given.

(3) For the purpose of subsection (2) above, the day on which the decision of the magistrates' court is given shall, where the court has adjourned the trial of an information after conviction, be the day on which the court sentences or otherwise deals with the offender.

(4) On the making of an application under this section in respect of a decision any right of the applicant to appeal against the decision to the Crown Court shall cease.

(5) If the justices are of opinion that an application under this section is frivolous, they may refuse to state a case, and, if the applicant so requires, shall give him a certificate stating that the application has been refused; but the justices shall not refuse to state a case if the application is made by or under the direction of the Attorney General.

(6) Where justices refuse to state a case, the High Court may, on the application of the person who applied for the case to be stated, make an order of mandamus requiring the justices to state a case.

SCHEDULE 1

5 Offences under the following provisions of the Offences against the Person Act 1861—

(a) section 16 (threats to kill);

(b) section 20 (inflicting bodily injury, with or without a weapon);

(c) section 26 (not providing apprentices or servants with food etc.);

(d) section 27 (abandoning or exposing child);

(e) section 34 (doing or omitting to do anything so as to endanger railway passengers);

(f) section 36 (assaulting a clergyman at a place of worship etc);

(g) section 38 (assault with intent to resist apprehension);

(h) section 47 (assault occasioning bodily harm ...);

(i) section 57 (bigamy);

(j) section 60 (concealing the birth of a child).

6 Offences under section 20 of the Telegraph Act 1868 (disclosing or intercepting messages).

19 Offences under section 36 of the Criminal Justice Act 1925 (forgery of passports etc.).

26 The following offences under the Criminal Law Act 1967—

(a) offences under section 4(1) (assisting offenders); and

(b) offences under section 5(1) (concealing arrestable offences and giving false information),

where the offence to which they relate is triable either way.

28 All indictable offences under the Theft Act 1968 except:—

(a) robbery, aggravated burglary, blackmail and assault with intent to rob;

(b) burglary comprising the commission of, or an intention to commit, an offence which is triable only on indictment;

(c) burglary in a dwelling if any person in the dwelling was subjected to violence or the threat of violence.

29 Offences under the following provisions of the Criminal Damage Act 1971—

(a) section 1(1) (destroying or damaging property);

(b) section 1(1) and (3) (arson);

(c) section 2 (threats to destroy or damage property);

(d) section 3 (possessing anything with intent to destroy or damage property).

33 Aiding, abetting, counselling or procuring the commission of any offence listed in the preceding paragraphs of this Schedule except paragraph 26.

Senior Courts Act 1981

48 Appeals to Crown Court

(1) The Crown Court may, in the course of hearing any appeal, correct any error or mistake in the order or judgment incorporating the decision which is the subject of the appeal.

(2) On the termination of the hearing of an appeal the Crown Court—

(a) may confirm, reverse or vary the decision appealed against; or

(b) may remit the matter with its opinion thereon to the authority whose decision is appealed against; or

(c) may make such other order in the matter as the court thinks just, and by such order exercise any power which the said authority might have exercised.

(3) Subsection (2) has effect subject to any enactment relating to any such appeal which expressly limits or restricts the powers of the court on the appeal.

(4) Subject to section 11(6) of the Criminal Appeal Act 1995, if the appeal is against a conviction or a sentence, the preceding provisions of this section shall be construed as including power to award any punishment, whether more or less severe than that awarded by the magistrates' court

whose decision is appealed against, if that is a punishment which that magistrates' court might have awarded.

(5) This section applies whether or not the appeal is against the whole of the decision.

(6) In this section 'sentence' includes any order made by a court when dealing with an offender, including—

(a) a hospital order under Part V of the Mental Health 1959 c. 72. Act 1959, with or without an order restricting discharge; and

(b) a recommendation for deportation made when dealing with an offender.

(7) The fact that an appeal is pending against an interim hospital order under the said Act of 1983 shall not affect the power of the magistrates' court that made it to renew or terminate the order or to deal with the appellant on its termination; and where the Crown Court quashes such an order but does not pass any sentence or make any other order in its place the Court may direct the appellant to be kept in custody or released on bail pending his being dealt with by that magistrates' court.

(8) Where the Crown Court makes an interim hospital order by virtue of subsection (2)—

(a) the power of renewing or terminating the order and of dealing with the appellant on its termination shall be exercisable by the magistrates' court whose decision is appealed against and not by the Crown Court; and

(b) that magistrates' court shall be treated for the purposes of section 38(7) of the said Act of 1983 (absconding offenders) as the court that made the order.

Police and Criminal Evidence Act 1984

1   Power of constable to stop and search persons, vehicles etc.

(1) A constable may exercise any power conferred by this section—

(a) in any place to which at the time when he proposes to exercise the power the public or any section of the public has access, on payment or otherwise, as of right or by virtue of express or implied permission; or

(b) in any other place to which people have ready access at the time when he proposes to exercise the power but which is not a dwelling.

(2) Subject to subsection (3) to (5) below, a constable—

(a) may search—

(i) any person or vehicle;

(ii) anything which is in or on a vehicle,

for stolen or prohibited articles, any article to which subsection (8A) below applies, or any firework to which subsection (8B) below applies; and

(b) may detain a person or vehicle for the purpose of such a search.

(3) This section does not give a constable power to search a person or vehicle or anything in or on a vehicle unless he has reasonable grounds for suspecting that he will find stolen or prohibited articles or any article to which subsection (8A) below applies, or any firework to which subsection (8B) below applies,

(4) If a person is in a garden or yard occupied with and used for the purposes of a dwelling or on other land so occupied and used, a constable may not search him in the exercise of the power conferred by this section unless the constable has reasonable grounds for believing—

(a) that he does not reside in the dwelling; and

(b) that he is not in the place in question with the express or implied permission of a person who resides in the dwelling.

(5) If a vehicle is in a garden or yard occupied with and used for the purposes of a dwelling or on other land so occupied and used, a constable may not search the vehicle or anything in or on it in the exercise of the power conferred by this section unless he has reasonable grounds for believing—

(a) that the person in charge of the vehicle does not reside in the dwelling; and

(b) that the vehicle is not in the place in question with the express or implied permission of a person who resides in the dwelling.

(6) If in the course of such a search a constable discovers an article which he has reasonable grounds for suspecting to be a stolen or prohibited article or any article to which subsection (8A) below applies or a firework to which subsection (8B) below applies, he may seize it.

(7) An article is prohibited for the purposes of this Part of this Act if it is—

(a) an offensive weapon; or

(b) an article—

(i) made or adapted for use in the course of or in connection with an offence to which this sub-paragraph applies; or

(ii) intended by the person having it with him for such use by him or by some other person.

(8) The offences to which subsection (7)(b)(i) above applies are—

(a) burglary;

(b) theft;

(c) offences under section 12 of the Theft Act 1968 (taking motor vehicle or other conveyance without authority);

(d) fraud (contrary to section 1 of the Fraud Act 2006);

(e) offences under section 1 of the Criminal Damage Act 1971 (destroying or damaging property).

(8A) This subsection applies to any article in relation to which a person has committed, or is committing or is going to commit an offence under section 139 of the Criminal Justice Act 1988.

(8B) This subsection applies to any firework which a person possesses in contravention of a prohibition imposed by fireworks regulations.

(8C) In this section—

(a) 'firework' shall be construed in accordance with the definition of 'fireworks' in section 1(1) of the Fireworks Act 2003; and

(b) 'fireworks regulations' has the same meaning as in that Act.

(9) In this Part of this Act 'offensive weapon' means any article—

(a) made or adapted for use for causing injury to persons; or

(b) intended by the person having it with him for such use by him or by some other person.

2 Provisions relating to search under section 1 and other powers

(1) A constable who detains a person or vehicle in the exercise—

(a) of the power conferred by section 1 above; or

(b) of any other power—

(i) to search a person without first arresting him; or

(ii) to search a vehicle without making an arrest,

need not conduct a search if it appears to him subsequently—

(i) that no search is required; or

(ii) that a search is impracticable.

(2) If a constable contemplates a search, other than a search of an unattended vehicle, in the exercise—

(a) of the power conferred by section 1 above; or

(b) of any other power, except the power conferred by section 6 below and the power conferred by section 27(2) of the Aviation Security Act 1982—

(i) to search a person without first arresting him; or

(ii) to search a vehicle without making an arrest,

it shall be his duty, subject to subsection (4) below, to take reasonable steps before he commences the search to bring to the attention of the appropriate person—

(i) if the constable is not in uniform, documentary evidence that he is a constable; and

(ii) whether he is in uniform or not, the matters specified in subsection (3) below;

and the constable shall not commence the search until he has performed that duty.

(3) The matters referred to in subsection (2)(ii) above are—
  (a) the constable's name and the name of the police station to which he is attached;
  (b) the object of the proposed search;
  (c) the constable's grounds for proposing to make it; and
  (d) the effect of section 3(7) or (8) below, as may be appropriate.

(4) A constable need not bring the effect of section 3(7) or (8) below to the attention of the appropriate person if it appears to the constable that it will not be practicable to make the record in section 3(1) below.

(5) In this section 'the appropriate person' means—
  (a) if the constable proposes to search a person, that person; and
  (b) if he proposes to search a vehicle, or anything in or on a vehicle, the person in charge of the vehicle.

(6) On completing a search of an unattended vehicle or anything in or on such a vehicle in the exercise of any such power as is mentioned in subsection (2) above a constable shall leave a notice—
  (a) stating that he has searched it;
  (b) giving the name of the police station to which he is attached;
  (c) stating that an application for compensation for any damage caused by the search may be made to that police station; and
  (d) stating the effect of section 3(8) below.

(7) The constable shall leave the notice inside the vehicle unless it is not reasonably practicable to do so without damaging the vehicle.

(8) The time for which a person or vehicle may be detained for the purposes of such a search is such time as is reasonably required to permit a search to be carried out either at the place where the person or vehicle was first detained or nearby.

(9) Neither the power conferred by section 1 above nor any other power to detain and search a person without first arresting him or to detain and search a vehicle without making an arrest is to be construed—
  (a) as authorising a constable to require a person to remove any of his clothing in public other than an outer coat, jacket or gloves; or
  (b) as authorising a constable not in uniform to stop a vehicle.

(10) This section and section 1 above apply to vessels, aircraft and hovercraft as they apply to vehicles.

3   Duty to make records concerning searches

(1) Where a constable has carried out a search in the exercise of any such power as is mentioned in section 2(1) above, other than a search—
  (a) under section 6 below; or
  (b) under section 27(2) of the Aviation Security Act 1982, he shall make a record of it in writing unless it is not practicable to do so.

(2) If a record of a search is required to be made by subsection (1) above—
  (a) in a case where the search results in a person being arrested and taken to a police station, the constable shall secure that the record is made as part of the person's custody record;
  (b) in any other case, the constable shall make the record on the spot, or, if that is not practicable, as soon as practicable after the completion of the search.

(6) The record of a search of a person or a vehicle—
  (a) shall state—
    (i)   the object of the search;
    (ii)   the grounds for making it;
    (iii) the date and time when it was made;
    (iv)   the place where it was made;

(v)   except in the case of a search of an unattended vehicle, the ethnic origins of the person searched or the person in charge of the vehicle searched (as the case may be); and

(b)   shall identify the constable who carried out the search

(6A) The requirement in subsection (6)(a)(v) above for a record to state a person's ethnic origins is a requirement to state—

(a)   the ethnic origins of the person as described by the person, and

(b)   if different, the ethnic origins of the person as perceived by the constable.

(7)   If a constable who conducted a search of a person made a record of it, the person who was searched shall be entitled to a copy of the record if he asks for one before the end of the period specified in subsection (9) below.

(8)   If—

(a)   the owner of a vehicle which has been searched or the person who was in charge of the vehicle at the time when it was searched asks for a copy of the record of the search before the end of the period specified in subsection (9) below; and

(b)   a record of the search of the vehicle has been made under this section,

the person who made the request shall be entitled to a copy.

(9)   The period mentioned in subsections (7) and (8) above is the period of 3 months beginning with the date on which the search was made.

(10) The requirements imposed by this section with regard to records of searches of vehicles shall apply also to records of searches of vessels, aircraft and hovercraft.

24   Arrest without warrant: constables

(1)   A constable may arrest without a warrant—

(a)   anyone who is about to commit an offence;

(b)   anyone who is in the act of committing an offence;

(c)   anyone whom he has reasonable grounds for suspecting to be about to commit an offence;

(d)   anyone whom he has reasonable grounds for suspecting to be committing an offence.

(2)   If a constable has reasonable grounds for suspecting that an offence has been committed, he may arrest without a warrant anyone whom he has reasonable grounds to suspect of being guilty of it.

(3)   If an offence has been committed, a constable may arrest without a warrant—

(a)   anyone who is guilty of the offence;

(b)   anyone whom he has reasonable grounds for suspecting to be guilty of it.

(4)   But the power of summary arrest conferred by subsection (1), (2) or (3) is exercisable only if the constable has reasonable grounds for believing that for any of the reasons mentioned in subsection (5) it is necessary to arrest the person in question.

(5)   The reasons are—

(a)   to enable the name of the person in question to be ascertained (in the case where the constable does not know, and cannot readily ascertain, the person's name, or has reasonable grounds for doubting whether a name given by the person as his name is his real name);

(b)   correspondingly as regards the person's address;

(c)   to prevent the person in question—

(i)   causing physical injury to himself or any other person;

(ii)   suffering physical injury;

(iii) causing loss of or damage to property;

(iv)   committing an offence against public decency (subject to subsection (6)); or

(v)   causing an unlawful obstruction of the highway;

(d)   to protect a child or other vulnerable person from the person in question;

(e)   to allow the prompt and effective investigation of the offence or of the conduct of the person in question;

(f) to prevent any prosecution for the offence from being hindered by the disappearance of the person in question.

(6) Subsection (5)(c)(iv) applies only where members of the public going about their normal business cannot reasonably be expected to avoid the person in question.

24A   Arrest without warrant: other persons

(1) A person other than a constable may arrest without a warrant—

(a) anyone who is in the act of committing an indictable offence;

(b) anyone whom he has reasonable grounds for suspecting to be committing an indictable offence.

(2) Where an indictable offence has been committed, a person other than a constable may arrest without a warrant—

(a) anyone who is guilty of the offence;

(b) anyone whom he has reasonable grounds for suspecting to be guilty of it.

(3) But the power of summary arrest conferred by subsection (1) or (2) is exercisable only if—

(a) the person making the arrest has reasonable grounds for believing that for any of the reasons mentioned in subsection (4) it is necessary to arrest the person in question; and

(b) it appears to the person making the arrest that it is not reasonably practicable for a constable to make it instead.

(4) The reasons are to prevent the person in question—

(a) causing physical injury to himself or any other person;

(b) suffering physical injury;

(c) causing loss of or damage to property; or

(d) making off before a constable can assume responsibility for him.

(5) This section does not apply in relation to an offence under Part 3 or 3A of the Public Order Act 1986.

27   Fingerprinting of certain offenders

(4) The Secretary of State may by regulations make provision for recording in national police records convictions for such offences as are specified in the regulations.

(4A) In subsection (4) 'conviction' includes—

(a) a caution within the meaning of Part 5 of the Police Act 1997; and

(b) a reprimand or warning given under section 65 of the Crime and Disorder Act 1998.

(5) Regulations under this section shall be made by statutory instrument and shall be subject to annulment in pursuance of a resolution of either House of Parliament.

28   Information to be given on arrest

(1) Subject to subsection (5) below, where a person is arrested, otherwise than by being informed that he is under arrest the arrest is not lawful unless the person arrested is informed that he is under arrest as soon as is practicable after his arrest.

(2) Where a person is arrested by a constable, subsection (1) above applies regardless of whether the fact of the arrest is obvious.

(3) Subject to subsection (5) below, no arrest is lawful unless the person arrested is informed of the ground for the arrest at the time of, or as soon as is practicable after, the arrest.

(4) Where a person is arrested by a constable, subsection (3) above applies regardless of whether the ground for the arrest is obvious.

(5) Nothing in this section is to be taken to require a person to be informed—

(a) that he is under arrest; or

(b) of the ground for the arrest,

if it was not reasonably practicable for him to be so informed by reason of his having escaped from arrest before the information could be given.

29   Voluntary attendance at police station etc.

Where for the purpose of assisting with an investigation a person attends voluntarily at a police station or at any other place where a constable is present or accompanies a constable to a police station or any such other place without having been arrested—

>   (a)   he shall be entitled to leave at will unless he is placed under arrest;
>   (b)   he shall be informed at once that he is under arrest if a decision is taken by a constable to prevent him from leaving at will.

30   Arrest elsewhere than at police station

>   (1)   Subsection (1A) applies where a person is, at any place other than a police station—
>   (a)   arrested by a constable for an offence, or
>   (b)   taken into custody by a constable after being arrested for an offence by a person other than a constable.

>   (1A)   The person must be taken by a constable to a police station as soon as practicable after the arrest.

>   (1B)   Subsection (1A) has effect subject to section 30A (release on bail) and subsection (7) (release without bail).

>   (2)   Subject to subsections (3) and (5) below, the police station to which an arrested person is taken under subsection (1A) above shall be a designated police station.

>   (3)   A constable to whom this subsection applies may take an arrested person to any police station unless it appears to the constable that it may be necessary to keep the arrested person in police detention for more than six hours.

>   (4)   Subsection (3) above applies—
>   (a)   to a constable who is working in a locality covered by a police station which is not a designated police station; and
>   (b)   to a constable belonging to a body of constables maintained by an authority other than a local policing body.

>   (5)   Any constable may take an arrested person to any police station if—
>   (a)   either of the following conditions is satisfied—
>   (i)   the constable has arrested him without the assistance of any other constable and no other constable is available to assist him;
>   (ii)   the constable has taken him into custody from a person other than a constable without the assistance of any other constable and no other constable is available to assist him; and
>   (b)   it appears to the constable that he will be unable to take the arrested person to a designated police station without the arrested person injuring himself, the constable or some other person.

>   (6)   If the first police station to which an arrested person is taken after his arrest is not a designated police station, he shall be taken to a designated police station not more than six hours after his arrival at the first police station unless he is released previously.

>   (7)   A person arrested by a constable at any place other than a police station must be released without bail if the condition in subsection (7A) is satisfied.

>   (7A)   The condition is that, at any time before the person arrested reaches a police station, a constable is satisfied that there are no grounds for keeping him under arrest or releasing him on bail under section 30A.

>   (8)   A constable who releases a person under subsection (7) above shall record the fact that he has done so.

>   (9)   The constable shall make the record as soon as is practicable after the release.

>   (10)   Nothing in subsection (1A) or in section 30A prevents a constable delaying taking a person to a police station or releasing him on bail if the condition in subsection (10A) is satisfied.

>   (10A)   The condition is that the presence of the person at a place (other than a police station) is necessary in order to carry out such investigations as it is reasonable to carry out immediately.

(11) Where there is any such delay the reasons for the delay must be recorded when the person first arrives at the police station or (as the case may be) is released on bail.

(12) Nothing in subsection (1A) or section 30A above shall be taken to affect—

(a) paragraphs 16(3) or 18(1) of Schedule 2 to the Immigration Act 1971;

(b) section 34(1) of the Criminal Justice Act 1972; or

(c) any provision of the Terrorism Act 2000.

(13) Nothing in subsection (10) above shall be taken to affect paragraph 18(3) of Schedule 2 to the Immigration Act 1971.

30A Bail elsewhere than at police station

(1) A constable may release on bail a person who is arrested or taken into custody in the circumstances mentioned in section 30(1).

(2) A person may be released on bail under subsection (1) at any time before he arrives at a police station.

(3) A person released on bail under subsection (1) must be required to attend a police station.

(3A) Where a constable releases a person on bail under subsection (1) —

(a) no recognizance for the person's surrender to custody shall be taken from the person,

(b) no security for the person's surrender to custody shall be taken from the person or from anyone else on the person's behalf,

(c) the person shall not be required to provide a surety or sureties for his surrender to custody, and

(d) no requirement to reside in a bail hostel may be imposed as a condition of bail.

(3B) Subject to subsection (3A), where a constable releases a person on bail under subsection (1) the constable may impose, as conditions of the bail, such requirements as appear to the constable to be necessary—

(a) to secure that the person surrenders to custody,

(b) to secure that the person does not commit an offence while on bail,

(c) to secure that the person does not interfere with witnesses or otherwise obstruct the course of justice, whether in relation to himself or any other person, or

(d) for the person's own protection or, if the person is under the age of 17, for the person's own welfare or in the person's own interests.

(4) Where a person is released on bail under subsection (1), a requirement may be imposed on the person as a condition of bail only under the preceding provisions of this section.

(5) The police station which the person is required to attend may be any police station.

37 Duties of custody officer before charge

(1) Where—

(a) a person is arrested for an offence—

(i) without a warrant; or

(ii) under a warrant not endorsed for bail,

the custody officer at each police station where he is detained after his arrest shall determine whether he has before him sufficient evidence to charge that person with the offence for which he was arrested and may detain him at the police station for such period as is necessary to enable him to do so.

(2) If the custody officer determines that he does not have such evidence before him, the person arrested shall be released either on bail or without bail, unless the custody officer has reasonable grounds for believing that his detention without being charged is necessary to secure or preserve evidence relating to an offence for which he is under arrest or to obtain such evidence by questioning him.

(3) If the custody officer has reasonable grounds for so believing, he may authorise the person arrested to be kept in police detention.

(4) Where a custody officer authorises a person who has not been charged to be kept in police detention, he shall, as soon as is practicable, make a written record of the grounds for the detention.

(5) Subject to subsection (6) below, the written record shall be made in the presence of the person arrested who shall at that time be informed by the custody officer of the grounds for his detention.

(6) Subsection (5) above shall not apply where the person arrested is, at the time when the written record is made—

    (a) incapable of understanding what is said to him;

    (b) violent or likely to become violent; or

    (c) in urgent need of medical attention.

(7) Subject to section 41(7) below, if the custody officer determines that he has before him sufficient evidence to charge the person arrested with the offence for which he was arrested, the person arrested—

    (a) shall be—

        (i) released without charge and on bail, or

        (ii) kept in police detention,

        for the purpose of enabling the Director of Public Prosecutions to make a decision under section 37B below,

    (b) shall be released without charge and on bail but not for that purpose,

    (c) shall be released without charge and without bail, or

    (d) shall be charged.

(7A) The decision as to how a person is to be dealt with under subsection (7) above shall be that of the custody officer.

(7B) Where a person is dealt with under subsection (7)(a) above, it shall be the duty of the custody officer to inform him that he is being released, or (as the case may be) detained, to enable the Director of Public Prosecutions to make a decision under section 37B below.

(8) Where—

    (a) a person is released under subsection (7)(b) or (c) above; and

    (b) at the time of his release a decision whether he should be prosecuted for the offence for which he was arrested has not been taken, it shall be the duty of the custody officer so to inform him.

(8A) Subsection (8B) applies if the offence for which the person is arrested is one in relation to which a sample could be taken under section 63B below and the custody officer—

    (a) is required in pursuance of subsection (2) above to release the person arrested and decides to release him on bail, or

    (b) decides in pursuance of subsection (7)(a) or (b) above to release the person without charge and on bail.

(8B) The detention of the person may be continued to enable a sample to be taken under section 63B, but this subsection does not permit a person to be detained for a period of more than 24 hours after the relevant time.

(9) If the person arrested is not in a fit state to be dealt with under subsection (7) above, he may be kept in police detention until he is.

(10) The duty imposed on the custody officer under subsection (1) above shall be carried out by him as soon as practicable after the person arrested arrives at the police station or, in the case of a person arrested at the police station, as soon as practicable after the arrest.

(15) In this Part of this Act—

'arrested juvenile' means a person arrested with or without a warrant who appears to be under the age of 17;

'endorsed for bail' means endorsed with a direction for bail in accordance with section 117(2) of the Magistrates' Courts Act 1980.

37A Guidance

(1) The Director of Public Prosecutions may issue guidance—

    (a) for the purpose of enabling custody officers to decide how persons should be dealt with under section 37(7) above or 37C(2) below, and

    (b) as to the information to be sent to the Director of Public Prosecutions under section 37B(1) below.

(2) The Director of Public Prosecutions may from time to time revise guidance issued under this section.

(3) Custody officers are to have regard to guidance under this section in deciding how persons should be dealt with under section 37(7) above or 37C (2) or 37CA (2) below.

(4) A report under section 9 of the Prosecution of Offences Act 1985 (report by DPP to Attorney General) must set out the provisions of any guidance issued, and any revisions to guidance made, in the year to which the report relates.

(5) The Director of Public Prosecutions must publish in such manner as he thinks fit—

    (a) any guidance issued under this section, and

    (b) any revisions made to such guidance.

(6) Guidance under this section may make different provision for different cases, circumstances or areas.

37B   Consultation with the Director of Public Prosecutions

(1) Where a person is dealt with under section 37(7)(a) above, an officer involved in the investigation of the offence shall, as soon as is practicable, send to the Director of Public Prosecutions such information as may be specified in guidance under section 37A above.

(2) The Director of Public Prosecutions shall decide whether there is sufficient evidence to charge the person with an offence.

(3) If he decides that there is sufficient evidence to charge the person with an offence, he shall decide—

    (a) whether or not the person should be charged and, if so, the offence with which he should be charged, and

    (b) whether or not the person should be given a caution and, if so, the offence in respect of which he should be given a caution.

(4) The Director of Public Prosecutions shall give written notice of his decision to an officer involved in the investigation of the offence.

(4A) Notice under subsection (4) above shall be in writing, but in the case of a person kept in police detention under section 37(7)(a) above it may be given orally in the first instance and confirmed in writing subsequently.

(5) If his decision is—

    (a) that there is not sufficient evidence to charge the person with an offence, or

    (b) that there is sufficient evidence to charge the person with an offence but that the person should not be charged with an offence or given a caution in respect of an offence,

a custody officer shall give the person notice in writing that he is not to be prosecuted.

(6) If the decision of the Director of Public Prosecutions is that the person should be charged with an offence, or given a caution in respect of an offence, the person shall be charged or cautioned accordingly.

(7) But if his decision is that the person should be given a caution in respect of the offence and it proves not to be possible to give the person such a caution, he shall instead be charged with the offence.

(8) For the purposes of this section, a person is to be charged with an offence either—

    (a) when he is in police detention after returning to a police station (whether because he has returned to answer bail, because he is detained under section 37(7)(a) above or for some other reason), or

    (b) in accordance with section 29 of the Criminal Justice Act 2003.

(9) In this section 'caution' includes—

    (a) a conditional caution within the meaning of Part 3 of the Criminal Justice Act 2003;

    (aa) a youth conditional caution within the meaning of Chapter 1 of Part 4 of the Crime and Disorder Act 1998, and

    (b) a youth caution under section 66ZA of that Act.

37C Breach of bail following release under section 37(7)(a)

(1) This section applies where—

(a) a person released on bail under section 37(7)(a) above or subsection (2)(b) below is arrested under section 46A below in respect of that bail, and

(b) at the time of his detention following that arrest at the police station mentioned in section 46A(2) below, notice under section 37B(4) above has not been given.

(2) The person arrested—

(a) shall be charged, or

(b) shall be released without charge, either on bail or without bail.

(3) The decision as to how a person is to be dealt with under subsection (2) above shall be that of a custody officer.

(4) A person released on bail under subsection (2)(b) above shall be released on bail subject to the same conditions (if any) which applied immediately before his arrest.

37CA Breach of bail following release under section 37(7)(b)

(1) This section applies where a person released on bail under section 37(7)(b) above or subsection (2)(b) below—

(a) is arrested under section 46A below in respect of that bail, and

(b) is being detained following that arrest at the police station mentioned in section 46A (2) below.

(2) The person arrested—

(a) shall be charged, or

(b) shall be released without charge, either on bail or without bail.

(3) The decision as to how a person is to be dealt with under subsection (2) above shall be that of a custody officer.

(4) A person released on bail under subsection (2)(b) above shall be released on bail subject to the same conditions (if any) which applied immediately before his arrest.

37D Release on bail under section 37: further provision

(1) Where a person is released on bail under section 37(7)(a) or section 37C(2)(b) or 37CA(2)(b) above, a custody officer may subsequently appoint a different time, or an additional time, at which the person is to attend at the police station to answer bail.

(2) The custody officer shall give the person notice in writing of the exercise of the power under subsection (1).

(3) The exercise of the power under subsection (1) shall not affect the conditions (if any) to which bail is subject.

(4) Where a person released on bail under section 37(7)(a) or 37C(2)(b) above returns to a police station to answer bail or is otherwise in police detention at a police station, he may be kept in police detention to enable him to be dealt with in accordance with section 37B or 37C above or to enable the power under subsection (1) above to be exercised.

(4A) Where a person released on bail under section 37(7)(b) or 37CA(2)(b) above returns to a police station to answer bail or is otherwise in police detention at a police station, he may be kept in police detention to enable him to be dealt with in accordance with section 37CA above or to enable the power under subsection (1) above to be exercised.

(5) If the person mentioned in subsection (4) or (4A) above is not in a fit state to enable him to be so dealt with as mentioned in that subsection or to enable that power under subsection (1) above to be exercised, he may be kept in police detention until he is.

(6) Where a person is kept in police detention by virtue of subsection (4), (4A) or (5) above, section 37(1) to (3) and (7) above (and section 40(8) below so far as it relates to section 37(1) to (3)) shall not apply to the offence in connection with which he was released on bail under section 37(7), 37C(2)(b) or 37CA(2)(b).

38   Duties of custody officer after charge

(1) Where a person arrested for an offence otherwise than under a warrant endorsed for bail is charged with an offence, the custody officer shall, subject to section 25 of the Criminal Justice and Public Order Act 1994, order his release from police detention, either on bail or without bail, unless—

    (a) if the person arrested is not an arrested juvenile—

        (i)   his name or address cannot be ascertained or the custody officer has reasonable grounds for doubting whether a name or address furnished by him as his name or address is his real name or address;

        (ii)   the custody officer has reasonable grounds for believing that the person arrested will fail to appear in court to answer to bail;

        (iii) in the case of a person arrested for an imprisonable offence, the custody officer has reasonable grounds for believing that the detention of the person arrested is necessary to prevent him from committing an offence;

        (iiia) in a case where a sample may be taken from the person under section 63B below, the custody officer has reasonable grounds for believing that the detention of the person is necessary to enable the sample to be taken from him;

        (iv)   in the case of a person arrested for an offence which is not an imprisonable offence, the custody officer has reasonable grounds for believing that the detention of the person arrested is necessary to prevent him from causing physical injury to any other person or from causing loss of or damage to property;

        (v)   the custody officer has reasonable grounds for believing that the detention of the person arrested is necessary to prevent him from interfering with the administration of justice or with the investigation of offences or of a particular offence; or

        (vi)   the custody officer has reasonable grounds for believing that the detention of the person arrested is necessary for his own protection;

    (b) if he is an arrested juvenile—

        (i)   any of the requirements of paragraph (a) above is satisfied (but, in the case of paragraph (a)(iiia) above, only if the arrested juvenile has attained the minimum age); or

        (ii)   the custody officer has reasonable grounds for believing that he ought to be detained in his own interests;

    (c) the offence with which the person is charged is murder.

(2) If the release of a person arrested is not required by subsection (1) above, the custody officer may authorise him to be kept in police detention but may not authorise a person to be kept in police detention by virtue of subsection (1)(a)(iiia) after the end of the period of six hours beginning when he was charged with the offence.

(2A) The custody officer, in taking the decisions required by subsection (1)(a) and (b) above (except (a)(i) and (vi) and (b)(ii)), shall have regard to the same considerations as those which a court is required to have regard to in taking the corresponding decisions under paragraph 2(1) of Part I of Schedule 1 to the Bail Act 1976 (disregarding paragraphs 1A and 2(2) of that Part).

(3) Where a custody officer authorises a person who has been charged to be kept in police detention, he shall, as soon as practicable, make a written record of the grounds for the detention.

(4) Subject to subsection (5) below, the written record shall be made in the presence of the person charged who shall at that time be informed by the custody officer of the grounds for his detention.

(5) Subsection (4) above shall not apply where the person charged is, at the time when the written record is made—

    (a) incapable of understanding what is said to him;

    (b) violent or likely to become violent; or

    (c) in urgent need of medical attention.

(6) Where a custody officer authorises an arrested juvenile to be kept in police detention under subsection (1) above, the custody officer shall, unless he certifies—

    (a) that, by reason of such circumstances as are specified in the certificate, it is impracticable for him to do so; or

(b) in the case of an arrested juvenile who has attained the age of 12 years, that no secure accommodation is available and that keeping him in other local authority accommodation would not be adequate to protect the public from serious harm from him, secure that the arrested juvenile is moved to local authority accommodation.

(6A) In this section—

'local authority accommodation' means accommodation provided by or on behalf of a local authority (within the meaning of the Children Act 1989);

'minimum age' means the age specified in section 63B(3)(b) below;

'secure accommodation' means accommodation provided for the purpose of restricting liberty;

'sexual offence' means an offence specified in Part 2 of Schedule 15 to the Criminal Justice Act 2003;

'violent offence' means murder or an offence specified in Part 1 of that Schedule;

and any reference, in relation to an arrested juvenile charged with a violent or sexual offence, to protecting the public from serious harm from him shall be construed as a reference to protecting members of the public from death or serious personal injury, whether physical or psychological, occasioned by further such offences committed by him.

(6B) Where an arrested juvenile is moved to local authority accommodation under subsection (6) above, it shall be lawful for any person acting on behalf of the authority to detain him.

(7) A certificate made under subsection (6) above in respect of an arrested juvenile shall be produced to the court before which he is first brought thereafter.

(7A) In this section 'imprisonable offence' has the same meaning as in Schedule 1 to the Bail Act 1976.

(8) In this Part of this Act 'local authority' has the same meaning as in the Children and Young Persons Act 1969.

39 Responsibilities in relation to persons detained

(1) Subject to subsections (2) and (4) below, it shall be the duty of the custody officer at a police station to ensure—

(a) that all persons in police detention at that station are treated in accordance with this Act and any code of practice issued under it and relating to the treatment of persons in police detention; and

(b) that all matters relating to such persons which are required by this Act or by such codes of practice to be recorded are recorded in the custody records relating to such persons.

(2) If the custody officer, in accordance with any code of practice issued under this Act, transfers or permits the transfer of a person in police detention—

(a) to the custody of a police officer investigating an offence for which that person is in police detention; or

(b) to the custody of an officer who has charge of that person outside the police station,

the custody officer shall cease in relation to that person to be subject to the duty imposed on him by subsection (1)(a) above; and it shall be the duty of the officer to whom the transfer is made to ensure that he is treated in accordance with the provisions of this Act and of any such codes of practice as are mentioned in subsection (1) above.

(3) If the person detained is subsequently returned to the custody of the custody officer, it shall be the duty of the officer investigating the offence to report to the custody officer as to the manner in which this section and the codes of practice have been complied with while that person was in his custody.

(4) If an arrested juvenile is moved to local authority accommodation under section 38(6) above, the custody officer shall cease in relation to that person to be subject to the duty imposed on him by subsection (1) above.

(6) Where—

(a) an officer of higher rank than the custody officer gives directions relating to a person in police detention; and

(b) the directions are at variance—

    (i)   with any decision made or action taken by the custody officer in the performance of a duty imposed on him under this Part of this Act; or

    (ii)   with any decision or action which would but for the directions have been made or taken by him in the performance of such a duty,

the custody officer shall refer the matter at once to an officer of the rank of superintendent or above who is responsible for the police station for which the custody officer is acting as custody officer.

40   Review of police detention

(1) Reviews of the detention of each person in police detention in connection with the investigation of an offence shall be carried out periodically in accordance with the following provisions of this section—

    (a) in the case of a person who has been arrested and charged, by the custody officer; and

    (b) in the case of a person who has been arrested but not charged, by an officer of at least the rank of inspector who has not been directly involved in the investigation.

(2) The officer to whom it falls to carry out a review is referred to in this section as a 'review officer'.

(3) Subject to subsection (4) below—

    (a) the first review shall be not later than six hours after the detention was first authorised;

    (b) the second review shall be not later than nine hours after the first;

    (c) subsequent reviews shall be at intervals of not more than nine hours.

(4) A review may be postponed—

    (a) if, having regard to all the circumstances prevailing at the latest time for it specified in subsection (3) above, it is not practicable to carry out the review at that time;

    (b) without prejudice to the generality of paragraph (a) above—

        (i)   if at that time the person in detention is being questioned by a police officer and the review officer is satisfied that an interruption of the questioning for the purpose of carrying out the review would prejudice the investigation in connection with which he is being questioned; or

        (ii)   if at that time no review officer is readily available.

(5) If a review is postponed under subsection (4) above it shall be carried out as soon as practicable after the latest time specified for it in subsection (3) above.

(6) If a review is carried out after postponement under subsection (4) above, the fact that it was so carried out shall not affect any requirement of this section as to the time at which any subsequent review is to be carried out.

(7) The review officer shall record the reasons for any postponement of a review in the custody record.

(8) Subject to subsection (9) below, where the person whose detention is under review has not been charged before the time of the review, section 37(1) to (6) above shall have effect in relation to him, but with the modifications specified in subsection (8A).

(8A) The modifications are—

    (a) the substitution of references to the person whose detention is under review for references to the person arrested;

    (b) the substitution of references to the review officer for references to the custody officer; and

    (c) in subsection (6), the insertion of the following paragraph after paragraph (a)— '(aa) asleep;'.

(9) Where a person has been kept in police detention by virtue of section 37(9) or 37D(5) above, section 37(1) to (6) shall not have effect in relation to him but it shall be the duty of the review officer to determine whether he is yet in a fit state.

(10) Where the person whose detention is under review has been charged before the time of the review, section 38(1) to (6B) above shall have effect in relation to him, but with the modifications specified in subsection (10A).

(10A) The modifications are—

(a) the substitution of a reference to the person whose detention is under review for any reference to the person arrested or to the person charged; and

(b) in subsection (5), the insertion of the following paragraph after *paragraph (a)*—

'(aa) asleep;'.

(11) Where—

(a) an officer of higher rank than the review officer gives directions relating to a person in police detention; and

(b) the directions are at variance—

(i) with any decision made or action taken by the review officer in the performance of a duty imposed on him under this Part of this Act; or

(ii) with any decision or action which would but for the directions have been made or taken by him in the performance of such a duty,

the review officer shall refer the matter at once to an officer of the rank of superintendent or above who is responsible for the police station for which the review officer is acting as review officer in connection with the detention.

(12) Before determining whether to authorise a person's continued detention the review officer shall give—

(a) that person (unless he is asleep); or

(b) any solicitor representing him who is available at the time of the review,

an opportunity to make representations to him about the detention.

(13) Subject to subsection (14) below, the person whose detention is under review or his solicitor may make representations under subsection (12) above either orally or in writing.

(14) The review officer may refuse to hear oral representations from the person whose detention is under review if he considers that he is unfit to make such representations by reason of his condition or behaviour.

40A   Use of telephone for review under s. 40

(1) A review under section 40(1)(b) may be carried out by means of a discussion, conducted by telephone, with one or more persons at the police station where the arrested person is held.

(2) But subsection (1) does not apply if—

(a) the review is of a kind authorised by regulations under section 45A to be carried out using video-conferencing facilities; and

(b) it is reasonably practicable to carry it out in accordance with those regulations.

(3) Where any review is carried out under this section by an officer who is not present at the station where the arrested person is held—

(a) any obligation of that officer to make a record in connection with the carrying out of the review shall have effect as an obligation to cause another officer to make the record;

(b) any requirement for the record to be made in the presence of the arrested person shall apply to the making of that record by that other officer; and

(c) the requirements under section 40(12) and (13) above for—

(i)   the arrested person, or

(ii) a solicitor representing him,

to be given any opportunity to make representations (whether in writing or orally) to that officer shall have effect as a requirement for that person, or such a solicitor, to be given an opportunity to make representations in a manner authorised by subsection (4) below.

(4) Representations are made in a manner authorised by this subsection—

(a) in a case where facilities exist for the immediate transmission of written representations to the officer carrying out the review, if they are made either—

(i)   orally by telephone to that officer; or

(ii)   in writing to that officer by means of those facilities; and

(b)   in any other case, if they are made orally by telephone to that officer.

(5)   In this section 'video-conferencing facilities' has the same meaning as in section 45A below.

41   Limits on period of detention without charge

(1)   Subject to the following provisions of this section and to sections 42 and 43 below, a person shall not be kept in police detention for more than 24 hours without being charged.

(2)   The time from which the period of detention of a person is to be calculated (in this Act referred to as 'the relevant time')—

(a)   in the case of a person to whom this paragraph applies, shall be—

(i)   the time at which that person arrives at the relevant police station; or

(ii)   the time 24 hours after the time of that person's arrest,

whichever is the earlier;

(b)   in the case of a person arrested outside England and Wales, shall be—

(i)   the time at which that person arrives at the first police station to which he is taken in the police area in England or Wales in which the offence for which he was arrested is being investigated; or

(ii)   the time 24 hours after the time of that person's entry into England and Wales, whichever is the earlier;

(c)   in the case of a person who—

(i)   attends voluntarily at a police station; or

(ii)   accompanies a constable to a police station without having been arrested, and is arrested at the police station, the time of his arrest;

(ca)   in the case of a person who attends a police station to answer bail granted under section 30A, the time when he arrives at the police station;

(d)   in any other case, except where subsection (5) below applies, shall be the time at which the person arrested arrives at the first police station to which he is taken after his arrest.

(3)   Subsection (2)(a) above applies to a person if—

(a)   his arrest is sought in one police area in England and Wales;

(b)   he is arrested in another police area; and

(c)   he is not questioned in the area in which he is arrested in order to obtain evidence in relation to an offence for which he is arrested;

and in sub-paragraph (i) of that paragraph 'the relevant police station' means the first police station to which he is taken in the police area in which his arrest was sought.

(4)   Subsection (2) above shall have effect in relation to a person arrested under section 31 above as if every reference in it to his arrest or his being arrested were a reference to his arrest or his being arrested for the offence for which he was originally arrested.

(5)   If—

(a)   a person is in police detention in a police area in England and Wales ('the first area'); and

(b)   his arrest for an offence is sought in some other police area in England and Wales ('the second area'); and

(c)   he is taken to the second area for the purposes of investigating that offence, without being questioned in the first area in order to obtain evidence in relation to it,

the relevant time shall be—

(i)   the time 24 hours after he leaves the place where he is detained in the first area; or

(ii)   the time at which he arrives at the first police station to which he is taken in the second area,

whichever is the earlier.

(6)   When a person who is in police detention is removed to hospital because he is in need of medical treatment, any time during which he is being questioned in hospital or on the way there or back by a police officer for the purpose of obtaining evidence relating to an offence shall be included in any

period which falls to be calculated for the purposes of this Part of this Act, but any other time while he is in hospital or on his way there or back shall not be so included.

(7) Subject to subsection (8) below, a person who at the expiry of 24 hours after the relevant time is in police detention and has not been charged shall be released at that time either on bail or without bail.

(8) Subsection (7) above does not apply to a person whose detention for more than 24 hours after the relevant time has been authorised or is otherwise permitted in accordance with section 42 or 43 below.

(9) A person released under subsection (7) above shall not be re-arrested without a warrant for the offence for which he was previously arrested unless new evidence justifying a further arrest has come to light since his release; but this subsection does not prevent an arrest under section 46A below.

42   Authorisation of continued detention

(1) Where a police officer of the rank of superintendent or above who is responsible for the police station at which a person is detained has reasonable grounds for believing that—

(a) the detention of that person without charge is necessary to secure or preserve evidence relating to an offence for which he is under arrest or to obtain such evidence by questioning him;

(b) an offence for which he is under arrest is an indictable offence; and

(c) the investigation is being conducted diligently and expeditiously,

he may authorise the keeping of that person in police detention for a period expiring at or before 36 hours after the relevant time.

(2) Where an officer such as is mentioned in subsection (1) above has authorised the keeping of a person in police detention for a period expiring less than 36 hours after the relevant time, such an officer may authorise the keeping of that person in police detention for a further period expiring not more than 36 hours after that time if the conditions specified in subsection (1) above are still satisfied when he gives the authorisation.

(3) If it is proposed to transfer a person in police detention to another police area, the officer determining whether or not to authorise keeping him in detention under subsection (1) above shall have regard to the distance and the time the journey would take.

(4) No authorisation under subsection (1) above shall be given in respect of any person—

(a) more than 24 hours after the relevant time; or

(b) before the second review of his detention under section 40 above has been carried out.

(5) Where an officer authorises the keeping of a person in police detention under subsection (1) above, it shall be his duty—

(a) to inform that person of the grounds for his continued detention; and

(b) to record the grounds in that person's custody record.

(6) Before determining whether to authorise the keeping of a person in detention under subsection (1) or (2) above, an officer shall give—

(a) that person; or

(b) any solicitor representing him who is available at the time when it falls to the officer to determine whether to give the authorisation,

an opportunity to make representations to him about the detention.

(7) Subject to subsection (8) below, the person in detention or his solicitor may make representations under subsection (6) above either orally or in writing.

(8) The officer to whom it falls to determine whether to give the authorisation may refuse to hear oral representations from the person in detention if he considers that he is unfit to make such representations by reason of his condition or behaviour.

(9) Where—

(a) an officer authorises the keeping of a person in detention under subsection (1) above; and

(b) at the time of the authorisation he has not yet exercised a right conferred on him by section 56 or 58 below,

the officer—
    (i)   shall inform him of that right;
    (ii)   shall decide whether he should be permitted to exercise it;
    (iii) shall record the decision in his custody record; and
    (iv)   if the decision is to refuse to permit the exercise of the right, shall also record the
           grounds for the decision in that record.

(10) Where an officer has authorised the keeping of a person who has not been charged in detention under subsection (1) or (2) above, he shall be released from detention, either on bail or without
bail, not later than 36 hours after the relevant time, unless—
    (a)   he has been charged with an offence; or
    (b)   his continued detention is authorised or otherwise permitted in accordance with section
          43 below.

(11) A person released under subsection (10) above shall not be re-arrested without a warrant
for the offence for which he was previously arrested unless new evidence justifying a further arrest
has come to light since his release; but this subsection does not prevent an arrest under section 46A
below.

43 Warrants of further detention

(1) Where, on an application on oath made by a constable and supported by an information, a
magistrates' court is satisfied that there are reasonable grounds for believing that the further detention of the person to whom the application relates is justified, it may issue a warrant of further detention authorising the keeping of that person in police detention.

(2) A court may not hear an application for a warrant of further detention unless the person to
whom the application relates—
    (a)   has been furnished with a copy of the information; and
    (b)   has been brought before the court for the hearing.

(3) The person to whom the application relates shall be entitled to be legally represented at the
hearing and, if he is not so represented but wishes to be so represented—
    (a)   the court shall adjourn the hearing to enable him to obtain representation; and
    (b)   he may be kept in police detention during the adjournment.

(4) A person's further detention is only justified for the purposes of this section or section 44
below if—
    (a)   his detention without charge is necessary to secure or preserve evidence relating to an
          offence for which he is under arrest or to obtain such evidence by questioning him;
    (b)   an offence for which he is under arrest is an indictable offence; and
    (c)   the investigation is being conducted diligently and expeditiously.

(5) Subject to subsection (7) below, an application for a warrant of further detention may be
made—
    (a)   at any time before the expiry of 36 hours after the relevant time; or
    (b)   in a case where—
        (i)   it is not practicable for the magistrates' court to which the application will be made to
               sit at the expiry of 36 hours after the relevant time; but
        (ii)   the court will sit during the 6 hours following the end of that period,
               at any time before the expiry of the said 6 hours.

(6) In a case to which subsection (5)(b) above applies—
    (a)   the person to whom the application relates may be kept in police detention until the ap-
          plication is heard; and
    (b)   the custody officer shall make a note in that person's custody record—
        (i)   of the fact that he was kept in police detention for more than 36 hours after the rel-
               evant time; and
        (ii)   of the reason why he was so kept.

(7) If—

    (a) an application for a warrant of further detention is made after the expiry of 36 hours after the relevant time; and

    (b) it appears to the magistrates' court that it would have been reasonable for the police to make it before the expiry of that period,

the court shall dismiss the application.

(8) Where on an application such as is mentioned in subsection (1) above a magistrates' court is not satisfied that there are reasonable grounds for believing that the further detention of the person to whom the application relates is justified, it shall be its duty—

    (a) to refuse the application; or

    (b) to adjourn the hearing of it until a time not later than 36 hours after the relevant time.

(9) The person to whom the application relates may be kept in police detention during the adjournment.

(10) A warrant of further detention shall—

    (a) state the time at which it is issued;

    (b) authorise the keeping in police detention of the person to whom it relates for the period stated in it.

(11) Subject to subsection (12) below, the period stated in a warrant of further detention shall be such period as the magistrates' court thinks fit, having regard to the evidence before it.

(12) The period shall not be longer than 36 hours.

(13) If it is proposed to transfer a person in police detention to a police area other than that in which he is detained when the application for a warrant of further detention is made, the court hearing the application shall have regard to the distance and the time the journey would take.

(14) Any information submitted in support of an application under this section shall state—

    (a) the nature of the offence for which the person to whom the application relates has been arrested;

    (b) the general nature of the evidence on which that person was arrested;

    (c) what inquiries relating to the offence have been made by the police and what further inquiries are proposed by them;

    (d) the reasons for believing the continued detention of that person to be necessary for the purposes of such further inquiries.

(15) Where an application under this section is refused, the person to whom the application relates shall forthwith be charged or, subject to subsection (16) below, released, either on bail or without bail.

(16) A person need not be released under subsection (15) above—

    (a) before the expiry of 24 hours after the relevant time; or

    (b) before the expiry of any longer period for which his continued detention is or has been authorised under section 42 above.

(17) Where an application under this section is refused, no further application shall be made under this section in respect of the person to whom the refusal relates, unless supported by evidence which has come to light since the refusal.

(18) Where a warrant of further detention is issued, the person to whom it relates shall be released from police detention, either on bail or without bail, upon or before the expiry of the warrant unless he is charged.

(19) A person released under subsection (18) above shall not be re-arrested without a warrant for the offence for which he was previously arrested unless new evidence justifying a further arrest has come to light since his release; but this subsection does not prevent an arrest under section 46A below.

44   Extension of warrants of further detention

(1) On an application on oath made by a constable and supported by an information a magistrates' court may extend a warrant of further detention issued under section 43 above if it is satisfied

that there are reasonable grounds for believing that the further detention of the person to whom the application relates is justified.

(2) Subject to subsection (3) below, the period for which a warrant of further detention may be extended shall be such period as the court thinks fit, having regard to the evidence before it.

(3) The period shall not—

(a) be longer than 36 hours; or

(b) end later than 96 hours after the relevant time.

(4) Where a warrant of further detention has been extended under subsection (1) above, or further extended under this subsection, for a period ending before 96 hours after the relevant time, on an application such as is mentioned in that subsection a magistrates' court may further extend the warrant if it is satisfied as there mentioned; and subsections (2) and (3) above apply to such further extensions as they apply to extensions under subsection (1) above.

(5) A warrant of further detention shall, if extended or further extended under this section, be endorsed with a note of the period of the extension.

(6) Subsections (2), (3) and (14) of section 43 above shall apply to an application made under this section as they apply to an application made under that section.

(7) Where an application under this section is refused, the person to whom the application relates shall forthwith be charged or, subject to subsection (8) below, released, either on bail or without bail.

(8) A person need not be released under subsection (7) above before the expiry of any period for which a warrant of further detention issued in relation to him has been extended or further extended on an earlier application made under this section.

45 Detention before charge—supplementary

(1) In sections 43 and 44 of this Act 'magistrates' court' means a court consisting of two or more justices of the peace sitting otherwise than in open court.

(2) Any reference in this Part of this Act to a period of time or a time of day is to be treated as approximate only.

45A Use of video-conferencing facilities for decisions about detention

(1) Subject to the following provisions of this section, the Secretary of State may by regulations provide that, in the case of an arrested person who is held in a police station, some or all of the functions mentioned in subsection (2) may be performed (notwithstanding anything in the preceding provisions of this Part) by an officer who—

(a) is not present in that police station; but

(b) has access to the use of video-conferencing facilities that enable him to communicate with persons in that station.

(2) Those functions are—

(a) the functions in relation to an arrested person taken to, or answering to bail at a police station that is not a designated police station which, in the case of an arrested person taken to a station that is a designated police station, are functions of a custody officer under section 37, 38 or 40 above; and

(b) the function of carrying out a review under section 40 (1)(b) above (review, by an officer of at least the rank of inspector, of the detention of person arrested but not charged).

(3) Regulations under this section shall specify the use to be made in the performance of the functions mentioned in subsection (2) above of the facilities mentioned in subsection (1) above.

(4) Regulations under this section shall not authorise the performance of any of the functions mentioned in subsection (2)(a) above by such an officer as is mentioned in subsection (1) above unless he is a custody officer for a designated police station.

(5) Where any functions mentioned in subsection (2) above are performed in a manner authorised by regulations under this section—

(a) any obligation of the officer performing those functions to make a record in connection with the performance of those functions shall have effect as an obligation to cause another officer to make the record; and

(b) any requirement for the record to be made in the presence of the arrested person shall apply to the making of that record by that other officer.

(6) Where the functions mentioned in subsection (2)(b) are performed in a manner authorised by regulations under this section, the requirements under section 40(12) and (13) above for—

(a) the arrested person, or

(b) a solicitor representing him,

to be given any opportunity to make representations (whether in writing or orally) to the person performing those functions shall have effect as a requirement for that person, or such a solicitor, to be given an opportunity to make representations in a manner authorised by subsection (7) below.

(7) Representations are made in a manner authorised by this subsection—

(a) in a case where facilities exist for the immediate transmission of written representations to the officer performing the functions, if they are made either—

(i) orally to that officer by means of the video-conferencing facilities used by him for performing those functions; or

(ii) in writing to that officer by means of the facilities available for the immediate transmission of the representations;

and

(b) in any other case if they are made orally to that officer by means of the video-conferencing facilities used by him for performing the functions.

(8) Regulations under this section may make different provision for different cases and may be made so as to have effect in relation only to the police stations specified or described in the regulations.

(9) Regulations under this section shall be made by statutory instrument and shall be subject to annulment in pursuance of a resolution of either House of Parliament.

(10) Any reference in this section to video-conferencing facilities, in relation to any functions, is a reference to any facilities (whether a live television link or other facilities) by means of which the functions may be performed with the officer performing them, the person in relation to whom they are performed and any legal representative of that person all able to both see and to hear each other.

46   Detention after charge

(1) Where a person—

(a) is charged with an offence; and

(b) after being charged—

(i) is kept in police detention; or

(ii) is detained by a local authority in pursuance of arrangements made under section 38(6) above,

he shall be brought before a magistrates' court in accordance with the provisions of this section.

(2) If he is to be brought before a magistrates' court in the local justice area in which the police station at which he was charged is situated, he shall be brought before such a court as soon as is practicable and in any event not later than the first sitting after he is charged with the offence.

(3) If no magistrates' court in that area is due to sit either on the day on which he is charged or on the next day, the custody officer for the police station at which he was charged shall inform the designated officer for the area that there is a person in the area to whom subsection (2) above applies.

(4) If the person charged is to be brought before a magistrates' court in a local justice area other than that in which the police station at which he was charged is situated, he shall be removed to that area as soon as is practicable and brought before such a court as soon as is practicable after his arrival in the area and in any event not later than the first sitting of a magistrates' court for that area after his arrival in the area.

(5) If no magistrates' court for that area is due to sit either on the day on which he arrives in the area or on the next day—

(a) he shall be taken to a police station in the area; and

(b) the custody officer at that station shall inform the designated officer in that area that there is a person in the area to whom subsection (4) applies.

(6) Subject to subsection (8) below, where the designated officer for a local justice area has been informed—

(a) under subsection (3) above that there is a person in the area to whom subsection (2) above applies; or

(b) under subsection (5) above that there is a person in the area to whom subsection (4) above applies,

the designated officer shall arrange for a magistrates' court to sit not later than the day next following the relevant day.

(7) In this section 'the relevant day'—

(a) in relation to a person who is to be brought before a magistrates' court in the local justice area in which the police station at which he was charged is situated, means the day on which he was charged; and

(b) in relation to a person who is to be brought before a magistrates' court in any other local justice area, means the day on which he arrives in the area.

(8) Where the day next following the relevant day is Christmas Day, Good Friday or a Sunday, the duty of the designated officer under subsection (6) above is a duty to arrange for a magistrates' court to sit not later than the first day after the relevant day which is not one of those days.

(9) Nothing in this section requires a person who is in hospital to be brought before a court if he is not well enough.

46A Power of arrest for failure to answer to police bail

(1) A constable may arrest without a warrant any person who, having been released on bail under this Part of this Act subject to a duty to attend at a police station, fails to attend at that police station at the time appointed for him to do so.

(1ZA) The reference in subsection (1) to a person who fails to attend at a police station at the time appointed for him to do so includes a reference to a person who—

(a) attends at a police station to answer to bail granted subject to the duty mentioned in section 47(3)(b),

(b) leaves the police station at any time before the beginning of proceedings in relation to a live link direction under section 57C of the Crime and Disorder Act 1998 in relation to him.

(1ZB) The reference in subsection (1) to a person who fails to attend at a police station at the time appointed for the person to do so includes a reference to a person who—

(a) attends at a police station to answer to bail granted subject to the duty mentioned in section 47(3)(b), but

(b) refuses to be searched under section 54B.

(1A) A person who has been released on bail under section 37(7)(a), 37C(2)(b) or 37CA(2)(b) above may be arrested without warrant by a constable if the constable has reasonable grounds for suspecting that the person has broken any of the conditions of bail.

(2) A person who is arrested under this section shall be taken to the police station appointed as the place at which he is to surrender to custody as soon as practicable after the arrest.

(3) For the purposes of—

(a) section 30 above (subject to the obligation in subsection (2) above), and

(b) section 31 above,

an arrest under this section shall be treated as an arrest for an offence.

47 Bail after arrest

(1) Subject to the following provisions of this section, a release on bail of a person under this Part of this Act shall be a release on bail granted in accordance with sections 3, 3A, 5 and 5A of the Bail Act 1976 as they apply to bail granted by a constable.

(1A) The normal powers to impose conditions of bail shall be available to him where a custody officer releases a person on bail under section 37(7)(A) above or section 38(1) above (including that subsection as applied by section 40(10) above) but not in any other cases.

In this subsection, 'the normal powers to impose conditions of bail' has the meaning given in section 3(6) of the Bail Act 1976.

(1B) No application may be made under section 5B of the Bail Act 1976 if a person is released on bail under section 37(7)(a) or 37C(2)(b) above.

(1C) Subsection (ID) to (IF) below apply where a person released on bail under section 37(7)(a) or 37C(2)(b) above is on bail subject to conditions.

(1D) The person shall not be entitled to make an application under section 43B of the Magistrates' Courts Act 1980.

(1E) A magistrates' court may, on an application by or on behalf of the person, vary the conditions of bail; and in this subsection 'vary' has the same meaning as in the Bail Act 1976.

(1F) Where a magistrates' court varies the conditions of bail under subsection (1E) above, that bail shall not lapse but shall continue subject to the conditions as so varied.

(2) Nothing in the Bail Act 1976 shall prevent the re-arrest without warrant of a person released on bail subject to a duty to attend at a police station if new evidence justifying a further arrest has come to light since his release.

(3) Subject to subsections (3A) and (4) below, in this Part of this Act references to 'bail' are references to bail subject to a duty—

    (a) to appear before a magistrates' court at such time and such place as the custody officer may appoint;

    (b) to attend at such police station at such time, as he may appoint for the purposes of—

        (i) proceedings in relation to a live link direction under section 57C of the Crime and Disorder Act 1998 (use of live link direction at preliminary hearings where accused is at police station); and

        (ii) any preliminary hearing in relation to which such a direction is given; or

    (c) to attend at such police station as the custody officer may appoint at such time as he may appoint for purposes other than those mentioned in paragraph (b).

(3A) Where a custody officer grants bail to a person subject to a duty to appear before a magistrates' court, he shall appoint for the appearance—

    (a) a date which is not later than the first sitting of the court after the person is charged with the offence; or

    (b) where he is informed by the designated officer for the relevant local justice area that the appearance cannot be accommodated until a later date, that later date.

(4) Where a custody officer has granted bail to a person subject to a duty to appear at a police station, the custody officer may give notice in writing to that person that his attendance at the police station is not required.

(6) Where a person who has been granted bail under this Part and either has attended at the police station in accordance with the grant of bail or has been arrested under section 46A above is detained at a police station, any time during which he was in police detention prior to being granted bail shall be included as part of any period which falls to be calculated under this Part of this Act.

(7) Where a person who was released on bail under this Part subject to a duty to attend at a police station is re-arrested, the provisions of this Part of this Act shall apply to him as they apply to a person arrested for the first time; but this subsection does not apply to a person who is arrested under section 46A above or has attended a police station in accordance with the grant of bail (and who accordingly is deemed by section 34(7) above to have been arrested for an offence) or to a person to whom section 46ZA(4) or (5) applies.

(8) In the Magistrates' Courts Act 1980—

(a) the following section shall be substituted for section 43—

43.—'Bail on arrest

(1) Where a person has been granted bail under the Police and Criminal Evidence Act 1984 subject to a duty to appear before a magistrates' court, the court before which he is to appear may appoint a later time as the time at which he is to appear and may enlarge the recognizances of any sureties for him at that time.

(2) The recognizance of any surety for any person granted bail subject to a duty to attend at a police station may be enforced as if it were conditioned for his appearance before a magistrates' court for the petty sessions area in which the police station named in the recognizance is situated.'; and

(b) the following subsection shall be substituted for section 117(3)—

'(3) Where a warrant has been endorsed for bail under subsection (1) above—

(a) where the person arrested is to be released on bail on his entering into a recognizance without sureties, it shall not be necessary to take him to a police station, but if he is so taken, he shall be released from custody on his entering into the recognizance; and

(b) where he is to be released on his entering into a recognizance with sureties, he shall be taken to a police station on his arrest, and the custody officer there shall (subject to his approving any surety tendered in compliance with the endorsement) release him from custody as directed in the endorsement.'.

47A Early administrative hearings conducted by justices' clerks

Where a person has been charged with an offence at a police station, any requirement imposed under this Part for the person to appear or be brought before a magistrates' court shall be taken to be satisfied if the person appears or is brought before a justices' clerk in order for the clerk to conduct a hearing under section 50 of the Crime and Disorder Act 1998 (early administrative hearings).

55 Intimate searches

(1) Subject to the following provisions of this section, if an officer of at least the rank of inspector has reasonable grounds for believing—

(a) that a person who has been arrested and is in police detention may have concealed on him anything which—

(i) he could use to cause physical injury to himself or others; and

(ii) he might so use while he is in police detention or in the custody of a court; or

(b) that such a person—

(i) may have a Class A drug concealed on him; and

(ii) was in possession of it with the appropriate criminal intent before his arrest,

he may authorise an intimate search of that person.

(2) An officer may not authorise an intimate search of a person for anything unless he has reasonable grounds for believing that it cannot be found without his being intimately searched.

(3) An officer may give an authorisation under subsection (1) above orally or in writing but, if he gives it orally, he shall confirm it in writing as soon as is practicable.

(3A) A drug offence search shall not be carried out unless the appropriate consent has been given in writing.

(3B) Where it is proposed that a drug offence search be carried out, an appropriate officer shall inform the person who is to be subject to it—

(a) of the giving of the authorisation for it; and

(b) of the grounds for giving the authorisation.

(4) An intimate search which is only a drug offence search shall be by way of examination by a suitably qualified person.

(5) Except as provided by subsection (4) above, an intimate search shall be by way of examination by a suitably qualified person unless an officer of at least the rank of inspector considers that this is not practicable.

(6) An intimate search which is not carried out as mentioned in subsection (5) above shall be carried out by a constable.

(7) A constable may not carry out an intimate search of a person of the opposite sex.

(8) No intimate search may be carried out except—

    (a) at a police station;

    (b) at a hospital;

    (c) at a registered medical practitioner's surgery; or

    (d) at some other place used for medical purposes.

(9) An intimate search which is only a drug offence search may not be carried out at a police station.

(10) If an intimate search of a person is carried out, the custody record relating to him shall state—

    (a) which parts of his body were searched; and

    (b) why they were searched.

(10A) If the intimate search is a drug offence search, the custody record relating to that person shall also state—

    (a) the authorisation by virtue of which the search was carried out;

    (b) the grounds for giving the authorisation; and

    (c) the fact that the appropriate consent was given.

(11) The information required to be recorded by subsections (10) and (10A) above shall be recorded as soon as practicable after the completion of the search.

(12) The custody officer at a police station may seize and retain anything which is found on an intimate search of a person, or cause any such thing to be seized and retained—

    (a) if he believes that the person from whom it is seized may use it—

        (i) to cause physical injury to himself or any other person;

        (ii) to damage property;

        (iii) to interfere with evidence; or

        (iv) to assist him to escape; or

    (b) if he has reasonable grounds for believing that it may be evidence relating to an offence.

(13) Where anything is seized under this section, the person from whom it is seized shall be told the reason for the seizure unless he is—

    (a) violent or likely to become violent; or

    (b) incapable of understanding what is said to him.

(13A) Where the appropriate consent to a drug offence search of any person was refused without good cause, in any proceedings against that person for an offence—

    (a) the court, in determining whether there is a case to answer;

    (b) a judge, in deciding whether to grant an application made by the accused under paragraph 2 of Schedule 3 to the Crime and Disorder Act 1998 (applications for dismissal); and

    (c) the court or jury, in determining whether that person is guilty of the offence charged, may draw such inferences from the refusal as appear proper.

(14) Every annual report—

    (a) under section 22 of the Police Act 1996; or

    (b) made by the Commissioner of Police of the Metropolis,

shall contain information about searches under this section which have been carried out in the area to which the report relates during the period to which it relates.

(15) The information about such searches shall include—

    (a) the total number of searches;

    (b) the number of searches conducted by way of examination by a suitably qualified person;

(c) the number of searches not so conducted but conducted in the presence of such a person; and

(d) the result of the searches carried out.

(16) The information shall also include, as separate items—

(a) the total number of drug offence searches; and

(b) the result of those searches.

(17) In this section—

'the appropriate criminal intent' means an intent to commit an offence under—

(a) section 5(3) of the Misuse of Drugs Act 1971 (possession of controlled drug with intent to supply to another); or

(b) section 68(2) of the Customs and Excise Management Act 1979 (exportation etc. with intent to evade a prohibition or restriction);

'appropriate officer' means—

(a) a constable,

(b) a person who is designated as a detention officer in pursuance of section 38 of the Police Reform Act 2002 if his designation applies paragraph 33D of Schedule 4 to that Act;

'Class A drug' has the meaning assigned to it by section 2(1)(b) of the Misuse of Drugs Act 1971;

'drug offence search' means an intimate search for a Class A drug which an officer has authorised by virtue of subsection (1)(b) above; and

'suitably qualified person' means—

(a) a registered medical practitioner; or

(b) a registered nurse.

55A   X-rays and ultrasound scans

(1) If an officer of at least the rank of inspector has reasonable grounds for believing that a person who has been arrested for an offence and is in police detention—

(a) may have swallowed a Class A drug, and

(b) was in possession of it with the appropriate criminal intent before his arrest,

the officer may authorise that an x-ray is taken of the person or an ultrasound scan is carried out on the person (or both).

(2) An x-ray must not be taken of a person and an ultrasound scan must not be carried out on him unless the appropriate consent has been given in writing.

(3) If it is proposed that an x-ray is taken or an ultrasound scan is carried out, an appropriate officer must inform the person who is to be subject to it—

(a) of the giving of the authorisation for it, and

(b) of the grounds for giving the authorisation.

(4) An x-ray may be taken or an ultrasound scan carried out only by a suitably qualified person and only at—

(a) a hospital,

(b) a registered medical practitioner's surgery, or

(c) some other place used for medical purposes.

(5) The custody record of the person must also state—

(a) the authorisation by virtue of which the x-ray was taken or the ultrasound scan was carried out,

(b) the grounds for giving the authorisation, and

(c) the fact that the appropriate consent was given.

(6) The information required to be recorded by subsection (5) must be recorded as soon as practicable after the x-ray has been taken or ultrasound scan carried out (as the case may be).

(7) Every annual report—

(a) under section 22 of the Police Act 1996, or

(b) made by the Commissioner of Police of the Metropolis,

must contain information about x-rays which have been taken and ultrasound scans which have been carried out under this section in the area to which the report relates during the period to which it relates.

(8) The information about such x-rays and ultrasound scans must be presented separately and must include—

(a) the total number of x-rays;

(b) the total number of ultrasound scans;

(c) the results of the x-rays;

(d) the results of the ultrasound scans.

(9) If the appropriate consent to an x-ray or ultrasound scan of any person is refused without good cause, in any proceedings against that person for an offence—

(a) the court, in determining whether there is a case to answer,

(b) a judge, in deciding whether to grant an application made by the accused under paragraph 2 of Schedule 3 to the Crime and Disorder Act 1998 (applications for dismissal), and

(c) the court or jury, in determining whether that person is guilty of the offence charged,

may draw such inferences from the refusal as appear proper.

(10) In this section 'the appropriate criminal intent', 'appropriate officer', 'Class A drug' and 'suitably qualified person' have the same meanings as in section 55 above.

56 Right to have someone informed when arrested

(1) Where a person has been arrested and is being held in custody in a police station or other premises, he shall be entitled, if he so requests, to have one friend or relative or other person who is known to him or who is likely to take an interest in his welfare told, as soon as is practicable except to the extent that delay is permitted by this section, that he has been arrested and is being detained there.

(2) Delay is only permitted—

(a) in the case of a person who is in police detention for an indictable offence; and

(b) if an officer of at least the rank of inspector authorises it.

(3) In any case the person in custody must be permitted to exercise the right conferred by subsection (1) above within 36 hours from the relevant time, as defined in section 41(2) above.

(4) An officer may give an authorisation under subsection (2) above orally or in writing but, if he gives it orally, he shall confirm it in writing as soon as is practicable.

(5) Subject to subsection (5A) below an officer may only authorise delay where he has reasonable grounds for believing that telling the named person of the arrest—

(a) will lead to interference with or harm to evidence connected with an indictable offence or interference with or physical injury to other persons; or

(b) will lead to the alerting of other persons suspected of having committed such an offence but not yet arrested for it; or

(c) will hinder the recovery of any property obtained as a result of such an offence.

(5A) An officer may also authorise delay where he has reasonable grounds for believing that—

(a) the person detained for the indictable offence has benefited from his criminal conduct, and

(b) the recovery of the value of the property constituting the benefit will be hindered by telling the named person of the arrest.

(5B) For the purposes of subsection (5A) above the question whether a person has benefited from his criminal conduct is to be decided in accordance with Part 2 of the Proceeds of Crime Act 2002.

(6) If a delay is authorised—

(a) the detained person shall be told the reason for it; and

(b) the reason shall be noted on his custody record.

(7) The duties imposed by subsection (6) above shall be performed as soon as is practicable.

(8) The rights conferred by this section on a person detained at a police station or other premises are exercisable whenever he is transferred from one place to another; and this section applies to each subsequent occasion on which they are exercisable as it applies to the first such occasion.

(9) There may be no further delay in permitting the exercise of the right conferred by subsection (1) above once the reason for authorising delay ceases to subsist.

(10) Nothing in this section applies to a person arrested or detained under the terrorism provisions.

58   Access to legal advice

(1) A person arrested and held in custody in a police station or other premises shall be entitled, if he so requests, to consult a solicitor privately at any time.

(2) Subject to subsection (3) below, a request under subsection (1) above and the time at which it was made shall be recorded in the custody record.

(3) Such a request need not be recorded in the custody record of a person who makes it at a time while he is at a court after being charged with an offence.

(4) If a person makes such a request, he must be permitted to consult a solicitor as soon as is practicable except to the extent that delay is permitted by this section.

(5) In any case he must be permitted to consult a solicitor within 36 hours from the relevant time, as defined in section 41(2) above.

(6) Delay in compliance with a request is only permitted—
    (a) in the case of a person who is in police detention for an indictable offence; and
    (b) if an officer of at least the rank of superintendent authorises it.

(7) An officer may give an authorisation under subsection (6) above orally or in writing but, if he gives it orally, he shall confirm it in writing as soon as is practicable.

(8) Subject to subsection (8A) below an officer may only authorise delay where he has reasonable grounds for believing that the exercise of the right conferred by subsection (1) above at the time when the person detained desires to exercise it—
    (a) will lead to interference with or harm to evidence connected with an indictable offence or interference with or physical injury to other persons; or
    (b) will lead to the alerting of other persons suspected of having committed such an offence but not yet arrested for it; or
    (c) will hinder the recovery of any property obtained as a result of such an offence.

(8A) An officer may also authorise delay where he has reasonable grounds for believing that—
    (a) the person detained for the indictable offence has benefited from his criminal conduct, and
    (b) the recovery of the value of the property constituting the benefit will be hindered by the exercise of the right conferred by subsection (1) above.

(8B) For the purposes of subsection (8A) above the question whether a person has benefited from his criminal conduct is to be decided in accordance with Part 2 of the Proceeds of Crime Act 2002.

(9) If delay is authorised—
    (a) the detained person shall be told the reason for it; and
    (b) the reason shall be noted on his custody record.

(10) The duties imposed by subsection (9) above shall be performed as soon as is practicable.

(11) There may be no further delay in permitting the exercise of the right conferred by subsection (1) above once the reason for authorising delay ceases to subsist.

(12) Nothing in this section applies to a person arrested or detained under the terrorism provisions.

61   Fingerprinting

(1) Except as provided by this section no person's fingerprints may be taken without the appropriate consent.

(2) Consent to the taking of a person's fingerprints must be in writing if it is given at a time when he is at a police station.

(3) The fingerprints of a person detained at a police station may be taken without the appropriate consent if—

    (a) he is detained in consequence of his arrest for a recordable offence; and

    (b) he has not had his fingerprints taken in the course of the investigation of the offence by the police.

(3A) Where a person mentioned in paragraph (a) of subsection (3) or (4) has already had his fingerprints taken in the course of the investigation of the offence by the police, that fact shall be disregarded for the purposes of that subsection if—

    (a) the fingerprints taken on the previous occasion do not constitute a complete set of his fingerprints; or

    (b) some or all of the fingerprints taken on the previous occasion are not of sufficient quality to allow satisfactory analysis, comparison or matching (whether in the case in question or generally).

(4) The fingerprints of a person detained at a police station may be taken without the appropriate consent if—

    (a) he has been charged with a recordable offence or informed that he will be reported for such an offence; and

    (b) he has not had his fingerprints taken in the course of the investigation of the offence by the police.

(4A) The fingerprints of a person who has answered to bail at a court or police station may be taken without the appropriate consent at the court or station if—

    (a) the court, or

    (b) an officer of at least the rank of inspector,

authorises them to be taken.

(4B) A court or officer may only give an authorisation under subsection (4A) if—

    (a) the person who has answered to bail has answered to it for a person whose fingerprints were taken on a previous occasion and there are reasonable grounds for believing that he is not the same person; or

    (b) the person who has answered to bail claims to be a different person from a person whose fingerprints were taken on a previous occasion.

(5) An officer may give an authorisation under subsection (4A) above orally or in writing but, if he gives it orally, he shall confirm it in writing as soon as is practicable.

(5A) The fingerprints of a person may be taken without the appropriate consent if (before or after the coming into force of this subsection) he has been arrested for a recordable offence and released and—

    (a) in the case of a person who is on bail, he has not had his fingerprints taken in the course of the investigation of the offence by the police; or

    (b) in any case, he has had his fingerprints taken in the course of that investigation but

        (i) subsection (3A)(a) or (b) above applies, or

        (ii) subsection (5C) below applies.

(5B) The fingerprints of a person not detained at a police station may be taken without the appropriate consent if (before or after the coming into force of this subsection) he has been charged with a recordable offence or informed that he will be reported for such an offence and—

    (a) he has not had his fingerprints taken in the course of the investigation of the offence by the police; or

    (b) he has had his fingerprints taken in the course of that investigation but

        (i) subsection (3A)(a) or (b) above applies, or

        (ii) subsection (5C) below applies.

(5C) This subsection applies where—

    (a) the investigation was discontinued but subsequently resumed, and

(b) before the resumption of the investigation the fingerprints were destroyed pursuant to section 63D(3) below.

(6) Any person's fingerprints may be taken without the appropriate consent if—

(a) he has been convicted of a recordable offence;

(b) he has been given a caution in respect of a recordable offence which, at the time of the caution, he has admitted, and either of the conditions mentioned in subsection (6ZA) below is met.

(6ZA) The conditions referred to in subsection (6) above are—

(a) the person has not had his fingerprints taken since he was convicted or cautioned;

(b) he has had his fingerprints taken since then but subsection (3A)(a) or (b) above applies.

(6ZB) Fingerprints may only be taken as specified in subsection (6) above with the authorisation of an officer of at least the rank of inspector.

(6ZC) An officer may only give an authorisation under subsection (6ZB) above if the officer is satisfied that taking the fingerprints is necessary to assist in the prevention or detection of crime.

(6A) A constable may take a person's fingerprints without the appropriate consent if—

(a) the constable reasonably suspects that the person is committing or attempting to commit an offence, or has committed or attempted to commit an offence; and

(b) either of the two conditions mentioned in subsection (6B) is met.

(6B) The conditions are that—

(a) the name of the person is unknown to, and cannot be readily ascertained by, the constable;

(b) the constable has reasonable grounds for doubting whether a name furnished by the person as his name is his real name.

(6C) The taking of fingerprints by virtue of subsection (6A) does not count for any of the purposes of this Act as taking them in the course of the investigation of an offence by the police.

(6D) Subject to this section, the fingerprints of a person may be taken without the appropriate consent if—

(a) under the law in force in a country or territory outside England and Wales the person has been convicted of an offence under that law (whether before or after the coming into force of this subsection and whether or not he has been punished for it);

(b) the act constituting the offence would constitute a qualifying offence if done in England and Wales (whether or not it constituted such an offence when the person was convicted); and

(c) either of the conditions mentioned in subsection (6E) below is met.

(6E) The conditions referred to in subsection (6D)(c) above are—

(a) the person has not had his fingerprints taken on a previous occasion under subsection (6D) above;

(b) he has had his fingerprints taken on a previous occasion under that subsection but subsection (3A)(a) or (b) above applies.

(6F) Fingerprints may only be taken as specified in subsection (6D) above with the authorisation of an officer of at least the rank of inspector.

(6G) An officer may only give an authorisation under subsection (6F) above if the officer is satisfied that taking the fingerprints is necessary to assist in the prevention or detection of crime.

(7) Where a person's fingerprints are taken without the appropriate consent by virtue of any power conferred by this section—

(a) before the fingerprints are taken, the person shall be informed of—

(i) the reason for taking the fingerprints;

(ii) the power by virtue of which they are taken; and

(iii) in a case where the authorisation of the court or an officer is required for the exercise of the power, the fact that the authorisation has been given; and

(b) those matters shall be recorded as soon as practicable after the fingerprints are taken.

(7A) If a person's fingerprints are taken at a police station, or by virtue of subsection (4A), (6A) at a place other than a police station, whether with or without the appropriate consent—

(a) before the fingerprints are taken, an officer shall inform him that they may be the subject of a speculative search; and

(b) the fact that the person has been informed of this possibility shall be recorded as soon as is practicable after the fingerprints have been taken.

(8) If he is detained at a police station when the fingerprints are taken, the matters referred to in subsection (7)(a)(i) to (iii) above and, in the case falling within subsection (7A) above, the fact referred to in paragraph (b) of that subsection shall be recorded on his custody record.

(8B) Any power under this section to take the fingerprints of a person without the appropriate consent, if not otherwise specified to be exercisable by a constable, shall be exercisable by a constable.

(9) Nothing in this section—

(a) affects any power conferred by paragraph 18(2) of Schedule 2 to the Immigration Act 1971; or

(b) applies to a person arrested or detained under the terrorism provisions.

(10) Nothing in this section applies to a person arrested under an extradition arrest power.

61A Impressions of footwear

(1) Except as provided by this section, no impression of a person's footwear may be taken without the appropriate consent.

(2) Consent to the taking of an impression of a person's footwear must be in writing if it is given at a time when he is at a police station.

(3) Where a person is detained at a police station, an impression of his footwear may be taken without the appropriate consent if—

(a) he is detained in consequence of his arrest for a recordable offence, or has been charged with a recordable offence, or informed that he will be reported for a recordable offence; and

(b) he has not had an impression taken of his footwear in the course of the investigation of the offence by the police.

(4) Where a person mentioned in paragraph (a) of subsection (3) above has already had an impression taken of his footwear in the course of the investigation of the offence by the police, that fact shall be disregarded for the purposes of that subsection if the impression of his footwear taken previously is—

(a) incomplete; or

(b) is not of sufficient quality to allow satisfactory analysis, comparison or matching (whether in the case in question or generally).

(5) If an impression of a person's footwear is taken at a police station, whether with or without the appropriate consent—

(a) before it is taken, an officer shall inform him that it may be the subject of a speculative search; and

(b) the fact that the person has been informed of this possibility shall be recorded as soon as is practicable after the impression has been taken, and if he is detained at a police station, the record shall be made on his custody record.

(6) In a case where, by virtue of subsection (3) above, an impression of a person's footwear is taken without the appropriate consent—

(a) he shall be told the reason before it is taken; and

(b) the reason shall be recorded on his custody record as soon as is practicable after the impression is taken.

(7) The power to take an impression of the footwear of a person detained at a police station without the appropriate consent shall be exercisable by any constable.

(8) Nothing in this section applies to any person—

(a) arrested or detained under the terrorism provisions;

(b) arrested under an extradition arrest power.

62   Intimate samples

(1)   Subject to section 63B below an intimate sample may be taken from a person in police detention only—

    (a)   if a police officer of at least the rank of inspector authorises it to be taken; and

    (b)   if the appropriate consent is given.

(1A)   An intimate sample may be taken from a person who is not in police detention but from whom, in the course of the investigation of an offence, two or more non-intimate samples suitable for the same means of analysis have been taken which have proved insufficient—

    (a)   if a police officer of at least the rank of inspector authorises it to be taken; and

    (b)   if the appropriate consent is given.

(2)   An officer may only give an authorisation under subsection (1) or (1A) above if he has reasonable grounds—

    (a)   for suspecting the involvement of the person from whom the sample is to be taken in a recordable offence; and

    (b)   for believing that the sample will tend to confirm or disprove his involvement.

(2A)   An intimate sample may be taken from a person where—

    (a)   two or more non-intimate samples suitable for the same means of analysis have been taken from the person under section 63(3E) below (persons convicted of offences outside England and Wales etc) but have proved insufficient;

    (b)   a police officer of at least the rank of inspector authorises it to be taken; and

    (c)   the appropriate consent is given.

(2B)   An officer may only give an authorisation under subsection (2A) above if the officer is satisfied that taking the sample is necessary to assist in the prevention or detection of crime.

(3)   An officer may give an authorisation under subsection (1) or (1A) or (2A) above orally or in writing but, if he gives it orally, he shall confirm it in writing as soon as is practicable.

(4)   The appropriate consent must be given in writing.

(5)   Before an intimate sample is taken from a person, an officer shall inform him of the following—

    (a)   the reason for taking the sample;

    (b)   the fact that authorisation has been given and the provision of this section under which it has been given; and

    (c)   if the sample was taken at a police station, the fact that the sample may be the subject of a speculative search.

(6)   The reason referred to in subsection (5)(a) above must include, except in a case where the sample is taken under subsection (2A) above, a statement of the nature of the offence in which it is suspected that the person has been involved.

(7)   After an intimate sample has been taken from a person, the following shall be recorded as soon as practicable—

    (a)   the matters referred to in subsection (5)(a) and (b) above;

    (b)   if the sample was taken at a police station, the fact that the person has been informed as specified in subsection (5)(c) above; and

    (c)   the fact that the appropriate consent was given.

(8)   If an intimate sample is taken from a person detained at a police station, the matters required to be recorded by subsection (7) above shall be recorded in his custody record.

(9)   In the case of an intimate sample which is a dental impression, the sample may be taken from a person only by a registered dentist.

(9A)   In the case of any other form of intimate sample, except in the case of a sample of urine, the sample may be taken from a person only by—

    (a)   a registered medical practitioner; or

    (b)   a registered health care professional.

(10) Where the appropriate consent to the taking of an intimate sample from a person was refused without good cause, in any proceedings against that person for an offence—

    (a)   the court, in determining—

        (ii) whether there is a case to answer; and

    (aa) a judge, in deciding whether to grant an application made by the accused under paragraph 2 of Schedule 3 to the Crime and Disorder Act 1998 (applications for dismissal); and

    (b)   the court or jury, in determining whether that person is guilty of the offence charged,

may draw such inferences from the refusal as appear proper.

(11) Nothing in this section applies to the taking of a specimen for the purposes of any provisions of sections 4 to 11 of the Road Traffic Act 1988 or of sections 26 to 38 of the Transport and Works Act 1992.

(12) Nothing in this section applies to a person arrested or detained under the terrorism provisions; and subsection (1A) shall not apply where the non-intimate samples mentioned in that subsection were taken under paragraph 10 of Schedule 8 to the Terrorism Act 2000.

63   Other samples

(1) Except as provided by this section, a non-intimate sample may not be taken from a person without the appropriate consent.

(2) Consent to the taking of a non-intimate sample must be given in writing.

(2A) A non-intimate sample may be taken from a person without the appropriate consent if two conditions are satisfied.

(2B) The first is that the person is in police detention in consequence of his arrest for a recordable offence.

(2C) The second is that—

    (a) he has not had a non-intimate sample of the same type and from the same part of the body taken in the course of the investigation of the offence by the police, or

    (b) he has had such a sample taken but it proved insufficient.

(3) A non-intimate sample may be taken from a person without the appropriate consent if—

    (a) he is being held in custody by the police on the authority of a court; and

    (b) an officer of at least the rank of inspector authorises it to be taken without the appropriate consent.

(3ZA) A non-intimate sample may be taken from a person without the appropriate consent if (before or after the coming into force of this subsection) he has been arrested for a recordable offence and released and—

    (a) in the case of a person who is on bail, he has not had a non-intimate sample of the same type and from the same part of the body taken from him in the course of the investigation of the offence by the police; or

    (b) in any case, he has had a non-intimate sample taken from him in the course of that investigation but—

        (i)   it was not suitable for the same means of analysis, or

        (ii) it proved insufficient, or;

        (iii) subsection (3AA) below applies.

(3A) A non-intimate sample may be taken from a person (whether or not he is in police detention or held in custody by the police on the authority of a court) without the appropriate consent if he has been charged with a recordable offence or informed that he will be reported for such an offence and—

    (a) he has not had a non-intimate sample taken from him in the course of the investigation of the offence by the police; or

    (b) he has had a non-intimate sample taken from him in the course of that investigation but—

        (i)   it was not suitable for the same means of analysis, or

> (ii) it proved insufficient; or
> (iii) subsection (3AA) below applies, or
(c) he has had a non-intimate sample taken from him in the course of that investigation and—
> (i) the sample has been destroyed pursuant to section 63R below or any other enactment, and
> (ii) it is disputed, in relation to any proceedings relating to the offence, whether a DNA profile relevant to the proceedings is derived from the sample.

(3AA) This subsection applies where the investigation was discontinued but subsequently resumed, and before the resumption of the investigation—
> (a) any DNA profile derived from the sample was destroyed pursuant to section 63D(3) below, and
> (b) the sample itself was destroyed pursuant to section 63R(4), (5) or (12) below.

(3B) Subject to this section, a non-intimate sample may be taken from a person without the appropriate consent if (before or after the coming into force of this subsection)—
> (a) he has been convicted of a recordable offence, or
> (b) he has been given a caution in respect of a recordable offence which, at the time of the caution, he has admitted and

either of the conditions mentioned in subsection (3BA) below is met.

(3BA) The conditions referred to in subsection (3B) above are—
> (a) a non-intimate sample has not been taken from the person since he was convicted or cautioned;
> (b) such a sample has been taken from him since then but—
> > (i) it was not suitable for the same means of analysis, or
> > (ii) it proved insufficient.

(3BB) A non-intimate sample may only be taken as specified in subsection (3B) above with the authorisation of an officer of at least the rank of inspector.

(3BC) An officer may only give an authorisation under subsection (3BB) above if the officer is satisfied that taking the sample is necessary to assist in the prevention or detection of crime.

(3C) A non-intimate sample may also be taken from a person without the appropriate consent if he is a person to whom section 2 of the Criminal Evidence (Amendment) Act 1997 applies (persons detained following acquittal on grounds of insanity or finding of unfitness to plead).

(3E) Subject to this section, a non-intimate sample may be taken without the appropriate consent from a person if—
> (a) under the law in force in a country or territory outside England and Wales the person has been convicted of an offence under that law (whether before or after the coming into force of this subsection and whether or not he has been punished for it);
> (b) the act constituting the offence would constitute a qualifying offence if done in England and Wales (whether or not it constituted such an offence when the person was convicted); and
> (c) either of the conditions mentioned in subsection (3F) below is met.

(3F) The conditions referred to in subsection (3E)(c) above are—
> (a) the person has not had a non-intimate sample taken from him on a previous occasion under subsection (3E) above;
> (b) he has had such a sample taken from him on a previous occasion under that subsection but—
> > (i) the sample was not suitable for the same means of analysis, or
> > (ii) it proved insufficient.

(3G) A non-intimate sample may only be taken as specified in subsection (3E) above with the authorisation of an officer of at least the rank of inspector.

(3H) An officer may only give an authorisation under subsection (3G) above if the officer is satisfied that taking the sample is necessary to assist in the prevention or detection of crime.

(4) An officer may only give an authorisation under subsection (3) above if he has reasonable grounds—

> (a) for suspecting the involvement of the person from whom the sample is to be taken in a recordable offence; and
> (b) for believing that the sample will tend to confirm or disprove his involvement.

(5) An officer may give an authorisation under subsection (3) above orally or in writing but, if he gives it orally, he shall confirm it in writing as soon as is practicable.

(5A) An officer shall not give an authorisation under subsection (3) above for the taking from any person of a non-intimate sample consisting of a skin impression if—

> (a) a skin impression of the same part of the body has already been taken from that person in the course of the investigation of the offence; and
> (b) the impression previously taken is not one that has proved insufficient.

(6) Where a non-intimate sample is taken from a person without the appropriate consent by virtue of any power conferred by this section—

> (a) before the sample is taken, an officer shall inform him of—
>>   (i)   the reason for taking the sample;
>>   (ii) the power by virtue of which it is taken; and
>>   (iii) in a case where the authorisation of an officer is required for the exercise of the power, the fact that the authorisation has been given; and
> (b) those matters shall be recorded as soon as practicable after the sample is taken.

(7) The reason referred to in subsection (6)(a)(i) above must include, except in a case where the non-intimate sample is taken under subsection (3B) or (3E) above, a statement of the nature of the offence in which it is suspected that the person has been involved.

(8A) In a case where by virtue of subsection (2A), (3A), (3B) or (3C) above a sample is taken from a person without the appropriate consent—

> (a) he shall be told the reason before the sample is taken; and
> (b) the reason shall be recorded as soon as practicable after the sample is taken.

(8B) If a non-intimate sample is taken from a person at a police station, whether with or without the appropriate consent—

> (a) before the sample is taken, an officer shall inform him that it may be the subject of a speculative search; and
> (b) the fact that the person has been informed of this possibility shall be recorded as soon as practicable after the sample has been taken.

(9) If a non-intimate sample is taken from a person detained at a police station, the matters required to be recorded by subsection (8), (8A) or (8B) above shall be recorded in his custody record.

(9ZA) The power to take a non-intimate sample from a person without the appropriate consent shall be exercisable by any constable.

(9A) Subsection (3B) above shall not apply

> (a) to any person convicted before 10th April 1995 unless he is a person to whom section 1 of the Criminal Evidence (Amendment) Act 1997 applies (persons imprisoned or detained by virtue of pre-existing conviction for sexual offence etc.).
> (b) a person given a caution before 10th April 1995.

(10) Nothing in this section applies to a person arrested or detained under the terrorism provisions.

(11) Nothing in this section applies to a person arrested under an extradition arrest power.

63A Fingerprints and samples: supplementary provisions

(1) Where a person has been arrested on suspicion of being involved in a recordable offence or has been charged with such an offence or has been informed that he will be reported for such an offence, fingerprints, impressions of footwear or samples or the information derived from

virtue of section 9(2) or 10(2) of the Drugs Act 2005;

samples taken under any power conferred by this Part of this Act from the person may be checked against—

(a) other fingerprints, impressions of footwear or samples to which the person seeking to check has access and which are held by or on behalf of any one or more relevant law-

Annex A   Summary of Main Stop and Search Powers

THIS TABLE RELATES TO STOP AND SEARCH POWERS ONLY. INDIVIDUAL STATUTES BELOW MAY CONTAIN OTHER POLICE POWERS OF ENTRY, SEARCH AND SEIZURE

Power	Object of search	Extent of search	Where exercisable
Unlawful articles general			
1. Public Stores Act 1875, s6.	HM Stores stolen or unlawfully obtained.	Persons, vehicles and vessels.	Anywhere where the constabulary powers are exercisable.
2. Firearms Act 1968, s47.	Firearms.	Persons and vehicles.	A public place, or anywhere in the case of reasonable suspicion of offences of carrying firearms with criminal intent or trespassing with firearms.
3. Misuse of Drugs Act 1971, s23.	Controlled drugs.	Persons and vehicles.	Anywhere.
4. Customs and Excise Management Act 1979, s163.	Goods: (a) on which duty has not been paid; (b) being unlawfully removed, imported or exported; (c) otherwise liable to forfeiture to HM Customs and Excise.	Vehicles and vessels only.	Anywhere.
5. Aviation Security Act 1982, s27(1).	Stolen or unlawfully obtained goods.	Airport employees and vehicles carrying airport employees or aircraft or any vehicle in a cargo area whether or not carrying an employee.	Any designated airport.
6. Police and Criminal Evidence Act 1984, s1.	Stolen goods; articles for use in certain Theft Act offences; offensive weapons, including bladed or sharply-pointed articles (except folding pocket knives with a bladed cutting edge not exceeding 3 inches); prohibited possession of a category 4 (display grade) firework, any person under 18 in possession of an adult firework in a public place.	Persons and vehicles.	Where there is public access.
	Criminal Damage: Articles made, adapted or intended for use in destroying or damaging property.	Persons and vehicles.	Where there is public access.

Power	Object of search	Extent of search	Where exercisable
Police and Criminal Evidence Act 1984, s6(3) (by a constable of the United Kingdom Atomic Energy Authority Constabulary in respect of property owned or controlled by British Nuclear Fuels plc).	HM Stores (in the form of goods and chattels belonging to British Nuclear Fuels plc).	Persons, vehicles and vessels.	Anywhere where the constabulary powers are exercisable.
7. Sporting events (Control of Alcohol etc.) Act 1985, s7.	Intoxicating liquor.	Persons, coaches and trains.	Designated sports grounds or coaches and trains travelling to or from a designated sporting event.
8. Crossbows Act 1987, s4.	Crossbows or parts of crossbows (except crossbows with a draw weight of less than 1.4 kilograms).	Persons and vehicles.	Anywhere except dwellings.
9. Criminal Justice Act 1988 s139B.	Offensive weapons, bladed or sharply pointed article.	Persons.	School premises.

Evidence of game and wildlife offences

Power	Object of search	Extent of search	Where exercisable
10. Poaching Prevention Act 1862, s2.	Game or poaching equipment.	Persons and vehicles.	A public place.
11. Deer Act 1991, s12.	Evidence of offences under the Act.	Persons and vehicles.	Anywhere except dwellings.
12. Conservation of Seals Act 1970, s4.	Seals or hunting equipment.	Vehicles only.	Anywhere.
13. Badgers Act 1992, s11.	Evidence of offences under the Act.	Persons and vehicles.	Anywhere.
14. Wildlife and Countryside Act 1981, s19.	Evidence of wildlife offences.	Persons and vehicles.	Anywhere except dwellings.

Other

Power	Object of search	Extent of search	Where exercisable
15. Paragraphs 6 & 8 of Schedule 5 to the Terrorism Prevention and Investigation Measures Act 2011.	Anything that contravenes measures specified in a TPIM notice.	Persons in respect of whom a TPIM notice is being served or is in force.	Anywhere.
16. Paragraph 10 of Schedule 5 to the Terrorism Prevention and Investigation Measures Act 2011.	Anything that could be used to threaten or harm any person.	Persons in respect of whom a TPIM notice is in force.	Anywhere.
17. *Not used*			
18. *Not used*			

Power	Object of search	Extent of search	Where exercisable
19. Section 60 Criminal Justice and Public Order Act 1994, *as amended by s.8 of the Knives Act 1997.*	Offensive weapons or dangerous instruments to prevent incidents of serious violence *or to deal with the carrying of such items.*	Persons and vehicles.	Anywhere within a locality authorised under subsection (1).

Annex B   Self-Defined Ethnic Classification Categories

White	**W**
A. White—British	W1
B. White—Irish	W2
C. Any other White background	W9
Mixed	**M**
D. White and Black Caribbean	M1
E. White and Black African	M2
F. White and Asian	M3
G. Any other Mixed Background	M9
Asian/Asian—British	**A**
H. Asian—Indian	A1
I. Asian—Pakistani	A2
J. Asian—Bangladeshi	A3
K. Any other Asian background	A9
Black/Black—British	**B**
L. Black—Caribbean	B1
M. Black African	B2
N. Any other Black background	B9
Other	**O**
O. Chinese	O1
P. Any other	O9
Not Stated	**NS**

Police and Criminal Evidence Act 1984, Code C 2014

REVISED CODE OF PRACTICE FOR THE DETENTION, TREATMENT AND QUESTIONING OF PERSONS BY POLICE OFFICERS

1   General

1.0 The powers and procedures in this Code must be used fairly, responsibly, with respect for the people to whom they apply and without unlawful discrimination. Under the Equality Act 2010, section 149, when police officers are carrying out their functions, they also have a duty to have due regard to the need to eliminate unlawful discrimination, harassment and victimisation, to advance equality of opportunity between people who share a relevant protected characteristic and people who do not share it, and to take steps to foster good relations between those persons. See *Notes 1A* and *1AA*.

1.1 All persons in custody must be dealt with expeditiously, and released as soon as the need for detention no longer applies.

1.1A A custody officer must perform the functions in this Code as soon as practicable. A custody officer will not be in breach of this Code if delay is justifiable and reasonable steps are taken to prevent unnecessary delay. The custody record shall show when a delay has occurred and the reason. See *Note 1H*.

1.2 This Code of Practice must be readily available at all police stations for consultation by:

- police officers;
- police staff;
- detained persons;
- members of the public.

1.3 The provisions of this Code:

- include the Annexes
- do not include the Notes for Guidance.

1.4 If an officer has any suspicion, or is told in good faith, that a person of any age may be mentally disordered or otherwise mentally vulnerable, in the absence of clear evidence to dispel that suspicion, the person shall be treated as such for the purposes of this Code. See *Note 1G*.

1.5 If anyone appears to be under 17, they shall in the absence of clear evidence that they are older, be treated as a juvenile for the purposes of this Code and any other Code.

2   Custody records

2.1A When a person:

- is brought to a police station under arrest
- is arrested at the police station having attended there voluntarily or
- attends a police station to answer bail

they must be brought before the custody officer as soon as practicable after their arrival at the station or, if applicable, following their arrest after attending the police station voluntarily. This applies to designated and non-designated police stations. A person is deemed to be 'at a police station' for these purposes if they are within the boundary of any building or enclosed yard which forms part of that police station.

2.1 A separate custody record must be opened as soon as practicable for each person brought to a police station under arrest or arrested at the station having gone there voluntarily or attending a police station in answer to street bail. All information recorded under this Code must be recorded as soon as practicable in the custody record unless otherwise specified. Any audio or video recording made in the custody area is not part of the custody record.

2.2 If any action requires the authority of an officer of a specified rank, subject to *paragraph 2.6A*, their name and rank must be noted in the custody record.

2.3 The custody officer is responsible for the custody record's accuracy and completeness and for making sure the record or copy of the record accompanies a detainee if they are transferred to another police station. The record shall show the:

- time and reason for transfer;
- time a person is released from detention.

2.3A If a person is arrested and taken to a police station as a result of a search in the exercise of any stop and search power to which PACE Code A (Stop and search) or the 'search powers code' issued under TACT applies, the officer carrying out the search is responsible for ensuring that the record of that stop and search is made as part of the person's custody record. The custody officer must then

3.4 (a) The custody officer shall:
- record the offence(s) that the detainee has been arrested for and the reason(s) for the arrest on the custody record. See *paragraph 10.3* and Code G *paragraphs 2.2* and *4.3*.
- note on the custody record any comment the detainee makes in relation to the arresting officer's account but shall not invite comment. If the arresting officer is not physically present when the detainee is brought to a police station, the arresting officer's account must be made available to the custody officer remotely or by a third party on the arresting officer's behalf. If the custody officer authorizes a person's detention, subject to paragraph 1.8, that officer must record the grounds for detention in the detainee's presence and at the same time, inform them of the grounds. The detainee must be informed of the grounds for their detention before they are questioned about any offence;
- note any comment the detainee makes in respect of the decision to detain them but shall not invite comment;
- not put specific questions to the detainee regarding their involvement in any offence, nor in respect of any comments they may make in response to the arresting officer's account or the decision to place them in detention. Such an exchange is likely to constitute an interview as in *paragraph 11.1A* and require the associated safeguards in section 11.

  Note: This *sub-paragraph* also applies to any further offences and grounds for detention which come to light whilst the person is detained.

  See *paragraph 11.13* in respect of unsolicited comments.

(b) Documents and materials which are essential to effectively challenging the lawfulness of the detainee's arrest and detention must be made available to the detainee or their solicitor. Documents and materials will be 'essential' for this purpose if they are capable of undermining the reasons and grounds which make the detainee's arrest and detention *necessary*. The decision about whether particular documents or materials must be made available for the purpose of this requirement therefore rests with the custody officer who determines whether detention is necessary, in consultation with the investigating officer who has the knowledge of the documents and materials in a particular case necessary to inform that decision. A note should be made in the detainee's custody record of the fact that documents or materials have been made available under this sub-paragraph and when. The investigating officer should make a separate note of what is made available and how it is made available in a particular case. This sub-paragraph also applies (with modifications) for the purposes of *sections 15 (Reviews and extensions of detention)* and *16 (Charging detained persons)*. See *Note 3ZA* and *paragraphs 15.0* and *16.7A*.

3.5 The custody officer or the custody staff as directed by the custody officer shall:
- (a) ask the detainee, whether at this time, they:
  - (i)   would like legal advice, see *paragraph 6.5*;
  - (ii) want someone informed of their detention, see *section 5*;
- (b) ask the detainee to sign the custody record to confirm their decisions in respect of (a);
- (c) determine whether the detainee:
  - (i)   is, or might be, in need of medical treatment or attention, see *section 9*;
  - (ii) requires:
    - an appropriate adult(see *paragraphs 1.4, 1.5, 1.5A and 3.15*);
    - help to check documentation (see *paragraph 3.20*);
    - an interpreter (see *paragraph 3.12* and *Note 13B*);
- (d) record the decision in respect of (c).

Where any duties under this paragraph have been carried out by custody staff at the direction of the custody officer, the outcomes shall, as soon as practicable, be reported to the custody officer who retains overall responsibility for the detainee's care and treatment and ensuring that it complies with this Code. See *Note 3F*.

3.6 When these needs are determined, the custody officer is responsible for initiating an assessment to consider whether the detainee is likely to present specific risks to custody staff or themselves. Such assessments should always include a check on the Police National Computer, to be carried out as soon as practicable, to identify any risks highlighted in relation to the detainee. Although such assessments are primarily the custody officer's responsibility, it may be necessary for them to consult and involve others, e.g. the arresting officer or an appropriate health care professional, see *paragraph 9.13*. Reasons for delaying the initiation or completion of the assessment must be recorded.

3.7 Chief Officers should ensure that arrangements for proper and effective risk assessments required by *paragraph 3.6* are implemented in respect of all detainees at police stations in their area.

3.8 Risk assessments must follow a structured process which clearly defines the categories of risk to be considered and the results must be incorporated in the detainee's custody record. The custody officer is responsible for making sure those responsible for the detainee's custody are appropriately briefed about the risks. If no specific risks are identified by the assessment, that should be noted in the custody record. See *Note 3E* and *paragraph 9.14*.

3.8A The content of any risk assessment and any analysis of the level of risk relating to the person's detention is not required to be shown or provided to the detainee or any person acting on behalf of the detainee. But information should not be withheld from any person acting on the detainee's behalf, for example, an appropriate adult, solicitor or interpreter, if to do so might put that person at risk.

3.9 The custody officer is responsible for implementing the response to any specific risk assessment, e.g.:
- reducing opportunities for self harm;
- calling a health care professional;
- increasing levels of monitoring or observation.
- reducing the risk to those who come into contact with the detainee.

See *Note 3E*.

3.10 Risk assessment is an ongoing process and assessments must always be subject to review if circumstances change.

3.11 If video cameras are installed in the custody area, notices shall be prominently displayed showing cameras are in use. Any request to have video cameras switched off shall be refused.

(b) Detained persons—special groups

3.12 If the detainee appears to be someone who does not speak or understand English or who has a hearing or speech impediment, the custody officer must ensure:
- (a) that without delay, an interpreter is called for assistance in the action under *paragraphs 3.1 to 3.5*. If the person appears to have a hearing or speech impediment, the reference *to* 'interpreter' includes appropriate assistance necessary to comply with *paragraphs 3.1 to 3.5*. See *paragraph 13.1C* if the detainee is in Wales. See *section 13* and *Note 13B*;
- (b) that in addition to the continuing rights set out in *paragraph 3.1(a)(i) to (iv)*, the detainee is told clearly about their right to interpretation and translation;
- (c) that the written notice given to the detainee in accordance with *paragraph 3.2* is in a language the detainee understands and includes the right to interpretation and translation together with information about the provisions in *section 13* and *Annex M*, which explain how the right applies (see *Note 3A*); and
- (d) that if the translation of the notice is not available, the information in the notice is given through an interpreter and a written translation provided without undue delay.

3.12A If the detainee is a citizen of an independent Commonwealth country or a national of a foreign country, including the Republic of Ireland, the custody officer must ensure that in addition to the continuing rights set out in *paragraph 3.1(a)(i) to (iv)*, they are informed as soon as practicable about their rights of communication with their High Commission, Embassy or Consulate set out in *section 7*. This right must be included in the written notice given to the detainee in accordance with *paragraph 3.2*.

3.13 If the detainee is a juvenile, the custody officer must, if it is practicable, ascertain the identity of a person responsible for their welfare. That person:

- may be:
  - ~ the parent or guardian;
  - ~ if the juvenile is in local authority or voluntary organisation care, or is otherwise being looked after under the Children Act 1989, a person appointed by that authority or organisation to have responsibility for the juvenile's welfare;
  - ~ any other person who has, for the time being, assumed responsibility for the juvenile's welfare.
- must be informed as soon as practicable that the juvenile has been arrested, why they have been arrested and where they are detained. This right is in addition to the juvenile's right in *section 5* not to be held incommunicado. See *Note 3C*.

Note: *Paragraph 1.5A* extends the obligations in this paragraph to 17-year-old detainees.

3.14 If a juvenile is known to be subject to a court order under which a person or organisation is given any degree of statutory responsibility to supervise or otherwise monitor them, reasonable steps must also be taken to notify that person or organisation (the 'responsible officer'). The responsible officer will normally be a member of a Youth Offending Team, except for a curfew order which involves electronic monitoring when the contractor providing the monitoring will normally be the responsible officer.

Note: *Paragraph 1.5A* extends the obligations in this paragraph to 17-year-old detainees.

3.15 If the detainee is a juvenile, mentally disordered or otherwise mentally vulnerable, the custody officer must, as soon as practicable:

- inform the appropriate adult, who in the case of a juvenile may or may not be a person responsible for their welfare, as in *paragraph 3.13*, of:
  - ~ the grounds for their detention;
  - ~ their whereabouts.
- ask the adult to come to the police station to see the detainee.

Note: *Paragraph 1.5A* extends the obligation to call someone to fulfil the role of the appropriate adult to 17-year-old detainees.

3.16 It is imperative that a mentally disordered or otherwise mentally vulnerable person, detained under the Mental Health Act 1983, section 136, be assessed as soon as possible. A police station should only be used as a place of safety as a last resort but if that assessment is to take place at the police station, an approved mental health professional and a registered medical practitioner shall be called to the station as soon as possible to carry it out. See *Note 9D*. The appropriate adult has no role in the assessment process and their presence is not required. Once the detainee has been assessed and suitable arrangements made for their treatment or care, they can no longer be detained under section 136. A detainee must be immediately discharged from detention under section 136 if a registered medical practitioner, having examined them, concludes they are not mentally disordered within the meaning of the Act.

3.17 If the appropriate adult is:

- already at the police station, the provisions of *paragraphs 3.1* to *3.5* must be complied with in the appropriate adult's presence;
- not at the station when these provisions are complied with, they must be complied with again in the presence of the appropriate adult when they arrive.

Note: *Paragraph 1.5A* extends the obligations in this paragraph to 17-year-old detainees.

3.18 The detainee shall be advised that:

- the duties of the appropriate adult include giving advice and assistance;
- they can consult privately with the appropriate adult at any time.

Note: *Paragraph 1.5A* extends the obligations in this paragraph to 17-year-old detainees.

3.19 If the detainee, or appropriate adult on the detainee's behalf, asks for a solicitor to be called to give legal advice, the provisions of *section 6* apply.

Note: *Paragraph 1.5A* extends the obligations in this paragraph to 17-year-old detainees.

3.20 If the detainee is blind, seriously visually impaired or unable to read, the custody officer shall make sure their solicitor, relative, appropriate adult or some other person likely to take an interest in them and not involved in the investigation is available to help check any documentation. When this Code requires written consent or signing the person assisting may be asked to sign instead, if the detainee prefers. This paragraph does not require an appropriate adult to be called solely to assist in checking and signing documentation for a person who is not a juvenile, or mentally disordered or otherwise mentally vulnerable (see *paragraph 3.15*).

(c) Persons attending a police station voluntarily

3.21 Anybody attending a police station or other location (see *paragraph 3.22*) voluntarily to assist police with an investigation of an offence may leave at will unless arrested. See *Note 1K*. The person may only be prevented from leaving at will if their arrest on suspicion of committing the offence is necessary in accordance with Code G. See *Code G Note 2G*.

If during an interview it is decided that their arrest is necessary, they must:
- be informed at once that they are under arrest and of the grounds and reasons as required by Code G, and
- be brought before the custody officer at the police station where they are arrested or, as the case may be, at the police station to which they are taken after being arrested elsewhere. The custody officer is then responsible for making sure that a custody record is opened and that they are notified of their rights in the same way as other detainees as required by this Code.
- If they are not arrested but are cautioned as in *section 10*, the person who gives the caution must, at the same time, inform them they are not under arrest, they are not obliged to remain at the station or other location but if they agree to remain, they may obtain free and independent legal advice if they want. They shall also be given a copy of the notice explaining the arrangements for obtaining legal advice and told that the right to legal advice includes the right to speak with a solicitor on the telephone and be asked if they want advice. If advice is requested, the interviewer is responsible for securing its provision without delay by contacting the Defence Solicitor Call Centre. The interviewer must ensure that the provisions of this Code and Codes E and F concerning the conduct and recording of interviews of suspects are followed insofar as they can be applied to suspects who are not under arrest. This includes determining whether they require an interpreter and the provision of interpretation and translation services. See *paragraphs 3.2* and *3.12*, *Note 6B* and *section 13*.

3.22 If the other location mentioned in *paragraph 3.21* is any place or premises for which the interviewer requires the person's informed consent to remain, for example, the person's home, then the references that the person is 'not obliged to remain' and that they 'may leave at will' mean that the person may also withdraw their consent and require the interviewer to leave.

(d) Documentation

3.23 The grounds for a person's detention shall be recorded, in the person's presence if practicable.

3.24 Action taken under *paragraphs 3.12* to *3.20* shall be recorded.

(e) Persons answering street bail

3.25 When a person is answering street bail, the custody officer should link any documentation held in relation to arrest with the custody record. Any further action shall be recorded on the custody record in accordance with *paragraphs 3.23* and *3.24* above.

Notes for guidance

3A The notice of entitlements should:
- *list the entitlements in this Code, including:*
  - *visits and contact with outside parties, including special provisions for Commonwealth citizens and foreign nationals;*
  - *reasonable standards of physical comfort;*

  - *adequate food and drink;*
  - *access to toilets and washing facilities, clothing, medical attention, and exercise when practicable.*
  * *mention the:*
    - *provisions relating to the conduct of interviews;*
    - *circumstances in which an appropriate adult should be available to assist the detainee and their statutory rights to make representation whenever the period of their detention is reviewed.*

3B In addition to notices in English, translations should be available in Welsh, the main minority ethnic languages and the principal European languages, whenever they are likely to be helpful. Audio versions of the notice should also be made available.

3C If the juvenile is in local authority or voluntary organisation care but living with their parents or other adults responsible for their welfare, although there is no legal obligation to inform them, they should normally be contacted, as well as the authority or organisation unless suspected of involvement in the offence concerned. Even if the juvenile is not living with their parents, consideration should be given to informing them.

3D The right to consult the Codes of Practice does not entitle the person concerned to delay unreasonably any necessary investigative or administrative action whilst they do so. Examples of action which need not be delayed unreasonably include:
  * *procedures requiring the provision of breath, blood or urine specimens under the Road Traffic Act 1988 or the Transport and Works Act 1992;*
  * *searching detainees at the police station;*
  * *taking fingerprints, footwear impressions or non-intimate samples without consent for evidential purposes.*

3E The Detention and Custody Authorised Professional Practice (APP) produced by the College of Policing (see http://www.app.college.police.uk*) provides more detailed guidance on risk assessments and identifies key risk areas which should always be considered.*

3F A custody officer or other officer who, in accordance with this Code, allows or directs the carrying out of any task or action relating to a detainee's care, treatment, rights and entitlements to another officer or any police staff must be satisfied that the officer or police staff concerned are suitable, trained and competent to carry out the task or action in question.

5 Right not to be held incommunicado

(a) Action

5.1 Subject to *paragraph 5.7B,* any person arrested and held in custody at a police station or other premises may, on request, have one person known to them or likely to take an interest in their welfare informed at public expense of their whereabouts as soon as practicable. If the person cannot be contacted the detainee may choose up to two alternatives. If they cannot be contacted, the person in charge of detention or the investigation has discretion to allow further attempts until the information has been conveyed. See *Notes 5C* and *5D.*

5.2 The exercise of the above right in respect of each person nominated may be delayed only in accordance with *Annex B.*

5.3 The above right may be exercised each time a detainee is taken to another police station.

5.4 If the detainee agrees, they may at the custody officer's discretion, receive visits from friends, family or others likely to take an interest in their welfare, or in whose welfare the detainee has an interest. See *Note 5B.*

5.5 If a friend, relative or person with an interest in the detainee's welfare enquires about their whereabouts, this information shall be given if the suspect agrees and *Annex B* does not apply. See *Note 5D.*

5.6 The detainee shall be given writing materials, on request, and allowed to telephone one person for a reasonable time, see *Notes 5A* and *5E.* Either or both these privileges may be denied or delayed if an officer of inspector rank or above considers sending a letter or making a telephone call may result in any of the consequences in:

> (a) *Annex B paragraphs 1 and 2* and the person is detained in connection with an indictable offence;
>
> (b) *Not used.*

Nothing in this paragraph permits the restrictions or denial of the rights in *paragraphs 5.1* and *6.1*.

5.7 Before any letter or message is sent, or telephone call made, the detainee shall be informed that what they say in any letter, call or message (other than in a communication to a solicitor) may be read or listened to and may be given in evidence. A telephone call may be terminated if it is being abused. The costs can be at public expense at the custody officer's discretion.

5.7A Any delay or denial of the rights in this section should be proportionate and should last no longer than necessary.

5.7B In the case of a person in police custody for specific purposes and periods in accordance with a direction under the Crime (Sentences) Act 1997, Schedule 1 (productions from prison etc.), the exercise of the rights in this section shall be subject to any additional conditions specified in the direction for the purpose of regulating the detainee's contact and communication with others whilst in police custody. See *Note 5F.*

(b) Documentation

5.8 A record must be kept of any:

> (a) request made under this section and the action taken;
>
> (b) letters, messages or telephone calls made or received or visit received;
>
> (c) refusal by the detainee to have information about them given to an outside enquirer. The detainee must be asked to countersign the record accordingly and any refusal recorded.

Notes for guidance

5A A person may request an interpreter to interpret a telephone call or translate a letter.

5B At the custody officer's discretion, visits should be allowed when possible, subject to having sufficient personnel to supervise a visit and any possible hindrance to the investigation.

5C If the detainee does not know anyone to contact for advice or support or cannot contact a friend or relative, the custody officer should bear in mind any local voluntary bodies or other organisations who might be able to help. Paragraph 6.1 applies if legal advice is required.

5D In some circumstances it may not be appropriate to use the telephone to disclose information under paragraphs 5.1 and 5.5.

5E The telephone call at paragraph 5.6 is in addition to any communication under paragraphs 5.1 and 6.1.

5F Prison Service Instruction 26/2012 (Production of Prisoners at the Request of Warranted Law Enforcement Agencies) provides detailed guidance and instructions for police officers and Governors and Directors of Prisons regarding applications for prisoners to be transferred to police custody and their safe custody and treatment while in police custody

6   Right to legal advice

(a) Action

6.1 Unless *Annex B* applies, all detainees must be informed that they may at any time consult and communicate privately with a solicitor, whether in person, in writing or by telephone, and that free independent legal advice is available. See *paragraph 3.1, Note 6B, 6B1, 6B2* and *Note 6J.*

6.2 *Not used.*

6.3 A poster advertising the right to legal advice must be prominently displayed in the charging area of every police station. See *Note 6H.*

6.4 No police officer should, at any time, do or say anything with the intention of dissuading a detainee from obtaining legal advice in accordance with this code, whether or not they have been arrested and are detained, from obtaining legal advice. See *Note 6ZA.*

6.5 The exercise of the right of access to legal advice may be delayed only as in *Annex B*. Whenever legal advice is requested, and unless *Annex B* applies, the custody officer must act without delay to secure the provision of such advice. If, on being informed or reminded of this right, the detainee declines to speak to a solicitor in person, the officer should point out that the right includes the right to speak with a solicitor on the telephone. If the detainee continues to waive this right or a detainee whose right to free legal advice is limited to telephone advice from the Criminal Defence Service (CDS) Direct (see *Note 6B*) declines to exercise that right, the officer should ask them why and any reasons should be recorded on the custody record or the interview record as appropriate. Reminders of the right to legal advice must be given as in *paragraphs 3.5, 11.2, 15.4, 16.4, 16.5, 2B of Annex A, 3 of Annex K* and *5 of Annex M* of this Code *and Code D, paragraphs 3.17(ii)* and *6.3*. Once it is clear a detainee does not want to speak to a solicitor in person or by telephone they should cease to be asked their reasons. See *Note 6K*.

6.5A In the case of a person who is a juvenile or is mentally disordered or otherwise mentally vulnerable, an appropriate adult should consider whether legal advice from a solicitor is required. If the person indicates that they do not want legal advice, the appropriate adult has the right to ask for a solicitor to attend if this would be in the best interests of the person. However, the detained person cannot be forced to see the solicitor if he is adamant that he does not wish to do so.

6.6 A detainee who wants legal advice may not be interviewed or continue to be interviewed until they have received such advice unless:

(a) *Annex B* applies, when the restriction on drawing adverse inferences from silence in *Annex C* will apply because the detainee is not allowed an opportunity to consult a solicitor; or

(b) an officer of superintendent rank or above has reasonable grounds for believing that:

(i) the consequent delay might:
- lead to interference with, or harm to, evidence connected with an offence;
- lead to interference with, or physical harm to, other people;
- lead to serious loss of, or damage to, property;
- lead to alerting other people suspected of having committed an offence but not yet arrested for it;
- hinder the recovery of property obtained in consequence of the commission of an offence.

See *Note 6A*

(ii) when a solicitor, including a duty solicitor, has been contacted and has agreed to attend, awaiting their arrival would cause unreasonable delay to the process of investigation.

Note: In these cases the restriction on drawing adverse inferences from silence in *Annex C* will apply because the detainee is not allowed an opportunity to consult a solicitor.

(c) the solicitor the detainee has nominated or selected from a list:

(i) cannot be contacted;

(ii) has previously indicated they do not wish to be contacted; or

(iii) having been contacted, has declined to attend; and
- the detainee has been advised of the Duty Solicitor Scheme but has declined to ask for the duty solicitor.
- in these circumstances the interview may be started or continued without further delay provided an officer of inspector rank or above has agreed to the interview proceeding.

Note: The restriction on drawing adverse inferences from silence in *Annex C* will not apply because the detainee is allowed an opportunity to consult the duty solicitor;

(d) the detainee changes their mind, about wanting legal advice or (as the case may be) about wanting a solicitor present at the interview and states that they no longer wish to speak to a solicitor. In these circumstances, the interview may be started or continued without delay provided that:.

(i) an officer of inspector rank or above:

- speaks to the detainee to enquire about the reasons for their change of mind (see *Note 6K*), and
- makes, or directs the making of, reasonable efforts to ascertain the solicitors expected time of arrival and to inform the solicitor that the suspect has stated that they wish to change their mind and the reason (if given);

(ii) the detainee's reason for their change of mind (if given) and the outcome of the action in (i) are recorded in the custody record;

(iii) the detainee, after being informed of the outcome of the action in (i) above, confirms in writing that they want the interview to proceed without speaking or further speaking to a solicitor or (as the case may be) without a solicitor being present and do not wish to wait for a solicitor by signing an entry to this effect in the custody record;

(iv) an officer of inspector rank or above is satisfied that it is proper for the interview to proceed in these circumstances and:

- gives authority in writing for the interview to proceed and, if the authority is not recorded in the custody record, the officer must ensure that the custody record shows the date and time of the authority and where it is recorded, and
- takes, or directs the taking of, reasonable steps to inform the solicitor that the authority has been given and the time when the interview is expected to commence and records or causes to be recorded, the outcome of this action in the custody record.

(v) When the interview starts and the interviewer reminds the suspect of their right to legal advice (see *paragraph 11.2*, Code E *paragraph 4.5* and Code F *paragraph 4.5*), the interviewer shall then ensure that the following is recorded in the written interview record or the interview record made in accordance with Code E or F:

- confirmation that the detainee has changed their mind about wanting legal advice or (as the case may be) about wanting a solicitor present and the reasons for it if given;
- the fact that authority for the interview to proceed has been given and, subject to *paragraph 2.6A*, the name of the authorising officer;
- that if the solicitor arrives at the station before the interview is completed, the detainee will be so informed without delay and *a break will be taken* to allow them to speak to the solicitor if they wish, unless *paragraph 6.6(a)* applies, and
- that at any time during the interview, the detainee may again ask for legal advice and that if they do, a break will be taken to allow them to speak to the solicitor, unless *paragraph 6.6(a), (b), or (c)* applies.

Note: In these circumstances the restriction on drawing adverse inferences from silence in *Annex C* will not apply because the detainee is allowed an opportunity to consult a solicitor if they wish.

6.7 If *paragraph 6.6(a)* applies, where the reason for authorising the delay ceases to apply, there may be no further delay in permitting the exercise of the right in the absence of a further authorisation unless *paragraph 6.6(b), (c)* or *(d)* applies. If *paragraph 6.6(b)(i)* applies, once sufficient information has been obtained to avert the risk, questioning must cease until the detainee has received legal advice unless *paragraph 6.6(a)*, (b)(ii), *(c)* or *(d)* applies.

6.8 A detainee who has been permitted to consult a solicitor shall be entitled on request to have the solicitor present when they are interviewed unless one of the exceptions in *paragraph 6.6* applies.

6.9 The solicitor may only be required to leave the interview if their conduct is such that the interviewer is unable properly to put questions to the suspect. See *Notes 6D* and *6E*.

6.10 If the interviewer considers a solicitor is acting in such a way, they will stop the interview and consult an officer not below superintendent rank, if one is readily available, and otherwise an officer not below inspector rank not connected with the investigation. After speaking to the solicitor, the officer consulted will decide if the interview should continue in the presence of that solicitor.

If they decide it should not, the suspect will be given the opportunity to consult another solicitor before the interview continues and that solicitor given an opportunity to be present at the interview. See *Note 6E*.

6.11 The removal of a solicitor from an interview is a serious step and, if it occurs, the officer of superintendent rank or above who took the decision will consider if the incident should be reported to the Law Society. If the decision to remove the solicitor has been taken by an officer below superintendent rank, the facts must be reported to an officer of superintendent rank or above who will similarly consider whether a report to the Law Society would be appropriate. When the solicitor concerned is a duty solicitor, the report should be both to the Law Society and to the Legal Services Commission.

6.12 'Solicitor' in this Code means:

- a solicitor who holds a current practising certificate
- an accredited or probationary representative included on the register of representatives maintained by the Legal Aid Agency.

6.12A An accredited or probationary representative sent to provide advice by, and on behalf of, a solicitor shall be admitted to the police station for this purpose unless an officer of inspector rank or above considers such a visit will hinder the investigation and directs otherwise. Hindering the investigation does not include giving proper legal advice to a detainee as in *Note 6D*. Once admitted to the police station, *paragraphs 6.6 to 6.10* apply.

6.13 In exercising their discretion under *paragraph 6.12A*, the officer should take into account in particular:

- whether:
  - ~ the identity and status of an accredited or probationary representative have been satisfactorily established;
  - ~ they are of suitable character to provide legal advice, e.g. a person with a criminal record is unlikely to be suitable unless the conviction was for a minor offence and not recent.
- any other matters in any written letter of authorisation provided by the solicitor on whose behalf the person is attending the police station. See *Note 6F*.

6.14 If the inspector refuses access to an accredited or probationary representative or a decision is taken that such a person should not be permitted to remain at an interview, the inspector must notify the solicitor on whose behalf the representative was acting and give them an opportunity to make alternative arrangements. The detainee must be informed and the custody record noted.

6.15 If a solicitor arrives at the station to see a particular person, that person must, unless *Annex B* applies, be so informed whether or not they are being interviewed and asked if they would like to see the solicitor. This applies even if the detainee has declined legal advice or, having requested it, subsequently agreed to be interviewed without receiving advice. The solicitor's attendance and the detainee's decision must be noted in the custody record.

(b) Documentation

6.16 Any request for legal advice and the action taken shall be recorded.

6.17 A record shall be made in the interview record if a detainee asks for legal advice and an interview is begun either in the absence of a solicitor or their representative, or they have been required to leave an interview.

Notes for guidance

6ZA No police officer or police staff shall indicate to any suspect, except to answer a direct question, that the period for which they are liable to be detained, or if not detained, the time taken to complete the interview, might be reduced:

- *if they do not ask for legal advice or do not want a solicitor present when they are interviewed; or*
- *if they have asked for legal advice or (as the case may be) asked for a solicitor to be present when they are interviewed but change their mind and agree to be interviewed without waiting for a solicitor.*

6A In considering if paragraph 6.6(b) applies, the officer should, if practicable, ask the solicitor for an estimate of how long it will take to come to the station and relate this to the time detention is permitted, the time of day (i.e. whether the rest period under paragraph 12.2 is imminent) and the requirements of other investigations. If the solicitor is on their way or is to set off immediately, it will not normally be appropriate to begin an interview before they arrive. If it appears necessary to begin an interview before the solicitor's arrival, they should be given an indication of how long the police would be able to wait before 6.6(b) applies so there is an opportunity to make arrangements for someone else to provide legal advice.

6B A detainee has a right to free legal advice and to be represented by a solicitor. This Note for Guidance explains the arrangements which enable detainees to obtain legal advice. An outline of these arrangements is also included in the Notice of Rights and Entitlements given to detainees in accordance with paragraph 3.2. The arrangements also apply, with appropriate modifications, to persons attending a police station or other location voluntarily who are cautioned prior to being interviewed. See paragraph 3.21.

When a detainee asks for free legal advice, the Defence Solicitor Call Centre (DSCC) must be informed of the request.

Free legal advice will be limited to telephone advice provided by CDS Direct if a detainee is:

* detained for a non-imprisonable offence,
* arrested on a bench warrant for failing to appear and being held for production before the court (except where the solicitor has clear documentary evidence available that would result in the client being released from custody),
* arrested for drink driving (driving/in charge with excess alcohol, failing to provide a specimen, driving/in charge whilst unfit through drink), or
* detained in relation to breach of police or court bail conditions

unless one or more exceptions apply, in which case the DSCC should arrange for advice to be given by a solicitor at the police station, for example:

* the police want to interview the detainee or carry out an eye-witness identification procedure;
* the detainee needs an appropriate adult;
* the detainee is unable to communicate over the telephone;
* the detainee alleges serious misconduct by the police;
* the investigation includes another offence not included in the list,
* the solicitor to be assigned is already at the police station.

When free advice is not limited to telephone advice, a detainee can ask for free advice from a solicitor they know or if they do not know a solicitor or the solicitor they know cannot be contacted, from the duty solicitor.

To arrange free legal advice, the police should telephone the DSCC. The call centre will decide whether legal advice should be limited to telephone advice from CDS Direct, or whether a solicitor known to the detainee or the duty solicitor should speak to the detainee.

When a detainee wants to pay for legal advice themselves:

* the DSCC will contact a solicitor of their choice on their behalf;
* they may, when free advice is only available by telephone from CDS Direct, still speak to a solicitor of their choice on the telephone for advice, but the solicitor would not be paid by legal aid and may ask the person to pay for the advice;
* they should be given an opportunity to consult a specific solicitor or another solicitor from that solicitor's firm. If this solicitor is not available, they may choose up to two alternatives. If these alternatives are not available, the custody officer has discretion to allow further attempts until a solicitor has been contacted and agreed to provide advice;
* they are entitled to a private consultation with their chosen solicitor on the telephone or the solicitor may decide to come to the police station;
* If their chosen solicitor cannot be contacted, the DSCC may still be called to arrange free legal advice.

Apart from carrying out duties necessary to implement these arrangements, an officer must not advise the suspect about any particular firm of solicitors.

6C Not used.

6D The solicitor's only role in the police station is to protect and advance the legal rights of their client. On occasions this may require the solicitor to give advice which has the effect of the client avoiding giving evidence which strengthens a prosecution case. The solicitor may intervene in order to seek clarification, challenge an improper question to their client or the manner in which it is put, advise their client not to reply to particular questions, or if they wish to give their client further legal advice. Paragraph 6.9 only applies if the solicitor's approach or conduct prevents or unreasonably obstructs proper questions being put to the suspect or the suspect's response being recorded. Examples of unacceptable conduct include answering questions on a suspect's behalf or providing written replies for the suspect to quote.

6E An officer who takes the decision to exclude a solicitor must be in a position to satisfy the court the decision was properly made. In order to do this they may need to witness what is happening.

6F If an officer of at least inspector rank considers a particular solicitor or firm of solicitors is persistently sending probationary representatives who are unsuited to provide legal advice, they should inform an officer of at least superintendent rank, who may wish to take the matter up with the Law Society.

6G Subject to the constraints of Annex B, a solicitor may advise more than one client in an investigation if they wish. Any question of a conflict of interest is for the solicitor under their professional code of conduct. If, however, waiting for a solicitor to give advice to one client may lead to unreasonable delay to the interview with another, the provisions of paragraph 6.6(b) may apply.

6H In addition to a poster in English, a poster or posters containing translations into Welsh, the main minority ethnic languages and the principal European languages should be displayed wherever they are likely to be helpful and it is practicable to do so.

6I Not used.

6J Whenever a detainee exercises their right to legal advice by consulting or communicating with a solicitor, they must be allowed to do so in private. This right to consult or communicate in private is fundamental. If the requirement for privacy is compromised because what is said or written by the detainee or solicitor for the purpose of giving and receiving legal advice is overheard, listened to, or read by others without the informed consent of the detainee, the right will effectively have been denied. When a detainee chooses to speak to a solicitor on the telephone, they should be allowed to do so in private unless this is impractical because of the design and layout of the custody area or the location of telephones. However, the normal expectation should be that facilities will be available, unless they are being used, at all police stations to enable detainees to speak in private to a solicitor either face to face or over the telephone.

6K A detainee is not obliged to give reasons for declining legal advice and should not be pressed to do so.

8 Conditions of detention

(a) Action

8.1 So far as it is practicable, not more than one detainee should be detained in each cell. See *Note 8C.*

8.2 Cells in use must be adequately heated, cleaned and ventilated. They must be adequately lit, subject to such dimming as is compatible with safety and security to allow people detained overnight to sleep. No additional restraints shall be used within a locked cell unless absolutely necessary and then only restraint equipment, approved for use in that force by the Chief Officer, which is reasonable and necessary in the circumstances having regard to the detainee's demeanour and with a view to ensuring their safety and the safety of others. If a detainee is deaf, mentally disordered or otherwise mentally vulnerable, particular care must be taken when deciding whether to use any form of approved restraints.

8.3 Blankets, mattresses, pillows and other bedding supplied shall be of a reasonable standard and in a clean and sanitary condition. See *Note 8A.*

8.4 Access to toilet and washing facilities must be provided.

8.5 If it is necessary to remove a detainee's clothes for the purposes of investigation, for hygiene, health reasons or cleaning, replacement clothing of a reasonable standard of comfort and cleanliness shall be provided. A detainee may not be interviewed unless adequate clothing has been offered.

8.6 At least two light meals and one main meal should be offered in any 24 hour period. See *Note 8B*. Drinks should be provided at meal times and upon reasonable request between meals. Whenever necessary, advice shall be sought from the appropriate health care professional, see *Note 9A*, on medical and dietary matters. As far as practicable, meals provided shall offer a varied diet and meet any specific dietary needs or religious beliefs the detainee may have. The detainee may, at the custody officer's discretion, have meals supplied by their family or friends at their expense. See *Note 8A*.

8.7 Brief outdoor exercise shall be offered daily if practicable.

8.8 A juvenile shall not be placed in a police cell unless no other secure accommodation is available and the custody officer considers it is not practicable to supervise them if they are not placed in a cell or that a cell provides more comfortable accommodation than other secure accommodation in the station. A juvenile may not be placed in a cell with a detained adult.

Note: *Paragraph 1.5A* extends these requirements to 17-year-old detainees.

(b) Documentation

8.9 A record must be kept of replacement clothing and meals offered.

8.10 If a juvenile is placed in a cell, the reason must be recorded.

Note: *Paragraph 1.5A* extends this requirement to 17-year-old detainees.

8.11 The use of any restraints on a detainee whilst in a cell, the reasons for it and, if appropriate, the arrangements for enhanced supervision of the detainee whilst so restrained, shall be recorded. See *paragraph 3.9*.

Notes for guidance

8A The provisions in paragraph 8.3 and 8.6 respectively are of particular importance in the case of a person likely to be detained for an extended period. In deciding whether to allow meals to be supplied by family or friends, the custody officer is entitled to take account of the risk of items being concealed in any food or package and the officer's duties and responsibilities under food handling legislation.

8B Meals should, so far as practicable, be offered at recognised meal times, or at other times that take account of when the detainee last had a meal.

8C The Detention and Custody Authorised Professional Practice (APP) produced by the College of Policing (see http://www.app.college.police.uk) provides more detailed guidance on matters concerning detainee healthcare and treatment and associated forensic issues which should be read in conjunction with sections 8 and 9 of this Code.

9 Care and treatment of detained persons

(a) General

9.1 Nothing in this section prevents the police from calling the police surgeon or, if appropriate, some other health care professional, to examine a detainee for the purposes of obtaining evidence relating to any offence in which the detainee is suspected of being involved. See *Note 9A* and *8C*.

9.2 If a complaint is made by, or on behalf of, a detainee about their treatment since their arrest, or it comes to notice that a detainee may have been treated improperly, a report must be made as soon as practicable to an officer of inspector rank or above not connected with the investigation. If the matter concerns a possible assault or the possibility of the unnecessary or unreasonable use of force, an appropriate health care professional must also be called as soon as practicable.

9.3 Detainees should be visited at least every hour. If no reasonably foreseeable risk was identified in a risk assessment, see *paragraphs 3.6–3.10*, there is no need to wake a sleeping detainee. Those suspected of being intoxicated through drink or drugs or having swallowed drugs, see *Note 9CA*, or whose level of consciousness causes concern must, subject to any clinical directions given by the appropriate health care professional, see *paragraph 9.13*:

- be visited and roused at least every half hour;
- have their condition assessed as in *Annex H*;
- and clinical treatment arranged if appropriate.

See *Notes 9B, 9C* and *9H*.

9.4 When arrangements are made to secure clinical attention for a detainee, the custody officer must make sure all relevant information which might assist in the treatment of the detainee's condition is made available to the responsible health care professional. This applies whether or not the health care professional asks for such information. Any officer or police staff with relevant information must inform the custody officer as soon as practicable.

(b) Clinical treatment and attention

9.5 The custody officer must make sure a detainee receives appropriate clinical attention as soon as reasonably practicable if the person:

  (a) appears to be suffering from physical illness; or

  (b) is injured; or

  (c) appears to be suffering from a mental disorder; or

  (d) appears to need clinical attention

9.5A This applies even if the detainee makes no request for clinical attention and whether or not they have already received clinical attention elsewhere. If the need for attention appears urgent, e.g. when indicated as in *Annex H*, the nearest available health care professional or an ambulance must be called immediately.

9.5B The custody officer must also consider the need for clinical attention as set out in Note for guidance 9C in relation to those suffering the effects of alcohol or drugs.

9.6 *Paragraph 9.5* is not meant to prevent or delay the transfer to a hospital if necessary of a person detained under the Mental Health Act 1983, *section 136*. See *Note 9D*. When an assessment under that Act takes place at a police station, see *paragraph 3.16*, the custody officer must consider whether an appropriate health care professional should be called to conduct an initial clinical check on the detainee. This applies particularly when there is likely to be any significant delay in the arrival of a suitably qualified medical practitioner.

9.7 If it appears to the custody officer, or they are told, that a person brought to a station under arrest may be suffering from an infectious disease or condition, the custody officer must take reasonable steps to safeguard the health of the detainee and others at the station. In deciding what action to take, advice must be sought from an appropriate health care professional. See *Note 9E*. The custody officer has discretion to isolate the person and their property until clinical directions have been obtained.

9.8 If a detainee requests a clinical examination, an appropriate health care professional must be called as soon as practicable to assess the detainee's clinical needs. If a safe and appropriate care plan cannot be provided, the police surgeon's advice must be sought. The detainee may also be examined by a medical practitioner of their choice at their expense.

9.9 If a detainee is required to take or apply any medication in compliance with clinical directions prescribed before their detention, the custody officer must consult the appropriate health care professional before the use of the medication. Subject to the restrictions in *paragraph 9.10*, the custody officer is responsible for the safekeeping of any medication and for making sure the detainee is given the opportunity to take or apply prescribed or approved medication. Any such consultation and its outcome shall be noted in the custody record.

9.10 No police officer may administer or supervise the self-administration of medically prescribed controlled drugs of the types and forms listed in the Misuse of Drugs Regulations 2001, Schedule 2 or 3. A detainee may only self-administer such drugs under the personal supervision of the registered medical practitioner authorising their use. Drugs listed in Schedule 4 or 5 may be distributed by the custody officer for self-administration if they have consulted the registered medical practitioner authorising their use, this may be done by telephone, and both parties are satisfied self-administration will not expose the detainee, police officers or anyone else to the risk of harm or injury.

9.11 When appropriate health care professionals administer drugs or authorise the use of other medications, or supervise their self-administration or consult with the custody officer about allowing self-administration of drugs listed in Schedule 4 or 5, it must be within current medicines legislation and the scope of practice as determined by their relevant statutory regulatory body.

9.12 If a detainee has in their possession, or claims to need, medication relating to a heart condition, diabetes, epilepsy or a condition of comparable potential seriousness then, even though *paragraph 9.5* may not apply, the advice of the appropriate health care professional must be obtained.

9.13 Whenever the appropriate health care professional is called in accordance with this section to examine or treat a detainee, the custody officer shall ask for their opinion about:

- any risks or problems which police need to take into account when making decisions about the detainee's continued detention;
- when to carry out an interview if applicable; and
- the need for safeguards.

9.14 When clinical directions are given by the appropriate health care professional, whether orally or in writing, and the custody officer has any doubts or is in any way uncertain about any aspect of the directions, the custody officer shall ask for clarification. It is particularly important that directions concerning the frequency of visits are clear, precise and capable of being implemented. See *Note 9F*.

(c) Documentation

9.15 A record must be made in the custody record of:

(a) the arrangements made for an examination by an appropriate health care professional under *paragraph 9.2* and of any complaint reported under that paragraph together with any relevant remarks by the custody officer;

(b) any arrangements made in accordance with *paragraph 9.5*;

(c) any request for a clinical examination under *paragraph 9.8* and any arrangements made in response;

(d) the injury, ailment, condition or other reason which made it necessary to make the arrangements in (a) to (c), see *Note 9G*;

(e) any clinical directions and advice, including any further clarifications, given to police by a health care professional concerning the care and treatment of the detainee in connection with any of the arrangements made in (a) to (c), see *Note 9F*;

(f) if applicable, the responses received when attempting to rouse a person using the procedure in *Annex H*, see *Note 9H*.

9.16 If a health care professional does not record their clinical findings in the custody record, the record must show where they are recorded. See *Note 9G*. However, information which is necessary to custody staff to ensure the effective ongoing care and well being of the detainee must be recorded openly in the custody record, see *paragraph 3.8* and *Annex G, paragraph 7*.

9.17 Subject to the requirements of section 4, the custody record shall include:

- a record of all medication a detainee has in their possession on arrival at the police station;
- a note of any such medication they claim to need but do not have with them.

Notes for guidance

9A A 'health care professional' means a clinically qualified person working within the scope of practice as determined by their relevant professional body. Whether a health care professional is 'appropriate' depends on the circumstances of the duties they carry out at the time.

9B Whenever possible juveniles and mentally vulnerable detainees should be visited more frequently. Note: Paragraph 1.5A extends this Note to 17-year-old detainees.

9C A detainee who appears drunk or behaves abnormally may be suffering from illness, the effects of drugs or may have sustained injury, particularly a head injury which is not apparent. A detainee needing or dependent on certain drugs, including alcohol, may experience harmful effects within a short time of being deprived of their supply. In these circumstances, when there is any doubt, police should always act urgently to call an appropriate health care professional or an ambulance. Paragraph 9.5 does not apply to minor ailments or injuries which do not need attention. However, all such ailments or injuries must be recorded in the custody record and any doubt must be resolved in favour of calling the appropriate health care professional.

9CA Paragraph 9.3 would apply to a person in police custody by order of a magistrates' court under the Criminal Justice Act 1988, section 152 (as amended by the Drugs Act 2005, section 8) to facilitate the recovery of evidence after being charged with drug possession or drug trafficking and suspected of having swallowed drugs. In the case of the healthcare needs of a person who has swallowed drugs, the custody officer subject to any clinical directions, should consider the necessity for rousing every half hour. This does not negate the need for regular visiting of the suspect in the cell.

9D Whenever practicable, arrangements should be made for persons detained for assessment under the Mental Health Act 1983, section 136 to be taken to a hospital. Chapter 10 of the Mental Health Act 1983 Code of Practice (as revised) provides more detailed guidance about arranging assessments under section 136 and transferring detainees from police stations to other places of safety 9E It is important to respect a person's right to privacy and information about their health must be kept confidential and only disclosed with their consent or in accordance with clinical advice when it is necessary to protect the detainee's health or that of others who come into contact with them.

9F The custody officer should always seek to clarify directions that the detainee requires constant observation or supervision and should ask the appropriate health care professional to explain precisely what action needs to be taken to implement such directions.

9G Paragraphs 9.15 and 9.16 do not require any information about the cause of any injury, ailment or condition to be recorded on the custody record if it appears capable of providing evidence of an offence.

9H The purpose of recording a person's responses when attempting to rouse them using the procedure in Annex H is to enable any change in the individual's consciousness level to be noted and clinical treatment arranged if appropriate.

10   Cautions

(a) When a caution must be given

10.1 A person whom there are grounds to suspect of an offence, see *Note 10A*, must be cautioned before any questions about an offence, or further questions if the answers provide the grounds for suspicion, are put to them if either the suspect's answers or silence, (i.e. failure or refusal to answer or answer satisfactorily) may be given in evidence to a court in a prosecution. A person need not be cautioned if questions are for other necessary purposes, e.g.:

    (a) solely to establish their identity or ownership of any vehicle;

    (b) to obtain information in accordance with any relevant statutory requirement, see *paragraph 10.9*;

    (c) in furtherance of the proper and effective conduct of a search, e.g. to determine the need to search in the exercise of powers of stop and search or to seek cooperation while carrying out a search; or

    (d) to seek verification of a written record as in *paragraph 11.13;*

    (e) *Not used.*

10.2 Whenever a person not under arrest is initially cautioned, or reminded they are under caution, that person must at the same time be told they are not under arrest and are free to leave if they want to. See *Note 10C*.

10.3 A person who is arrested, or further arrested, must be informed at the time, or as soon as practicable thereafter, that they are under arrest and the grounds for their arrest, see *paragraph 3.4, Note 10B* and *Code G, paragraphs 2.2* and *4.3.*

10.4 As per *Code G, section 3*, a person who is arrested, or further arrested, must also be cautioned unless:

    (a) it is impracticable to do so by reason of their condition or behaviour at the time;

    (b) they have already been cautioned immediately prior to arrest as in *paragraph 10.1.*

(b) Terms of the cautions

10.5 The caution which must be given on:

    (a) arrest; or

    (b) all other occasions before a person is charged or informed they may be prosecuted, see *section 16,* should, unless the restriction on drawing adverse inferences from silence applies, see *Annex C*, be in the following terms:

> 'You do not have to say anything. But it may harm your defence if you do not mention when questioned something which you later rely on in Court. Anything you do say may be given in evidence.'

. . .

See *Note 10G*.

10.6 *Annex C, paragraph 2* sets out the alternative terms of the caution to be used when the restriction on drawing adverse inferences from silence applies.

10.7 Minor deviations from the words of any caution given in accordance with this Code do not constitute a breach of this Code, provided the sense of the relevant caution is preserved. See *Note 10D*.

10.8 After any break in questioning under caution, the person being questioned must be made aware they remain under caution. If there is any doubt the relevant caution should be given again in full when the interview resumes. See *Note 10E*.

10.9 When, despite being cautioned, a person fails to co-operate or to answer particular questions which may affect their immediate treatment, the person should be informed of any relevant consequences and that those consequences are not affected by the caution. Examples are when a person's refusal to provide:

- their name and address when charged may make them liable to detention;
- particulars and information in accordance with a statutory requirement, e.g. under the Road Traffic Act 1988, may amount to an offence or may make the person liable to a further arrest.

(c) Special warnings under the Criminal Justice and Public Order Act 1994, sections 36 and 37

10.10 When a suspect interviewed at a police station or authorised place of detention after arrest fails or refuses to answer certain questions, or to answer satisfactorily, after due warning, see *Note 10F*, a court or jury may draw such inferences as appear proper under the Criminal Justice and Public Order Act 1994, sections 36 and 37. Such inferences may only be drawn when:

    (a) the restriction on drawing adverse inferences from silence, see *Annex C*, does not apply; and

    (b) the suspect is arrested by a constable and fails or refuses to account for any objects, marks or substances, or marks on such objects found:

- on their person;
- in or on their clothing or footwear;
- otherwise in their possession; or
- in the place they were arrested;

    (c) the arrested suspect was found by a constable at a place at or about the time the offence for which that officer has arrested them is alleged to have been committed, and the suspect fails or refuses to account for their presence there. When the restriction on drawing adverse inferences from silence applies, the suspect may still be asked to account for any of the matters in (b) or (c) but the special warning described in *paragraph 10.11* will not apply and must not be given.

10.11 For an inference to be drawn when a suspect fails or refuses to answer a question about one of these matters or to answer it satisfactorily, the suspect must first be told in ordinary language:

    (a) what offence is being investigated;

    (b) what fact they are being asked to account for;

    (c) this fact may be due to them taking part in the commission of the offence;

    (d) a court may draw a proper inference if they fail or refuse to account for this fact;

    (e) a record is being made of the interview and it may be given in evidence if they are brought to trial.

(d) Juveniles and persons who are mentally disordered or otherwise mentally vulnerable

10.11A The information required in *paragraph 10.11* must not be given to a suspect who is a juvenile or who is mentally disordered or otherwise mentally vulnerable unless the appropriate adult is present.

10.12 If a juvenile or a person who is mentally disordered or otherwise mentally vulnerable is cautioned in the absence of the appropriate adult, the caution must be repeated in the adult's presence.

10.12A *Paragraph 1.5A extends the requirements in paragraphs 10.11A and 10.12 to 17-year-old detainees.*

(e) Documentation

10.13 A record shall be made when a caution is given under this section, either in the interviewer's pocket book or in the interview record.

Notes for guidance

10A There must be some reasonable, objective grounds for the suspicion, based on known facts or information which are relevant to the likelihood the offence has been committed and the person to be questioned committed it.

10B An arrested person must be given sufficient information to enable them to understand that they have been deprived of their liberty and the reason they have been arrested, e.g. when a person is arrested on suspicion of committing an offence they must be informed of the suspected offence's nature, when and where it was committed. The suspect must also be informed of the reason or reasons why the arrest is considered necessary. Vague or technical language should be avoided.

10C The restriction on drawing inferences from silence, see Annex C, paragraph 1, does not apply to a person who has not been detained and who therefore cannot be prevented from seeking legal advice if they want, see paragraph 3.21.

10D If it appears a person does not understand the caution, the person giving it should explain it in their own words.

10E It may be necessary to show to the court that nothing occurred during an interview break or between interviews which influenced the suspect's recorded evidence. After a break in an interview or at the beginning of a subsequent interview, the interviewing officer should summarise the reason for the break and confirm this with the suspect.

10F The Criminal Justice and Public Order Act 1994, sections 36 and 37 apply only to suspects who have been arrested by a constable or Customs and Excise officer and are given the relevant warning by the police or customs officer who made the arrest or who is investigating the offence. They do not apply to any interviews with suspects who have not been arrested.

10G Nothing in this Code requires a caution to be given or repeated when informing a person not under arrest they may be prosecuted for an offence. However, a court will not be able to draw any inferences under the Criminal Justice and Public Order Act 1994, section 34, if the person was not cautioned.

11   Interviews—general

(a) Action

11.1A An interview is the questioning of a person regarding their involvement or suspected involvement in a criminal offence or offences which, under *paragraph 10.1*, must be carried out under caution. Whenever a person is interviewed they must be informed of the nature of the offence, or further offence. Procedures under the Road Traffic Act 1988, section 7 or the Transport and Works Act 1992, section 31 do not constitute interviewing for the purpose of this Code.

11.1 Following a decision to arrest a suspect, they must not be interviewed about the relevant offence except at a police station or other authorised place of detention, unless the consequent delay would be likely to:

    (a) lead to:

- interference with, or harm to, evidence connected with an offence;
- interference with, or physical harm to, other people; or
- serious loss of, or damage to, property;

    (b) lead to alerting other people suspected of committing an offence but not yet arrested for it; or

    (c) hinder the recovery of property obtained in consequence of the commission of an offence.

Interviewing in any of these circumstances shall cease once the relevant risk has been averted or the necessary questions have been put in order to attempt to avert that risk.

11.2 Immediately prior to the commencement or re-commencement of any interview at a police station or other authorised place of detention, the interviewer should remind the suspect of their entitlement to free legal advice and that the interview can be delayed for legal advice to be obtained, unless one of the exceptions in *paragraph 6.6* applies. It is the interviewer's responsibility to make sure all reminders are recorded in the interview record.

11.3 *Not used.*

11.4 At the beginning of an interview the interviewer, after cautioning the suspect, see section 10, shall put to them any significant statement or silence which occurred in the presence and hearing of a police officer or other police staff before the start of the interview and which have not been put to the suspect in the course of a previous interview. See *Note 11A*. The interviewer shall ask the suspect whether they confirm or deny that earlier statement or silence and if they want to add anything.

11.4A A significant statement is one which appears capable of being used in evidence against the suspect, in particular a direct admission of guilt. A significant silence is a failure or refusal to answer a question or answer satisfactorily when under caution, which might, allowing for the restriction on drawing adverse inferences from silence, see *Annex C*, give rise to an inference under the Criminal Justice and Public Order Act 1994, Part III.

11.5 No interviewer may try to obtain answers or elicit a statement by the use of oppression. Except as in *paragraph 10.9*, no interviewer shall indicate, except to answer a direct question, what action will be taken by the police if the person being questioned answers questions, makes a statement or refuses to do either. If the person asks directly what action will be taken if they answer questions, make a statement or refuse to do either, the interviewer may inform them what action the police propose to take provided that action is itself proper and warranted.

11.6 The interview or further interview of a person about an offence with which that person has not been charged or for which they have not been informed they may be prosecuted, must cease when:

    (a) the officer in charge of the investigation is satisfied all the questions they consider relevant to obtaining accurate and reliable information about the offence have been put to the suspect, this includes allowing the suspect an opportunity to give an innocent explanation and asking questions to test if the explanation is accurate and reliable, e.g. to clear up ambiguities or clarify what the suspect said;

    (b) the officer in charge of the investigation has taken account of any other available evidence; and

    (c) the officer in charge of the investigation, or in the case of a detained suspect, the custody officer, see *paragraph 16.1*, reasonably believes there is sufficient evidence to provide a realistic prospect of conviction for that offence. See *Note 11B*.

This paragraph does not prevent officers in revenue cases or acting under the confiscation provisions of the Criminal Justice Act 1988 or the Drug Trafficking Act 1994 from inviting suspects to complete a formal question and answer record after the interview is concluded.

(b) Interview records

11.7 (a) An accurate record must be made of each interview, whether or not the interview takes place at a police station.

    (b) The record must state the place of interview, the time it begins and ends, any interview breaks and, subject to *paragraph 2.6A*, the names of all those present; and must be made on the forms provided for this purpose or in the interviewer's pocket book or in accordance with the Codes of Practice E or F;

    (c) Any written record must be made and completed during the interview, unless this would not be practicable or would interfere with the conduct of the interview, and must constitute either a verbatim record of what has been said or, failing this, an account of the interview which adequately and accurately summarises it.

11.8 If a written record is not made during the interview it must be made as soon as practicable after its completion.

11.9 Written interview records must be timed and signed by the maker.

11.10 If a written record is not completed during the interview the reason must be recorded in the interview record.

11.11 Unless it is impracticable, the person interviewed shall be given the opportunity to read the interview record and to sign it as correct or to indicate how they consider it inaccurate. If the person interviewed cannot read or refuses to read the record or sign it, the senior interviewer present shall read it to them and ask whether they would like to sign it as correct or make their mark or to indicate how they consider it inaccurate. The interviewer shall certify on the interview record itself what has occurred. See *Note 11E*.

11.12 If the appropriate adult or the person's solicitor is present during the interview, they should also be given an opportunity to read and sign the interview record or any written statement taken down during the interview.

Note: *Paragraph 1.5A* extends the requirement in this paragraph to interviews of 17-year-old suspects.

11.13 A written record shall be made of any comments made by a suspect, including unsolicited comments, which are outside the context of an interview but which might be relevant to the offence. Any such record must be timed and signed by the maker. When practicable the suspect shall be given the opportunity to read that record and to sign it as correct or to indicate how they consider it inaccurate. See *Note 11E*.

11.14 Any refusal by a person to sign an interview record when asked in accordance with this Code must itself be recorded.

(c) Juveniles and mentally disordered or otherwise mentally vulnerable people

11.15 A juvenile or person who is mentally disordered or otherwise mentally vulnerable must not be interviewed regarding their involvement or suspected involvement in a criminal offence or offences, or asked to provide or sign a written statement under caution or record of interview, in the absence of the appropriate adult unless *paragraphs 11.1, 11.18 to 11.20* apply. See *Note 11C*.

11.16 Juveniles may only be interviewed at their place of education in exceptional circumstances and only when the principal or their nominee agrees. Every effort should be made to notify the parent(s) or other person responsible for the juvenile's welfare and the appropriate adult, if this is a different person, that the police want to interview the juvenile and reasonable time should be allowed to enable the appropriate adult to be present at the interview. If awaiting the appropriate adult would cause unreasonable delay, and unless the juvenile is suspected of an offence against the educational establishment, the principal or their nominee can act as the appropriate adult for the purposes of the interview.

Note: *Paragraph 1.5A* extends the requirement in this paragraph to 17-year-old suspects.

11.17 If an appropriate adult is present at an interview, they shall be informed:
- they are not expected to act simply as an observer; and
- the purpose of their presence is to:
  - ~ advise the person being interviewed;
  - ~ observe whether the interview is being conducted properly and fairly;
  - ~ facilitate communication with the person being interviewed.

(d) Vulnerable suspects—urgent interviews at police stations

11.18 The following persons may not be interviewed unless an officer of superintendent rank or above considers delay will lead to the consequences in *paragraph 11.1(a) to (c)*, and is satisfied the interview would not significantly harm the person's physical or mental state (see *Annex G*):

    (a) an interview of a juvenile or person who is mentally disordered or otherwise mentally vulnerable if at the time of the interview the appropriate adult is not present;

(b) an interview of anyone other than in (a) who at the time of the interview appears unable to:
   • appreciate the significance of questions and their answers; or
   • understand what is happening because of the effects of drink, drugs or any illness, ailment or condition;

(c) an interview, without an interpreter being present, a person whom the custody officer has determined requires an interpreter (see *paragraphs 3.5(c)(ii)* and *3.12*) which is carried out by an interviewer speaking the suspect's own language or (as the case may be) otherwise establishing effective communication which is sufficient to enable the necessary questions to be asked and answered in order to avert the consequences. See *paragraphs 13.2* and *13.5*.

11.19 These interviews may not continue once sufficient information has been obtained to avert the consequences in *paragraph 11.1(a)* to *(c)*.

11.20 A record shall be made of the grounds for any decision to interview a person under *paragraph 11.18*.

Notes for guidance

11A Paragraph 11.4 does not prevent the interviewer from putting significant statements and silences to a suspect again at a later stage or a further interview.

11B The Criminal Procedure and Investigations Act 1996 Code of Practice, paragraph 3.4 states 'In conducting an investigation, the investigator should pursue all reasonable lines of enquiry, whether these point towards or away from the suspect. What is reasonable will depend on the particular circumstances.' Interviewers should keep this in mind when deciding what questions to ask in an interview.

11C Although juveniles or people who are mentally disordered or otherwise mentally vulnerable are often capable of providing reliable evidence, they may, without knowing or wishing to do so, be particularly prone in certain circumstances to provide information that may be unreliable, misleading or self-incriminating. Special care should always be taken when questioning such a person, and the appropriate adult should be involved if there is any doubt about a person's age, mental state or capacity. Because of the risk of unreliable evidence it is also important to obtain corroboration of any facts admitted whenever possible.

11D Juveniles should not be arrested at their place of education unless this is unavoidable. When a juvenile is arrested at their place of education, the principal or their nominee must be informed.

11E Significant statements described in paragraph 11.4 will always be relevant to the offence and must be recorded. When a suspect agrees to read records of interviews and other comments and sign them as correct, they should be asked to endorse the record with, e.g. 'I agree that this is a correct record of what was said' and add their signature. If the suspect does not agree with the record, the interviewer should record the details of any disagreement and ask the suspect to read these details and sign them to the effect that they accurately reflect their disagreement. Any refusal to sign should be recorded.

12 Interviews in police stations

(a) Action

12.1 If a police officer wants to interview or conduct enquiries which require the presence of a detainee, the custody officer is responsible for deciding whether to deliver the detainee into the officer's custody. An investigating officer who is given custody of a detainee takes over responsibility for the detainee's care and safe custody for the purposes of this Code until they return the detainee to the custody officer when they must report the manner in which they complied with the Code whilst having custody of the detainee.

12.2 Except as below, in any period of 24 hours a detainee must be allowed a continuous period of at least 8 hours for rest, free from questioning, travel or any interruption in connection with the investigation concerned. This period should normally be at night or other appropriate time which takes account of when the detainee last slept or rested. If a detainee is arrested at a police station after going there voluntarily, the period of 24 hours runs from the time of their arrest and not the time of arrival at the police station. The period may not be interrupted or delayed, except:

(a) when there are reasonable grounds for believing not delaying or interrupting the period would:

    (i) involve a risk of harm to people or serious loss of, or damage to, property;

    (ii) delay unnecessarily the person's release from custody; or

    (iii) otherwise prejudice the outcome of the investigation;

(b) at the request of the detainee, their appropriate adult or legal representative;

(c) when a delay or interruption is necessary in order to:

    (i) comply with the legal obligations and duties arising under section 15;

    (ii) to take action required under section 9 or in accordance with medical advice.

If the period is interrupted in accordance with (a), a fresh period must be allowed.

Interruptions under (b) and (c), do not require a fresh period to be allowed.

12.3 Before a detainee is interviewed the custody officer, in consultation with the officer in charge of the investigation and appropriate health care professionals as necessary, shall assess whether the detainee is fit enough to be interviewed. This means determining and considering the risks to the detainee's physical and mental state if the interview took place and determining what safeguards are needed to allow the interview to take place. See *Annex G*. The custody officer shall not allow a detainee to be interviewed if the custody officer considers it would cause significant harm to the detainee's physical or mental state. Vulnerable suspects listed at *paragraph 11.18* shall be treated as always being at some risk during an interview and these persons may not be interviewed except in accordance with *paragraphs 11.18* to *11.20*.

12.4 As far as practicable interviews shall take place in interview rooms which are adequately heated, lit and ventilated.

12.5 A suspect whose detention without charge has been authorised under PACE, because the detention is necessary for an interview to obtain evidence of the offence for which they have been arrested, may choose not to answer questions but police do not require the suspect's consent or agreement to interview them for this purpose. If a suspect takes steps to prevent themselves being questioned or further questioned, e.g. by refusing to leave their cell to go to a suitable interview room or by trying to leave the interview room, they shall be advised their consent or agreement to interview is not required. The suspect shall be cautioned as in section 10, and informed if they fail or refuse to co-operate, the interview may take place in the cell and that their failure or refusal to cooperate may be given in evidence. The suspect shall then be invited to co-operate and go into the interview room.

12.6 People being questioned or making statements shall not be required to stand.

12.7 Before the interview commences each interviewer shall, subject to *paragraph 2.6A*, identify themselves and any other persons present to the interviewee.

12.8 Breaks from interviewing should be made at recognised meal times or at other times that take account of when an interviewee last had a meal. Short refreshment breaks shall be provided at approximately two hour intervals, subject to the interviewer's discretion to delay a break if there are reasonable grounds for believing it would:

(i) involve a:

    • risk of harm to people;

    • serious loss of, or damage to, property;

(ii) unnecessarily delay the detainee's release;

(iii) otherwise prejudice the outcome of the investigation.

See *Note 12B*.

12.9 If during the interview a complaint is made by or on behalf of the interviewee concerning the provisions of this Code, the interviewer should:

(i) record it in the interview record;

(ii) inform the custody officer, who is then responsible for dealing with it as in section 9.

(b) Documentation

12.10 A record must be made of the:

- time a detainee is not in the custody of the custody officer, and why
- reason for any refusal to deliver the detainee out of that custody

12.11 A record shall be made of:

(a) the reasons it was not practicable to use an interview room; and

(b) any action taken as in *paragraph 12.5*.

The record shall be made on the custody record or in the interview record for action taken whilst an interview record is being kept, with a brief reference to this effect in the custody record.

12.12 Any decision to delay a break in an interview must be recorded, with reasons, in the interview record.

12.13 All written statements made at police stations under caution shall be written on forms provided for the purpose.

12.14 All written statements made under caution shall be taken in accordance with *Annex D*. Before a person makes a written statement under caution at a police station they shall be reminded about the right to legal advice. See *Note 12A*.

Notes for guidance

12A It is not normally necessary to ask for a written statement if the interview was recorded in writing and the record signed in accordance with paragraph 11.11 or audibly or visually recorded in accordance with Code E or F. Statements under caution should normally be taken in these circumstances only at the person's express wish. A person may however be asked if they want to make such a statement.

12B Meal breaks should normally last at least 45 minutes and shorter breaks after two hours should last at least 15 minutes. If the interviewer delays a break in accordance with paragraph 12.8 and prolongs the interview, a longer break should be provided. If there is a short interview, and another short interview is contemplated, the length of the break may be reduced if there are reasonable grounds to believe this is necessary to avoid any of the consequences in paragraph 12.8(i) to (iii).

13   Interpreters

(a) General

Chief officers are responsible for making arrangements to provide appropriately qualified independent persons to act as interpreters and to provide translations of essential documents for:

(a) detained suspects who, in accordance with *paragraph 3.5(c)(ii)*, the custody officer has determined require an interpreter, and

(b) suspects who are not under arrest but are cautioned as in *section 10* who, in accordance with *paragraph 3.21*, the interviewer has determined require an interpreter. In these cases, the responsibilities of the custody officer are, if appropriate, assigned to the interviewer. An interviewer who has any doubts about whether an interpreter is required or about how the provisions of this section should be applied to a suspect who is not under arrest should seek advice from an officer of the rank of sergeant or above.

If the suspect has a hearing or speech impediment, references to 'interpreter' and 'interpretation' in this Code include appropriate assistance necessary to establish effective communication with that person. See *paragraph 13.1C* below if the person is in Wales.

13.1A The arrange*ments must* comply with the minimum requirements set out in Directive 2010/64/EU of the European Parliament and of the Council of 20 October 2010 on the right to interpretation and translation in criminal proceedings (see *Note 13A*). The provisions *of this* Code implement the requirements for those to whom this Code applies. These requirements include the following:

- That the arrangements made and the quality of interpretation and translation provided shall be sufficient to 'safeguard the fairness of the proceedings, in particular by ensuring that suspected or accused persons have knowledge of the cases against them and are able to exercise their right of defence'. This term which is used by the Directive means that the suspect must be able to understand their position and be able to communicate effectively with police officers, interviewers, solicitors and appropriate adults as provided for by this and any other Code in the same way as a suspect who can speak and 46 Police and Criminal Evidence Act 1984 Code C understand English and who does not have a hearing or speech impediment and who would therefore not require an interpreter.

- The provision of a written translation of all documents considered essential for the person to exercise their right of defence and to '*safeguard the fairness of the proceedings*' as described above. For the purposes of this Code, this includes any decision to authorise a person to be detained and details of any offence(s) with which the person has been charged or for which they have been told they may be prosecuted, see *Annex M*.
- Procedures to help determine:
  - ~ whether a suspect can speak and understand English and needs the assistance of an interpreter, *see paragraph 13.1* and *Notes 13B and 13C*; and
  - ~ whether another interpreter should be called or another translation should be provided when a suspect complains about the quality of either or both, see *paragraphs 13.10A* and *13.10C*.

13.1B All reasonable attempts should be made to make the suspect understand that interpretation and translation will be provided at public expense.

13.1C *With regard to persons in* Wales, nothing in this or any other Code affects the application of the Welsh Language Schemes produced by police and crime commissioners in Wales in accordance with the Welsh Language Act 1993. See paragraphs *3.12 and 13.1*.

(b) Foreign languages

13.2 Unless *paragraphs 11.1, 11.18(c)* apply, a suspect who for the purposes of this Code requires an interpreter because they do not appear to speak or understand English (see *paragraphs 3.5(c)(ii)* and *3.12*) must not be interviewed in the absence of a person capable of interpreting.

13.2A An interpreter should also be called if a juvenile is interviewed and their parent or guardian, present as the appropriate adult, does not appear to speak or understand English, unless the interview is urgent and *paragraphs 11.1 or 11.18(c)* apply.

Note: *Paragraph 1.5A* extends the requirement in this paragraph to interviews of 17-year-old suspects.

13.3 When a written record of the interview is made (see *paragraph 11.7*), the interviewer shall make sure the interpreter makes a note of the interview at the time in the person's language for use in the event of the interpreter being called to give evidence, and certifies its accuracy. The interviewer should allow sufficient time for the interpreter to note each question and answer after each is put, given and interpreted. The person should be allowed to read the record or have it read to them and sign it as correct or indicate the respects in which they consider it inaccurate. If the interview is audibly recorded or visually recorded, the arrangements in Code E or F apply.

13.4 In the case of a person making a statement to a police officer or other police staff other than in English:

  (a) the interpreter shall record the statement in the language it is made;
  (b) the person shall be invited to sign it;
  (c) an official English translation shall be made in due course.

(c) Interviewing suspects who have a hearing or speech impediment

13.5 Unless *paragraphs 11.1 or 11.18(c)* (urgent interviews) apply, a suspect who for the purposes of this Code requires an interpreter or other appropriate assistance to enable effective communication with them because they appear to have a hearing or speech impediment (see *paragraphs 3.5(c)(ii)* and *3.12*) must not be interviewed in the absence of an independent person capable of interpreting or without that assistance.13.6 An interpreter should also be called if a juvenile is interviewed and the parent or guardian present as the appropriate adult appears to be deaf or there is doubt about their hearing or speaking ability, unless they agree in writing to the interview proceeding without one or *paragraphs 11.1, 11.18 to 11.20* apply.

13.7 The interviewer shall make sure the interpreter is allowed to read the interview record and certify its accuracy in the event of the interpreter being called to give evidence. If the interview is audibly recorded or visually recorded, the arrangements in Code E or F apply.

(d) Additional rules for detained persons

13.8 *Not used.*

13.9 If *paragraph 6.1* applies and the detainee cannot communicate with the solicitor because of language, hearing or speech difficulties, an interpreter must be called. A police officer or any other police staff may not be used for this purpose.

13.10 After the custody officer has determined that a detainee requires an interpreter (see *paragraph 3.5(c)(ii)*) and following the initial action in *paragraphs 3.1 to 3.5*, arrangements must also be made for an interpreter to:

- explain the grounds and reasons for any authorisation for their *continued* detention, before or after charge and any information about the authorisation given to them by the authorising officer and which is recorded in the custody record. See *paragraphs 15.3, 15.4* and *15.16(a)* and *(b)*;
- be present at the magistrates' court for the hearing of an application for a warrant of further detention or any extension or further extension of such warrant to explain any grounds and reasons for the application and any information about the authorisation of their further detention given to them by the court (see PACE, sections 43 and 44 and *paragraphs 15.2* and *15.16(c)*), and
- explain any offence with which the detainee is charged or for which they are informed they may be prosecuted and any other information about the offence given to them by or on behalf of the custody officer, see *paragraphs 16.1* and *16.3*.

13.10A If a detainee complains that they are not satisfied with the quality of interpretation, the custody officer or (as the case may be) the interviewer, is responsible for deciding whether a different interpreter should be called in accordance with the procedures set out in the arrangements made by the chief officer, *see paragraph 13.1A*.

(e) Translations of essential documents

13.10B Written translations, oral translations and oral summaries of essential documents in a language the detainee understands shall be provided in accordance with *Annex M* (Translations of documents and records).

13.10C If a detainee complains that they are not satisfied with the quality of the translation, the custody officer or (as the case may be) the interviewer, is responsible for deciding whether a further translation should be provided in accordance with the procedures set out in the arrangements made by the chief officer, see *paragraph 13.1A*.

(f) Decisions not to provide interpretation and translation.

13.10D If a suspect challenges a decision:

- made by the custody officer or (as the case may be) by the interviewer, in accordance with this Code (see *paragraphs 3.5(c)(ii)* and *3.21)* that they do not require an interpreter; or
- made in accordance with *paragraphs 13.10A, 13.10B* or *13.10C* not to provide a different interpreter or another translation or not to translate a requested document, the matter shall be reported to an inspector to deal with as a complaint for the purposes of *paragraph 9.2* or *12.9* if the challenge is made during an interview.

(g) Documentation

13.11 The following must be recorded in the custody record or, as applicable, the interview record:

- (a) Action taken to call an interpreter;
- (b) Action taken when a detainee is not satisfied about the standard of interpretation or translation provided, see *paragraphs 13.10A* and *13.10C*;

(c) When an urgent interview is carried out in accordance with *paragraph 13.2* or *13.5* in the absence of an interpreter;

(d) When a detainee has been assisted by an interpreter for the purpose of providing or being given information or being interviewed;

(e) Action taken in accordance with Annex M when:
- a written translation of an essential document is provided;
- an oral translation or oral summary of an essential document is provided instead of a written translation and the authorising officer's reason(s) why this would not prejudice the fairness of the proceedings (see *Annex M, paragraph 3*);
- a suspect waives their right to a translation of an essential document (see *Annex M, paragraph 4*);
- when representations that a document which is not included in the table is essential and that a translation should be provided are refused and the reason for the refusal (see *Annex M, paragraph 8*).

Notes for Guidance

13A Chief officers have discretion when determining the individuals or organisations they use to provide interpretation and translation services for their forces provided that these services are compatible with the requirements of the Directive. One example which chief officers may wish to consider is the Ministry of Justice Framework Agreement for interpretation and translation services. 49

13B A procedure for determining whether a person needs an interpreter might involve a telephone interpreter service or using cue cards or similar visual aids which enable the detainee to indicate their ability to speak and understand English and their preferred language. This could be confirmed through an interpreter who could also assess the extent to which the person can speak and understand English.

13C There should also be a procedure for determining whether a suspect who requires an interpreter requires assistance in accordance with paragraph 3.20 to help them check and if applicable, sign any documentation.

14   Questioning—special restrictions

14.1 If a person is arrested by one police force on behalf of another and the lawful period of detention in respect of that offence has not yet commenced in accordance with PACE, section 41 no questions may be put to them about the offence while they are in transit between the forces except to clarify any voluntary statement they make.

14.2 If a person is in police detention at a hospital they may not be questioned without the agreement of a responsible doctor. See *Note 14A*.

Note for guidance

14A If questioning takes place at a hospital under paragraph 14.2, or on the way to or from a hospital, the period of questioning concerned counts towards the total period of detention permitted.

15   Reviews and extensions of detention

(a) Persons detained under PACE

15.1 The review officer is responsible under PACE, section 40 for periodically determining if a person's detention, before or after charge, continues to be necessary. This requirement continues throughout the detention period and except as in *paragraph 15.10*, the review officer must be present at the police station holding the detainee. See *Notes 15A* and *15B*.

15.2 Under PACE, section 42, an officer of superintendent rank or above who is responsible for the station holding the detainee may give authority any time after the second review to extend the maximum period the person may be detained without charge by up to 12 hours. Further detention without charge may be authorised only by a magistrates' court in accordance with PACE, sections 43 and 44. See *Notes 15C, 15D* and *15E*.

15.2A An authorisation under section 42(1) of PACE extends the maximum period of detention permitted before charge for indictable offences from 24 hours to 36 hours. Detaining a juvenile or mentally vulnerable person for longer than 24 hours will be dependent on the circumstances of the case and with regard to the person's:

    (a) special vulnerability;

    (b) the legal obligation to provide an opportunity for representations to be made prior to a decision about extending detention;

    (c) the need to consult and consider the views of any appropriate adult; and

    (d) any alternatives to police custody.

15.3 Before deciding whether to authorise continued detention the officer responsible under *paragraphs 15.1* or *15.2* shall give an opportunity to make representations about the detention to:

    (a) the detainee, unless in the case of a review as in *paragraph 15.1*, the detainee is asleep;

    (b) the detainee's solicitor if available at the time; and

    (c) the appropriate adult if available at the time.

15.3A Other people having an interest in the detainee's welfare may also make representations at the authorising officer's discretion.

15.3B Subject to *paragraph 15.10*, the representations may be made orally in person or by telephone or in writing. The authorising officer may, however, refuse to hear oral representations from the detainee if the officer considers them unfit to make representations because of their condition or behaviour. See *Note 15C*.

15.3C The decision on whether the review takes place in person or by telephone or by video conferencing (see *Note 15G*) is a matter for the review officer. In determining the form the review may take, the review officer must always take full account of the needs of the person in custody. The benefits of carrying out a review in person should always be considered, based on the individual circumstances of each case with specific additional consideration if the person is:

    (a) a juvenile (and the age of the juvenile); or

        Note: *Paragraph 1.5A* extends this sub-paragraph to 17-year-old detainees.

    (b) Suspected of being mentally vulnerable; or

    (c) in need of medical attention for other than routine minor ailments; or

    (d) subject to presentational or community issues around their detention.

15.4 Before conducting a review or determining whether to extend the maximum period of detention without charge, the officer responsible must make sure the detainee is reminded of their entitlement to free legal advice, see *paragraph 6.5*, unless in the case of a review the person is asleep.

15.5 If, after considering any representations, the review officer under paragraph 15.1 decides to keep the detainee in detention or the superintendent under paragraph 15.2 extends the maximum period they may be detained without charge, any comment made by the detainee shall be recorded. If applicable, the officer shall be informed of the comment as soon as practicable. See also *paragraphs 11.4* and *11.13*.

15.6 No officer shall put specific questions to the detainee:

    • regarding their involvement in any offence; or

    • in respect of any comments they may make:

      ~ when given the opportunity to make representations; or

      ~ in response to a decision to keep them in detention or extend the maximum period of detention.

Such an exchange could constitute an interview as in *paragraph 11.1A* and would be subject to the associated safeguards in section 11 and, in respect of a person who has been charged, *paragraph 16.5*. See also *paragraph 11.13*.

15.7 A detainee who is asleep at a review, see *paragraph 15.1*, and whose continued detention is authorised must be informed about the decision and reason as soon as practicable after waking.

15.8 *Not used.*

(b) Telephone review of detention

15.9 PACE, section 40A provides that the officer responsible under section 40 for reviewing the detention of a person who has not been charged, need not attend the police station holding the detainee and may carry out the review by telephone.

15.9A PACE, section 45A(2) provides that the officer responsible under section 40 for reviewing the detention of a person who has not been charged, need not attend the police station holding the detainee and may carry out the review by video conferencing facilities. (See *Note 15G*).

15.9B A telephone review is not permitted where facilities for review by video conferencing exist and it is practicable to use them.

15.9C The review officer can decide at any stage that a telephone review or review by video conferencing should be terminated and that the review will be conducted in person. The reasons for doing so should be noted in the custody record. See *Note 15F*.

15.10 When a telephone review is carried out by telephone or video conferencing facilities, an officer at the station holding the detainee shall be required by the review officer to fulfil that officer's obligations under PACE section 40 or this Code by:

  (a) making any record connected with the review in the detainee's custody record;

  (b) if applicable, making a record in (a) in the presence of the detainee; and

  (c) for a review by telephone, giving the detainee information about the review.

15.11 When a review is carried out by telephone or by video conferencing facilities, the requirement in *paragraph 15.3* will be satisfied:

  (a) if facilities exist for the immediate transmission of written representations to the review officer, e.g. fax or email message, by allowing those who are given the opportunity to make representations:

    (i) orally by telephone or (as the case may be) by means of the video conferencing facilities; or

    (ii) in writing using those facilities for the immediate transmission of written representations; and

  (b) in all other cases, by allowing those who are given the opportunity to make their representations, to make their representations orally by telephone or by the means of video conferencing facilities.

(c) Documentation

15.12 It is the officer's responsibility to make sure all reminders given under *paragraph 15.4* are noted in the custody record.

15.13 The grounds for, and extent of, any delay in conducting a review shall be recorded.

15.14 When a review is carried out by telephone or video conferencing facilities, a record shall be made of:

  (a) the reason the review officer did not attend the station holding the detainee;

  (b) the place the review officer was;

  (c) the method representations, oral or written, were made to the review officer, see *paragraph 15.11*.

15.15 Any written representations shall be retained.

15.16 A record shall be made as soon as practicable of:

  (a) the outcome of each review of detention before or after charge, and if *paragraph 15.7* applies, of when the person was informed and by whom;

  (b) the outcome of any determination under PACE, section 42 by a superintendent whether to extend the maximum period of detention without charge beyond 24 hours from the relevant time. If an authorisation is given, the record shall state the number of hours and minutes by which the detention period is extended or further extended.

  (c) the outcome of each application under PACE, section 43, for a warrant of further detention or under section 44, for an extension or further extension of that warrant. If a warrant for further detention is granted under section 43 or extended or further extended under 44, the record shall state the detention period authorised by the warrant and the date and time it was granted or (as the case may be) the period by which the warrant is extended or further extended.

Note: Any period during which a person is released on bail does not count towards the maximum period of detention without charge allowed under PACE, sections 41 to 44.

Notes for guidance

15A Review officer for the purposes of:

- PACE, sections 40, 40A and 45A means, in the case of a person arrested but not charged, an officer of at least inspector rank not directly involved in the investigation and, if a person has been arrested and charged, the custody officer;

15B The detention of persons in police custody not subject to the statutory review requirement in paragraph 15.1 should still be reviewed periodically as a matter of good practice. Such reviews can be carried out by an officer of the rank of sergeant or above. The purpose of such reviews is to check the particular power under which a detainee is held continues to apply, any associated conditions are complied with and to make sure appropriate action is taken to deal with any changes. This includes the detainee's prompt release when the power no longer applies, or their transfer if the power requires the detainee be taken elsewhere as soon as the necessary arrangements are made. Examples include persons:

(a) arrested on warrant because they failed to answer bail to appear at court;

(b) arrested under the Bail Act 1976, section 7(3) for breaching a condition of bail granted after charge;

(c) in police custody for specific purposes and periods under the Crime (Sentences) Act 1997, Schedule 1;

(d) convicted, or remand prisoners, held in police stations on behalf of the Prison Service under the Imprisonment (Temporary Provisions) Act 1980, section 6;

(e) being detained to prevent them causing a breach of the peace;

(f) detained at police stations on behalf of the Immigration Service.

(g) detained by order of a magistrates' court under the Criminal Justice Act 1988, section 152 (as amended by the Drugs Act 2005, section 8) to facilitate the recovery of evidence after being charged with drug possession or drug trafficking and suspected of having swallowed drugs.

The detention of persons remanded into police detention by order of a court under the Magistrates' Courts Act 1980, section 128 is subject to a statutory requirement to review that detention. This is to make sure the detainee is taken back to court no later than the end of the period authorised by the court or when the need for their detention by police ceases, whichever is the sooner.

15C In the case of a review of detention, but not an extension, the detainee need not be woken for the review. However, if the detainee is likely to be asleep, e.g. during a period of rest allowed as in paragraph 12.2, at the latest time a review or authorisation to extend detention may take place, the officer should, if the legal obligations and time constraints permit, bring forward the procedure to allow the detainee to make representations.

A detainee not asleep during the review must be present when the grounds for their continued detention are recorded and must at the same time be informed of those grounds unless the review officer considers the person is incapable of understanding what is said, violent or likely to become violent or in urgent need of medical attention.

15D An application to a Magistrates' Court under PACE, sections 43 or 44 for a warrant of further detention or its extension should be made between 10am and 9pm, and if possible during normal court hours. It will not usually be practicable to arrange for a court to sit specially outside the hours of 10am to 9pm. If it appears a special sitting may be needed outside normal court hours but between 10am and 9pm, the clerk to the justices should be given notice and informed of this possibility, while the court is sitting if possible.

15E In paragraph 15.2, the officer responsible for the station holding the detainee includes a super-intendent or above who, in accordance with their force operational policy or police regulations, is given that responsibility on a temporary basis whilst the appointed long-term holder is off duty or otherwise unavailable.

15F The provisions of PACE, section 40A allowing telephone reviews do not apply to reviews of detention after charge by the custody officer. When video conferencing is not required, they allow the use of a telephone to carry out a review of detention before charge. The procedure under PACE, section 42 must be done in person.

15G The use of video conferencing facilities for decisions about detention under section 45A of PACE is subject to the introduction of regulations by the Secretary of State.

16 Charging detained persons

(a) Action

16.1 When the officer in charge of the investigation reasonably believes there is sufficient evidence to provide a realistic prospect of conviction for the offence (see *paragraph 11.6*), they shall without delay, and subject to the following qualification, inform the custody officer who will be responsible for considering whether the detainee should be charged. See *Notes 11B* and *16A*. When a person is detained in respect of more than one offence it is permissible to delay informing the custody officer until the above conditions are satisfied in respect of all the offences, but see *paragraph 11.6*. If the detainee is a juvenile, mentally disordered or otherwise mentally vulnerable, any resulting action shall be taken in the presence of the appropriate adult if they are present at the time. See *Notes 16B* and *16C*.

16.1A Where guidance issued by the Director of Public Prosecutions under section 37A is in force the custody officer must comply with that Guidance in deciding how to act in dealing with the detainee. See *Notes 16AA* and *16AB*.

16.1B Where in compliance with the DPP's Guidance the custody officer decides that the case should be immediately referred to the CPS to make the charging decision, consultation should take place with a Crown Prosecutor as soon as is reasonably practicable. Where the Crown Prosecutor is unable to make the charging decision on the information available at that time, the detainee may be released without charge and on bail (with conditions if necessary) under section 37(7)(a). In such circumstances, the detainee should be informed that they are being released to enable the Director of Public Prosecutions to make a decision under section 37B.

16.2 When a detainee is charged with or informed they may be prosecuted for an offence, see *Note 16B*, they shall, unless the restriction on drawing adverse inferences from silence applies, see *Annex C*, be cautioned as follows:

'*You do not have to say anything. But it may harm your defence if you do not mention now something which you later rely on in court. Anything you do say may be given in evidence.*'

Where the use of the Welsh Language is appropriate, a constable may provide the caution directly in Welsh in the following terms:

'*Does dim rhaid i chi ddweud dim byd. Ond gall niweidio eich amddiffyniad os na fyddwch chi'n sôn, yn awr, am rywbeth y byddwch chi'n dibynnu arno nes ymlaen yn y llys. Gall unrhyw beth yr ydych yn ei ddweud gael ei roi fel tystiolaeth.*'

Annex C, paragraph 2 sets out the alternative terms of the caution to be used when the restriction on drawing adverse inferences from silence applies.

16.3 When a detainee is charged they shall be given a written notice showing particulars of the offence and, subject to *paragraph 2.6A*, the officer's name and the case reference number. As far as possible the particulars of the charge shall be stated in simple terms, but they shall also show the precise offence in law with which the detainee is charged. The notice shall begin: '*You are charged with the offence(s) shown below.*' Followed by the caution.

If the detainee is a juvenile, mentally disordered or otherwise mentally vulnerable, the notice should be given to the appropriate adult.

Note: *Paragraph 1.5A* provides that a copy of the notice should be given to the person called to fulfil the role of the appropriate adult when a 17-year-old detainee is charged.

16.4 If, after a detainee has been charged with or informed they may be prosecuted for an offence, an officer wants to tell them about any written statement or interview with another person relating to such an offence, the detainee shall either be handed a true copy of the written statement or the content of the interview record brought to their attention. Nothing shall be done to invite any reply or comment except to:

    (a) caution the detainee, 'You do not have to say anything, but anything you do say may be given in evidence.';

          Where the use of the Welsh Language is appropriate, caution the detainee in the following terms:

          'Does dim rhaid i chi ddweud dim byd, ond gall unrhyw beth yr ydych yn ei ddweud gael ei roi fel tystiolaeth.'
          and

    (b) remind the detainee about their right to legal advice.

16.4A If the detainee:

- cannot read, the document may be read to them
- is a juvenile, mentally disordered or otherwise mentally vulnerable, the appropriate adult shall also be given a copy, or the interview record shall be brought to their attention.

Note: *Paragraph 1.5A* requires a copy of the record to be given to, or brought to the attention of, the person called to fulfil the role of the appropriate adult for a 17-year-old detainee.

16.5 A detainee may not be interviewed about an offence after they have been charged with, or informed they may be prosecuted for it, unless the interview is necessary:

- to prevent or minimise harm or loss to some other person, or the public
- to clear up an ambiguity in a previous answer or statement
- in the interests of justice for the detainee to have put to them, and have an opportunity to comment on, information concerning the offence which has come to light since they were charged or informed they might be prosecuted

Before any such interview, the interviewer shall:

    (a) caution the detainee, 'You do not have to say anything, but anything you do say may be given in evidence.'

          Where the use of the Welsh Language is appropriate, the interviewer shall caution the detainee, *'Does dim rhaid i chi ddweud dim byd, ond gall unrhyw beth yr ydych yn ei ddweud gael ei roi fel tystiolaeth.'*

    (b) remind the detainee about their right to legal advice. See *Note 16B.*

16.6 The provisions of *paragraphs 16.2 to 16.5* must be complied with in the appropriate adult's presence if they are already at the police station. If they are not at the police station then these provisions must be complied with again in their presence when they arrive unless the detainee has been released. See *Note 16C.*

16.7 When a juvenile is charged with an offence and the custody officer authorises their continued detention after charge, the custody officer must try to make arrangements for the juvenile to be taken into the care of a local authority to be detained pending appearance in court unless the custody officer certifies it is impracticable to do so or, in the case of a juvenile of at least 12 years old, no secure accommodation is available and there is a risk to the public of serious harm from that juvenile, in accordance with PACE, section 38(6). See *Note 16D.*

Note: The 16 year old maximum age limit for transfer to local authority accommodation, the power of the local authority to detain the person transferred and take over responsibility for that person from the police are determined by section 38 of PACE. For this reason, this paragraph and Note 16D do not apply to detainees who appear to have attained the age of 17, see *paragraph 1.5A(a).*

(b) Documentation

16.8 A record shall be made of anything a detainee says when charged.

16.9 Any questions put in an interview after charge and answers given relating to the offence shall be recorded in full during the interview on forms for that purpose and the record signed by the detainee or, if they refuse, by the interviewer and any third parties present. If the questions are audibly recorded or visually recorded the arrangements in Code E or F apply.

16.10 If arrangements for a juvenile's transfer into local authority care as in *paragraph 16.7* are not made, the custody officer must record the reasons in a certificate which must be produced before the court with the juvenile. See *Note 16D.*

Notes for guidance

16A The custody officer must take into account alternatives to prosecution under the Crime and Disorder Act 1998, reprimands and warning applicable to persons under 18, and in national guidance on the cautioning of offenders, for persons aged 18 and over.

16AA When a person is arrested under the provisions of the Criminal Justice Act 2003 which allow a person to be re-tried after being acquitted of a serious offence which is a qualifying offence specified in Schedule 5 to that Act and not precluded from further prosecution by virtue of section 75(3) of that Act the detention provisions of PACE are modified and make an officer of the rank of superintendent or above who has not been directly involved in the investigation responsible for determining whether the evidence is sufficient to charge.

16AB Where Guidance issued by the Director of Public Prosecutions under section 37B is in force, a custody officer who determines in accordance with that Guidance that there is sufficient evidence to charge the detainee, may detain that person for no longer than is reasonably necessary to decide how that person is to be dealt with under PACE, section 37(7)(a) to (d), including, where appropriate, consultation with the Duty Prosecutor. The period is subject to the maximum period of detention before charge determined by PACE, sections 41 to 44. Where in accordance with the Guidance the case is referred to the CPS for decision, the custody officer should ensure that an officer involved in the investigation sends to the CPS such information as is specified in the Guidance.

16B The giving of a warning or the service of the Notice of Intended Prosecution required by the Road Traffic Offenders Act 1988, section 1 does not amount to informing a detainee they may be prosecuted for an offence and so does not preclude further questioning in relation to that offence.

16C There is no power under PACE to detain a person and delay action under paragraphs 16.2 to 16.5 solely to await the arrival of the appropriate adult. Reasonable efforts should therefore be made to give the appropriate adult sufficient notice of the time the decision (charge etc.) is to be implemented so that they can be present. If the appropriate adult is not, or cannot be, present at that time, the detainee should be released on bail to return for the decision to be implemented when the adult is present, unless the custody officer determines that the absence of the appropriate adult makes the detainee unsuitable for bail for this purpose. After charge, bail cannot be refused, or release on bail delayed, simply because an appropriate adult is not available, unless the absence of that adult provides the custody officer with the necessary grounds to authorise detention after charge under PACE, section 38.

16D Except as in paragraph 16.7, neither a juvenile's behaviour nor the nature of the offence provides grounds for the custody officer to decide it is impracticable to arrange the juvenile's transfer to local authority care. Similarly, the lack of secure local authority accommodation does not make it impracticable to transfer the juvenile. The availability of secure accommodation is only a factor in relation to a juvenile aged 12 or over when the local authority accommodation would not be adequate to protect the public from serious harm from them. The obligation to transfer a juvenile to local authority accommodation applies as much to a juvenile charged during the daytime as to a juvenile to be held overnight, subject to a requirement to bring the juvenile before a court under PACE, section 46.

This Note does not apply to 17-year-old detainees (see paragraph 16.7).

ANNEX B DELAY IN NOTIFYING ARREST OR ALLOWING ACCESS TO LEGAL ADVICE

A Persons detained under PACE

1. The exercise of the rights in section 5 or section 6, or both, may be delayed if the person is in police detention, as in PACE, section 118(2), in connection with an indictable offence, has not yet been charged with an offence and an officer of superintendent rank or above, or inspector rank or above only for the rights in section 5, has reasonable grounds for believing their exercise will:

    (i) lead to:
- interference with, or harm to, evidence connected with an indictable offence; or
- interference with, or physical harm to, other people; or

    (ii) lead to alerting other people suspected of having committed an indictable offence but not yet arrested for it; or

    (iii) hinder the recovery of property obtained in consequence of the commission of such an offence.

2. These rights may also be delayed if the officer has reasonable grounds to believe that:

    (i) the person detained for an indictable offence has benefited from their criminal conduct (decided in accordance with Part 2 of the Proceeds of Crime Act 2002); and

    (ii) the recovery of the value of the property constituting that benefit will be hindered by the exercise of either right.

3. Authority to delay a detainee's right to consult privately with a solicitor may be given only if the authorising officer has reasonable grounds to believe the solicitor the detainee wants to consult will, inadvertently or otherwise, pass on a message from the detainee or act in some other way which will have any of the consequences specified under *paragraphs 1* or *2*. In these circumstances the detainee must be allowed to choose another solicitor. See *Note B3*.

4. If the detainee wishes to see a solicitor, access to that solicitor may not be delayed on the grounds they might advise the detainee not to answer questions or the solicitor was initially asked to attend the police station by someone else. In the latter case the detainee must be told the solicitor has come to the police station at another person's request, and must be asked to sign the custody record to signify whether they want to see the solicitor.

5. The fact the grounds for delaying notification of arrest may be satisfied does not automatically mean the grounds for delaying access to legal advice will also be satisfied.

6. These rights may be delayed only for as long as grounds exist and in no case beyond 36 hours after the relevant time as in PACE, section 41. If the grounds cease to apply within this time, the detainee must, as soon as practicable, be asked if they want to exercise either right, the custody record must be noted accordingly, and action taken in accordance with the relevant section of the Code.

7. A detained person must be permitted to consult a solicitor for a reasonable time before any court hearing.

B *Not used*

C Documentation

13. The grounds for action under this Annex shall be recorded and the detainee informed of them as soon as practicable.

14. Any reply given by a detainee under *paragraphs 6* or *11* must be recorded and the detainee asked to endorse the record in relation to whether they want to receive legal advice at this point.

D Cautions and special warnings

15. When a suspect detained at a police station is interviewed during any period for which access to legal advice has been delayed under this Annex, the court or jury may not draw adverse inferences from their silence.

Notes for guidance

B1   Even if Annex B applies in the case of a juvenile, or a person who is mentally disordered or otherwise mentally vulnerable, action to inform the appropriate adult and the person responsible for a juvenile's welfare if that is a different person, must nevertheless be taken as in paragraph 3.13 and 3.15.

B2   In the case of Commonwealth citizens and foreign nationals, see Note 7A.

B3   A decision to delay access to a specific solicitor is likely to be a rare occurrence and only when it can be shown the suspect is capable of misleading that particular solicitor and there is more than a substantial risk that the suspect will succeed in causing information to be conveyed which will lead to one or more of the specified consequences

Police and Criminal Evidence Act 1984, Code D 2011

CODE OF PRACTICE FOR THE IDENTIFICATION OF PERSONS BY POLICE OFFICERS

3   Identification of a suspect by an eye-witness

(A)   Identification of a suspect by an eye-witness

3.0 This part applies when an eye-witness has seen the offender committing the crime or in any other circumstances which tend to prove or disprove the involvement of the person they saw in the crime, for example, close to the scene of the crime, immediately before or immediately after it was committed. It sets out the procedures to be used to test the ability of that eye-witness to identify a person suspected of involvement in the offence as the person they saw on the previous occasion. Except where stated, this part does not apply to the procedures described in Part B and Note 3AA.

3.1 A record shall be made of the suspect's description as first given by a potential witness. This record must:

   (a) be made and kept in a form which enables details of that description to be accurately produced from it, in a visible and legible form, which can be given to the suspect or the suspect's solicitor in accordance with this Code; and

   (b) unless otherwise specified, be made before the witness takes part in any identification procedures under *paragraphs 3.5 to 3.10, 3.21 or 3.23*.

A copy of the record shall where practicable, be given to the suspect or their solicitor before any procedures under *paragraphs 3.5 to 3.10, 3.21 or 3.23* are carried out. See *Note 3E*.

(a)   Cases when the suspect's identity is not known

3.2 In cases when the suspect's identity is not known, a witness may be taken to a particular neighbourhood or place to see whether they can identify the person they saw. Although the number, age, sex, race, general description and style of clothing of other people present at the location and the way in which any identification is made cannot be controlled, the principles applicable to the formal procedures under *paragraphs 3.5 to 3.10* shall be followed as far as practicable. For example:

   (a) where it is practicable to do so, a record should be made of the witness' description of the suspect, as in *paragraph 3.1(a)*, before asking the witness to make an identification;

   (b) care must be taken not to direct the witness' attention to any individual unless, taking into account all the circumstances, this cannot be avoided. However, this does not prevent a witness being asked to look carefully at the people around at the time or to look towards a group or in a particular direction, if this appears necessary to make sure that the witness does not overlook a possible suspect simply because the witness is looking in the opposite direction and also to enable the witness to make comparisons between any suspect and others who are in the area; See *Note 3F*.

   (c) where there is more than one witness, every effort should be made to keep them separate and witnesses should be taken to see whether they can identify a person independently;

(d) once there is sufficient information to justify the arrest of a particular individual for suspected involvement in the offence, e.g., after a witness makes a positive identification, the provisions set out from *paragraph 3.4* onwards shall apply for any other witnesses in relation to that individual;

(e) the officer or police staff accompanying the witness must record, in their pocket book, the action taken as soon as, and in as much detail, as possible. The record should include: the date, time and place of the relevant occasion the witness claims to have previously seen the suspect; where any identification was made; how it was made and the conditions at the time (e.g., the distance the witness was from the suspect, the weather and light); if the witness's attention was drawn to the suspect; the reason for this; and anything said by the witness or the suspect about the identification or the conduct of the procedure.

3.3 A witness must not be shown photographs, computerised or artist's composite likenesses or similar likenesses or pictures (including 'E-fit' images) if the identity of the suspect is known to the police and the suspect is available to take part in a video identification, an identification parade or a group identification. If the suspect's identity is not known, the showing of such images to a witness to obtain identification evidence must be done in accordance with *Annex E*.

(b) Cases when the suspect is known and available

3.4 If the suspect's identity is known to the police and they are available, the identification procedures set out in *paragraphs 3.5* to *3.10* may be used. References in this section to a suspect being 'known' mean there is sufficient information known to the police to justify the arrest of a particular person for suspected involvement in the offence. A suspect being 'available' means they are immediately available or will be within a reasonably short time and willing to take an effective part in at least one of the following which it is practicable to arrange:

- video identification;
- identification parade; or
- group identification.

Video identification

3.5 A 'video identification' is when the witness is shown moving images of a known suspect, together with similar images of others who resemble the suspect. Moving images must be used unless:

- the suspect is known but not available (see *paragraph 3.21* of this Code); or
- in accordance with *paragraph 2A* of *Annex A* of this Code, the identification officer does not consider that replication of a physical feature can be achieved or that it is not possible to conceal the location of the feature on the image of the suspect.

The identification officer may then decide to make use of video identification but using still images.

3.6 Video identifications must be carried out in accordance with *Annex A*.

Identification parade

3.7 An 'identification parade' is when the witness sees the suspect in a line of others who resemble the suspect.

3.8 Identification parades must be carried out in accordance with *Annex B*.

Group identification

3.9 A 'group identification' is when the witness sees the suspect in an informal group of people.

3.10 Group identifications must be carried out in accordance with *Annex C*.

Arranging identification procedures

3.11 Except for the provisions in *paragraph 3.19*, the arrangements for, and conduct of, the identification procedures in *paragraphs 3.5* to *3.10* and circumstances in which an identification procedure must be held shall be the responsibility of an officer not below inspector rank who is not involved with the investigation, 'the identification officer'. Unless otherwise specified, the identification officer may allow another officer or police staff, see *paragraph 2.21*, to make arrangements for, and conduct, any of these identification procedures. In delegating these procedures, the identification officer must be able to supervise effectively and either intervene or be contacted for advice. No officer or any other person involved with the investigation of the case against the suspect, beyond the extent required by these procedures, may take any part in these procedures or act as the identification officer. This does not prevent the identification officer from consulting the officer in charge of the investigation to determine which procedure to use. When an identification procedure is required, in the interest of fairness to suspects and witnesses, it must be held as soon as practicable.

Circumstances in which an identification procedure must be held

3.12 Whenever:

    (i) a witness has identified a suspect or purported to have identified them prior to any identification procedure set out in *paragraphs 3.5* to *3.10* having been held; or

    (ii) there is a witness available, who expresses an ability to identify the suspect, or where there is a reasonable chance of the witness being able to do so, and they have not been given an opportunity to identify the suspect in any of the procedures set out in *paragraphs 3.5* to *3.10*, and the suspect disputes being the person the witness claims to have seen, an identification procedure shall be held unless it is not practicable or it would serve no useful purpose in proving or disproving whether the suspect was involved in committing the offence. For example:

- where the suspect admits being at the scene of the crime and gives an account of what took place and the eye-witness does not see anything which contradicts that.
- when it is not disputed that the suspect is already known to the witness who claims to have recognised them when seeing them commit the crime.

3.13 An eye witness identification procedure may also be held if the officer in charge of the investigation considers it would be useful.

Selecting an identification procedure

3.14 If, because of *paragraph 3.12*, an identification procedure is to be held, the suspect shall initially be offered a video identification unless:

    (a) a video identification is not practicable; or

    (b) an identification parade is both practicable and more suitable than a video identification; or

    (c) *paragraph 3.16* applies.

The identification officer and the officer in charge of the investigation shall consult each other to determine which option is to be offered. An identification parade may not be practicable because of factors relating to the witnesses, such as their number, state of health, availability and travelling requirements. A video identification would normally be more suitable if it could be arranged and completed sooner than an identification parade. Before an option is offered the suspect must also be reminded of their entitlement to have free legal advice, see Code C, *paragraph 6.5*.

3.15 A suspect who refuses the identification procedure first offered shall be asked to state their reason for refusing and may get advice from their solicitor and/or if present, their appropriate adult. The suspect, solicitor and/or appropriate adult shall be allowed to make representations about why another procedure should be used. A record should be made of the reasons for refusal and any representations made. After considering any reasons given, and representations made, the identification officer shall, if appropriate, arrange for the suspect to be offered an alternative which the officer considers suitable and practicable. If the officer decides it is not suitable and practicable to offer an alternative identification procedure, the reasons for that decision shall be recorded.

3.16 A group identification may initially be offered if the officer in charge of the investigation considers it is more suitable than a video identification or an identification parade and the identification officer considers it practicable to arrange.

Notice to suspect

3.17 Unless *paragraph 3.20* applies, before a video identification, an identification parade or group identification is arranged, the following shall be explained to the suspect:

(i)   the purposes of the video identification, identification parade or group identification;

(ii)   their entitlement to free legal advice; see Code C, *paragraph 6.5*;

(iii)   the procedures for holding it, including their right to have a solicitor or friend present;

(iv)   that they do not have to consent to or co-operate in a video identification, identification parade or group identification;

(v)   that if they do not consent to, and co-operate in, a video identification, identification parade or group identification, their refusal may be given in evidence in any subsequent trial and police may proceed covertly without their consent or make other arrangements to test whether a witness can identify them, see *paragraph 3.21*;

(vi)   whether, for the purposes of the video identification procedure, images of them have previously been obtained, see *paragraph 3.20*, and if so, that they may co-operate in providing further, suitable images to be used instead;

(vii)   if appropriate, the special arrangements for juveniles;

(viii)   if appropriate, the special arrangements for mentally disordered or otherwise mentally vulnerable people;

(ix)   that if they significantly alter their appearance between being offered an identification procedure and any attempt to hold an identification procedure, this may be given in evidence if the case comes to trial, and the identification officer may then consider other forms of identification, see *paragraph 3.21* and *Note 3C*;

(x)   that a moving image or photograph may be taken of them when they attend for any identification procedure;

(xi)   whether, before their identity became known, the witness was shown photographs, a computerised or artist's composite likeness or similar likeness or image by the police, see *Note 3B*;

(xii)   that if they change their appearance before an identification parade, it may not be practicable to arrange one on the day or subsequently and, because of the appearance change, the identification officer may consider alternative methods of identification, see *Note 3C*;

(xiii)   that they or their solicitor will be provided with details of the description of the suspect as first given by any witnesses who are to attend the video identification, identification parade, group identification or confrontation, see *paragraph 3.1*.

3.18 This information must also be recorded in a written notice handed to the suspect. The suspect must be given a reasonable opportunity to read the notice, after which, they should be asked to sign a second copy to indicate if they are willing to co-operate with the making of a video or take part in the identification parade or group identification. The signed copy shall be retained by the identification officer.

3.19 The duties of the identification officer under *paragraphs 3.17* and *3.18* may be performed by the custody officer or other officer not involved in the investigation if:

(a)   it is proposed to release the suspect in order that an identification procedure can be arranged and carried out and an inspector is not available to act as the identification officer, see *paragraph 3.11*, before the suspect leaves the station; or

(b)   it is proposed to keep the suspect in police detention whilst the procedure is arranged and carried out and waiting for an inspector to act as the identification officer, see *paragraph 3.11*, would cause unreasonable delay to the investigation.

The officer concerned shall inform the identification officer of the action taken and give them the signed copy of the notice. See *Note 3C*.

3.20 If the identification officer and officer in charge of the investigation suspect, on reasonable grounds that if the suspect was given the information and notice as in *paragraphs 3.17* and

3.18, they would then take steps to avoid being seen by a witness in any identification procedure, the identification officer may arrange for images of the suspect suitable for use in a video identification procedure to be obtained before giving the information and notice. If suspect's images are obtained in these circumstances, the suspect may, for the purposes of a video identification procedure, co-operate in providing new images which if suitable, would be used instead, see *paragraph 3.17(vi)*.

(c) Cases when the suspect is known but not available

3.21   When a known suspect is not available or has ceased to be available, see *paragraph 3.4*, the identification officer may make arrangements for a video identification (see *Annex A*). If necessary, the identification officer may follow the video identification procedures but using still images. Any suitable moving or still images may be used and these may be obtained covertly if necessary. Alternatively, the identification officer may make arrangements for a group identification. See *Note 3D*. These provisions may also be applied to juveniles where the consent of their parent or guardian is either refused or reasonable efforts to obtain that consent have failed (see *paragraph 2.12*).

3.22   Any covert activity should be strictly limited to that necessary to test the ability of the witness to identify the suspect.

3.23   The identification officer may arrange for the suspect to be confronted by the witness if none of the options referred to in *paragraphs 3.5* to *3.10* or *3.21* are practicable. A 'confrontation' is when the suspect is directly confronted by the witness. A confrontation does not require the suspect's consent. Confrontations must be carried out in accordance with *Annex D*.

3.24   Requirements for information to be given to, or sought from, a suspect or for the suspect to be given an opportunity to view images before they are shown to a witness, do not apply if the suspect's lack of co-operation prevents the necessary action.

(d) Documentation

3.25   A record shall be made of the video identification, identification parade, group identification or confrontation on forms provided for the purpose.

3.26   If the identification officer considers it is not practicable to hold a video identification or identification parade requested by the suspect, the reasons shall be recorded and explained to the suspect.

3.27   A record shall be made of a person's failure or refusal to co-operate in a video identification, identification parade or group identification and, if applicable, of the grounds for obtaining images in accordance with *paragraph 3.20*.

(e) Showing films and photographs of incidents and information released to the media

3.28   Nothing in this Code inhibits showing films photographs or other images to the public through the national or local media, or to police officers for the purposes of recognition and tracing suspects. However, when such material is shown to obtain evidence of recognition, the procedures in Part B will apply. See *Note 3AA*.

3.29   When a broadcast or publication is made, see *paragraph 3.28*, a copy of the relevant material released to the media for the purposes of recognising or tracing the suspect, shall be kept. The suspect or their solicitor shall be allowed to view such material before any procedures under *paragraphs 3.5* to *3.10, 3.21* or *3.23* of Part A are carried out, provided it is practicable and would not unreasonably delay the investigation. Each eye-witness involved in the procedure shall be asked, after they have taken part, whether they have seen any film, photograph or image relating to the offence or any description of the suspect which has been broadcast or published in any national or local media or on any social networking site and if they have, they should be asked to give details of the circumstances, such as the date and place as relevant. Their replies shall be recorded. This paragraph does not affect any separate requirement under the Criminal Procedure and Investigations Act 1996 to retain material in connection with criminal investigations.

(f) Destruction and retention of photographs taken or used in identification procedures

3.30 PACE, section 64A, see *paragraph 5.12*, provides powers to take photographs of suspects and allows these photographs to be used or disclosed only for purposes related to the prevention or detection of crime, the investigation of offences or the conduct of prosecutions by, or on behalf of, police or other law enforcement and prosecuting authorities inside and outside the United Kingdom or the enforcement of a sentence. After being so used or disclosed, they may be retained but can only be used or disclosed for the same purposes.

3.31 Subject to *paragraph 3.33*, the photographs (and all negatives and copies), of suspects not taken in accordance with the provisions in *paragraph 5.12* which are taken for the purposes of, or in connection with, the identification procedures in *paragraphs 3.5* to *3.10*, 3.21 or *3.23* must be destroyed unless the suspect:

    (a) is charged with, or informed they may be prosecuted for, a recordable offence;

    (b) is prosecuted for a recordable offence;

    (c) is cautioned for a recordable offence or given a warning or reprimand in accordance with the Crime and Disorder Act 1998 for a recordable offence; or

    (d) gives informed consent, in writing, for the photograph or images to be retained for purposes described in *paragraph 3.30*.

3.32 When *paragraph 3.31* requires the destruction of any photograph, the person must be given an opportunity to witness the destruction or to have a certificate confirming the destruction if they request one within five days of being informed that the destruction is required.

3.33 Nothing in *paragraph 3.31* affects any separate requirement under the Criminal Procedure and Investigations Act 1996 to retain material in connection with criminal investigations.

(B) Evidence of recognition by showing films, photographs and other images

3.34 This Part of this section applies when, for the purposes of obtaining evidence of recognition, any person, including a police officer:

    (a) views the image of an individual in a film, photograph or any other visual medium; and

    (b) is asked whether they recognise that individual as someone who is known to them.

See *Notes 3AA* and *3G*

3.35 The films, photographs and other images shall be shown on an individual basis to avoid any possibility of collusion and to provide safeguards against mistaken recognition (see *Note 3G*), the showing shall as far as possible follow the principles for video identification if the suspect is known, see *Annex A*, or identification by photographs if the suspect is not known, see *Annex E*.

3.36 A record of the circumstances and conditions under which the person is given an opportunity to recognise the individual must be made and the record must include:

    (a) Whether the person knew or was given information concerning the name or identity of any suspect.

    (b) What the person has been told *before* the viewing about the offence, the person(s) depicted in the images or the offender and by whom.

    (c) How and by whom the witness was asked to view the image or look at the individual.

    (d) Whether the viewing was alone or with others and if with others, the reason for it.

    (e) The arrangements under which the person viewed the film or saw the individual and by whom those arrangements were made.

    (f) Whether the viewing of any images was arranged as part of a mass circulation to police and the public or for selected persons.

    (g) The date time and place images were viewed or further viewed or the individual was seen.

    (h) The times between which the images were viewed or the individual was seen.

    (i) How the viewing of images or sighting of the individual was controlled and by whom.

    (j) Whether the person was familiar with the location shown in any images or the place where they saw the individual and if so, why.

(k) Whether or not on this occasion, the person claims to recognise any image shown, or any individual seen, as being someone known to them, and if they do:

    (i)   the reason

    (ii) the words of recognition

    (iii) any expressions of doubt

    (iv) what features of the image or the individual triggered the recognition.

3.37 The record under paragraph 3.36 may be made by:

- the person who views the image or sees the individual and makes the recognition.
- the officer or police staff in charge of showing the images to the person or in charge of the conditions under which the person sees the individual.

Notes for guidance

3AA The eye-witness identification procedures in Part A should not be used to test whether a witness can recognise a person as someone they know and would be able to give evidence of recognition along the lines that 'On (describe date, time location) I saw an image of an individual who I recognised as AB.' In these cases, the procedures in Part B shall apply.

3A Except for the provisions of Annex E, paragraph 1, a police officer who is a witness for the purposes of this part of the Code is subject to the same principles and procedures as a civilian witness.

3B When a witness attending an identification procedure has previously been shown photographs, or been shown or provided with computerised or artist's composite likenesses, or similar likenesses or pictures, it is the officer in charge of the investigation's responsibility to make the identification officer aware of this.

3C The purpose of paragraph 3.19 is to avoid or reduce delay in arranging identification procedures by enabling the required information and warnings, see sub-paragraphs 3.17(ix) and 3.17(xii), to be given at the earliest opportunity.

3D Paragraph 3.21 would apply when a known suspect deliberately makes themselves 'unavailable' in order to delay or frustrate arrangements for obtaining identification evidence. It also applies when a suspect refuses or fails to take part in a video identification, an identification parade or a group identification, or refuses or fails to take part in the only practicable options from that list. It enables any suitable images of the suspect, moving or still, which are available or can be obtained, to be used in an identification procedure. Examples include images from custody and other CCTV systems and from visually recorded interview records, see Code F Note for guidance 2D.

3E When it is proposed to show photographs to a witness in accordance with Annex E, it is the responsibility of the officer in charge of the investigation to confirm to the officer responsible for supervising and directing the showing, that the first description of the suspect given by that witness has been recorded. If this description has not been recorded, the procedure under Annex E must be postponed. See Annex E paragraph 2

3F The admissibility and value of identification evidence obtained when carrying out the procedure under paragraph 3.2 may be compromised if:

    (a) before a person is identified, the witness' attention is specifically drawn to that person; or

    (b) the suspect's identity becomes known before the procedure.

3G The admissibility and value of evidence of recognition obtained when carrying out the procedures in Part B may be compromised if before the person is recognised, the witness who has claimed to know them is given or is made, or becomes aware of, information about the person which was not previously known to them personally but which they have purported to rely on to support their claim that the person is in fact known to them.

4   Identification by fingerprints and footwear impressions

(A) Taking fingerprints in connection with a criminal investigation

(a) General

4.1 References to 'fingerprints' means any record, produced by any method, of the skin pattern and other physical characteristics or features of a person's:

    (i)   fingers; or

    (ii) palms.

(b) Action

4.2 A person's fingerprints may be taken in connection with the investigation of an offence only with their consent or if *paragraph 4.3* applies. If the person is at a police station consent must be in writing.

4.3 PACE, section 61, provides powers to take fingerprints without consent from any person over the age of ten years:

- (a) under section 61(3), from a person detained at a police station in consequence of being arrested for a recordable offence, see *Note 4A*, if they have not had their fingerprints taken in the course of the investigation of the offence unless those previously taken fingerprints are not a complete set or some or all of those fingerprints are not of sufficient quality to allow satisfactory analysis, comparison or matching.
- (b) under section 61(4), from a person detained at a police station who has been charged with a recordable offence, see *Note 4A*, or informed they will be reported for such an offence if they have not had their fingerprints taken in the course of the investigation of the offence unless those previously taken fingerprints are not a complete set or some or all of those fingerprints are not of sufficient quality to allow satisfactory analysis, comparison or matching.
- (c) under section 61(4A), from a person who has been bailed to appear at a court or police station if the person:
    - (i) has answered to bail for a person whose fingerprints were taken previously and there are reasonable grounds for believing they are not the same person; or
    - (ii) who has answered to bail claims to be a different person from a person whose fingerprints were previously taken;
    and in either case, the court or an officer of inspector rank or above, authorises the fingerprints to be taken at the court or police station;
- (ca) under section 61(5A) from a person who has been arrested for a recordable offence and released if the person:
    - (i) is on bail and has not had their fingerprints taken in the course of the investigation of the offence, or;
    - (ii) has had their fingerprints taken in the course of the investigation of the offence, but they do not constitute a complete set or some, or all, of the fingerprints are not of sufficient quality to allow satisfactory analysis, comparison or matching.
- (cb) under section 61(5B) from a person not detained at a police station who has been charged with a recordable offence or informed they will be reported for such an offence if they have not had their fingerprints taken in the course of the investigation or their fingerprints have been taken in the course of the investigation of the offence, but they do not constitute a complete set or some, or all, of the fingerprints are not of sufficient quality to allow satisfactory analysis, comparison or matching.
- (d) under section 61(6), from a person who has been:
    - (i) convicted of a recordable offence;
    - (ii) given a caution in respect of a recordable offence which, at the time of the caution, the person admitted; or
    - (iii) warned or reprimanded under the Crime and Disorder Act 1998, section 65, for a recordable offence.
- (e) under section 61(6A) from a person a constable reasonably suspects is committing or attempting to commit, or has committed or attempted to commit, any offence if either:
    - the person's name is unknown and cannot be readily ascertained by the constable; or
    - the constable has reasonable grounds for doubting whether a name given by the person is their real name.
    Note: fingerprints taken under this power are not regarded as having been taken in the course of the investigation of an offence.
    [See *Note 4C*]

(f)   under section 61(6D) from a person who has been convicted outside England and Wales of an offence which if committed in England and Wales would be a qualifying offence as defined by PACE, section 65A (see *Note 4AB*) if:

(i)   the person's fingerprints have not been taken previously under this power or their fingerprints have been so taken on a previous occasion but they do not constitute a complete set or some, or all, of the fingerprints are not of sufficient quality to allow satisfactory analysis, comparison or matching; and

(ii)   a police officer of inspector rank or above is satisfied that taking fingerprints is necessary to assist in the prevention or detection of crime and authorises them to be taken.

4.4 PACE, section 63A(4) and Schedule 2A provide powers to:

(a)   make a requirement (in accordance with Annex G) for a person to attend a police station to have their fingerprints taken in the exercise of certain powers in paragraph 4.3 above when that power applies at the time the fingerprints would be taken in accordance with the requirement. Those powers are:

(i)   section 61(5A)—Persons arrested for a recordable offence and released, see paragraph 4.3(ca): The requirement may not be made more than six months from the day the investigating officer was informed that the fingerprints previously taken were incomplete or below standard.

(ii)   section 61(5B)—Persons charged etc. with a recordable offence, see paragraph 4.3(cb): The requirement may not be made more than six months from:

- the day the person was charged or reported if fingerprints have not been taken since then; or
- the day the investigating officer was informed that the fingerprints previously taken were incomplete or below standard.

(iii)   section 61(6)—Person convicted, cautioned, warned or reprimanded for a recordable offence in England and Wales, see paragraph 4.3(d): Where the offence for which the person was convicted etc is also a qualifying offence (see *Note 4AB*), there is no time limit for the exercise of this power. Where the conviction etc. is for a recordable offence which is not a qualifying offence, the requirement may not be made more than two years from:

- the day the person was convicted, cautioned, warned or reprimanded, or the day Schedule 2A comes into force (if later), if fingerprints have not been taken since then; or
- the day an officer from the force investigating the offence was informed that the fingerprints previously taken were incomplete or below standard or the day Schedule 2A comes into force (if later).

(v)   section 61(6D)—A person who has been convicted of a qualifying offence (see *Note 4AB*) outside England and Wales, see paragraph 4.3(g): There is no time limit for making the requirement.

Note: A person who has had their fingerprints taken under any of the powers in section 61 mentioned in paragraph 4.3 on two occasions in relation to any offence may not be required under Schedule 2A to attend a police station for their fingerprints to be taken again under section 61 in relation to that offence, unless authorised by an officer of inspector rank or above. The fact of the authorisation and the reasons for giving it must be recorded as soon as practicable.

(b)   arrest, without warrant, a person who fails to comply with the requirement.

4.5 A person's fingerprints may be taken, as above, electronically.

4.6 Reasonable force may be used, if necessary, to take a person's fingerprints without their consent under the powers as in *paragraphs 4.3* and *4.4*.

4.7 Before any fingerprints are taken:

    (a) without consent under any power mentioned in *paragraphs 4.3* and *4.4* above, the person must be informed of:

        (i) the reason their fingerprints are to be taken;

        (ii) the power under which they are to be taken; and

        (iii) the fact that the relevant authority has been given if any power mentioned in *paragraph 4.3(c), (d)* or *(f)* applies

    (b) with or without consent at a police station or elsewhere, the person must be informed:

        (i) that their fingerprints may be subject of a speculative search against other fingerprints, see *Note 4B*; and

        (ii) that their fingerprints may be retained in accordance with *Annex F, Part (a)* unless they were taken under the power mentioned in paragraph 4.3(e) when they must be destroyed after they have being checked (See *Note 4C*).

(c) Documentation

4.8A A record must be made as soon as practicable after the fingerprints are taken, of:

- the matters in paragraph 4.7(a)(i) to (iii) and the fact that the person has been informed of those matters; and
- the fact that the person has been informed of the matters in paragraph 4.7(b) (i) and (ii).

The record must be made in the person's custody record if they are detained at a police station when the fingerprints are taken.

4.8 If force is used, a record shall be made of the circumstances and those present.

4.9 *Not used.*

(B) Taking fingerprints in connection with immigration enquiries

Action

4.10 A person's fingerprints may be taken and retained for the purposes of immigration law enforcement and control in accordance with powers and procedures other than under PACE and for which the UK Border Agency (not the police) are responsible. Details of these powers and procedures which are under the Immigration Act 1971, Schedule 2 and Immigration and Asylum Act 1999, section 141, including modifications to the PACE Codes of Practice are contained in Chapter 24 of the Operational Instructions and Guidance manual which is published by the UK Border Agency (See *Note 4D*).

4.11 *Not used.*

4.12 *Not used.*

4.13 *Not used.*

4.14 *Not used.*

4.15 *Not used.*

(C) Taking footwear impressions in connection with a criminal investigation

(a) Action

4.16 Impressions of a person's footwear may be taken in connection with the investigation of an offence only with their consent or if *paragraph 4.17* applies. If the person is at a police station consent must be in writing.

4.17 PACE, section 61A, provides power for a police officer to take footwear impressions without consent from any person over the age of ten years who is detained at a police station:

    (a) in consequence of being arrested for a recordable offence, see *Note 4A*; or if the detainee has been charged with a recordable offence, or informed they will be reported for such an offence; and

    (b) the detainee has not had an impression of their footwear taken in the course of the investigation of the offence unless the previously taken impression is not complete or is not of sufficient quality to allow satisfactory analysis, comparison or matching (whether in the case in question or generally).

4.18 Reasonable force may be used, if necessary, to take a footwear impression from a detainee without consent under the power in *paragraph 4.17.*

4.19 Before any footwear impression is taken with, or without, consent as above, the person must be informed:

(a) of the reason the impression is to be taken;

(b) that the impression may be retained and may be subject of a speculative search against other impressions, see *Note 4B*, unless destruction of the impression is required in accordance with *Annex F*, Part (a); and

(c) that if their footwear impressions are required to be destroyed, they may witness their destruction as provided for in *Annex F*, Part (a).

(b) Documentation

4.20 A record must be made as soon as possible, of the reason for taking a person's footwear impressions without consent. If force is used, a record shall be made of the circumstances and those present.

4.21 A record shall be made when a person has been informed under the terms of *paragraph 4.19(b)*, of the possibility that their footwear impressions may be subject of a speculative search.

Notes for guidance

4A References to 'recordable offences' in this Code relate to those offences for which convictions, cautions, reprimands and warnings may be recorded in national police records. See PACE, section 27(4). The recordable offences current at the time when this Code was prepared, are any offences which carry a sentence of imprisonment on conviction (irrespective of the period, or the age of the offender or actual sentence passed) as well as the non-imprisonable offences under the Vagrancy Act 1824 sections 3 and 4 (begging and persistent begging), the Street Offences Act 1959, section 1 (loitering or soliciting for purposes of prostitution), the Road Traffic Act 1988, section 25 (tampering with motor vehicles), the Criminal Justice and Public Order Act 1994, section 167 (touting for hire car services) and others listed in the National Police Records (Recordable Offences) Regulations 2000 as amended.

4AB A qualifying offence is one of the offences specified in PACE, section 65A. These indictable offences which concern the use or threat of violence or unlawful force against persons, sexual offences and offences against children include, for example, murder, manslaughter, false imprisonment, kidnapping and other offences such as:

- *sections 4, 16, 18, 20 to 24 or 47 of the Offences Against the Person Act 1861;*
- *sections 16 to 18 of the Firearms Act 1968;*
- *sections 9 or 10 of the Theft Act 1968 or under section 12A of that Act involving an accident which caused a person's death;*
- *section 1 of the Criminal Damage Act 1971 required to be charged as arson;*
- *section 1 of the Protection of Children Act 1978 and;*
- *sections 1 to 19, 25, 26, 30 to 41, 47 to 50, 52, 53, 57 to 59, 61 to 67, 69 and 70 of the Sexual Offences Act 2003.*

4B Fingerprints, footwear impressions or a DNA sample (and the information derived from it) taken from a person arrested on suspicion of being involved in a recordable offence, or charged with such an offence, or informed they will be reported for such an offence, may be subject of a speculative search. This means the fingerprints, footwear impressions or DNA sample may be checked against other fingerprints, footwear impressions and DNA records held by, or on behalf of, the police and other law enforcement authorities in, or outside, the UK, or held in connection with, or as a result of, an investigation of an offence inside or outside the UK. Fingerprints, footwear impressions and samples taken from a person suspected of committing a recordable offence but not arrested, charged or informed they will be reported for it, may be subject to a speculative search only if the person consents in writing. The following is an example of a basic form of words:

> 'I consent to my fingerprints, footwear impressions and DNA sample and information derived from it being retained and used only for purposes related to the prevention and detection of a crime, the investigation of an offence or the conduct of a prosecution either nationally or internationally.
>
> I understand that my fingerprints, footwear impressions or DNA sample may be checked against other fingerprint, footwear impressions and DNA records held by or on behalf of relevant law enforcement authorities, either nationally or internationally.
>
> I understand that once I have given my consent for my fingerprints, footwear impressions or DNA sample to be retained and used I cannot withdraw this consent.'

See Annex F regarding the retention and use of fingerprints and footwear impressions taken with consent for elimination purposes.

4C The power under section 61(6A) of PACE described in paragraph 4.3(e) allows fingerprints of a suspect who has not been arrested to be taken in connection with any offence (whether recordable or not) using a mobile device and then checked on the street against the database containing the national fingerprint collection. Fingerprints taken under this power cannot be retained after they have been checked. The results may make an arrest for the suspected offence based on the name condition unnecessary (See Code G paragraph 2.9(a)) and enable the offence to be disposed of without arrest, for example, by summons/charging by post, penalty notice or words of advice. If arrest for a non-recordable offence is necessary for any other reasons, this power may also be exercised at the station. Before the power is exercised, the officer should:

- inform the person of the nature of the suspected offence and why they are suspected of committing it.
- give them a reasonable opportunity to establish their real name before deciding that their name is unknown and cannot be readily ascertained or that there are reasonable grounds to doubt that a name they have given is their real name.
- as applicable, inform the person of the reason why their name is not know and cannot be readily ascertained or of the grounds for doubting that a name they have given is their real name, including, for example, the reason why a particular document the person has produced to verify their real name, is not sufficient.

4D Powers to take fingerprints without consent for immigration purposes are given to police and immigration officers under the:

- (a) Immigration Act 1971, Schedule 2, paragraph 18(2), when it is reasonably necessary for the purposes of identifying a person detained under the Immigration Act 1971, Schedule 2, paragraph 16 (Detention of person liable to examination or removal), and
- (b) Immigration and Asylum Act 1999, section 141(7) when a person:
  - fails without reasonable excuse to produce, on arrival, a valid passport with a photograph or some other document satisfactorily establishing their identity and nationality;
  - is refused entry to the UK but is temporarily admitted if an immigration officer reasonably suspects the person might break a residence or reporting condition;
  - is subject to directions for removal from the UK;
  - has been arrested under the Immigration Act 1971, Schedule 2, paragraph 17;
  - has made a claim for asylum
  - is a dependant of any of the above.

The Immigration and Asylum Act 1999, section 142(3), also gives police and immigration officers power to arrest without warrant, a person who fails to comply with a requirement imposed by the Secretary of State to attend a specified place for fingerprinting.

5 Examinations to establish identity and the taking of photographs

(A) Detainees at police stations

(a) Searching or examination of detainees at police stations

5.1 PACE, section 54A (1), allows a detainee at a police station to be searched or examined or both, to establish:

(a) whether they have any marks, features or injuries that would tend to identify them as a person involved in the commission of an offence and to photograph any identifying marks, see *paragraph 5.5*; or

(b) their identity, see *Note 5A*.

A person detained at a police station to be searched under a stop and search power, see Code A, is not a detainee for the purposes of these powers.

5.2 A search and/or examination to find marks under section 54A (1) (a) may be carried out without the detainee's consent, see *paragraph 2.12*, only if authorised by an officer of at least inspector rank when consent has been withheld or it is not practicable to obtain consent, see *Note 5D*.

5.3 A search or examination to establish a suspect's identity under section 54A (1) (b) may be carried out without the detainee's consent, see *paragraph 2.12*, only if authorised by an officer of at least inspector rank when the detainee has refused to identify themselves or the authorising officer has reasonable grounds for suspecting the person is not who they claim to be.

5.4 Any marks that assist in establishing the detainee's identity, or their identification as a person involved in the commission of an offence, are identifying marks. Such marks may be photographed with the detainee's consent, see *paragraph 2.12*; or without their consent if it is withheld or it is not practicable to obtain it, see *Note 5D*.

5.5 A detainee may only be searched, examined and photographed under section 54A, by a police officer of the same sex.

5.6 Any photographs of identifying marks, taken under section 54A, may be used or disclosed only for purposes related to the prevention or detection of crime, the investigation of offences or the conduct of prosecutions by, or on behalf of, police or other law enforcement and prosecuting authorities inside, and outside, the UK. After being so used or disclosed, the photograph may be retained but must not be used or disclosed except for these purposes, see *Note 5B*.

5.7 The powers, as in *paragraph 5.1*, do not affect any separate requirement under the Criminal Procedure and Investigations Act 1996 to retain material in connection with criminal investigations.

5.8 Authority for the search and/or examination for the purposes of *paragraphs 5.2* and *5.3* may be given orally or in writing. If given orally, the authorising officer must confirm it in writing as soon as practicable. A separate authority is required for each purpose which applies.

5.9 If it is established a person is unwilling to co-operate sufficiently to enable a search and/or examination to take place or a suitable photograph to be taken, an officer may use reasonable force to:

(a) search and/or examine a detainee without their consent; and

(b) photograph any identifying marks without their consent.

5.10 The thoroughness and extent of any search or examination carried out in accordance with the powers in section 54A must be no more than the officer considers necessary to achieve the required purpose. Any search or examination which involves the removal of more than the person's outer clothing shall be conducted in accordance with Code C, *Annex A, paragraph 11*.

5.11 An intimate search may not be carried out under the powers in section 54A.

(b) Photographing detainees at police stations and other persons elsewhere than at a police station

5.12 Under PACE, section 64A, an officer may photograph :

(a) any person whilst they are detained at a police station; and

(b) any person who is elsewhere than at a police station and who has been:—

(i) arrested by a constable for an offence;

(ii) taken into custody by a constable after being arrested for an offence by a person other than a constable;

(iiia) given a direction by a constable under section 27 of the Violent Crime Reduction Act 2006.

(iii) made subject to a requirement to wait with a community support officer under *paragraph 2(3)* or *(3B)* of Schedule 4 to the Police Reform Act 2002;

(iv) given a penalty notice by a constable in uniform under Chapter 1 of Part 1 of the Criminal Justice and Police Act 2001, a penalty notice by a constable under section 444A of the Education Act 1996, or a fixed penalty notice by a constable in uniform under section 54 of the Road Traffic Offenders Act 1988;

(v) given a notice in relation to a relevant fixed penalty offence (within the meaning of *paragraph 1* of Schedule 4 to the Police Reform Act 2002) by a community support officer by virtue of a designation applying that paragraph to him;

(vi) given a notice in relation to a relevant fixed penalty offence (within the meaning of paragraph 1 of Schedule 5 to the Police Reform Act 2002) by an accredited person by virtue of accreditation specifying that that paragraph applies to him; or

(vii) given a direction to leave and not return to a specified location for up to 48 hours by a police constable (under section 27 of the Violent Crime Reduction Act 2006).

5.12A Photographs taken under PACE, section 64A:

(a) may be taken with the person's consent, or without their consent if consent is withheld or it is not practicable to obtain their consent, see *Note 5E*; and

(b) may be used or disclosed only for purposes related to the prevention or detection of crime, the investigation of offences or the conduct of prosecutions by, or on behalf of, police or other law enforcement and prosecuting authorities inside and outside the United Kingdom or the enforcement of any sentence or order made by a court when dealing with an offence. After being so used or disclosed, they may be retained but can only be used or disclosed for the same purposes. See *Note 5B*.

5.13 The officer proposing to take a detainee's photograph may, for this purpose, require the person to remove any item or substance worn on, or over, all, or any part of, their head or face. If they do not comply with such a requirement, the officer may remove the item or substance.

5.14 If it is established the detainee is unwilling to co-operate sufficiently to enable a suitable photograph to be taken and it is not reasonably practicable to take the photograph covertly, an officer may use reasonable force, see *Note 5F*.

(a) to take their photograph without their consent; and

(b) for the purpose of taking the photograph, remove any item or substance worn on, or over, all, or any part of, the person's head or face which they have failed to remove when asked.

5.15 For the purposes of this Code, a photograph may be obtained without the person's consent by making a copy of an image of them taken at any time on a camera system installed anywhere in the police station.

(c) Information to be given

5.16 When a person is searched, examined or photographed under the provisions as in *paragraph 5.1* and 5.12, or their photograph obtained as in *paragraph 5.15*, they must be informed of the:

(a) purpose of the search, examination or photograph;

(b) grounds on which the relevant authority, if applicable, has been given; and

(c) purposes for which the photograph may be used, disclosed or retained. This information must be given before the search or examination commences or the photograph is taken, except if the photograph is:

(i) to be taken covertly;

(ii) obtained as in *paragraph 5.15*, in which case the person must be informed as soon as practicable after the photograph is taken or obtained.

(d) Documentation

5.17 A record must be made when a detainee is searched, examined, or a photograph of the person, or any identifying marks found on them, are taken. The record must include the:

(a) identity, subject to *paragraph 2.18*, of the officer carrying out the search, examination or taking the photograph;

(b) purpose of the search, examination or photograph and the outcome;

(c) detainee's consent to the search, examination or photograph, or the reason the person was searched, examined or photographed without consent;

(d) giving of any authority as in *paragraphs 5.2* and *5.3*, the grounds for giving it and the authorising officer.

5.18 If force is used when searching, examining or taking a photograph in accordance with this section, a record shall be made of the circumstances and those present.

(B) Persons at police stations not detained

5.19 When there are reasonable grounds for suspecting the involvement of a person in a criminal offence, but that person is at a police station **voluntarily** and not detained, the provisions of *paragraphs 5.1* to *5.18* should apply, subject to the modifications in the following paragraphs.

5.20 References to the 'person being detained' and to the powers mentioned in *paragraph 5.1* which apply only to detainees at police stations shall be omitted.

5.21 Force may not be used to:

(a) search and/or examine the person to:

(i) discover whether they have any marks that would tend to identify them as a person involved in the commission of an offence; or

(ii) establish their identity, see *Note 5A*;

(b) take photographs of any identifying marks, see *paragraph 5.4*; or

(c) take a photograph of the person.

5.22 Subject to *paragraph 5.24*, the photographs of persons or of their identifying marks which are not taken in accordance with the provisions mentioned in *paragraphs 5.1* or *5.12*, must be destroyed (together with any negatives and copies) unless the person:

(a) is charged with, or informed they may be prosecuted for, a recordable offence;

(b) is prosecuted for a recordable offence;

(c) is cautioned for a recordable offence or given a warning or reprimand in accordance with the Crime and Disorder Act 1998 for a recordable offence; or

(d) gives informed consent, in writing, for the photograph or image to be retained as in *paragraph 5.6*.

5.23 When *paragraph 5.22* requires the destruction of any photograph, the person must be given an opportunity to witness the destruction or to have a certificate confirming the destruction provided they so request the certificate within five days of being informed the destruction is required.

5.24 Nothing in *paragraph 5.22* affects any separate requirement under the Criminal Procedure and Investigations Act 1996 to retain material in connection with criminal investigations.

Notes for guidance

5A The conditions under which fingerprints may be taken to assist in establishing a person's identity, are described in section 4.

5B Examples of purposes related to the prevention or detection of crime, the investigation of offences or the conduct of prosecutions include:

(a) *checking the photograph against other photographs held in records or in connection with, or as a result of, an investigation of an offence to establish whether the person is liable to arrest for other offences;*

(b) *when the person is arrested at the same time as other people, or at a time when it is likely that other people will be arrested, using the photograph to help establish who was arrested, at what time and where;*

(c) when the real identity of the person is not known and cannot be readily ascertained or there are reasonable grounds for doubting a name and other personal details given by the person, are their real name and personal details. In these circumstances, using or disclosing the photograph to help to establish or verify their real identity or determine whether they are liable to arrest for some other offence, e.g. by checking it against other photographs held in records or in connection with, or as a result of, an investigation of an offence;

(d) when it appears any identification procedure in section 3 may need to be arranged for which the person's photograph would assist;

(e) when the person's release without charge may be required, and if the release is:

   (i)   on bail to appear at a police station, using the photograph to help verify the person's identity when they answer their bail and if the person does not answer their bail, to assist in arresting them; or

   (ii) without bail, using the photograph to help verify their identity or assist in locating them for the purposes of serving them with a summons to appear at court in criminal proceedings;

(f) when the person has answered to bail at a police station and there are reasonable grounds for doubting they are the person who was previously granted bail, using the photograph to help establish or verify their identity;

(g) when the person arrested on a warrant claims to be a different person from the person named on the warrant and a photograph would help to confirm or disprove their claim;

(h) when the person has been charged with, reported for, or convicted of, a recordable offence and their photograph is not already on record as a result of (a) to (f) or their photograph is on record but their appearance has changed since it was taken and the person has not yet been released or brought before a court.

5C   There is no power to arrest a person convicted of a recordable offence solely to take their photograph. The power to take photographs in this section applies only where the person is in custody as a result of the exercise of another power, e.g. arrest for fingerprinting under PACE, section 27.

5D   Examples of when it would not be practicable to obtain a detainee's consent, see paragraph 2.12, to a search, examination or the taking of a photograph of an identifying mark include:

(a) when the person is drunk or otherwise unfit to give consent;

(b) when there are reasonable grounds to suspect that if the person became aware a search or examination was to take place or an identifying mark was to be photographed, they would take steps to prevent this happening, e.g. by violently resisting, covering or concealing the mark etc and it would not otherwise be possible to carry out the search or examination or to photograph any identifying mark;

(c) in the case of a juvenile, if the parent or guardian cannot be contacted in sufficient time to allow the search or examination to be carried out or the photograph to be taken.

5E   Examples of when it would not be practicable to obtain the person's consent, see paragraph 2.12, to a photograph being taken include:

(a) when the person is drunk or otherwise unfit to give consent;

(b) when there are reasonable grounds to suspect that if the person became aware a photograph, suitable to be used or disclosed for the use and disclosure described in paragraph 5.6, was to be taken, they would take steps to prevent it being taken, e.g. by violently resisting, covering or distorting their face etc, and it would not otherwise be possible to take a suitable photograph;

(c) when, in order to obtain a suitable photograph, it is necessary to take it covertly; and

(d) in the case of a juvenile, if the parent or guardian cannot be contacted in sufficient time to allow the photograph to be taken.

5F   The use of reasonable force to take the photograph of a suspect elsewhere than at a police station must be carefully considered. In order to obtain a suspect's consent and co-operation to remove an item of religious headwear to take their photograph, a constable should consider whether in the circumstances of the situation the removal of the headwear and the taking of the photograph should be by an officer of the same sex as the person. It would be appropriate for these actions to be conducted out of public view.

6 Identification by body samples and impressions

(A) General

6.1 References to:

(a) an 'intimate sample' mean a dental impression or sample of blood, semen or any other tissue fluid, urine, or pubic hair, or a swab taken from any part of a person's genitals or from a person's body orifice other than the mouth;

(b) a 'non-intimate sample' means:

(i) a sample of hair, other than pubic hair, which includes hair plucked with the root, see *Note 6A*;

(ii) a sample taken from a nail or from under a nail;

(iii) a swab taken from any part of a person's body other than a part from which a swab taken would be an intimate sample;

(iv) saliva;

(v) a skin impression which means any record, other than a fingerprint, which is a record, in any form and produced by any method, of the skin pattern and other physical characteristics or features of the whole, or any part of, a person's foot or of any other part of their body.

(B) Action

(a) Intimate samples

6.2 PACE, section 62, provides that intimate samples may be taken under:

(a) section 62(1), from a person in police detention only:

(i) if a police officer of inspector rank or above has reasonable grounds to believe such an impression or sample will tend to confirm or disprove the suspect's involvement in a recordable offence, see *Note 4A*, and gives authorisation for a sample to be taken; and

(ii) with the suspect's written consent;

(b) section 62(1A), from a person not in police detention but from whom two or more non-intimate samples have been taken in the course of an investigation of an offence and the samples, though suitable, have proved insufficient if:

(i) a police officer of inspector rank or above authorises it to be taken; and

(ii) the person concerned gives their written consent. See *Notes 6B* and *6C*.

(c) section 62(2A), from a person convicted outside England and Wales of an offence which if committed in England and Wales would be qualifying offence as defined by PACE, section 65A (see *Note 4AB*) from whom two or more non-intimate samples taken under section 63(3E) (see paragraph 6.6(h)) have proved insufficient if:

(i) a police officer of inspector rank or above is satisfied that taking the sample is necessary to assist in the prevention or detection of crime and authorises it to be taken; and

(ii) the person concerned gives their written consent.

6.2A PACE, section 63A(4) and Schedule 2A provide powers to:

(a) make a requirement (in accordance with Annex G) for a person to attend a police station to have an intimate sample taken in the exercise of one of the following powers in paragraph 6.2 when that power applies at the time the sample is to be taken in accordance with the requirement or after the person's arrest if they fail to comply with the requirement:

(i) section 62(1A)—Persons from whom two or more non-intimate samples have been taken and proved to be insufficient, see paragraph 6.2(b): There is no time limit for making the requirement.

(ii) section 62(2A)—Persons convicted outside England and Wales from whom two or more non-intimate samples taken under section 63(3E) (see paragraph 6.6(h)) have proved insufficient, see *paragraph 6.2(c)*: There is no time limit for making the requirement.

6.3 Before a suspect is asked to provide an intimate sample, they must be:

(a) informed:

    (i) of the reason, including the nature of the suspected offence (except if taken under *paragraph 6.2(c)* from a person convicted outside England and Wales.

    (ii) that authorisation has been given and the provisions under which given;

    (iii) that a sample taken at a police station may be subject of a speculative search;

(b) warned that if they refuse without good cause their refusal may harm their case if it comes to trial, see *Note 6D*. If the suspect is in police detention and not legally represented, they must also be reminded of their entitlement to have free legal advice, see Code C, *paragraph 6.5*, and the reminder noted in the custody record. If *paragraph 6.2(b)* applies and the person is attending a station voluntarily, their entitlement to free legal advice as in Code C, *paragraph 3.21* shall be explained to them. 6.4 Dental impressions may only be taken by a registered dentist. Other intimate samples, except for samples of urine, may only be taken by a registered medical practitioner or registered nurse or registered paramedic.

(b) Non-intimate samples

6.5 A non-intimate sample may be taken from a detainee only with their written consent or if *paragraph 6.6* applies.

6.6 (aa) A non-intimate sample may be taken from a person without the appropriate consent in the following circumstances:

    (i) under section 63(2A) where the person is in police detention as a consequence of his arrest for a recordable offence and he has not had a non-intimate sample of the same type and from the same part of the body taken in the course of the investigation of the offence by the police or he has had such a sample taken but it proved insufficient.

    (ii) Under section 63(3)(a) where he is being held in custody by the police on the authority of a court and an officer of at least the rank of inspector authorises it to be taken.

(b) under section 63(3A), from a person charged with a recordable offence or informed they will be reported for such an offence: and

    (i) that person has not had a non-intimate sample taken from them in the course of the investigation; or

    (ii) if they have had a sample taken, it proved unsuitable or insufficient for the same form of analysis, see *Note 6B*; or

(c) under section 63(3B), from a person convicted of a recordable offence after the date on which that provision came into effect. PACE, section 63A, describes the circumstances in which a police officer may require a person convicted of a recordable offence to attend a police station for a non-intimate sample to be taken.

6.7 Reasonable force may be used, if necessary, to take a non-intimate sample from a person without their consent under the powers mentioned in *paragraph 6.6*.

6.8 Before any intimate sample is taken with consent or non-intimate sample is taken with, or without, consent, the person must be informed:

(a) of the reason for taking the sample;

(b) of the grounds on which the relevant authority has been given;

(c) that the sample or information derived from the sample may be retained and subject of a speculative search, see *Note 6E*, unless their destruction is required as in *Annex F*, Part A.

6.9 When clothing needs to be removed in circumstances likely to cause embarrassment to the person, no person of the opposite sex who is not a registered medical practitioner or registered health care professional shall be present, (unless in the case of a juvenile, mentally disordered or mentally vulnerable person, that person specifically requests the presence of an appropriate adult of the opposite sex who is readily available) nor shall anyone whose presence is unnecessary. However, in the case of a juvenile, this is subject to the overriding proviso that such a removal of clothing may take place in the absence of the appropriate adult only if the juvenile signifies, in their presence, that they prefer the adult's absence and they agree.

(c) Documentation

6.10 A record of the reasons for taking a sample or impression and, if applicable, of its destruction must be made as soon as practicable. If force is used, a record shall be made of the circumstances and those present. If written consent is given to the taking of a sample or impression, the fact must be recorded in writing.

6.11 A record must be made of a warning given as required by *paragraph 6.3*.

6.12 A record shall be made of the fact that a person has been informed as in *paragraph 6.8(c)* that samples may be subject of a speculative search.

Notes for guidance

6A *When hair samples are taken for the purpose of DNA analysis (rather than for other purposes such as making a visual match), the suspect should be permitted a reasonable choice as to what part of the body the hairs are taken from. When hairs are plucked, they should be plucked individually, unless the suspect prefers otherwise and no more should be plucked than the person taking them reasonably considers necessary for a sufficient sample.*

6B (a) *An insufficient sample is one which is not sufficient either in quantity or quality to provide information for a particular form of analysis, such as DNA analysis. A sample may also be insufficient if enough information cannot be obtained from it by analysis because of loss, destruction, damage or contamination of the sample or as a result of an earlier, unsuccessful attempt at analysis.*

(b) *An unsuitable sample is one which, by its nature, is not suitable for a particular form of analysis.*

6C *Nothing in paragraph 6.2 prevents intimate samples being taken for elimination purposes with the consent of the person concerned but the provisions of paragraph 2.12 relating to the role of the appropriate adult, should be applied. Paragraph 6.2(b) does not, however, apply where the non-intimate samples were previously taken under the Terrorism Act 2000, Schedule 8, paragraph 10.*

6D *In warning a person who is asked to provide an intimate sample as in paragraph 6.3, the following form of words may be used:*

'You do not have to provide this sample/allow this swab or impression to be taken, but I must warn you that if you refuse without good cause, your refusal may harm your case if it comes to trial.'

6E *Fingerprints or a DNA sample and the information derived from it taken from a person arrested on suspicion of being involved in a recordable offence, or charged with such an offence, or informed they will be reported for such an offence, may be subject of a speculative search. This means they may be checked against other fingerprints and DNA records held by, or on behalf of, the police and other law enforcement authorities in or outside the UK or held in connection with, or as a result of, an investigation of an offence inside or outside the UK. Fingerprints and samples taken from any other person, e.g. a person suspected of committing a recordable offence but who has not been arrested, charged or informed they will be reported for it, may be subject to a speculative search only if the person consents in writing to their fingerprints being subject of such a search. The following is an example of a basic form of words:*

'I consent to my fingerprints/DNA sample and information derived from it being retained and used only for purposes related to the prevention and detection of a crime, the investigation of an offence or the conduct of a prosecution either nationally or internationally.

I understand that this sample may be checked against other fingerprint/DNA records held by or on behalf of relevant law enforcement authorities, either nationally or internationally.

I understand that once I have given my consent for the sample to be retained and used I cannot withdraw this consent.'

See Annex F regarding the retention and use of fingerprints and samples taken with consent for elimination purposes.

6F Samples of urine and non-intimate samples taken in accordance with sections 63B and 63C of PACE may not be used for identification purposes in accordance with this Code. See Code C Note for guidance 17D.

ANNEX A   VIDEO IDENTIFICATION

(a) General

1. The arrangements for obtaining and ensuring the availability of a suitable set of images to be used in a video identification must be the responsibility of an identification officer, who has no direct involvement with the case.

2. The set of images must include the suspect and at least eight other people who, so far as possible, resemble the suspect in age, general appearance and position in life. Only one suspect shall appear in any set unless there are two suspects of roughly similar appearance, in which case they may be shown together with at least twelve other people.

2A If the suspect has an unusual physical feature, e.g., a facial scar, tattoo or distinctive hairstyle or hair colour which does not appear on the images of the other people that are available to be used, steps may be taken to:

    (a) conceal the location of the feature on the images of the suspect and the other people; or

    (b) replicate that feature on the images of the other people.

For these purposes, the feature may be concealed or replicated electronically or by any other method which it is practicable to use to ensure that the images of the suspect and other people resemble each other. The identification officer has discretion to choose whether to conceal or replicate the feature and the method to be used. If an unusual physical feature has been described by the witness, the identification officer should, if practicable, have that feature replicated. If it has not been described, concealment may be more appropriate.

2B If the identification officer decides that a feature should be concealed or replicated, the reason for the decision and whether the feature was concealed or replicated in the images shown to any witness shall be recorded.

2C If the witness requests to view an image where an unusual physical feature has been concealed or replicated without the feature being concealed or replicated, the witness may be allowed to do so.

3. The images used to conduct a video identification shall, as far as possible, show the suspect and other people in the same positions or carrying out the same sequence of movements. They shall also show the suspect and other people under identical conditions unless the identification officer reasonably believes:

    (a) because of the suspect's failure or refusal to co-operate or other reasons, it is not practicable for the conditions to be identical; and

    (b) any difference in the conditions would not direct a witness' attention to any individual image.

4. The reasons identical conditions are not practicable shall be recorded on forms provided for the purpose.

5. Provision must be made for each person shown to be identified by number.

6. If police officers are shown, any numerals or other identifying badges must be concealed. If a prison inmate is shown, either as a suspect or not, then either all, or none of, the people shown should be in prison clothing.

7. The suspect or their solicitor, friend, or appropriate adult must be given a reasonable opportunity to see the complete set of images before it is shown to any witness. If the suspect has a reasonable objection to the set of images or any of the participants, the suspect shall be asked to state the reasons for the objection. Steps shall, if practicable, be taken to remove the grounds for objection. If this is not practicable, the suspect and/or their representative shall be told why their objections cannot be met and the objection, the reason given for it and why it cannot be met shall be recorded on forms provided for the purpose.

8. Before the images are shown in accordance with *paragraph 7*, the suspect or their solicitor shall be provided with details of the first description of the suspect by any witnesses who are to attend the video identification. When a broadcast or publication is made, as in *paragraph 3.28*, the suspect or their solicitor must also be allowed to view any material released to the media by the police for the purpose of recognising or tracing the suspect, provided it is practicable and would not unreasonably delay the investigation.

9. The suspect's solicitor, if practicable, shall be given reasonable notification of the time and place the video identification is to be conducted so a representative may attend on behalf of the suspect. If a solicitor has not been instructed, this information shall be given to the suspect. The suspect may not be present when the images are shown to the witness(es). In the absence of the suspect's representative, the viewing itself shall be recorded on video. No unauthorised people may be present.

(b) Conducting the video identification

10. The identification officer is responsible for making the appropriate arrangements to make sure, before they see the set of images, witnesses are not able to communicate with each other about the case, see any of the images which are to be shown, see, or be reminded of, any photograph or description of the suspect or be given any other indication as to the suspect's identity, or overhear a witness who has already seen the material. There must be no discussion with the witness about the composition of the set of images and they must not be told whether a previous witness has made any identification.

11. Only one witness may see the set of images at a time. Immediately before the images are shown, the witness shall be told that the person they saw on a specified earlier occasion may, or may not, appear in the images they are shown and that if they cannot make a positive identification, they should say so. The witness shall be advised that at any point, they may ask to see a particular part of the set of images or to have a particular image frozen for them to study. Furthermore, it should be pointed out to the witness that there is no limit on how many times they can view the whole set of images or any part of them. However, they should be asked not to make any decision as to whether the person they saw is on the set of images until they have seen the whole set at least twice.

12. Once the witness has seen the whole set of images at least twice and has indicated that they do not want to view the images, or any part of them, again, the witness shall be asked to say whether the individual they saw in person on a specified earlier occasion has been shown and, if so, to identify them by number of the image. The witness will then be shown that image to confirm the identification, see *paragraph 17*.

13. Care must be taken not to direct the witness' attention to any one individual image or give any indication of the suspect's identity. Where a witness has previously made an identification by photographs, or a computerised or artist's composite or similar likeness, the witness must not be reminded of such a photograph or composite likeness once a suspect is available for identification by other means in accordance with this Code. Nor must the witness be reminded of any description of the suspect.

14. After the procedure, each witness shall be asked whether they have seen any broadcast or published films or photographs, or any descriptions of suspects relating to the offence and their reply shall be recorded.

(c) Image security and destruction

15. Arrangements shall be made for all relevant material containing sets of images used for specific identification procedures to be kept securely and their movements accounted for. In particular, no-one involved in the investigation shall be permitted to view the material prior to it being shown to any witness.

16. As appropriate, *paragraph 3.30* or *3.31* applies to the destruction or retention of relevant sets of images.

(d) Documentation

17. A record must be made of all those participating in, or seeing, the set of images whose names are known to the police.

18. A record of the conduct of the video identification must be made on forms provided for the purpose. This shall include anything said by the witness about any identifications or the conduct of the procedure and any reasons it was not practicable to comply with any of the provisions of this Code governing the conduct of video identifications.

ANNEX B   IDENTIFICATION PARADES

(a) General

1. A suspect must be given a reasonable opportunity to have a solicitor or friend present, and the suspect shall be asked to indicate on a second copy of the notice whether or not they wish to do so.

2. An identification parade may take place either in a normal room or one equipped with a screen permitting witnesses to see members of the identification parade without being seen. The procedures for the composition and conduct of the identification parade are the same in both cases, subject to *paragraph 8* (except that an identification parade involving a screen may take place only when the suspect's solicitor, friend or appropriate adult is present or the identification parade is recorded on video).

3. Before the identification parade takes place, the suspect or their solicitor shall be provided with details of the first description of the suspect by any witnesses who are attending the identification parade. When a broadcast or publication is made as in *paragraph 3.28*, the suspect or their solicitor should also be allowed to view any material released to the media by the police for the purpose of recognising or tracing the suspect, provided it is practicable to do so and would not unreasonably delay the investigation.

(b) Identification parades involving prison inmates

4. If a prison inmate is required for identification, and there are no security problems about the person leaving the establishment, they may be asked to participate in an identification parade or video identification.

5. An identification parade may be held in a Prison Department establishment but shall be conducted, as far as practicable under normal identification parade rules. Members of the public shall make up the identification parade unless there are serious security, or control, objections to their admission to the establishment. In such cases, or if a group or video identification is arranged within the establishment, other inmates may participate. If an inmate is the suspect, they are not required to wear prison clothing for the identification parade unless the other people taking part are other inmates in similar clothing, or are members of the public who are prepared to wear prison clothing for the occasion.

(c) Conduct of the identification parade

6. Immediately before the identification parade, the suspect must be reminded of the procedures governing its conduct and cautioned in the terms of Code C, *paragraphs 10.5 or 10.6*, as appropriate.

7. All unauthorised people must be excluded from the place where the identification parade is held.

8. Once the identification parade has been formed, everything afterwards, in respect of it, shall take place in the presence and hearing of the suspect and any interpreter, solicitor, friend or appropriate adult who is present (unless the identification parade involves a screen, in which case everything said to, or by, any witness at the place where the identification parade is held, must be said in the hearing and presence of the suspect's solicitor, friend or appropriate adult or be recorded on video).

9. The identification parade shall consist of at least eight people (in addition to the suspect) who, so far as possible, resemble the suspect in age, height, general appearance and position in life. Only one suspect shall be included in an identification parade unless there are two suspects of roughly similar appearance, in which case they may be paraded together with at least twelve other people. In no circumstances shall more than two suspects be included in one identification parade and where there are separate identification parades, they shall be made up of different people.

10. If the suspect has an unusual physical feature, e.g., a facial scar, tattoo or distinctive hair-style or hair colour which cannot be replicated on other members of the identification parade, steps may be taken to conceal the location of that feature on the suspect and the other members of the identification parade if the suspect and their solicitor, or appropriate adult, agree. For example, by use of a plaster or a hat, so that all members of the identification parade resemble each other in general appearance.

11. When all members of a similar group are possible suspects, separate identification parades shall be held for each unless there are two suspects of similar appearance when they may appear on the same identification parade with at least twelve other members of the group who are not suspects. When police officers in uniform form an identification parade any numerals or other identifying badges shall be concealed.

12. When the suspect is brought to the place where the identification parade is to be held, they shall be asked if they have any objection to the arrangements for the identification parade or to any of the other participants in it and to state the reasons for the objection. The suspect may obtain advice from their solicitor or friend, if present, before the identification parade proceeds. If the suspect has a reasonable objection to the arrangements or any of the participants, steps shall, if practicable, be taken to remove the grounds for objection. When it is not practicable to do so, the suspect shall be told why their objections cannot be met and the objection, the reason given for it and why it cannot be met, shall be recorded on forms provided for the purpose.

13. The suspect may select their own position in the line, but may not otherwise interfere with the order of the people forming the line. When there is more than one witness, the suspect must be told, after each witness has left the room, that they can, if they wish, change position in the line. Each position in the line must be clearly numbered, whether by means of a number laid on the floor in front of each identification parade member or by other means.

14. Appropriate arrangements must be made to make sure, before witnesses attend the identification parade, they are not able to:
   (i)   communicate with each other about the case or overhear a witness who has already seen the identification parade;
   (ii)   see any member of the identification parade;
   (iii) see, or be reminded of, any photograph or description of the suspect or be given any other indication as to the suspect's identity; or
   (iv)   see the suspect before or after the identification parade.

15. The person conducting a witness to an identification parade must not discuss with them the composition of the identification parade and, in particular, must not disclose whether a previous witness has made any identification.

16. Witnesses shall be brought in one at a time. Immediately before the witness inspects the identification parade, they shall be told the person they saw on a specified earlier occasion may, or may not, be present and if they cannot make a positive identification, they should say so. The witness must also be told they should not make any decision about whether the person they saw is on the identification parade until they have looked at each member at least twice.

17. When the officer or police staff (see *paragraph 3.11*) conducting the identification procedure is satisfied the witness has properly looked at each member of the identification parade, they shall ask the witness whether the person they saw on a specified earlier occasion is on the identification parade and, if so, to indicate the number of the person concerned, see *paragraph 28*.

18. If the witness wishes to hear any identification parade member speak, adopt any specified posture or move, they shall first be asked whether they can identify any person(s) on the identification parade on the basis of appearance only. When the request is to hear members of the identification parade speak, the witness shall be reminded that the participants in the identification parade have been chosen on the basis of physical appearance only. Members of the identification parade may then be asked to comply with the witness' request to hear them speak, see them move or adopt any specified posture.

19. If the witness requests that the person they have indicated remove anything used for the purposes of *paragraph 10* to conceal the location of an unusual physical feature, that person may be asked to remove it.

20. If the witness makes an identification after the identification parade has ended, the suspect and, if present, their solicitor, interpreter or friend shall be informed. When this occurs, consideration should be given to allowing the witness a second opportunity to identify the suspect.

21 After the procedure, each witness shall be asked whether they have seen any broadcast or published films or photographs or any descriptions of suspects relating to the offence and their reply shall be recorded.

22. When the last witness has left, the suspect shall be asked whether they wish to make any comments on the conduct of the identification parade.

(d) Documentation

23. A video recording must normally be taken of the identification parade. If that is impracticable, a colour photograph must be taken. A copy of the video recording or photograph shall be supplied, on request, to the suspect or their solicitor within a reasonable time.

24. As appropriate, *paragraph 3.30* or *3.31*, should apply to any photograph or video taken as in *paragraph 23*.

25. If any person is asked to leave an identification parade because they are interfering with its conduct, the circumstances shall be recorded.

26. A record must be made of all those present at an identification parade whose names are known to the police.

27. If prison inmates make up an identification parade, the circumstances must be recorded.

28. A record of the conduct of any identification parade must be made on forms provided for the purpose. This shall include anything said by the witness or the suspect about any identifications or the conduct of the procedure, and any reasons it was not practicable to comply with any of this Code's provisions.

ANNEX C   GROUP IDENTIFICATION

(a) General

1. The purpose of this Annex is to make sure, as far as possible, group identifications follow the principles and procedures for identification parades so the conditions are fair to the suspect in the way they test the witness' ability to make an identification.

2. Group identifications may take place either with the suspect's consent and cooperation or covertly without their consent.

3. The location of the group identification is a matter for the identification officer, although the officer may take into account any representations made by the suspect, appropriate adult, their solicitor or friend.

4. The place where the group identification is held should be one where other people are either passing by or waiting around informally, in groups such that the suspect is able to join them and be capable of being seen by the witness at the same time as others in the group. For example people leaving an escalator, pedestrians walking through a shopping centre, passengers on railway and bus stations, waiting in queues or groups or where people are standing or sitting in groups in other public places.

5. If the group identification is to be held covertly, the choice of locations will be limited by the places where the suspect can be found and the number of other people present at that time. In these cases, suitable locations might be along regular routes travelled by the suspect, including buses or trains or public places frequented by the suspect.

6. Although the number, age, sex, race and general description and style of clothing of other people present at the location cannot be controlled by the identification officer, in selecting the

location the officer must consider the general appearance and numbers of people likely to be present. In particular, the officer must reasonably expect that over the period the witness observes the group, they will be able to see, from time to time, a number of others whose appearance is broadly similar to that of the suspect.

7. A group identification need not be held if the identification officer believes, because of the unusual appearance of the suspect, none of the locations it would be practicable to use satisfy the requirements of *paragraph 6* necessary to make the identification fair.

8. Immediately after a group identification procedure has taken place (with or without the suspect's consent), a colour photograph or video should be taken of the general scene, if practicable, to give a general impression of the scene and the number of people present. Alternatively, if it is practicable, the group identification may be video recorded.

9. If it is not practicable to take the photograph or video in accordance with *paragraph 8*, a photograph or film of the scene should be taken later at a time determined by the identification officer if the officer considers it practicable to do so.

10. An identification carried out in accordance with this Code remains a group identification even though, at the time of being seen by the witness, the suspect was on their own rather than in a group.

11. Before the group identification takes place, the suspect or their solicitor shall be provided with details of the first description of the suspect by any witnesses who are to attend the identification. When a broadcast or publication is made, as in *paragraph 3.28*, the suspect or their solicitor should also be allowed to view any material released by the police to the media for the purposes of recognising or tracing the suspect, provided that it is practicable and would not unreasonably delay the investigation.

12. After the procedure, each witness shall be asked whether they have seen any broadcast or published films or photographs or any descriptions of suspects relating to the offence and their reply recorded.

(b) Identification with the consent of the suspect

13. A suspect must be given a reasonable opportunity to have a solicitor or friend present. They shall be asked to indicate on a second copy of the notice whether or not they wish to do so.

14. The witness, the person carrying out the procedure and the suspect's solicitor, appropriate adult, friend or any interpreter for the witness, may be concealed from the sight of the individuals in the group they are observing, if the person carrying out the procedure considers this assists the conduct of the identification.

15. The person conducting a witness to a group identification must not discuss with them the forthcoming group identification and, in particular, must not disclose whether a previous witness has made any identification.

16. Anything said to, or by, the witness during the procedure about the identification should be said in the presence and hearing of those present at the procedure.

17. Appropriate arrangements must be made to make sure, before witnesses attend the group identification, they are not able to:
   (i) communicate with each other about the case or overhear a witness who has already been given an opportunity to see the suspect in the group;
   (ii) see the suspect; or
   (iii) see, or be reminded of, any photographs or description of the suspect or be given any other indication of the suspect's identity.

18. Witnesses shall be brought one at a time to the place where they are to observe the group. Immediately before the witness is asked to look at the group, the person conducting the procedure shall tell them that the person they saw may, or may not, be in the group and that if they cannot make a positive identification, they should say so. The witness shall be asked to observe the group in which the suspect is to appear. The way in which the witness should do this will depend on whether the group is moving or stationary.

Moving group

19. When the group in which the suspect is to appear is moving, e.g. leaving an escalator, the provisions of *paragraphs 20* to *24* should be followed.

20. If two or more suspects consent to a group identification, each should be the subject of separate identification procedures. These may be conducted consecutively on the same occasion.

21. The person conducting the procedure shall tell the witness to observe the group and ask them to point out any person they think they saw on the specified earlier occasion.

22. Once the witness has been informed as in *paragraph 21* the suspect should be allowed to take whatever position in the group they wish.

23. When the witness points out a person as in *paragraph 21* they shall, if practicable, be asked to take a closer look at the person to confirm the identification. If this is not practicable, or they cannot confirm the identification, they shall be asked how sure they are that the person they have indicated is the relevant person.

24. The witness should continue to observe the group for the period which the person conducting the procedure reasonably believes is necessary in the circumstances for them to be able to make comparisons between the suspect and other individuals of broadly similar appearance to the suspect as in *paragraph 6*.

Stationary groups

25. When the group in which the suspect is to appear is stationary, e.g. people waiting in a queue, the provisions of *paragraphs 26* to *29* should be followed.

26. If two or more suspects consent to a group identification, each should be subject to separate identification procedures unless they are of broadly similar appearance when they may appear in the same group. When separate group identifications are held, the groups must be made up of different people.

27. The suspect may take whatever position in the group they wish. If there is more than one witness, the suspect must be told, out of the sight and hearing of any witness, that they can, if they wish, change their position in the group.

28. The witness shall be asked to pass along, or amongst, the group and to look at each person in the group at least twice, taking as much care and time as possible according to the circumstances, before making an identification. Once the witness has done this, they shall be asked whether the person they saw on the specified earlier occasion is in the group and to indicate any such person by whatever means the person conducting the procedure considers appropriate in the circumstances. If this is not practicable, the witness shall be asked to point out any person they think they saw on the earlier occasion.

29. When the witness makes an indication as in *paragraph 28*, arrangements shall be made, if practicable, for the witness to take a closer look at the person to confirm the identification. If this is not practicable, or the witness is unable to confirm the identification, they shall be asked how sure they are that the person they have indicated is the relevant person.

All cases

30. If the suspect unreasonably delays joining the group, or having joined the group, deliberately conceals themselves from the sight of the witness, this may be treated as a refusal to co-operate in a group identification.

31. If the witness identifies a person other than the suspect, that person should be informed what has happened and asked if they are prepared to give their name and address. There is no obligation upon any member of the public to give these details. There shall be no duty to record any details of any other member of the public present in the group or at the place where the procedure is conducted.

32. When the group identification has been completed, the suspect shall be asked whether they wish to make any comments on the conduct of the procedure.

33. If the suspect has not been previously informed, they shall be told of any identifications made by the witnesses.

(c) Identification without the suspect's consent

34. Group identifications held covertly without the suspect's consent should, as far as practicable, follow the rules for conduct of group identification by consent.

35. A suspect has no right to have a solicitor, appropriate adult or friend present as the identification will take place without the knowledge of the suspect.

36. Any number of suspects may be identified at the same time.

(d) Identifications in police stations

37. Group identifications should only take place in police stations for reasons of safety, security or because it is not practicable to hold them elsewhere.

38. The group identification may take place either in a room equipped with a screen permitting witnesses to see members of the group without being seen, or anywhere else in the police station that the identification officer considers appropriate.

39. Any of the additional safeguards applicable to identification parades should be followed if the identification officer considers it is practicable to do so in the circumstances.

(e) Identifications involving prison inmates

40. A group identification involving a prison inmate may only be arranged in the prison or at a police station.

41. When a group identification takes place involving a prison inmate, whether in a prison or in a police station, the arrangements should follow those in *paragraphs 37 to 39*. If a group identification takes place within a prison, other inmates may participate. If an inmate is the suspect, they do not have to wear prison clothing for the group identification unless the other participants are wearing the same clothing.

(f) Documentation

42. When a photograph or video is taken as in *paragraph 8* or *9*, a copy of the photograph or video shall be supplied on request to the suspect or their solicitor within a reasonable time.

43. *Paragraph 3.30* or *3.31*, as appropriate, shall apply when the photograph or film taken in accordance with *paragraph 8* or *9* includes the suspect.

44. A record of the conduct of any group identification must be made on forms provided for the purpose. This shall include anything said by the witness or suspect about any identifications or the conduct of the procedure and any reasons why it was not practicable to comply with any of the provisions of this Code governing the conduct of group identifications.

ANNEX D   CONFRONTATION BY A WITNESS

1. Before the confrontation takes place, the witness must be told that the person they saw may, or may not, be the person they are to confront and that if they are not that person, then the witness should say so.

2. Before the confrontation takes place the suspect or their solicitor shall be provided with details of the first description of the suspect given by any witness who is to attend. When a broadcast or publication is made, as in *paragraph 3.28*, the suspect or their solicitor should also be allowed to view any material released to the media for the purposes of recognising or tracing the suspect, provided it is practicable to do so and would not unreasonably delay the investigation.

3. Force may not be used to make the suspect's face visible to the witness.

4. Confrontation must take place in the presence of the suspect's solicitor, interpreter or friend unless this would cause unreasonable delay.

5. The suspect shall be confronted independently by each witness, who shall be asked 'Is this the person?'. If the witness identifies the person but is unable to confirm the identification, they shall be asked how sure they are that the person is the one they saw on the earlier occasion.

6. The confrontation should normally take place in the police station, either in a normal room or one equipped with a screen permitting a witness to see the suspect without being seen. In both cases,

the procedures are the same except that a room equipped with a screen may be used only when the suspect's solicitor, friend or appropriate adult is present or the confrontation is recorded on video.

7. After the procedure, each witness shall be asked whether they have seen any broadcast or published films or photographs or any descriptions of suspects relating to the offence and their reply shall be recorded.

ANNEX E   SHOWING PHOTOGRAPHS

(a) Action

1. An officer of sergeant rank or above shall be responsible for supervising and directing the showing of photographs. The actual showing may be done by another officer or police staff, see *paragraph 3.11.*

2. The supervising officer must confirm the first description of the suspect given by the witness has been recorded before they are shown the photographs. If the supervising officer is unable to confirm the description has been recorded they shall postpone showing the photographs.

3. Only one witness shall be shown photographs at any one time. Each witness shall be given as much privacy as practicable and shall not be allowed to communicate with any other witness in the case.

4. The witness shall be shown not less than twelve photographs at a time, which shall, as far as possible, all be of a similar type.

5. When the witness is shown the photographs, they shall be told the photograph of the person they saw may, or may not, be amongst them and if they cannot make a positive identification, they should say so. The witness shall also be told they should not make a decision until they have viewed at least twelve photographs. The witness shall not be prompted or guided in any way but shall be left to make any selection without help.

6. If a witness makes a positive identification from photographs, unless the person identified is otherwise eliminated from enquiries or is not available, other witnesses shall not be shown photographs. But both they, and the witness who has made the identification, shall be asked to attend a video identification, an identification parade or group identification unless there is no dispute about the suspect's identification.

7. If the witness makes a selection but is unable to confirm the identification, the person showing the photographs shall ask them how sure they are that the photograph they have indicated is the person they saw on the specified earlier occasion.

8. When the use of a computerised or artist's composite or similar likeness has led to there being a known suspect who can be asked to participate in a video identification, appear on an identification parade or participate in a group identification, that likeness shall not be shown to other potential witnesses.

9. When a witness attending a video identification, an identification parade or group identification has previously been shown photographs or computerised or artist's composite or similar likeness (and it is the responsibility of the officer in charge of the investigation to make the identification officer aware that this is the case), the suspect and their solicitor must be informed of this fact before the identification procedure takes place.

10. None of the photographs shown shall be destroyed, whether or not an identification is made, since they may be required for production in court. The photographs shall be numbered and a separate photograph taken of the frame or part of the album from which the witness made an identification as an aid to reconstituting it.

(b) Documentation

11. Whether or not an identification is made, a record shall be kept of the showing of photographs on forms provided for the purpose. This shall include anything said by the witness about any identification or the conduct of the procedure, any reasons it was not practicable to comply with any

of the provisions of this Code governing the showing of photographs and the name and rank of the supervising officer.

12. The supervising officer shall inspect and sign the record as soon as practicable.

ANNEX G   REQUIREMENT FOR A PERSON TO ATTEND A POLICE STATION FOR FINGERPRINTS AND SAMPLES

1. A requirement under Schedule 2A for a person to attend a police station to have fingerprints or samples taken:

    (a) must give the person a period of at least seven days within which to attend the police station; and

    (b) may direct them to attend at a specified time of day or between specified times of day.

2. When specifying the period and times of attendance, the officer making the requirements must consider whether the fingerprints or samples could reasonably be taken at a time when the person is required to attend the police station for any other reason. See Note G1.

3. An officer of the rank of inspector or above may authorise a period shorter than 7 days if there is an urgent need for person's fingerprints or sample for the purposes of the investigation of an offence. The fact of the authorisation and the reasons for giving it must be recorded as soon as practicable.

4. The constable making a requirement and the person to whom it applies may agree to vary it so as to specify any period within which, or date or time at which, the person is to attend. However, variation shall not have effect for the purposes of enforcement, unless it is confirmed by the constable in writing.

Notes for Guidance

G1   The specified period within which the person is to attend need not fall within the period allowed (if applicable) for making the requirement.

G2   To justify the arrest without warrant of a person who fails to comply with a requirement, (see paragraph 4.4(b) above), the officer making the requirement, or confirming a variation, should be prepared to explain how, when and where the requirement was made or the variation was confirmed and what steps were taken to ensure the person understood what to do and the consequences of not complying with the requirement.

Police and Criminal Evidence Act 1984, Code E 2016

REVISED CODE OF PRACTICE ON AUDIO RECORDING INTERVIEWS WITH SUSPECTS

3   Interviews to be audio recorded

3.1 Subject to *paragraph 3.4*, audio recording shall be used for any interview:

    (a) with a person cautioned under Code C, *section 10* in respect of any *indictable* offence, including an offence triable either way, except when:

        (i) that person has been arrested and the interview takes place elsewhere than at a police station in accordance with *Code C paragraph 11.1* for which a written record would be required.

        (ii) the conditions in *paragraph 3.3A* are satisfied and authority not to audio record the interview is given by:

            • the custody officer in the case of a detained suspect, or

            • an officer of the rank of sergeant or above in the case of a suspect who has not been arrested and to whom *paragraphs 3.21* and *3.22* of Code C (Persons attending a police station or elsewhere voluntarily) apply; or

        (iii) the conditions in Part 1 of the Annex to this Code are satisfied, in which case the interview must be conducted and recorded in writing, in accordance with *section 11 of Code C*.

(*See Note 3A.*)
    (b) which takes place as a result of an interviewer exceptionally putting further questions to a suspect about an offence described in *paragraph 3.1(a)* after they have been charged with, or told they may be prosecuted for, that offence, see Code C, *paragraph 16.5*.
    (c) when an interviewer wants to tell a person, after they have been charged with, or informed they may be prosecuted for, an offence described in *paragraph 3.1(a)*, about any written statement or interview with another person, see Code C, *paragraph 16.4*.

3.2 The Terrorism Act 2000 and the Counter-Terrorism Act 2008 make separate provisions for a Code of Practice for the video recording with sound of:
- interviews of persons detained under section 41 of, or Schedule 7 to, the 2000 Act; and
- post-charge questioning of persons authorised under section 22 or 23 of the 2008 Act.

The provisions of this Code do not apply to such interviews. (See *Note 3C*.)

3.3 *Not used*

3.3A The conditions referred to in *paragraph 3.1(a)(ii)* are:
    (a) it is not reasonably practicable to audio record, or as the case may be, continue to audio record, the interview because of equipment failure or the unavailability of a suitable interview room or recording equipment; and
    (b) the authorising officer considers, on reasonable grounds, that the interview or continuation of the interview should not be delayed until the failure has been rectified or until a suitable room or recording equipment becomes available.

In these cases:
- the interview must be recorded or continue to be recorded in writing in accordance with Code C, *section 11*; and
- the authorising officer shall record the specific reasons for not audio recording and the interviewer is responsible for ensuring that the written interview record shows the date and time of the authority, the authorising officer and where the authority is recorded. (See *Note 3B*.)

3.4 If a detainee refuses to go into or remain in a suitable interview room, see Code C *paragraph 12.5*, and the custody officer considers, on reasonable grounds, that the interview should not be delayed the interview may, at the custody officer's discretion, be conducted in a cell using portable recording equipment or, if none is available, recorded in writing as in Code C, *section 11*. The reasons for this shall be recorded.

3.5 The whole of each interview shall be audio recorded, including the taking and reading back of any statement.

3.6 A sign or indicator which is visible to the suspect must show when the recording equipment is recording.

Notes for guidance

3A Nothing in this Code is intended to preclude audio recording at police discretion of interviews at police stations with people cautioned in respect of offences not covered by paragraph 3.1, or responses made by persons after they have been charged with, or told they may be prosecuted for, an offence, provided this Code is complied with.

3B A decision not to audio record an interview for any reason may be the subject of comment in court. The authorising officer should be prepared to justify that decision.

3C If, during the course of an interview under this Code, it becomes apparent that the interview should be conducted under the terrorism code for the video recording with sound of interviews, the interview should only continue in accordance with that code.

3D Attention is drawn to the provisions set out in Code C about the matters to be considered when deciding whether a detained person is fit to be interviewed.

3E Code C sets out the circumstances in which a suspect may be questioned about an offence after being charged with it.

3F Code C sets out the procedures to be followed when a person's attention is drawn after charge, to a statement made by another person. One method of bringing the content of an interview with another person to the notice of a suspect may be to play them a recording of that interview.

4 The interview

(a) General

4.1 The provisions of Code C:

- *sections 10* and *11*, and the applicable Notes for guidance apply to the conduct of interviews to which this Code applies
- *paragraphs 11.7* to *11.14* apply only when a written record is needed.

4.2 Code C, *paragraphs 10.10, 10.11* and *Annex C* describe the restriction on drawing adverse inferences from a suspect's failure or refusal to say anything about their involvement in the offence when interviewed or after being charged or informed they may be prosecuted, and how it affects the terms of the caution and determines if and by whom a special warning under sections 36 and 37 can be given.

(b) Commencement of interviews

4.3 When the suspect is brought into the interview room the interviewer shall, without delay but in the suspect's sight, load the recorder with new recording media and set it to record. The recording media must be unwrapped or opened in the suspect's presence.

This paragraph does not apply to interviews recorded using a secure digital network, see paragraphs 7.4 and 7.5.)

4.4 The interviewer should tell the suspect about the recording process and point out the sign or indicator which shows that the recording equipment is activated and recording. (see paragraph 3.6) The interviewer shall:

- (a) say the interview is being audibly recorded
- (b) subject to *paragraph 2.3*, give their name and rank and that of any other interviewer present;
- (c) ask the suspect and any other party present, e.g. the appropriate adult, a solicitor, or interpreter, to identify themselves;
- (d) state the date, time of commencement and place of the interview; and
- (e) state the suspect will be given a notice about what will happen to the copies of the recording. *(This sub-paragraph does not apply to interviews recorded using a secure digital network, see paragraphs 7.4 and 7.6 to 7.7.)*

4.4A Any person entering the interview room after the interview has commenced shall be invited by the interviewer to identify themselves for the purpose of the audio recording and state the reason why they have entered the interview room.
See *Note 4A*.

4.5 The interviewer shall:

- caution the suspect, see Code C, section 10; and
- if they are detained, remind them of their entitlement to free legal advice, see Code C, *paragraph 11.2*; or
- if they are not detained under arrest, explain this and their entitlement to free legal advice, see Code C, *paragraph 3.21*.

4.6 The interviewer shall put to the suspect any significant statement or silence; see Code C, *paragraph 11.4*.

(c) Interviews with suspects who appear to have a hearing impediment

4.7 If the suspect appears to have impaired hearing, the interviewer shall make a written note of the interview in accordance with Code C, at the same time as audio recording it in accordance with this Code. (See *Notes 4B* and *4C*.)

(d) Objections and complaints by the suspect

4.8 If the suspect objects to the interview being audibly recorded at the outset, during the interview or during a break, the interviewer shall explain that the interview is being audibly recorded and that this Code requires the suspect's objections to be recorded on the audio recording. When any objections have been audibly recorded or the suspect has refused to have their objections recorded, the interviewer shall say they are turning off the recorder, give their reasons and turn it off. The interviewer shall then make a written record of the interview as in Code C, section 11. If, however, the interviewer reasonably considers they may proceed to question the suspect with the audio recording still on, the interviewer may do so. This procedure also applies in cases where the suspect has previously objected to the interview being visually recorded, see Code F 4.8, and the investigating officer has decided to audibly record the interview. See *Note 4D*.

4.9 If in the course of an interview a complaint is made by or on behalf of the person being questioned concerning the provisions of this Code or Code C, the interviewer shall act as in Code C, *paragraph 12.9*. (See *Notes 4E* and *4F*.)

4.10 If the suspect indicates they want to tell the interviewer about matters not directly connected with the offence and they are unwilling for these matters to be audio recorded, the suspect should be given the opportunity to tell the interviewer at the end of the formal interview.

(e) Changing recording media

4.11 When the recorder shows the recording media only has a short time left, the interviewer shall tell the suspect the recording media are coming to an end and round off that part of the interview. If the interviewer leaves the room for a second set of recording media, the suspect shall not be left unattended. The interviewer will remove the recording media from the recorder and insert the new recording media which shall be unwrapped or opened in the suspect's presence. The recorder should be set to record on the new media. To avoid confusion between the recording media, the interviewer shall mark the media with an identification number immediately after they are removed from the recorder.

(*This paragraph does not apply to interviews recorded using a secure digital network as this does not use removable media, see paragraphs 1.6(c), 7.4 and 7.14 to 7.15.*)

(f) Taking a break during interview

4.12 When a break is taken, the fact that a break is to be taken, the reason for it and the time shall be recorded on the audio recording.

4.12A When the break is taken and the interview room vacated by the suspect, the recording media shall be removed from the recorder and the procedures for the conclusion of an interview followed, see *paragraph 4.18*.

4.13 When a break is a short one and both the suspect and an interviewer remain in the interview room, the recording may be stopped. There is no need to remove the recording media and when the interview recommences the recording should continue on the same recording media. The time the interview recommences shall be recorded on the audio recording.

4.14 After any break in the interview the interviewer must, before resuming the interview, remind the person being questioned that they remain under caution or, if there is any doubt, give the caution in full again. See *Note 4G*.

(*Paragraphs 4.12 to 4.14 do not apply to interviews recorded using a secure digital network, see paragraphs 7.4 and 7.8 to 7.10.*)

(g) Failure of recording equipment

4.15 If there is an equipment failure which can be rectified quickly, e.g. by inserting new recording media, the interviewer shall follow the appropriate procedures as in *paragraph 4.11*. When the recording is resumed the interviewer shall explain what happened and record the time the interview recommences. If, however, it will not be possible to continue recording on that recorder and no replacement recorder is readily available, the interview may continue without being audibly recorded. If this happens, the interviewer shall seek the custody officer's authority as in *paragraph 3.3*. See *Note 4H*.

(h) Removing recording media from the recorder

4.16 When recording media is removed from the recorder during the interview, they shall be retained and the procedures in paragraph 4.18 followed.

(*This paragraph does not apply to interviews recorded using a secure digital network as this does not use removable media, see 1.6(c), 7.4 and 7.14 to 7.15.*)

(i) Conclusion of interview

4.17 At the conclusion of the interview, the suspect shall be offered the opportunity to clarify anything he or she has said and asked if there is anything they want to add.

4.18 At the conclusion of the interview, including the taking and reading back of any written statement, the time shall be recorded and the recording shall be stopped. The interviewer shall seal the master recording with a master recording label and treat it as an exhibit in accordance with force standing orders. The interviewer shall sign the label and ask the suspect and any third party present during the interview to sign it. If the suspect or third party refuse to sign the label an officer of at least inspector rank, or if not available the custody officer, shall be called into the interview room and asked, subject to *paragraph 2.3*, to sign it.

4.19 The suspect shall be handed a notice which explains:

- how the audio recording will be used
- the arrangements for access to it
- that if the person is charged or informed they will be prosecuted, a copy of the audio record-ing will be supplied as soon as practicable or as otherwise agreed between the suspect and the police.

Notes for guidance

4A For the purpose of voice identification the interviewer should ask the suspect and any other people present to identify themselves.

4B This provision is to give a person who is deaf or has impaired hearing equivalent rights of access to the full interview record as far as this is possible using audio recording.

4C The provisions of Code C, section 13 on interpreters for deaf persons or for interviews with suspects who have difficulty understanding English continue to apply. However, in an audibly recorded interview the requirement on the interviewer to make sure the interpreter makes a separate note of the interview applies only to paragraph 4.7 (interviews with deaf persons).

4D The interviewer should remember that a decision to continue recording against the wishes of the suspect may be the subject of comment in court.

4E If the custody officer is called to deal with the complaint, the recorder should, if possible, be left on until the custody officer has entered the room and spoken to the person being interviewed. Continuation or termination of the interview should be at the interviewer's discretion pending action by an inspector under Code C, paragraph 9.2.

4F If the complaint is about a matter not connected with this Code or Code C, the decision to continue is at the interviewer's discretion. When the interviewer decides to continue the interview, they shall tell the suspect the complaint will be brought to the custody officer's attention at the conclusion of the interview. When the interview is concluded the interviewer must, as soon as practicable, inform the custody officer about the existence and nature of the complaint made.

4G The interviewer should remember that it may be necessary to show to the court that nothing occurred during a break or between interviews which influenced the suspect's recorded evidence. After a break or at the beginning of a subsequent interview, the interviewer should consider summarising on the record the reason for the break and confirming this with the suspect.

4H Where the interview is being recorded and the media or the recording equipment fails the officer conducting the interview should stop the interview immediately. Where part of the interview is unaffected by the error and is still accessible on the media, that media shall be copied and sealed in the suspect's pres-ence and the interview recommenced using new equipment/media as required. Where the content of the interview has been lost in its entirety the media should be sealed in the suspect's presence and the interview begun again. If the recording equipment cannot be fixed or no replacement is immediately available the interview should be recorded in accordance with Code C, section 11.

5 After the interview

5.1 The interviewer shall make a note in their pocket book that the interview has taken place, was audibly recorded, its time, duration and date and the master recording's identifica-tion number.

5.2 If no proceedings follow in respect of the person whose interview was recorded, the recording media must be kept securely as in *paragraph 6.1* and *Note 6A*.

(This section (paragraphs 5.1, 5.2 and Note 5A) does not apply to interviews recorded using a secure digital network, see paragraphs 7.4 and 7.14 to 7.15.)

Note for guidance

5A Any written record of an audibly recorded interview should be made in accordance with national guidelines approved by the Secretary of State.

6   Media security

6.1 The officer in charge of each police station at which interviews with suspects are recorded shall make arrangements for master recordings to be kept securely and their movements accounted for on the same basis as material which may be used for evidential purposes, in accordance with force standing orders. See *Note 6A*.

(b) Breaking master recording seal for criminal proceedings

6.2 A police officer has no authority to break the seal on a master recording required for criminal trial or appeal proceedings. If it is necessary to gain access to the master recording, the police officer shall arrange for its seal to be broken in the presence of a representative of the Crown Prosecution Service. The defendant or their legal adviser should be informed and given a reasonable opportunity to be present. If the defendant or their legal representative is present they shall be invited to reseal and sign the master recording. If either refuses or neither is present this should be done by the representative of the Crown Prosecution Service. See *Notes 6B* and *6C*.

(c) Breaking master recording seal: other cases

6.3 If no criminal proceedings result or the criminal trial and, if applicable, appeal proceedings to which the interview relates have been concluded, the chief officer of police is responsible for establishing arrangements for breaking the seal on the master recording, if necessary.

6.3A Subject to paragraph 6.3C, a representative of each party must be given a reasonable opportunity to be present when the seal is broken and the master recording copied and re-sealed.

6.3B If one or more of the parties is not present when the master copy seal is broken because they cannot be contacted or refuse to attend or paragraph 6.6 applies, arrangements should be made for an independent person such as a custody visitor, to be present. Alternatively, or as an additional safeguard, arrangement should be made for a film or photographs to be taken of the procedure.

6.3C Paragraph 6.3A does not require a person to be given an opportunity to be present when;
- (a) it is necessary to break the master copy seal for the proper and effective further investigation of the original offence or the investigation of some other offence; and
- (b) the officer in charge of the investigation has reasonable grounds to suspect that allowing an opportunity might prejudice any such an investigation or criminal proceedings which may be brought as a result or endanger any person. (See *Note 6E*.)

(d) Documentation

6.4 When the master recording seal is broken, a record must be made of the procedure followed, including the date, time, place and persons present.

(This section (paragraphs 6.1 to 6.4 and Notes 6A to 6E) does not apply to interviews recorded using a secure digital network, see paragraphs 7.4 and 7.14 to 7.15.)

Notes for guidance

6A This section is concerned with the security of the master recording sealed at the conclusion of the interview. Care must be taken of working copies of recordings because their loss or destruction may lead to the need to access master recordings.

6B If the recording has been delivered to the crown court for their keeping after committal for trial the crown prosecutor will apply to the chief clerk of the crown court centre for the release of the recording for unsealing by the crown prosecutor.

6C Reference to the Crown Prosecution Service or to the crown prosecutor in this part of the Code should be taken to include any other body or person with a statutory responsibility for prosecution for whom the police conduct any audibly recorded interviews.

6D The most common reasons for needing access to master copies that are not required for criminal proceedings arise from civil actions and complaints against police and civil actions between individuals arising out of allegations of crime investigated by police.

6E Paragraph 6.3C could apply, for example, when one or more of the outcomes or likely outcomes of the investigation might be: (i) the prosecution of one or more of the original suspects; (ii) the prosecution of someone previously not suspected, including someone who was originally a witness; and (iii) any original suspect being treated as a prosecution witness and when premature disclosure of any police action, particularly through contact with any parties involved, could lead to a real risk of compromising the investigation and endangering witnesses.

7 Recording of interviews by secure digital network

7.1 A secure digital network does not use removable media and this section specifies the provisions which will apply when a secure digital network is used.

7.2 Not used

7.3 The following requirements are solely applicable to the use of a secure digital network for the recording of interviews.

(a) Application of section 1 to 6 of Code E

7.4 Sections 1 to 6 of Code E above apply except for the following paragraphs:

- Paragraph 2.2 under 'Recording and sealing of master recordings';
- Paragraph 4.3 under '(b) Commencement of interviews';
- Paragraph 4.4 (e) under '(b) Commencement of interviews';
- Paragraphs 4.11–4.19 '(e) Changing recording media', '(f) Taking a break during interview', '(g) Failure of recording equipment', '(h) Removing recording media from the recorder' and '(i) Conclusion of interview'; and
- Paragraphs 6.1–6.4 and *Notes 6A* to *6C* under 'Media security'

(b) Commencement of interview

7.5 When the suspect is brought into the interview room, the interviewer shall without delay and in the sight of the suspect, switch on the recording equipment and enter the information necessary to log on to the secure network and start recording.

7.6 The interviewer must then inform the suspect that the interview is being recorded using a secure digital network and that recording commenced.

7.7 In addition to the requirements of *paragraph 4.4 (a–d)* above, the interviewer must inform the person that:

- they will be given access to the recording of the interview in the event that they are charged or informed that they will be prosecuted but if they are not charged or informed that they will be prosecuted they will only be given access as agreed with the police or on the order of a court; and
- they will be given a written notice at the end of the interview setting out their rights to access the recording and what will happen to the recording.

(c) Taking a break during interview

7.8 When a break is taken, the fact that the break is taken, the reason for it and the time shall be recorded on the audio recording. The recording shall be stopped and the procedures in *paragraphs 7.12 and 7.13* for the conclusion of an interview followed.

7.9 When the interview recommences the procedures in *paragraphs 7.5 to 7.7* for commencing an interview shall be followed to create a new file to record the continuation of the interview. The time the interview recommences shall be recorded on the audio recording.

7.10 After any break in the interview the interviewer must, before resuming the interview, remind the person being questioned that they remain under caution or, if there is any doubt, give the caution in full again. See *Note for guidance 4G*.

(d) Failure of recording equipment

7.11 If there is an equipment failure which can be rectified quickly, e.g. by commencing a new secure digital network recording, the interviewer shall follow the appropriate procedures as in *paragraph 7.8*. When the recording is resumed the interviewer shall explain what happened and record the time the interview recommences. If, however, it is not possible to continue recording on the secure digital network the interview should be recorded on removable media as in *paragraph 4.3* unless the necessary equipment is not available. If this happens the interview may continue without being audibly recorded and the interviewer shall seek the custody officer's authority as in *paragraph 3.3*. See Note for guidance 4H.

(e) Conclusion of interview

7.12 At the conclusion of the interview, the suspect shall be offered the opportunity to clarify anything he or she has said and asked if there is anything they want to add.

7.13 At the conclusion of the interview, including the taking and reading back of any written statement:
  (a) the time shall be orally recorded
  (b) the suspect shall be handed a notice (see *Note 7A*) which explains:
    • how the audio recording will be used
    • the arrangements for access to it
    • that if they are charged or informed they will be prosecuted, they will be given access to the recording of the interview either electronically or by being given a copy on removable recording media, but if they are not charged or informed that they will be prosecuted, they will only be given access as agreed with the police or on the order of a court.
  (c) the suspect must be asked to confirm that he or she has received a copy of the notice at *subparagraph (b)* above. If the suspect fails to accept or to acknowledge receipt of the notice, the interviewer will state for the recording that a copy of the notice has been provided to the suspect and that he or she has refused to take a copy of the notice or has refused to acknowledge receipt.
  (d) the time shall be recorded and the interviewer shall notify the suspect that the recording is being saved to the secure network. The interviewer must save the recording in the presence of the suspect. The suspect should then be informed that the interview is terminated.

(f) After the interview

7.14 The interviewer shall make a note in their pocket book that the interview has taken place and, that it was audibly recorded, the time it commenced, its duration and date and the identification number of the original recording.

7.15 If no proceedings follow in respect of the person whose interview was recorded, the recordings must be kept securely as in *paragraphs 7.16* and *7.17*.
  (See *Note 5A*.)

(g) Security of secure digital network interview records

7.16 Interview record files are stored in read only format on non-removable storage devices, for example, hard disk drives, to ensure their integrity. The recordings are first saved locally to a secure non-removable device before being transferred to the remote network device. If for any reason the network connection fails, the recording remains on the local device and will be transferred when the network connections are restored.

Police and Criminal Evidence Act 1984, Code F 2013

CODE OF PRACTICE ON VISUAL RECORDING WITH SOUND OF INTERVIEWS WITH SUSPECTS

2 Recording and sealing of master recordings

2.1 *Not used*

2.2 The camera(s) shall be placed in the interview room so as to ensure coverage of as much of the room as is practicably possible whilst the interviews are taking place. (See *Note 2A*)

2.3 When the recording medium is placed in the recorder and it is switched on to record, the correct date and time, in hours, minutes and seconds, will be superimposed automatically, second by second, during the whole recording, *see Note 2B*. See section 7 regarding the use of a secure digital network to record the interview.

2.4 One recording, referred to in this code as the master copy, will be sealed before it leaves the presence of the suspect. A second copy will be used as a working copy. (See *Note 2C and 2D*).

2.5 Nothing in this code requires the identity of an officer to be recorded or disclosed if:

    (a) *Not used*

    (b) otherwise where the officer reasonably believes that recording or disclosing their name might put them in danger.

In these cases, the officer will have their back to the camera and shall use their warrant or other identification number and the name of the police station to which they are attached. Such instances and the reasons for them shall be recorded in the custody record. (See *Note 2E)*

Notes for guidance

2A Interviewers will wish to arrange that, as far as possible, visual recording arrangements are unobtrusive. It must be clear to the suspect, however, that there is no opportunity to interfere with the recording equipment or the recording media.

2B In this context, the certified recording medium should be capable of having an image of the date and time superimposed as the interview is recorded.

2C The purpose of sealing the master recording before it leaves the presence of the suspect is to establish their confidence that the integrity of the copy is preserved.

2D The visual recording of the interview may be used for identification procedures in accordance with paragraph 3.21 or Annex E of Code D.

2E The purpose of the paragraph 2.5(b) is to protect police officers and others involved in the investigation of serious organised crime or the arrest of particularly violent suspects when there is reliable information that those arrested or their associates may threaten or cause harm to the officers, their families or their personal property. In cases of doubt, an officer of inspector rank should be consulted.

3 Interviews to be visually recorded

3.1 Subject to *paragraph 3.2* below, if an interviewer is deciding whether to make a visual recording these are the areas where it might be appropriate:

    (a) with a suspect in respect of an indictable offence (including an offence triable either way) (see *Notes 3A* and *3B);*

    (b) which takes place as a result of an interviewer exceptionally putting further questions to a suspect about an offence described in sub-paragraph (a) above after they have been charged with, or informed they may be prosecuted for, that offence [see *Note 3C*];

    (c) in which an interviewer wishes to bring to the notice of a person, after that person has been charged with, or informed they may be prosecuted for an offence described in sub-paragraph (a) above, any written statement made by another person, or the content of an interview with another person [see *Note 3D*];

    (d) with, or in the presence of, a deaf or deaf/blind or speech impaired person who uses sign language to communicate;

    (e) with, or in the presence of anyone who requires an 'appropriate adult'; or

    (f) in any case where the suspect or their representative requests that the interview be recorded visually.

    3.2 The Terrorism Act 2000 and the Counter-Terrorism Act 2008 make separate provision for a Code of Practice for the video recording with sound of:

- interviews of persons detained under section 41 of, or Schedule 7 to, the 2000 Act; and
- post-charge questioning of persons authorised under section 22 or 23 of the 2008 Act.

The provisions of this code do not therefore apply to such interviews [see *Note 3E*].

    3.3 Following a decision by an interviewer to *visually record* any interview mentioned in paragraph 3.1 above, the custody officer in the case of a detained person, or a sergeant in the case of a suspect who has not been arrested, may authorise the interviewer not to make a *visual record* and for the purpose of this Code (F), the provisions of Code E *paragraphs 3.1, 3.2, 3.3, 3.3A* and *3.4* shall apply as appropriate. However, authority not to make a *visual recording* does not detract in any way from the requirement for *audio recording*. This would require a further authorisation not to make in accordance with Code E. (See *Note 3F*.)

    3.5 The whole of each interview shall be recorded visually, including the taking and reading back of any statement.

    3.6 A visible sign or indicator which is visible to the suspect must show when the visual recording equipment is recording.

Notes for guidance

3A Nothing in the code is intended to preclude visual recording at police discretion of interviews at police stations with people cautioned in respect of offences not covered by paragraph 3.1, or responses made by interviewees after they have been charged with, or informed they may be prosecuted for, an offence, provided that this code is complied with.

3B Attention is drawn to the provisions set out in Code C about the matters to be considered when deciding whether a detained person is fit to be interviewed.

3C Code C sets out the circumstances in which a suspect may be questioned about an offence after being charged with it.

3D Code C sets out the procedures to be followed when a person's attention is drawn after charge, to a statement made by another person. One method of bringing the content of an interview with another person to the notice of a suspect may be to play him a recording of that interview.

3E When it only becomes clear during the course of an interview which is being visually recorded that the interviewee may have committed an offence to which paragraph 3.2 applies, the interviewing officer should turn off the recording equipment and the interview should continue in accordance with the provisions of the Terrorism Act 2000.

3F A decision not to record an interview visually for any reason may be the subject of comment in court. The authorising officer should therefore be prepared to justify their decision in each case.

4 The Interview

(a) General

    4.1 The provisions of Code C in relation to cautions and interviews and the Notes for guidance applicable to those provisions shall apply to the conduct of interviews to which this Code applies.

    4.2 Particular attention is drawn to those parts of Code C that describe the restrictions on drawing adverse inferences from a suspect's failure or refusal to say anything about their involvement in the offence when interviewed, or after being charged or informed they may be prosecuted and how those restrictions affect the terms of the caution and determine whether a special warning under sections 36 and 37 of the Criminal Justice and Public Order Act 1994 can be given.

(b) Commencement of interviews

4.3 When the suspect is brought into the interview room the interviewer shall without delay, but in sight of the suspect, load the recording equipment and set it to record.

The recording media must be unwrapped or otherwise opened in the presence of the suspect. [See *Note 4A*]

4.4 The interviewer shall then tell the suspect formally about the visual recording and point out the sign or indicator which shows that the recording equipment is activated and recording (see *paragraph 3.6*). The interviewer shall:

   (a) explain the interview is being visually recorded;
   (b) subject to *paragraph 2.5*, give his or her name and rank, and that of any other interviewer present;
   (c) ask the suspect and any other party present (e.g. his solicitor) to identify themselves.
   (d) state the date, time of commencement and place of the interview; and
   (e) state that the suspect will be given a notice about what will happen to the recording.

See *Note 4AA*

4.4A Any person entering the interview room after the interview has commenced shall be invited by the interviewer to identify themselves for the purpose of the recording and state the reason why they have entered the interview room.

4.5 The interviewer shall then caution the suspect, see Code C, section 10 and:
   • if they are detained, remind them of their entitlement to free legal advice, see Code C *paragraph 11.2*, or
   • if they are not detained under arrest, explain this and their entitlement to free legal advice, see Code C *paragraph 3.21*.

4.6 The interviewer shall then put to the suspect any significant statement or silence, see Code C, *paragraph 11.4.*.

(c) Interviews suspects who appear to require an interpreter

4.7 The provisions of Code C on interpreters for suspects who do not appear to speak or understand English, or who appear to have a hearing or speech impediment, continue to apply.

(d) Objections and complaints by the suspect

4.8 If the suspect raises objections to the interview being visually recorded either at the outset or during the interview or during a break in the interview, the interviewer shall explain the fact that the interview is being visually recorded and that the provisions of this code require that the suspect's objections shall be recorded on the visual recording. When any objections have been visually recorded or the suspect has refused to have their objections recorded, the interviewer shall say that they are turning off the recording equipment, give their reasons and turn it off. If a separate audio recording is being maintained, the officer shall ask the person to record the reasons for refusing to agree to visual recording of the interview. *Paragraph 4.8* of Code E will apply if the person objects to audio recording of the interview. The officer shall then make a written record of the interview. If the interviewer reasonably considers they may proceed to question the suspect with the visual recording still on, the interviewer may do so. See *Note 4G*.

4.9 If in the course of an interview a complaint is made by the person being questioned, or on their behalf, concerning the provisions of this code or of Code C, then the interviewer shall act in accordance with Code C, record it in the interview record and inform the custody officer. [See *4B and 4C*].

4.10 If the suspect indicates that they wish to tell the interviewer about matters not directly connected with the offence of which they are suspected and that they are unwilling for these matters to be recorded, the suspect shall be given the opportunity to tell the interviewer about these matters after the conclusion of the formal interview.

(e) Changing the recording media

4.11 In instances where the recording medium is not of sufficient length to record all of the interview with the suspect, further certified recording medium will be used. When the recording equipment indicates that the recording medium has only a short time left to run, the interviewer shall advise the suspect and round off that part of the interview.

If the interviewer wishes to continue the interview but does not already have further certified recording media with him, they shall obtain a set. The suspect should not be left unattended in the interview room. The interviewer will remove the recording media from the recording equipment and insert the new ones which have been unwrapped or otherwise opened in the suspect's presence. The recording equipment shall then be set to record. Care must be taken, particularly when a number of sets of recording media have been used, to ensure that there is no confusion between them. This could be achieved by marking the sets of recording media with consecutive identification numbers.

(f) Taking a break during the interview

4.12 When a break is to be taken during the course of an interview and the interview room is to be vacated by the suspect, the fact that a break is to be taken, the reason for it and the time shall be recorded. The recording equipment must be turned off and the recording media removed. The procedures for the conclusion of an interview set out in *paragraph 4.19*, below, should be followed.

4.12A When the break is taken and the interview room vacated by the suspect, the recording media shall be removed from the recorder and the procedures for the conclusion of an interview followed. (See *paragraph 4.18*.)

4.13 When a break is to be a short one, and both the suspect and a police officer are to remain in the interview room, the fact that a break is to be taken, the reasons for it and the time shall be recorded on the recording media. The recording equipment may be turned off, but there is no need to remove the recording media. When the interview is recommenced the recording shall continue on the same recording media and the time at which the interview recommences shall be recorded.

4.14 When there is a break in questioning under caution, the interviewing officer must ensure that the person being questioned is aware that they remain under caution. If there is any doubt, the caution must be given again in full when the interview resumes. [See *Notes 4D and 4E*].

(g) Failure of recording equipment

4.15 If there is a failure of equipment which can be rectified quickly, the appropriate procedures set out in *paragraph 4.12* shall be followed. When the recording is resumed the interviewer shall explain what has happened and record the time the interview recommences. If, however, it is not possible to continue recording on that particular recorder and no alternative equipment is readily available, the interview may continue without being recorded visually. In such circumstances, the procedures set out in *paragraph 3.3* of this code for seeking the authority of the custody officer will be followed. [See *Note 4F*].

(h) Removing used recording media from recording equipment

4.16 Where used recording media are removed from the recording equipment during the course of an interview, they shall be retained and the procedures set out in *paragraph 4.18* below followed.

(i) Conclusion of interview

4.17 Before the conclusion of the interview, the suspect shall be offered the opportunity to clarify anything he or she has said and asked if there is anything that they wish to add.

4.18 At the conclusion of the interview, including the taking and reading back of any written statement, the time shall be recorded and the recording equipment switched off. The master tape or CD shall be removed from the recording equipment, sealed with a master copy label and treated as an exhibit in accordance with the force standing orders. The interviewer shall sign the label and also ask the suspect and any appropriate adults or other third party present during the interview to sign it. If the suspect or third party refuses to sign the label, an officer of at least the rank of inspector, or if one is not available, the custody officer or, if the suspect has not been arrested, a sergeant, shall be called into the interview room and asked subject to paragraph 2.5, to sign it.

4.19 The suspect shall be handed a notice which explains the use which will be made of the recording and the arrangements for access to it. The notice will also advise the suspect that a copy of the tape shall be supplied as soon as practicable if the person is charged or informed that he will be prosecuted.

Notes for guidance

4AA For the purpose of voice identification the interviewer should ask the suspect and any other people present to identify themselves.

4A The interviewer should attempt to estimate the likely length of the interview and ensure that an appropriate quantity of certified recording media and labels with which to seal the master copies are available in the interview room.

4B Where the custody officer, or in the case of a person who has not been arrested, a sergeant, is called to deal with the complaint, wherever possible the recording equipment should be left to run until the custody officer has entered the interview room and spoken to the person being interviewed. Continuation or termination of the interview should be at the discretion of the interviewing officer pending action by an inspector as set out in Code C paragraph 9.2.

4C Where the complaint is about a matter not connected with this code or Code C, the decision to continue with the interview is at the interviewer's discretion. Where the interviewer decides to continue with the interview, the person being interviewed shall be told that the complaint will be brought to the attention of the custody officer at the conclusion of the interview. When the interview is concluded, the interviewer must, as soon as practicable, inform the custody officer or sergeant of the existence and nature of the complaint made.

4D In considering whether to caution again after a break, the officer should bear in mind that he may have to satisfy a court that the person understood that he was still under caution when the interview resumed.

4E The officer should bear in mind that it may be necessary to satisfy the court that nothing occurred during a break in an interview or between interviews which influenced the suspect's recorded evidence. On the re-commencement of an interview, the officer should consider summarising on the tape or CD the reason for the break and confirming this with the suspect.

4F Where the interview is being recorded and the media or the recording equipment fails, the interviewer should stop the interview immediately. Where part of the interview is unaffected by the error and is still accessible on the media, that part shall be copied and sealed in the suspect's presence as a master copy and the interview recommenced using new equipment/media as required. Where the content of the interview has been lost in its entirety, the media should be sealed in the suspect's presence and the interview begun again. If the recording equipment cannot be fixed or no replacement is immediately available, the interview should be audio recorded in accordance with Code E. 4G The interviewer should be aware that a decision to continue recording against the wishes of the suspect may be the subject of comment in court.

5   After the Interview

5.1 The interviewer shall make a note in his or her pocket book of the fact that the interview has taken place and has been recorded, its time, duration and date and the identification number of the master copy of the recording media.

5.2 Where no proceedings follow in respect of the person whose interview was recorded, the recording media must nevertheless be kept securely in accordance with *paragraph 6.1* and *Note 6A*.

Note for guidance

5A Any written record of a recorded interview shall be made in accordance with national guidelines for police officers, police staff and CPS prosecutors concerned with the preparation, processing and submission of files.

6 Master copy security

(a) General

6.1 The officer in charge of the police station at which interviews with suspects are recorded or as the case may be, where recordings of interviews carried out elsewhere than at a police station are held, shall make arrangements for the master copies to be kept securely and their movements accounted for on the same basis as other material which may be used for evidential purposes, in accordance with force standing orders [See *Note 6A*].

(b) Breaking master copy seal for criminal proceedings

6.2 A police officer has no authority to break the seal on a master copy which is required for criminal trial or appeal proceedings. If it is necessary to gain access to the master copy, the police officer shall arrange for its seal to be broken in the presence of a representative of the Crown Prosecution Service. The defendant or their legal adviser shall be informed and given a reasonable opportunity to be present. If the defendant or their legal representative is present they shall be invited to reseal and sign the master copy. If either refuses or neither is present, this shall be done by the representative of the Crown Prosecution Service. [See *Notes 6B* and *6C*].

(c) Breaking master copy seal: other cases

6.3 The chief officer of police is responsible for establishing arrangements for breaking the seal of the master copy where no criminal proceedings result, or the criminal proceedings, to which the interview relates, have been concluded and it becomes necessary to break the seal. These arrangements should be those which the chief officer considers are reasonably necessary to demonstrate to the person interviewed and any other party who may wish to use or refer to the interview record that the master copy has not been tampered with and that the interview record remains accurate. [See *Note 6D*]

6.4 Subject to *paragraph 6.6*, a representative of each party must be given a reasonable opportunity to be present when the seal is broken, the master copy copied and resealed.

6.5 If one or more of the parties is not present when the master copy seal is broken because they cannot be contacted or refuse to attend or *paragraph 6.6* applies, arrangements should be made for an independent person such as a custody visitor, to be present. Alternatively, or as an additional safeguard, arrangement should be made for a film or photographs to be taken of the procedure.

6.6 *Paragraph 6.4* does not require a person to be given an opportunity to be present when:

    (a) it is necessary to break the master copy seal for the proper and effective further investigation of the original offence or the investigation of some other offence; and

    (b) the officer in charge of the investigation has reasonable grounds to suspect that allowing an opportunity might prejudice any such an investigation or criminal proceedings which may be brought as a result or endanger any person. [See *Note 6E*]

(d) Documentation

6.7 When the master copy seal is broken, copied and re-sealed, a record must be made of the procedure followed, including the date time and place and persons present.

Notes for guidance

6A This section is concerned with the security of the master copy which will have been sealed at the conclusion of the interview. Care should, however, be taken of working copies since their loss or destruction may lead unnecessarily to the need to have access to master copies.

6B If the master recording has been delivered to the Crown Court for their keeping after committal for trial the Crown Prosecutor will apply to the Chief Clerk of the Crown Court Centre for its release for unsealing by the Crown Prosecutor.

6C Reference to the Crown Prosecution Service or to the Crown Prosecutor in this part of the code shall be taken to include any other body or person with a statutory responsibility for prosecution for whom the police conduct any recorded interviews.

6D The most common reasons for needing access to master copies that are not required for criminal proceedings arise from civil actions and complaints against police and civil actions between individuals arising out of allegations of crime investigated by police.

6E Paragraph 6.6 could apply, for example, when one or more of the outcomes or likely outcomes of the investigation might be: (i) the prosecution of one or more of the original suspects, (ii) the prosecution of someone previously not suspected, including someone who was originally a witness; and (iii) any original suspect being treated as a prosecution witness and when premature disclosure of any police action, particularly through contact with any parties involved, could lead to a real risk of compromising the investigation and endangering witnesses.

Police and Criminal Evidence Act 1984, Code G 2012

CODE OF PRACTICE FOR THE STATUTORY POWER OF ARREST BY POLICE OFFICERS

2   Elements of arrest under section 24 PACE

2.1 A lawful arrest requires two elements:

A person's involvement or suspected involvement or attempted involvement in the commission of a criminal offence;

AND

Reasonable grounds for believing that the person's arrest is necessary.

- Both elements must be satisfied, and
- It can never be necessary to arrest a person unless there are reasonable grounds to suspect them of committing an offence.

2.2 The arrested person must be informed they have been arrested, even if this fact is obvious, and of the relevant circumstances of the arrest in relation to both elements. The custody officer must be informed of these matters on arrival at the police station. See *paragraphs 2.9, 3.3* and *Note 3* and *Code C paragraph 3.4.*

Involvement in the commission of an offence

2.3 A constable may arrest without warrant in relation to any offence (see *Notes 1* and *1A*) anyone;

- who is about to commit an offence *or* is in the act of committing an offence
- whom the officer has reasonable grounds for suspecting is about to commit an offence or to be committing an offence
- whom the officer has reasonable grounds to suspect of being guilty of an offence which he *or* she has reasonable grounds for suspecting has been committed
- anyone who is guilty of an offence which has been committed or anyone whom the officer has reasonable grounds for suspecting to be guilty of that offence.

2.3A There must be some reasonable, objective grounds for the suspicion, based on known facts and information which are relevant to the likelihood the offence has been committed and the person liable to arrest committed it. See *Notes 2* and *2A.*

Necessity criteria

2.4 The power of arrest is *only* exercisable if the constable has reasonable grounds for believing that it is necessary to arrest the person. The statutory criteria for what may constitute necessity are set out in *paragraph 2.9* and it remains an operational decision at the discretion of the constable to decide:

- which one or more necessity criteria (if any) applied to the individual; and
- if any criteria do apply, whether to arrest, grant street bail after arrest, report for summons or for charging by post, issue a penalty notice or take any other action if open to the officer.

2.5 In applying the criteria, the arresting officer has to be satisfied that at least one of the reasons supporting the need for arrest is satisfied.

2.6 Extending the power of arrest to all offences provides a constable with the ability to use that power to deal with any situation. However applying the necessity criteria requires the constable to examine and justify the reason or reasons why a person needs to be arrested or (as the case may be) further arrested, for an offence for the custody officer to decide whether to authorise their detention for that offence. See *Note 2C*.

2.7 The criteria in paragraph 2.9 below which are set out in section 24 of PACE as substituted by section 110 of the Serious Organised Crime and Police Act 2005 *are* exhaustive. However, the circumstances that may satisfy those criteria remain a matter for the operational discretion of individual officers. Some examples are given below of what those circumstances might be and what officers might consider when deciding whether to arrest is necessary.

2.8 In considering the individual circumstances, the constable must take into account the situation of the victim, the nature of the offence, the circumstances of the suspect and the needs of the investigative process.

2.9   When it is practicable to tell a person why their arrest is necessary (as required by paragraphs 2.2, 3.3 and *Note 3*), the constable should outline the facts, information and other circumstances which provide the grounds for believing that their arrest is necessary and which the officer considers satisfy one or more of the statutory criteria in sub-paragraphs (a) to (f), namely:

(a) to enable the name of the person in question to be ascertained (in the case where the constable does not know, and cannot readily ascertain, the person's name, or has reasonable grounds for doubting whether a name given by the person as his name is his real name)

An officer might decide that a person's name cannot be readily ascertained if they fail or refuse to give it when asked, particularly after being warned that failure or refusal is likely to make their arrest necessary (see *Note 2D*). Grounds to doubt a name given may arise if the person appears reluctant or hesitant when asked to give their name or to verify the name they have given.

Where mobile fingerprinting is available and the suspect's name cannot be ascertained or is doubted, the officer should consider using the power under section 61(6A) of PACE (see *Code D paragraph 4.3(e)*) to take and check the fingerprints of a suspect as this may avoid the need to arrest solely to enable their name to be ascertained.

(b) correspondingly as regards the person's address an address:

An officer might decide that a person's address cannot be readily ascertained if they fail or refuse to give it when asked, particularly after being warned that such a failure or refusal is likely to make their arrest necessary. See *Note 2D*. Grounds to doubt an address given may arise if the person appears reluctant or hesitant when asked to give their address or is unable to provide verifiable details of the locality they claim to live in.

When considering reporting to consider summons or charging by post as alternatives to arrest, an address would be satisfactory if the person will be at it for a sufficiently long period for it to be possible to serve them with the summons or requisition and charge; or, that some other person at that address specified by the person will accept service on their behalf. When considering issuing a penalty notice, the address should be one where the person will be in the event of enforcement action if the person does not pay the penalty or is convicted and fined after a court hearing.

(c) to prevent the person in question—

(i)   causing physical injury to himself or any other person;

This might apply where the suspect has already used or threatened violence against others and it is thought likely that they may assault others if they are not arrested. See *Note 2D*

    (ii)   suffering physical injury;

        This might apply where the suspect's behaviour and actions are believed likely to provoke, or have provoked, others to want to assault the suspect unless the suspect is arrested for their own protection. See *Note 2D*

    (iii) causing loss or damage to property;

        This might apply where the suspect is a known persistent offender with a history of serial offending against property (theft and criminal damage) and it is thought likely that they may continue offending if they are not arrested.

    (iv) committing an offence against public decency (only applies where members of the public going about their normal business cannot reasonably be expected to avoid the person in question);

        This might apply when an offence against public decency is being committed in a place to which the public have access and is likely to be repeated in that or some other public place at a time when the public are likely to encounter the suspect. See *Note 2D*

    (v)   causing an unlawful obstruction of the highway;

        This might apply to any offence where its commission causes an unlawful obstruction which it is believed may continue or be repeated if the person is not arrested, particularly if the person has been warned that they are causing an obstruction. See *Note 2D*

(d) to protect a child or other vulnerable person from the person in question

    This might apply when the health (physical or mental) or welfare of a child or vulnerable person is likely to be harmed or is at risk of being harmed, if the person is not arrested in cases where it is not practicable and appropriate to make alternative arrangements to prevent the suspect from having any harmful or potentially harmful contact with the child or vulnerable person.

(e) to allow the prompt and effective investigation of the offence or of the conduct of the person in question. See *Note 2E*

    This may arise when it is thought likely that unless the person is arrested and then either taken in custody to the police station or granted 'street bail' to attend the station later, see *Note 2J*, further action considered necessary to properly investigate their involvement in the offence would be frustrated, unreasonably delayed or otherwise hindered and therefore be impracticable. Examples of such actions include:

    (i)   interviewing the suspect on occasions when the person's voluntary attendance is not considered to be a practicable alternative to arrest, because for example:

        • it is thought unlikely that the person would attend the police station voluntarily to be interviewed.

        • it is necessary to interview the suspect about the outcome of other investigative action for which their arrest is necessary, see (ii) to (v) below.

        • arrest would enable the special warning to be given in accordance with Code C paragraphs 10.10 and 10.11 when the suspect is found:

          – in possession of incriminating objects, or at a place where such objects are found;

          – at or near the scene of the crime at or about the time it was committed.

        • the person has made false statements and/or presented false evidence;

        • it is thought likely that the person:

          – may steal or destroy evidence;

          – may collude or make contact with, co-suspects or conspirators;

          – may intimidate or threaten or make contact with, witnesses.

    See *Notes 2F and 2G*

    (ii) when considering arrest in connection with the investigation of an indictable offence, there is a need:

- to enter and search without a search warrant any premises occupied or controlled by the arrested person or where the person was when arrested or immediately before the arrest;
- to prevent the arrested person from having contact with others;
- to detain the arrested person for than 24 hours before charge.

    (iii) when considering arrest in connection with any recordable offence and it is necessary to secure or preserve evidence of that offence by taking fingerprints, footwear impressions or samples from the suspect for evidential comparison or matching with other material relating to that offence, for example, from the crime scene. See *Note 2H*

    (iv) when considering arrest in connection with any offence and it is necessary to search, examine or photograph the person to obtain evidence. See *Note 2H*

    (v) when considering arrest in connection with an offence to which the statutory Class A drug testing requirements in Code C section 17 apply, to enable testing when it is thought that drug misuse might have caused or contributed to the offence. See *Note 2I*.

  (f) to prevent any prosecution for the offence from being hindered by the disappearance of the person in question.

    This may arise when it is though that:

- if the person is not arrested they are unlikely to attend court if they are prosecuted;
- the address given is not a satisfactory address for service of a summons or a written charge and requisition to appear at court because the person will not be at it for a sufficiently long period for the summons or charge and requisition to be served and no other person at that specified address will accept service on their behalf.

3 Information to be given on arrest

(a) Cautions—when a caution must be given (taken from Code C section 10)

3.1 Code C paragraphs 10.1 and 10.2 set out the requirement for a person whom there are grounds to suspect of an offence (see *Note 2*) to be cautioned before being questioned or further questioned about an offence. 3.2 *Not used*

3.3 A person who is arrested, or further arrested, must be informed at the time, or if not, as soon as practicable thereafter, that they are under arrest and the grounds for their arrest, see *paragraphs 2.2* and *Note 3*.

3.4 A person who is arrested, or further arrested, must be cautioned unless:

  (a) it is impracticable to do so by reason of their condition or behaviour at the time;

  (b) they have already been cautioned immediately prior to arrest as in *paragraph 3.1*.

  (c) Terms of the caution (Taken from Code C section 10)

3.5 The caution, which must be given on arrest, should be in the following terms:

'You do not have to say anything. But it may harm your defence if you do not mention when questioned something which you later rely on in Court. Anything you do say may be given in evidence.'

Where the use of the Welsh Language is appropriate, a constable may provide the caution directly in Welsh in the following terms:

'Does dim rhaid i chi ddweud dim byd. Ond gall niweidio eich amddiffyniad os na fyddwch chi'n sôn, wrth gael eich holi, am rywbeth y byddwch chi'n dibynnu arno nes ymlaen yn y Llys. Gall unrhyw beth yr ydych yn ei ddweud gael ei roi fel tystiolaeth.'

See *Note 4*

3.6 Minor deviations from the words of any caution given in accordance with this Code do not constitute a breach of this Code, provided the sense of the relevant caution is preserved. See *Note 5*.

3.7 *Not used.*

4 Records of arrest

(a) General

4.1 The arresting officer is required to record in his pocket book or by other methods used for recording information:

- the nature and circumstances of the offence leading to the arrest
- the reason or reasons why arrest was necessary
- the giving of the caution
- anything said by the person at the time of arrest

4.2 Such a record should be made at the time of the arrest unless impracticable to do. If not made at that time, the record should then be completed as soon as possible thereafter.

4.3 On arrival at the police station or after being first arrested at the police station, the arrested person must be brought before the custody officer as soon as practicable and a custody officer must be opened in accordance with section 2 of Code C. The information given by the arresting officer on the circumstances and reason or reasons for arrest shall be recorded as part of the custody record. Alternatively, a copy of the record made by the officer in accordance with *paragraph 4.1* above shall be attached as part of the custody record.

See *paragraph 2.2* and *Code C paragraphs 3.4* and *10.3*.

4.4 The custody record will serve as a record of the arrest. Copies of the custody record will be provided in accordance with *paragraphs 2.4* and *2.4A* of Code C and access for inspection of the original record in accordance with *paragraph 2.5* of Code C.

(b) Interviews and arrests

4.5 Records of interview, significant statements or silences will be treated in the same way as set out in sections 10 and 11 of Code C and in Codes E and F (audio and visual recording of interviews).

Notes for guidance

1 For the purposes of this Code, 'offence' means any statutory or common law offence for which a person may be tried by a magistrates' court or the Crown court and punished if convicted. Statutory offences include assault, rape, criminal damage, theft, robbery, burglary, fraud, possession of controlled drugs and offences under road traffic, liquor licensing, gambling and immigration legislation and local government byelaws. Common law offences include murder, manslaughter, kidnapping, false imprisonment, perverting the course of justice and escape from lawful custody.

1A This code does not apply to powers of arrest conferred on constables under any arrest warrant, for example, a warrant issued under the Magistrates' Courts Act 1980, sections 1 or 13, or the Bail Act 1976, section 7(1), or to the powers of constables to arrest without warrant other than under section 24 of PACE for an offence. These other powers to arrest without warrant do not depend on the arrested person committing any specific offence and include:

- *PACE, section 46A, arrest of person who fails to answer police bail to attend police station or is suspected of breaching any condition of that bail for the custody officer to decide whether they should be kept in police detention which applies whether or not the person commits an offence under section 6 of the Bail Act 1976 (e.g. failing without reasonable cause to surrender to custody);*
- *Bail Act 1976, section 7(3), arrest of person bailed to attend court who Is suspected of breaching, or is believed likely to breach, any condition of bail to take them to court for bail to be re-considered;*
- *Children & Young Persons Act 1969, section 32(1A) (absconding)—arrest*
- *to return the person to the place where they are required to reside;*
- *Immigration Act 1971, Schedule 2 to arrest a person liable to examination to determine their right to remain in the UK;*
- *Mental Health Act 1983, section 136 to remove person suffering from mental disorder to place of safety for assessment;*

- *Prison Act 1952, section 49, arrest to return person unlawfully at large to the prison etc. where they are liable to be detained;*
- *Road Traffic Act 1988, section 6D arrest of driver following the outcome of a preliminary road-side test requirement to enable the driver to be required to provide an evidential sample;*
- *Common law power to stop or prevent a Breach of the Peace—after arrest a person aged 18 or over may be brought before a justice of the peace court to show cause why they should not be bound over to keep the peace–not criminal proceedings.*

1B Juveniles should not be arrested at their place of education unless this is unavoidable. When a juvenile is arrested at their place of education, the principal or their nominee must be informed. (From Code C Note 11D)

2 Facts and information relevant to a person's suspected involvement in an offence should not be confined to those which tend to indicate the person has committed or attempted to commit the offence. Before making a decision to arrest, a constable should take account of any facts and information that are available, including claims of innocence made by the person, that might dispel the suspicion.

2A Particular examples of facts and information which might point to a person's innocence and may tend to dispel suspicion include those which relate to the statutory defence provided by the Criminal Law Act 1967, section 3(1) which allows the use of reasonable force in the prevention of crime or making an arrest and the common law of self-defence. This may be relevant when a person appears, or claims, to have been acting reasonably in defence of themselves or others or to prevent their property or the property of others from being stolen, destroyed or damaged, particularly if the offence alleged is based on the use of unlawful force, e.g. a criminal assault. When investigating allegations involving the use of force by school staff, the power given to all school staff under the Education and Inspections Act 2006, section 93, to use reasonable force to prevent their pupils from committing any offence, injuring persons, damaging property or prejudicing the maintenance of good order and discipline may be similarly relevant. The Association of Chief Police Officers and the Crown Prosecution Service have published joint guidance to help the public understand the meaning of reasonable force and what to expect from the police and CPS in cases which involve claims of self defence. Separate advice for school staff on their powers to use reasonable force is available from the Department for Education

2B If a constable who is dealing with an allegation of crime and considering the need to arrest becomes an investigator for the purposes of the Code of Practice under the Criminal Procedure and Investigations Act 1996, the officer should, in accordance with paragraph 3.5 of that Code, 'pursue all reasonable lines of inquiry, whether these point towards or away from the suspect. What is reasonable in each case will depend on the particular circumstances.'

2C For a constable to have reasonable grounds for believing it necessary to arrest, he or she is not required to be satisfied that there is no viable alternative to arrest. However, it does mean that in all cases, the officer should consider that arrest is the practical, sensible and proportionate option in all the circumstances at the time the decision is made. This applies equally to a person in police detention after being arrested for an offence who is suspected of involvement in a further offence and the necessity to arrest them for that further offence is being considered.

2D Although a warning is not expressly required, officers should if practicable, consider whether a warning which points out their offending behaviour, and explains why, if they do not stop, the resulting consequences may make their arrest necessary. Such a warning might:
- *if heeded, avoid the need to arrest, or*
- *if it is ignored, support the need to arrest and also help prove the mental element of certain offences, for example, the person's intent or awareness, or help to rebut a defence that they were acting reasonably.*

A person who is warned that they may be liable to arrest if their real name and address cannot be ascertained, should be given a reasonable opportunity to establish their real name and address before deciding that either or both are unknown and cannot be readily ascertained or that there are reasonable grounds to doubt that a name and address they have given is their real name and address. They should be told why their name is not known and cannot be readily ascertained and (as the case may be) of the grounds for doubting that a name and address they have given is their real name and address, including, for example, the reason why a particular document the person has produced to verify their real name and/or address, is not sufficient.

2E The meaning of 'prompt' should be considered on a case by case basis taking account of all the circumstances. It indicates that the progress of the investigation should not be delayed to the extent that it would adversely affect the effectiveness of the investigation. The arresting officer also has discretion to release the arrested person on 'street bail' as an alternative to taking the person directly to the station. See Note 2J.

2F An officer who believes that it is necessary to interview the person suspected of committing the offence must then consider whether their arrest is necessary in order to carry out the interview. The officer is not required to interrogate the suspect to determine whether they will attend a police station voluntarily to be interviewed but they must consider whether the suspect's voluntary attendance is a practicable alternative for carrying out the interview. If it is, then arrest would not be necessary. Conversely, an officer who considers this option but is not satisfied that it is a practicable alternative, may have reasonable grounds for deciding that the arrest is necessary at the outset 'on the street'. Without such considerations, the officer would not be able to establish that arrest was necessary in order to interview. Circumstances which suggest that a person's arrest 'on the street' would not be necessary to interview them might be where the officer:

- is satisfied as to their identity and address and that they will attend the police station voluntarily to be interviewed, either immediately or by arrangement at a future date and time; and
- is not aware of any other circumstances which indicate that voluntary attendance would not be a practicable alternative. See paragraph 2.9(e)(i) to (v).

When making arrangements for the person's voluntary attendance, the officer should tell the person:

- that to properly investigate their suspected involvement in the offence they must be interviewed under caution at the police station, but in the circumstances their arrest for this purpose will not be necessary if they attend the police station voluntarily to be interviewed;
- that if they attend voluntarily, they will be entitled to free legal advice before, and to have a solicitor present at, the interview;
- that the date and time of the interview will take account of their circumstances and the needs of the investigation; and
- that if they do not agree to attend voluntarily at a time which meets the needs of the investigation, or having so agreed, fail to attend, or having attended, fail to remain for the interview to be completed, their arrest will be necessary to enable them to be interviewed.

2G When the person attends the police station voluntarily for interview by arrangement as in Note 2F above, their arrest on arrival at the station prior to interview would only be justified if:

- new information coming to light after the arrangements were made indicates that from that time, voluntary attendance ceased to be a practicable alternative and the person's arrest became necessary; and
- it was not reasonably practicable for the person to be arrested before they attended the station.

If a person who attends the police station voluntarily to be interviewed decides to leave before the interview is complete, the police would at that point be entitled to consider whether their arrest was necessary to carry out the interview. The possibility that the person might decide to leave during the interview is therefore not a valid reason for arresting them before the interview has commenced. See Code C paragraph 3.21.

2H The necessity criteria do not permit arrest solely to enable the routine taking, checking (speculative searching) and retention of fingerprints, samples, footwear impressions and photographs when there are no prior grounds to believe that checking and comparing the fingerprints etc. Or taking a photograph would provide relevant evidence of the person's involvement in the offence concerned or would help to ascertain or verify their real identity.

2I The necessity criteria do not permit arrest for an offence solely because it happens to be one of the statutory drug testing 'trigger offences' (see Code C Note 17E) when there is no suspicion that Class A drug misuse might have caused or contributed to the offence.

2J Having determined that the necessity criteria have been met and having made the arrest, the officer can then consider the use of street bail on the basis of the effective and efficient progress of the *investigation of the offence in question. It gives the officer discretion to compel the person to attend a police station at a date/time that best suits the overall needs of the particular investigation. Its use is not confined to dealing with child care issues or allowing officers to attend to more urgent operational duties and granting street bail does not retrospectively negate the need to arrest.*

3 An arrested person must be given sufficient information to enable them to understand they have been deprived of their liberty and the reason they have been arrested, as soon as practicable after the arrest, e.g. when a person is arrested on suspicion of committing an offence they must be informed of the nature of the suspected offence and when and where it was committed. The suspect must also be informed of the reason or reasons why arrest is considered necessary. Vague or technical language should be avoided. When explaining why one or more of the arrest criteria apply, it is not necessary to disclose any specific details that might undermine or otherwise adversely affect any investigative processes. An example might be the conduct of a formal interview when prior disclosure of such details might give the suspect an opportunity to fabricate an innocent explanation or to otherwise conceal lies from the interviewer.

4 Nothing in this Code requires a caution to be given or repeated when informing a person not under arrest they may be prosecuted for an offence. However, a court will not be able to draw any inferences under the Criminal Justice and Public Order Act 1994, section 34, if the person was not cautioned.

5 If it appears a person does not understand the caution, the person giving it should explain it in their own words.

6 Certain powers available as the result of an arrest—for example, entry and search of premises, detention without charge beyond 24 hours, holding a person incommunicado and delaying access to legal advice—only apply in respect of indictable offences and are subject to the specific requirements on authorisation as set out in PACE and the relevant Code of Practice.

Prosecution of Offences Act 1985

1   The Crown Prosecution Service

(1) There shall be a prosecuting service for England and Wales (to be known as the 'Crown Prosecution Service') consisting of—

  (a) the Director of Public Prosecutions, who shall be head of the Service;

  (b) the Chief Crown Prosecutors, designated under subsection (4) below, each of whom shall be the member of the Service responsible to the Director for supervising the operation of the Service in his area; and

  (c) the other staff appointed by the Director under this section.

(2) The Director shall appoint such staff for the Service as, with the approval of the Treasury as to numbers, remuneration and other terms and conditions of service, he considers necessary for the discharge of his functions.

(3) The Director may designate any member of the Service who has a general qualification (within the meaning of section 71 of the Courts and Legal Services Act 1990) for the purposes of this subsection, and any person so designated shall be known as a Crown Prosecutor.

(4) The Director shall divide England and Wales into areas and, for each of those areas, designate a Crown Prosecutor for the purposes of this subsection and any person so designated shall be known as a Chief Crown Prosecutor.

(5) The Director may, from time to time, vary the division of England and Wales made for the purposes of subsection (4) above.

(6) Without prejudice to any functions which may have been assigned to him in his capacity as a member of the Service, every Crown Prosecutor shall have all the powers of the Director as to the institution and conduct of proceedings but shall exercise those powers under the direction of the Director.

(7) Where any enactment (whenever passed)—

(a) prevents any step from being taken without the consent of the Director or without his consent or the consent of another; or

(b) requires any step to be taken by or in relation to the Director;

any consent given by or, as the case may be, step taken by or in relation to, a Crown Prosecutor shall be treated, for the purposes of that enactment, as given by or, as the case may be, taken by or in relation to the Director.

2   The Director of Public Prosecutions

(1) The Director of Public Prosecutions shall be appointed by the Attorney General.

(2) The Director must be a person who has a 10 year general qualification within the meaning of section 71 of the Courts and Legal Services Act 1990.

(3) There shall be paid to the Director such remuneration as the Attorney General may, with the approval of the Treasury, determine.

3   Functions of the Director

(1) The Director shall discharge his functions under this or any other enactment under the superintendence of the Attorney General.

(2) It shall be the duty of the Director, subject to any provisions contained in the Criminal Justice Act 1987—

(a) to take over the conduct of all criminal proceedings, other than specified proceedings, instituted on behalf of a police force (whether by a member of that force or by any other person);

(aa) to take over the conduct of any criminal proceedings instituted by an immigration officer (as defined for the purposes of the Immigration Act 1971) acting in his capacity as such an officer,

(ac) to take over the conduct of any criminal proceedings instituted on behalf of the National Crime Agency;

(b) to institute and have the conduct of criminal proceedings in any case where it appears to him that—

(i) the importance or difficulty of the case makes it appropriate that proceedings should be instituted by him; or

(ii) it is otherwise appropriate for proceedings to be instituted by him;

(ba) to institute and have the conduct of any criminal proceedings in any case where the proceedings relate to the subject-matter of a report a copy of which has been sent to him under paragraph 23 or 24 of Schedule 3 of the Police Reform Act 2002 (c. 30) (reports on investigations into conduct of persons serving with the police);

(bc) where it appears to him appropriate to do so, to institute and have the conduct of any criminal proceedings relating to a criminal investigation by the National Crime Agency;

(c) to take over the conduct of all binding over proceedings instituted on behalf of a police force (whether by a member of that force or by any other person);

(d) to take over the conduct of all proceedings begun by summons issued under section 3 of the Obscene Publications Act 1959 (forfeiture of obscene articles);

(e) to give, to such extent as he considers appropriate, advice to police forces on all matters relating to criminal offences;

(ea) to have the conduct of any extradition proceedings;

(eb) to give, to such extent as he considers appropriate, and to such persons as he considers appropriate, advice on any matters relating to extradition proceedings or proposed extradition proceedings

(ec) to give, to such extent as he considers appropriate, advice to immigration officers on matters relating to criminal offences;

(ed) to give advice, to such extent as he considers appropriate and to such person as he considers appropriate, in relation to—

(i) criminal investigations by the National Crime Agency, or

(ii) criminal proceedings arising out of such investigations;

(ee) to give, to such extent as he considers appropriate, and to such persons as he considers appropriate, advice on matters relating to—

(i) a criminal investigation by the Revenue and Customs; or

(ii) criminal proceedings instituted in England and Wales relating to a criminal investigation by the Revenue and Customs;

(f) to appear for the prosecution, when directed by the court to do so, on any appeal under—

(i) section 1 of the Administration of Justice Act 1960 (appeal from the High Court in criminal cases):

(ii) Part I or Part II of the Criminal Appeal Act 1968 (appeals from the Crown Court to the criminal division of the Court of Appeal and thence to the Supreme Court; or

(iii) section 108 of the Magistrates' Courts Act 1980 (right of appeal to Crown Court) as it applies, by virtue of subsection (5) of section 12 of the Contempt of Court Act 1981, to orders made under section 12 (contempt of magistrates' courts);

(fa) to have the conduct of applications for orders under section 1C of the Crime and Disorder Act 1998 (orders made on conviction of certain offences), section 6 of the Violent Crime Reduction Act 2006 (orders on conviction in criminal proceedings) and section 14A of the Football Spectators Act 1989 (banning orders made on conviction of certain offences);

(faa) where it appears to him appropriate to do so, to have the conduct of applications made by him for orders under section 14B of the Football Spectators Act 1989 (banning orders made on complaint);

(fb) where it appears to him appropriate to do so, to have the conduct of applications under section 1CA(3) of the Crime and Disorder Act 1998 for the variation or discharge of orders made under section 1C of that Act;

(fc) where it appears to him appropriate to do so, to appear on any application under section 1CA of that Act made by a person subject to an order under section 1C of that Act for the variation or discharge of the order;

(ff) to discharge such duties as are conferred on him by, or in relation to, Part 5 or 8 of the Proceeds of Crime Act 2002 (c. 29) (civil recovery of the proceeds etc. of unlawful conduct, civil recovery investigations and disclosure orders in relation to confiscation investigations);

(g) to discharge such other functions as may from time to time be assigned to him by the Attorney General in pursuance of this paragraph.

(2A) Subsection (2)(ea) above does not require the Director to have the conduct of any extradition proceedings in respect of a person if he has received a request not to do so and—

(a) in a case where the proceedings are under Part 1 of the Extradition Act 2003, the request is made by the authority which issued the Part 1 warrant in respect of the person;

(b) in a case where the proceedings are under Part 2 of that Act, the request is made on behalf of the territory to which the person's extradition has been requested.

(3) In this section—

'the court' means—

(a) in the case of an appeal to or from the criminal division of the Court of Appeal, that division;

(b) in the case of an appeal from a Divisional Court of the Queen's Bench Division, the Divisional Court; and

(c) in the case of an appeal against an order of a magistrates' court, the Crown Court;

'criminal investigation' means any process—

(i) for considering whether an offence has been committed;

(ii) for discovering by whom an offence has been committed; or

(iii) as a result of which an offence is alleged to have been committed;

'police force' means any police force maintained by a local policing body and any other body of constables for the time being specified by order made by the Secretary of State for the purposes of this section; and

'specified proceedings' means proceedings which fall within any category for the time being specified by order made by the Attorney General for the purposes of this section.

(3A)   In this section a reference to the Revenue and Customs is a reference to—

    (a)   the Commissioners for Her Majesty's Revenue and Customs;

    (b)   an officer of Revenue and Customs; or

    (c)   a person acting on behalf of the Commissioners or an officer of Revenue and Customs.

(4)   The power to make orders under subsection (3) above shall be exercisable by statutory instrument subject to annulment in pursuance of a resolution of either House of Parliament.

10   Guidelines for Crown Prosecutors

(1)   The Director shall issue a Code for Crown Prosecutors giving guidance on general principles to be applied by them—

    (a)   in determining, in any case—

       (i)   whether proceedings for an offence should be instituted or, where proceedings have been instituted, whether they should be discontinued; or

       (ii)   what charges should be preferred; and

    (b)   in considering, in any case, representations to be made by them to any magistrates' court about the mode of trial suitable for that case.

(2)   The Director may from time to time make alterations in the Code.

(3)   The provisions of the Code shall be set out in the Director's report under section 9 of this Act for the year in which the Code is issued; and any alteration in the Code shall be set out in his report under that section for the year in which the alteration is made.

Bail (Amendment) Act 1993

1   Prosecution right of appeal

(1)   Where a magistrates' court grants bail to a person who is charged with, or convicted of, an offence punishable by imprisonment, the prosecution may appeal to a judge of the Crown Court against the granting of bail.

(1A)   Where a magistrates' court grants bail to a person in connection with extradition proceedings, the prosecution may appeal to a judge of the High Court against the granting of bail.

(1B)   Where a judge of the Crown Court grants bail to a person who is charged with, or convicted of, an offence punishable by imprisonment, the prosecution may appeal to the High Court against the granting of bail.

(1C)   An appeal under subsection (1B) may not be made where a judge of the Crown Court has granted bail on an appeal under subsection (1).

(2)   Subsection (1) and (1B) above applies only where the prosecution is conducted—

    (a)   by or on behalf of the Director of Public Prosecutions; or

    (b)   by a person who falls within such class or description of person as may be prescribed for the purposes of this section by order made by the Secretary of State.

(3)   An appeal under subsection (1) (1A) or (1B) may be made only if—

    (a)   the prosecution made representations that bail should not be granted; and

    (b)   the representations were made before it was granted.

(4)   In the event of the prosecution wishing to exercise the right of appeal set out in subsection (1), (1A) or (1B) above, oral notice of appeal shall be given to the court which has granted bail at the conclusion of the proceedings in which bail has been granted and before the release from custody of the person concerned.

(5) Written notice of appeal shall thereafter be served on the court which has granted bail and the person concerned within two hours of the conclusion of such proceedings.

(6) Upon receipt from the prosecution of oral notice of appeal from its decision to grant bail the court which has granted bail shall remand in custody the person concerned, until the appeal is determined or otherwise disposed of.

(7) Where the prosecution fails, within the period of two hours mentioned in subsection (5) above, to serve one or both of the notices required by that subsection, the appeal shall be deemed to have been disposed of.

(8) The hearing of an appeal under subsection (1),(1A) or (1B) above against a decision of the court to grant bail shall be commenced within forty-eight hours, excluding weekends and any public holiday (that is to say, Christmas Day, Good Friday or a bank holiday), from the date on which oral notice of appeal is given.

(9) At the hearing of any appeal by the prosecution under this section, such appeal shall be by way of re-hearing, and the judge hearing any such appeal may remand the person concerned in custody or may grant bail subject to such conditions (if any) as he thinks fit.

(10) In relation to a person under the age of 18

(a) the references in subsections (1) and (1B) above to an offence punishable by imprisonment are to be read as a references to an offence which would be so punishable in the case of an adult; and

(b) the references in subsections (6) and (9) above to remand in custody are to be read subject to the provisions of Chapter 3 of Part 3 of the Legal Aid, Sentencing and Punishment of Offenders Act 2012 (remands of children otherwise than on bail).

(11) The power to make an order under subsection (2) above shall be exercisable by statutory instrument and any instrument shall be subject to annulment in pursuance of a resolution of either House of Parliament.

(12) In this section—

'extradition proceedings' means proceedings under the Extradition Act 2003;

'magistrates' court' and 'court' in relation to extradition proceedings means a District Judge (Magistrates' Courts) designated in accordance with section 67 or section 139 of the Extradition Act 2003;

'prosecution' in relation to extradition proceedings means the person acting on behalf of the territory to which extradition is sought.

Criminal Justice and Public Order Act 1994

25   No bail for defendants charged with or convicted of homicide or rape after previous conviction of such offences

(1) A person who in any proceedings has been charged with or convicted of an offence to which this section applies in circumstances to which it applies shall be granted bail in those proceedings only if the court or, as the case may be, the constable considering the grant of bail is of the opinion that there are exceptional circumstances which justify it.

(2) This section applies, subject to subsection (3) below, to the following offences, that is to say—

(a)   murder;

(b)   attempted murder;

(c)   manslaughter;

(d)   rape under the law of Scotland;

(e)   an offence under section 1 of the Sexual Offences Act 1956 (rape);

(f)   an offence under section 1 of the Sexual Offences Act 2003 (rape);

(g)   an offence under section 2 of that Act (assault by penetration);

(h)   an offence under section 4 of that Act (causing a person to engage in sexual activity without consent), where the activity caused involved penetration within subsection (4) (a) to (d) of that section;

(i)   an offence under section 5 of that Act (rape of a child under 13);

(j)   an offence under section 6 of that Act (assault of a child under 13 by penetration);

(k)   an offence under section 8 of that Act (causing or inciting a child under 13 to engage in sexual activity), where an activity involving penetration within subsection (3)(a) to (d) of that section was caused;

(l)   an offence under section 30 of that Act (sexual activity with a person with a mental disorder impeding choice), where the touching involved penetration within subsection (3)(a) to (d) of that section;

(m)   an offence under section 31 of that Act (causing or inciting a person, with a mental disorder impeding choice, to engage in sexual activity), where an activity involving penetration within subsection (3)(a) to (d) of that section was caused;

(ma)   an offence under Article 5 of the Sexual Offences (Northern Ireland) Order 2008 (rape);

(mb)   an offence under Article 6 of that Order (assault by penetration);

(mc)   an offence under Article 8 of that Order (causing a person to engage in sexual activity without consent) where the activity caused involved penetration within paragraph (4)(a) to (d) of that Article;

(md)   an offence under Article 12 of that Order (rape of a child under 13);

(me)   an offence under Article 13 of that Order (assault of a child under 13 by penetration);

(mf)   an offence under Article 15 of that Order (causing or inciting a child under 13 to engage in sexual activity) where an activity involving penetration within paragraph (2)(a) to (d) of that Article was caused;

(mg)   an offence under Article 43 of that Order (sexual activity with a person with a mental disorder impeding choice) where the touching involved penetration within paragraph (3)(a) to (d) of that Article;

(mh)   an offence under Article 44 of that Order (causing or inciting a person, with a mental disorder impeding choice, to engage in sexual activity) where an activity involving penetration within paragraph (3)(a) to (d) of that Article was caused;

(n)   an attempt to commit an offence within any of paragraphs (d) to (mh).

(3)   This section applies in the circumstances described in subsection (3A) or (3B) only.

(3A)   This section applies where—

(a)   the person has been previously convicted by or before a court in any part of the United Kingdom of any offence within subsection (2) or of culpable homicide, and

(b)   if that previous conviction is one of manslaughter or culpable homicide—

(i)   the person was then a child or young person, and was sentenced to long-term detention under any of the relevant enactments, or

(ii)   the person was not then a child or young person, and was sentenced to imprisonment or detention.

(3B)   This section applies where—

(a)   the person has been previously convicted by or before a court in another member State of any relevant foreign offence corresponding to an offence within subsection (2) or to culpable homicide, and

(b)   if the previous conviction is of a relevant foreign offence corresponding to the offence of manslaughter or culpable homicide—

(i)   the person was then a child or young person, and was sentenced to detention for a period in excess of 2 years, or

(ii)   the person was not then a child or young person, and was sentenced to detention.

(4)   This section applies whether or not an appeal is pending against conviction or sentence.

(5)   In this section—

'conviction' includes—
  (a) a finding that a person is not guilty by reason of insanity;
  (b) a finding under section 4A(3) of the Criminal Procedure (Insanity) Act 1964 (cases of un-fitness to plead) that a person did the act or made the omission charged against him; and
  (c) a conviction of an offence for which an order is made discharging the offender absolutely or conditionally;
and 'convicted' shall be construed accordingly;
'the relevant enactments' means—
  (a) as respects England and Wales, section 91 of the Powers of Criminal Courts (Sentencing) Act 2000;
  (b) as respects Scotland, sections 205(1) to (3) and 208 of the Criminal Procedure (Scotland) Act 1995;
  (c) as respects Northern Ireland, section 73(2) of the Children and Young Persons Act (Northern Ireland) 1968; and
'relevant foreign offence', in relation to a member State other than the United Kingdom, means an offence under the law in force in that member State.

(5A) For the purposes of subsection (3B), a relevant foreign offence corresponds to another offence if the relevant foreign offence would have constituted that other offence if it had been done in any part of the United Kingdom at the time when the relevant foreign offence was committed.

(6) This section does not apply in relation to proceedings instituted before its commencement.

Inferences from accused's silence

34 Effect of accused's failure to mention facts when questioned or charged

(1) Where, in any proceedings against a person for an offence, evidence is given that the accused—
  (a) at any time before he was charged with the offence, on being questioned under caution by a constable trying to discover whether or by whom the offence had been committed, failed to mention any fact relied on in his defence in those proceedings; or
  (b) on being charged with the offence or officially informed that he might be prosecuted for it, failed to mention any such fact; or
  (c) at any time after being charged with the offence, on being questioned under section 22 of the Counter-Terrorism Act 2008 (post-charge questioning), failed to mention any such fact,
being a fact which in the circumstances existing at the time the accused could reasonably have been expected to mention when so questioned, charged or informed, as the case may be, subsection (2) below applies.

(2) Where this subsection applies—
  (b) a judge, in deciding whether to grant an application made by the accused under para-graph 2 of Schedule 3 to the Crime and Disorder Act 1998;
  (c) the court, in determining whether there is a case to answer; and
  (d) the court or jury, in determining whether the accused is guilty of the offence charged,
may draw such inferences from the failure as appear proper.

(2A) Where the accused was at an authorised place of detention at the time of the failure, subsec-tions (1) and (2) above do not apply if he had not been allowed an opportunity to consult a solicitor prior to being questioned, charged or informed as mentioned in subsection (1) above.

(3) Subject to any directions by the court, evidence tending to establish the failure may be given before or after evidence tending to establish the fact which the accused is alleged to have failed to mention.

(4) This section applies in relation to questioning by persons (other than constables) charged with the duty of investigating offences or charging offenders as it applies in relation to questioning by constables; and in subsection (1) above 'officially informed' means informed by a constable or any such person.

(5) This section does not—

(a) prejudice the admissibility in evidence of the silence or other reaction of the accused in the face of anything said in his presence relating to the conduct in respect of which he is charged, in so far as evidence thereof would be admissible apart from this section; or

(b) preclude the drawing of any inference from any such silence or other reaction of the accused which could properly be drawn apart from this section.

(6) This section does not apply in relation to a failure to mention a fact if the failure occurred before the commencement of this section.

35 Effect of accused's silence at trial

(1) At the trial of any person for an offence, subsections (2) and (3) below apply unless—

(a) the accused's guilt is not in issue; or

(b) it appears to the court that the physical or mental condition of the accused makes it undesirable for him to give evidence;

but subsection (2) below does not apply if, at the conclusion of the evidence for the prosecution, his legal representative informs the court that the accused will give evidence or, where he is unrepresented, the court ascertains from him that he will give evidence.

(2) Where this subsection applies, the court shall, at the conclusion of the evidence for the prosecution, satisfy itself (in the case of proceedings on indictment with a jury, in the presence of the jury) that the accused is aware that the stage has been reached at which evidence can be given for the defence and that he can, if he wishes, give evidence and that, if he chooses not to give evidence, or having been sworn, without good cause refuses to answer any question, it will be permissible for the court or jury to draw such inferences as appear proper from his failure to give evidence or his refusal, without good cause, to answer any question.

(3) Where this subsection applies, the court or jury, in determining whether the accused is guilty of the offence charged, may draw such inferences as appear proper from the failure of the accused to give evidence or his refusal, without good cause, to answer any question.

(4) This section does not render the accused compellable to give evidence on his own behalf, and he shall accordingly not be guilty of contempt of court by reason of a failure to do so.

(5) For the purposes of this section a person who, having been sworn, refuses to answer any question shall be taken to do so without good cause unless—

(a) he is entitled to refuse to answer the question by virtue of any enactment, whenever passed or made, or on the ground of privilege; or

(b) the court in the exercise of its general discretion excuses him from answering it.

(7) This section applies—

(a) in relation to proceedings on indictment for an offence, only if the person charged with the offence is arraigned on or after the commencement of this section;

(b) in relation to proceedings in a magistrates' court, only if the time when the court begins to receive evidence in the proceedings falls after the commencement of this section.

36 Effect of accused's failure or refusal to account for objects, substances or marks

(1) Where—

(a) a person is arrested by a constable, and there is—

(i) on his person; or

(ii) in or on his clothing or footwear; or

(iii) otherwise in his possession; or

(iv) in any place in which he is at the time of his arrest,

any object, substance or mark, or there is any mark on any such object; and

(b) that or another constable investigating the case reasonably believes that the presence of the object, substance or mark may be attributable to the participation of the person arrested in the commission of an offence specified by the constable; and

  (c) the constable informs the person arrested that he so believes, and requests him to account for the presence of the object, substance or mark; and

  (d) the person fails or refuses to do so,

then if, in any proceedings against the person for the offence so specified, evidence of those matters is given, subsection (2) below applies.

  (2) Where this subsection applies—

  (b) a judge, in deciding whether to grant an application made by the accused under paragraph 2 of Schedule 3 to the Crime and Disorder Act 1998;

  (c) the court, in determining whether there is a case to answer; and

  (d) the court or jury, in determining whether the accused is guilty of the offence charged,

may draw such inferences from the failure or refusal as appear proper.

  (3) Subsections (1) and (2) above apply to the condition of clothing or footwear as they apply to a substance or mark thereon.

  (4) Subsections (1) and (2) above do not apply unless the accused was told in ordinary language by the constable when making the request mentioned in subsection (1)(c) above what the effect of this section would be if he failed or refused to comply with the request.

  (4A) Where the accused was at an authorised place of detention at the time of the failure or refusal, subsections (1) and (2) above do not apply if he had not been allowed an opportunity to consult a solicitor prior to the request being made.

  (5) This section applies in relation to officers of customs and excise as it applies in relation to constables.

  (6) This section does not preclude the drawing of any inference from a failure or refusal of the accused to account for the presence of an object, substance or mark or from the condition of clothing or footwear which could properly be drawn apart from this section.

  (7) This section does not apply in relation to a failure or refusal which occurred before the commencement of this section.

37 Effect of accused's failure or refusal to account for presence at a particular place

  (1) Where—

  (a) a person arrested by a constable was found by him at a place at or about the time the offence for which he was arrested is alleged to have been committed; and

  (b) that or another constable investigating the offence reasonably believes that the presence of the person at that place and at that time may be attributable to his participation in the commission of the offence; and

  (c) the constable informs the person that he so believes, and requests him to account for that presence; and

  (d) the person fails or refuses to do so,

then if, in any proceedings against the person for the offence, evidence of those matters is given, subsection (2) below applies.

  (2) Where this subsection applies—

  (b) a judge, in deciding whether to grant an application made by the accused under paragraph 2 of Schedule 3 to the Crime and Disorder Act 1998;

  (c) the court, in determining whether there is a case to answer; and

  (d) the court or jury, in determining whether the accused is guilty of the offence charged,

may draw such inferences from the failure or refusal as appear proper.

  (3) Subsections (1) and (2) do not apply unless the accused was told in ordinary language by the constable when making the request mentioned in subsection (1)(c) above what the effect of this section would be if he failed or refused to comply with the request.

  (3A) Where the accused was at an authorised place of detention at the time of the failure or refusal, subsections (1) and (2) do not apply if he had not been allowed an opportunity to consult a solicitor prior to the request being made.

(4) This section applies in relation to officers of customs and excise as it applies in relation to constables.

(5) This section does not preclude the drawing of any inference from a failure or refusal of the accused to account for his presence at a place which could properly be drawn apart from this section.

(6) This section does not apply in relation to a failure or refusal which occurred before the commencement of this section.

60 Powers to stop and search in anticipation of, or after, violence

(1) If a police officer of or above the rank of inspector reasonably believes—

(a) that incidents involving serious violence may take place in any locality in his police area, and that it is expedient to give an authorisation under this section to prevent their occurrence,

(aa) that—

(i) an incident involving serious violence has taken place in England and Wales in his police area;

(ii) a dangerous instrument or offensive weapon used in the incident is being carried in any locality in his police area by a person; and

(iii) it is expedient to give an authorisation under this section to find the instrument or weapon; or

(b) that persons are carrying dangerous instruments or offensive weapons in any locality in his police area without good reason,

he may give an authorisation that the powers conferred by this section are to be exercisable at any place within that locality for a specified period not exceeding 24 hours.

(3) If it appears to an officer of or above the rank of superintendent that it is expedient to do so, having regard to offences which have, or are reasonably suspected to have, been committed in connection with any activity falling within the authorisation, he may direct that the authorisation shall continue in being for a further 24 hours.

(3A) If an inspector gives an authorisation under subsection (1) he must, as soon as it is practicable to do so, cause an officer of or above the rank of superintendent to be informed.

(4) This section confers on any constable in uniform power—

(a) to stop any pedestrian and search him or anything carried by him for offensive weapons or dangerous instruments;

(b) to stop any vehicle and search the vehicle, its driver and any passenger for offensive weapons or dangerous instruments.

(5) A constable may, in the exercise of the powers conferred by subsection (4) above stop any person or vehicle and make any search he thinks fit whether or not he has any grounds for suspecting that the person or vehicle is carrying weapons or articles of that kind.

(6) If in the course of a search under this section a constable discovers a dangerous instrument or an article which he has reasonable grounds for suspecting to be an offensive weapon, he may seize it.

(7) This section applies (with the necessary modifications) to ships, aircraft and hovercraft as it applies to vehicles.

(8) A person who fails

(a) to stop, or to stop the vehicle,

when required to do so by a constable in the exercise of his powers under this section shall be liable on summary conviction to imprisonment for a term not exceeding one month or to a fine not exceeding level 3 on the standard scale or both.

(9) Subject to subsection (9ZA) any authorisation under this section shall be in writing signed by the officer giving it and shall specify the grounds on which it is given and the locality in which and the period during which the powers conferred by this section are exercisable and a direction under subsection (3) above shall also be given in writing or, where that is not practicable, recorded in writing as soon as it is practicable to do so.

(9ZA) An authorisation under subsection (1)(aa) need not be given in writing where it is not practicable to do so but any oral authorisation must state the matters which would otherwise have to be specified under subsection (9) and must be recorded in writing as soon as it is practicable to do so.

(9A) The preceding provisions of this section, so far as they relate to an authorisation by a member of the British Transport Police Force (including one who for the time being has the same powers and privileges as a member of a police force for a police area), shall have effect as if the references to a locality in his police area were references to a place in England and Wales specified in section 31(1) (a) to (f) of the Railways and Transport Safety Act 2003 and as if the reference in subsection (1)(aa) (i) above to his police area were a reference to any place falling within section 31(1)(a) to (f) of the Act of 2003.

(10) Where a vehicle is stopped by a constable under this section, the driver shall be entitled to obtain a written statement that the vehicle was stopped under the powers conferred by this section if he applies for such a statement not later than the end of the period of twelve months from the day on which the vehicle was stopped as respects a pedestrian who is stopped and searched under this section.

(10A) A person who is searched by a constable under this section shall be entitled to obtain a written statement that he was searched under the powers conferred by this section if he applies for such a statement not later than the end of the period of twelve months from the day on which he was searched.

(11) In this section—

'dangerous instruments' means instruments which have a blade or are sharply pointed;

'offensive weapon' has the meaning given by section 1(9) of the Police and Criminal Evidence Act 1984 or, in relation to Scotland, section 47(4) of the Criminal Law (Consolidation) (Scotland) Act 1995 but in subsections (1)(aa), (4), (5) and (6) above and subsection (11A) below includes, in the case of an incident of the kind mentioned in subsection (1)(aa)(i) above, any article used in the incident to cause or threaten injury to any person or otherwise to intimidate; and

'vehicle' includes a caravan as defined in section 29(1) of the Caravan Sites and Control of Development Act 1960.

(11A) For the purposes of this section, a person carries a dangerous instrument or an offensive weapon if he has it in his possession.

(12) The powers conferred by this section are in addition to and not in derogation of, any power otherwise conferred.

Criminal Appeal Act 1995

8   The Commission

(1) There shall be a body corporate to be known as the Criminal Cases Review Commission.

(2) The Commission shall not be regarded as the servant or agent of the Crown or as enjoying any status, immunity or privilege of the Crown; and the Commission's property shall not be regarded as property of, or held on behalf of, the Crown.

(3) The Commission shall consist of not fewer than eleven members.

(4) The members of the Commission shall be appointed by Her Majesty on the recommendation of the Prime Minister.

(5) At least one third of the members of the Commission shall be persons who are legally qualified; and for this purpose a person is legally qualified if—

  (a) he has a ten year general qualification, within the meaning of section 71 of the Courts and Legal Services Act 1990, or

  (b) he is a member of the Bar of Northern Ireland, or solicitor of the Supreme Court of Northern Ireland, of at least ten years' standing.

(6) At least two thirds of the members of the Commission shall be persons who appear to the Prime Minister to have knowledge or experience of any aspect of the criminal justice system and of them at least one shall be a person who appears to him to have knowledge or experience of any aspect of the criminal justice system in Northern Ireland; and for the purposes of this subsection the criminal justice system includes, in particular, the investigation of offences and the treatment of offenders.

(7) Schedule 1 (further provisions with respect to the Commission) shall have effect.

13 Conditions for making of references

(1) A reference of a conviction, verdict, finding or sentence shall not be made under any of sections 9 to 12B unless—

(a) the Commission consider that there is a real possibility that the conviction, verdict, finding or sentence would not be upheld were the reference to be made,

(b) the Commission so consider—

(i) in the case of a conviction, verdict or finding, because of an argument, or evidence, not raised in the proceedings which led to it or on any appeal or application for leave to appeal against it, or

(ii) in the case of a sentence, because of an argument on a point of law, or information, not so raised, and

(c) an appeal against the conviction, verdict, finding or sentence has been determined or leave to appeal against it has been refused.

(2) Nothing in subsection (1)(b)(i) or (c) shall prevent the making of a reference if it appears to the Commission that there are exceptional circumstances which justify making it.

Criminal Evidence (Amendment) Act 1997

Extension of power to take non-intimate body samples without consent

1 Persons imprisoned or detained by virtue of pre-existing conviction for sexual offence etc

(1) This section has effect for removing, in relation to persons to whom this section applies, the restriction on the operation of section 63(3B) of the Police and Criminal Evidence Act 1984 (power to take non-intimate samples without the appropriate consent from persons convicted of recordable offences)—

(a) which is imposed by the subsection (10) inserted in section 63 by section 55(6) of the Criminal Justice and Public Order Act 1994, and

(b) by virtue of which section 63(3B) does not apply to persons convicted before 10th April 1995.

(2) Accordingly, in section 63 of the 1984 Act, for the subsection (10) referred to in subsection (1) above there shall be substituted—

'(9A) Subsection (3B) above shall not apply to any person convicted before 10th April 1995 unless he is a person to whom section 1 of the Criminal Evidence (Amendment) Act 1997 applies (persons imprisoned or detained by virtue of pre-existing conviction for sexual offence etc.).'

(3) This section applies to a person who was convicted of a recordable offence before 10th April 1995 if—

(a) that offence was one of the offences listed in Schedule 1 to this Act (which lists certain sexual, violent and other offences), and

(b) he has at any time served or at the relevant time he is serving a sentence of imprisonment in respect of that offence.

(4) This section also applies to a person who was convicted of a recordable offence before 10th April 1995 if—

(a) that offence was one of the offences listed in Schedule 1 to this Act, and

(b) he has been detained or at the relevant time he is detained under Part III of the Mental Health Act 1983 in pursuance of—

(i) a hospital order or interim hospital order made following that conviction.

Expressions used in this subsection and in the Mental Health Act 1983 have the same meaning as in that Act.

(5) Where a person convicted of a recordable offence before 10th April 1995 was, following his conviction for that and any other offence or offences, sentenced to two or more terms of imprisonment (whether taking effect consecutively or concurrently), he shall be treated for the purposes of this section as serving a sentence of imprisonment in respect of that offence at any time when serving any of those terms.

(6) For the purposes of this section, references to a person serving a sentence of imprisonment include references—

(a) to his being detained in any institution to which the Prison Act 1952 applies in pursuance of any other sentence or order for detention imposed by a court in criminal proceedings, or

(b) to his being detained (otherwise than in any such institution) in pursuance of directions of the Secretary of State under section 92 of the Powers of Criminal Courts (Sentencing) Act 2000,

and any reference to a term of imprisonment shall be construed accordingly.

2   Persons detained following acquittal on grounds of insanity or finding of unfitness to plead

(1) This section has effect for enabling non-intimate samples to be taken from persons under section 63 of the 1984 Act without the appropriate consent where they are persons to whom this section applies.

(2) Accordingly, in section 63 of the 1984 Act—

(a) after subsection (3B) there shall be inserted—

'(3C) A non-intimate sample may also be taken from a person without the appropriate consent if he is a person to whom section 2 of the Criminal Evidence (Amendment) Act 1997 applies (persons detained following acquittal on grounds of insanity or finding of unfitness to plead).'; and

(b) in subsection (8A) (giving of reason for taking sample without appropriate consent), for 'or (3B)' there shall be substituted ', (3B) or (3C) above'.

(3) This section applies to a person if—

(a) he has at any time been detained or at the relevant time he is detained under Part III of the Mental Health Act 1983 in pursuance of an order made under—

(i) section 5(2)(a) of the Criminal Procedure (Insanity) Act 1964 or section 6 or 14 of the Criminal Appeal Act 1968 (findings of insanity or unfitness to plead), or

(ii) section 37(3) of the Mental Health Act 1983 (power of magistrates' court to make hospital order without convicting accused); and

(b) that order was made on or after the date of the passing of this Act in respect of a recordable offence.

(4) This section also applies to a person if—

(a) he has at any time been detained or at the relevant time he is detained under Part III of the Mental Health Act 1983 in pursuance of an order made under—

(i) any of the provisions mentioned in subsection (3)(a), or

(ii) section 5(1) of the Criminal Procedure (Insanity) Act 1964 as originally enacted; and

(b) that order was made before the date of the passing of this Act in respect of any offence listed in Schedule 1 to this Act.

(5) Subsection (4)(a)(i) does not apply to any order made under section 14(2) of the Criminal Appeal Act 1968 as originally enacted.

(6) For the purposes of this section an order falling within subsection (3) or (4) shall be treated as having been made in respect of an offence of a particular description—

    (a) if, where the order was made following—

        (i) a finding of not guilty by reason of insanity, or

        (ii) a finding that the person in question was under a disability and did the act or made the omission charged against him, or

        (iii) a finding for the purposes of section 37(3) of the Mental Health Act 1983 that the person in question did the act or made the omission charged against him, or

        (iv) (in the case of an order made under section 5(1) of the Criminal Procedure (Insanity) Act 1964 as originally enacted) a finding that he was under a disability,

        that finding was recorded in respect of an offence of that description; or

    (b) if, where the order was made following the Court of Appeal forming such opinion as is mentioned in section 6(1) or 14(1) of the Criminal Appeal Act 1968, that opinion was formed on an appeal brought in respect of an offence of that description.

(7) In this section any reference to an Act 'as originally enacted' is a reference to that Act as it had effect without any of the amendments made by the Criminal Procedure (Insanity and Unfitness to Plead) Act 1991.

Youth Justice and Criminal Evidence Act 1999

59 Restriction on use of answers etc. obtained under compulsion

Schedule 3, which amends enactments providing for the use of answers and statements given under compulsion so as to restrict in criminal proceedings their use in evidence against the persons giving them, shall have effect.

Police Reform Act 2002

9 The Independent Police Complaints Commission

(1) There shall be a body corporate to be known as the Independent Police Complaints Commission (in this Part referred to as 'the Commission').

(2) The Commission shall consist of—

    (a) a chairman appointed by Her Majesty; and

    (b) not less than five other members appointed by the Secretary of State.

(3) A person shall not be appointed as the chairman of the Commission, or as another member of the Commission, if—

    (a) he holds or has held office as a constable in any part of the United Kingdom;

    (b) he is or has been under the direction and control of a chief officer or of any person holding an equivalent office in Scotland or Northern Ireland;

    (c) he is a person in relation to whom a designation under section 39 is or has been in force;

    (d) he is a person in relation to whom an accreditation under section 41 or 41A is or has been in force;

    (da) he has been the chairman or a member of, or a member of the staff of, the Serious Organised Crime Agency;

    (db) he has been—

        (i) the chairman or chief executive of, or

        (ii) another member of, or

        (iii) another member of the staff of,

        the National Policing Improvement Agency;

(dc) the person is, or has been, a National Crime Agency officer;

(e) he has been a member of the National Criminal Intelligence Service or the National Crime Squad; or

(f) he is or has at any time been a member of a body of constables which at the time of his membership is or was a body of constables in relation to which any procedures are or were in force by virtue of an agreement or order under—

  (i) section 26 of this Act; or

  (ii) section 78 of the 1996 Act or section 96 of the 1984 Act (which made provision corresponding to that made by section 26 of this Act).

(4) An appointment made in contravention of subsection (3) shall have no effect.

(5) The Commission shall not—

(a) be regarded as the servant or agent of the Crown; or

(b) enjoy any status, privilege or immunity of the Crown;

and the Commission's property shall not be regarded as property of, or property held on behalf of, the Crown.

(6) Schedule 2 (which makes further provision in relation to the Commission) shall have effect.

(7) The Police Complaints Authority shall cease to exist on such day as the Secretary of State may by order appoint.

10 General functions of the Commission

(1) The functions of the Commission shall be—

(a) to secure the maintenance by the Commission itself, and by local policing bodies and chief officers, of suitable arrangements with respect to the matters mentioned in subsection (2);

(b) to keep under review all arrangements maintained with respect to those matters;

(c) to secure that arrangements maintained with respect to those matters comply with the requirements of the following provisions of this Part, are efficient and effective and contain and manifest an appropriate degree of independence;

(d) to secure that public confidence is established and maintained in the existence of suitable arrangements with respect to those matters and with the operation of the arrangements that are in fact maintained with respect to those matters;

(e) to make such recommendations, and to give such advice, for the modification of the arrangements maintained with respect to those matters, and also of police practice in relation to other matters, as appear, from the carrying out by the Commission of its other functions, to be necessary or desirable;

(f) to such extent as it may be required to do so by regulations made by the Secretary of State, to carry out functions in relation to bodies of constables maintained otherwise than by local policing bodies which broadly correspond to those conferred on the Commission in relation to police forces by the preceding paragraphs of this subsection; and

(g) to carry out functions in relation to the National Crime Agency which correspond to those conferred on the Commission in relation to police forces by paragraph (e) of this subsection.

(2) Those matters are—

(a) the handling of complaints made about the conduct of persons serving with the police;

(b) the recording of matters from which it appears that there may have been conduct by such persons which constitutes or involves the commission of a criminal offence or behaviour justifying disciplinary proceedings;

(ba) the recording of matters from which it appears that a person has died or suffered serious injury during, or following, contact with a person serving with the police;

(c) the manner in which any such complaints or any such matters as are mentioned in paragraph (b) or (ba) are investigated or otherwise handled and dealt with.

(3) The Commission shall also have the functions which are conferred on it by—

 (b) any agreement or order under section 26 of this Act (other bodies of constables);

 (bc) any regulations under section 26C of this Act (the National Crime Agency);

 (c) any regulations under section 39 of this Act (police powers for contracted-out staff); or

 (d) any regulations or arrangements relating to disciplinary or similar proceedings against persons serving with the police, or against members of any body of constables maintained otherwise than by a local policing body.

(4) It shall be the duty of the Commission—

 (a) to exercise the powers and perform the duties conferred on it by the following provisions of this Part in the manner that it considers best calculated for the purpose of securing the proper carrying out of its functions under subsections (1) and (3); and

 (b) to secure that arrangements exist which are conducive to, and facilitate, the reporting of misconduct by persons in relation to whose conduct the Commission has functions.

(5) It shall also be the duty of the Commission—

 (a) to enter into arrangements with the chief inspector of constabulary for the purpose of securing co-operation, in the carrying out of their respective functions, between the Commission and the inspectors of constabulary; and

 (b) to provide those inspectors with all such assistance and co-operation as may be required by those arrangements, or as otherwise appears to the Commission to be appropriate, for facilitating the carrying out by those inspectors of their functions.

(6) Subject to the other provisions of this Part, the Commission may do anything which appears to it to be calculated to facilitate, or is incidental or conducive to, the carrying out of its functions.

(7) The Commission may, in connection with the making of any recommendation or the giving of any advice to any person for the purpose of carrying out—

 (a) its function under subsection (1)(e),

 (b) any corresponding function conferred on it by virtue of subsection (1)(f), or

 (c) its function under subsection (1)(g) or (h),

impose any such charge on that person for anything done by the Commission for the purposes of, or in connection with the carrying out of that function as it thinks fit.

11   Reports to the Secretary of State

(1) As soon as practicable after the end of each of its financial years, the Commission shall make a report to the Secretary of State on the carrying out of its functions during that year.

(2) The Commission shall also make such reports to the Secretary of State about matters relating generally to the carrying out of its functions as he may, from time to time, require.

(3) The Commission may, from time to time, make such other reports to the Secretary of State as it considers appropriate for drawing his attention to matters which—

 (a) have come to the Commission's notice; and

 (b) are matters that it considers should be drawn to his attention by reason of their gravity or of other exceptional circumstances.

(4) The Commission shall prepare such reports containing advice and recommendations as it thinks appropriate for the purpose of carrying out—

 (a) its function under subsection (1)(e) of section 10; or

 (b) any corresponding function conferred on it by virtue of subsection (1)(f) of that section.

(5) Where the Secretary of State receives any report under this section, he shall—

 (a) in the case of every annual report under subsection (1), and

 (b) in the case of any other report, if and to the extent that he considers it appropriate to do so,

 lay a copy of the report before Parliament and cause the report to be published.

(6) The Commission shall send a copy of every annual report under subsection (1)—

 (a) to every local policing body;

(d) to every authority that is maintaining a body of constables in relation to which any proce-
    dures are for the time being in force by virtue of any agreement or order under section 26
    or by virtue of subsection (9) of that section; and

(f) to the National Crime Agency.

(7) The Commission shall send a copy of every report under subsection (3)—

(a) to any local policing body that appears to the Commission to be concerned; and

(b) to the chief officer of police of any police force that appears to it to be concerned.

(8) Where a report under subsection (3) relates to the National Crime Agency, the Commission
shall send a copy of that report to the Agency.

(9) Where a report under subsection (3) relates to a body of constables maintained by an authority other than a local policing body, the Commission shall send a copy of that report—

(a) to that authority; and

(b) to the person having the direction and control of that body of constables.

(10) The Commission shall send a copy of every report under subsection (4) to—

(a) the Secretary of State;

(b) every local policing body;

(c) every chief officer;

(f) every authority that is maintaining a body of constables in relation to which any proce-
    dures are for the time being in force by virtue of any agreement or order under section 26
    or by virtue of subsection (9) of that section;

(g) every person who has the direction and control of such a body of constables; and

(i) the National Crime Agency.

(11) The Commission shall send a copy of every report made or prepared by it under subsection
(3) or (4) to such of the persons (in addition to those specified in the preceding subsections) who—

(a) are referred to in the report, or

(b) appear to the Commission otherwise to have a particular interest in its contents,

as the Commission thinks fit.

Application of Part 2

12   Complaints, matters and persons to which Part 2 applies

(1) In this Part references to a complaint are references (subject to the following provisions of
this section) to any complaint about the conduct of a person serving with the police which is made
(whether in writing or otherwise) by—

(a) a member of the public who claims to be the person in relation to whom the conduct took
    place;

(b) a member of the public not falling within paragraph (a) who claims to have been ad-
    versely affected by the conduct;

(c) a member of the public who claims to have witnessed the conduct;

(d) a person acting on behalf of a person falling within any of paragraphs (a) to (c).

(2) In this Part 'conduct matter' means (subject to the following provisions of this section, section
28A and any regulations made under it, paragraph 2(4) of Schedule 3 and any regulations made by
virtue of section 23(2)(d)) any matter which is not and has not been the subject of a complaint but in
the case of which there is an indication (whether from the circumstances or otherwise) that a person
serving with the police may have—

(a) committed a criminal offence; or

(b) behaved in a manner which would justify the bringing of disciplinary proceedings.

(2A) In this Part 'death or serious injury matter' (or 'DSI matter' for short) means subject to section 28A and any regulations made under it any circumstances (other than those which are or have
been the subject of a complaint or which amount to a conduct matter)—

(a) in or in consequence of which a person has died or has sustained serious injury; and

(b) in relation to which the requirements of either subsection (2B) or subsection (2C) are
    satisfied.

(2B) The requirements of this subsection are that at the time of the death or serious injury the person—

    (a) had been arrested by a person serving with the police and had not been released from that arrest; or

    (b) was otherwise detained in the custody of a person serving with the police.

(2C) The requirements of this subsection are that—

    (a) at or before the time of the death or serious injury the person had contact (of whatever kind, and whether direct or indirect) with a person serving with the police who was acting in the execution of his duties; and

    (b) there is an indication that the contact may have caused (whether directly or indirectly) or contributed to the death or serious injury.

(2D) In subsection (2A) the reference to a person includes a person serving with the police, but in relation to such a person 'contact' in subsection (2C) does not include contact that he has whilst acting in the execution of his duties.

(3) The complaints that are complaints for the purposes of this Part by virtue of subsection (1)(b) do not, except in a case falling within subsection (4), include any made by or on behalf of a person who claims to have been adversely affected as a consequence only of having seen or heard the conduct, or any of the alleged effects of the conduct.

(4) A case falls within this subsection if—

    (a) it was only because the person in question was physically present, or sufficiently nearby, when the conduct took place or the effects occurred that he was able to see or hear the conduct or its effects; or

    (b) the adverse effect is attributable to, or was aggravated by, the fact that the person in relation to whom the conduct took place was already known to the person claiming to have suffered the adverse effect.

(5) For the purposes of this section a person shall be taken to have witnessed conduct if, and only if—

    (a) he acquired his knowledge of that conduct in a manner which would make him a competent witness capable of giving admissible evidence of that conduct in criminal proceedings; or

    (b) he has in his possession or under his control anything which would in any such proceedings constitute admissible evidence of that conduct.

(6) For the purposes of this Part a person falling within subsection 1(a) to (c) to shall not be taken to have authorised another person to act on his behalf unless—

    (a) that other person is for the time being designated for the purposes of this Part by the Commission as a person through whom complaints may be made, or he is of a description of persons so designated; or

    (b) the other person has been given, and is able to produce, the written consent to his so acting of the person on whose behalf he acts.

(7) For the purposes of this Part, a person is serving with the police if—

    (a) he is a member of a police force;

    (aa) he is a civilian employee of a police force;

    (b) he is an employee of the Common Council of the City of London who is under the direction and control of a chief officer; or

    (c) he is a special constable who is under the direction and control of a chief officer.

(8) The Secretary of State may make regulations providing that, for the purposes of this Part and of any regulations made under this Part—

    (a) a contractor,

    (b) a sub-contractor of a contractor, or

    (c) an employee of a contractor or a sub-contractor,

is to be treated as a person serving with the police.

(9)　Regulations under subsection (8) may make modifications to this Part, and to any regulations made under this Part, in its application to those persons.

(10)　In subsection (8) 'contractor' means a person who has entered into a contract with a local policing body or a chief officer to provide services to a chief officer.

Handling of complaints and conduct matters etc.

13　Handling of complaints and conduct matters etc.

Schedule 3 (which makes provision for the handling of complaints and conduct matters and DSI matters, and for the carrying out of investigations) shall have effect.

Co-operation, assistance and information

15　General duties of local policing bodies, chief officers and inspectors

(1)　It shall be the duty of—

(a)　every local policing body maintaining a police force,

(b)　the chief officer of police of every police force, and

(c)　every inspector of constabulary carrying out any of his functions in relation to a police force,

to ensure that it or he is kept informed, in relation to that force, about all matters falling within subsection (2).

(1A)　It shall be the duty of the National Crime Agency to ensure that it is kept informed, in relation to the agency, about all matters falling within subsection (2).

(2)　Those matters are—

(a)　matters with respect to which any provision of this Part has effect;

(b)　anything which is done under or for the purposes of any such provision; and

(c)　any obligations to act or refrain from acting that have arisen by or under this Part but have not yet been complied with, or have been contravened.

(2A)　Subsection (2B) applies in a case where it appears to a local policing body that—

(a)　an obligation to act or refrain from acting has arisen by or under this Part,

(b)　that obligation is an obligation of the chief officer of police of the police force which is maintained by the local policing body, and

(c)　the chief officer has not yet complied with that obligation, or has contravened it.

(2B)　The local policing body may direct the chief officer to take such steps as the local policing body thinks appropriate.

(2C)　The chief officer must comply with any direction given under subsection (2B).

(3)　Where—

(a)　a local policing body maintaining any police force requires the chief officer of that force or of any other force to provide a member of his force for appointment under paragraph 16, 17 or 18 of Schedule 3,

(b)　the chief officer of police of any police force requires the chief officer of police of any other police force to provide a member of that other force for appointment under any of those paragraphs, or

(c)　a local policing body or chief officer requires the Director General of the National Crime Agency to provide a National Crime Agency officer for appointment under any of those paragraphs,

it shall be the duty of the chief officer to whom the requirement is addressed or of the Director General to comply with it.

(4)　It shall be the duty of—

(a)　every local policing body maintaining a police force,

(b)　the chief officer of police of every police force, and

(c)　the National Crime Agency,

to provide the Commission and every member of the Commission's staff with all such assistance as the Commission or that member of staff may reasonably require for the purposes of, or in connection with, the carrying out of any investigation by the Commission under this Part.

(5) It shall be the duty of—

    (a) every local policing body maintaining a police force,

    (b) the chief officer of every police force, and

    (c) the National Crime Agency

to ensure that a person appointed under paragraph 16, 17 or 18 of Schedule 3 to carry out an investigation is given all such assistance and co-operation in the carrying out of that investigation as that person may reasonably require

(6) The duties imposed by subsections (4) and (5) on a local policing body maintaining a police force and on the chief officer of such a force and on the National Crime Agency have effect—

    (a) irrespective of whether the investigation relates to the conduct of a person who is or has been a member of that force or a National Crime Agency officer; and

    (b) irrespective of who has the person appointed to carry out the investigation under his direction and control;

but a chief officer of a third force may be required to give assistance and co-operation under subsection (5) only with the approval of the chief officer of the force to which the person who requires it belongs.

(7) In subsection (6) 'third force', in relation to an investigation, means a police force other than—

    (a) the force to which the person carrying out the investigation belongs; or

    (b) the force to which the person whose conduct is under investigation belonged at the time of the conduct;

and where the person whose conduct is under investigation was a National Crime Agency officer at the time of his conduct, 'third force' means any police force other than the force to which the person carrying out the investigation belongs.

(8) Where the person who requires assistance and co-operation under subsection (5) is a National Crime Agency officer, a chief officer of a third force may be required to give that assistance and co-operation only with the approval of the Director General of the Agency.

(8B) In subsections (8) and (8A) 'third force', in relation to an investigation, means any police force other than the force to which the person whose conduct is under investigation belonged at the time of the conduct.

(9) Where—

    (a) the person carrying out an investigation is not a National Crime Agency officer; and

    (b) the person whose conduct is under investigation was not a National Crime Agency officer at the time of the conduct,

the Agency may be required to give assistance and co-operation under subsection (5) only with the approval of the relevant directing officer.

(10) In subsection (9) 'the relevant directing officer'—

    (a) in a case where the person who requires assistance and cooperation belongs to a police force, means the chief officer of that force.

16 Payment for assistance with investigations

(1) This section applies where—

    (a) one police force is required to provide assistance to another in connection with an investigation under this Part; or

    (b) a police force is required to provide assistance in such a connection to the Commission.

(2) For the purposes of this section—

    (a) assistance is required to be provided by one police force to another in connection with an investigation under this Part if the chief officer of the first force ('the assisting force') complies with a requirement under section 15(3) or (5) that is made in connection with

    (i)   an investigation relating to the conduct of a person who, at the time of the conduct, was a member of the other force, or

    (ii)   an investigation of a DSI matter in relation to which the relevant officer was, at the time of the death or serious injury, a member of the other force; and

  (b) assistance is required to be provided in such a connection by a police force ('the assisting force') to the Commission if the chief officer of that force complies with a requirement under section 15(4) that is made in connection with

    (i)   an investigation relating to the conduct of a person who, at the time of the conduct, was not a member of that force, or

    (ii)   an investigation of a DSI matter in relation to which the relevant officer was, at the time of the death or serious injury, not a member of that force.

(3) Where the assistance is required to be provided by one police force to another, the local policing body maintaining that other police force shall pay to the local policing body maintaining the assisting force such contribution (if any) towards the costs of the assistance—

  (a) as may be agreed between them; or

  (b) in the absence of an agreement, as may be determined in accordance with any arrangements which—

    (i)   have been agreed to by local policing bodies generally; and

    (ii)   are for the time being in force with respect to the making of contributions towards the costs of assistance provided, in connection with investigations under this Part, by one police force to another; or

  (c) in the absence of any such arrangements, as may be determined by the Secretary of State.

(4) Where the assistance is required to be provided by a police force to the Commission, the Commission shall pay to the local policing body maintaining the assisting force such contribution (if any) towards the costs of the assistance—

  (a) as may be agreed between the Commission and that body; or

  (b) in the absence of an agreement, as may be determined in accordance with any arrangements which—

    (i)   have been agreed to by local policing bodies generally and by the Commission; and

    (ii)   are for the time being in force with respect to the making of contributions towards the costs of assistance provided, in connection with investigations under this Part, to the Commission; or

  (c) in the absence of any such arrangements, as may be determined by the Secretary of State.

(5) In this section (subject to subsection (6))—

  (a) references to a police and to a local policing body maintaining a police force include references to the National Crime Agency; and

  (b) in relation to that Agency, references to the chief officer are references to the Director General.

(6) This section shall have effect in relation to cases in which assistance is required to be provided by the National Crime Agency as if—

  (a) the reference in subsection (3)(b) to local policing bodies generally included a reference to the Agency; and

  (b) the reference in subsection (4)(b) to local policing bodies generally were a reference to the Agency.

(7) This section is without prejudice to the application of section 24 of the 1996 Act (assistance given voluntarily by one force to another) in a case in which assistance is provided, otherwise than in pursuance of any duty imposed by section 15 of this Act, in connection with an investigation under this Part.

17 Provision of information to the Commission

(1) It shall be the duty of—

    (a) every local policing body, and

    (b) every chief officer,

at such times, in such circumstances and in accordance with such other requirements as may be set out in regulations made by the Secretary of State, to provide the Commission with all such information and documents as may be specified or described in regulations so made.

(2) It shall also be the duty of every local policing body and of every chief officer—

    (a) to provide the Commission with all such other information and documents specified or described in a notification given by the Commission to that body or chief officer, and

    (b) to produce or deliver up to the Commission all such evidence and other things so specified or described,

as appear to the Commission to be required by it for the purposes of the carrying out of any of its functions.

(3) Anything falling to be provided, produced or delivered up by any person in pursuance of a requirement imposed under subsection (2) must be provided, produced or delivered up in such form, in such manner and within such period as may be specified in—

    (a) the notification imposing the requirement; or

    (b) in any subsequent notification given by the Commission to that person for the purposes of this subsection.

(4) Nothing in this section shall require a local policing body or chief officer—

    (a) to provide the Commission with any information or document, or to produce or deliver up any other thing, before the earliest time at which it is practicable for that body or chief officer to do so; or

    (b) to provide, produce or deliver up anything at all in a case in which it never becomes practicable for that body or chief officer to do so.

(5) A requirement imposed by any regulations or notification under this section may authorise or require information or documents to which it relates to be provided to the Commission electronically.

18 Inspections of police premises on behalf of the Commission

(1) Where—

    (a) the Commission requires—

        (i)   a local policing body maintaining any police force, or

        (ii) the chief officer of police of any such force,

        to allow a person nominated for the purpose by the Commission to have access to any premises occupied for the purposes of that force and to documents and other things on those premises, and

    (b) the requirement is imposed for any of the purposes mentioned in subsection (2),

it shall be the duty of the body or, as the case may be, of the chief officer to secure that the required access is allowed to the nominated person.

(2) Those purposes are—

    (a) the purposes of any examination by the Commission of the efficiency and effectiveness of the arrangements made by the force in question for handling complaints or dealing with recordable conduct matters or DSI matters;

    (b) the purposes of any investigation by the Commission under this Part or of any investigation carried out under its supervision or management.

(3) A requirement imposed under this section for the purposes mentioned in subsection (2)(a) must be notified to the body or chief officer at least 48 hours before the time at which access is required.

(4) Where—

    (a) a requirement imposed under this section for the purposes mentioned in subsection (2)(a) requires access to any premises, document or thing to be allowed to any person, but

    (b) there are reasonable grounds for not allowing that person to have the required access at the time at which he seeks to have it, the obligation to secure that the required access is allowed shall have effect as an obligation to secure that the access is allowed to that person at the earliest practicable time after there cease to be any such grounds as that person may specify.

(5) The provisions of this section are in addition to, and without prejudice to—

    (a) the rights of entry, search and seizure that are or may be conferred on—

        (i) a person designated for the purposes of paragraph 19 of Schedule 3, or

        (ii) any person who otherwise acts on behalf of the Commission, in his capacity as a constable or as a person with the powers and privileges of a constable; or

    (b) the obligations of local policing bodies and chief officers under sections 15 and 17.

19 Use of investigatory powers by or on behalf of the Commission

(1) The Secretary of State may by order make such provision as he thinks appropriate for the purpose of authorising—

    (a) the use of directed and intrusive surveillance, and

    (b) the conduct and use of covert human intelligence sources,

for the purposes of, or for purposes connected with, the carrying out of the Commission's functions.

(2) An order under this section may, for the purposes of or in connection with any such provision as is mentioned in subsection (1), provide for—

    (a) Parts 2 and 4 the Regulation of Investigatory Powers Act 2000 (c. 23) (surveillance and covert human intelligence sources and scrutiny of investigatory powers), and

    (b) Part 3 of the 1997 Act (authorisations in respect of property),

to have effect with such modifications as may be specified in the order.

(3) The Secretary of State shall not make an order containing (with or without any other provision) any provision authorised by this section unless a draft of that order has been laid before Parliament and approved by a resolution of each House.

(4) Expressions used in this section and in Part 2 of the Regulation of Investigatory Powers Act 2000 have the same meanings in this section as in that Part.

20 Duty to keep the complainant informed

(1) In any case in which there is an investigation of a complaint in accordance with the provisions of Schedule 3—

    (a) by the Commission, or

    (b) under its management,

it shall be the duty of the Commission to provide the complainant with all such information as will keep him properly informed, while the investigation is being carried out and subsequently, of all the matters mentioned in subsection (4).

(2) In any case in which there is an investigation of a complaint in accordance with the provisions of Schedule 3—

    (a) by the appropriate authority on its own behalf, or

    (b) under the supervision of the Commission,

it shall be the duty of the appropriate authority to provide the complainant with all such information as will keep him properly informed, while the investigation is being carried out and subsequently, of all the matters mentioned in subsection (4).

(3) Where subsection (2) applies, it shall be the duty of the Commission to give the appropriate authority all such directions as it considers appropriate for securing that that authority complies with its duty under that subsection; and it shall be the duty of the appropriate authority to comply with any direction given to it under this subsection.

(4) The matters of which the complainant must be kept properly informed are—

    (a) the progress of the investigation;

    (b) any provisional findings of the person carrying out the investigation;

    (c) whether any report has been submitted under paragraph 22 of Schedule 3;

    (d) the action (if any) that is taken in respect of the matters dealt with in any such report; and

    (e) the outcome of any such action.

(5) The duties imposed by this section on the Commission and the appropriate authority in relation to any complaint shall be performed in such manner, and shall have effect subject to such exceptions, as may be provided for by regulations made by the Secretary of State.

(6) The Secretary of State shall not by regulations provide for any exceptions from the duties imposed by this section except so far as he considers it necessary to do so for the purpose of—

(a) preventing the premature or inappropriate disclosure of information that is relevant to, or may be used in, any actual or prospective criminal proceedings;

(b) preventing the disclosure of information in any circumstances in which it has been determined in accordance with the regulations that its non-disclosure—

(i) is in the interests of national security;

(ii) is for the purposes of the prevention or detection of crime, or the apprehension or prosecution of offenders;

(iii) is required on proportionality grounds; or

(iv) is otherwise necessary in the public interest.

(7) The non-disclosure of information is required on proportionality grounds if its disclosure would cause, directly or indirectly, an adverse effect which would be disproportionate to the benefits arising from its disclosure.

(8) Regulations under this section may include provision framed by reference to the opinion of, or a determination by, the Commission or any local policing body or chief officer.

(9) It shall be the duty of a person appointed to carry out an investigation under this Part to provide the Commission or, as the case may be, the appropriate authority with all such information as the Commission or that authority may reasonably require for the purpose of performing its duty under this section.

21 Duty to provide information for other persons

(1) A person has an interest in being kept properly informed about the handling of a complaint, recordable conduct matter or DSI matter if—

(a) it appears to the Commission or to an appropriate authority that he is a person falling within subsection (2) or 2A; and

(b) that person has indicated that he consents to the provision of information to him in accordance with this section and that consent has not been withdrawn.

(2) A person falls within this subsection if (in the case of a complaint or recordable conduct matter)—

(a) he is a relative of a person whose death is the alleged result from the conduct complained of or to which the recordable conduct matter relates;

(b) he is a relative of a person whose serious injury is the alleged result from that conduct and that person is incapable of making a complaint;

(c) he himself has suffered serious injury as the alleged result of that conduct.

(2A) A person falls within this subsection if (in the case of a DSI matter)—

(a) he is a relative of the person who has died;

(b) he is a relative of the person who has suffered serious injury and that person is incapable of making a complaint;

(c) he himself is the person who has suffered serious injury.

(3) A person who does not fall within subsection (2) or (2A) has an interest in being kept properly informed about the handling of a complaint, recordable conduct matter or DSI matter if—

(a) the Commission or an appropriate authority considers that he has an interest in the handling of the complaint, recordable conduct matter or DSI matter which is sufficient to make it appropriate for information to be provided to him in accordance with this section; and

(b) he has indicated that he consents to the provision of information to him in accordance with this section.

(4) In relation to a complaint, this section confers no rights on the complainant.

(5) A person who has an interest in being kept properly informed about the handling of a complaint, conduct matter or DSI matter is referred to in this section as an 'interested person'.

(6) In any case in which there is an investigation of the complaint, recordable conduct matter or DSI matter in accordance with the provisions of Schedule 3—

(a) by the Commission, or

(b) under its management,

it shall be the duty of the Commission to provide the interested person with all such information as will keep him properly informed, while the investigation is being carried out and subsequently, of all the matters mentioned in subsection (9).

(7) In any case in which there is an investigation of the complaint, recordable conduct matter or DSI matter in accordance with the provisions of Schedule 3—

(a) by the appropriate authority on its own behalf, or

(b) under the supervision of the Commission,

it shall be the duty of the appropriate authority to provide the interested person with all such information as will keep him properly informed, while the investigation is being carried out and subsequently, of all the matters mentioned in subsection (9).

(8) Where subsection (7) applies, it shall be the duty of the Commission to give the appropriate authority all such directions as it considers appropriate for securing that that authority complies with its duty under that subsection; and it shall be the duty of the appropriate authority to comply with any direction given to it under this subsection.

(9) The matters of which the interested person must be kept properly informed are—

(a) the progress of the investigation;

(b) any provisional findings of the person carrying out the investigation;

(ba) whether the Commission or the appropriate authority has made a determination under paragraph 21A of Schedule 3;

(c) whether any report has been submitted under paragraph 22 or 24A of Schedule 3;

(d) the action (if any) that is taken in respect of the matters dealt with in any such report; and

(e) the outcome of any such action.

(10) The duties imposed by this section on the Commission and the appropriate authority in relation to any complaint, recordable conduct matter or DSI matter shall be performed in such manner, and shall have effect subject to such exceptions, as may be provided for by regulations made by the Secretary of State.

(11) Subsections (6) to (9) of section 20 apply for the purposes of this section as they apply for the purposes of that section.

(12) In this section 'relative' means a person of a description prescribed in regulations made by the Secretary of State.

Guidance and regulations

22 Power of the Commission to issue guidance

(1) The Commission may issue guidance—

(a) to local policing bodies

(b) to chief officers, and

(c) to persons who are serving with the police otherwise than as chief officers,

concerning the exercise or performance, by the persons to whom the guidance is issued, of any of the powers or duties specified in subsection (2).

(2) Those powers and duties are—

(a) those that are conferred or imposed by or under this Part; and

(b) those that are otherwise conferred or imposed but relate to—

(i) the handling of complaints;

(ii) the means by which recordable conduct matters or DSI matters are dealt with; or

(iii) the detection or deterrence of misconduct by persons serving with the police.

(3) Before issuing any guidance under this section, the Commission shall consult with—

    (a) such persons as appear to the Commission to represent the views of police and crime commissioners;

    (aa) the Mayor's Office for Policing and Crime;

    (ab) the Common Council;

    (b) the Association of Chief Police Officers; and

    (c) such other persons as it thinks fit.

(4) The approval of the Secretary of State shall be required for the issue by the Commission of any guidance under this section.

(5) Without prejudice to the generality of the preceding provisions of this section, the guidance that may be issued under this section includes—

    (a) guidance about the handling of complaints which have not yet been recorded and about dealing with recordable conduct matters or DSI matters that have not been recorded;

    (b) guidance about the procedure to be followed by the appropriate authority when recording a complaint or any recordable conduct matter or DSI matter;

    (c) guidance about—

        (i) how to decide whether a complaint is suitable for being subjected to local resolution;

    (d) guidance about how to protect the scene of an incident or alleged incident which—

        (i) is or may become the subject-matter of a complaint; or

        (ii) is or may involve a recordable conduct matter or DSI matter;

    (e) guidance about the circumstances in which it is appropriate (where it is lawful to do so)—

        (i) to disclose to any person, or to publish, any information about an investigation of a complaint, conduct matter or DSI matter; or

        (ii) to provide any person with, or to publish, any report or other document relating to such an investigation;

    (f) guidance about the matters to be included in a memorandum under paragraph 23 or 25 of Schedule 3 and about the manner in which, and the place at which, such a memorandum is to be delivered to the Commission.

(6) Nothing in this section shall authorise the issuing of any guidance about a particular case.

(7) It shall be the duty of every person to whom any guidance under this section is issued to have regard to that guidance in exercising or performing the powers and duties to which the guidance relates.

(8) A failure by a person to whom guidance under this section is issued to have regard to the guidance shall be admissible in evidence in any disciplinary proceedings or on any appeal from a decision taken in any such proceedings.

23   Regulations

(1) The Secretary of State may make regulations as to the procedure to be followed under any provision of this Part.

(2) Without prejudice to the generality of the power conferred by subsection (1) or of any other power to make regulations conferred by any provision of this Part, the Secretary of State may also by regulations provide—

    (a) for the appropriate authority, in the case of a complaint against any person, to be required, in accordance with procedures provided for in the regulations—

        (i) to supply the person complained against with a copy of the complaint; and

        (ii) to supply the complainant with a copy of the record made of that complaint;

    (b) for the matters to be taken into account in making any determination as to which procedure to adopt for handling complaints and dealing with recordable conduct matters and DSI matters;

    (c) for any procedure for the purposes of this Part to be discontinued where—

        (i) a complaint is withdrawn;

        (ii) the complainant indicates that he does not wish any further steps to be taken; or

    (iii) the whole or part of the investigation of the complaint has been postponed until the conclusion of criminal proceedings and the complainant fails to indicate after the conclusion of those proceedings that he wishes the investigation to be resumed;

and for the manner in which any such withdrawal or indication is to be effected or given, and for the circumstances in which it is to be taken as effected or given;

(d) for requiring the subject-matter of a complaint that has been withdrawn to be treated for the purposes of this Part, in the cases and to the extent specified in the regulations, as a recordable conduct matter;

(e) for the manner in which any procedure for the purposes of this Part is to be discontinued in a case where it is discontinued in accordance with the regulations, and for the consequences of any such discontinuance;

(f) for the circumstances in which any investigation or other procedure under this Part may be or must be suspended to allow any other investigation or proceedings to continue, and for the consequences of such a suspension;

(g) for the regulation of the appointment of persons to carry out investigations under this Part or to assist with the carrying out of such investigations, for limiting the persons who may be appointed and for the regulation of the carrying out of any such investigation;

(h) for combining into a single investigation the investigation of any complaint, conduct matter or DSI matter with the investigation or investigations of any one or more, or any combination, of the following—

    (i)   complaints (whether relating to the same or different conduct),

    (ii)   conduct matters; or

    (iii) DSI matters,

and for splitting a single investigation into two or more separate investigations;

(i) for the procedure to be followed in cases in which the Commission relinquishes the supervision or management of any investigation and for the consequences of its doing so;

(j) for the manner in which any reference of a complaint, conduct matter or DSI matter to the Commission is to be made;

(k) for applying the provisions of this Part with such modifications as the Secretary of State thinks fit in cases where a complaint or recordable conduct matter relates to the conduct of a person who has ceased to be a person serving with the police since the time of the conduct;

(l) for applying the provisions of this Part with such modifications as the Secretary of State thinks fit in cases where a complaint or conduct matter relates to the conduct of a person—

    (i)   whose identity is unascertained at the time at which a complaint is made or a conduct matter is recorded;

    (ii)   whose identity is not ascertained during, or subsequent to, the investigation of a complaint or recordable conduct matter;

(m) for the Commission—

    (i)   to be required to notify actions and decisions it takes in consequence of the receipt of a memorandum under paragraph 23 or 25 of Schedule 3; and

    (ii)   to be authorised to provide information in relation to the matters notified;

(n) for the records to be kept by local policing bodies and chief officers—

    (i)   with respect to complaints and purported complaints;

    (ii)   with respect to recordable conduct matters or DSI matters; and

    (iii) with respect to the exercise and performance of their powers and duties under this Part;

(o) for the Commission to be required to establish and maintain a register of such information provided to it in accordance with this Part as may be of a description specified in the regulations and for regulating the extent to which information stored on that register, may be published or otherwise disclosed to any person by the Commission;

(p) for chief officers to have power to delegate the exercise or performance of powers and duties conferred or imposed on them by or under this Part;

(q) for the manner in which any notification for the purposes of any provision of this Part is to be given and the time at which, or period within which, any such notification must be given.

(r) for enabling representations on behalf of a person to whose conduct an investigation relates to be made to the Commission by a person who is not that person's legal representative but is of a description specified in the regulations.

24 Consultation on regulations

Before making any regulations under this Part, the Secretary of State shall consult with—

(a) the Commission;

(b) such persons as appear to the Secretary of State to represent the views of police and crime commissioners;

(ba) the Mayor's Office for Policing and Crime;

(bb) the Common Council;

(c) the Association of Chief Police Officers; and

(d) such other persons as he thinks fit.

Conduct of persons in other forms of police service

26 Forces maintained otherwise than by local policing bodies

(1) Notwithstanding any provision made by or under any enactment passed or made before this Act—

(a) the Commission, and

(b) an authority other than a local policing body which maintains a body of constables,

shall each have power to enter into an agreement with the other for the establishment and maintenance in relation to that body of constables of procedures corresponding or similar to any of those provided for by or under this Part.

(2) If it appears to the Secretary of State appropriate to do so in relation to any body of constables maintained otherwise than by a local policing body to establish any such corresponding or similar procedures, he may by order—

(a) provide for the establishment and maintenance of such procedures in relation to that body of constables; and

(b) in a case in which procedures in relation to that body of constables have effect by virtue of subsection (9) or have previously been established by virtue of this section—

(i) provide for those procedures to be superseded by the provision made by the order; and

(ii) make transitional provision in connection with the replacement of the superseded procedures.

(3) It shall be the duty of the Secretary of State to secure that procedures are established and maintained under subsection (2) in relation to each of the following—

(a) the Ministry of Defence Police; and

(b) the British Transport Police Force.

(4) An agreement under this section shall not be made, varied or terminated except with the approval of the Secretary of State.

(5) An agreement or order under this section in relation to any body of constables may contain provision for enabling the Commission to bring and conduct, or otherwise participate or intervene in, any proceedings which are identified by the agreement or order as disciplinary proceedings in relation to members of that body of constables.

(6) An agreement or order under this section in relation to any body of constables may provide for the application of procedures in relation to persons who are not themselves constables but are employed for the purposes of that body of constables and in relation to the conduct of such persons, as well as in relation to members of that body of constables and their conduct.

(7) Before making an order under this section the Secretary of State shall consult with both—

    (a) the Commission; and

    (b) the authority maintaining the body of constables to whom the order relates.

(8) Procedures established in accordance with any agreement or order under this section shall have no effect in relation to anything done outside England and Wales by any constable or any person employed for the purposes of a body of constables.

(9) Where, immediately before the coming into force of this section, any procedures have effect in relation to any body of constables by virtue of—

    (a) section 78 of the 1996 Act (which made provisions similar to that made by this section), or

    (b) paragraph 13 of Schedule 8 to that Act (transitional provisions),

those procedures shall continue to have effect thereafter (notwithstanding the repeal by this Act of Chapter 1 of Part 4 of the 1996 Act and of that paragraph) until superseded by procedures established by virtue of any agreement or order under this section.

(10) Subsection (9) has effect subject to the provisions of any order made under section 28.

27 Conduct of the Commission's staff

(1) The Secretary of State shall by regulations make provision for the manner in which the following cases are to be handled or dealt with—

    (a) cases in which allegations of misconduct are made against members of the Commission's staff; and

    (b) cases in which there is otherwise an indication that there may have been misconduct by a member of the Commission's staff.

(2) Regulations under this section may apply, with such modifications as the Secretary of State thinks fit, any provision made by or under this Part.

(3) Regulations under this section may provide for it to be the duty of any person on whom functions are conferred by the regulations to have regard, in the carrying out of those functions, to any guidance given by such persons and in such manner as may be specified in the regulations.

(4) Before making any regulations under this section the Secretary of State shall consult with the Commission.

Transitional provisions

28 Transitional arrangements connected with establishing the Commission etc.

(1) The Secretary of State may, in connection with the coming into force of any provision of this Part, by order make such transitional provision and savings (including provision modifying this Part) as he thinks fit.

(2) The Secretary of State may, for the purpose of facilitating the carrying out by the Commission of its functions, or in connection with the coming into force of any provision of this Part, by order make such provision as he thinks fit—

    (a) for the transfer and apportionment of property; and

    (b) for the transfer, apportionment and creation of rights and liabilities.

(3) The provision that may be made by an order under this section shall include provision that—

    (a) pending the coming into force of any repeal by this Act of an enactment contained in Chapter 1 of Part 4 of the 1996 Act (complaints), or

    (b) for transitional purposes connected with the coming into force of any such repeal,

the functions of the Police Complaints Authority under an enactment so contained are to be carried out by the Commission.

(4) The provision that may be made by an order under this section shall also include transitional provision in connection with the repeal by this Act of the reference to the Police Complaints Authority in Schedule 1 to the Superannuation Act 1972 (c. 11).

(5) An order under this section may—

    (a) provide for the Secretary of State, or any other person nominated by or in accordance with the order, to determine any matter requiring determination under or in consequence of the order; and

    (b) make provision as to the payment of fees charged, or expenses incurred, by any person nominated to determine any matter by virtue of paragraph (a).

(6) Where a person—

    (a) ceases to be a member of the Police Complaints Authority by reason of its abolition, and

    (b) does not become a member of the Commission,

the Secretary of State may make a payment to that person of such amount as the Secretary of State may, with the consent of the Treasury, determine.

Interpretation of Part 2

29   Interpretation of Part 2

(1) In this Part—

'the appropriate authority'—

    (a) in relation to a person serving with the police or in relation to any complaint, conduct matter or investigation relating to the conduct of such a person, means—

        (i)   if that person is the chief officer or an acting chief officer, the local policing body for the area of the police force of which he is a member; and

        (ii) if he is not the chief officer or an acting chief officer, the chief officer under whose direction and control he is; and

    (b) in relation to a death or serious injury matter, means—

        (i)   if the relevant officer is the chief officer or an acting chief officer, the local policing body for the area of the police force of which he is a member; and

        (ii) if he is not the chief officer or an acting chief officer, the chief officer under whose direction and control he is;

and, for the purposes of this definition, 'acting chief officer' means a person exercising or performing functions of a chief constable in accordance with section 41 of the Police Reform and Social Responsibility Act 2011; a person exercising powers or duties of the Commissioner of Police of the Metropolis in accordance with section 44 or 45(4) of that Act; or a person exercising duties of the Commissioner of Police for the City of London in accordance with section 25 of the City of London Police Act 1839;

'chief officer' means the chief officer of police of any police force;

'the Commission' has the meaning given by section 9(1);

'complainant' shall be construed in accordance with subsection (2);

'complaint' has the meaning given by section 12;

'conduct' includes acts, omissions, statements and decisions (whether actual, alleged or inferred);

'conduct matter' has the meaning given by section 12;

'death or serious injury matter' and 'DSI matter' have the meaning given by section 12;

'disciplinary proceedings' means—

    (a) in relation to a member of a police force or a special constable, proceedings under any regulations made by virtue of section 50 or 51 of the 1996 Act and identified as disciplinary proceedings by those regulations; and

    (b) in relation to a person serving with the police who is not a member of a police force or a special constable, proceedings identified as such by regulations made by the Secretary of State for the purposes of this Part;

'document' means anything in which information of any description is recorded;

'information' includes estimates and projections, and statistical analyses;

'local resolution', in relation to a complaint, means the handling of that complaint in accordance with a procedure which—

    (a) does not involve a formal investigation; and

    (b) is laid down by regulations under paragraph 8 of Schedule 3 for complaints which it has been decided, in accordance with paragraph 6 of that Schedule, to subject to local resolution;

'person complained against', in relation to a complaint, means the person whose conduct is the subject-matter of the complaint;

'recordable conduct matter' means (subject to any regulations under section 23(2)(d))—

    (a)   a conduct matter that is required to be recorded by the appropriate authority under paragraph 10 or 11 of Schedule 3 or has been so recorded; or

    (aa) a conduct matter that is required to be recorded by the appropriate authority under section 28A(8) or has been so recorded;

'relevant force', in relation to the appropriate authority, means—

    (a)   if that authority is a local policing body, the police force which the body is responsible for maintaining; and

    (b)   if that authority is the chief officer of police of a police force, his force;

'serious injury' means a fracture, a deep cut, a deep laceration or an injury causing damage to an internal organ or the impairment of any bodily function;

'serving with the police', in relation to any person, shall be construed in accordance with section 12(7) to (10).

(1A) In this Part 'the relevant officer', in relation to a DSI matter, means the person serving with the police (within the meaning of section 12(7) to (10))—

    (a)   who arrested the person who has died or suffered serious injury,

    (b)   in whose custody that person was at the time of the death or serious injury, or

    (c)   with whom that person had the contact in question;

and where there is more than one such person it means, subject to subsection (1B), the one who so dealt with him last before the death or serious injury occurred.

(1B) Where it cannot be determined which of two or more persons serving with the police dealt with a person last before a death or serious injury occurred, the relevant officer is the most senior of them.

(2) References in this Part, in relation to anything which is or purports to be a complaint, to the complainant are references—

    (a)   except in the case of anything which is or purports to be a complaint falling within section 12(1)(d), to the person by whom the complaint or purported complaint was made; and

    (b)   in that case, to the person on whose behalf the complaint or purported complaint was made;

but where any person is acting on another's behalf for the purposes of any complaint or purported complaint, anything that is to be or may be done under this Part by or in relation to the complainant may be done, instead, by or in relation to the person acting on the complainant's behalf.

(3) Subject to subsection (4), references in this Part, in relation to any conduct or anything purporting to be a complaint about any conduct, to a member of the public include references to any person falling within any of the following paragraphs (whether at the time of the conduct or at any subsequent time)—

    (a)   a person serving with the police;

    (ca) a National Crime Agency officer; or

    (d)   a person engaged on relevant service, within the meaning of section 97(1)(a) or (d) of the 1996 Act (temporary service of various kinds).

(4) In this Part references, in relation to any conduct or to anything purporting to be a complaint about any conduct, to a member of the public do not include references to—

    (a)   a person who, at the time when the conduct is supposed to have taken place, was under the direction and control of the same chief officer as the person whose conduct it was; or

    (b)   a person who—

        (i)   at the time when the conduct is supposed to have taken place, in relation to him, or

        (ii) at the time when he is supposed to have been adversely affected by it, or to have witnessed it,

    was on duty in his capacity as a person falling within subsection (3)(a) to (d).

(5) For the purposes of this Part a person is adversely affected if he suffers any form of loss or damage, distress or inconvenience, if he is put in danger or if he is otherwise unduly put at risk of being adversely affected.

(6) References in this Part to the investigation of any complaint or matter by the appropriate authority on its own behalf, under the supervision of the Commission, under the management of the Commission or by the Commission itself shall be construed as references to its investigation in accordance with paragraph 16, 17, 18 or, as the case may be, 19 of Schedule 3.

(7) The Commissioner of Police for the City of London shall be treated for the purposes of this Part as if he were a member of the City of London police force.

Criminal Justice Act 2003

22   Conditional cautions

(1) An authorised person may give a conditional caution to a person aged 18 or over ('the offender') if each of the five requirements in section 23 is satisfied.

(2) In this Part 'conditional caution' means a caution which is given in respect of an offence committed by the offender and which has conditions attached to it with which the offender must comply.

(3) The conditions which may be attached to any conditional caution are those which have one or more of the following objects—

   (a) facilitating the rehabilitation of the offender;
   (b) ensuring that the offender makes reparation for the offence;
   (c) punishing the offender.

(3A) The conditions which may be attached to a conditional caution include—

   (a) (subject to section 23A) a condition that the offender pay a financial penalty;
   (b) a condition that the offender attend at a specified place at specified times.

'Specified' means specified in the condition.

(3D) A conditional caution given to a relevant foreign offender may have conditions attached to it that have one or more of the objects mentioned in subsection (3E) (whether or not in addition to conditions with one or more of the objects mentioned in subsection (3)).

(3E) The objects are—

   (a) bringing about the departure of the relevant foreign offender from the United Kingdom;
   (b) ensuring that the relevant foreign offender does not return to the United Kingdom for a period of time.

(3F) If a relevant foreign offender is given a conditional caution with a condition attached to it with the object of ensuring that the offender does not return to the United Kingdom for a period of time, the expiry of that period does not of itself give rise to any right on the part of the offender to return to the United Kingdom.

(3G) In this section 'relevant foreign offender' means—

   (a) an offender directions for whose removal from the United Kingdom have been, or may be, given under—
      (i)   Schedule 2 to the Immigration Act 1971, or
      (ii) section 10 of the Immigration and Asylum Act 1999, or
   (b) an offender against whom a deportation order under section 5 of the Immigration Act 1971 is in force.

(4) In this Part 'authorised person' means—

   (a) a constable,
   (b) an investigating officer, or
   (c) a person authorised by a relevant prosecutor for the purposes of this section.

23   The five requirements

(1) The first requirement is that the authorised person has evidence that the offender has committed an offence.

(2) The second requirement is that a relevant prosecutor or the authorised person decides—

(a) that there is sufficient evidence to charge the offender with the offence, and

(b) that a conditional caution should be given to the offender in respect of the offence.

(3) The third requirement is that the offender admits to the authorised person that he committed the offence.

(4) The fourth requirement is that the authorised person explains the effect of the conditional caution to the offender and warns him that failure to comply with any of the conditions attached to the caution may result in his being prosecuted for the offence.

(5) The fifth requirement is that the offender signs a document which contains—

(a) details of the offence,

(b) an admission by him that he committed the offence,

(c) his consent to being given the conditional caution, and

(d) the conditions attached to the caution.

24   Failure to comply with conditions

(1) If the offender fails, without reasonable excuse, to comply with any of the conditions attached to the conditional caution, criminal proceedings may be instituted against the person for the offence in question.

(2) The document mentioned in section 23(5) is to be admissible in such proceedings.

(3) Where such proceedings are instituted, the conditional caution is to cease to have effect.

25   Code of practice

(1) The Secretary of State must prepare a code of practice in relation to conditional cautions.

(2) The code may, in particular, include provision as to—

(a) the circumstances in which conditional cautions may be given,

(b) the procedure to be followed in connection with the giving of such cautions,

(c) the conditions which may be attached to such cautions and the time for which they may have effect,

(d) the category of constable or investigating officer by whom such cautions may be given,

(e) the persons who may be authorised by a relevant prosecutor for the purposes of section 22,

(f) the form which such cautions are to take and the manner in which they are to be given and recorded,

(g) the places where such cautions may be given,

(ga) the provision which may be made in a condition under section 23A(5)(b),

(h) the monitoring of compliance with conditions attached to such cautions

(i) the exercise of the power of arrest conferred by section 24A(1), and

(j) who is to decide how a person should be dealt with under section 24A(2).

(3) After preparing a draft of the code the Secretary of State—

(a) must publish the draft,

(b) must consider any representations made to him about the draft, and

(c) may amend the draft accordingly,

but he may not publish or amend the draft without the consent of the Attorney General.

(4) After the Secretary of State has proceeded under subsection (3) he must lay the code before each House of Parliament.

(5) When he has done so he may bring the code into force by order.

(6) The Secretary of State may from time to time revise a code of practice brought into force under this section.

(7) Subsections (3) to (6) are to apply (with appropriate modifications) to a revised code as they apply to an original code.

26 Assistance of National Probation Service

(1) Section 1 of the Criminal Justice and Court Services Act 2000 (c. 43) (purposes of Chapter 1) is amended as follows.

(2) After subsection (1) there is inserted—

'(1A) This Chapter also has effect for the purposes of providing for—

(a) authorised persons to be given assistance in determining whether conditional cautions should be given and which conditions to attach to conditional cautions, and

(b) the supervision and rehabilitation of persons to whom conditional cautions are given.'

(3) After subsection (3) there is inserted—

'(4) In this section "authorised person" and "conditional caution" have the same meaning as in Part 3 of the Criminal Justice Act 2003.'

27 Interpretation of Part 3

In this Part—

'authorised person' has the meaning given by section 22(4),

'conditional caution' has the meaning given by section 22(2),

'investigating officer' means an officer of Revenue and Customs, appointed in accordance with section 2(1) of the Commissioners for Revenue and Customs Act 2005, or a person designated as an investigating officer under section 38 of the Police Reform Act 2002 (c. 30),

'the offender' has the meaning given by section 22(1),

'relevant prosecutor' means—

(a) the Attorney General,

(b) the Director of the Serious Fraud Office,

(c) the Director of Public Prosecutions,

(d) a Secretary of State, or

(g) a person who is specified in an order made by the Secretary of State as being a relevant prosecutor for the purposes of this Part.

57 Introduction

(1) In relation to a trial on indictment, the prosecution is to have the rights of appeal for which provision is made by this Part.

(2) But the prosecution is to have no right of appeal under this Part in respect of—

(a) a ruling that a jury be discharged, or

(b) a ruling from which an appeal lies to the Court of Appeal by virtue of any other enactment.

(3) An appeal under this Part is to lie to the Court of Appeal.

(4) Such an appeal may be brought only with the leave of the judge or the Court of Appeal.

58 General right of appeal in respect of rulings

(1) This section applies where a judge makes a ruling in relation to a trial on indictment at an applicable time and the ruling relates to one or more offences included in the indictment.

(2) The prosecution may appeal in respect of the ruling in accordance with this section.

(3) The ruling is to have no effect whilst the prosecution is able to take any steps under subsection (4).

(4) The prosecution may not appeal in respect of the ruling unless—

(a) following the making of the ruling, it—

(i) informs the court that it intends to appeal, or

(ii) requests an adjournment to consider whether to appeal, and

(b) if such an adjournment is granted, it informs the court following the adjournment that it intends to appeal.

(5) If the prosecution requests an adjournment under subsection (4)(a)(ii), the judge may grant such an adjournment.

(6) Where the ruling relates to two or more offences—

(a) any one or more of those offences may be the subject of the appeal, and

(b) if the prosecution informs the court in accordance with subsection (4) that it intends to appeal, it must at the same time inform the court of the offence or offences which are the subject of the appeal.

(7) Where—

(a) the ruling is a ruling that there is no case to answer, and

(b) the prosecution, at the same time that it informs the court in accordance with subsection (4) that it intends to appeal, nominates one or more other rulings which have been made by a judge in relation to the trial on indictment at an applicable time and which relate to the offence or offences which are the subject of the appeal,

that other ruling, or those other rulings, are also to be treated as the subject of the appeal.

(8) The prosecution may not inform the court in accordance with subsection (4) that it intends to appeal, unless, at or before that time, it informs the court that it agrees that, in respect of the offence or each offence which is the subject of the appeal, the defendant in relation to that offence should be acquitted of that offence if either of the conditions mentioned in subsection (9) is fulfilled.

(9) Those conditions are—

(a) that leave to appeal to the Court of Appeal is not obtained, and

(b) that the appeal is abandoned before it is determined by the Court of Appeal.

(10) If the prosecution informs the court in accordance with subsection (4) that it intends to appeal, the ruling mentioned in subsection (1) is to continue to have no effect in relation to the offence or offences which are the subject of the appeal whilst the appeal is pursued.

(11) If and to the extent that a ruling has no effect in accordance with this section—

(a) any consequences of the ruling are also to have no effect,

(b) the judge may not take any steps in consequence of the ruling, and

(c) if he does so, any such steps are also to have no effect.

(12) Where the prosecution has informed the court of its agreement under subsection (8) and either of the conditions mentioned in subsection (9) is fulfilled, the judge or the Court of Appeal must order that the defendant in relation to the offence or each offence concerned be acquitted of that offence.

(13) In this section 'applicable time', in relation to a trial on indictment, means any time (whether before or after the commencement of the trial) before the time when the judge starts his summing-up to the jury.

(14) The reference in subsection (13) to the time when the judge starts his summing-up to the jury includes the time when the judge would start his summing-up to the jury but for the making of an order under Part 7.

59 Expedited and non-expedited appeals

(1) Where the prosecution informs the court in accordance with section 58(4) that it intends to appeal, the judge must decide whether or not the appeal should be expedited.

(2) If the judge decides that the appeal should be expedited, he may order an adjournment.

(3) If the judge decides that the appeal should not be expedited, he may—

(a) order an adjournment, or

(b) discharge the jury (if one has been sworn).

(4) If he decides that the appeal should be expedited, he or the Court of Appeal may subsequently reverse that decision and, if it is reversed, the judge may act as mentioned in subsection (3)(a) or (b).

60 Continuation of proceedings for offences not affected by ruling

(1) This section applies where the prosecution informs the court in accordance with section 58(4) that it intends to appeal.

(2) Proceedings may be continued in respect of any offence which is not the subject of the appeal.

61   Determination of appeal by Court of Appeal

(1) On an appeal under section 58, the Court of Appeal may confirm, reverse or vary any ruling to which the appeal relates.

(2) Subsections (3) to (5) apply where the appeal relates to a single ruling.

(3) Where the Court of Appeal confirms the ruling, it must, in respect of the offence or each offence which is the subject of the appeal, order that the defendant in relation to that offence be acquitted of that offence.

(4) Where the Court of Appeal reverses or varies the ruling, it must, in respect of the offence or each offence which is the subject of the appeal, do any of the following—

    (a) order that proceedings for that offence may be resumed in the Crown Court,

    (b) order that a fresh trial may take place in the Crown Court for that offence,

    (c) order that the defendant in relation to that offence be acquitted of that offence.

(5) But the Court of Appeal may not make an order under subsection (4)(a) or (b) in respect of an offence unless it considers that the defendant could not receive a fair trial if an order were made under subsection (4)(a) or (b).

(6) Subsections (7) and (8) apply where the appeal relates to a ruling that there is no case to answer and one or more other rulings.

(7) Where the Court of Appeal confirms the ruling that there is no case to answer, it must, in respect of the offence or each offence which is the subject of the appeal, order that the defendant in relation to that offence be acquitted of that offence.

(8) Where the Court of Appeal reverses or varies the ruling that there is no case to answer, it must in respect of the offence or each offence which is the subject of the appeal, make any of the orders mentioned in subsection (4)(a) to (c) (but subject to subsection (5)).

67   Reversal of rulings

The Court of Appeal may not reverse a ruling on an appeal under this Part unless it is satisfied—

    (a) that the ruling was wrong in law,

    (b) that the ruling involved an error of law or principle, or

    (c) that the ruling was a ruling that it was not reasonable for the judge to have made.

75   Cases that may be retried

(1) This Part applies where a person has been acquitted of a qualifying offence in proceedings—

    (a) on indictment in England and Wales,

    (b) on appeal against a conviction, verdict or finding in proceedings on indictment in England and Wales, or

    (c) on appeal from a decision on such an appeal.

(2) A person acquitted of an offence in proceedings mentioned in subsection (1) is treated for the purposes of that subsection as also acquitted of any qualifying offence of which he could have been convicted in the proceedings because of the first-mentioned offence being charged in the indictment, except an offence—

    (a) of which he has been convicted,

    (b) of which he has been found not guilty by reason of insanity, or

    (c) in respect of which, in proceedings where he has been found to be under a disability (as defined by section 4 of the Criminal Procedure (Insanity) Act 1964 (c. 84)), a finding has been made that he did the act or made the omission charged against him.

(3) References in subsections (1) and (2) to a qualifying offence do not include references to an offence which, at the time of the acquittal, was the subject of an order under section 77(1) or (3).

(4) This Part also applies where a person has been acquitted, in proceedings elsewhere than in the United Kingdom, of an offence under the law of the place where the proceedings were held, if the commission of the offence as alleged would have amounted to or included the commission (in the United Kingdom or elsewhere) of a qualifying offence.

(5) Conduct punishable under the law in force elsewhere than in the United Kingdom is an offence under that law for the purposes of subsection (4), however it is described in that law.

(6) This Part applies whether the acquittal was before or after the passing of this Act.

(7) References in this Part to acquittal are to acquittal in circumstances within subsection (1) or (4).

(8) In this Part 'qualifying offence' means an offence listed in Part 1 of Schedule 5.

76   Application to Court of Appeal

(1) A prosecutor may apply to the Court of Appeal for an order—

    (a) quashing a person's acquittal in proceedings within section 75(1), and

    (b) ordering him to be retried for the qualifying offence.

(2) A prosecutor may apply to the Court of Appeal, in the case of a person acquitted elsewhere than in the United Kingdom, for—

    (a) a determination whether the acquittal is a bar to the person being tried in England and Wales for the qualifying offence, and

    (b) if it is, an order that the acquittal is not to be a bar.

(3) A prosecutor may make an application under subsection (1) or (2) only with the written consent of the Director of Public Prosecutions.

(4) The Director of Public Prosecutions may give his consent only if satisfied that—

    (a) there is evidence as respects which the requirements of section 78 appear to be met,

    (b) it is in the public interest for the application to proceed, and

    (c) any trial pursuant to an order on the application would not be inconsistent with obligations of the United Kingdom under Article 31 or 34 of the Treaty on European Union (as it had effect before 1 December 2009) or Article 82, 83 or 85 of the Treaty on the Functioning of the European Union relating to the principle of *ne bis in idem*.

(5) Not more than one application may be made under subsection (1) or (2) in relation to an acquittal.

77   Determination by Court of Appeal

(1) On an application under section 76(1), the Court of Appeal—

    (a) if satisfied that the requirements of sections 78 and 79 are met, must make the order applied for;

    (b) otherwise, must dismiss the application.

(2) Subsections (3) and (4) apply to an application under section 76(2).

(3) Where the Court of Appeal determines that the acquittal is a bar to the person being tried for the qualifying offence, the court—

    (a) if satisfied that the requirements of sections 78 and 79 are met, must make the order applied for;

    (b) otherwise, must make a declaration to the effect that the acquittal is a bar to the person being tried for the offence.

(4) Where the Court of Appeal determines that the acquittal is not a bar to the person being tried for the qualifying offence, it must make a declaration to that effect.

78   New and compelling evidence

(1) The requirements of this section are met if there is new and compelling evidence against the acquitted person in relation to the qualifying offence.

(2) Evidence is new if it was not adduced in the proceedings in which the person was acquitted (nor, if those were appeal proceedings, in earlier proceedings to which the appeal related).

(3) Evidence is compelling if—

    (a) it is reliable,

    (b) it is substantial, and

    (c) in the context of the outstanding issues, it appears highly probative of the case against the acquitted person.

(4) The outstanding issues are the issues in dispute in the proceedings in which the person was acquitted and, if those were appeal proceedings, any other issues remaining in dispute from earlier proceedings to which the appeal related.

(5) For the purposes of this section, it is irrelevant whether any evidence would have been admissible in earlier proceedings against the acquitted person.

79   Interests of justice

(1) The requirements of this section are met if in all the circumstances it is in the interests of justice for the court to make the order under section 77.

(2) That question is to be determined having regard in particular to—

    (a) whether existing circumstances make a fair trial unlikely;

    (b) for the purposes of that question and otherwise, the length of time since the qualifying offence was allegedly committed;

    (c) whether it is likely that the new evidence would have been adduced in the earlier proceedings against the acquitted person but for a failure by an officer or by a prosecutor to act with due diligence or expedition;

    (d) whether, since those proceedings or, if later, since the commencement of this Part, any officer or prosecutor has failed to act with due diligence or expedition.

(3) In subsection (2) references to an officer or prosecutor include references to a person charged with corresponding duties under the law in force elsewhere than in England and Wales.

(4) Where the earlier prosecution was conducted by a person other than a prosecutor, subsection (2)(c) applies in relation to that person as well as in relation to a prosecutor.

82   Restrictions on publication in the interests of justice

(1) Where it appears to the Court of Appeal that the inclusion of any matter in a publication would give rise to a substantial risk of prejudice to the administration of justice in a retrial, the court may order that the matter is not to be included in any publication while the order has effect.

(2) In subsection (1) 'retrial' means the trial of an acquitted person for a qualifying offence pursuant to any order made or that may be made under section 77.

(3) The court may make an order under this section only if it appears to it necessary in the interests of justice to do so.

(4) An order under this section may apply to a matter which has been included in a publication published before the order takes effect, but such an order—

    (a) applies only to the later inclusion of the matter in a publication (whether directly or by inclusion of the earlier publication), and

    (b) does not otherwise affect the earlier publication.

(5) After notice of an application has been given under section 80(1) relating to the acquitted person and the qualifying offence, the court may make an order under this section only—

    (a) of its own motion, or

    (b) on the application of the Director of Public Prosecutions.

(6) Before such notice has been given, an order under this section—

    (a) may be made only on the application of the Director of Public Prosecutions, and

    (b) may not be made unless, since the acquittal concerned, an investigation of the commission by the acquitted person of the qualifying offence has been commenced by officers.

(7) The court may at any time, of its own motion or on an application made by the Director of Public Prosecutions or the acquitted person, vary or revoke an order under this section.

(8) Any order made under this section before notice of an application has been given under section 80(1) relating to the acquitted person and the qualifying offence must specify the time when it ceases to have effect.

(9) An order under this section which is made or has effect after such notice has been given ceases to have effect, unless it specifies an earlier time—

    (a) when there is no longer any step that could be taken which would lead to the acquitted person being tried pursuant to an order made on the application, or

    (b) if he is tried pursuant to such an order, at the conclusion of the trial.

(10) Nothing in this section affects any prohibition or restriction by virtue of any other enactment on the inclusion of any matter in a publication or any power, under an enactment or otherwise, to impose such a prohibition or restriction.

(11) In this section—

'programme service' has the same meaning as in the Broadcasting Act 1990 (c. 42),

'publication' includes any speech, writing, relevant programme or other communication in whatever form, which is addressed to the public at large or any section of the public (and for this purpose every relevant programme is to be taken to be so addressed), but does not include an indictment or other document prepared for use in particular legal proceedings,

'relevant programme' means a programme included in a programme service.

84 Retrial

(1) Where a person—

    (a) is tried pursuant to an order under section 77(1), or

    (b) is tried on indictment pursuant to an order under section 77(3),

the trial must be on an indictment preferred by direction of the Court of Appeal.

(2) After the end of 2 months after the date of the order, the person may not be arraigned on an indictment preferred in pursuance of such a direction unless the Court of Appeal gives leave.

(3) The Court of Appeal must not give leave unless satisfied that—

    (a) the prosecutor has acted with due expedition, and

    (b) there is a good and sufficient cause for trial despite the lapse of time since the order under section 77.

(4) Where the person may not be arraigned without leave, he may apply to the Court of Appeal to set aside the order and—

    (a) for any direction required for restoring an earlier judgment and verdict of acquittal of the qualifying offence, or

    (b) in the case of a person acquitted elsewhere than in the United Kingdom, for a declaration to the effect that the acquittal is a bar to his being tried for the qualifying offence.

(5) An indictment under subsection (1) may relate to more than one offence, or more than one person, and may relate to an offence which, or a person who, is not the subject of an order or declaration under section 77.

(6) Evidence given at a trial pursuant to an order under section 77(1) or (3) must be given orally if it was given orally at the original trial, unless—

    (a) all the parties to the trial agree otherwise,

    (b) section 116 applies, or

    (c) the witness is unavailable to give evidence, otherwise than as mentioned in subsection (2) of that section, and section 114(1)(d) applies.

(7) At a trial pursuant to an order under section 77(1), paragraph 5 of Schedule 3 to the Crime and Disorder Act 1998 (c. 37) (use of depositions) does not apply to a deposition read as evidence at the original trial.

98 'Bad character'

References in this Chapter to evidence of a person's 'bad character' are to evidence of, or of a disposition towards, misconduct on his part, other than evidence which—

    (a) has to do with the alleged facts of the offence with which the defendant is charged, or

    (b) is evidence of misconduct in connection with the investigation or prosecution of that offence.

99 Abolition of common law rules

(1) The common law rules governing the admissibility of evidence of bad character in criminal proceedings are abolished.

(2) Subsection (1) is subject to section 118(1) in so far as it preserves the rule under which in criminal proceedings a person's reputation is admissible for the purposes of proving his bad character.

100 Non-defendant's bad character

(1) In criminal proceedings evidence of the bad character of a person other than the defendant is admissible if and only if—

    (a) it is important explanatory evidence,

(b) it has substantial probative value in relation to a matter which—
    (i)   is a matter in issue in the proceedings, and
    (ii) is of substantial importance in the context of the case as a whole, or
(c) all parties to the proceedings agree to the evidence being admissible.

(2) For the purposes of subsection (1)(a) evidence is important explanatory evidence if—
(a) without it, the court or jury would find it impossible or difficult properly to understand other evidence in the case, and
(b) its value for understanding the case as a whole is substantial.

(3) In assessing the probative value of evidence for the purposes of subsection (1)(b) the court must have regard to the following factors (and to any others it considers relevant)—
(a) the nature and number of the events, or other things, to which the evidence relates;
(b) when those events or things are alleged to have happened or existed;
(c) where—
    (i)   the evidence is evidence of a person's misconduct, and
    (ii) it is suggested that the evidence has probative value by reason of similarity between that misconduct and other alleged misconduct,
the nature and extent of the similarities and the dissimilarities between each of the alleged instances of misconduct;
(d) where—
    (i)   the evidence is evidence of a person's misconduct,
    (ii)   it is suggested that that person is also responsible for the misconduct charged, and
    (iii) the identity of the person responsible for the misconduct charged is disputed,
the extent to which the evidence shows or tends to show that the same person was responsible each time.

(4) Except where subsection (1)(c) applies, evidence of the bad character of a person other than the defendant must not be given without leave of the court.

101   Defendant's bad character

(1) In criminal proceedings evidence of the defendant's bad character is admissible if, but only if—
(a) all parties to the proceedings agree to the evidence being admissible,
(b) the evidence is adduced by the defendant himself or is given in answer to a question asked by him in cross-examination and intended to elicit it,
(c) it is important explanatory evidence,
(d) it is relevant to an important matter in issue between the defendant and the prosecution,
(e) it has substantial probative value in relation to an important matter in issue between the defendant and a co-defendant,
(f) it is evidence to correct a false impression given by the defendant, or
(g) the defendant has made an attack on another person's character.

(2) Sections 102 to 106 contain provision supplementing subsection (1).

(3) The court must not admit evidence under subsection (1)(d) or (g) if, on an application by the defendant to exclude it, it appears to the court that the admission of the evidence would have such an adverse effect on the fairness of the proceedings that the court ought not to admit it.

(4) On an application to exclude evidence under subsection (3) the court must have regard, in particular, to the length of time between the matters to which that evidence relates and the matters which form the subject of the offence charged.

102   'Important explanatory evidence'

For the purposes of section 101(1)(c) evidence is important explanatory evidence if—
(a) without it, the court or jury would find it impossible or difficult properly to understand other evidence in the case, and
(b) its value for understanding the case as a whole is substantial.

103 'Matter in issue between the defendant and the prosecution'

(1) For the purposes of section 101(1)(d) the matters in issue between the defendant and the prosecution include—

(a) the question whether the defendant has a propensity to commit offences of the kind with which he is charged, except where his having such a propensity makes it no more likely that he is guilty of the offence;

(b) the question whether the defendant has a propensity to be untruthful, except where it is not suggested that the defendant's case is untruthful in any respect.

(2) Where subsection (1)(a) applies, a defendant's propensity to commit offences of the kind with which he is charged may (without prejudice to any other way of doing so) be established by evidence that he has been convicted of—

(a) an offence of the same description as the one with which he is charged, or

(b) an offence of the same category as the one with which he is charged.

(3) Subsection (2) does not apply in the case of a particular defendant if the court is satisfied, by reason of the length of time since the conviction or for any other reason, that it would be unjust for it to apply in his case.

(4) For the purposes of subsection (2)—

(a) two offences are of the same description as each other if the statement of the offence in a written charge or indictment would, in each case, be in the same terms;

(b) two offences are of the same category as each other if they belong to the same category of offences prescribed for the purposes of this section by an order made by the Secretary of State.

(5) A category prescribed by an order under subsection (4)(b) must consist of offences of the same type.

(6) Only prosecution evidence is admissible under section 101(1)(d).

(7) Where—

(a) a defendant has been convicted of an offence under the law of any country outside England and Wales ('the previous offence'), and

(b) the previous offence would constitute an offence under the law of England and Wales ('the corresponding offence') if it were done in England and Wales at the time of the trial for the offence with which the defendant is now charged ('the current offence'),

subsection (8) applies for the purpose of determining if the previous offence and the current offence are of the same description or category.

(8) For the purposes of subsection (2)—

(a) the previous offence is of the same description as the current offence if the corresponding offence is of that same description, as set out in subsection (4)(a);

(b) the previous offence is of the same category as the current offence if the current offence and the corresponding offence belong to the same category of offences prescribed as mentioned in subsection (4)(b).

(9) For the purposes of subsection (10) 'foreign service offence' means an offence which—

(a) was the subject of proceedings under the service law of a country outside the United Kingdom, and

(b) would constitute an offence under the law of England and Wales or a service offence ('the corresponding domestic offence') if it were done in England and Wales by a member of Her Majesty's forces at the time of the trial for the offence with which the defendant is now charged ('the current offence').

(10) Where a defendant has been found guilty of a foreign service offence ('the previous service offence'), for the purposes of subsection (2)—

(a) the previous service offence is an offence of the same description as the current offence if the corresponding domestic offence is of that same description, as set out in subsection (4)(a);

(b) the previous service offence is an offence of the same category as the current offence if the current offence and the corresponding domestic offence belong to the same category of offences prescribed as mentioned in subsection (4)(b).

(11) In this section—

'Her Majesty's forces' has the same meaning as in the Armed Forces Act 2006;

'service law', in relation to a country outside the United Kingdom, means the law governing all or any of the naval, military or air forces of that country.

104 'Matter in issue between the defendant and a co-defendant'

(1) Evidence which is relevant to the question whether the defendant has a propensity to be untruthful is admissible on that basis under section 101(1)(e) only if the nature or conduct of his defence is such as to undermine the co-defendant's defence.

(2) Only evidence—

(a) which is to be (or has been) adduced by the co-defendant, or

(b) which a witness is to be invited to give (or has given) in cross-examination by the co-defendant,

is admissible under section 101(1)(e).

105 'Evidence to correct a false impression'

(1) For the purposes of section 101(1)(f)—

(a) the defendant gives a false impression if he is responsible for the making of an express or implied assertion which is apt to give the court or jury a false or misleading impression about the defendant;

(b) evidence to correct such an impression is evidence which has probative value in correcting it.

(2) A defendant is treated as being responsible for the making of an assertion if—

(a) the assertion is made by the defendant in the proceedings (whether or not in evidence given by him),

(b) the assertion was made by the defendant—

(i) on being questioned under caution, before charge, about the offence with which he is charged, or

(ii) on being charged with the offence or officially informed that he might be prosecuted for it,

and evidence of the assertion is given in the proceedings,

(c) the assertion is made by a witness called by the defendant,

(d) the assertion is made by any witness in cross-examination in response to a question asked by the defendant that is intended to elicit it, or is likely to do so, or

(e) the assertion was made by any person out of court, and the defendant adduces evidence of it in the proceedings.

(3) A defendant who would otherwise be treated as responsible for the making of an assertion shall not be so treated if, or to the extent that, he withdraws it or disassociates himself from it.

(4) Where it appears to the court that a defendant, by means of his conduct (other than the giving of evidence) in the proceedings, is seeking to give the court or jury an impression about himself that is false or misleading, the court may if it appears just to do so treat the defendant as being responsible for the making of an assertion which is apt to give that impression.

(5) In subsection (4) 'conduct' includes appearance or dress.

(6) Evidence is admissible under section 101(1)(f) only if it goes no further than is necessary to correct the false impression.

(7) Only prosecution evidence is admissible under section 101(1)(f).

106 'Attack on another person's character'

(1) For the purposes of section 101(1)(g) a defendant makes an attack on another person's character if—

(a) he adduces evidence attacking the other person's character,

(b) he (or any legal representative appointed under section 38(4) of the Youth Justice and Criminal Evidence Act 1999 (c. 23) to cross-examine a witness in his interests) asks questions in cross-examination that are intended to elicit such evidence, or are likely to do so, or

(c) evidence is given of an imputation about the other person made by the defendant—

    (i) on being questioned under caution, before charge, about the offence with which he is charged, or

    (ii) on being charged with the offence or officially informed that he might be prosecuted for it.

(2) In subsection (1) 'evidence attacking the other person's character' means evidence to the effect that the other person—

(a) has committed an offence (whether a different offence from the one with which the defendant is charged or the same one), or

(b) has behaved, or is disposed to behave, in a reprehensible way;

and 'imputation about the other person' means an assertion to that effect.

(3) Only prosecution evidence is admissible under section 101(1)(g).

107 Stopping the case where evidence contaminated

(1) If on a defendant's trial before a judge and jury for an offence—

(a) evidence of his bad character has been admitted under any of paragraphs (c) to (g) of section 101(1), and

(b) the court is satisfied at any time after the close of the case for the prosecution that—

    (i) the evidence is contaminated, and

    (ii) the contamination is such that, considering the importance of the evidence to the case against the defendant, his conviction of the offence would be unsafe,

the court must either direct the jury to acquit the defendant of the offence or, if it considers that there ought to be a retrial, discharge the jury.

(2) Where—

(a) a jury is directed under subsection (1) to acquit a defendant of an offence, and

(b) the circumstances are such that, apart from this subsection, the defendant could if acquitted of that offence be found guilty of another offence,

the defendant may not be found guilty of that other offence if the court is satisfied as mentioned in subsection (1)(b) in respect of it.

(3) If—

(a) a jury is required to determine under section 4A(2) of the Criminal Procedure (Insanity) Act 1964 (c. 84) whether a person charged on an indictment with an offence did the act or made the omission charged,

(b) evidence of the person's bad character has been admitted under any of paragraphs (c) to (g) of section 101(1), and

(c) the court is satisfied at any time after the close of the case for the prosecution that—

    (i) the evidence is contaminated, and

    (ii) the contamination is such that, considering the importance of the evidence to the case against the person, a finding that he did the act or made the omission would be unsafe,

the court must either direct the jury to acquit the defendant of the offence or, if it considers that there ought to be a rehearing, discharge the jury.

(4) This section does not prejudice any other power a court may have to direct a jury to acquit a person of an offence or to discharge a jury.

(5) For the purposes of this section a person's evidence is contaminated where—

(a) as a result of an agreement or understanding between the person and one or more others, or

(b) as a result of the person being aware of anything alleged by one or more others whose evidence may be, or has been, given in the proceedings,

the evidence is false or misleading in any respect, or is different from what it would otherwise have been.

108   Offences committed by defendant when a child

(1) Section 16(2) and (3) of the Children and Young Persons Act 1963 (c. 37) (offences committed by person under 14 disregarded for purposes of evidence relating to previous convictions) shall cease to have effect.

(2) In proceedings for an offence committed or alleged to have been committed by the defendant when aged 21 or over, evidence of his conviction for an offence when under the age of 14 is not admissible unless—

   (a) both of the offences are triable only on indictment, and

   (b) the court is satisfied that the interests of justice require the evidence to be admissible.

(2A) Subsection (2B) applies where—

   (a) the defendant has been convicted of an offence under the law of any country outside England and Wales ('the previous offence'),and

   (b) the previous offence would constitute an offence under the law of England and Wales ('the corresponding offence') if it were done in England and Wales at the time of the proceedings for the offence with which the defendant is now charged.

(2B) For the purposes of subsection (2), the previous offence is to be regarded as triable only on indictment if the corresponding offence is so triable.

(3) Subsection (2) applies in addition to section 101.

109   Assumption of truth in assessment of relevance or probative value

(1) Subject to subsection (2), a reference in this Chapter to the relevance or probative value of evidence is a reference to its relevance or probative value on the assumption that it is true.

(2) In assessing the relevance or probative value of an item of evidence for any purpose of this Chapter, a court need not assume that the evidence is true if it appears, on the basis of any material before the court (including any evidence it decides to hear on the matter), that no court or jury could reasonably find it to be true.

110   Court's duty to give reasons for rulings

(1) Where the court makes a relevant ruling—

   (a) it must state in open court (but in the absence of the jury, if there is one) its reasons for the ruling;

   (b) if it is a magistrates' court, it must cause the ruling and the reasons for it to be entered in the register of the court's proceedings.

(2) In this section 'relevant ruling' means—

   (a) a ruling on whether an item of evidence is evidence of a person's bad character;

   (b) a ruling on whether an item of such evidence is admissible under section 100 or 101 (including a ruling on an application under section 101(3));

   (c) a ruling under section 107.

118   Preservation of certain common law categories of admissibility

(1) The following rules of law are preserved.

Public information etc

1 Any rule of law under which in criminal proceedings—

   (a) published works dealing with matters of a public nature (such as histories, scientific works, dictionaries and maps) are admissible as evidence of facts of a public nature stated in them,

   (b) public documents (such as public registers, and returns made under public authority with respect to matters of public interest) are admissible as evidence of facts stated in them,

   (c) records (such as the records of certain courts, treaties, Crown grants, pardons and commissions) are admissible as evidence of facts stated in them, or

   (d) evidence relating to a person's age or date or place of birth may be given by a person without personal knowledge of the matter.

Reputation as to character

2 Any rule of law under which in criminal proceedings evidence of a person's reputation is admissible for the purpose of proving his good or bad character.

Note: The rule is preserved only so far as it allows the court to treat such evidence as proving the matter concerned.

Reputation or family tradition

3 Any rule of law under which in criminal proceedings evidence of reputation or family tradition is admissible for the purpose of proving or disproving—

    (a) pedigree or the existence of a marriage,

    (b) the existence of any public or general right, or

    (c) the identity of any person or thing.

Note: The rule is preserved only so far as it allows the court to treat such evidence as proving or disproving the matter concerned.

Res gestae

4 Any rule of law under which in criminal proceedings a statement is admissible as evidence of any matter stated if—

    (a) the statement was made by a person so emotionally overpowered by an event that the possibility of concoction or distortion can be disregarded,

    (b) the statement accompanied an act which can be properly evaluated as evidence only if considered in conjunction with the statement, or

    (c) the statement relates to a physical sensation or a mental state (such as intention or emotion).

Confessions etc

5 Any rule of law relating to the admissibility of confessions or mixed statements in criminal proceedings.

Admissions by agents etc

6 Any rule of law under which in criminal proceedings—

    (a) an admission made by an agent of a defendant is admissible against the defendant as evidence of any matter stated, or

    (b) a statement made by a person to whom a defendant refers a person for information is admissible against the defendant as evidence of any matter stated.

Common enterprise

7 Any rule of law under which in criminal proceedings a statement made by a party to a common enterprise is admissible against another party to the enterprise as evidence of any matter stated.

Expert evidence

8 Any rule of law under which in criminal proceedings an expert witness may draw on the body of expertise relevant to his field.

(2) With the exception of the rules preserved by this section, the common law rules governing the admissibility of hearsay evidence in criminal proceedings are abolished.

Serious Organised Crime and Police Act 2005

112   Power to direct a person to leave a place

(1) A constable may direct a person to leave a place if he believes, on reasonable grounds, that the person is in the place at a time when he would be prohibited from entering it by virtue of—

    (a) an order to which subsection (2) applies, or

    (b) a condition to which subsection (3) applies.

(2) This subsection applies to an order which—

   (a) was made, by virtue of any enactment, following the person's conviction of an offence, and

   (b) prohibits the person from entering the place or from doing so during a period specified in the order.

(3) This subsection applies to a condition which—

   (a) was imposed, by virtue of any enactment, as a condition of the person's release from a prison in which he was serving a sentence of imprisonment following his conviction of an offence, and

   (b) prohibits the person from entering the place or from doing so during a period specified in the condition.

(4) A direction under this section may be given orally.

(5) Any person who knowingly contravenes a direction given to him under this section is guilty of an offence and liable on summary conviction to imprisonment for a term not exceeding 51 weeks or to a fine not exceeding level 4 on the standard scale, or to both.

(8) In subsection (3)(a)—

   (a) 'sentence of imprisonment' and 'prison' are to be construed in accordance with section 62(5) of the Criminal Justice and Court Services Act 2000 (c. 43);

   (b) the reference to a release from prison includes a reference to a temporary release.

(9) In this section, 'place' includes an area.

(10) This section applies whether or not the order or condition mentioned in subsection (1) was made or imposed before or after the commencement of this section.

Part II

Sentencing

Prevention of Crime Act 1953

1 Prohibition of the carrying of offensive weapons without lawful authority or reasonable excuse

(1) Any person who without lawful authority or reasonable excuse, the proof whereof shall lie on him, has with him in any public place any offensive weapon shall be guilty of an offence, and shall be liable—

    (a) on summary conviction, to imprisonment for a term not exceeding six months or a fine not exceeding the prescribed sum or both;

    (b) on conviction on indictment, to imprisonment for a term not exceeding four years or a fine, or both.

(2) Where any person is convicted of an offence under subsection (1) of this section the court may make an order for the forfeiture or disposal of any weapon in respect of which the offence was committed.

(2A) Subsection (2B) applies where—

    (a) a person is convicted of an offence under subsection (1) committed after this subsection is commenced, and

    (b) when the offence was committed, the person was aged 16 or over and had at least one relevant conviction (see section 1ZA).

(2B) Where this subsection applies, the court must impose an appropriate custodial sentence (with or without a fine) unless the court is of the opinion that there are particular circumstances which—

    (a) relate to the offence, to the previous offence or to the offender, and

    (b) would make it unjust to do so in all the circumstances.

(2C) In this section 'appropriate custodial sentence' means—

    (a) in the case of a person who is aged 18 or over when convicted, a sentence of imprisonment for a term of at least 6 months;

    (b) in the case of a person who is aged at least 16 but under 18 when convicted, a detention and training order of at least 4 months.

(2D) In considering whether it is of the opinion mentioned in subsection (2B) in the case of a person aged 16 or 17, the court must have regard to its duty under section 44 of the Children and Young Persons Act 1933 (general considerations).

(2E) Where—

    (a) an appropriate custodial sentence has been imposed on a person under subsection (2B), and

    (b) a relevant conviction without which subsection (2B) would not have applied has been subsequently set aside on appeal,

notice of appeal against the sentence may be given at any time within 28 days from the date on which the conviction was set aside (despite anything in section 18 of the Criminal Appeal Act 1968 (initiating procedure)).

(2F) Where an offence is found to have been committed over a period of two or more days, or at some time during a period of two or more days, it shall be taken for the purposes of this section to have been committed on the last of those days.

(2G) In relation to times before the coming into force of paragraph 180 of Schedule 7 to the Criminal Justice and Court Services Act 2000, the reference in subsection (2C)(a) to a sentence of imprisonment, in relation to an offender aged under 21 at the time of conviction, is to be read as a reference to a sentence of detention in a young offender institution.

(4) In this section 'public place' includes any highway and any other premises or place to which at the material time the public have or are permitted to have access, whether on payment or otherwise; and 'offensive weapon' means any article made or adapted for use for causing injury to the person, or intended by the person having it with him for such use by him or by some other person.

Murder (Abolition of Death Penalty) Act 1965

1   Abolition of death penalty for murder

(1) No person shall suffer death for murder, and a person convicted of murder shall be sentenced to imprisonment for life.

(3) For the purpose of any proceedings on or subsequent to a person's trial on a charge of capital murder, that charge and any plea or finding of guilty of capital murder shall be treated as being or having been a charge, or a plea or finding of guilty, of murder only; and if at the commencement of this Act a person is under sentence of death for murder, the sentence shall have effect as a sentence of imprisonment for life.

Firearms Act 1968

51A   Minimum sentence for certain offences under s. 5

(1) This section applies where—

(a) an individual is convicted of—

  (i)   an offence under section 5(1)(a), (ab), (aba), (ac), (ad), (ae), (af) or (c) of this Act,

  (ii) an offence under section 5(1A)(a) of this Act, or

  (iii) an offence under any of the provisions of this Act listed in subsection (1A) in respect of a firearm or ammunition specified in section 5(1)(a), (ab), (aba), (ac), (ad), (ae), (af) or (c) or section 5(1A)(a) of this Act, and

(b) the offence was committed after the commencement of this section and at a time when he was aged 16 or over.

(1A) The provisions are—

(za) section 5(2A) (manufacture, sale or transfer of firearm, or possession etc for sale or transfer);

(a)   section 16 (possession of firearm with intent to injure);

(b)   section 16A (possession of firearm with intent to cause fear of violence);

(c)   section 17 (use of firearm to resist arrest);

(d)   section 18 (carrying firearm with criminal intent);

(e)   section 19 (carrying a firearm in a public place);

(f)   section 20(1) (trespassing in a building with firearm).

(2) The court shall impose an appropriate custodial sentence (or order for detention) for a term of at least the required minimum term (with or without a fine) unless the court is of the opinion that there are exceptional circumstances relating to the offence or to the offender which justify its not doing so.

(3) Where an offence is found to have been committed over a period of two or more days, or at some time during a period of two or more days, it shall be taken for the purposes of this section to have been committed on the last of those days.

(4) In this section 'appropriate custodial sentence (or order for detention)' means—

    (a) in relation to England and Wales—

        (i) in the case of an offender who is aged 18 or over when convicted, a sentence of imprisonment, and

        (ii) in the case of an offender who is aged under 18 at that time, a sentence of detention under section 91 of the Powers of Criminal Courts (Sentencing) Act 2000;

    (b) in relation to Scotland—

        (i) in the case of an offender who is aged 21 or over when convicted, a sentence of imprisonment,

        (ii) in the case of an offender who is aged under 21 at that time (not being an offender mentioned in sub-paragraph (iii)), a sentence of detention under section 207 of the Criminal Procedure (Scotland) Act 1995, and

        (iii) in the case of an offender who is aged under 18 at that time and is subject to a supervision requirement, an order for detention under section 44, or sentence of detention under section 208, of that Act.

(5) In this section 'the required minimum term' means—

    (a) in relation to England and Wales—

        (i) in the case of an offender who was aged 18 or over when he committed the offence, five years, and

        (ii) in the case of an offender who was under 18 at that time, three years, and

    (b) in relation to Scotland—

        (i) in the case of an offender who was aged 21 or over when he committed the offence, five years, and

        (ii) in the case of an offender who was aged under 21 at that time, three years.

52 Forfeiture and disposal of firearms; cancellation of certificate by convicting court

(1) Where a person—

    (a) is convicted of an offence under this Act (other than an offence under section 22(3) or an offence relating specifically to air weapons) or is convicted of a crime for which he is sentenced to imprisonment, or detention in a detention centre or in a young offenders' institution in Scotland or is subject to a detention and training order; or

    (b) has been ordered to enter into a recognizance to keep the peace or to be of good behaviour, a condition of which is that he shall not possess, use or carry a firearm; or

    (c) is subject to a community order containing a requirement that he shall not possess, use or carry a firearm; or

    (d) has, in Scotland, been ordained to find caution a condition of which is that he shall not possess, use or carry a firearm,

the court by or before which he is convicted, or by which the order is made, may make such order as to the forfeiture or disposal of any firearm or ammunition found in his possession as the court thinks fit and may cancel any firearm certificate or shot gun certificate held by him.

(1A) In subsection (1)(c) 'community order' means—

    (a) a community order within the meaning of Part 12 of the Criminal Justice Act 2003, or a youth rehabilitation order within the meaning of Part 1 of the Criminal Justice and Immigration Act 2008, made in England and Wales, or

    (b) a community payback order under section 227A of the Criminal Procedure (Scotland) Act 1995 (c. 46).

(2) Where the court cancels a certificate under this section—

    (a) the court shall cause notice to be sent to the chief officer of police by whom the certificate was granted; and

(b) the chief officer of police shall by notice in writing require the holder of the certificate to surrender it; and

(c) it is an offence for the holder to fail to surrender the certificate within twenty-one days from the date of the notice given him by the chief officer of police.

(3) A constable may seize and detain any firearm or ammunition which may be the subject of an order for forfeiture under this section.

(4) A court of summary jurisdiction or, in Scotland, the sheriff may, on the application of the chief officer of police, order any firearm or ammunition seized and detained by a constable under this Act to be destroyed or otherwise disposed of.

(5) In this section references to ammunition include references to a primer to which section 35 of the Violent Crime Reduction Act 2006 applies and to an empty cartridge case incorporating such a primer.

Justices of the Peace Act 1968

1   Appointment of justices, oaths of office, etc

(7) It is hereby declared that any court of record having a criminal jurisdiction has, as ancillary to that jurisdiction, the power to bind over to keep the peace, and power to bind over to be of good behaviour, a person who or whose case is before the court, by requiring him to enter into his own recognisances or to find sureties or both, and committing him to prison if he does not comply.

Misuse of Drugs Act 1971

27   Forfeiture

(1) Subject to subsection (2) below, the court by or before which a person is convicted of an offence under this Act or an offence falling within subsection (3) below or an offence to which section 1 of the Criminal Justice (Scotland) Act 1987 relates or a drug trafficking offence, as defined in Article 2(2) of the Proceeds of Crime (Northern Ireland) Order 1996 may order anything shown to the satisfaction of the court to relate to the offence, to be forfeited and either destroyed or dealt with in such other manner as the court may order.

(2) The court shall not order anything to be forfeited under this section, where a person claiming to be the owner of or otherwise interested in it applies to be heard by the court, unless an opportunity has been given to him to show cause why the order should not be made.

(3) An offence falls within this subsection if it is an offence which is specified in—

(a) paragraph 1 of Schedule 2 to the Proceeds of Crime Act 2002 (drug trafficking offences), or

(b) so far as it relates to that paragraph, paragraph 10 of that Schedule.

Magistrates' Courts Act 1980

32   Penalties on summary conviction for offences triable either way

(1) On summary conviction of any of the offences triable either way listed in Schedule 1 to this Act a person shall be liable to imprisonment for a term not exceeding 6 months or to a fine not exceeding the prescribed sum or both, except that—

(a) a magistrates' court shall not have power to impose imprisonment for an offence so listed if the Crown Court would not have that power in the case of an adult convicted of it on indictment.

(2) For any offence triable either way which is not listed in Schedule 1 to this Act, being an offence under a relevant enactment, the maximum fine which may be imposed on summary conviction shall by virtue of this subsection be the prescribed sum unless the offence is one for which by virtue of an enactment other than this subsection a larger fine may be imposed on summary conviction.

(3) Where, by virtue of any relevant enactment, a person summarily convicted of an offence triable either way would, apart from this section, be liable to a maximum fine of one amount in the case of a first conviction and of a different amount in the case of a second or subsequent conviction, subsection (2) above shall apply irrespective of whether the conviction is a first, second or subsequent one.

(4) Subsection (2) above shall not affect so much of any enactment as (in whatever words) makes a person liable on summary conviction to a fine not exceeding a specified amount for each day on which a continuing offence is continued after conviction or the occurrence of any other specified event.

(5) Subsection (2) above shall not apply on summary conviction of any of the following offences:—

  (a) offences under section 5(2) of the Misuse of Drugs Act 1971 (having possession of a controlled drug) where the controlled drug in relation to which the offence was committed was a Class B or Class C drug;

  (b) offences under the following provisions of that Act, where the controlled drug in relation to which the offence was committed was a Class C drug, namely—

    (i) section 4(2) (production, or being concerned in the production, of a controlled drug);

    (ii) section 4(3) (supplying or offering a controlled drug or being concerned in the doing of either activity by another);

    (iii) section 5(3) (having possession of a controlled drug with intent to supply it to another);

    (iv) section 8 (being the occupier, or concerned in the management, of premises and permitting or suffering certain activities to take place there);

    (v) section 12(6) (contravention of direction prohibiting practitioner etc. from possessing, supplying etc. controlled drugs); or

    (vi) section 13(3) (contravention of direction prohibiting practitioner etc. from prescribing, supplying etc. controlled drugs).

(6) Where, as regards any offence triable either way, there is under any enactment (however framed or worded) a power by subordinate instrument to restrict the amount of the fine which on summary conviction can be imposed in respect of that offence—

  (a) subsection (2) above shall not affect that power or override any restriction imposed in the exercise of that power; and

  (b) the amount to which that fine may be restricted in the exercise of that power shall be any amount less than the maximum fine which could be imposed on summary conviction in respect of the offence apart from any restriction so imposed.

(8) In subsection (5) above 'controlled drug', 'Class B drug' and 'Class C drug' have the same meaning as in the Misuse of Drugs Act 1971.

(9) In this section—

'fine' includes a pecuniary penalty but does not include a pecuniary forfeiture or pecuniary compensation;

'the prescribed sum' means £5,000 or such sum as is for the time being substituted in this definition by an order in force under section 143(1) below;

'relevant enactment' means an enactment contained in the Criminal Law Act 1977 or in any Act passed before, or in the same Session as, that Act.

(10) Section 85 of the Legal Aid, Sentencing and Punishment of Offenders Act 2012 (removal of limit on certain fines on conviction by magistrates' court) makes provision that affects the application of this section.

115 Binding over to keep the peace or be of good behaviour

(1) The power of a magistrates' court on the complaint of any person to adjudge any other person to enter into a recognizance, with or without sureties, to keep the peace or to be of good behaviour towards the complainant shall be exercised by order on complaint.

(2) Where a complaint is made under this section, the power of the court to remand the defendant under subsection (5) of section 55 above shall not be subject to the restrictions imposed by subsection (6) of that section.

(3) If any person ordered by a magistrates' court under subsection (1) above to enter into a recognizance, with or without sureties, to keep the peace or to be of good behaviour fails to comply with the order, the court may commit him to custody for a period not exceeding 6 months or until he sooner complies with the order.

Protection from Harassment Act 1997

5 Restraining orders on conviction

(1) A court sentencing or otherwise dealing with a person ('the defendant') convicted of an offence may (as well as sentencing him or dealing with him in any other way) make an order under this section.

(2) The order may, for the purpose of protecting the victim or victims of the offence, or any other person mentioned in the order, from conduct which—

(a) amounts to harassment, or

(b) will cause a fear of violence,

prohibit the defendant from doing anything described in the order.

(3) The order may have effect for a specified period or until further order.

(3A) In proceedings under this section both the prosecution and the defence may lead, as further evidence, any evidence that would be admissible in proceedings for an injunction under section 3.

(4) The prosecutor, the defendant or any other person mentioned in the order may apply to the court which made the order for it to be varied or discharged by a further order.

(4A) Any person mentioned in the order is entitled to be heard on the hearing of an application under subsection (4).

(5) If without reasonable excuse the defendant does anything which he is prohibited from doing by an order under this section, he is guilty of an offence.

(6) A person guilty of an offence under this section is liable—

(a) on conviction on indictment, to imprisonment for a term not exceeding five years, or a fine, or both, or

(b) on summary conviction, to imprisonment for a term not exceeding six months, or a fine not exceeding the statutory maximum, or both.

(7) A court dealing with a person for an offence under this section may vary or discharge the order in question by a further order.

Crime and Disorder Act 1998

8 Parenting orders

(1) This section applies where, in any court proceedings—

(a) a child safety order is made in respect of a child or the court determines on an application under section 12(6) below that a child has failed to comply with any requirement included in such an order;

(aa) a parental compensation order is made in relation to a child's behaviour;

(b) an injunction is granted under section 1 of the Anti-social Behaviour, Crime and Policing Act 2014, an order is made under section 22 of that Act or a sexual harm prevention order is made in respect of a child or young person;

(c) a child or young person is convicted of an offence; or

(d) a person is convicted of an offence under section 443 (failure to comply with school attendance order) or section 444 (failure to secure regular attendance at school of registered pupil) of the Education Act 1996.

(2) Subject to subsection (3) and section 9(1) below, if in the proceedings the court is satisfied that the relevant condition is fulfilled, it may make a parenting order in respect of a person who is a parent or guardian of the child or young person or, as the case may be, the person convicted of the offence under section 443 or 444 ('the parent').

(3) A court shall not make a parenting order unless it has been notified by the Secretary of State that arrangements for implementing such orders are available in the area in which it appears to the court that the parent resides or will reside and the notice has not been withdrawn.

(4) A parenting order is an order which requires the parent—

(a) to comply, for a period not exceeding twelve months, with such requirements as are specified in the order, and

(b) subject to subsection (5) below, to attend, for a concurrent period not exceeding three months, such counselling or guidance programme as may be specified in directions given by the responsible officer.

(5) A parenting order may, but need not, include such a requirement as is mentioned in subsection (4)(b) above in any case where a parenting order under this section or any other enactment has been made in respect of the parent on a previous occasion.

(6) The relevant condition is that the parenting order would be desirable in the interests of preventing—

(a) in a case falling within paragraph (a), (aa) or (b) of subsection (1) above, any repetition of the kind of behaviour which led to the order being made or the injunction granted;

(b) in a case falling within paragraph (c) of that subsection, the commission of any further offence by the child or young person;

(c) in a case falling within paragraph (d) of that subsection, the commission of any further offence under section 443 or 444 of the Education Act 1996.

(7) The requirements that may be specified under subsection (4)(a) above are those which the court considers desirable in the interests of preventing any such repetition or, as the case may be, the commission of any such further offence.

(7A) A counselling or guidance programme which a parent is required to attend by virtue of subsection (4)(b) above may be or include a residential course but only if the court is satisfied—

(a) that the attendance of the parent at a residential course is likely to be more effective than his attendance at a non-residential course in preventing any such repetition or, as the case may be, the commission of any such further offence, and

(b) that any interference with family life which is likely to result from the attendance of the parent at a residential course is proportionate in all the circumstances.

(8) In this section and section 9 below 'responsible officer', in relation to a parenting order, means one of the following who is specified in the order, namely—

(a) an officer of a local probation board or an officer of a provider of probation services;

(b) a social worker of a local authority; and

(bb) a person nominated by a person appointed as director of children's services under section 18 of the Children Act 2004 or by a person appointed as chief education officer under section 532 of the Education Act 1996.

(c) a member of a youth offending team.

(9) In this section 'sexual harm prevention order' means an order under section 103A of the Sexual Offences Act 2003 (sexual harm prevention orders).

9 Parenting orders: supplemental

(1) Where a person under the age of 16 is convicted of an offence, the court by or before which he is so convicted—

(a) if it is satisfied that the relevant condition is fulfilled, shall make a parenting order; and

(b) if it is not so satisfied, shall state in open court that it is not and why it is not.

(1A) The requirements of subsection (1) do not apply where the court makes a referral order in respect of the offence.

(1B) If an injunction under section 1 of the Anti-social Behaviour, Crime and Policing Act 2014 is granted or an order is made under section 22 of that Act is made in respect of a person under the age of 16 the court which grants the injunction or makes the order—

(a) must make a parenting order if it is satisfied that the relevant condition is fulfilled;

(b) if it is not so satisfied, must state in open court that it is not and why it is not.

(2) Before making a parenting order—

(a) in a case falling within paragraph (a) of subsection (1) of section 8 above;

(b) in a case falling within paragraph (b) or (c) of that subsection, where the person concerned is under the age of 16; or

(c) in a case falling within paragraph (d) of that subsection, where the person to whom the offence related is under that age,

a court shall obtain and consider information about the person's family circumstances and the likely effect of the order on those circumstances.

(2A) In a case where a court proposes to make both a referral order in respect of a child or young person convicted of an offence and a parenting order, before making the parenting order the court shall obtain and consider a report by an appropriate officer—

(a) indicating the requirements proposed by that officer to be included in the parenting order;

(b) indicating the reasons why he considers those requirements would be desirable in the interests of preventing the commission of any further offence by the child or young person; and

(c) if the child or young person is aged under 16, containing the information required by subsection (2) above.

(2B) In subsection (2A) above 'an appropriate officer' means—

(a) an officer of a local probation board or an officer of a provider of probation services;

(b) a social worker of a local authority; or

(c) a member of a youth offending team

(3) Before making a parenting order, a court shall explain to the parent in ordinary language—

(a) the effect of the order and of the requirements proposed to be included in it;

(b) the consequences which may follow (under subsection (7) below) if he fails to comply with any of those requirements; and

(c) that the court has power (under subsection (5) below) to review the order on the application either of the parent or of the responsible officer.

(4) Requirements specified in, and directions given under, a parenting order shall, as far as practicable, be such as to avoid—

(a) any conflict with the parent's religious beliefs; and

(b) any interference with the times, if any, at which he normally works or attends an educational establishment.

(5) If while a parenting order is in force it appears to the court which made it, on the application of the responsible officer or the parent, that it is appropriate to make an order under this subsection, the court may make an order discharging the parenting order or varying it—

(a) by cancelling any provision included in it; or

(b) by inserting in it (either in addition to or in substitution for any of its provisions) any provision that could have been included in the order if the court had then had power to make it and were exercising the power.

(6) Where an application under subsection (5) above for the discharge of a parenting order is dismissed, no further application for its discharge shall be made under that subsection by any person except with the consent of the court which made the order.

(7) If while a parenting order is in force the parent without reasonable excuse fails to comply with any requirement included in the order, or specified in directions given by the responsible officer, he shall be liable on summary conviction to a fine not exceeding level 3 on the standard scale.

(7A) In this section 'referral order' means an order under section 16(2) or (3) of the Powers of Criminal Courts (Sentencing) Act 2000 (referral of offender to youth offender panel).

Powers of Criminal Courts (Sentencing) Act 2000

12 Absolute and conditional discharge

(1) Where a court by or before which a person is convicted of an offence (not being an offence the sentence for which is fixed by law or falls to be imposed under a provision mentioned in subsection (1A)) is of the opinion, having regard to the circumstances including the nature of the offence and the character of the offender, that it is inexpedient to inflict punishment, the court may make an order either—

    (a) discharging him absolutely; or

    (b) if the court thinks fit, discharging him subject to the condition that he commits no offence during such period, not exceeding three years from the date of the order, as may be specified in the order.

(1A) The provisions referred to in subsection (1) are—

    (a) section 1(2B) or 1A(5) of the Prevention of Crime Act 1953;

    (b) section 51A(2) of the Firearms Act 1968;

    (c) section 139(6B), 139A(5B) or 139AA(7) of the Criminal Justice Act 1988;

    (d) section 110(2) or 111(2) of this Act;

    (e) section 224A, 225(2) or 226(2) of the Criminal Justice Act 2003;

    (f) section 29(4) or (6) of the Violent Crime Reduction Act 2006.

(2) Subsection (1)(b) above has effect subject to section 66ZB(6) of the Crime and Disorder Act 1998 (effect of youth cautions).

(3) An order discharging a person subject to such a condition as is mentioned in subsection (1)(b) above is in this Act referred to as an 'order for conditional discharge'; and the period specified in any such order is in this Act referred to as 'the period of conditional discharge'.

(5) If (by virtue of section 13 below) a person conditionally discharged under this section is sentenced for the offence in respect of which the order for conditional discharge was made, that order shall cease to have effect.

(6) On making an order for conditional discharge, the court may, if it thinks it expedient for the purpose of the offender's reformation, allow any person who consents to do so to give security for the good behaviour of the offender.

(7) Nothing in this section shall be construed as preventing a court, on discharging an offender absolutely or conditionally in respect of any offence, or imposing any disqualification on the offender or from making in respect of the offence an order under section 130, 143 or 148 below (compensation orders, deprivation orders and restitution orders) or from making in respect of the offence an unlawful profit order under section 4 of the Prevention of Social Housing Fraud Act 2013.

(8) Nothing in this section shall be construed as preventing a court, on discharging an offender absolutely or conditionally in respect of an offence, from—

    (a) making an order under section 21A of the Prosecution of Offences Act 1985 (criminal courts charge), or

    (b) making an order for costs against the offender.

13 Commission of further offence by person conditionally discharged

(1) If it appears to the Crown Court, where that court has jurisdiction in accordance with subsection (2) below, or to a justice of the peace having jurisdiction in accordance with that subsection, that a person in whose case an order for conditional discharge has been made—

    (a) has been convicted by a court in Great Britain of an offence committed during the period of conditional discharge, and

    (b) has been dealt with in respect of that offence,

that court or justice may, subject to subsection (3) below, issue a summons requiring that person to appear at the place and time specified in it or a warrant for his arrest.

(2) Jurisdiction for the purposes of subsection (1) above may be exercised—

    (a) if the order for conditional discharge was made by the Crown Court, by that court;

    (b) if the order was made by a magistrates' court, by a justice of the peace.

(3) A justice of the peace shall not issue a summons under this section except on information and shall not issue a warrant under this section except on information in writing and on oath.

(4) A summons or warrant issued under this section shall direct the person to whom it relates to appear or to be brought before the court by which the order for conditional discharge was made.

(5) If a person in whose case an order for conditional discharge has been made by the Crown Court is convicted by a magistrates' court of an offence committed during the period of conditional discharge, the magistrates' court—

    (a) may commit him to custody or release him on bail until he can be brought or appear before the Crown Court; and

    (b) if it does so, shall send to the Crown Court a copy of the minute or memorandum of the conviction entered in the register, signed by the designated officer by whom the register is kept.

(6) Where it is proved to the satisfaction of the court by which an order for conditional discharge was made that the person in whose case the order was made has been convicted of an offence committed during the period of conditional discharge, the court may deal with him, for the offence for which the order was made, in any way in which it could deal with him if he had just been convicted by or before that court of that offence.

(7) If a person in whose case an order for conditional discharge has been made by a magistrates' court—

    (a) is convicted before the Crown Court of an offence committed during the period of conditional discharge, or

    (b) is dealt with by the Crown Court for any such offence in respect of which he was committed for sentence to the Crown Court,

the Crown Court may deal with him, for the offence for which the order was made, in any way in which the magistrates' court could deal with him if it had just convicted him of that offence.

(8) If a person in whose case an order for conditional discharge has been made by a magistrates' court is convicted by another magistrates' court of any offence committed during the period of conditional discharge, that other court may, with the consent of the court which made the order, deal with him, for the offence for which the order was made, in any way in which the court could deal with him if it had just convicted him of that offence.

(9) Where an order for conditional discharge has been made by a magistrates' court in the case of an offender under 18 years of age in respect of an offence triable only on indictment in the case of an adult, any powers exercisable under subsection (6), (7) or (8) above by that or any other court in respect of the offender after he attains the age of 18 shall be powers to do either or both of the following—

    (a) to impose a fine not exceeding £5,000 for the offence in respect of which the order was made;

    (b) to deal with the offender for that offence in any way in which a magistrates' court could deal with him if it had just convicted him of an offence punishable with imprisonment for a term not exceeding six months.

(10) The reference in subsection (6) above to a person's having been convicted of an offence committed during the period of conditional discharge is a reference to his having been so convicted by a court in Great Britain.

14 Effect of discharge

(1) Subject to subsection (2) below, a conviction of an offence for which an order is made under section 12 above discharging the offender absolutely or conditionally shall be deemed not to be a conviction for any purpose other than the purposes of the proceedings in which the order is made and of any subsequent proceedings which may be taken against the offender under section 13 above.

(2) Where the offender was aged 18 or over at the time of his conviction of the offence in question and is subsequently sentenced (under section 13 above) for that offence, subsection (1) above shall cease to apply to the conviction.

(3) Without prejudice to subsections (1) and (2) above, the conviction of an offender who is discharged absolutely or conditionally under section 12 above shall in any event be disregarded for the purposes of any enactment or instrument which—

(a) imposes any disqualification or disability upon convicted persons; or

(b) authorises or requires the imposition of any such disqualification or disability.

(4) Subsections (1) to (3) above shall not affect—

(a) any right of an offender discharged absolutely or conditionally under section 12 above to rely on his conviction in bar of any subsequent proceedings for the same offence;

(b) the restoration of any property in consequence of the conviction of any such offender; or

(c) the operation, in relation to any such offender, of any enactment or instrument in force on 1st July 1974 which is expressed to extend to persons dealt with under section 1(1) of the Probation of Offenders Act 1907 as well as to convicted persons.

(5) In subsections (3) and (4) above—

'enactment' includes an enactment contained in a local Act; and

'instrument' means an instrument having effect by virtue of an Act.

(6) Subsection (1) above has effect subject to section 50(1A) of the Criminal Appeal Act 1968 and section 108(1A) of the Magistrates' Courts Act 1980 (rights of appeal); and this subsection shall not be taken to prejudice any other enactment that excludes the effect of subsection (1) or (3) above for particular purposes.

(7) Without prejudice to paragraph 1(3) of Schedule 11 to this Act (references to provisions of this Act to be construed as including references to corresponding old enactments), in this section—

(a) any reference to an order made under section 12 above discharging an offender absolutely or conditionally includes a reference to an order which was made under any provision of Part I of the Powers of Criminal Courts Act 1973 (whether or not reproduced in this Act) discharging the offender absolutely or conditionally;

(b) any reference to an offender who is discharged absolutely or conditionally under section 12 includes a reference to an offender who was discharged absolutely or conditionally under any such provision.

15 Discharge: Supplementary

(1) The Secretary of State may by order direct that subsection (1) of section 12 above shall be amended by substituting, for the maximum period specified in that subsection as originally enacted or as previously amended under this subsection, such period as may be specified in the order.

(2) Where an order for conditional discharge has been made on appeal, for the purposes of section 13 above it shall be deemed—

(a) if it was made on an appeal brought from a magistrates' court, to have been made by that magistrates' court;

(b) if it was made on an appeal brought from the Crown Court or from the criminal division of the Court of Appeal, to have been made by the Crown Court.

(3) In proceedings before the Crown Court under section 13 above, any question whether any person in whose case an order for conditional discharge has been made has been convicted of an

offence committed during the period of conditional discharge shall be determined by the court and not by the verdict of a jury.

16   Duty and power to refer certain young offenders to youth offender panels

(1) This section applies where a youth court or other magistrates' court is dealing with a person aged under 18 for an offence and—

(a) neither the offence nor any connected offence is one for which the sentence is fixed by law;

(b) the court is not, in respect of the offence or any connected offence, proposing to impose a custodial sentence on the offender or make a hospital order (within the meaning of the Mental Health Act 1983) in his case; and

(c) the court is not proposing to discharge him, whether absolutely or conditionally, in respect of the offence.

(2) If—

(a) the compulsory referral conditions are satisfied in accordance with section 17 below, and

(b) referral is available to the court,

the court shall sentence the offender for the offence by ordering him to be referred to a youth offender panel.

(3) If—

(a) the discretionary referral conditions are satisfied in accordance with section 17 below, and

(b) referral is available to the court,

the court may sentence the offender for the offence by ordering him to be referred to a youth offender panel.

(4) For the purposes of this Part an offence is connected with another if the offender falls to be dealt with for it at the same time as he is dealt with for the other offence (whether or not he is convicted of the offences at the same time or by or before the same court).

(5) For the purposes of this section referral is available to a court if—

(a) the court has been notified by the Secretary of State that arrangements for the implementation of referral orders are available in the area in which it appears to the court that the offender resides or will reside; and

(b) the notice has not been withdrawn.

(6) An order under subsection (2) or (3) above is in this Act referred to as a 'referral order'.

(7) No referral order may be made in respect of any offence committed before the commencement of section 1 of the Youth Justice and Criminal Evidence Act 1999.

17   The referral conditions

(1) For the purposes of section 16(2) above and subsection (2) below the compulsory referral conditions are satisfied in relation to an offence if the offence is an offence punishable with imprisonment and the offender—

(a) pleaded guilty to the offence and to any connected offence; and

(b) has never been—

(i)   convicted by or before a court in the United Kingdom of any offence other than the offence and any connected offence, or

(ii) convicted by or before a court in another member State of any offence.

(2) For the purposes of section 16(3) above, the discretionary referral conditions are satisfied in relation to an offence if—

(a) the compulsory referral conditions are not satisfied in relation to the offence; and

(b) the offender pleaded guilty—

(i)   to the offence; or

(ii) if the offender is being dealt with by the court for the offence and any connected offence, to at least one of those offences

(3) The Secretary of State may by regulations make such amendments of this section as he considers appropriate for altering in any way the descriptions of offenders in the case of which the compulsory referral conditions or the discretionary referral conditions fall to be satisfied for the purposes of section 16(2) or (3) above (as the case may be).

(4) Any description of offender having effect for those purposes by virtue of such regulations may be framed by reference to such matters as the Secretary of State considers appropriate, including (in particular) one or more of the following—

    (a) the offender's age;

    (b) how the offender has pleaded;

    (c) the offence (or offences) of which the offender has been convicted;

    (d) the offender's previous convictions (if any);

    (e) how (if at all) the offender has been previously punished or otherwise dealt with by any court; and

    (f) any characteristics or behaviour of, or circumstances relating to, any person who has at any time been charged in the same proceedings as the offender (whether or not in respect of the same offence).

18 Making of referral orders: general

(1) A referral order shall—

    (a) specify the youth offending team responsible for implementing the order;

    (b) require the offender to attend each of the meetings of a youth offender panel to be established by the team for the offender; and

    (c) specify the period for which any youth offender contract taking effect between the offender and the panel under section 23 below is to have effect (which must not be less than three nor more than twelve months).

(2) The youth offending team specified under subsection (1)(a) above shall be the team having the function of implementing referral orders in the area in which it appears to the court that the offender resides or will reside.

(3) On making a referral order the court shall explain to the offender in ordinary language—

    (a) the effect of the order; and

    (b) the consequences which may follow—

        (i)   if no youth offender contract takes effect between the offender and the panel under section 23 below; or

        (ii) if the offender breaches any of the terms of any such contract.

(3A) Where a court makes a referral order in respect of an offender who is subject to an earlier referral order, the court may direct that any youth offender contract under the later order is not to take effect under section 23 until the earlier order is revoked or discharged.

(4) Subsections (5) to (7) below apply where, in dealing with an offender for two or more connected offences, a court makes a referral order in respect of each, or each of two or more, of the offences.

(5) The orders shall have the effect of referring the offender to a single youth offender panel; and the provision made by them under subsection (1) above shall accordingly be the same in each case, except that the periods specified under subsection (1)(c) may be different.

(6) The court may direct that the period so specified in either or any of the orders is to run concurrently with or be additional to that specified in the other or any of the others; but in exercising its power under this subsection the court must ensure that the total period for which such a contract as is mentioned in subsection (1)(c) above is to have effect does not exceed twelve months.

(7) Each of the orders mentioned in subsection (4) above shall, for the purposes of this Part, be treated as associated with the other or each of the others.

19 Making of referral orders: effect on court's other sentencing powers

(1) Subsections (2) to (5) below apply where a court makes a referral order in respect of an offence.

(2) The court may not deal with the offender for the offence in any of the prohibited ways.

(3) The court—

    (a) shall, in respect of any connected offence, either sentence the offender by making a referral order or make an order discharging him absolutely; and

    (b) may not deal with the offender for any such offence in any of the prohibited ways.

(4) For the purposes of subsections (2) and (3) above the prohibited ways are—

    (a) imposing a sentence which consists of or includes a youth rehabilitation order on the offender;

    (b) ordering him to pay a fine;

    (ba) making an order under section 1(2A) of the Street Offences Act 1959 in respect of the offender;

    (c) making a reparation order in respect of him; and

    (d) making an order discharging him conditionally.

(5) The court may not make, in connection with the conviction of the offender for the offence or any connected offence—

    (a) an order binding him over to keep the peace or to be of good behaviour;

    (b) an order under section 150 below (binding over of parent or guardian)

(6) Subsections (2), (3) and (5) above do not affect the exercise of any power to deal with the offender conferred by paragraph 5 (offender referred back to court by panel) or paragraph 14 (powers of a court where offender convicted while subject to referral) of Schedule 1 to this Act.

(7) Where section 16(2) above requires a court to make a referral order, the court may not under section 1 above defer passing sentence on him, but section 16(2) and subsection (3)(a) above do not affect any power or duty of a magistrates' court under—

    (a) section 8 above (remission to youth court, or another such court, for sentence);

    (b) section 10(3) of the Magistrates' Courts Act 1980 (adjournment for inquiries); or

    (c) section 35, 38, 43 or 44 of the Mental Health Act 1983 (remand for reports, interim hospital orders and committal to Crown Court for restriction order).

20 Making of referral orders: attendance of parents etc

(1) A court making a referral order may make an order requiring—

    (a) the appropriate person, or

    (b) in a case where there are two or more appropriate persons, any one or more of them,

to attend the meetings of the youth offender panel.

(2) Where an offender is aged under 16 when a court makes a referral order in his case—

    (a) the court shall exercise its power under subsection (1) above so as to require at least one appropriate person to attend meetings of the youth offender panel; and

    (b) if the offender falls within subsection (6) below, the person or persons so required to attend those meetings shall be or include a representative of the local authority mentioned in that subsection.

(3) The court shall not under this section make an order requiring a person to attend meetings of the youth offender panel—

    (a) if the court is satisfied that it would be unreasonable to do so; or

    (b) to an extent which the court is satisfied would be unreasonable.

(4) Except where the offender falls within subsection (6) below, each person who is a parent or guardian of the offender is an 'appropriate person' for the purposes of this section.

(5) Where the offender falls within subsection (6) below, each of the following is an 'appropriate person' for the purposes of this section—

    (a) a representative of the local authority mentioned in that subsection; and

    (b) each person who is a parent or guardian of the offender with whom the offender is allowed to live.

(6) An offender falls within this subsection if he is (within the meaning of the Children Act 1989) a child who is looked after by a local authority.

(7) If, at the time when a court makes an order under this section—

    (a) a person who is required by the order to attend meetings of a youth offender panel is not present in court, or

    (b) a local authority whose representative is so required to attend such meetings is not represented in court,

the court must send him or (as the case may be) the authority a copy of the order forthwith.

21   Establishment of panels

(1) Where a referral order has been made in respect of an offender (or two or more associated referral orders have been so made), it is the duty of the youth offending team specified in the order (or orders)—

    (a) to establish a youth offender panel for the offender;

    (b) to arrange for the first meeting of the panel to be held for the purposes of section 23 below; and

    (c) subsequently to arrange for the holding of any further meetings of the panel required by virtue of section 25 below (in addition to those required by virtue of any other provision of this Part).

(2) A youth offender panel shall—

    (a) be constituted,

    (b) conduct its proceedings, and

    (c) discharge its functions under this Part (and in particular those arising under section 23 below),

in accordance with guidance given from time to time by the Secretary of State.

(3) At each of its meetings a panel shall, however, consist of at least—

    (a) one member appointed by the youth offending team from among its members; and

    (b) two members so appointed who are not members of the team.

(4) The Secretary of State may by regulations make provision requiring persons appointed as members of a youth offender panel to have such qualifications, or satisfy such other criteria, as are specified in the regulations.

(5) Where it appears to the court which made a referral order that, by reason of either a change or a prospective change in the offender's place or intended place of residence, the youth offending team for the time being specified in the order ('the current team') either does not or will not have the function of implementing referral orders in the area in which the offender resides or will reside, the court may amend the order so that it instead specifies the team which has the function of implementing such orders in that area ('the new team').

(6) Where a court so amends a referral order—

    (a) subsection (1)(a) above shall apply to the new team in any event;

    (b) subsection (1)(b) above shall apply to the new team if no youth offender contract has (or has under paragraph (c) below been treated as having) taken effect under section 23 below between the offender and a youth offender panel established by the current team;

    (c) if such a contract has (or has previously under this paragraph been treated as having) so taken effect, it shall (after the amendment) be treated as if it were a contract which had taken effect under section 23 below between the offender and the panel being established for the offender by the new team.

(7) References in this Part to the meetings of a youth offender panel (or any such meeting) are to the following meetings of the panel (or any of them)—

    (a) the first meeting held in pursuance of subsection (1)(b) above;

    (b) any further meetings held in pursuance of section 25 below;

    (c) any progress meeting held under section 26 below; and

    (d) the final meeting held under section 27 below.

22 Attendance at panel meetings

(1) The specified team shall, in the case of each meeting of the panel established for the offender, notify—

(a) the offender, and

(b) any person to whom an order under section 20 above applies,

of the time and place at which he is required to attend that meeting.

(2) If the offender fails to attend any part of such a meeting the panel may—

(a) adjourn the meeting to such time and place as it may specify; or

(b) end the meeting and refer the offender back to the appropriate court;

and subsection (1) above shall apply in relation to any such adjourned meeting.

(2A) If—

(a) a parent or guardian of the offender fails to comply with an order under section 20 above (requirement to attend the meetings of the panel), and

(b) the offender is aged under 18 at the time of the failure,

the panel may refer that parent or guardian to a youth court acting in the local justice area in which it appears to the panel that the offender resides or will reside.

(3) One person aged 18 or over chosen by the offender, with the agreement of the panel, shall be entitled to accompany the offender to any meeting of the panel (and it need not be the same person who accompanies him to every meeting).

(4) The panel may allow to attend any such meeting—

(a) any person who appears to the panel to be a victim of, or otherwise affected by, the offence, or any of the offences, in respect of which the offender was referred to the panel;

(b) any person who appears to the panel to be someone capable of having a good influence on the offender.

(5) Where the panel allows any such person as is mentioned in subsection (4)(a) above ('the victim') to attend a meeting of the panel, the panel may allow the victim to be accompanied to the meeting by one person chosen by the victim with the agreement of the panel.

23 First meeting: agreement of contract with offender

(1) At the first meeting of the youth offender panel established for an offender the panel shall seek to reach agreement with the offender on a programme of behaviour the aim (or principal aim) of which is the prevention of re-offending by the offender.

(2) The terms of the programme may, in particular, include provision for any of the following—

(a) the offender to make financial or other reparation to any person who appears to the panel to be a victim of, or otherwise affected by, the offence, or any of the offences, for which the offender was referred to the panel;

(b) the offender to attend mediation sessions with any such victim or other person;

(c) the offender to carry out unpaid work or service in or for the community;

(d) the offender to be at home at times specified in or determined under the programme;

(e) attendance by the offender at a school or other educational establishment or at a place of work;

(f) the offender to participate in specified activities (such as those designed to address offending behaviour, those offering education or training or those assisting with the rehabilitation of persons dependent on, or having a propensity to misuse, alcohol or drugs);

(g) the offender to present himself to specified persons at times and places specified in or determined under the programme;

(h) the offender to stay away from specified places or persons (or both);

(i) enabling the offender's compliance with the programme to be supervised and recorded.

(3) The programme may not, however, provide—

(a) for the electronic monitoring of the offender's whereabouts; or

(b) for the offender to have imposed on him any physical restriction on his movements.

(4) No term which provides for anything to be done to or with any such victim or other affected person as is mentioned in subsection (2)(a) above may be included in the programme without the consent of that person.

(5) Where a programme is agreed between the offender and the panel, the panel shall cause a written record of the programme to be produced forthwith—

(a) in language capable of being readily understood by, or explained to, the offender; and

(b) for signature by him.

(6) Once the record has been signed—

(a) by the offender, and

(b) by a member of the panel on behalf of the panel,

the terms of the programme, as set out in the record, take effect as the terms of a 'youth offender contract' between the offender and the panel; and the panel shall cause a copy of the record to be given or sent to the offender.

. . .

27A   Revocation of referral order where offender making good progress etc

(1) This section applies where, having regard to circumstances which have arisen since a youth offender contract took effect under section 23 above, it appears to the youth offender panel to be in the interests of justice for the referral order (or each of the referral orders) to be revoked.

(2) The panel may refer the offender back to the appropriate court requesting it—

(a) to exercise only the power conferred by sub-paragraph (2) of paragraph 5 of Schedule 1 to this Act to revoke the order (or each of the orders); or

(b) to exercise both—

(i)   the power conferred by that sub-paragraph to revoke the order (or each of the orders); and

(ii) the power conferred by sub-paragraph (4) of that paragraph to deal with the offender for the offence in respect of which the revoked order was made.

(3) The circumstances in which the panel may make a referral under subsection (2) above include the offender's making good progress under the contract.

(4) Where—

(a) the panel makes a referral under subsection (2) above in relation to any offender and any youth offender contract, and

(b) the appropriate court decides not to exercise the power conferred by paragraph 5(2) of Schedule 1 to this Act in consequence of that referral,

the panel may not make a further referral under that subsection in relation to that offender and contract during the relevant period except with the consent of the appropriate court.

(5) In subsection (4) above 'the relevant period' means the period of 3 months beginning with the date on which the appropriate court made the decision mentioned in paragraph (b) of that subsection.

27B   Extension of period for which young offender contract has effect

(1) This section applies where at any time—

(a) a youth offender contract has taken effect under section 23 above for a period which is less than twelve months;

(b) that period has not ended; and

(c) having regard to circumstances which have arisen since the contract took effect, it appears to the youth offender panel to be in the interests of justice for the length of that period to be extended.

(2) The panel may refer the offender back to the appropriate court requesting it to extend the length of that period.

(3) The requested period of extension must not exceed three months

28 Offender or parent referred back to court: offender convicted while subject to referral order

Schedule 1 to this Act, which—

    (a) in Parts 1 and 1ZA makes provision for what is to happen when a youth offender panel refers an offender back to the appropriate court; and

    (aa) in Part 1A makes provision for what is to happen when a youth offender panel refers a parent or guardian to the court under section 22(2A) above, and

    (b) in Part II makes provision for what is to happen when an offender is convicted of further offences while for the time being subject to a referral order,

shall have effect.

29 Functions of youth offending teams

    (1) The functions of a youth offending team responsible for implementing a referral order include, in particular, arranging for the provision of such administrative staff, accommodation or other facilities as are required by the youth offender panel established in pursuance of the order.

    . . .

30 Regulations under Part III

    (1) Any power of the Secretary of State to make regulations under section 17(3) or 21(4) above or paragraph 13(8) of Schedule 1 to this Act shall be exercisable by statutory instrument.

    . . .

32 Definitions for purposes of Part III

In this Part—

    'the appropriate court' shall be construed in accordance with paragraph 1(2) of Schedule 1 to this Act;

    'associated', in relation to referral orders, shall be construed in accordance with section 18(7) above;

    'connected', in relation to offences, shall be construed in accordance with section 16(4) above;

    'meeting', in relation to a youth offender panel, shall be construed in accordance with section 21(7) above;

    'the specified team', in relation to an offender to whom a referral order applies (or two or more associated referral orders apply), means the youth offending team for the time being specified in the order (or orders).

33 Meaning of 'youth community order' and 'community sentence'

    (1) In this Act 'youth community order' means any of the following orders—

      (c) an attendance centre order;

36B Electronic monitoring of requirements in youth community orders

    (1) Subject to subsections (2) and (3) below, a youth community order may include requirements for securing the electronic monitoring of the offender's compliance with any other requirements imposed by the order.

    (2) A court shall not include in a youth community order a requirement under subsection (1) above unless the court—

    (a) has been notified by the Secretary of State that electronic monitoring arrangements are available in the relevant areas specified in subsections (7) to (10) below; and

    (b) is satisfied that the necessary provision can be made under those arrangements.

    (3) Where—

    (a) it is proposed to include in an exclusion order a requirement for securing electronic monitoring in accordance with this section; but

    (b) there is a person (other than the offender) without whose co-operation it will not be practicable to secure the monitoring,

the requirement shall not be included in the order without that person's consent.

(5) An order which includes requirements under subsection (1) above shall include provision for making a person responsible for the monitoring; and a person who is made so responsible shall be of a description specified in an order made by the Secretary of State.

(6) The Secretary of State may make rules for regulating—

(a) the electronic monitoring of compliance with requirements included in a youth community order; and

(b) without prejudice to the generality of paragraph (a) above, the functions of persons made responsible for securing the electronic monitoring of compliance with requirements included in the order.

(7) In the case of a curfew order or an exclusion order, the relevant area is the area in which the place proposed to be specified in the order is situated.

In this subsection, 'place', in relation to an exclusion order, has the same meaning as in section 40A below.

(9) In the case of a supervision order or an action plan order, the relevant area is the local justice area proposed to be specified in the order.

(10) In the case of an attendance centre order, the relevant area is the local justice area in which the attendance centre proposed to be specified in the order is situated.

60 Attendance centre orders

(1) Where—

(b) a court would have power, but for section 89 below (restrictions on imprisonment of young offenders and defaulters), to commit a person aged under 21 to prison in default of payment of any sum of money or for failing to do or abstain from doing anything required to be done or left undone, or

(c) a court has power to commit a person aged at least 21 but under 25 to prison in default of payment of any sum of money,

the court may, if it has been notified by the Secretary of State that an attendance centre is available for the reception of persons of his description, order him to attend at such a centre, to be specified in the order, for such number of hours as may be so specified.

(2) An order under subsection (1) above is in this Act referred to as an 'attendance centre order'.

(3) The aggregate number of hours for which an attendance centre order may require a person to attend at an attendance centre shall not be less than 12 except where—

(a) he is aged under 14; and

(b) the court is of the opinion that 12 hours would be excessive, having regard to his age or any other circumstances.

(4) The aggregate number of hours shall not exceed 12 except where the court is of the opinion, having regard to all the circumstances, that 12 hours would be inadequate, and in that case—

(a) shall not exceed 24 where the person is aged under 16; and

(b) shall not exceed 36 where the person is aged 16 or over but under 21 or (where subsection (1)(c) above applies) under 25.

(5) A court may make an attendance centre order in respect of a person before a previous attendance centre order made in respect of him has ceased to have effect, and may determine the number of hours to be specified in the order without regard—

(a) to the number specified in the previous order; or

(b) to the fact that order is still in effect.

(6) An attendance centre order shall not be made unless the court is satisfied that the attendance centre to be specified in it is reasonably accessible to the person concerned, having regard to his age, the means of access available to him and any other circumstances.

(7) The times at which a person is required to attend at an attendance centre shall, as for as practicable, be such as to avoid—

(a) any conflict with his religious beliefs or with the requirements of any other youth community order to which he may be subject; and

(b) any interference with the times, if any, at which he normally works or attends school or any other educational establishment.

(8) The first time at which the person is required to attend at an attendance centre shall be a time at which the centre is available for his attendance in accordance with the notification of the Secretary of State, and shall be specified in the order.

(9) The subsequent times shall be fixed by the officer in charge of the centre, having regard to the person's circumstances.

(10) A person shall not be required under this section to attend at an attendance centre on more than one occasion on any day, or for more than three hours on any occasion.

(11) Where a court makes an attendance centre order, the designated officer for the court shall—

(a) deliver or send a copy of the order to the officer in charge of the attendance centre specified in it; and

(b) deliver a copy of the order to the person in respect of whom it is made or send a copy by registered post or the recorded delivery service addressed to his last or usual place of abode.

(12) Where a person ('the defaulter') has been ordered to attend at an attendance centre in default of the payment of any sum of money—

(a) on payment of the whole sum to any person authorised to receive it, the attendance centre order shall cease to have effect;

(b) on payment of a part of the sum to any such person, the total number of hours for which the defaulter is required to attend at the centre shall be reduced proportionately, that is to say by such number of complete hours as bears to the total number the proportion most nearly approximating to, without exceeding, the proportion which the part bears to the whole sum.

61 Breach, revocation and amendment of attendance centre orders

Schedule 5 to this Act (which makes provision for dealing with failures to comply with attendance centre orders, for revoking such orders with or without the substitution of other sentences and for amending such orders) shall have effect.
. . .

73 Reparation orders

(1) Where a child or young person (that is to say, any person aged under 18) is convicted of an offence other than one for which the sentence is fixed by law, the court by or before which he is convicted may make an order requiring him to make reparation specified in the order—

(a) to a person or persons so specified; or

(b) to the community at large;

and any person so specified must be a person identified by the court as a victim of the offence or a person otherwise affected by it.

(2) An order under subsection (1) above is in this Act referred to as a 'reparation order'.

(3) In this section and section 74 below 'make reparation', in relation to an offender, means make reparation for the offence otherwise than by the payment of compensation; and the requirements that may be specified in a reparation order are subject to section 74(1) to (3).

(4) The court shall not make a reparation order in respect of the offender if it proposes—

(a) to pass on him a custodial sentence; or

(b) to make in respect of him a youth rehabilitation order or a referral order.

(4A) The court shall not make a reparation order in respect of the offender at a time when a youth rehabilitation order is in force in respect of him unless when it makes the reparation order it revokes the youth rehabilitation order.

(4B) Where a youth rehabilitation order is revoked under subsection (4A), paragraph 24 of Schedule 2 to the Criminal Justice and Immigration Act 2008 (breach, revocation or amendment of youth rehabilitation order) applies to the revocation.

(5) Before making a reparation order, a court shall obtain and consider a written report by an officer of a local probation board, an officer of a provider of probation services, a social worker of a local authority or a member of a youth offending team indicating—

(a) the type of work that is suitable for the offender; and

(b) the attitude of the victim or victims to the requirements proposed to be included in the order.

(6) The court shall not make a reparation order unless it has been notified by the Secretary of State that arrangements for implementing such orders are available in the area proposed to be named in the order under section 74(4) below and the notice has not been withdrawn.

(8) The court shall give reasons if it does not make a reparation order in a case where it has power to do so.

74 Requirements and provisions of reparation order, and obligations of person subject to it

(1) A reparation order shall not require the offender—

(a) to work for more than 24 hours in aggregate; or

(b) to make reparation to any person without the consent of that person.

(2) Subject to subsection (1) above, requirements specified in a reparation order shall be such as in the opinion of the court are commensurate with the seriousness of the offence, or the combination of the offence and one or more offences associated with it.

(3) Requirements so specified shall, as far as practicable, be such as to avoid—

(a) any conflict with the offender's religious beliefs or with the requirements of any youth community order to which he may be subject; and

(b) any interference with the times, if any, at which he normally works or attends school or any other educational establishment.

(4) A reparation order shall name the local justice area in which it appears to the court making the order (or to the court amending under Schedule 8 to this Act any provision included in the order in pursuance of this subsection) that the offender resides or will reside.

(5) In this Act 'responsible officer', in relation to an offender subject to a reparation order, means one of the following who is specified in the order, namely—

(a) an officer of a local probation board or an officer of a provider of probation services (as the case may be);

(b) a social worker of a local authority;

(c) a member of a youth offending team.

(6) Where a reparation order specifies an officer of a local probation board under subsection (5) above, the officer specified must be an officer appointed for or assigned to the local justice area named in the order.

(6A) Where a reparation order specifies an officer of a provider of probation services under subsection (5) above, the officer specified must be an officer acting in the local justice area named in the order.

(7) Where a reparation order specifies under that subsection—

(a) a social worker of a local authority, or

(b) a member of a youth offending team,

the social worker or member specified must be a social worker of, or a member of a youth offending team established by, the local authority within whose area it appears to the court that the offender resides or will reside.

(8) Any reparation required by a reparation order—

(a) shall be made under the supervision of the responsible officer; and

(b) shall be made within a period of three months from the date of the making of the order.

75 Breach, revocation and amendment of reparation orders

Schedule 8 to this Act (which makes provision for dealing with failures to comply with reparation orders and for revoking and amending such orders) shall have effect

76   Meaning of 'custodial sentence'

(1) In this Act 'custodial sentence' means—

    (a)   a sentence of imprisonment (as to which, see section 89(1)(a) below);

    (b)   a sentence of detention under section 90 or 91 below;

    (bb) a sentence of detention for public protection under section 226 of the Criminal Justice Act 2003;

    (bc) a sentence of detention under section 226B or 228 of that Act;

    (c)   a sentence of custody for life under section 93 or 94 below;

    (d)   a sentence of detention in a young offender institution (under section 96 below or otherwise); or

    (e)   a detention and training order (under section 100 below).

(2) In subsection (1) above 'sentence of imprisonment' does not include a committal for contempt of court or any kindred offence.

77   Liability to imprisonment on conviction on indictment

Where a person is convicted on indictment of an offence against any enactment and is for that offence liable to be sentenced to imprisonment, but the sentence is not by any enactment either limited to a specified term or expressed to extend to imprisonment for life, the person so convicted shall be liable to imprisonment for not more than two years.

78   General limit on magistrates' court's power to impose imprisonment or detention in a young offender institution

(1) A magistrates' court shall not have power to impose imprisonment, or detention in a young offender institution, for more than six months in respect of any one offence.

(2) Unless expressly excluded, subsection (1) above shall apply even if the offence in question is one for which a person would otherwise be liable on summary conviction to imprisonment or detention in a young offender institution for more than six months.

(3) Subsection (1) above is without prejudice to section 133 of the Magistrates' Courts Act 1980 (consecutive terms of imprisonment).

(4) Any power of a magistrates' court to impose a term of imprisonment for non-payment of a fine, or for want of sufficient goods to satisfy a fine, shall not be limited by virtue of subsection (1) above.

(4A) In subsection (4) the reference to want of sufficient goods to satisfy a fine is a reference to circumstances where—

    (a)   there is power to use the procedure in Schedule 12 to the Tribunals, Courts and Enforcement Act 2007 to recover the fine from a person, but

    (b)   it appears, after an attempt has been made to exercise the power, that the person's goods are insufficient to pay the amount outstanding (as defined by paragraph 50(3) of that Schedule).

(5) In subsection (4) above 'fine' includes a pecuniary penalty but does not include a pecuniary forfeiture or pecuniary compensation.

(6) In this section 'impose imprisonment' means pass a sentence of imprisonment or fix a term of imprisonment for failure to pay any sum of money, or for want of sufficient distress to satisfy any sum of money, or for failure to do or abstain from doing anything required to be done or left undone.

(7) Section 132 of the Magistrates' Courts Act 1980 contains provision about the minimum term of imprisonment which may be imposed by a magistrates' court.

82A   Determination of tariffs

(1) This section applies if a court passes a life sentence in circumstances where the sentence is not fixed by law.

(2) The court shall, unless it makes an order under subsection (4) below, order that the provisions of section 28(5) to (8) of the Crime (Sentences) Act 1997 (referred to in this section as the 'early

release provisions') shall apply to the offender as soon as he has served the part of his sentence which is specified in the order.

(3) The part of his sentence shall be such as the court considers appropriate taking into account—

(a) the seriousness of the offence, or of the combination of the offence and one or more offences associated with it;

(b) the effect that the following would have if the court had sentenced the offender to a term of imprisonment—

(i)   section 240ZA of the Criminal Justice Act 2003 (crediting periods of remand in custody);

(ii) section 246 of the Armed Forces Act 2006 (equivalent provision for service courts);

(iii) any direction which the court would have given under section 240A of the Criminal Justice Act 2003 (crediting periods of remand on bail subject to certain types of condition);

(c) the early release provisions as compared with section 244(1) of the Criminal Justice Act 2003

(4) If the offender was aged 21 or over when he committed the offence and the court is of the opinion that, because of the seriousness of the offence or of the combination of the offence and one or more offences associated with it, no order should be made under subsection (2) above, the court shall order that, the early release provisions shall not apply to the offender.

(7) In this section—

'court' includes the Court Martial;

'life sentence' means a sentence mentioned in subsection (2) of section 34 of the Crime (Sentences) Act 1997 other than a sentence mentioned in paragraph (d) or (e) of that subsection.

(8) So far as this section relates to sentences passed by the Court Martial, section 167(1) below does not apply.

83   Restriction on imposing custodial sentences on persons not legally represented

(1) A magistrates' court on summary conviction, or the Crown Court on committal for sentence or on conviction on indictment, shall not pass a sentence of imprisonment on a person who—

(a) is not legally represented in that court, and

(b) has not been previously sentenced to that punishment by a court in any part of the United Kingdom,

unless he is a person to whom subsection (3) below applies.

(2) A magistrates' court on summary conviction, or the Crown Court on committal for sentence or on conviction on indictment, shall not—

(a) pass a sentence of detention under section 90 or 91 below,

(b) pass a sentence of custody for life under section 93 or 94 below,

(c) pass a sentence of detention in a young offender institution, or

(d) make a detention and training order,

on or in respect of a person who is not legally represented in that court unless he is a person to whom subsection (3) below applies.

(3) This subsection applies to a person if either—

(a) representation was made available to him for the purposes of the proceedings under Part 1 of the Legal Aid, Sentencing and Punishment of Offenders Act 2012 but was withdrawn because of his conduct or because it appeared that his financial resources were such that he was not eligible for such representation;

(aa) he applied for such representation and the application was refused because it appeared that his financial resources were such that he was not eligible for such representation; or

(b) having been informed of his right to apply for such representation and having had the opportunity to do so, he refused or failed to apply.

(4) For the purposes of this section a person is to be treated as legally represented in a court if, but only if, he has the assistance of counsel or a solicitor to represent him in the proceedings in that court at some time after he is found guilty and before he is sentenced.

(5) For the purposes of subsection (1)(b) above a previous sentence of imprisonment which has been suspended and which has not taken effect under section 119 below or under section 19 of the Treatment of Offenders Act (Northern Ireland) 1968 shall be disregarded.

(6) In this section 'sentence of imprisonment' does not include a committal for contempt of court or any kindred offence.

89   Restriction on imposing imprisonment on persons under 21

(1) Subject to subsection (2) below, no court shall—

(a) pass a sentence of imprisonment on a person for an offence if he is aged under 21 when convicted of the offence; or

(b) commit a person aged under 21 to prison for any reason.

(2) Nothing in subsection (1) above shall prevent the committal to prison of a person aged under 21 who is—

(a) remanded in custody;

(b) committed in custody for sentence; or

(c) sent in custody for trial under section 51 or 51A of the Crime and Disorder Act 1998

90   Offenders who commit murder etc. when under 18: duty to detain at Her Majesty's pleasure

Where a person convicted of murder or any other offence the sentence for which is fixed by law as life imprisonment appears to the court to have been aged under 18 at the time the offence was committed, the court shall (notwithstanding anything in this or any other Act) sentence him to be detained during Her Majesty's pleasure.

91   Offenders under 18 convicted of certain serious offences: power to detain for specified period

(1) Subsection (3) below applies where a person aged under 18 is convicted on indictment of—

(a) an offence punishable in the case of a person aged 21 or over with imprisonment for 14 years or more, not being an offence the sentence for which is fixed by law; or

(b) an offence under section 3 of the Sexual Offences Act 2003 (in this section, 'the 2003 Act') (sexual assault); or

(c) an offence under section 13 of the 2003 Act (child sex offences committed by children or young person's); or

(d) an offence under section 25 of the 2003 Act (sexual activity with a child family member); or

(e) an offence under section 26 of the 2003 Act (inciting a child family member to engage in sexual activity).

(1A) Subsection (3) below also applies where—

(a) a person aged under 18 is convicted on indictment of an offence—

(i)   under subsection (1)(a), (ab), (aba), (ac), (ad), (ae), (af) or (c) of section 5 of the Firearms Act 1968 (prohibited weapons), or

(ii)   under subsection (1A)(a) of that section,

(b) the offence was committed after the commencement of section 51A of that Act and for the purposes of subsection (3) of that section at a time when he was aged 16 or over, and

(c) the court is of the opinion mentioned in section 51A(2) of that Act (exceptional circumstances which justify its not imposing required custodial sentence).

(1B) Subsection (3) below also applies where—

(a) a person aged under 18 is convicted on indictment of an offence under the Firearms Act 1968 that is listed in section 51A(1A)(b), (e) or (f) of that Act and was committed in respect of a firearm or ammunition specified in section 5(1)(a), (ab), (aba), (ac), (ad), (ae), (af) or (c) or section 5(1A)(a) of that Act;

(b) the offence was committed after the commencement of section 30 of the Violent Crime Reduction Act 2006 and for the purposes of section 51A(3) of the Firearms Act 1968 at a time when he was aged 16 or over; and

(c) the court is of the opinion mentioned in section 51A(2) of the Firearms Act 1968.

(1C) Subsection (3) below also applies where—

(a) a person aged under 18 is convicted of an offence under section 28 of the Violent Crime Reduction Act 2006 (using someone to mind a weapon);

(b) section 29(3) of that Act applies (minimum sentences in certain cases); and

(c) the court is of the opinion mentioned in section 29(6) of that Act (exceptional circumstances which justify not imposing the minimum sentence).

(3) If the court is of the opinion that neither a youth rehabilitation order nor a detention and training order is suitable, the court may sentence the offender to be detained for such period, not exceeding the maximum term of imprisonment with which the offence is punishable in the case of a person aged 21 or over, as may be specified in the sentence.

(4) Subsection (3) above is subject to (in particular) section 152 and 153 of the Criminal Justice Act 2003

(5) Where—

(a) subsection (2) of section 51A of the Firearms Act 1968, or

(b) subsection (6) of section 29 of the Violent Crime Reduction Act 2006,

requires the imposition of a sentence of detention under this section for a term of at least the term provided for in that section, the court shall sentence the offender to be detained for such period, of at least the term so provided for but not exceeding the maximum term of imprisonment with which the offence is punishable in the case of a person aged 18 or over, as may be specified in the sentence.

92 Detention under sections 90 and 91: place of detention etc

(1) A person sentenced to be detained under section 90 or 91 above shall be liable to be detained in such place and under such conditions—

(a) as the Secretary of State may direct; or

(b) as the Secretary of State may arrange with any person.

(2) A person detained pursuant to the directions or arrangements made by the Secretary of State under this section shall be deemed to be in legal custody.

93 Duty to impose custody for life in certain cases where offender under 21

Where a person aged under 21 is convicted of murder or any other offence the sentence for which is fixed by law as imprisonment for life, the court shall sentence him to custody for life unless he is liable to be detained under section 90 above.

94 Power to impose custody for life in certain other cases where offender at least 18 but under 21

(1) Where a person aged at least 18 but under 21 is convicted of an offence—

(a) for which the sentence is not fixed by law, but

(b) for which a person aged 21 or over would be liable to imprisonment for life,

the court shall, if it considers that a sentence for life would be appropriate, sentence him to custody for life.

(2) Subsection (1) above is subject to (in particular) sections 79 and 80 above, but this subsection does not apply in relation to a sentence which falls to be imposed under section 109(2) below.

95 Custody for life: place of detention

(1) Subject to section 22(2)(b) of the Prison Act 1952 (removal to hospital etc.), an offender sentenced to custody for life shall be detained in a young offender institution unless a direction under subsection (2) below is in force in relation to him.

(2) The Secretary of State may from time to time direct that an offender sentenced to custody for life shall be detained in a prison or remand centre instead of a young offender institution.

96 Detention in a young offender institution for other cases where offender at least 18 but under 21

Subject to sections 90, 93 and 94 above, where—

(a) a person aged at least 18 but under 21 is convicted of an offence which is punishable with imprisonment in the case of a person aged 21 or over, and

(b) the court is of the opinion that either or both of paragraphs (a) and (b) of section 79(2) above apply or the case falls within section 79(3),

the sentence that the court is to pass is a sentence of detention in a young offender institution.

97 Term of detention in a young offender institution, and consecutive sentences

(1) The maximum term of detention in a young offender institution that a court may impose for an offence is the same as the maximum term of imprisonment that it may impose for that offence.

(2) A court shall not pass a sentence for an offender's detention in a young offender institution for less than 21 days.

(4) Where—

(a) an offender is convicted of more than one offence for which he is liable to a sentence of detention in a young offender institution, or

(b) an offender who is serving a sentence of detention in a young offender institution is convicted of one or more further offences for which he is liable to such a sentence,

the court shall have the same power to pass consecutive sentences of detention in a young offender institution as if they were sentences of imprisonment.

(5) Subject to section 84 above (restriction on consecutive sentences for released prisoners), where an offender who—

(a) is serving a sentence of detention in a young offender institution, and

(b) is aged 21 or over,

is convicted of one or more further offences for which he is liable to imprisonment, the court shall have the power to pass one or more sentences of imprisonment to run consecutively upon the sentence of detention in a young offender institution.

98 Detention in a young offender institution: place of detention

(1) Subject to section 22(2)(b) of the Prison Act 1952 (removal to hospital etc.), an offender sentenced to detention in a young offender institution shall be detained in such an institution unless a direction under subsection (2) below is in force in relation to him.

(2) The Secretary of State may from time to time direct that an offender sentenced to detention in a young offender institution shall be detained in a prison or remand centre instead of a young offender institution.

99 Conversion of sentence of detention to sentence of imprisonment

(1) Subject to the following provisions of this section, where an offender has been sentenced by a relevant sentence of detention to a term of detention and either—

(a) he has attained the age of 21, or

(b) he has attained the age of 18 and has been reported to the Secretary of State by the independent monitoring board of the institution in which he is detained as exercising a bad influence on the other inmates of the institution or as behaving in a disruptive manner to the detriment of those inmates,

the Secretary of State may direct that he shall be treated as if he had been sentenced to imprisonment for the same term.

(2) Where the Secretary of State gives a direction under subsection (1) above in relation to an offender, the portion of the term of detention imposed under the relevant sentence of detention which he has already served shall be deemed to have been a portion of a term of imprisonment.

(3) Where the Secretary of State gives a direction under subsection (1) above in relation to an offender serving a sentence of detention for public protection under section 226 of the Criminal

Justice Act 2003 the offender shall be treated as if he had been sentenced under section 225 of that Act.

(3A) Where the Secretary of State gives a direction under subsection (1) above in relation to an offender serving an extended sentence of detention imposed under Chapter 5 of Part 12 of the Criminal Justice Act 2003—

(a) if the sentence was imposed under section 226B of that Act, the offender shall be treated as if the offender had been sentenced under section 226A of that Act, and

(b) if the sentence was imposed under section 228 of that Act, the offender shall be treated as if the offender had been sentenced under section 227 of that Act.

(4) Rules under section 47 of the Prison Act 1952 may provide that any award for an offence against discipline made in respect of an offender serving a relevant sentence of detention shall continue to have effect after a direction under subsection (1) has been given in relation to him.

(5) In this section 'relevant sentence of detention' means—

(a) a sentence of detention under section 90, 91 or 96 above,

(aa) a sentence of detention under section 209 or 218 of the Armed Forces Act 2006,

(b) a sentence of detention for public protection under section 226 or, in the case of a person aged at least 18 but under 21, a sentence of custody for life or detention in a young offender institution under section 225 of the Criminal Justice Act 2003, or

(c) an extended sentence of detention under section 228 or, in the case of a person aged at least 18 but under 21, an extended sentence of detention in a young offender institution under section 226B or 227 of that Act.

(6) References in this section to a sentence under section 226, 226B or 228 of the Criminal Justice Act 2003 include such a sentence passed as a result of section 221, 221A or 222 of the Armed Forces Act 2006.

100   Offenders under 18: detention and training orders

(1) Subject to sections 90 and 91 above, sections 226 and 226B of the Criminal Justice Act 2003, and subsection (2) below, where—

(a) a child or young person (that is to say, any person aged under 18) is convicted of an offence which is punishable with imprisonment in the case of a person aged 21 or over, and

(b) the court is of the opinion that subsection (2) of section 152 of the Criminal Justice Act 2003 applies or the case falls within subsection (3) of that section,

the sentence that the court is to pass is a detention and training order.

(1A) Subsection (1) applies with the omission of paragraph (b) in the case of an offence the sentence for which falls to be imposed under these provisions—

(a) section 1(2B) or 1A(5) of the Prevention of Crime Act 1953 (minimum sentence for certain offences involving offensive weapons);

(b) section 139(6B), 139A(5B) or 139AA(7) of the Criminal Justice Act 1988 (minimum sentence for certain offences involving article with blade or point or offensive weapon).

(2) A court shall not make a detention and training order—

(a) in the case of an offender under the age of 15 at the time of the conviction, unless it is of the opinion that he is a persistent offender;

(b) in the case of an offender under the age of 12 at that time, unless—

(i) it is of the opinion that only a custodial sentence would be adequate to protect the public from further offending by him; and

(ii) the offence was committed on or after such date as the Secretary of State may by order appoint.

(3) A detention and training order is an order that the offender in respect of whom it is made shall be subject, for the term specified in the order, to a period of detention and training followed by a period of supervision.

101   Term of order, consecutive terms and taking account of remands

(1) Subject to subsection (2) below, the term of a detention and training order made in respect of an offence (whether by a magistrates' court or otherwise) shall be 4, 6, 8, 10, 12, 18 or 24 months.

(2) The term of a detention and training order may not exceed the maximum term of imprisonment that the Crown Court could (in the case of an offender aged 21 or over) impose for the offence.

(3) Subject to subsections (4) and (6) below, a court making a detention and training order may order that its term shall commence on the expiry of the term of any other detention and training order made by that or any other court.

(4) A court shall not make in respect of an offender a detention and training order the effect of which would be that he would be subject to detention and training orders for a term which exceeds 24 months.

(5) Where the term of the detention and training orders to which an offender would otherwise be subject exceeds 24 months, the excess shall be treated as remitted.

(6) A court making a detention and training order shall not order that its term shall commence on the expiry of the term of a detention and training order under which the period of supervision has already begun (under section 103(1) below).

(7) Where a detention and training order ('the new order') is made in respect of an offender who is subject to a detention and training order under which the period of supervision has begun ('the old order'), the old order shall be disregarded in determining—

(a) for the purposes of subsection (4) above whether the effect of the new order would be that the offender would be subject to detention and training orders for a term which exceeds 24 months; and

(b) for the purposes of subsection (5) above whether the term of the detention and training orders to which the offender would (apart from that subsection) be subject exceeds 24 months.

(8) In determining the term of a detention and training order for an offence, the court shall take account of any period for which the offender has been remanded—

(a) in custody, or

(b) on bail subject to a qualifying curfew condition and an electronic monitoring condition (within the meaning of section 240A of the Criminal Justice Act 2003),

in connection with the offence, or any other offence the charge for which was founded on the same facts or evidence.

(9) Where a court proposes to make detention and training orders in respect of an offender for two or more offences—

(a) subsection (8) above shall not apply; but

(b) in determining the total term of the detention and training orders it proposes to make in respect of the offender, the court shall take account of the total period (if any) for which he has been remanded as mentioned in that subsection in connection with any of those offences, or any other offence the charge for which was founded on the same facts or evidence.

(10) Once a period of remand has, under subsection (8) or (9) above, been taken account of in relation to a detention and training order made in respect of an offender for any offence or offences, it shall not subsequently be taken account of (under either of those subsections) in relation to such an order made in respect of the offender for any other offence or offences.

(11) Any reference in subsection (8) or (9) above to an offender's being remanded in custody is a reference to his being—

(a) held in police detention;

(b) remanded in or committed to custody by an order of a court;

(c) remanded to youth detention accommodation under section 91(4) of the Legal Aid, Sentencing and Punishment of Offenders Act 2012; or

(d) remanded, admitted or removed to hospital under section 35, 36, 38 or 48 of the Mental Health Act 1983.

(12) A person is in police detention for the purposes of subsection (11) above—

(a) at any time when he is in police detention for the purposes of the Police and Criminal Evidence Act 1984; and

(b) at any time when he is detained under section 41 of the Terrorism Act 2000.

(12A) Section 243 of the Criminal Justice Act 2003 (persons extradited to the United Kingdom) applies in relation to a person sentenced to a detention and training order as it applies in relation to a fixed-term prisoner, with the reference in subsection (2A) of that section to section 240ZA being read as a reference to subsection (8) above.

(13) For the purpose of any reference in sections 102 to 105 and 106B below to the term of a detention and training order, consecutive terms of such orders and terms of such orders which are wholly or partly concurrent shall be treated as a single term if—

(a) the orders were made on the same occasion; or

(b) where they were made on different occasions, the offender has not been released (by virtue of subsection (2), (3), (4) or (5) of section 102 below) at any time during the period beginning with the first and ending with the last of those occasions.

102　The period of detention and training

(1) An offender shall serve the period of detention and training under a detention and training order in such youth detention accommodation as may be determined by the Secretary of State

(2) Subject to subsections (3) to (5) below, the period of detention and training under a detention and training order shall be one-half of the term of the order.

(3) The Secretary of State may at any time release the offender if he is satisfied that exceptional circumstances exist which justify the offender's release on compassionate grounds.

(4) The Secretary of State may release the offender—

(a) in the case of an order for a term of 8 months or more but less than 18 months, at any time during the period of one month ending with the half-way point of the term of the order; and

(b) in the case of an order for a term of 18 months or more, at any time during the period of two months ending with that point.

(5) If a youth court so orders on an application made by the Secretary of State for the purpose, the Secretary of State shall release the offender—

(a) in the case of an order for a term of 8 months or more but less than 18 months, one month after the half-way point of the term of the order; and

(b) in the case of an order for a term of 18 months or more, one month or two months after that point.

(6) An offender detained in pursuance of a detention and training order shall be deemed to be in legal custody.

103　The period of supervision

(1) The period of supervision of an offender who is subject to a detention and training order—

(a) shall begin with the offender's release, whether at the half-way point of the term of the order or otherwise; and

(b) subject to subsection (2) below, shall end when the term of the order ends.

(2) Subject to subsection (2A), the Secretary of State may by order provide that the period of supervision shall end at such point during the term of a detention and training order as may be specified in the order under this subsection.

(2A) An order under subsection (2) may not include provision about cases in which—

(a) the offender is aged 18 or over at the half-way point of the term of the detention and training order, and

(b) the order was imposed in respect of an offence committed on or after the day on which section 6(4) of the Offender Rehabilitation Act 2014 came into force.

(3) During the period of supervision, the offender shall be under the supervision of—

    (a) an officer of a local probation board or an officer of a provider of probation services; or

    (c) a member of a youth offending team;

and the category of person to supervise the offender shall be determined from time to time by the Secretary of State.

(4) Where the supervision is to be provided by an officer of a local probation board, the officer of a local probation board shall be an officer appointed for or assigned to the local justice area within which the offender resides for the time being.

(4A) Where the supervision is to be provided by an officer of a provider of probation services, the officer of a provider of probation services shall be an officer acting in the local justice area within which the offender resides for the time being.

(5) Where the supervision is to be provided by—

    (b) a member of a youth offending team,

the member shall be a member of a youth offending team established by, the local authority within whose area the offender resides for the time being.

(6) The offender shall be given a notice from the Secretary of State specifying—

    (a) the category of person for the time being responsible for his supervision; and

    (b) any requirements with which he must for the time being comply.

(7) A notice under subsection (6) above shall be given to the offender—

    (a) before the commencement of the period of supervision; and

    (b) before any alteration in the matters specified in subsection (6)(a) or (b) above comes into effect.

104   Breach of supervision requirements

(1) Where a detention and training order is in force in respect of an offender and it appears on information to a justice of the peace that the offender has failed to comply with requirements under section 103(6)(b) above, the justice—

    (a) may issue a summons requiring the offender to appear at the place and time specified in the summons; or

    (b) if the information is in writing and on oath, may issue a warrant for the offender's arrest

(2) Any summons or warrant issued under this section shall direct the offender to appear or be brought—

    (a) before a youth court acting in the local justice in which the offender resides; or

    (b) if it is not known where the offender resides, before a youth court acting in the same local justice area as the justice who issued the summons or warrant.

(3) If it is proved to the satisfaction of the youth court before which an offender appears or is brought under this section that he has failed to comply with requirements under section 103(6)(b) above, that court may—

    (a) order the offender to be detained, in such youth detention accommodation as the Secretary of State may determine, for such period, not exceeding the maximum period found under subsection (3A) below, as the court may specify;

    (aa) order the offender to be subject to such period of supervision, not exceeding the maximum period found under subsection (3A) below, as the court may specify; or

    (b) impose on the offender a fine not exceeding level 3 on the standard scale.

(3A) The maximum period referred to in subsection (3)(a) and (aa) above is the shorter of—

    (a) three months, and

    (b) the period beginning with the date of the offender's failure and ending with the last day of the term of the detention and training order.

(3B) For the purposes of subsection (3A) above a failure that is found to have occurred over two or more days is to be taken to have occurred on the first of those days.

(3C) A court may order a period of detention or supervision, or impose a fine, under subsection (3) above before or after the end of the term of the detention and training order.

(3D) A period of detention or supervision ordered under subsection (3) above—

(a) begins on the date the order is made, and

(b) may overlap to any extent with the period of supervision under the detention and training order.

(4) An offender detained in pursuance of an order under subsection (3)(a) above shall be deemed to be in legal custody

(4A) Where an order under subsection (3)(a) above is made in the case of a person who has attained the age of 18, the order has effect to require the person to be detained in prison for the period specified by the court.

(5) A fine imposed under subsection (3)(b) above shall be deemed, for the purposes of any enactment, to be a sum adjudged to be paid by a conviction.

(5A) Sections 104A and 104B below make further provision about the operation of orders under subsection (3) above.

(6) An offender may appeal to the Crown Court against any order made under subsection (3)(a), (aa) or (b) above.

104A Application of sections 103 to 105 in relation to orders under section 104(3)(aa)

(1) Subsections (3) to (7) of section 103 above apply in relation to a period of supervision to which an offender is subject by virtue of an order under section 104(3)(aa) above as they apply to the period of supervision under a detention and training order.

(2) In the application of section 103 above by virtue of subsection (1) above, subsection (7)(a) of that section is to be read as requiring a notice to be given to the offender as soon as is reasonably practicable after the order under section 104(3)(aa) above is made.

(3) Section 104 above and section 105 below apply where an offender is subject to a period of supervision under section 104(3)(aa) above as they apply where a detention and training order is in force in respect of an offender.

(4) In the application of section 104 above by virtue of subsection (3) above—

(a) the references in that section to section 103(6)(b) above are to be read as references to that provision as applied by subsection (1) above,

(b) the references in subsections (3A)(b) and (3C) of that section to the term of the detention and training order are to be read as references to the term of the period of supervision under section 104(3)(aa) above, and

(c) the reference in subsection (3D)(b) of that section to the period of supervision under the detention and training order is to be read as including a reference to the period of supervision under section 104(3)(aa) above.

(5) In the application of section 105 below by virtue of subsection (3) above—

(a) paragraph (a) of subsection (1) of that section is to be read as if the words 'after his release and' were omitted, and

(b) the reference in that paragraph to the date on which the term of the detention and training order ends is to be read as a reference to the date on which the period of supervision under section 104(3)(aa) ends.

104B Interaction of orders under section 104(3)(a) with other sentences

(1) Where a court makes a detention and training order in the case of an offender who is subject to a period of detention under section 104(3)(a) above, the detention and training order takes effect—

(a) at the beginning of the day on which it is made, or

(b) if the court so orders, at the time when the period of detention under section 104(3)(a) above ends.

(2) Where a court orders an offender who is subject to a detention and training order to be subject to a period of detention under section 104(3)(a) above for a failure to comply with

requirements under a different detention and training order, the period of detention takes effect as follows—

    (a) if the offender has been released by virtue of subsection (2), (3), (4) or (5) of section 102 above, at the beginning of the day on which the order for the period of detention is made, and

    (b) if not, either as mentioned in paragraph (a) above or, if the court so orders, at the time when the offender would otherwise be released by virtue of subsection (2), (3), (4) or (5) of section 102 above.

  (3) Subject to subsection (4) below, where at any time an offender is subject concurrently—

    (a) to a detention and training order, and

    (b) to a period of detention under section 104(3)(a) above,

the offender is to be treated for the purposes of sections 102 to 105 of this Act as if the offender were subject only to the detention and training order.

  (4) Nothing in subsection (3) above requires the offender to be released in respect of either the order or the period of detention unless and until the offender is required to be released in respect of each of them.

  (5) The Secretary of State may by regulations make provision about the interaction between a period of detention under section 104(3)(a) above and a custodial sentence in a case where—

    (a) an offender who is subject to such a period of detention becomes subject to a custodial sentence, or

    (b) an offender who is subject to a custodial sentence becomes subject to such a period of detention.

  (6) The provision that may be made by regulations under subsection (5) above includes—

    (a) provision as to the time at which the period of detention under section 104(3)(a) above or the custodial sentence is to take effect;

    (b) provision for the offender to be treated, for the purposes of the enactments specified in the regulations, as subject only to the period of detention or the custodial sentence;

    (c) provision about the effect of enactments relating to the person's release from detention or imprisonment in a case where that release is not to take effect immediately by virtue of provision in the regulations.

  (7) The power of the Secretary of State to make regulations under subsection (5) above—

    (a) is exercisable by statutory instrument;

    (b) includes power to make supplementary, incidental, transitional, transitory or saving provision.

  (8) A statutory instrument containing regulations under subsection (5) above is subject to annulment in pursuance of a resolution of either House of Parliament.

105   **Offences during currency of order**

  (1) This section applies to a person subject to a detention and training order if—

    (a) after his release and before the date on which the term of the order ends, he commits an offence punishable with imprisonment in the case of a person aged 21 or over ('the new offence'); and

    (b) whether before or after that date, he is convicted of the new offence.

  (2) Subject to section 8(6) above (duty of adult magistrates' court to remit young offenders to youth court for sentence), the court by or before which a person to whom this section applies is convicted of the new offence may, whether or not it passes any other sentence on him, order him to be detained in such youth detention accommodation as the Secretary of State may determine for the whole or any part of the period which—

    (a) begins with the date of the court's order; and

    (b) is equal in length to the period between the date on which the new offence was committed and the date mentioned in subsection (1) above.

(3)　The period for which a person to whom this section applies is ordered under subsection (2) above to be detained in youth detention accommodation—

(a)　shall, as the court may direct, either be served before and be followed by, or be served concurrently with, any sentence imposed for the new offence; and

(b)　in either case, shall be disregarded in determining the appropriate length of that sentence.

(4)　Where the new offence is found to have been committed over a period of two or more days, or at some time during a period of two or more days, it shall be taken for the purposes of this section to have been committed on the last of those days.

(5)　A person detained in pursuance of an order under subsection (2) above shall be deemed to be in legal custody.

106　Interaction with sentences of detention in a young offender institution

(1)　Where a court passes a sentence of detention in a young offender institution in the case of an offender who is subject to a detention and training order, the sentence shall take effect as follows—

(a)　if the offender has been released by virtue of subsection (2), (3), (4) or (5) of section 102 above, at the beginning of the day on which it is passed;

(b)　if not, either as mentioned in paragraph (a) above or, if the court so orders, at the time when the offender would otherwise be released by virtue of subsection (2), (3), (4) or (5) of section 102.

(4)　Subject to subsection (5) below, where at any time an offender is subject concurrently—

(a)　to a detention and training order, and

(b)　to a sentence of detention in a young offender institution,

he shall be treated for the purposes of sections 102 to 105 above and of section 98 above (place of detention), Chapter IV of this Part (return to detention) and Chapter 6 of Part 12 of the Criminal Justice Act 2003 (release, licences, supervision and recall) as if he were subject only to the one of them that was imposed on the later occasion.

(5)　Nothing in subsection (4) above shall require the offender to be released in respect of either the order or the sentence unless and until he is required to be released in respect of each of them.

(6)　Where, by virtue of any enactment giving a court power to deal with a person in a way in which a court on a previous occasion could have dealt with him, a detention and training order for any term is made in the case of a person who has attained the age of 18, the person shall be treated as if he had been sentenced to detention in a young offender institution for the same term.

106A　Interaction with sentences of detention

(1)　In this section—

‘the 2003 Act’ means the Criminal Justice Act 2003;

‘sentence of detention’ means—

(a)　a sentence of detention under section 91 above or section 209 of the Armed Forces Act 2006, or

(b)　a sentence of detention under section 226B or 228 of the 2003 Act (extended sentence for certain violent or sexual offences: persons under 18);

and references in this section to a sentence of detention under section 226B or 228 of the 2003 Act include such a sentence passed as a result of section 221A or 222 of the Armed Forces Act 2006.

(2)　Where a court passes a sentence of detention in the case of an offender who is subject to a detention and training order, the sentence shall take effect as follows—

(a)　if the offender has at any time been released by virtue of subsection (2), (3), (4) or (5) of section 102 above, at the beginning of the day on which the sentence is passed, and

(b)　if not, either as mentioned in paragraph (a) above or, if the court so orders, at the time when the offender would otherwise be released by virtue of subsection (2), (3), (4) or (5) of section 102.

(3) Where a court makes a detention and training order in the case of an offender who is subject to a sentence of detention, the order shall take effect as follows—

(a) if the offender has at any time been released under Chapter 6 of Part 12 of the 2003 Act (release on licence of fixed-term prisoners), at the beginning of the day on which the order is made, and

(b) if not, either as mentioned in paragraph (a) above or, if the court so orders, at the time when the offender would otherwise be released under that Chapter.

(4) Where an order under section 102(5) above is made in the case of a person in respect of whom a sentence of detention is to take effect as mentioned in subsection (2)(b) above, the order is to be expressed as an order that the period of detention attributable to the detention and training order is to end at the time determined under section 102(5)(a) or (b) above.

(5) In determining for the purposes of subsection (3)(b) the time when an offender would otherwise be released under Chapter 6 of Part 12 of the 2003 Act, section 246 of that Act (power of Secretary of State to release prisoners on licence before he is required to do so) is to be disregarded.

(6) Where by virtue of subsection (3)(b) above a detention and training order made in the case of a person who is subject to a sentence of detention under section 226B or 228 of the 2003 Act is to take effect at the time when he would otherwise be released under Chapter 6 of Part 12 of that Act, any direction by the Parole Board under subsection (5)(b) of section 246A or (as the case may be) subsection (2)(b) of section 247 of that Act in respect of him is to be expressed as a direction that the Board would, but for the detention and training order, have directed his release under that section.

(7) Subject to subsection (9) below, where at any time an offender is subject concurrently—

(a) to a detention and training order, and

(b) to a sentence of detention,

he shall be treated for the purposes of the provisions specified in subsection (8) below as if he were subject only to the sentence of detention.

(8) Those provisions are—

(a) sections 102 to 105 above,

(b) section 92 above, section 235 of the 2003 Act and section 210 of the Armed Forces Act 2006 (place of detention etc),

(c) Chapter 6 of Part 12 of the 2003 Act, and

(d) section 214 of the Armed Forces Act 2006 (offences committed during a detention and training order under that Act).

(9) Nothing in subsection (7) above shall require the offender to be released in respect of either the order or the sentence unless and until he is required to be released in respect of each of them.

106B   Further supervision after end of term of detention and training order

(1) This section applies where a detention and training order is made in respect of an offender if—

(a) the offender is aged 18 or over at the half-way point of the term of the order,

(b) the term of the order is less than 24 months, and

(c) the order was imposed in respect of an offence committed on or after the day on which section 6(4) of the Offender Rehabilitation Act 2014 came into force.

(2) The following provisions of the Criminal Justice Act 2003 (which relate to supervision after end of sentence) apply as they apply in cases described in section 256AA(1) of that Act—

(a) sections 256AA(2) to (11), 256AB and 256AC,

(b) sections 256D and 256E, and

(c) Schedule 19A,

but with the following modifications.

(3) 'The supervision period', in relation to the offender, is the period which—

(a) begins on the expiry of the term of the detention and training order, and

(b) ends on the expiry of the period of 12 months beginning immediately after the half-way point of the term of the order.

(4) 'The supervisor', in relation to the offender, must be—

    (a) an officer of a provider of probation services, or

    (b) a member of the youth offending team established by the local authority in whose area the offender resides for the time being.

(5) The power under section 256AB(4) includes power to make provision about the supervision requirements that may be imposed under section 256AA as applied by this section and to amend this Act.

(6) Subsection (7) applies where the term of the detention and training order is determined by section 101(13) (consecutive and concurrent orders).

(7) The offender is subject to supervision under section 256AA (as applied by this section) if that section (as applied) so requires in respect of one or more of the consecutive or concurrent orders.

107   Meaning of 'youth detention accommodation' and references to terms

(1) In sections 102, 104 and 105 above 'youth detention accommodation' means—

    (a) a secure training centre;

    (aa) a secure college;

    (b) a young offender institution;

    (c) accommodation provided by or on behalf of a local authority for the purpose of restricting the liberty of children and young persons;

    (d) accommodation provided for that purpose under subsection (5) of section 82 of the Children Act 1989 (financial support by the Secretary of State); or

    (e) such other accommodation or descriptions of accommodation as the Secretary of State may by order specify.

(2) In sections 102 to 105 and 106B above references to the term of a detention and training order shall be construed in accordance with section 101(13) above.

(3) For the purposes of sections 103(2A) and 106B(1), where an offence is found to have been committed over a period of 2 or more days, or at some time during a period of 2 or more days, it must be taken to have been committed on the last of those days.

110   Minimum of seven years for third class A drug trafficking offence

(1) This section applies where—

    (a) a person is convicted of a class A drug trafficking offence committed after 30th September 1997;

    (b) at the time when that offence was committed, he was 18 or over and had 2 relevant drug convictions; and

    (c) one of those other offences was committed after he had been convicted of the other.

(2) The court shall impose an appropriate custodial sentence for a term of at least seven years except where the court is of the opinion that there are particular circumstances which—

    (a) relate to any of the offences or to the offender; and

    (b) would make it unjust to do so in all the circumstances.

(2A) For the purposes of subsection (1)—

    (a) a 'relevant drug conviction' means—

       (i) a conviction in any part of the United Kingdom of a class A drug trafficking offence, or

       (ii) a conviction in another member State of an offence which was committed after the relevant date and would, if done in the United Kingdom at the time of the conviction, have constituted a class A drug trafficking offence; and

    (b) 'the relevant date' means the date on which this subsection comes into force.

(4) Where—

    (a) a person is charged with a class A drug trafficking offence (which, apart from this subsection, would be triable either way), and

    (b) the circumstances are such that, if he were convicted of the offence, he could be sentenced for it under subsection (2) above,

the offence shall be triable only on indictment.

(5) In this section 'class A drug trafficking offence' means a drug trafficking offence committed in respect of a class A drug; and for this purpose—

'class A drug' has the same meaning as in the Misuse of Drugs Act 1971;

'drug trafficking offence' means an offence which is specified in—

(a) paragraph 1 of Schedule 2 to the Proceeds of Crime Act 2002 (drug trafficking offences), or

(b) so far as it relates to that paragraph, paragraph 10 of that Schedule.

(6) In this section 'an appropriate custodial sentence' means—

(a) in relation to a person who is 21 or over when convicted of the offence mentioned in sub-section (1)(a) above, a sentence of imprisonment;

(b) in relation to a person who is under 21 at that time, a sentence of detention in a young offender institution.

111 Minimum of three years for third domestic burglary

(1) This section applies where—

(a) a person is convicted of a domestic burglary committed after 30th November 1999;

(b) at the time when that burglary was committed, he was 18 or over and had 2 relevant domestic burglary convictions; and

(c) one of those other burglaries was committed after he had been convicted of the other, and both of them were committed after the relevant date.

(2) The court shall impose an appropriate custodial sentence for a term of at least three years except where the court is of the opinion that there are particular circumstances which—

(a) relate to any of the offences or to the offender; and

(b) would make it unjust to do so in all the circumstances.

(2A) For the purposes of subsection (1)—

(a) a 'relevant domestic burglary conviction' means—

(i) a conviction in England and Wales of a domestic burglary, or

(ii) a conviction in any other part of the United Kingdom or any other member State of an offence which would, if done in England and Wales at the time of the conviction, have constituted domestic burglary;

(b) 'the relevant date', in relation to a relevant domestic burglary conviction, means—

(i) in respect of a conviction in England and Wales, 30 November 1999, and

(ii) in any other case, the day on which this subsection comes into force.

(4) Where—

(a) a person is charged with a domestic burglary which, apart from this subsection, would be triable either way, and

(b) the circumstances are such that, if he were convicted of the burglary, he could be sentenced for it under subsection (2) above,

the burglary shall be triable only on indictment.

(5) In this section 'domestic burglary' means a burglary committed in respect of a building or part of a building which is a dwelling.

(6) In this section 'an appropriate custodial sentence' means —

(a) in relation to a person who is 21 or over when convicted of the offence mentioned in sub-section (1)(a) above, a sentence of imprisonment;

(b) in relation to a person who is under 21 at that time, a sentence of detention in a young offender institution.

112 Appeals where previous convictions set aside

(1) This section applies where—

(a) a sentence has been imposed on any person under subsection (2) of section 110 or 111 above; and

(b) any previous conviction of his without which that section would not have applied has been subsequently set aside on appeal.

(2) Notwithstanding anything in section 18 of the Criminal Appeal Act 1968, notice of appeal against the sentence may be given at any time within 28 days from the date on which the previous conviction was set aside.

113   Certificates of convictions for purposes of Chapter III

(1) Where—

    (a) on any date after 30th September 1997 a person is convicted in England and Wales of a class A drug trafficking offence, or on any date after 30th November 1999 a person is convicted in England and Wales of a domestic burglary, and

    (b) the court by or before which he is so convicted states in open court that he has been convicted of such an offence on that date, and

    (c) that court subsequently certifies that fact,

the certificate shall be evidence, for the purposes of the relevant section of this Chapter, that he was convicted of such an offence on that date.

(1A) Where—

    (a) a person is convicted—

        (i) in any part of the United Kingdom other than England and Wales of a class A drug trafficking offence,

        (ii) in any member State other than the United Kingdom of a corresponding drug trafficking offence, or

        (iii) in any part of the United Kingdom other than England and Wales, or in any other member State, of a corresponding domestic burglary offence,

    (b) in the case of a conviction by or before a court in the United Kingdom, it is stated in open court that the person has been convicted of such an offence on that date, and

    (c) the court by or before which the person is convicted certifies, by way of a certificate signed by the proper officer of the court, the fact that the person has been convicted of such an offence on that date,

the certificate is evidence, for the purposes of the relevant section of this Chapter, that the person was convicted of such an offence on that date.

(2) Where—

    (a) after 30th September 1997 a person is convicted in England and Wales of a class A drug trafficking offence or after 30th November 1999 a person is convicted in England and Wales of a domestic burglary, and

    (b) the court by or before which he is so convicted states in open court that the offence was committed on a particular day or over, or at some time during, a particular period, and

    (c) that court subsequently certifies that fact,

the certificate shall be evidence, for the purposes of the relevant section of this Chapter, that the offence was committed on that day or over, or at some time during, that period.

(2A) Where—

    (a) a person is convicted—

        (i) in any part of the United Kingdom other than England and Wales of a class A drug trafficking offence,

        (ii) in any member State other than the United Kingdom of a corresponding drug trafficking offence, or

        (iii) in any part of the United Kingdom other than England and Wales, or in any other member State, of a corresponding domestic burglary offence,

    (b) in the case of a conviction by or before a court in the United Kingdom, it is stated in open court that the offence was committed on a particular day or over, or at some time during, a particular period, and

    (c) the court by or before which the person is convicted certifies, by way of a certificate signed by the proper officer of the court, that the offence was committed on a particular day or over, or at some time during, a particular period, the certificate is evidence, for the purposes of the relevant section of this Chapter, that the offence was committed on that day or over, or at some time during, that period.

(3) In this section—

'proper officer' means the clerk of the court, that clerk's deputy or any other person having custody of the court record;

'class A drug trafficking offence' and 'domestic burglary' have the same meanings as in sections 110 and 111 respectively;

'corresponding drug trafficking offence' means an offence within section 110(2A)(a)(ii);

'corresponding domestic burglary offence' means an offence within section 111(2A)(a)(ii); and

'the relevant section of this Chapter', in relation to any such offence, shall be construed accordingly.

114   Offences under service law

(1) Where—
- (a) a person has at any time been convicted of an offence under section 42 of the Armed Forces Act 2006, and
- (b) the corresponding offence under the law of England and Wales (within the meaning given by that section) was a class A drug trafficking offence or a domestic burglary,

the relevant section of this Chapter shall have effect as if he had at that time been convicted in England and Wales of that corresponding offence.

(1A) Where—
- (a) a person has at any time been found guilty of a member State service offence committed after the relevant date, and
- (b) the corresponding UK offence was a class A drug trafficking offence or a domestic burglary,

the relevant section of this Chapter and subsection (1) above shall have effect as if the person had at that time been convicted in England and Wales of that corresponding UK offence.

(1B) For the purposes of subsection (1A)—
- (a) 'member State service offence' means an offence which—
  - (i) was the subject of proceedings under the service law of a member State other than the United Kingdom, and
  - (ii) at the time it was done would have constituted an offence under the law of any part of the United Kingdom, or an offence under section 42 of the Armed Forces Act 2006, if it had been done in any part of the United Kingdom by a member of Her Majesty's forces ('the corresponding UK offence');
- (b) 'relevant date' means—
  - (i) where the corresponding UK offence was a class A drug trafficking offence, the relevant date referred to in section 110(2A)(b), and
  - (ii) where the corresponding UK offence was a domestic burglary, the relevant date referred to in section 111(2A)(b)(ii);
- (c) 'Her Majesty's forces' has the same meaning as in the Armed Forces Act 2006;
- (d) 'service law', in relation to a member State other than the United Kingdom, means the law governing all or any of the naval, military or air forces of that State.

(2) Subsection (3) of section 113 applies for the purposes of this section as it applies for the purposes of that section.

(3) Section 48 of the Armed Forces Act 2006 (attempts, conspiracy, encouragement and assistance and aiding and abetting outside England and Wales) applies for the purposes of this section as if the reference in subsection (3)(b) of that section to any of the following provisions of that Act were a reference to this section.

(4) Where—
- (a) the corresponding UK offence is an offence under section 42 of the Armed Forces Act 2006 by reason of section 43, 45, 46 or 47 of that Act (attempting, conspiring to commit, inciting, aiding, abetting, counselling or procuring criminal conduct); and

(b) the act to which it relates ('the contemplated act') is not an act that is (or that if done would have been) punishable by the law of England and Wales;

for the purposes of subsections (1A) and (1B) it must be assumed that the contemplated act amounted to the offence under the law of England and Wales that it would have amounted to if it had been the equivalent act in England or Wales.

115   Determination of day when offence committed

Where an offence is found to have been committed over a period of two or more days, or at some time during a period of two or more days, it shall be taken for the purposes of sections 110 and 111 above to have been committed on the last of those days.

130   Compensation orders against convicted persons

(1) A court by or before which a person is convicted of an offence, instead of or in addition to dealing with him in any other way, may, on application or otherwise, make an order (in this Act referred to as a 'compensation order') requiring him—

(a) to pay compensation for any personal injury, loss or damage resulting from that offence or any other offence which is taken into consideration by the court in determining sentence; or

(b) to make payments for funeral expenses or bereavement in respect of a death resulting from any such offence, other than a death due to an accident arising out of the presence of a motor vehicle on a road;

but this is subject to the following provisions of this section and to section 131 below.

(2) Where the person is convicted of an offence the sentence for which is fixed by law or falls to be imposed under a provision mentioned in subsection (2ZA), subsection (1) above shall have effect as if the words 'instead of or' were omitted.

(2ZA) The provisions referred to in subsection (2) are—

(a) section 1(2B) or 1A(5) of the Prevention of Crime Act 1953;

(b) section 51A(2) of the Firearms Act 1968;

(c) section 139(6B), 139A(5B) or 139AA(7) of the Criminal Justice Act 1988;

(d) section 110(2) or 111(2) of this Act;

(e) section 224A, 225(2) or 226(2) of the Criminal Justice Act 2003;

(f) section 29(4) or (6) of the Violent Crime Reduction Act 2006.

(2A) A court must consider making a compensation order in any case where this section empowers it to do so.

(3) A court shall give reasons, on passing sentence, if it does not make a compensation order in a case where this section empowers it to do so.

(4) Compensation under subsection (1) above shall be of such amount as the court considers appropriate, having regard to any evidence and to any representations that are made by or on behalf of the accused or the prosecutor.

(5) In the case of an offence under the Theft Act 1968 or Fraud Act 2006, where the property in question is recovered, any damage to the property occurring while it was out of the owner's possession shall be treated for the purposes of subsection (1) above as having resulted from the offence, however and by whomever the damage was caused.

(6) A compensation order may only be made in respect of injury, loss or damage (other than loss suffered by a person's dependants in consequence of his death) which was due to an accident arising out of the presence of a motor vehicle on a road, if—

(a) it is in respect of damage which is treated by subsection (5) above as resulting from an offence under the Theft Act 1968 or Fraud Act 2006; or

(b) it is in respect of injury, loss or damage as respects which—

(i)   the offender is uninsured in relation to the use of the vehicle; and

(ii) compensation is not payable under any arrangements to which the Secretary of State is a party.

(7) Where a compensation order is made in respect of injury, loss or damage due to an accident arising out of the presence of a motor vehicle on a road, the amount to be paid may include an amount

representing the whole or part of any loss of or reduction in preferential rates of insurance attributable to the accident.

(8) A vehicle the use of which is exempted from insurance by section 144 of the Road Traffic Act 1988 is not uninsured for the purposes of subsection (6) above.

(9) A compensation order in respect of funeral expenses may be made for the benefit of anyone who incurred the expenses.

(10) A compensation order in respect of bereavement may be made only for the benefit of a person for whose benefit a claim for damages for bereavement could be made under section 1A of the Fatal Accidents Act 1976; and the amount of compensation in respect of bereavement shall not exceed the amount for the time being specified in section 1A(3) of that Act.

(11) In determining whether to make a compensation order against any person, and in determining the amount to be paid by any person under such an order, the court shall have regard to his means so far as they appear or are known to the court.

(12) Where the court considers—

(a) that it would be appropriate both to impose a fine and to make a compensation order, but

(b) that the offender has insufficient means to pay both an appropriate fine and appropriate compensation,

the court shall give preference to compensation (though it may impose a fine as well).

131 Limit on amount payable under compensation order of magistrates' court in case of young offender

(A1) This section applies if (but only if) a magistrates' court has convicted a person aged under 18 ('the offender') of an offence or offences.

(1) The compensation to be paid under a compensation order made by the court in respect of the offence, or any one of the offences, shall not exceed £5,000.

(2) The compensation or total compensation to be paid under a compensation order or compensation orders made by the court in respect of any offence or offence taken into consideration in determining sentence shall not exceed the difference (if any) between—

(a) the amount or total amount which under subsection (1) above is the maximum for the offence or offences of which the offender has been convicted; and

(b) the amount or total amounts (if any) which are in fact ordered to be paid in respect of that offence or those offences.

132 Compensation orders: appeals etc

(1) A person in whose favour a compensation order is made shall not be entitled to receive the amount due to him until (disregarding any power of a court to grant leave to appeal out of time) there is no further possibility of an appeal on which the order could be varied or set aside.

(2) Criminal Procedure Rules may make provision regarding the way in which the magistrates' court for the time being having functions (by virtue of section 41(1) of the Administration of Justice Act 1970) in relation to the enforcement of a compensation order is to deal with money paid in satisfaction of the order where the entitlement of the person in whose favour it was made is suspended.

(3) The Court of Appeal may by order annul or vary any compensation order made by the court of trial, although the conviction is not quashed; and the order, if annulled, shall not take effect and, if varied, shall take effect as varied.

(4) Where the Supreme Court restores a conviction, it may make any compensation order which the court of trial could have made.

(4A) Where an order is made in respect of a person under subsection (3) or (4) above, the Court of Appeal or the Supreme Court shall make such order for the payment of a surcharge under section 161A of the Criminal Justice Act 2003, or such variation of the order of the Crown Court under that section, as is necessary to secure that the person's liability under that section is the same as it would be if he were being dealt with by the Crown Court.

(5) Where a compensation order has been made against any person in respect of an offence taken into consideration in determining his sentence—

(a) the order shall cease to have effect if he successfully appeals against his conviction of the offence or, if more than one, all the offences, of which he was convicted in the proceedings in which the order was made;

(b) he may appeal against the order as if it were part of the sentence imposed in respect of the offence or, if more than one, any of the offences, of which he was so convicted.

133 Review of compensation orders

(1) The magistrates' court for the time being having functions in relation to the enforcement of a compensation order (in this section referred to as 'the appropriate court') may, on the application of the person against whom the compensation order was made, discharge the order or reduce the amount which remains to be paid; but this is subject to subsections (2) to (4) below.

(2) The appropriate court may exercise a power conferred by subsection (1) above only—

(a) at a time when (disregarding any power of a court to grant leave to appeal out of time) there is no further possibility of an appeal on which the compensation order could be varied or set aside; and

(b) at a time before the person against whom the compensation order was made has paid into court the whole of the compensation which the order requires him to pay.

(3) The appropriate court may exercise a power conferred by subsection (1) above only if it appears to the court—

(a) that the injury, loss or damage in respect of which the compensation order was made has been held in civil proceedings to be less than it was taken to be for the purposes of the order; or

(b) in the case of a compensation order in respect of the loss of any property, that the property has been recovered by the person in whose favour the order was made; or

(c) that the means of the person against whom the compensation order was made are insufficient to satisfy in full both the order and any or all of the following made against him in the same proceedings—

(i) a confiscation order under Part 6 of the Criminal Justice Act 1988 or Part 2 of the Proceeds of Crime Act 2002;

(ii) an unlawful profit order under section 4 of the Prevention of Social Housing Fraud Act 2013;

(iii) a slavery and trafficking reparation order under section 8 of the Modern Slavery Act 2015; or

(d) that the person against whom the compensation order was made has suffered a substantial reduction in his means which was unexpected at the time when the order was made, and that his means seem unlikely to increase for a considerable period.

(4) Where the compensation order was made by the Crown Court, the appropriate court shall not exercise any power conferred by subsection (1) above in a case where it is satisfied as mentioned in paragraph (c) or (d) of subsection (3) above unless it has first obtained the consent of the Crown Court.

(5) Where the compensation order has been made on appeal, for the purposes of subsection (4) above it shall be deemed—

(a) if it was made on an appeal brought from a magistrates' court, to have been made by that magistrates' court;

(b) if it was made on an appeal brought from the Crown Court or from the criminal division of the Court of Appeal, to have been made by the Crown Court.

. . .

135 Limit on fines imposed by magistrates' courts in respect of young offenders

(1) Where a person aged under 18 is found guilty by a magistrates' court of an offence for which, apart from this section, the court would have power to impose a fine of an amount exceeding £1,000, the amount of any fine imposed by the court shall not exceed £1,000.

(2) In relation to a person aged under 14, subsection (1) above shall have effect as if for '£1,000', in both places where it occurs, there were substituted '£250'.

136 Power to order statement as to financial circumstances of parent or guardian

(1) Before exercising its powers under section 137 below (power to order parent or guardian to pay fine, costs, compensation or surcharge) against the parent or guardian of an individual who has been convicted of an offence, the court may make a financial circumstances order with respect to the parent or (as the case may be) guardian.

(2) In this section 'financial circumstances order' has the meaning given by subsection (3) of section 162 of the Criminal Justice Act 2003, and subsections (4) to (6) of that section shall apply in relation to a financial circumstances order made under this section as they apply in relation to such an order made under that section.

137 Power to order parent or guardian to pay fine, costs, compensation or surcharge

(1) Where—

  (a) a child or young person (that is to say, any person aged under 18) is convicted of any offence for the commission of which a fine or costs may be imposed or a compensation order may be made, and

  (b) the court is of the opinion that the case would best be met by the imposition of a fine or costs or the making of such an order, whether with or without any other punishment,

the court shall order that the fine, compensation or costs awarded be paid by the parent or guardian of the child or young person instead of by the child or young person himself, unless the court is satisfied—

  (i) that the parent or guardian cannot be found; or

  (ii) that it would be unreasonable to make an order for payment, having regard to the circumstances of the case.

(1A) Where but for this subsection a court would order a child or young person to pay a surcharge under section 161A of the Criminal Justice Act 2003, the court shall order that the surcharge be paid by the parent or guardian of the child or young person instead of by the child or young person himself, unless the court is satisfied—

  (a) that the parent or guardian cannot be found; or

  (b) that it would be unreasonable to make an order for payment, having regard to the circumstances of the case.

(2) Where but for this subsection a court would impose a fine on a child or young person under—

  (za) paragraph 6(2)(a) or 8(2)(a) of Schedule 2 to the Criminal Justice and Immigration Act 2008 (breach of youth rehabilitation order),

  (b) paragraph 2(1)(a) of Schedule 5 to this Act (breach of attendance centre order or attendance centre rules),

  (d) paragraph 2(2)(a) of Schedule 8 to this Act (breach of reparation order),

  (e) section 104(3)(b) above (breach of requirements of supervision under a detention and training order), or

  (f) section 4(3)(b) of the Criminal Justice and Public Order Act 1994 (breach of requirements of supervision under a secure training order),

the court shall order that the fine be paid by the parent or guardian of the child or young person instead of by the child or young person himself, unless the court is satisfied—

  (i) that the parent or guardian cannot be found; or

     (ii) that it would be unreasonable to make an order for payment, having regard to the circumstances of the case.

    (3) In the case of a young person aged 16 or over, subsections (1) to (2) above shall have effect as if, instead of imposing a duty, they conferred a power to make such an order as is mentioned in those subsections.

    (4) Subject to subsection (5) below, no order shall be made under this section without giving the parent or guardian an opportunity of being heard.

    (5) An order under this section may be made against a parent or guardian who, having been required to attend, has failed to do so.

    (6) A parent or guardian may appeal to the Crown Court against an order under this section made by a magistrates' court.

    (7) A parent or guardian may appeal to the Court of Appeal against an order under this section made by the Crown Court, as if he had been convicted on indictment and the order were a sentence passed on his conviction.

    (8) In relation to a child or young person for whom a local authority have parental responsibility and who—

      (a) is in their care, or

      (b) is provided with accommodation by them in the exercise of any functions (in particular those under the Children Act 1989) which are social services functions within the meaning of the Local Authority Social Services Act 1970,

references in this section to his parent or guardian shall be construed as references to that authority.

    (9) In subsection (8) above 'local authority' and 'parental responsibility' have the same meanings as in the Children Act 1989.

138 Fixing of fine, compensation or surcharge to be paid by parent or guardian

    (1) For the purposes of any order under section 137 above made against the parent or guardian of a child or young person—

      (za) subsection (3) of section 161A of the Criminal Justice Act 2003 (surcharges) and subsection (4A) of section 164 of that Act (fixing of fines) shall have effect as if any reference in those subsections to the offender's means were a reference to those of the parent or guardian;

      (a) section 164 of the Criminal Justice Act 2003 (fixing of fines) shall have effect as if any reference in subsections (1) to (4) to the financial circumstances of the offender were a reference to the financial circumstances of the parent or guardian, and as if subsection (5) were omitted;

      (b) section 130(11) above (determination of compensation order) shall have effect as if any reference to the means of the person against whom the compensation order is made were a reference to the financial circumstances of the parent or guardian; and

      (c) section 130(12) above (preference to be given to compensation if insufficient means to pay both compensation and a fine) shall have effect as if the reference to the offender were a reference to the parent or guardian;

but in relation to an order under section 137 made against a local authority this subsection has effect subject to subsection (2) below.

    (2) For the purposes of any order under section 137 above made against a local authority, section 164(1) of the Criminal Justice Act 2003 and section 130(11) above shall not apply.

    (3) For the purposes of any order under section 137 above, where the parent or guardian of an offender who is a child or young person—

      (a) has failed to comply with an order under section 136 above, or

      (b) has otherwise failed to co-operate with the court in its inquiry into his financial circumstances,

and the court considers that it has insufficient information to make a proper determination of the parent's or guardian's financial circumstances, it may make such determination as it thinks fit.

    (4) Where a court has, in fixing the amount of a fine, determined the financial circumstances of a parent or guardian under subsection (3) above, subsections (2) to (4) section 165 of the Criminal

Justice Act 2003 (remission of fines) shall (so far as applicable) have effect as they have effect in the case mentioned in section 165(1), but as if the reference in section 165(2) to the offender's financial circumstances were a reference to the financial circumstances of the parent or guardian.

(5) In this section 'local authority' has the same meaning as in the Children Act 1989.

139   Powers and duties of Crown Court in relation to fines and forfeited recognizances

(1) Subject to the provisions of this section, if the Crown Court imposes a fine on any person or forfeits his recognizance, the court may make an order—

    (a) allowing time for the payment of the amount of the fine or the amount due under the recognizance;

    (b) directing payment of that amount by instalments of such amounts and on such dates as may be specified in the order;

    (c) in the case of a recognizance, discharging the recognizance or reducing the amount due under it.

(2) Subject to the provisions of this section, if the Crown Court imposes a fine on any person or forfeits his recognizance, the court shall make an order fixing a term of imprisonment or of detention under section 108 above (detention of persons aged 18 to 20 for default) which he is to undergo if any sum which he is liable to pay is not duly paid or recovered:

(3) No person shall on the occasion when a fine is imposed on him or his recognizance is forfeited by the Crown Court be committed to prison or detained in pursuance of an order under subsection (2) above unless—

    (a) in the case of an offence punishable with imprisonment, he appears to the court to have sufficient means to pay the sum forthwith;

    (b) it appears to the court that he is unlikely to remain long enough at a place of abode in the United Kingdom to enable payment of the sum to be enforced by other methods; or

    (c) on the occasion when the order is made the court sentences him to immediate imprisonment, custody for life or detention in a young offender institution for that or another offence, or so sentences him for an offence in addition to forfeiting his recognizance, or he is already serving a sentence of custody for life or a term—

        (i) of imprisonment;

        (ii) of detention in a young offender institution; or

        (iii) of detention under section 108 above.

(4) The periods set out in the second column of the following Table shall be the maximum periods of imprisonment or detention under subsection (2) above applicable respectively to the amounts set out opposite them.

Table

An amount not exceeding £200	7 days
An amount exceeding £200 but not exceeding £500	14 days
An amount exceeding £500 but not exceeding £1,000	28 days
An amount exceeding £1,000 but not exceeding £2,500	45 days
An amount exceeding £2,500 but not exceeding £5,000	3 months
An amount exceeding £5,000 but not exceeding £10,000	6 months
An amount exceeding £10,000 but not exceeding £20,000	12 months
An amount exceeding £20,000 but not exceeding £50,000	18 months
An amount exceeding £50,000 but not exceeding £100,000	2 years
An amount exceeding £100,000 but not exceeding £250,000	3 years
An amount exceeding £250,000 but not exceeding £1 million	5 years
An amount exceeding £1 million	10 years

(5) Where any person liable for the payment of a fine or a sum due under a recognizance to which this section applies is sentenced by the court to, or is serving or otherwise liable to serve, a term of imprisonment or detention in a young offender institution or a term of detention under section 108 above, the court may order that any term of imprisonment or detention fixed under subsection (2) above shall not being to run until after the end of the first-mentioned term.

(6) The power conferred by this section to discharge a recognizance or reduce the amount due under it shall be in addition to the powers conferred by any other Act relating to the discharge, cancellation, mitigation or reduction of recognizances or sums forfeited under recognizances.

(7) Subject to subsection (8) below, the powers conferred by this section shall not be taken as restricted by any enactment which authorises the Crown Court to deal with an offender in any way in which a magistrates' court might have dealt with him or could deal with him.

(8) Any term fixed under subsection (2) above as respects a fine imposed in pursuance of such an enactment, that is to say a fine which the magistrates' court could have imposed, shall not exceed the period applicable to that fine (if imposed by the magistrates' court) under section 149(1) of the Customs and Excise Management Act 1979 (maximum periods of imprisonment in default of payment of certain fines).

(9) This section shall not apply to a fine imposed by the Crown Court on appeal against a decision of a magistrates' court, but subsections (2) to (4) above shall apply in relation to a fine imposed or recognizance forfeited by the criminal division of the Court of Appeal, or by the Supreme Court on appeal from that division, as they apply in relation to a fine imposed or recognizance forfeited by the Crown Court, and the references to the Crown Court in subsections (2) and (3) above shall be construed accordingly.

(10) For the purposes of any reference in this section, however expressed, to the term of imprisonment or other detention to which a person has been sentenced or which, or part of which, he has served, consecutive terms and terms which are wholly or partly concurrent shall, unless the context otherwise requires, be treated as a single term.

(11) Any reference in this section, however expressed, to a previous sentence shall be construed as a reference to a previous sentence passed by a court in Great Britain.

140   Enforcement of fines imposed and recognizances forfeited by Crown Court

(1) Subject to subsection (5) below, a fine imposed or a recognizance forfeited by the Crown Court shall be treated for the purposes of collection, enforcement and remission of the fine or other sum as having been imposed or forfeited—

(a) by a magistrates' court specified in an order made by the Crown Court, or

(b) if no such order is made, by the magistrates' court by which the offender was sent to the Crown Court for trial under section 51 or 51A of the Crime and Disorder Act 1998,

and, in the case of a fine, as having been so imposed on conviction by the magistrates' court in question.

(2) Subsection (3) below applies where a magistrates' court issues a warrant of commitment on a default in the payment of—

(a) a fine imposed by the Crown Court; or

(b) a sum due under a recognizance forfeited by the Crown Court.

(3) In such a case, the term of imprisonment or detention under section 108 above specified in the warrant of commitment as the term which the offender is liable to serve shall be—

(a) the term fixed by the Crown Court under section 139(2) above, or

(b) if that term has been reduced under section 79(2) of the Magistrates' Courts Act 1980 (part payment) or section 85(2) of that Act (remission), that term as so reduced,

notwithstanding that that term exceeds the period applicable to the case under section 149(1) of the Customs and Excise Management Act 1979 (maximum periods of imprisonment in default of payment of certain fines).

(4) Subsections (1) to (3) above shall apply in relation to a fine imposed or recognizance forfeited by the criminal division of the Court of Appeal, or by the Supreme Court on appeal from that division, as they apply in relation to a fine imposed or recognizance forfeited by the Crown Court; and references in those subsections to the Crown Court (except the references in subsection (1)(b)) shall be construed accordingly.

(5) A magistrates' court shall not, under section 85(1) or 120 of the Magistrates' Courts Act 1980 as applied by subsection (1) above, remit the whole or any part of a fine imposed by, or sum due under a recognizance forfeited by—

(a) the Crown Court,

(b) the criminal division of the Court of Appeal, or

(c) the Supreme Court on appeal from that division,

without the consent of the Crown Court.

(6) Any fine or other sum the payment of which is enforceable by a magistrates' court by virtue of this section shall be treated for the purposes of the Justices of the Peace Act 1997 and, in particular, section 60 of that Act (application of fines and fees) as having been imposed by a magistrates' court, or as being due under a recognizance forfeited by such a court.

141 Power of Crown Court to allow time for payment, or payment by instalments, of costs and compensation

Where the Crown Court makes any such order as is mentioned in Part I of Schedule 9 to the Administration of Justice Act 1970 (orders against accused for the payment of costs or compensation), the court may—

(a) allow time for the payment of the sum due under the order;

(b) direct payment of that sum by instalments of such amounts and on such dates as the court may specify.

. . .

143 Powers to deprive offender of property used etc. for purposes of crime

(1) Where a person is convicted of an offence and the court by or before which he is convicted is satisfied that any property which has been lawfully seized from him, or which was in his possession or under his control at the time when he was apprehended for the offence or when a summons in respect of it was issued—

(a) has been used for the purpose of committing, or facilitating the commission of, any offence, or

(b) was intended by him to be used for that purpose,

the court may (subject to subsection (5) below) make an order under this section in respect of that property.

(2) Where a person is convicted of an offence and the offence, or an offence which the court has taken into consideration in determining his sentence, consists of unlawful possession of property which—

(a) has been lawfully seized from him, or

(b) was in his possession or under his control at the time when he was apprehended for the offence of which he has been convicted or when a summons in respect of that offence was issued,

the court may (subject to subsection (5) below) make an order under this section in respect of that property.

(3) An order under this section shall operate to deprive the offender of his rights, if any, in the property to which it relates, and the property shall (if not already in their possession) be taken into the possession of the police.

(4) Any power conferred on a court by subsection (1) or (2) above may be exercised—

(a) whether or not the court also deals with the offender in any other way in respect of the offence of which he has been convicted; and

(b) without regard to any restrictions on forfeiture in any enactment contained in an Act passed before 29th July 1988.

(5) In considering whether to make an order under this section in respect of any property, a court shall have regard—

  (a) to the value of the property; and

  (b) to the likely financial and other effects on the offender of the making of the order (taken together with any other order that the court contemplates making).

(6) Where a person commits an offence to which this subsection applies by—

  (a) driving, attempting to drive, or being in charge of a vehicle, or

  (b) failing to comply with a requirement made under section 7 or 7A of the Road Traffic Act 1988 (failure to provide specimen for analysis or laboratory test or to give permission for such a test) in the course of an investigation into whether the offender had committed an offence while driving, attempting to drive or being in charge of a vehicle, or

  (c) failing, as the driver of a vehicle, to comply with subsection (2) or (3) of section 170 of the Road Traffic Act 1988 (duty to stop and give information or report accident),

the vehicle shall be regarded for the purposes of subsection (1) above (and section 144(1)(b) below) as used for the purpose of committing the offence (and for the purpose of committing any offence of aiding, abetting, counselling or procuring the commission of the offence).

(7) Subsection (6) above applies to—

  (a) an offence under the Road Traffic Act 1988 which is punishable with imprisonment;

  (b) an offence of manslaughter; and

  (c) an offence under section 35 of the Offences Against the Person Act 1861 (wanton and furious driving).

(8) Facilitating the commission of an offence shall be taken for the purposes of subsection (1) above to include the taking of any steps after it has been committed for the purpose of disposing of any property to which it relates or of avoiding apprehension or detection.

144 Property which is in possession of police by virtue of section 143

(1) The Police (Property) Act 1897 shall apply, with the following modifications, to property which is in the possession of the police by virtue of section 143 above—

  (a) no application shall be made under section 1(1) of that Act by any claimant of the property after the end of six months from the date on which the order in respect of the property was made under section 143 above; and

  (b) no such application shall succeed unless the claimant satisfies the court either—

    (i) that he had not consented to the offender having possession of the property; or

    (ii) where an order is made under subsection (1) of section 143 above, that he did not know, and had no reason to suspect, that the property was likely to be used for the purpose mentioned in that subsection.

(2) In relation to property which is in the possession of the police by virtue of section 143 above, the power to make regulations under section 2 of the Police (Property) Act 1897 (disposal of property in cases where the owner of the property has not been ascertained and no order of a competent court has been made with respect to it) shall, subject to subsection (3) below, include power to make regulations for disposal (including disposal by vesting in the relevant authority) in cases where no application by a claimant of the property has been made within the period specified in subsection (1)(a) above or no such application has succeeded.

(3) The regulations may not provide for the vesting in the relevant authority of property in relation to which an order has been made under section 145 below (court order as to application of proceeds of forfeited property).

(4) Nothing in subsection (2A)(a) or (3) of section 2 of the Police (Property) Act 1897 limits the power to make regulations under that section by virtue of subsection (2) above.

(5) In this section 'relevant authority' has the meaning given by section 2(2B) of the Police (Property) Act 1897.

145   Application of proceeds of forfeited property

(1) Where a court makes an order under section 143 above in a case where—

(a) the offender has been convicted of an offence which has resulted in a person suffering personal injury, loss or damage, or

(b) any such offence is taken into consideration by the court in determining sentence,

the court may also make an order that any proceeds which arise from the disposal of the property and which do not exceed a sum specified by the court shall be paid to that person.

(2) The court may make an order under this section only if it is satisfied that but for the inadequacy of the offender's means it would have made a compensation order under which the offender would have been required to pay compensation of an amount not less than the specified amount.

(3) An order under this section has no effect—

(a) before the end of the period specified in section 144(1)(a) above; or

(b) if a successful application under section 1(1) of the Police (Property) Act 1897 has been made.

146   Driving disqualification for any offence

(1) The court by or before which a person is convicted of an offence committed after 31st December 1997 may, instead of or in addition to dealing with him in any other way, order him to be disqualified, for such period as it thinks fit, for holding or obtaining a driving licence.

(2) Where the person is convicted of an offence the sentence for which is fixed by law or falls to be imposed under a provision mentioned in subsection (2A), subsection (1) above shall have effect as if the words 'instead of or' were omitted.

(2A) The provisions referred to in subsection (2) are—

(a) section 1(2B) or 1A(5) of the Prevention of Crime Act 1953;

(b) section 51A(2) of the Firearms Act 1968;

(c) section 139(6B), 139A(5B) or 139AA(7) of the Criminal Justice Act 1988;

(d) section 110(2) or 111(2) of this Act;

(e) section 224A, 225(2) or 226(2) of the Criminal Justice Act 2003;

(f) section 29(4) or (6) of the Violent Crime Reduction Act 2006.

(3) A court shall not make an order under subsection (1) above unless the court has been notified by the Secretary of State that the power to make such orders is exercisable by the court and the notice has not been withdrawn.

(4) A court which makes an order under this section disqualifying a person for holding or obtaining a driving licence shall require him to produce—

(a) any such licence held by him;

(aa) in the case where he holds a Northern Ireland licence (within the meaning of Part 3 of the Road Traffic Act 1988), his Northern Ireland licence; or

(b) in the case where he holds a Community licence (within the meaning of Part III of the Road Traffic Act 1988), his Community licence.

(5) In this section—

'driving licence' means a licence to drive a motor vehicle granted under Part III of the Road Traffic Act 1988;

147   Driving disqualification where vehicle used for purposes of crime

(1) This section applies where a person—

(a) is convicted before the Crown Court of an offence punishable on indictment with imprisonment for a term of two years or more; or

(b) having been convicted by a magistrates' court of such an offence, is committed under section 3 above to the Crown Court for sentence.

(2) This section also applies where a person is convicted by or before any court of common assault or of any other offence involving an assault (including an offence of aiding, abetting, counselling or procuring, or inciting to the commission of, an offence).

(3) If, in a case to which this section applies by virtue of subsection (1) above, the Crown Court is satisfied that a motor vehicle was used (by the person convicted or by anyone else) for the purpose of committing, or facilitating the commission of, the offence in question, the court may order the person convicted to be disqualified, for such period as the court thinks fit, for holding or obtaining a driving licence.

(4) If, in a case to which this section applies by virtue of subsection (2) above, the court is satisfied that the assault was committed by driving a motor vehicle, the court may order the person convicted to be disqualified, for such period as the court thinks fit, for holding or obtaining a driving licence.

(5) A court which makes an order under this section disqualifying a person for holding or obtaining a driving licence shall require him to produce—

(a)   any such licence held by him;

(aa) in the case where he holds a Northern Ireland licence (within the meaning of Part 3 of the Road Traffic Act 1988), his Northern Ireland licence; or

(b)   in the case where he holds a Community licence (within the meaning of Part III of the Road Traffic Act 1988), his Community licence.

(6) Facilitating the commission of an offence shall be taken for the purposes of this section to include the taking of any steps after it has been committed for the purpose of disposing of any property to which it relates or of avoiding apprehension or detection.

(7) In this section 'driving licence' has the meaning given by section 146(5) above.

147A Extension of disqualification where custodial sentence also imposed

(1) This section applies where a person is convicted of an offence for which the court—

(a)   imposes a custodial sentence, and

(b)   orders the person to be disqualified under section 146 or 147 for holding or obtaining a driving licence.

(2) The order under section 146 or 147 must provide for the person to be disqualified for the appropriate extension period, in addition to the discretionary disqualification period.

(3) The discretionary disqualification period is the period for which, in the absence of this section, the court would have disqualified the person under section 146 or 147.

(4) The appropriate extension period is—

(a)   where an order under section 82A(2) of this Act (determination of tariffs) is made in relation to the custodial sentence, a period equal to the part of the sentence specified in that order;

(b)   in the case of a detention and training order under section 100 of this Act (offenders under 18: detention and training orders), a period equal to half the term of that order;

(c)   where an order under section 181 of the Criminal Justice Act 2003 (prison sentences of less than 12 months) is made in relation to the custodial sentence, a period equal to the custodial period specified pursuant to section 181(3)(a) of that Act less any relevant discount;

(d)   where an order under section 183 of that Act (intermittent custody orders) is made in relation to the custodial sentence, a period equal to the number of custodial days specified pursuant to section 183(1)(a) of that Act less any relevant discount;

(e)   where section 227 of that Act (extended sentence for certain violent or sexual offences: persons 18 or over) applies in relation to the custodial sentence, a period equal to half the term imposed pursuant to section 227(2C)(a) of the Criminal Justice Act 2003;

(f)   where section 228 of that Act (extended sentence for certain violent or sexual offences: persons under 18) applies in relation to the custodial sentence, a period equal to half the term imposed pursuant to section 228(2B)(a) of that Act;

(fa) in the case of a sentence under section 236A of that Act (special custodial sentence for certain offenders of particular concern), a period equal to half of the term imposed pursuant to section 236A(2)(a) of that Act;

(g) where an order under section 269(2) of that Act (determination of minimum term in relation to mandatory life sentence: early release) is made in relation to the custodial sentence, a period equal to the part of the sentence specified in that order;

(h) in any other case, a period equal to half the custodial sentence imposed.

(5) If a period determined under subsection (4) includes a fraction of a day, that period is to be rounded up to the nearest number of whole days.

(7) This section does not apply where—

(a) the custodial sentence was a suspended sentence,

(b) the court has made an order under section 269(4) of the Criminal Justice Act 2003 (determination of minimum term in relation to mandatory life sentence: no early release) in relation to the custodial sentence, or

(c) the court has made an order under section 82A(4) of this Act (determination of minimum term in relation to discretionary life sentence: no early release) in relation to the custodial sentence.

(8) Subsection (9) applies where an amending order provides that the proportion of a prisoner's sentence referred to in section 244(3)(a) or 247(2) of the Criminal Justice Act 2003 (release of prisoners in certain circumstances) is to be read as a reference to another proportion ('the new proportion').

(9) The Secretary of State may by order—

(a) if the amending order makes provision in respect of section 244(3)(a) of that Act, provide that the proportion specified in subsection (4)(h) of this section is to be read, in the case of a custodial sentence to which the amending order applies, as a reference to the new proportion;

(b) if the amending order makes provision in respect of section 247(2) of that Act, provide that the proportion specified in subsection (4)(e) and (f) of this section is to be read, in the case of a custodial sentence to which the amending order applies, as a reference to the new proportion.

(10) In this section—

'amending order' means an order under section 267 of the Criminal Justice Act 2003 (alteration by order of relevant proportion of sentence);

'driving licence' means a licence to drive a motor vehicle granted under Part 3 of the Road Traffic Act 1988;

'suspended sentence' has the meaning given by section 189 of the Criminal Justice Act 2003.

147B   Effect of custodial sentence in other cases

(1) This section applies where a person is convicted of an offence for which a court proposes to order the person to be disqualified under section 146 or 147 for holding or obtaining a driving licence and—

(a) the court proposes to impose on the person a custodial sentence (other than a suspended sentence) for another offence, or

(b) at the time of sentencing for the offence, a custodial sentence imposed on the person on an earlier occasion has not expired.

(2) In determining the period for which the person is to be disqualified under section 146 or 147, the court must have regard to the consideration in subsection (3) if and to the extent that it is appropriate to do so.

(3) The consideration is the diminished effect of disqualification as a distinct punishment if the person who is disqualified is also detained in pursuance of a custodial sentence.

(4) If the court proposes to order the person to be disqualified under section 146 or 147 and to impose a custodial sentence for the same offence, the court may not in relation to that disqualification take that custodial sentence into account for the purposes of subsection (2).

(5) In this section 'suspended sentence' has the same meaning as in section 147A.

148   Restitution orders

(1) This section applies where goods have been stolen, and either—

    (a) a person is convicted of any offence with reference to the theft (whether or not the stealing is the gist of his offence); or

    (b) a person is convicted of any other offence, but such an offence as is mentioned in paragraph (a) above is taken into consideration in determining his sentence.

(2) Where this section applies, the court by or before which the offender is convicted may on the conviction (whether or not the passing of sentence is in other respects deferred) exercise any of the following powers—

    (a) the court may order anyone having possession or control of the stolen goods to restore them to any person entitled to recover them from him; or

    (b) on the application of a person entitled to recover from the person convicted any other goods directly or indirectly representing the stolen goods (as being the proceeds of any disposal or realisation of the whole or part of them or of goods so representing them), the court may order those other goods to be delivered or transferred to the applicant; or

    (c) the court may order that a sum not exceeding the value of the stolen goods shall be paid, out of any money of the person convicted which was taken out of his possession on his apprehension, to any person who, if those goods were in the possession of the person convicted, would be entitled to recover them from him;

and in this subsection 'the stolen goods' means the goods referred to in subsection (1) above.

(3) Where the court has power on a person's conviction to make an order against him both under paragraph (b) and under paragraph (c) of subsection (2) above with reference to the stealing of the same goods, the court may make orders under both paragraphs provided that the person in whose favour the orders are made does not thereby recover more than the value of those goods.

(4) Where the court on a person's conviction makes an order under subsection (2)(a) above for the restoration of any goods, and it appears to the court that the person convicted—

    (a) has sold the goods to a person acting in good faith, or

    (b) has borrowed money on the security of them from a person so acting,

the court may order that there shall be paid to the purchaser or lender, out of any money of the person convicted which was taken out of his possession on his apprehension, a sum not exceeding the amount paid for the purchase by the purchaser or, as the case may be, the amount owed to the lender in respect of the loan.

(5) The court shall not exercise the powers conferred by this section unless in the opinion of the court the relevant facts sufficiently appear from evidence given at the trial or the available documents, together with admissions made by or on behalf of any person in connection with any proposed exercise of the powers.

(6) In subsection (5) above 'the available documents' means—

    (a) any written statements or admissions which were made for use, and would have been admissible, as evidence at the trial; and

    (b) such documents as were served on the offender in pursuance of regulations made under paragraph 1 of Schedule 3 to the Crime and Disorder Act 1998.

(7) Any order under this section shall be treated as an order for the restitution of property within the meaning of section 30 of the Criminal Appeal Act 1968 (which relates to the effect on such orders of appeals).

(8) Subject to subsection (9) below, references in this section to stealing shall be construed in accordance with section 1(1) of the Theft Act 1968 (read with the provisions of that Act relating to the construction of section 1(1)).

(9) Subsections (1) and (4) of section 24 of that Act (interpretation of certain provisions) shall also apply in relation to this section as they apply in relation to the provisions of that Act relating to goods which have been stolen.

(10) In this section and section 149 below, 'goods', except in so far as the context otherwise requires, includes money and every other description of property (within the meaning of the Theft Act 1968) except land, and includes things severed from the land by stealing.

(11) An order may be made under this section in respect of money owed by the Crown.

. . .

150 Binding over of parent or guardian

(1) Where a child or young person (that is to say, any person aged under 18) is convicted of an offence, the powers conferred by this section shall be exercisable by the court by which he is sentenced for that offence, and where the offender is aged under 16 when sentenced it shall be the duty of that court—

    (a) to exercise those powers if it is satisfied, having regard to the circumstances of the case, that their exercise would be desirable in the interests of preventing the commission by him of further offences; and

    (b) if it does not exercise them, to state in open court that it is not satisfied as mentioned in paragraph (a) above and why it is not so satisfied;

but this subsection has effect subject to section 19(5) above and paragraph 13(5) of Schedule 1 to this Act (cases where referral orders made or extended).

(2) The powers conferred by this section are as follows—

    (a) with the consent of the offender's parent or guardian, to order the parent or guardian to enter into a recognizance to take proper care of him and exercise proper control over him; and

    (b) if the parent or guardian refuses consent and the court considers the refusal unreasonable, to order the parent or guardian to pay a fine not exceeding £1,000;

and where the court has passed on the offender a sentence which consists of or includes a youth rehabilitation order, it may include in the recognizance a provision that the offender's parent or guardian ensure that the offender complies with the requirements of that sentence.

(3) An order under this section shall not require the parent or guardian to enter into a recognizance for an amount exceeding £1,000.

(4) An order under this section shall not require the parent or guardian to enter into a recognizance—

    (a) for a period exceeding three years; or

    (b) where the offender will attain the age of 18 in a period shorter than three years, for a period exceeding that shorter period.

(5) Section 120 of the Magistrates' Courts Act 1980 (forfeiture of recognizances) shall apply in relation to a recognizance entered into in pursuance of an order under this section as it applies in relation to a recognizance to keep the peace.

(6) A fine imposed under subsection (2)(b) above shall be deemed, for the purposes of any enactment, to be a sum adjudged to be paid by a conviction.

(7) In fixing the amount of a recognizance under this section, the court shall take into account among other things the means of the parent or guardian so far as they appear or are known to the court; and this subsection applies whether taking into account the means of the parent or guardian has the effect of increasing or reducing the amount of the recognizance.

(8) A parent or guardian may appeal to the Crown Court against an order under this section made by a magistrates' court.

(9) A parent or guardian may appeal to the Court of Appeal against an order under this section made by the Crown Court, as if he had been convicted on indictment and the order were a sentence passed on his conviction.

(10) A court may vary or revoke an order made by it under this section if, on the application of the parent or guardian, it appears to the court, having regard to any change in the circumstances since the order was made, to be in the interests of justice to do so.

(11) For the purposes of this section, taking 'care' of a person includes giving him protection and guidance and 'control' includes discipline.

Criminal Justice Act 2003

142 Purposes of sentencing

(1) Any court dealing with an offender in respect of his offence must have regard to the following purposes of sentencing—

    (a) the punishment of offenders,

    (b) the reduction of crime (including its reduction by deterrence),

    (c) the reform and rehabilitation of offenders,

    (d) the protection of the public, and

    (e) the making of reparation by offenders to persons affected by their offences.

(2) Subsection (1) does not apply—

    (a) in relation to an offender who is aged under 18 at the time of conviction,

    (b) to an offence the sentence for which is fixed by law,

    (c) to an offence the sentence for which falls to be imposed under a provision mentioned in subsection (2AA) or

    (d) in relation to the making under Part 3 of the Mental Health Act 1983 (c. 20) of a hospital order (with or without a restriction order), an interim hospital order, a hospital direction or a limitation direction.

(2AA) The provisions referred to in subsection (2)(c) are—

    (a) section 1(2B) or 1A(5) of the Prevention of Crime Act 1953 (minimum sentence for certain offences involving offensive weapons);

    (b) section 51A(2) of the Firearms Act 1968 (minimum sentence for certain firearms offences);

    (c) section 139(6B), 139A(5B) or 139AA(7) of the Criminal Justice Act 1988 (minimum sentence for certain offences involving article with blade or point or offensive weapon);

    (d) section 110(2) or 111(2) of the Sentencing Act (minimum sentence for certain drug trafficking and burglary offences);

    (e) section 224A of this Act (life sentence for second listed offence for certain dangerous offenders);

    (f) section 225(2) or 226(2) of this Act (imprisonment or detention for life for certain dangerous offenders);

    (g) section 29(4) or (6) of the Violent Crime Reduction Act 2006 (minimum sentence in certain cases of using someone to mind a weapon).

(3) In this Chapter 'sentence', in relation to an offence, includes any order made by a court when dealing with the offender in respect of his offence; and 'sentencing' is to be construed accordingly.

143 Determining the seriousness of an offence

(1) In considering the seriousness of any offence, the court must consider the offender's culpability in committing the offence and any harm which the offence caused, was intended to cause or might forseeably have caused.

(2) In considering the seriousness of an offence ('the current offence') committed by an offender who has one or more previous convictions, the court must treat each previous conviction as an aggravating factor if (in the case of that conviction) the court considers that it can reasonably be so treated having regard, in particular, to—

    (a) the nature of the offence to which the conviction relates and its relevance to the current offence, and

    (b) the time that has elapsed since the conviction.

(3) In considering the seriousness of any offence committed while the offender was on bail, the court must treat the fact that it was committed in those circumstances as an aggravating factor.

(4) Any reference in subsection (2) to a previous conviction is to be read as a reference to—

    (a) a previous conviction by a court in the United Kingdom,

    (aa) a previous conviction by a court in another member State of a relevant offence under the law of that State,

(b)   a previous conviction of a service offence within the meaning of the Armed Forces Act 2006 ('conviction' here including anything that under section 376(1) and (2) of that Act is to be treated as a conviction), or

(c)   a finding of guilt in respect of a member State service offence.

(5)   Subsections (2) and (4) do not prevent the court from treating—

(a)   a previous conviction by a court outside both the United Kingdom and any other member State, or

(b)   a previous conviction by a court in any member State (other than the United Kingdom) of an offence which is not a relevant offence,

as an aggravating factor in any case where the court considers it appropriate to do so.

(6)   For the purposes of this section—

(a)   an offence is 'relevant' if the offence would constitute an offence under the law of any part of the United Kingdom if it were done in that part at the time of the conviction of the defendant for the current offence,

(b)   'member State service offence' means an offence which—

(i)   was the subject of proceedings under the service law of a member State other than the United Kingdom, and

(ii)   would constitute an offence under the law of any part of the United Kingdom, or a service offence (within the meaning of the Armed Forces Act 2006), if it were done in any part of the United Kingdom, by a member of Her Majesty's forces, at the time of the conviction of the defendant for the current offence,

(c)   'Her Majesty's forces' has the same meaning as in the Armed Forces Act 2006, and

(d)   'service law', in relation to a member State other than the United Kingdom, means the law governing all or any of the naval, military or air forces of that State.

144   Reduction in sentences for guilty pleas

(1)   In determining what sentence to pass on an offender who has pleaded guilty to an offence in proceedings before that or another court, a court must take into account—

(a)   the stage in the proceedings for the offence at which the offender indicated his intention to plead guilty, and

(b)   the circumstances in which this indication was given.

(2)   In the case of an offender who—

(a)   is convicted of an offence the sentence for which falls to be imposed under a provision mentioned in subsection (3), and

(b)   is aged 18 or over when convicted,

nothing in that provision prevents the court, after taking into account any matter referred to in subsection (1) of this section, from imposing any sentence which is not less than 80 per cent of that specified in that provision.

(3)   The provisions referred to in subsection (2) are—

section 1(2B) or 1A(5) of the Prevention of Crime Act 1953;

section 110(2) of the Sentencing Act;

section 111(2) of the Sentencing Act;

section 139(6B), 139A(5B) or 139AA(7) of the Criminal Justice Act 1988.

(4)   In the case of an offender who—

(a)   is convicted of an offence the sentence for which falls to be imposed under a provision mentioned in subsection (5), and

(b)   is aged 16 or 17 when convicted,

nothing in that provision prevents the court from imposing any sentence that it considers appropriate after taking into account any matter referred to in subsection (1) of this section.

(5)   The provisions referred to in subsection (4) are—

section 1(2B) or 1A(5) of the Prevention of Crime Act 1953;

section 139(6B), 139A(5B) or 139AA(7) of the Criminal Justice Act 1988.

145   Increase in sentences for racial or religious aggravation

(1) This section applies where a court is considering the seriousness of an offence other than one under sections 29 to 32 of the Crime and Disorder Act 1998 (c. 37) (racially or religiously aggravated assaults, criminal damage, public order offences and harassment etc).

(2) If the offence was racially or religiously aggravated, the court—

(a) must treat that fact as an aggravating factor, and

(b) must state in open court that the offence was so aggravated.

(3) Section 28 of the Crime and Disorder Act 1998 (meaning of 'racially or religiously aggravated') applies for the purposes of this section as it applies for the purposes of sections 29 to 32 of that Act.

146   Increase in sentences for aggravation related to disability, sexual orientation or transgender identity

(1) This section applies where the court is considering the seriousness of an offence committed in any of the circumstances mentioned in subsection (2).

(2) Those circumstances are—

(a) that, at the time of committing the offence, or immediately before or after doing so, the offender demonstrated towards the victim of the offence hostility based on—

(i)   the sexual orientation (or presumed sexual orientation) of the victim,

(ii)   a disability (or presumed disability) of the victim, or

(iii) the victim being (or being presumed to be) transgender, or

(b) that the offence is motivated (wholly or partly)—

(i)   by hostility towards persons who are of a particular sexual orientation,

(ii)   by hostility towards persons who have a disability or a particular disability

(iii) by hostility towards persons who are transgender.

(3) The court—

(a) must treat the fact that the offence was committed in any of those circumstances as an aggravating factor, and

(b) must state in open court that the offence was committed in such circumstances.

(4) It is immaterial for the purposes of paragraph (a) or (b) of subsection (2) whether or not the offender's hostility is also based, to any extent, on any other factor not mentioned in that paragraph.

(5) In this section 'disability' means any physical or mental impairment.

(6) In this section references to being transgender include references to being transsexual, or undergoing, proposing to undergo or having undergone a process or part of a process of gender reassignment.

147   Meaning of 'community sentence' etc.

(1) In this Part 'community sentence' means a sentence which consists of or includes—

(a) a community order (as defined by section 177)

(c) a youth rehabilitation order.

148   Restrictions on imposing community sentences

(1) A court must not pass a community sentence on an offender unless it is of the opinion that the offence, or the combination of the offence and one or more offences associated with it, was serious enough to warrant such a sentence.

(2) Where a court passes a community sentence —

(a) the particular requirement or requirements forming part of the community order, or, as the case may be, youth rehabilitation order, comprised in the sentence must be such as, in the opinion of the court, is, or taken together are, the most suitable for the offender, and

(b) the restrictions on liberty imposed by the order must be such as in the opinion of the court are commensurate with the seriousness of the offence, or the combination of the offence and one or more offences associated with it.

(2A) Subsection (2) is subject to section 177(2A) (community orders: punitive elements) and to paragraph 3(4) of Schedule 1 to the Criminal Justice and Immigration Act 2008 (youth rehabilitation order with intensive supervision and surveillance).

(4) Subsections (1) and (2) (b) have effect subject to section 151(2).

(5) The fact that by virtue of any provision of this section—

    (a) a community sentence may be passed in relation to an offence; or

    (b) particular restrictions on liberty may be imposed by a community order or youth rehabilitation order.

149 Passing of community sentence on offender remanded in custody

(1) In determining the restrictions on liberty to be imposed by a community order or youth rehabilitation order in respect of an offence, the court may have regard to any period for which the offender has been remanded in custody in connection with the offence or any other offence the charge for which was founded on the same facts or evidence.

(2) In subsection (1) 'remanded in custody' has the meaning given by section 242(2).

150 Community sentence not available where sentence fixed by law etc.

(1) The power to make a community order or youth rehabilitation order is not exercisable in respect of an offence for which the sentence—

    (a) is fixed by law,

    (b) falls to be imposed under section 51A(2) of the Firearms Act 1968 (c. 27) (required custodial sentence for certain firearms offences),

    (c) falls to be imposed under section 110(2) or 111(2) of the Sentencing Act (requirement to impose custodial sentences for certain repeated offences committed by offenders aged 18 or over),

    (ca) falls to be imposed under section 29(4) or (6) of the Violent Crime Reduction Act 2006 (required custodial sentence in certain cases of using someone to mind a weapon),

    (cb) falls to be imposed under section 224A of this Act (life sentence for second listed offence for certain dangerous offenders), or

    (d) falls to be imposed under section 225(2) or 226(2) of this Act (requirement to impose sentence of imprisonment for life or detention for life).

(2) The power to make a community order is not exercisable in respect of an offence for which the sentence—

    (a) falls to be imposed under section 1(2B) or 1A(5) of the Prevention of Crime Act 1953 (minimum sentence for certain offences involving offensive weapons), or

    (b) falls to be imposed under section 139(6B), 139A(5B) or 139AA(7) of the Criminal Justice Act 1988 (minimum sentence for certain offences involving article with blade or point or offensive weapon).

150A Community order available only for offences punishable with imprisonment or for persistent offenders previously fined

(1) The power to make a community order is only exercisable in respect of an offence if—

    (a) the offence is punishable with imprisonment; or

    (b) in any other case, section 151(2) confers power to make such an order.

(2) For the purposes of this section and section 151 an offence triable either way that was tried summarily is to be regarded as punishable with imprisonment only if it is so punishable by the sentencing court (and for this purpose section 148(1) is to be disregarded).

152 General restrictions on imposing discretionary custodial sentences

(1) This section applies where a person is convicted of an offence punishable with a custodial sentence other than one—

    (a) fixed by law, or

    (b) falling to be imposed under a provision mentioned in subsection (1A).

(1A) The provisions referred to in subsection (1)(b) are—
- (a) section 1(2B) or 1A(5) of the Prevention of Crime Act 1953;
- (b) section 51A(2) of the Firearms Act 1968;
- (c) section 139(6B), 139A(5B) or 139AA(7) of the Criminal Justice Act 1988;
- (d) section 110(2) or 111(2) of the Sentencing Act;
- (e) section 224A, 225(2) or 226(2) of this Act;
- (f) section 29(4) or (6) of the Violent Crime Reduction Act 2006.

(2) The court must not pass a custodial sentence unless it is of the opinion that the offence, or the combination of the offence and one or more offences associated with it, was so serious that neither a fine alone nor a community sentence can be justified for the offence.

(3) Nothing in subsection (2) prevents the court from passing a custodial sentence on the offender if—
- (a) he fails to express his willingness to comply with a requirement which is proposed by the court to be included in a community order and which requires an expression of such willingness, or
- (b) he fails to comply with an order under section 161(2) (pre-sentence drug testing).

153   Length of discretionary custodial sentences: general provision

(1) This section applies where a court passes a custodial sentence other than one fixed by law or imposed under section 224A, 225 or 226

(2) Subject to the provisions listed in subsection (3), the custodial sentence must be for the shortest term (not exceeding the permitted maximum) that in the opinion of the court is commensurate with the seriousness of the offence, or the combination of the offence and one or more offences associated with it.

(3) The provisions referred to in subsection (2) are—
- (a) sections 1(2B) and 1A(5) of the Prevention of Crime Act 1953;
- (b) section 51A(2) of the Firearms Act 1968;
- (c) sections 139(6B), 139A(5B) and 139AA(7) of the Criminal Justice Act 1988;
- (d) sections 110(2) and 111(2) of the Sentencing Act;
- (e) sections 226A(4) and 226B(2) of this Act;
- (f) section 29(4) or (6) of the Violent Crime Reduction Act 2006.

156   Pre-sentence reports and other requirements

(1) In forming any such opinion as is mentioned in section 148(1) or (2)(b), section 152(2) or section 153(2), or in section 1(4)(b) or (c) of the Criminal Justice and Immigration Act 2008 (youth rehabilitation orders with intensive supervision and surveillance or fostering), a court must take into account all such information as is available to it about the circumstances of the offence or (as the case may be) of the offence and the offence or offences associated with it, including any aggravating or mitigating factors.

(2) In forming any such opinion as is mentioned in section 148(2)(a), the court may take into account any information about the offender which is before it.

(3) Subject to subsection (4), a court must obtain and consider a pre-sentence report before—
- (a) in the case of a custodial sentence, forming any such opinion as is mentioned in section 152(2), section 153(2), section 225(1)(b), section 226(1)(b), section 226A(1)(b) or section 226B(1)(b), or
- (b) in the case of a community sentence, forming any such opinion as is mentioned in section 148(1) or (2)(b), or in section 1(4)(b) or (c) of the Criminal Justice and Immigration Act 2008,or any opinion as to the suitability for the offender of the particular requirement or requirements to be imposed by the community order or youth rehabilitation order.

(4) Subsection (3) does not apply if, in the circumstances of the case, the court is of the opinion that it is unnecessary to obtain a pre-sentence report.

(5) In a case where the offender is aged under 18, the court must not form the opinion mentioned in subsection (4) unless—
- (a) there exists a previous pre-sentence report obtained in respect of the offender, and

(b) the court has had regard to the information contained in that report, or, if there is more than one such report, the most recent report.

(6) No custodial sentence or community sentence is invalidated by the failure of a court to obtain and consider a pre-sentence report before forming an opinion referred to in subsection (3), but any court on an appeal against such a sentence—

(a) must, subject to subsection (7), obtain a pre-sentence report if none was obtained by the court below, and

(b) must consider any such report obtained by it or by that court.

(7) Subsection (6)(a) does not apply if the court is of the opinion—

(a) that the court below was justified in forming an opinion that it was unnecessary to obtain a pre-sentence report, or

(b) that, although the court below was not justified in forming that opinion, in the circumstances of the case at the time it is before the court, it is unnecessary to obtain a pre-sentence report.

(8) In a case where the offender is aged under 18, the court must not form the opinion mentioned in subsection (7) unless—

(a) there exists a previous pre-sentence report obtained in respect of the offender, and

(b) the court has had regard to the information contained in that report, or, if there is more than one such report, the most recent report.

(9) References in subsections (1) and (3) to a court forming the opinions mentioned in sections 152(2) and 153(2) include a court forming those opinions for the purposes of section 224A(3).

(10) The reference in subsection (1) to a court forming the opinion mentioned in section 153(2) includes a court forming that opinion for the purposes of section 226A(6) or 226B(4).

157   Additional requirements in case of mentally disordered offender

(1) Subject to subsection (2), in any case where the offender is or appears to be mentally disordered, the court must obtain and consider a medical report before passing a custodial sentence other than one fixed by law.

(2) Subsection (1) does not apply if, in the circumstances of the case, the court is of the opinion that it is unnecessary to obtain a medical report.

(3) Before passing a custodial sentence other than one fixed by law on an offender who is or appears to be mentally disordered, a court must consider—

(a) any information before it which relates to his mental condition (whether given in a medical report, a pre-sentence report or otherwise), and

(b) the likely effect of such a sentence on that condition and on any treatment which may be available for it.

(4) No custodial sentence which is passed in a case to which subsection (1) applies is invalidated by the failure of a court to comply with that subsection, but any court on an appeal against such a sentence—

(a) must obtain a medical report if none was obtained by the court below, and

(b) must consider any such report obtained by it or by that court.

(5) In this section 'mentally disordered', in relation to any person, means suffering from a mental disorder within the meaning of the Mental Health Act 1983 (c. 20).

(6) In this section 'medical report' means a report as to an offender's mental condition made or submitted orally or in writing by a registered medical practitioner who is approved for the purposes of section 12 of the Mental Health Act 1983 by the Secretary of State or by another person by virtue of section 12ZA or 12ZB of that Act as having special experience in the diagnosis or treatment of mental disorder.

(7) Nothing in this section is to be taken to limit the generality of section 156.

158   Meaning of 'pre-sentence report'

(1) In this Part 'pre-sentence report' means a report which—

(a) with a view to assisting the court in determining the most suitable method of dealing with an offender, is made or submitted by an appropriate officer, and

   (b) contains information as to such matters, presented in such manner, as may be prescribed by rules made by the Secretary of State.

   (1A) Subject to any rules made under subsection (1)(b) and to subsection (1B), the court may accept a pre-sentence report given orally in open court.

   (1B) But a pre-sentence report that—

   (a) relates to an offender aged under 18, and

   (b) is required to be obtained and considered before the court forms an opinion mentioned in section 156(3)(a),

must be in writing.

   (2) In subsection (1) 'an appropriate officer' means—

   (a) where the offender is aged 18 or over, an officer of a local probation board or an officer of a provider of probation services, and

   (b) where the offender is aged under 18, an officer of a local probation board, an officer of a provider of probation services, a social worker of a local authority or a member of a youth offending team.

159   Disclosure of pre-sentence reports

   (1) This section applies where the court obtains a pre-sentence report, other than a report given orally in open court.

   (2) Subject to subsections (3) and (4), the court must give a copy of the report—

   (a) to the offender or his legal representative

   (b) if the offender is aged under 18, to any parent or guardian of his who is present in court, and

   (c) to the prosecutor, that is to say, the person having the conduct of the proceedings in respect of the offence.

   (3) If the offender is aged under 18 and it appears to the court that the disclosure to the offender or to any parent or guardian of his of any information contained in the report would be likely to create a risk of significant harm to the offender, a complete copy of the report need not be given to the offender or, as the case may be, to that parent or guardian.

   (4) If the prosecutor is not of a description prescribed by order made by the Secretary of State, a copy of the report need not be given to the prosecutor if the court considers that it would be inappropriate for him to be given it.

   (5) No information obtained by virtue of subsection (2)(c) may be used or disclosed otherwise than for the purpose of—

   (a) determining whether representations as to matters contained in the report need to be made to the court, or

   (b) making such representations to the court.

   (6) In relation to an offender aged under 18 for whom a local authority have parental responsibility and who—

   (a) is in their care, or

   (b) is provided with accommodation by them in the exercise of any social services functions,

references in this section to his parent or guardian are to be read as references to that authority.

   (7) In this section and section 160—

   'harm' has the same meaning as in section 31 of the Children Act 1989 (c. 41);

   'local authority' and 'parental responsibility' have the same meanings as in that Act;

   'social services functions', in relation to a local authority, has the meaning given by section 1A of the Local Authority Social Services Act 1970 (c. 42).

161A   Court's duty to order payment of surcharge

   (1) A court when dealing with a person for one or more offences must also (subject to subsections (2) and (3)) order him to pay a surcharge.

   (2) Subsection (1) does not apply in such cases as may be prescribed by an order made by the Secretary of State.

(3) Where a court dealing with an offender considers—

    (a) that it would be appropriate to make one or more of a compensation order, an unlawful profit order and a slavery and trafficking reparation order, but

    (b) that he has insufficient means to pay both the surcharge and appropriate amounts under such of those orders as it would be appropriate to make,

the court must reduce the surcharge accordingly (if necessary to nil).

(4) For the purposes of this section a court does not 'deal with' a person if it—

    (a) discharges him absolutely, or

    (b) makes an order under the Mental Health Act 1983 in respect of him.

(5) In this section —

'slavery and trafficking reparation order' means an order under section 8 of the Modern Slavery Act 2015, and

'unlawful profit order' means an unlawful profit order under section 4 of the Prevention of Social Housing Fraud Act 2013.

161B   Amount of surcharge

(1) The surcharge payable under section 161A is such amount as the Secretary of State may specify by order.

(2) An order under this section may provide for the amount to depend on—

    (a) the offence or offences committed,

    (b) how the offender is otherwise dealt with (including, where the offender is fined, the amount of the fine),

    (c) the age of the offender.

This is not to be read as limiting section 330(3) (power to make different provision for different purposes etc).

162   Powers to order statement as to offender's financial circumstances

(1) Where an individual has been convicted of an offence, the court may, before sentencing him, make a financial circumstances order with respect to him.

(2) Where a magistrates' court has been notified in accordance with section 12(4) of the Magistrates' Courts Act 1980 (c. 43) that an individual desires to plead guilty without appearing before the court, the court may make a financial circumstances order with respect to him.

(3) In this section 'a financial circumstances order' means, in relation to any individual, an order requiring him to give to the court, within such period as may be specified in the order, such a statement of his assets and other financial circumstances as the court may require.

(4) An individual who without reasonable excuse fails to comply with a financial circumstances order is liable on summary conviction to a fine not exceeding level 3 on the standard scale.

(5) If an individual, in furnishing any statement in pursuance of a financial circumstances order—

    (a) makes a statement which he knows to be false in a material particular,

    (b) recklessly furnishes a statement which is false in a material particular, or

    (c) knowingly fails to disclose any material fact,

he is liable on summary conviction to a fine not exceeding level 4 on the standard scale.

(6) Proceedings in respect of an offence under subsection (5) may, notwithstanding anything in section 127(1) of the Magistrates' Courts Act 1980 (c. 43) (limitation of time), be commenced at any time within two years from the date of the commission of the offence or within six months from its first discovery by the prosecutor, whichever period expires the earlier.

163   General power of Crown Court to fine offender convicted on indictment

Where a person is convicted on indictment of any offence, other than an offence for which the sentence is fixed by law or falls to be imposed under section 110(2)or 111(2) of the Sentencing Act or under section 224A, 225(2) or 226(2) of this Act, the court, if not precluded from sentencing an offender by its exercise of some other power, may impose a fine instead of or in addition to dealing with him in any other way in which the court has power to deal with him, subject however to any enactment requiring the offender to be dealt with in a particular way.

164   Fixing of fines

(1) Before fixing the amount of any fine to be imposed on an offender who is an individual, a court must inquire into his financial circumstances.

(2) The amount of any fine fixed by a court must be such as, in the opinion of the court, reflects the seriousness of the offence.

(3) In fixing the amount of any fine to be imposed on an offender (whether an individual or other person), a court must take into account the circumstances of the case including, among other things, the financial circumstances of the offender so far as they are known, or appear, to the court.

(4) Subsection (3) applies whether taking into account the financial circumstances of the offender has the effect of increasing or reducing the amount of the fine.

(4A) In applying subsection (3), a court must not reduce the amount of a fine on account of any surcharge it orders the offender to pay under section 161A, except to the extent that he has insufficient means to pay both.

(5) Where—

    (a) an offender has been convicted in his absence in pursuance of section 11 or 12 of the Magistrates' Courts Act 1980 (c. 43) (non-appearance of accused), or

    (aa) an offender has been convicted in the offender's absence in proceedings conducted in accordance with section 16A of the Magistrates' Courts Act 1980 (trial by single justice on the papers),

    (b) an offender—

        (i) has failed to furnish a statement of his financial circumstances in response to a request which is an official request for the purposes of section 20A of the Criminal Justice Act 1991 (c.53) (offence of making false statement as to financial circumstances),

        (ii) has failed to comply with an order under section 162(1), or

        (iii) has otherwise failed to co-operate with the court in its inquiry into his financial circumstances,

and the court considers that it has insufficient information to make a proper determination of the financial circumstances of the offender, it may make such determination as it thinks fit.

165   Remission of fines

(1) This section applies where a court has, in fixing the amount of a fine, determined the offender's financial circumstances under section 164(5).

(2) If, on subsequently inquiring into the offender's financial circumstances, the court is satisfied that had it had the results of that inquiry when sentencing the offender it would—

    (a) have fixed a smaller amount, or

    (b) not have fined him,

it may remit the whole or part of the fine.

(3) Where under this section the court remits the whole or part of a fine after a term of imprisonment has been fixed under section 139 of the Sentencing Act (powers of Crown Court in relation to fines) or section 82(5) of the Magistrates' Courts Act 1980 (magistrates' powers in relation to default) it must reduce the term by the corresponding proportion.

(4) In calculating any reduction required by subsection (3), any fraction of a day is to be ignored.

(5) Where—

    (a) under this section the court remits the whole or part of a fine, and

    (b) the offender was ordered under section 161A to pay a surcharge the amount of which was set by reference to the amount of the fine,

the court must determine how much the surcharge would have been if the fine had not included the amount remitted, and remit the balance of the surcharge.

166 Savings for powers to mitigate sentences and deal appropriately with mentally disordered offenders

(1) Nothing in—
  (a) section 148 (imposing community sentences),
  (b) section 152, 153 or 157 (imposing custodial sentences),
  (c) section 156 (pre-sentence reports and other requirements),
  (d) section 164 (fixing of fines),
  (e) paragraph 3 of Schedule 1 to the Criminal Justice and Immigration Act 2008 (youth rehabilitation order with intensive supervision and surveillance), or
  (f) paragraph 4 of Schedule 1 to that Act (youth rehabilitation order with fostering),
prevents a court from mitigating an offender's sentence by taking into account any such matters as, in the opinion of the court, are relevant in mitigation of sentence.

(2) Section 152(2) does not prevent a court, after taking into account such matters, from passing a community sentence even though it is of the opinion that the offence, or the combination of the offence and one or more offences associated with it, was so serious that a community sentence could not normally be justified for the offence.

(3) Nothing in the sections mentioned in subsection (1)(a) to (f) prevents a court—
  (a) from mitigating any penalty included in an offender's sentence by taking into account any other penalty included in that sentence, and
  (b) in the case of an offender who is convicted of one or more other offences, from mitigating his sentence by applying any rule of law as to the totality of sentences.

(4) Subsections (2) and (3) are without prejudice to the generality of subsection (1).

(5) Nothing in the sections mentioned in subsection (1)(a) to (f) is to be taken—
  (a) as requiring a court to pass a custodial sentence, or any particular custodial sentence, on a mentally disordered offender, or
  (b) as restricting any power (whether under the Mental Health Act 1983 (c. 20) or otherwise) which enables a court to deal with such an offender in the manner it considers to be most appropriate in all the circumstances.

(6) In subsection (5) 'mentally disordered', in relation to a person, means suffering from a mental disorder within the meaning of the Mental Health Act 1983.

174 Duty to give reasons for and to explain effect of sentence

(1) A court passing sentence on an offender has the duties in subsections (2) and (3).

(2) The court must state in open court, in ordinary language and in general terms, the court's reasons for deciding on the sentence.

(3) The court must explain to the offender in ordinary language—
  (a) the effect of the sentence,
  (b) the effects of non-compliance with any order that the offender is required to comply with and that forms part of the sentence,
  (c) any power of the court to vary or review any order that forms part of the sentence, and
  (d) the effects of failure to pay a fine, if the sentence consists of or includes a fine.

(4) Criminal Procedure Rules may—
  (a) prescribe cases in which either duty does not apply, and
  (b) make provision about how an explanation under subsection (3) is to be given.

(5) Subsections (6) to (8) are particular duties of the court in complying with the duty in subsection (2).

(6) The court must identify any definitive sentencing guidelines relevant to the offender's case and—
  (a) explain how the court discharged any duty imposed on it by section 125 of the Coroners and Justice Act 2009 (duty to follow guidelines unless satisfied it would be contrary to the interests of justice to do so);
  (b) where the court was satisfied it would be contrary to the interests of justice to follow the guidelines, state why.

(7) Where, as a result of taking into account any matter referred to in section 144(1) (guilty pleas), the court imposes a punishment on the offender which is less severe than the punishment it would otherwise have imposed, the court must state that fact.

(8) Where the offender is under 18 and the court imposes a sentence that may only be imposed in the offender's case if the court is of the opinion mentioned in—

    (a) section 1(4)(a) to (c) of the Criminal Justice and Immigration Act 2008 and section 148(1) of this Act (youth rehabilitation order with intensive supervision and surveillance or with fostering), or

    (b) section 152(2) of this Act (discretionary custodial sentence),

the court must state why it is of that opinion.

(9) In this section 'definitive sentencing guidelines' means sentencing guidelines issued by the Sentencing Council for England and Wales under section 120 of the Coroners and Justice Act 2009 as definitive guidelines, as revised by any subsequent guidelines so issued.

175 Duty to publish information about sentencing

In section 95 of the Criminal Justice Act 1991 (c. 53) (information for financial and other purposes) in subsection (1)before the 'or' at the end of paragraph (a) there is inserted—

    '(aa) enabling such persons to become aware of the relative effectiveness of different sentences—

        (i) in preventing re-offending, and

        (ii) in promoting public confidence in the criminal justice system;'.

176 Interpretation of Chapter 1

In this Chapter—

    'sentence' and 'sentencing' are to be read in accordance with section 142(3);

    'youth rehabilitation order' has the meaning given by section 1(1) of the Criminal Justice and Immigration Act 2008;

    'youth rehabilitation order with fostering' has the meaning given by paragraph 4 of Schedule 1 to that Act;

    'youth rehabilitation order with intensive supervision and surveillance' has the meaning given by paragraph 3 of Schedule 1 to that Act.

177 Community orders

(1) Where a person aged 18 or over is convicted of an offence, the court by or before which he is convicted may make an order (in this Part referred to as a 'community order') imposing on him any one or more of the following requirements—

    (a) an unpaid work requirement (as defined by section 199),

    (aa) a rehabilitation activity requirement (as defined by section 200A),

    (d) a prohibited activity requirement (as defined by section 203),

    (e) a curfew requirement (as defined by section 204),

    (f) an exclusion requirement (as defined by section 205),

    (g) a residence requirement (as defined by section 206),

    (ga) a foreign travel prohibition requirement (as defined by section 206A),

    (h) a mental health treatment requirement (as defined by section 207),

    (i) a drug rehabilitation requirement (as defined by section 209),

    (j) an alcohol treatment requirement (as defined by section 212),

    (l) in a case where the offender is aged under 25, an attendance centre requirement (as defined by section 214).

(2) Subsection (1) has effect subject to sections 150 and 218 and to the following provisions of Chapter 4 relating to particular requirements—

    (a) section 199(3) (unpaid work requirement),

    (c) section 202(4) and (5) (programme requirement),

    (d) section 203(2) (prohibited activity requirement),

    (e) section 207(3) (mental health treatment requirement),

(f) section 209(2) (drug rehabilitation requirement), and

(g) section 212(2) and (3) (alcohol treatment requirement).

(2A) Where the court makes a community order, the court must—

(a) include in the order at least one requirement imposed for the purpose of punishment, or

(b) impose a fine for the offence in respect of which the community order is made, or

(c) comply with both of paragraphs (a) and (b).

(2B) Subsection (2A) does not apply where there are exceptional circumstances which—

(a) relate to the offence or to the offender,

(b) would make it unjust in all the circumstances for the court to comply with subsection (2A)(a) in the particular case, and

(c) would make it unjust in all the circumstances for the court to impose a fine for the offence concerned.

(3) Where the court makes a community order imposing a curfew requirement or an exclusion requirement, the court must also impose an electronic monitoring requirement (as defined by section 215) unless—

(a) it is prevented from doing so by section 215(2) or 218(4), or

(b) in the particular circumstances of the case, it considers it inappropriate to do so.

(4) Where the court makes a community order imposing an unpaid work requirement, a rehabilitation activity requirement, a programme requirement, a prohibited activity requirement, a residence requirement, a foreign travel prohibition requirement, a mental health treatment requirement, a drug rehabilitation requirement, an alcohol treatment requirement or an attendance centre requirement, the court may also impose an electronic monitoring requirement unless prevented from doing so by section 215(2) or 218(4).

(5) A community order must specify a date ('the end date'), not more than three years after the date of the order, by which all the requirements in it must have been complied with

(5A) If a community order imposes two or more different requirements falling within subsection (1), the order may also specify a date by which each of those requirements must have been complied with; and the last of those dates must be the same as the end date.

(5B) Subject to section 200(3) (duration of community order imposing unpaid work requirement), a community order ceases to be in force on the end date.

(6) Before making a community order imposing two or more different requirements falling within subsection (1), the court must consider whether, in the circumstances of the case, the requirements are compatible with each other.

178   Power to provide for court review of community orders

(1) The Secretary of State may by order—

(a) enable or require a court making a community order to provide for the community order to be reviewed periodically by that or another court,

(b) enable a court to amend a community order so as to include or remove a provision for review by a court, and

(c) make provision as to the timing and conduct of reviews and as to the powers of the court on a review.

(2) An order under this section may, in particular, make provision in relation to community orders corresponding to any provision made by sections 191 and 192 in relation to suspended sentence orders.

(3) An order under this section may repeal or amend any provision of this Part.

179   Breach, revocation or amendment of community order

Schedule 8(which relates to failures to comply with the requirements of community orders and to the revocation or amendment of such orders) shall have effect.

. . .

189 Suspended sentences of imprisonment

(1) If a court passes a sentence of imprisonment or, in the case of a person aged at least 18 but under 21, a sentence of detention in a young offender institution for a term of least 14 days but not more than 2 years, it may make an order providing that the sentence of imprisonment or detention in a young offender institution is not to take effect unless—

    (a) during a period specified in the order for the purposes of this paragraph ('the operational period') the offender commits another offence in the United Kingdom (whether or not punishable with imprisonment), and

    (b) a court having power to do so subsequently orders under paragraph 8 of Schedule 12 that the original sentence is to take effect.

(1A) An order under subsection (1) may also provide that the offender must comply during a period specified in the order for the purposes of this subsection ('the supervision period') with one or more requirements falling within section 190(1) and specified in the order.

(1B) Where an order under subsection (1) contains provision under subsection (1A), it must provide that the sentence of imprisonment or detention in a young offender institution will also take effect if—

    (a) during the supervision period the offender fails to comply with a requirement imposed under subsection (1A), and

    (b) a court having power to do so subsequently orders under paragraph 8 of Schedule 12 that the original sentence is to take effect.

(2) Where two or more sentences imposed on the same occasion are to be served consecutively, the power conferred by subsection (1) is not exercisable in relation to any of them unless the aggregate of the terms of the sentences does not exceed 2 years.

(3) The supervision period (if any) and the operational period must each be a period of not less than six months and not more than two years beginning with the date of the order.

(4) Where an order under subsection (1) imposes one or more community requirements, the supervision period must not end later than the operational period.

(5) A court which passes a suspended sentence on any person for an offence may not impose a community sentence in his case in respect of that offence or any other offence of which he is convicted by or before the court or for which he is dealt with by the court.

(6) Subject to any provision to the contrary contained in the Criminal Justice Act 1967 (c. 80), the Sentencing Act or any other enactment passed or instrument made under any enactment after 31st December 1967, a suspended sentence which has not taken effect under paragraph 8 of Schedule 12 is to be treated as a sentence of imprisonment or in the case of a person aged at least 18 but under 21, a sentence of detention in a young offender institution for the purposes of all enactments and instruments made under enactments.

(7) In this Part—

    (a) 'suspended sentence order' means an order under subsection (1),

    (b) 'suspended sentence' means a sentence to which a suspended sentence order relates, and

    (c) 'community requirement', in relation to a suspended sentence order, means a requirement imposed under subsection (1A)

190 Imposition of requirements by suspended sentence order

(1) The requirements falling within this subsection are—

    (a) an unpaid work requirement (as defined by section 199),

    (aa) a rehabilitation activity requirement (as defined by section 200A),

    (c) a programme requirement (as defined by section 202),

    (d) a prohibited activity requirement (as defined by section 203),

    (e) a curfew requirement (as defined by section 204),

    (f) an exclusion requirement (as defined by section 205),

    (g) a residence requirement (as defined by section 206),

(ga) a foreign travel prohibition requirement (as defined by section 206A),

(h) a mental health treatment requirement (as defined by section 207),

(i) a drug rehabilitation requirement (as defined by section 209),

(j) an alcohol treatment requirement (as defined by section 212),

(l) in a case where the offender is aged under 25, an attendance centre requirement (as defined by section 214).

(2) Section 189(1A) has effect subject to section 218 and to the following provisions of Chapter 4 relating to particular requirements—

(a) section 199(3) (unpaid work requirement),

(d) section 203(2) (prohibited activity requirement),

(e) section 207(3) (mental health treatment requirement),

(f) section 209(2) (drug rehabilitation requirement), and

(g) section 212(2) and (3) (alcohol treatment requirement).

(3) Where the court makes a suspended sentence order imposing a curfew requirement or an exclusion requirement, it must also impose an electronic monitoring requirement (as defined by section 215) unless—

(a) the court is prevented from doing so by section 215(2) or 218(4), or

(b) in the particular circumstances of the case, it considers it inappropriate to do so.

(4) Where the court makes a suspended sentence order imposing an unpaid work requirement, a rehabilitation activity requirement, a programme requirement, a prohibited activity requirement, a residence requirement, a foreign travel prohibition requirement, a mental health treatment requirement, a drug rehabilitation requirement, an alcohol treatment requirement or an attendance centre requirement, the court may also impose an electronic monitoring requirement unless the court is prevented from doing so by section 215(2) or 218(4).

(5) Before making a suspended sentence order imposing two or more different requirements falling within subsection (1), the court must consider whether, in the circumstances of the case, the requirements are compatible with each other.

191 Power to provide for review of suspended sentence order

(1) A suspended sentence order that imposes one or more community requirements may—

(a) provide for the order to be reviewed periodically at specified intervals,

(b) provide for each review to be made, subject to section 192(4), at a hearing held for the purpose by the court responsible for the order (a 'review hearing'),

(c) require the offender to attend each review hearing, and

(d) provide for an officer of a provider of probation services to make to the court responsible for the order, before each review, a report on the offender's progress in complying with the community requirements of the order.

(2) Subsection (1) does not apply in the case of an order imposing a drug rehabilitation requirement (provision for such a requirement to be subject to review being made by section 210).

(3) In this section references to the court responsible for a suspended sentence order are references—

(a) where a court is specified in the order in accordance with subsection (4), to that court;

(b) in any other case, to the court by which the order is made.

(4) Where the area specified in a suspended sentence order made by a magistrates' court is not the area for which the court acts, the court may, if it thinks fit, include in the order provision specifying for the purpose of subsection (3) a magistrates' court which acts for the area specified in the order.

(5) Where a suspended sentence order has been made on an appeal brought from the Crown Court or from the criminal division of the Court of Appeal, it is to be taken for the purposes of subsection (3)(b) to have been made by the Crown Court.

192 Periodic reviews of suspended sentence order

(1) At a review hearing (within the meaning of subsection (1) of section 191) the court may, after considering the officer's report referred to in that subsection ('the review officer's report'), amend the

community requirements of the suspended sentence order, or any provision of the order which relates to those requirements.

(2) The court—

    (a) may not amend the community requirements of the order so as to impose a requirement of a different kind unless the offender expresses his willingness to comply with that requirement,

    (b) may not amend a mental health treatment requirement, a drug rehabilitation requirement or an alcohol treatment requirement unless the offender expresses his willingness to comply with the requirement as amended,

    (c) may amend the supervision period only if the period as amended complies with section 189(3) and (4),

    (d) may not amend the operational period of the suspended sentence, and

    (e) except with the consent of the offender, may not amend the order while an appeal against the order is pending.

(3) For the purposes of subsection (2)(a)—

    (a) a community requirement falling within any paragraph of section 190(1) is of the same kind as any other community requirement falling within that paragraph, and

    (b) an electronic monitoring requirement is a community requirement of the same kind as any requirement falling within section 190(1) to which it relates.

(4) If before a review hearing is held at any review the court, after considering the review officer's report, is of the opinion that the offender's progress in complying with the community requirements of the order is satisfactory, it may order that no review hearing is to be held at that review; and if before a review hearing is held at any review, or at a review hearing, the court, after considering that report, is of that opinion, it may amend the suspended sentence order so as to provide for each subsequent review to be held without a hearing.

(5) If at a review held without a hearing the court, after considering the review officer's report, is of the opinion that the offender's progress under the order is no longer satisfactory, the court may require the offender to attend a hearing of the court at a specified time and place.

(6) If at a review hearing the court is of the opinion that the offender has without reasonable excuse failed to comply with any of the community requirements of the order, the court may adjourn the hearing for the purpose of dealing with the case under paragraph 8 of Schedule 12.

(7) At a review hearing the court may amend the suspended sentence order so as to vary the intervals specified under section 191(1).

(8) In this section any reference to the court, in relation to a review without a hearing, is to be read—

    (a) in the case of the Crown Court, as a reference to a judge of the court, and

    (b) in the case of a magistrates' court, as a reference to a justice of the peace.

193 Breach, revocation or amendment of suspended sentence order, and effect of further conviction

Schedule 12 (which relates to the breach, revocation or amendment of the community requirements of suspended sentence orders, and to the effect of any further conviction) shall have effect.

194 Transfer of suspended sentence orders to Scotland or Northern Ireland

Schedule 13 (transfer of suspended sentence orders to Scotland or Northern Ireland) shall have effect.

195 Interpretation of Chapter 3

In this Chapter—

'the operational period', in relation to a suspended sentence, has the meaning given by section 189(1)(a);

'sentence of imprisonment' does not include a committal for contempt of court or any kindred offence;

'the supervision period', in relation to a suspended sentence, has the meaning given by section 189(1A).

196 Meaning of 'relevant order etc'

(1) In this Chapter 'relevant order' means—

    (a) a community order, or

    (c) a suspended sentence order

(1A) In this Chapter 'suspended sentence order' means a suspended sentence order that imposes one or more community requirements.

197 Meaning of 'the responsible officer'

(1) For the purposes of this Part, 'the responsible officer', in relation to an offender to whom a relevant order relates, means the person who is for the time being responsible for discharging the functions conferred by this Part on the responsible officer in accordance with arrangements made by the Secretary of State.

(2) The responsible officer must be—

    (a) an officer of a provider of probation services, or

    (b) a person responsible for monitoring the offender in accordance with an electronic monitoring requirement imposed by the relevant order.

198 Duties of responsible officer

(1) Where a relevant order has effect, it is the duty of the responsible officer—

    (a) to make any arrangements that are necessary in connection with the requirements imposed by the order, and

    (b) to promote the offender's compliance with those requirements.

199 Unpaid work requirement

(1) In this Part 'unpaid work requirement', in relation to a relevant order, means a requirement that the offender must perform unpaid work in accordance with section 200.

(2) The number of hours which a person may be required to work under an unpaid work requirement must be specified in the relevant order and must be in the aggregate—

    (a) not less than 40, and

    (b) not more than 300.

(3) A court may not impose an unpaid work requirement in respect of an offender unless after hearing (if the courts thinks necessary) an officer of a local probation board or an officer of a provider of probation services, the court is satisfied that the offender is a suitable person to perform work under such a requirement.

(5) Where the court makes relevant orders in respect of two or more offences of which the offender has been convicted on the same occasion and includes unpaid work requirements in each of them, the court may direct that the hours of work specified in any of those requirements is to be concurrent with or additional to those specified in any other of those orders, but so that the total number of hours which are not concurrent does not exceed the maximum specified in subsection (2)(b).

200 Obligations of person subject to unpaid work requirement

(1) An offender in respect of whom an unpaid work requirement of a relevant order is in force must perform for the number of hours specified in the order such work at such times as he may be instructed by the responsible officer.

(2) Subject to paragraph 20 of Schedule 8 and paragraph 18 of Schedule 12 (power to extend order), the work required to be performed under an unpaid work requirement of a community order or a suspended sentence order must be performed during a period of twelve months.

(3) Unless revoked, a community order imposing an unpaid work requirement remains in force until the offender has worked under it for the number of hours specified in it.

(4) Where an unpaid work requirement is imposed by a suspended sentence order, the supervision period as defined by section 189(1A) continues until the offender has worked under the order for the number of hours specified in the order, but does not continue beyond the end of the operational period as defined by section 189(1)(a).

200A   Rehabilitation activity requirement

(1) In this Part 'rehabilitation activity requirement', in relation to a relevant order, means a requirement that, during the relevant period, the offender must comply with any instructions given by the responsible officer to attend appointments or participate in activities or both.

(2) A relevant order imposing a rehabilitation activity requirement must specify the maximum number of days for which the offender may be instructed to participate in activities.

(3) Any instructions given by the responsible officer must be given with a view to promoting the offender's rehabilitation; but this does not prevent the responsible officer giving instructions with a view to other purposes in addition to rehabilitation.

(4) The responsible officer may instruct the offender to attend appointments with the responsible officer or with someone else.

(5) The responsible officer, when instructing the offender to participate in activities, may require the offender to—

    (a) participate in specified activities and, while doing so, comply with instructions given by the person in charge of the activities, or

    (b) go to a specified place and, while there, comply with any instructions given by the person in charge of the place.

(6) The references in subsection (5)(a) and (b) to instructions given by a person include instructions given by anyone acting under the person's authority.

(7) The activities that responsible officers may instruct offenders to participate in include—

    (a) activities forming an accredited programme (see section 202(2));

    (b) activities whose purpose is reparative, such as restorative justice activities.

(8) For the purposes of subsection (7)(b) an activity is a restorative justice activity if—

    (a) the participants consist of, or include, the offender and one or more of the victims,

    (b) the aim of the activity is to maximise the offender's awareness of the impact of the offending concerned on the victims, and

    (c) the activity gives a victim or victims an opportunity to talk about, or by other means express experience of, the offending and its impact.

(9) In subsection (8) 'victim' means a victim of, or other person affected by, the offending concerned.

(10) Where compliance with an instruction would require the co-operation of a person other than the offender, the responsible officer may give the instruction only if that person agrees.

(11) In this section 'the relevant period' means—

    (a) in relation to a community order, the period for which the community order remains in force, and

    (b) in relation to a suspended sentence order, the supervision period as defined by section 189(1A).

202   Programme requirement

(1) In this Part 'programme requirement', in relation to a relevant order, means a requirement that the offender must participate in accordance with this section in an accredited programme on the number of days specified in the order.

(2) In this Part 'accredited programme' means a programme that is for the time being accredited by the Secretary of State for the purposes of this section

(3) In this section—

    (a) 'programme' means a systematic set of activities, and

(6) A programme requirement operates to require the offender—

    (a) in accordance with instructions given by the responsible officer, to participate in the accredited programme that is from time to time specified by the responsible officer at the place that is so specified on the number of days specified in the order, and

    (b) while at that place, to comply with instructions given by, or under the authority of, the person in charge of the programme.

203   Prohibited activity requirement

(1) In this Part 'prohibited activity requirement', in relation to a relevant order, means a requirement that the offender must refrain from participating in activities specified in the order—

(a) on a day or days so specified, or

(b) during a period so specified.

(2) A court may not include a prohibited activity requirement in a relevant order unless it has consulted an officer of a local probation board or an officer of a provider of probation services.

(3) The requirements that may by virtue of this section be included in a relevant order include a requirement that the offender does not possess, use or carry a firearm within the meaning of the Firearms Act 1968 (c. 27).

204   Curfew requirement

(1) In this Part 'curfew requirement', in relation to a relevant order, means a requirement that the offender must remain, for periods specified in the relevant order, at a place so specified.

(2) A relevant order imposing a curfew requirement may specify different places or different periods for different days, but may not specify periods which amount to less than two hours or more than sixteen hours in any day.

(3) A community order or suspended sentence order which imposes a curfew requirement may not specify periods which fall outside the period of twelve months beginning with the day on which it is made.

(6) Before making a relevant order imposing a curfew requirement, the court must obtain and consider information about the place proposed to be specified in the order (including information as to the attitude of persons likely to be affected by the enforced presence there of the offender).

205   Exclusion requirement

(1) In this Part 'exclusion requirement', in relation to a relevant order, means a provision prohibiting the offender from entering a place specified in the order for a period so specified.

(2) Where the relevant order is a community order, the period specified must not be more than two years.

(3) An exclusion requirement—

(a) may provide for the prohibition to operate only during the periods specified in the order, and

(b) may specify different places for different periods or days.

(4) In this section 'place' includes an area.

206   Residence requirement

(1) In this Part, 'residence requirement', in relation to a community order or a suspended sentence order, means a requirement that, during a period specified in the relevant order, the offender must reside at a place specified in the order.

(2) If the order so provides, a residence requirement does not prohibit the offender from residing, with the prior approval of the responsible officer, at a place other than that specified in the order.

(3) Before making a community order or suspended sentence order containing a residence requirement, the court must consider the home surroundings of the offender.

(4) A court may not specify a hostel or other institution as the place where an offender must reside, except on the recommendation of an officer of a local probation board or an officer of a provider of probation services.

206A   Foreign travel prohibition requirement

(1) In this Part 'foreign travel prohibition requirement', in relation to a relevant order, means a requirement prohibiting the offender from travelling, on a day or days specified in the order, or for a period so specified—

(a) to any country or territory outside the British Islands specified or described in the order,

(b) to any country or territory outside the British Islands other than a country or territory specified or described in the order, or

(c) to any country or territory outside the British Islands.

(2) A day specified under subsection (1) may not fall outside the period of 12 months beginning with the day on which the relevant order is made.

(3) A period specified under that subsection may not exceed 12 months beginning with the day on which the relevant order is made.

207   **Mental health treatment requirement**

(1) In this Part, 'mental health treatment requirement', in relation to a community order or suspended sentence order, means a requirement that the offender must submit, during a period or periods specified in the order, to treatment by or under the direction of a registered medical practitioner or a registered psychologist (or both, for different periods) with a view to the improvement of the offender's mental condition.

(2) The treatment required must be such one of the following kinds of treatment as may be specified in the relevant order—

(a) treatment as a resident patient in a care home within the meaning of the Care Standards Act 2000 (c. 14) an independent hospital or a hospital within the meaning of the Mental Health Act 1983 (c. 20), but not in hospital premises where high security psychiatric services within the meaning of that Act are provided;

(b) treatment as a non-resident patient at such institution or place as may be specified in the order;

(c) treatment by or under the direction of such registered medical practitioner or registered psychologist (or both) as may be so specified;

but the nature of the treatment is not to be specified in the order except as mentioned in paragraph (a), (b) or (c).

(3) A court may not by virtue of this section include a mental health treatment requirement in a relevant order unless—

(a) the court is satisfied that the mental condition of the offender—

(i) is such as requires and may be susceptible to treatment, but

(ii) is not such as to warrant the making of a hospital order or guardianship order within the meaning of the Mental Health Act 1983;

(b) the court is also satisfied that arrangements have been or can be made for the treatment intended to be specified in the order (including arrangements for the reception of the offender where he is to be required to submit to treatment as a resident patient); and

(c) the offender has expressed his willingness to comply with such a requirement.

(4) While the offender is under treatment as a resident patient in pursuance of a mental health requirement of a relevant order, his responsible officer shall carry out the supervision of the offender to such extent only as may be necessary for the purpose of the revocation or amendment of the order.

(4A) In subsection (2) 'independent hospital'—

(a) in relation to England, means a hospital as defined by section 275 of the National Health Service Act 2006 that is not a health service hospital as defined by that section; and

(b) in relation to Wales, has the same meaning as in the Care Standards Act 2000.

(6) In this section and section 208, 'registered psychologist' means a person registered in the part of the register maintained under the Health and Social Work Professions Order 2001 which relates to practitioner psychologists.

208   **Mental health treatment at place other than that specified in order**

(1) Where the medical practitioner or registered psychologist by whom or under whose direction an offender is being treated for his mental condition in pursuance of a mental health treatment requirement is of the opinion that part of the treatment can be better or more conveniently given in or at an institution or place which—

(a) is not specified in the relevant order, and

(b) is one in or at which the treatment of the offender will be given by or under the direction of a registered medical practitioner or registered psychologist,

he may, with the consent of the offender, make arrangements for him to be treated accordingly.

(2) Such arrangements as are mentioned in subsection (1) may provide for the offender to receive part of his treatment as a resident patient in an institution or place notwithstanding that the institution or place is not one which could have been specified for that purpose in the relevant order.

(3) Where any such arrangements as are mentioned in subsection (1) are made for the treatment of an offender—

(a) the medical practitioner or registered psychologist by whom the arrangements are made shall give notice in writing to the offender's responsible officer, specifying the institution or place in or at which the treatment is to be carried out; and

(b) the treatment provided for by the arrangements shall be deemed to be treatment to which he is required to submit in pursuance of the relevant order.

209 Drug rehabilitation requirement

(1) In this Part 'drug rehabilitation requirement', in relation to a community order or suspended sentence order, means a requirement that during a period specified in the order ('the treatment and testing period') the offender—

(a) must submit to treatment by or under the direction of a specified person having the necessary qualifications or experience with a view to the reduction or elimination of the offender's dependency on or propensity to misuse drugs, and

(b) for the purpose of ascertaining whether he has any drug in his body during that period, must provide samples of such description as may be so determined, at such times or in such circumstances as may (subject to the provisions of the order) be determined by the responsible officer or by the person specified as the person by or under whose direction the treatment is to be provided.

(2) A court may not impose a drug rehabilitation requirement unless—

(a) it is satisfied—

(i) that the offender is dependent on, or has a propensity to misuse, drugs, and

(ii) that his dependency or propensity is such as requires and may be susceptible to treatment,

(b) it is also satisfied that arrangements have been or can be made for the treatment intended to be specified in the order (including arrangements for the reception of the offender where he is to be required to submit to treatment as a resident),

(c) the requirement has been recommended to the court as being suitable or the offender by an officer of a local probation board or an officer of a provider of probation services, and

(d) the offender expresses his willingness to comply with the requirement.

(4) The required treatment for any particular period must be—

(a) treatment as a resident in such institution or place as may be specified in the order, or

(b) treatment as a non-resident in or at such institution or place, and at such intervals, as may be so specified;

but the nature of the treatment is not to be specified in the order except as mentioned in paragraph (a) or (b) above.

(5) The function of making a determination as to the provision of samples under provision included in the community order or suspended sentence order by virtue of subsection (1)(b) is to be exercised in accordance with guidance given from time to time by the Secretary of State.

(6) A community order or suspended sentence order imposing a drug rehabilitation requirement must provide that the results of tests carried out on any samples provided by the offender in pursuance of the requirement to a person other than the responsible officer are to be communicated to the responsible officer.

(7) In this section 'drug' means a controlled drug as defined by section 2 of the Misuse of Drugs Act 1971 (c. 38).

210   Drug rehabilitation requirement: provision for review by court

(1)   A community order or suspended sentence order imposing a drug rehabilitation requirement may (and must if the treatment and testing period is more than 12 months)—

(a)   provide for the requirement to be reviewed periodically at intervals of not less than one month,

(b)   provide for each review of the requirement to be made, subject to section 211(6), at a hearing held for the purpose by the court responsible for the order (a 'review hearing'),

(c)   require the offender to attend each review hearing,

(d)   provide for an officer of a provider of probation services to make to the court responsible for the order, before each review, a report in writing on the offender's progress under the requirement, and

(e)   provide for each such report to include the test results communicated to the responsible officer under section 209(6) or otherwise and the views of the treatment provider as to the treatment and testing of the offender.

(2)   In this section references to the court responsible for a community order or suspended sentence order imposing a drug rehabilitation requirement are references—

(a)   where a court is specified in the order in accordance with subsection (3), to that court;

(b)   in any other case, to the court by which the order is made.

(3)   Where the area specified in a community order or suspended sentence order which is made by a magistrates' court and imposes a drug rehabilitation requirement is not the area for which the court acts, the court may, if it thinks fit, include in the order provision specifying for the purposes of subsection (2) a magistrates' court which acts for the area specified in the order.

(4)   Where a community order or suspended sentence order imposing a drug rehabilitation requirement has been made on an appeal brought from the Crown Court or from the criminal division of the Court of Appeal, for the purposes of subsection (2)(b) it shall be taken to have been made by the Crown Court.

211   Periodic review of drug rehabilitation requirement

(1)   At a review hearing (within the meaning given by subsection (1) of section 210) the court may, after considering the officer's report referred to in that subsection, amend the community order or suspended sentence order, so far as it relates to the drug rehabilitation requirement.

(2)   The court—

(a)   may not amend the drug rehabilitation requirement unless the offender expresses his willingness to comply with the requirement as amended, and

(c)   except with the consent of the offender, may not amend any requirement or provision of the order while an appeal against the order is pending.

(3)   If the offender fails to express his willingness to comply with the drug rehabilitation requirement as proposed to be amended by the court, the court may—

(a)   revoke the community order, or the suspended sentence order and the suspended sentence to which it relates, and

(b)   deal with him, for the offence in respect of which the order was made, in any way in which he could have been dealt with for that offence by the court which made the order if the order had not been made.

(4)   In dealing with the offender under subsection (3)(b), the court—

(a)   shall take into account the extent to which the offender has complied with the requirements of the order, and

(b)   may impose a custodial sentence (where the order was made in respect of an offence punishable with such a sentence) notwithstanding anything in section 152(2).

(6)   If at a review hearing (as defined by section 210(1)(b)) the court, after considering the officer's report, is of the opinion that the offender's progress under the requirement is satisfactory, the court may so amend the order as to provide for each subsequent review to be made by the court without a hearing.

(7) If at a review without a hearing the court, after considering the officer's report, is of the opinion that the offender's progress under the requirement is no longer satisfactory, the court may require the offender to attend a hearing of the court at a specified time and place.

(8) At that hearing the court, after considering that report, may—

(a) exercise the powers conferred by this section as if the hearing were a review hearing, and

(b) so amend the order as to provide for each subsequent review to be made at a review hearing.

(9) In this section any reference to the court, in relation to a review without a hearing, is to be read—

(a) in the case of the Crown Court, as a reference to a judge of the court;

(b) in the case of a magistrates' court, as a reference to a justice of the peace.

212 Alcohol treatment requirement

(1) In this Part 'alcohol treatment requirement', in relation to a community order or suspended sentence order, means a requirement that the offender must submit during a period specified in the order to treatment by or under the direction of a specified person having the necessary qualifications or experience with a view to the reduction or elimination of the offender's dependency on alcohol.

(2) A court may not impose an alcohol treatment requirement in respect of an offender unless it is satisfied—

(a) that he is dependent on alcohol,

(b) that his dependency is such as requires and may be susceptible to treatment, and

(c) that arrangements have been or can be made for the treatment intended to be specified in the order (including arrangements for the reception of the offender where he is to be required to submit to treatment as a resident).

(3) A court may not impose an alcohol treatment requirement unless the offender expresses his willingness to comply with its requirements.

(5) The treatment required by an alcohol treatment requirement for any particular period must be—

(a) treatment as a resident in such institution or place as may be specified in the order,

(b) treatment as a non-resident in or at such institution or place, and at such intervals, as may be so specified, or

(c) treatment by or under the direction of such person having the necessary qualification or experience as may be so specified;

but the nature of the treatment shall not be specified in the order except as mentioned in paragraph (a), (b) or (c) above.

214 Attendance centre requirement

(1) In this Part 'attendance centre requirement', in relation to a relevant order, means a requirement that the offender must attend at an attendance centre for such number of hours as may be specified in the relevant order.

(2) The aggregate number of hours for which the offender may be required to attend at an attendance centre must not be less than 12 or more than 36.

(3) The court may not impose an attendance centre requirement unless the court is satisfied that an attendance centre which is available for persons of the offender's description is reasonably accessible to the offender concerned, having regard to the means of access available to him and any other circumstances.

(3A) The attendance centre at which the offender is required to attend is to be notified to the offender by the responsible officer from time to time.

(3B) When choosing an attendance centre, the responsible officer must consider—

(a) the accessibility of the attendance centre to the offender, having regard to the means of access available to the offender and any other circumstances, and

(b) the description of persons for whom it is available.

(4) The first time at which the offender is required to attend at the attendance centre is a time notified to the offender by the responsible officer.

(5) The subsequent hours are to be fixed by the officer in charge of the centre, having regard to the offender's circumstances.

(6) An offender may not be required under this section to attend at an attendance centre on more than one occasion on any day, or for more than three hours on any occasion.

(7) A requirement to attend at an attendance centre for any period on any occasion operates as a requirement, during that period, to engage in occupation, or receive instruction, under the supervision of and in accordance with instructions given by, or under the authority of, the officer in charge of the centre, whether at the centre or elsewhere.

215 Electronic monitoring requirement

(1) In this Part 'electronic monitoring requirement', in relation to a relevant order, means a requirement for securing the electronic monitoring of the offender's compliance with other requirements imposed by the order during a period specified in the order, or determined by the responsible officer in accordance with the relevant order.

(2) Where—

(a) it is proposed to include in a relevant order a requirement for securing electronic monitoring in accordance with this section, but

(b) there is a person (other than the offender) without whose co-operation it will not be practicable to secure the monitoring,

the requirement may not be included in the order without that person's consent.

(3) A relevant order which includes an electronic monitoring requirement must include provision for making a person responsible for the monitoring; and a person who is made so responsible must be of a description specified in an order made by the Secretary of State.

(4) Where an electronic monitoring requirement is required to take effect during a period determined by the responsible officer in accordance with the relevant order, the responsible officer must, before the beginning of that period, notify—

(a) the offender,

(b) the person responsible for the monitoring, and

(c) any person falling within subsection (2)(b),

of the time when the period is to begin.

216 Local justice area to be specified in relevant order

(1) A community order or suspended sentence order must specify the local justice area in which the offender resides or will reside.

217 Requirement to avoid conflict with religious beliefs, etc

(1) The court must ensure, as far as practicable, that any requirement imposed by a relevant order is such as to avoid—

(a) any conflict with the offender's religious beliefs or with the requirements of any other relevant order to which he may be subject; and

(b) any interference with the times, if any, at which he normally works or attends any educational establishment.

(2) The responsible officer in relation to an offender to whom a relevant order relates must ensure, as far as practicable, that any instruction given or requirement imposed by him in pursuance of the order is such as to avoid the conflict or interference mentioned in subsection (1).

(3) The Secretary of State may by order provide that subsection (1) or (2) is to have effect with such additional restrictions as may be specified in the order.

218 Availability of arrangements in local area

(1) A court may not include an unpaid work requirement in a relevant order unless the court is satisfied that provision for the offender to work under such a requirement can be made under the

arrangements for persons to perform work under such a requirement which exist in the local justice area in which he resides or will reside.

(3) A court may not include an attendance centre requirement in a relevant order in respect of an offender unless the court has been notified by the Secretary of State that an attendance centre is available for persons of his description.

(4) A court may not include an electronic monitoring requirement in a relevant order in respect of an offender unless the court—

    (a) has been notified by the Secretary of State that electronic monitoring arrangements are available in the relevant area (see subsections (5) to (7)), and

    (b) is satisfied that the necessary provision can be made under those arrangements.

(5) In the case of a relevant order containing a curfew requirement or an exclusion requirement, the relevant area for the purposes of subsection (4) is the area in which the place proposed to be specified in the order is situated.

(6) In the case of a relevant order containing an attendance centre requirement, the relevant area for the purposes of subsection (4) is an area in which there is an attendance centre which is available for persons of the offender's description and which the court is satisfied is reasonably accessible to the offender.

(7) In the case of any other relevant order, the relevant area for the purposes of subsection (4) is the local justice area proposed to be specified in the order.

(8) In subsection (5) 'place', in relation to an exclusion requirement, has the same meaning as in section 205.

220   Duty of offender to keep in touch with responsible officer

(1) An offender in respect of whom a community order or a suspended sentence order is in force—

    (a) must keep in touch with the responsible officer in accordance with such instructions as he may from time to time be given by that officer.

(2) The obligation imposed by subsection (1) is enforceable as if it were a requirement imposed by the order.

220A   Duty to obtain permission before changing residence

(1) An offender in respect of whom a relevant order is in force must not change residence without permission given in accordance with this section by—

    (a) the responsible officer, or

    (b) a court.

(2) The appropriate court may, on an application by the offender, give permission in a case in which the responsible officer has refused.

(3) A court may also give permission in any proceedings before it under Schedule 8 or 12 (breach or amendment of orders etc).

(4) The grounds on which the responsible officer or court may refuse an application for permission are that, in the opinion of the officer or court, the change in residence—

    (a) is likely to prevent the offender complying with a requirement imposed by the relevant order, or

    (b) would hinder the offender's rehabilitation.

(5) The obligation imposed by subsection (1) is enforceable as if it were a requirement imposed by the relevant order.

(6) This section does not apply if the relevant order includes a residence requirement imposed under section 206.

(7) For cases in which a relevant order has to be amended because of permission given under this section, see paragraph 16 of Schedule 8 and paragraph 14 of Schedule 12 (amendment to reflect change in local justice area).

(8) In this section 'the appropriate court' has the same meaning as in paragraph 16 of Schedule 8 or paragraph 14 of Schedule 12.

221   Provision of attendance centres

(1) The Secretary of State may continue to provide attendance centres.

(2) In this Part 'attendance centre' means a place at which offenders aged under 25 may be required to attend and be given under supervision appropriate occupation or instruction in pursuance of—

    (a)   attendance centre requirements of relevant orders, or

    (aa) attendance centre requirements of youth rehabilitation orders, within the meaning of Part 1 of the Criminal Justice and Immigration Act 2008,

    (b)   attendance centre orders under section 60 of the Sentencing Act

    (c)   default orders under section 300 of this Act, or

    (d)   youth default orders under section 39 of the Criminal Justice and Immigration Act 2008.

(3) For the purpose of providing attendance centres, the Secretary of State may make arrangements with any local authority or local policing body for the use of premises of that authority or body.

222   Rules

(1) The Secretary of State may make rules for regulating—

    (a)   the supervision of persons who are subject to relevant orders,

    (b)   without prejudice to the generality of paragraph (a), the functions of responsible officers in relation to offenders subject to relevant orders,

    (c)   the arrangements to be made by local probation boards or providers of probation services for persons subject to unpaid work requirements to perform work and the performance of such work,

    (d)   the provision and carrying on of attendance centres,

    (e)   the attendance of persons subject to rehabilitation activity requirements or attendance centre requirements, or to attendance centre requirements imposed by youth rehabilitation orders under Part 1 of the Criminal Justice and Immigration Act 2008, at the places at which they are required to attend, including hours of attendance, reckoning days of attendance and the keeping of attendance records,

    (f)   electronic monitoring in pursuance of an electronic monitoring requirement, and

    (g)   without prejudice to the generality of paragraph (f), the functions of persons made responsible for securing electronic monitoring in pursuance of such a requirement.

(2) Rules under subsection (1)(c) may, in particular, make provision—

    (a)   limiting the number of hours of work to be done by a person on any one day,

    (b)   as to the reckoning of hours worked and the keeping of work records, and

    (c)   for the payment of travelling and other expenses in connection with the performance of work.

223   Power to amend limits

(1) The Secretary of State may by order amend—

    (a)   subsection (2) of section 199 (unpaid work requirement), or

    (b)   subsection (2) of section 204 (curfew requirement),

by substituting, for the maximum number of hours for the time being specified in that subsection, such other number of hours as may be specified in the order.

(2) The Secretary of State may by order amend any of the provisions mentioned in subsection (3) by substituting, for any period for the time being specified in the provision, such other period as may be specified in the order.

(3) Those provisions are—

    (a)   section 204(3) (curfew requirement);

    (b)   section 205(2) (exclusion requirement).

Chapter 5 Dangerous Offenders

224   Meaning of 'specified offence' etc

(1) An offence is a 'specified offence' for the purposes of this Chapter if it is a specified violent offence or a specified sexual offence.

(2) An offence is a 'serious offence' for the purposes of this Chapter if and only if—

(a) it is a specified offence, and

(b) it is, apart from section 224A, punishable in the case of a person aged 18 or over by—

(i) imprisonment for life or, in the case of a person aged at least 18 but under 21, custody for life, or

(ii) imprisonment or, in the case of a person aged at least 18 but under 21, detention in a young offender institution, for a determinate period of ten years or more.

(3) In this Chapter—

'serious harm' means death or serious personal injury, whether physical or psychological;

'specified violent offence' means an offence specified in Part 1 of Schedule 15;

'specified sexual offence' means an offence specified in Part 2 of that Schedule.

224A   Life sentence for second listed offence

(1) This section applies where—

(a) a person aged 18 or over is convicted of an offence listed in Part 1 of Schedule 15B,

(b) the offence was committed after this section comes into force, and

(c) the sentence condition and the previous offence condition are met.

(2) The court must impose a sentence of imprisonment for life or, in the case of a person aged at least 18 but under 21, custody for life under section 94 of the Sentencing Act unless the court is of the opinion that there are particular circumstances which—

(a) relate to the offence, to the previous offence referred to in subsection (4) or to the offender, and

(b) would make it unjust to do so in all the circumstances

(3) The sentence condition is that, but for this section, the court would, in compliance with sections 152(2) and 153(2), impose a sentence of imprisonment for 10 years or more or, if the person is aged at least 18 but under 21, a sentence of detention in a young offender institution for such a period, disregarding any extension period imposed under section 226A.

(4) The previous offence condition is that —

(a) at the time the offence was committed, the offender had been convicted of an offence listed in Schedule 15B ('the previous offence'), and

(b) a relevant life sentence or a relevant sentence of imprisonment or detention for a determinate period was imposed on the offender for the previous offence

(5) A life sentence is relevant for the purposes of subsection (4)(b) if—

(a) the offender was not eligible for release during the first 5 years of the sentence, or

(b) the offender would not have been eligible for release during that period but for the reduction of the period of ineligibility to take account of a relevant pre-sentence period.

(6) An extended sentence imposed under this Act (including one imposed as a result of the Armed Forces Act 2006) is relevant for the purposes of subsection (4)(b) if the appropriate custodial term imposed was 10 years or more.

(7) Any other extended sentence is relevant for the purposes of subsection (4)(b) if the custodial term imposed was 10 years or more.

(8) Any other sentence of imprisonment or detention for a determinate period is relevant for the purposes of subsection (4)(b) if it was for a period of 10 years or more.

(9) An extended sentence or other sentence of imprisonment or detention is also relevant if it would have been relevant under subsection (7) or (8) but for the reduction of the sentence, or any part of the sentence, to take account of a relevant pre-sentence period.

(10) For the purposes of subsections (4) to (9)

'extended sentence' means—

    (a) a sentence imposed under section 85 of the Sentencing Act or under section 226A, 226B, 227 or 228 of this Act (including one imposed as a result of section 219A, 220, 221A or 222 of the Armed Forces Act 2006), or

    (b) an equivalent sentence imposed under the law of Scotland, Northern Ireland or a member State (other than the United Kingdom);

'life sentence' means—

    (a) a life sentence as defined in section 34 of the Crime (Sentences) Act 1997, or

    (b) an equivalent sentence imposed under the law of Scotland, Northern Ireland or a member State (other than the United Kingdom);

'relevant pre-sentence period', in relation to the previous offence referred to in subsection (4), means any period which the offender spent in custody or on bail before the sentence for that offence was imposed;

'sentence of imprisonment or detention' includes any sentence of a period in custody (however expressed).

(11) An offence the sentence for which is imposed under this section is not to be regarded as an offence the sentence for which is fixed by law.

(12) Where an offence is found to have been committed over a period of two or more days, or at some time during a period of two or more days, it must be taken for the purposes of subsections (1)(b) and (4)(a) to have been committed on the last of those days.

225 Life sentence for serious offences

(1) This section applies where—

    (a) a person aged 18 or over is convicted of a serious offence committed after the commencement of this section, and

    (b) the court is of the opinion that there is a significant risk to members of the public of serious harm occasioned by the commission by him of further specified offences.

(2) If—

    (a) the offence is one in respect of which the offender would apart from this section be liable to imprisonment for life, and

    (b) the court considers that the seriousness of the offence, or of the offence and one or more offences associated with it, is such as to justify the imposition of a sentence of imprisonment for life,

the court must impose a sentence of imprisonment for life or in the case of a person aged at least 18 but under 21, a sentence of custody for life.

(5) An offence the sentence for which is imposed under this section is not to be regarded as an offence the sentence for which is fixed by law.

226 Detention for life for serious offences committed by those under 18

(1) This section applies where—

    (a) a person aged under 18 is convicted of a serious offence committed after the commencement of this section, and

    (b) the court is of the opinion that there is a significant risk to members of the public of serious harm occasioned by the commission by him of further specified offences.

(2) If—

    (a) the offence is one in respect of which the offender would apart from this section be liable to a sentence of detention for life under section 91 of the Sentencing Act, and

    (b) the court considers that the seriousness of the offence, or of the offence and one or more offences associated with it, is such as to justify the imposition of a sentence of detention for life,

the court must impose a sentence of detention for life under that section.

(5) An offence the sentence for which is imposed under this section is not to be regarded as an offence the sentence for which is fixed by law.

226A   Extended sentence for certain violent or sexual offences: persons 18 or over

(1) This section applies where—

    (a) a person aged 18 or over is convicted of a specified offence (whether the offence was committed before or after this section comes into force),

    (b) the court considers that there is a significant risk to members of the public of serious harm occasioned by the commission by the offender of further specified offences,

    (c) the court is not required by section 224A or 225(2) to impose a sentence of imprisonment for life, and

    (d) condition A or B is met.

(2) Condition A is that, at the time the offence was committed, the offender had been convicted of an offence listed in Schedule 15B.

(3) Condition B is that, if the court were to impose an extended sentence of imprisonment, the term that it would specify as the appropriate custodial term would be at least 4 years.

(4) The court may impose an extended sentence of imprisonment on the offender.

(5) An extended sentence of imprisonment is a sentence of imprisonment the term of which is equal to the aggregate of—

    (a) the appropriate custodial term, and

    (b) a further period (the 'extension period') for which the offender is to be subject to a licence.

(6) The appropriate custodial term is the term of imprisonment that would (apart from this section) be imposed in compliance with section 153(2).

(7) The extension period must be a period of such length as the court considers necessary for the purpose of protecting members of the public from serious harm occasioned by the commission by the offender of further specified offences, subject to subsections (7A) to (9).

(7A) The extension period must be at least 1 year.

(8) The extension period must not exceed—

    (a) 5 years in the case of a specified violent offence, and

    (b) 8 years in the case of a specified sexual offence.

(9) The term of an extended sentence of imprisonment imposed under this section in respect of an offence must not exceed the term that, at the time the offence was committed, was the maximum term permitted for the offence.

(10) In subsections (1)(a) and (8), references to a specified offence, a specified violent offence and a specified sexual offence include an offence that—

    (a) was abolished before 4 April 2005, and

    (b) would have constituted such an offence if committed on the day on which the offender was convicted of the offence.

(11) Where the offence mentioned in subsection (1)(a) was committed before 4 April 2005—

    (a) subsection (1)(c) has effect as if the words 'by section 224A or 225(2)' were omitted, and

    (b) subsection (6) has effect as if the words 'in compliance with section 153(2)' were omitted.

(12) In the case of a person aged at least 18 but under 21, this section has effect as if—

    (a) the reference in subsection (1)(c) to imprisonment for life were to custody for life, and

    (b) other references to imprisonment (including in the expression 'extended sentence of imprisonment') were to detention in a young offender institution.

226B   Extended sentence for certain violent or sexual offences: persons under 18

(1) This section applies where—

    (a) a person aged under 18 is convicted of a specified offence (whether the offence was committed before or after this section comes into force),

(b) the court considers that there is a significant risk to members of the public of serious harm occasioned by the commission by the offender of further specified offences,

(c) the court is not required by section 226(2) to impose a sentence of detention for life under section 91 of the Sentencing Act, and

(d) if the court were to impose an extended sentence of detention, the term that it would specify as the appropriate custodial term would be at least 4 years.

(2) The court may impose an extended sentence of detention on the offender.

(3) An extended sentence of detention is a sentence of detention the term of which is equal to the aggregate of—

(a) the appropriate custodial term, and

(b) a further period (the 'extension period') for which the offender is to be subject to a licence.

(4) The appropriate custodial term is the term of detention that would (apart from this section) be imposed in compliance with section 153(2).

(5) The extension period must be a period of such length as the court considers necessary for the purpose of protecting members of the public from serious harm occasioned by the commission by the offender of further specified offences, subject to subsections (5A) to (7).

(5A) The extension period must be at least 1 year.

(6) The extension period must not exceed—

(a) 5 years in the case of a specified violent offence, and

(b) 8 years in the case of a specified sexual offence.

(7) The term of an extended sentence of detention imposed under this section in respect of an offence may not exceed the term that, at the time the offence was committed, was the maximum term of imprisonment permitted for the offence in the case of a person aged 21 or over.

(8) In subsections (1)(a) and (6), references to a specified offence, a specified violent offence and a specified sexual offence include an offence that—

(a) was abolished before 4 April 2005, and

(b) would have constituted such an offence if committed on the day on which the offender was convicted of the offence.

(9) Where the offence mentioned in subsection (1)(a) was committed before 4 April 2005—

(a) subsection (1) has effect as if paragraph (c) were omitted, and

(b) subsection (4) has effect as if the words 'in compliance with section 153(2)' were omitted.

229 The assessment of dangerousness

(1) This section applies where—

(a) a person has been convicted of a specified offence, and

(b) it falls to a court to assess under any of sections 225 to 228 whether there is a significant risk to members of the public of serious harm occasioned by the commission by him of further such offences.

(2) The court in making the assessment referred to in subsection (1)(b)—

(a) must take into account all such information as is available to it about the nature and circumstances of the offence,

(aa) may take into account all such information as is available to it about the nature and circumstances of any other offences of which the offender has been convicted by a court anywhere in the world,

(b) may take into account any information which is before it about any pattern of behaviour of which any of the offences mentioned in paragraph (a) or (aa) forms part, and

(c) may take into account any information about the offender which is before it.

(2A) The reference in subsection (2)(aa) to a conviction by a court includes a reference to—

(a) a conviction of an offence in any service disciplinary proceedings, and

(b) a conviction of a service offence within the meaning of the Armed Forces Act 2006 ('conviction' here including anything that under section 376(1) and (2) of that Act is to be treated as a conviction).

(2B) For the purposes of subsection (2A)(a) 'service disciplinary proceedings' means—

    (a) any proceedings under the Army Act 1955, the Air Force Act 1955 or the Naval Discipline Act 1957 (whether before a court-martial or any other court or person authorised under any of those Acts to award a punishment in respect of any offence), and

    (b) any proceedings before a Standing Civilian Court;

and 'conviction' includes the recording of a finding that a charge in respect of the offence has been proved.

...

235   Detention under sections 226, 226B and 228

A person sentenced to be detained under section 226, 226B or 228 is liable to be detained in such place, and under such conditions, as may be determined by the Secretary of State or by such other person as may be authorised by him for the purpose.

236A   Special custodial sentence for certain offenders of particular concern

(1) Subsection (2) applies where—

    (a) a person is convicted of an offence listed in Schedule 18A (whether the offence was committed before or after this section comes into force),

    (b) the person was aged 18 or over when the offence was committed, and

    (c) the court does not impose one of the following for the offence—

        (i) a sentence of imprisonment for life, or

        (ii) an extended sentence under section 226A.

(2) If the court imposes a sentence of imprisonment for the offence, the term of the sentence must be equal to the aggregate of—

    (a) the appropriate custodial term, and

    (b) a further period of 1 year for which the offender is to be subject to a licence.

(3) The 'appropriate custodial term' is the term that, in the opinion of the court, ensures that the sentence is appropriate.

(4) The term of a sentence of imprisonment imposed under this section for an offence must not exceed the term that, at the time the offence was committed, was the maximum term permitted for the offence.

(5) The references in subsections (1)(c) and (2) to a sentence imposed for the offence include a sentence imposed for the offence and one or more offences associated with it.

(6) The Secretary of State may by order amend Schedule 18A by—

    (a) adding offences, or

    (b) varying or omitting offences listed in the Schedule.

(7) An order under subsection (6) may, in particular, make provision that applies in relation to the sentencing of a person for an offence committed before the provision comes into force.

(8) In the case of a person aged under 21, this section applies as if the references to imprisonment were to detention in a young offender institution.

237   Meaning of 'fixed-term prisoner' etc

(1) In this Chapter 'fixed-term prisoner' means—

    (a) a person serving a sentence of imprisonment for a determinate term, or

    (b) a person serving a determinate sentence of detention under section 91 or 96 of the Sentencing Act or under section 226A, 226B, 227, 228 or 236A of this Act and 'fixed-term sentence' means a sentence falling within paragraph (a) or (b).

(1B) In this Chapter—

    (a) references to a sentence of imprisonment include such a sentence passed by a service court;

    (b) references to a sentence of detention under section 91 of the Sentencing Act include a sentence of detention under section 209 of the Armed Forces Act 2006 or section 240A;

(ba) references to a sentence under section 226A of this Act include a sentence under that section passed as a result of section 219A of the Armed Forces Act 2006;

(bb) references to a sentence under section 226B of this Act include a sentence under that section passed as a result of section 221A of the Armed Forces Act 2006;

(c) references to a sentence under section 227 of this Act include a sentence under that section passed as a result of section 220 of the Armed Forces Act 2006; and

(d) references to a sentence under section 228 of this Act include a sentence under that section passed as a result of section 222 of that Act; and

(e) references to a sentence under section 236A of this Act include a sentence under that section passed as a result of section 224A of that Act.

(1C) Nothing in subsection (1B) has the effect that section 240ZA or 265 (provision equivalent to which is made by the Armed Forces Act 2006) or section 240A applies to a service court.

(2) In this Chapter, unless the context otherwise requires, 'prisoner' includes a person serving a sentence falling within subsection (1)(b); and 'prison' includes any place where a person serving such a sentence is liable to be detained.

(3) In this Chapter, references to a sentence of detention under section 96 of the Sentencing Act or section 226A, 227 or 236A of this Act are references to a sentence of detention in a young offender institution.

238   Power of court to recommend licence conditions for certain prisoners

(1) A court which sentences an offender to a term of imprisonment or detention in a young offender institution of twelve months or more in respect of any offence may, when passing sentence, recommend to the Secretary of State particular conditions which in its view should be included in any licence granted to the offender under this Chapter on his release from prison.

(2) In exercising his powers under section 250(4)(b)in respect of an offender, the Secretary of State must have regard to any recommendation under subsection (1).

(3) A recommendation under subsection (1) is not to be treated for any purpose as part of the sentence passed on the offender.

(4) This section does not apply in relation to a sentence of detention under section 91 of the Sentencing Act or section 226B of this Act.

239   The Parole Board

(1) The Parole Board is to continue to be, by that name, a body corporate and as such is—

(a) to be constituted in accordance with this Chapter, and

(b) to have the functions conferred on it by this Chapter in respect of fixed-term prisoners and by Chapter 2 of Part 2 of the Crime (Sentences) Act 1997 (c. 43) (in this Chapter referred to as 'the 1997 Act') in respect of life prisoners within the meaning of that Chapter.

(2) It is the duty of the Board to advise the Secretary of State with respect to any matter referred to it by him which is to do with the early release or recall of prisoners.

(3) The Board must, in dealing with cases as respects which it makes recommendations under this Chapter or under Chapter 2 of Part 2 of the 1997 Act, consider—

(a) any documents given to it by the Secretary of State, and

(b) any other oral or written information obtained by it;

and if in any particular case the Board thinks it necessary to interview the person to whom the case relates before reaching a decision, the Board may authorise one of its members to interview him and must consider the report of the interview made by that member.

(4) The Board must deal with cases as respects which it gives directions under this Chapter or under Chapter 2 of Part 2 of the 1997 Act on consideration of all such evidence as may be adduced before it.

(5) Without prejudice to subsections (3) and (4), the Secretary of State may make rules with respect to the proceedings of the Board, including proceedings authorising cases to be dealt with by a prescribed number of its members or requiring cases to be dealt with at prescribed times.

(6) The Secretary of State may also give to the Board directions as to the matters to be taken into account by it in discharging any functions under this Chapter or under Chapter 2 of Part 2 of the 1997 Act; and in giving any such directions the Secretary of State must have regard to—

(a) the need to protect the public from serious harm from offenders, and

(b) the desirability of preventing the commission by them of further offences and of securing their rehabilitation.

(7) Schedule 19 shall have effect with respect to the Board.

240ZA Time remanded in custody to count as time served: terms of imprisonment and detention

(1) This section applies where—

(a) an offender is serving a term of imprisonment in respect of an offence, and

(b) the offender has been remanded in custody (within the meaning given by section 242) in connection with the offence or a related offence.

(2) It is immaterial for that purpose whether, for all or part of the period during which the offender was remanded in custody, the offender was also remanded in custody in connection with other offences (but see subsection (5)).

(3) The number of days for which the offender was remanded in custody in connection with the offence or a related offence is to count as time served by the offender as part of the sentence.

But this is subject to subsections (4) to (6).

(4) If, on any day on which the offender was remanded in custody, the offender was also detained in connection with any other matter, that day is not to count as time served.

(5) A day counts as time served—

(a) in relation to only one sentence, and

(b) only once in relation to that sentence.

(6) A day is not to count as time served as part of any automatic release period served by the offender (see section 255B(1)).

(7) For the purposes of this section a suspended sentence—

(a) is to be treated as a sentence of imprisonment when it takes effect under paragraph 8(2) (a) or (b) of Schedule 12, and

(b) is to be treated as being imposed by the order under which it takes effect.

(8) In this section 'related offence' means an offence, other than the offence for which the sentence is imposed ('offence A'), with which the offender was charged and the charge for which was founded on the same facts or evidence as offence A.

(9) For the purposes of the references in subsections (3) and (5) to the term of imprisonment to which a person has been sentenced (that is to say, the reference to the offender's 'sentence'), consecutive terms and terms which are wholly or partly concurrent are to be treated as a single term if—

(a) the sentences were passed on the same occasion, or

(b) where they were passed on different occasions, the person has not been released at any time during the period beginning with the first and ending with the last of those occasions.

(10) The reference in subsection (4) to detention in connection with any other matter does not include remand in custody in connection with another offence but includes—

(a) detention pursuant to any custodial sentence;

(b) committal in default of payment of any sum of money;

(c) committal for want of sufficient distress to satisfy any sum of money;

(d) committal for failure to do or abstain from doing anything required to be done or left undone.

(11) This section applies to a determinate sentence of detention under section 91 or 96 of the Sentencing Act or section 226A, 226B, 227, 228 or 236A of this Act as it applies to an equivalent sentence of imprisonment.

240A   Time remanded on bail to count towards time served: terms of imprisonment and detention

(1) This section applies where—

(a) a court sentences an offender to imprisonment for a term in respect of an offence,

(b) the offender was remanded on bail by a court in course of or in connection with proceedings for the offence, or any related offence, after the coming into force of section 21 of the Criminal Justice and Immigration Act 2008, and

(c) the offender's bail was subject to a qualifying curfew condition and an electronic monitoring condition ('the relevant conditions').

(2) Subject to subsections (3A) and (3B), the court must direct that the credit period is to count as time served by the offender as part of the sentence.

(3) The credit period is calculated by taking the following steps.

Step 1

Add—

(a) the day on which the offender's bail was first subject to the relevant conditions (and for this purpose a condition is not prevented from being a relevant condition by the fact that it does not apply for the whole of the day in question), and

(b) the number of other days on which the offender's bail was subject to those conditions (but exclude the last of those days if the offender spends the last part of it in custody).

Step 2

Deduct the number of days on which the offender, whilst on bail subject to the relevant conditions, was also—

(a) subject to any requirement imposed for the purpose of securing the electronic monitoring of the offender's compliance with a curfew requirement, or

(b) on temporary release under rules made under section 47 of the Prison Act 1952.

Step 3

From the remainder, deduct the number of days during that remainder on which the offender has broken either or both of the relevant conditions.

Step 4

Divide the result by 2.

Step 5

If necessary, round up to the nearest whole number.

(3A) A day of the credit period counts as time served—

(a) in relation to only one sentence, and

(b) only once in relation to that sentence.

(3B) A day of the credit period is not to count as time served as part of any automatic release period served by the offender (see section 255B(1)).

(8) Where the court gives a direction under subsection (2) it shall state in open court—

(a) the number of days on which the offender was subject to the relevant conditions, and

(b) the number of days (if any) which it deducted under each of steps 2 and 3.

(11) Subsections (7) to (9) and (11) of section 240ZA apply for the purposes of this section as they apply for the purposes of that section but as if—

(a) in subsection (7)—

(i)   the reference to a suspended sentence is to be read as including a reference to a sentence to which an order under section 118(1) of the Sentencing Act relates;

(ii) in paragraph (a) after 'Schedule 12' there were inserted 'or section 119(1)(a) or (b) of the Sentencing Act'; and

(b) in subsection (9) the references to subsections (3) and (5) of section 240ZA are to be read as a reference to subsection (2) of this section and, in paragraph (b), after 'Chapter' there were inserted 'or Part 2 of the Criminal Justice Act 1991'.

(12) In this section—

'electronic monitoring condition' means any electronic monitoring requirements imposed under section 3(6ZAA) of the Bail Act 1976 for the purpose of securing the electronic monitoring of a person's compliance with a qualifying curfew condition;

'curfew requirement' means a requirement (however described) to remain at one or more specified places for a specified number of hours in any given day, provided that the requirement is imposed by a court or the Secretary of State and arises as a result of a conviction;

'qualifying curfew condition' means a condition of bail which requires the person granted bail to remain at one or more specified places for a total of not less than 9 hours in any given day

241 Effect of section 240ZA or direction under section 240A on release on licence

(1) In determining for the purposes of this Chapter whether a person to whom section 240ZA applies or a direction under section 240A relates—

    (a) has served, or would (but for his release) have served, a particular proportion of his sentence, or

    (b) has served a particular period,

the number of days specified in section 240ZA or in the direction under section 240A are to be treated as having been served by him as part of that sentence or period.

(1A) In subsection (1) the reference to section 240ZA includes section 246 of the Armed Forces Act 2006.

242 Interpretation of sections 240ZA, 240A and 241

(1) For the purposes of sections 240ZA, 240A and 241, the definition of 'sentence of imprisonment' in section 305 applies as if for the words from the beginning of the definition to the end of paragraph (a) there were substituted—

'"sentence of imprisonment" does not include a committal—

    (a) in default of payment of any sum of money, other than one adjudged to be paid on a conviction';

and references in those sections to sentencing an offender to imprisonment, and to an offender's sentence, are to be read accordingly.

(2) References in sections 240ZA and 241 to an offender's being remanded in custody are references to his being—

    (a) remanded in or committed to custody by order of a court,

    (b) remanded to youth detention accommodation under section 91(4) of the Legal Aid, Sentencing and Punishment of Offenders Act 2012, or

    (c) remanded, admitted or removed to hospital under section 35, 36, 38 or 48 of the Mental Health Act 1983 (c. 20).

243 Persons extradited to the United Kingdom

(1) A fixed-term prisoner is an extradited prisoner for the purposes of this section if—

    (a) he was tried for the offence in respect of which his sentence was imposed or he received that sentence—

        (i) after having been extradited to the United Kingdom, and

        (ii) without having first been restored or had an opportunity of leaving the United Kingdom, and

    (b) he was for any period kept in custody while awaiting his extradition to the United Kingdom as mentioned in paragraph (a).

(2) In the case of an extradited prisoner, the court must specify in open court the number of days for which the prisoner was kept in custody while awaiting extradition.

(2A) Section 240ZA applies to days specified under subsection (2) as if they were days for which the prisoner was remanded in custody in connection with the offence or a related offence.

243A   Duty to release certain prisoners serving less than 12 months

(1) This section applies to a fixed-term prisoner if—

   (a) the prisoner is serving a sentence which is for a term of 1 day, or

   (b) the prisoner—

      (i)   is serving a sentence which is for a term of less than 12 months, and

      (ii) is aged under 18 on the last day of the requisite custodial period.

(1A) This section also applies to a fixed-term prisoner if—

   (a) the prisoner is serving a sentence which is for a term of less than 12 months, and

   (b) the sentence was imposed in respect of an offence committed before the day on which section 1 of the Offender Rehabilitation Act 2014 came into force.

(2) As soon as a prisoner to whom this section applies has served the requisite custodial period for the purposes of this section, it is the duty of the Secretary of State to release that person unconditionally.

(3) For the purposes of this section 'the requisite custodial period' is—

   (a) in relation to a person serving one sentence, one-half of the sentence, and

   (b) in relation to a person serving two or more concurrent or consecutive sentences, the period determined under sections 263(2) and 264(2).

(4) This section is subject to—

   (a) section 256B (supervision of young offenders after release), and

   (b) paragraph 8 of Schedule 20B (transitional cases).

244   Duty to release prisoners

(1) As soon as a fixed-term prisoner, other than a prisoner to whom section 243A, 244A, 246A or 247 applies, has served the requisite custodial period for the purposes of this section, it is the duty of the Secretary of State to release him on licence under this section.

(1A) Subsection (1) does not apply if the prisoner has been released on licence under section 246 or 248 and recalled under section 254 (provision for the release of such persons being made by sections 255B and 255C).

(3) For the purposes of this section 'the requisite custodial period' means—

   (a) in relation to a prisoner serving one sentence, one-half of the sentence,

   (b) in relation to a person serving two or more concurrent or consecutive sentences, the period determined under sections 263(2) and 264(2).

(4) This section is subject to paragraphs 5, 6, 8, 25 and 28 of Schedule 20B (transitional cases).

244A   Release on licence of prisoners serving sentence under section 236A

(1) This section applies to a prisoner ('P') who is serving a sentence imposed under section 236A.

(2) The Secretary of State must refer P's case to the Board—

   (a) as soon as P has served the requisite custodial period, and

   (b) where there has been a previous reference of P's case to the Board under this subsection and the Board did not direct P's release, not later than the second anniversary of the disposal of that reference.

(3) It is the duty of the Secretary of State to release P on licence under this section as soon as—

   (a) P has served the requisite custodial period, and

   (b) the Board has directed P's release under this section.

(4) The Board must not give a direction under subsection (3) unless—

   (a) the Secretary of State has referred P's case to the Board, and

   (b) the Board is satisfied that it is not necessary for the protection of the public that P should be confined.

(5) It is the duty of the Secretary of State to release P on licence under this section as soon as P has served the appropriate custodial term, unless P has previously been released on licence under this section and recalled under section 254 (provision for the release of such persons being made by sections 255A to 255C).

(6) For the purposes of this section—

'the appropriate custodial term' means the term determined as such by the court under section 236A;

'the requisite custodial period' means—

(a) in relation to a person serving one sentence, one-half of the appropriate custodial term, and

(b) in relation to a person serving two or more concurrent or consecutive sentences, the period determined under sections 263(2) and 264(2).

246 Power to release prisoners on licence before required to do so

(1) Subject to subsections (2) to (4), the Secretary of State may—

(a) release on licence under this section a fixed-term prisoner at any time during the period of 135 days ending with the day on which the prisoner will have served the requisite custodial period

(2) Subsection (1)(a) does not apply in relation to a prisoner unless—

(a) the length of the requisite custodial period is at least 6 weeks, and

(b) he has served—

(i) at least 4 weeks of that period, and

(ii) at least one-half of that period.

(4) Subsection (1) does not apply where—

(a) the sentence is imposed under section 226A, 227, 228 or 236A,

(aa) the sentence is for a term of 4 years or more,

(b) the sentence is for an offence under section 1 of the Prisoners (Return to Custody) Act 1995 (c. 16),

(c) the prisoner is subject to a hospital order, hospital direction or transfer direction under section 37, 45A or 47 of the Mental Health Act 1983 (c. 20),

(d) the sentence was imposed by virtue of paragraph 9(1)(b) or (c) or 10(1)(b) or (c) of Schedule 8in a case where the prisoner has failed to comply with a curfew requirement of a community order,

(e) the prisoner is subject to the notification requirements of Part 2 of the Sexual Offences Act 2003 (c. 42),

(f) the prisoner is liable to removal from the United Kingdom,

(g) the prisoner has been released on licence under this section at any time, and has been recalled to prison under section 255(1)(a) (and the revocation has not been cancelled under section 255(3)),

(ga) the prisoner has at any time been released on licence under section 34A of the Criminal Justice Act 1991 and has been recalled to prison under section 38A(1)(a) of that Act (and the revocation of the licence has not been cancelled under section 38A(3) of that Act);

(h) the prisoner has been released on licence under section 248 during the currency of the sentence, and has been recalled to prison under section 254,

(ha) the prisoner has at any time been returned to prison under section 40 of the Criminal Justice Act 1991 or section 116 of the Sentencing Act, or

(i) in the case of a prisoner to whom section 240ZA applies or a direction under section 240A relates, the interval between the date on which the sentence was passed and the date on which the prisoner will have served the requisite custodial period is less than 14 days.

(4ZA) Where subsection (4)(aa) applies to a prisoner who is serving two or more terms of imprisonment, the reference to the term of the sentence is—

(a) if the terms are partly concurrent, a reference to the period which begins when the first term begins and ends when the last term ends;

(b) if the terms are to be served consecutively, a reference to the aggregate of the terms.

(4A) In subsection (4)—

    (a) the reference in paragraph (d) to a community order includes a service community order or overseas community order under the Armed Forces Act 2006; and

    (b) the reference in paragraph (i) to section 240ZA includes section 246 of that Act.

(5) The Secretary of State may by order—

    (a) amend the number of days for the time being specified in subsection (1)(a) or (4)(i),

    (b) amend the number of weeks for the time being specified in subsection (2)(a) or (b)(i), and

    (c) amend the fraction for the time being specified in subsection (2)(b)(ii).

(6) In this section—

'the requisite custodial period' in relation to a person serving any sentence, has the meaning given by paragraph (a) or (b) of section 243A(3) or (as the case may be) paragraph (a) or (d) of section 244(3);

'term of imprisonment' includes a determinate sentence of detention under section 91 or 96 of the Sentencing Act or under section 226A, 226B, 227, 228 or 236A of this Act.

246A Release on licence of prisoners serving extended sentence under section 226A or 226B

(1) This section applies to a prisoner ('P') who is serving an extended sentence imposed under section 226A or 226B.

(2) It is the duty of the Secretary of State to release P on licence under this section as soon as P has served the requisite custodial period for the purposes of this section if—

    (a) the sentence was imposed before the coming into force of section 4 of the Criminal Justice and Courts Act 2015,

    (b) the appropriate custodial term is less than 10 years, and

    (c) the sentence was not imposed in respect of an offence listed in Parts 1 to 3 of Schedule 15B or in respect of offences that include one or more offences listed in those Parts of that Schedule.

(3) In any other case, it is the duty of the Secretary of State to release P on licence in accordance with subsections (4) to (7).

(4) The Secretary of State must refer P's case to the Board—

    (a) as soon as P has served the requisite custodial period, and

    (b) where there has been a previous reference of P's case to the Board under this subsection and the Board did not direct P's release, not later than the second anniversary of the disposal of that reference.

(5) It is the duty of the Secretary of State to release P on licence under this section as soon as—

    (a) P has served the requisite custodial period, and

    (b) the Board has directed P's release under this section.

(6) The Board must not give a direction under subsection (5) unless—

    (a) the Secretary of State has referred P's case to the Board, and

    (b) the Board is satisfied that it is no longer necessary for the protection of the public that P should be confined.

(7) It is the duty of the Secretary of State to release P on licence under this section as soon as P has served the appropriate custodial term, unless P has previously been released on licence under this section and recalled under section 254 (provision for the release of such persons being made by section 255C).

(8) For the purposes of this section—

'appropriate custodial term' means the term determined as such by the court under section 226A or 226B (as appropriate);

'the requisite custodial period' means—

    (a) in relation to a person serving one sentence, two-thirds of the appropriate custodial term, and

    (b) in relation to a person serving two or more concurrent or consecutive sentences, the period determined under sections 263(2) and 264(2).

247 Release on licence of prisoner serving extended sentence under section 227 or 228

(1) This section applies to a prisoner who is serving an extended sentence imposed under section 227 or 228.

(2) As soon as—

(a) a prisoner to whom this section applies has served the requisite custodial period,

it is the duty of the Secretary of State to release him on licence.

(7) In this section—

'the appropriate custodial term' means the period determined by the court as the appropriate custodial term under section 227 or 228.

'the requisite custodial period' means—

(a) in relation to a person serving one sentence, one half of the appropriate custodial term, and

(b) in relation to a person serving two or more concurrent or consecutive sentences, the period determined under sections 263(2) and 264(2).

(8) In its application to a person serving a sentence imposed before 14 July 2008, this section is subject to the modifications set out in paragraph 15 of Schedule 20B (transitional cases).

248 Power to release prisoners on compassionate grounds

(1) The Secretary of State may at any time release a fixed-term prisoner on licence if he is satisfied that exceptional circumstances exist which justify the prisoner's release on compassionate grounds.

249 Duration of licence

(1) Subject to subsection (3), where a fixed-term prisoner, other than one to whom section 243A applies, is released on licence, the licence shall, subject to any revocation under section 254 or 255, remain in force for the remainder of his sentence.

(1A) Where a prisoner to whom section 243A applies is released on licence, the licence shall, subject to any revocation under section 254 or 255, remain in force until the date on which, but for the release, the prisoner would have served one-half of the sentence.

This is subject to subsection (3).

(3) Subsections (1) and (1A) have effect subject to sections 263(2) (concurrent terms) and sections 264(3C)(a) and 264B (consecutive terms)

(5) This section is subject to paragraphs 17, 19 and 26 of Schedule 20B (transitional cases).

250 Licence conditions

(1) In this section—

(a) 'the standard conditions' means such conditions as may be prescribed for the purposes of this section as standard conditions, and

(b) 'prescribed' means prescribed by the Secretary of State by order.

(4) Any licence under this Chapter in respect of a prisoner serving a sentence of imprisonment or detention in a young offender institution (including a sentence imposed under section 226A, 227 or 236A) or any sentence of detention under section 91 or 96 of the Sentencing Act or section 226A, 226B, 227, 228 or 236A of this Act—

(a) must include the standard conditions, and

(b) may include—

(i) any condition authorised by section 62, 64 or 64A of the Criminal Justice and Court Services Act 2000 or section 28 of the Offender Management Act 2007, and

(ii) such other conditions of a kind prescribed by the Secretary of State for the purposes of this paragraph as the Secretary of State may for the time being specify in the licence.

(5) A licence under section 246 must also include a curfew condition complying with section 253.

(5A) Subsection (5B) applies to a licence granted, either on initial release or after recall to prison, to—

(a) a prisoner serving an extended sentence imposed under section 226A or 226B, other than a sentence that meets the conditions in section 246A(2) (release without direction of the Board), or

(b) a prisoner serving a sentence imposed under section 236A.

(5B) The Secretary of State must not—

(a) include a condition referred to in subsection (4)(b)(ii) in the licence, either on release or subsequently, or

(b) vary or cancel any such condition included in the licence,

unless the Board directs the Secretary of State to do so.

(8) In exercising his powers to prescribe standard conditions or the other conditions referred to in subsection (4)(b)(ii), the Secretary of State must have regard to the following purposes of the supervision of offenders while on licence under this Chapter—

(a) the protection of the public,

(b) the prevention of re-offending, and

(c) securing the successful re-integration of the prisoner into the community.

252   Duty to comply with licence conditions

(1) A person subject to a licence under this Chapter must comply with such conditions as may for the time being be specified in the licence.

(2) But where—

(a) the licence relates to a sentence of imprisonment passed by a service court, and

(c) the person is residing outside the British Islands,

the conditions specified in the licence apply to him only so far as it is practicable for him to comply with them where he is residing.

253   Curfew condition to be included in licence under section 246, 255B or 255C

(1) For the purposes of this Chapter, a curfew condition is a condition which—

(a) requires the released person to remain, for periods for the time being specified in the condition, at a place for the time being so specified (which may be premises approved by the Secretary of State under section 13 of the Offender Management Act 2007 (c. 21)), and

(b) includes a requirement, imposed under section 62 of the Criminal Justice and Court Services Act 2000, to submit to electronic monitoring of his whereabouts during the periods for the time being so specified.

(2) The curfew condition may specify different places or different periods for different days, but may not specify periods which amount to less than 9 hours in any one day (excluding for this purpose the first and last days of the period for which the condition is in force).

(3) The curfew condition is to remain in force until the date when the released person would (but for his release) fall to be released unconditionally under section 243A or on licence under section 244.

(6) Nothing in this section is to be taken to require the Secretary of State to ensure that arrangements are made for the electronic monitoring of released persons' whereabouts in any particular part of England and Wales.

254   Recall of prisoners while on licence

(1) The Secretary of State may, in the case of any prisoner who has been released on licence under this Chapter, revoke his licence and recall him to prison.

(2) A person recalled to prison under subsection (1)—

(a) may make representations in writing with respect to his recall, and

(b) on his return to prison, must be informed of the reasons for his recall and of his right to make representations.

(2A) The Secretary of State, after considering any representations under subsection (2)(a) or any other matters, may cancel a revocation under this section.

(2B) The Secretary of State may cancel a revocation under subsection (2A) only if satisfied that the person recalled has complied with all the conditions specified in the licence.

(2C) Where the revocation of a person's licence is cancelled under subsection (2A), the person is to be treated as if the recall under subsection (1) had not happened.

(6) On the revocation of the licence of any person under this section, he shall be liable to be detained in pursuance of his sentence and, if at large, is to be treated as being unlawfully at large.

(7) Nothing in this section applies in relation to a person recalled under section 255.

255   Recall of prisoners released early under section 246

(1) If it appears to the Secretary of State, as regards a person released on licence under section 246—

(a) that he has failed to comply with the curfew condition included in the licence, or

(b) that his whereabouts can no longer be electronically monitored at the place for the time being specified in the curfew condition included in his licence,

the Secretary of State may, if the curfew condition is still in force, revoke the licence and recall the person to prison under this section.

(2) A person whose licence under section 246 is revoked under this section—

(a) may make representations in writing with respect to the revocation, and

(b) on his return to prison, must be informed of the reasons for the revocation and of his right to make representations.

(3) The Secretary of State, after considering any representations under subsection (2)(a) or any other matters, may cancel a revocation under this section.

(4) Where the revocation of a person's licence is cancelled under subsection (3), the person is to be treated for the purposes of section 246as if he had not been recalled to prison under this section.

(5) On the revocation of a person's licence under section 246, he is liable to be detained in pursuance of his sentence and, if at large, is to be treated as being unlawfully at large.

255ZA   Offence of remaining unlawfully at large after recall

(1) A person recalled to prison under section 254 or 255 commits an offence if the person—

(a) has been notified of the recall orally or in writing, and

(b) while unlawfully at large fails, without reasonable excuse, to take all necessary steps to return to prison as soon as possible.

(2) A person is to be treated for the purposes of subsection (1)(a) as having been notified of the recall if—

(a) written notice of the recall has been delivered to an appropriate address, and

(b) a period specified in the notice has elapsed.

(3) In subsection (2) 'an appropriate address' means—

(a) an address at which, under the person's licence, the person is permitted to reside or stay, or

(b) an address nominated, in accordance with the person's licence, for the purposes of this section.

(4) A person is also to be treated for the purposes of subsection (1)(a) as having been notified of the recall if—

(a) the person's licence requires the person to keep in touch in accordance with any instructions given by an officer of a provider of probation services,

(b) the person has failed to comply with such an instruction, and

(c) the person has not complied with such an instruction for at least 6 months.

(5) A person who is guilty of an offence under this section is liable—

(a) on conviction on indictment to imprisonment for a term not exceeding 2 years or a fine (or both);

(b) on summary conviction to imprisonment for a term not exceeding 12 months or a fine (or both).

(6) In relation to an offence committed before section 154(1) comes into force, the reference in subsection (5)(b) to 12 months is to be read as a reference to 6 months.

(7) In relation to an offence committed before section 85 of the Legal Aid, Sentencing and Punishment of Offenders Act 2012 comes into force, the reference in subsection (5)(b) to a fine is to be read as a reference to a fine not exceeding the statutory maximum.

255A   Further release after recall: introductory

(1) This section applies for the purpose of identifying which of sections 255B and 255C governs the further release of a person who has been recalled under section 254.

(2) The Secretary of State must, on recalling a person other than an extended sentence prisoner, consider whether the person is suitable for automatic release.

(4) A person is suitable for automatic release only if the Secretary of State is satisfied that the person will not present a risk of serious harm to members of the public if released at the end of the automatic release period.

(5) The person must be dealt with—

(a) in accordance with section 255B if suitable for automatic release;

(b) in accordance with section 255C otherwise,

but that is subject, where applicable, to section 243A(2) (unconditional release).

(6) For the purposes of this section, a person returns to custody when that person, having been recalled, is detained (whether or not in prison) in pursuance of the sentence.

(7) An 'extended sentence prisoner' is a prisoner serving an extended sentence imposed under—

(a) section 226A, 226B, 227 or 228 of this Act, or

(b) section 85 of the Sentencing Act;

and paragraph (b) includes (in accordance with paragraph 1(3) of Schedule 11 to the Sentencing Act) a reference to section 58 of the Crime and Disorder Act 1998.

(8) 'Automatic release' means release at the end of the automatic release period.

(9) In the case of a person recalled under section 254 while on licence under a provision of this Chapter other than section 246, 'the automatic release period' means—

(a) where the person is serving a sentence of less than 12 months, the period of 14 days beginning with the day on which the person returns to custody;

(b) where the person is serving a sentence of 12 months or more, the period of 28 days beginning with that day.

(10) In the case of a person recalled under section 254 while on licence under section 246, 'the automatic release period' means whichever of the following ends later—

(a) the period described in subsection (9)(a) or (b) (as appropriate);

(b) the requisite custodial period which the person would have served under section 243A or 244 but for the earlier release.

255B   Automatic release

(1) A prisoner who is suitable for automatic release ('P') must—

(a) on return to prison, be informed that he or she will be released under this section (subject to subsections (8) and (9)), and

(b) at the end of the automatic release period (as defined in section 255A(9) and (10)), be released by the Secretary of State on licence under this Chapter (unless P is released before that date under subsection (2) or (5)).

(2) The Secretary of State may, at any time after P is returned to prison, release P again on licence under this Chapter.

(3) The Secretary of State must not release P under subsection (2) unless the Secretary of State is satisfied that it is not necessary for the protection of the public that P should remain in prison until the end of the period mentioned in subsection (1)(b).

(4) If P makes representations under section 254(2) before the end of that period, the Secretary of State must refer P's case to the Board on the making of those representations.

(5) Where on a reference under subsection (4) the Board directs P's immediate release on licence under this Chapter, the Secretary of State must give effect to the direction.

(6) Subsection (7) applies if P is recalled before the date on which P would (but for the earlier release) have served the requisite custodial period for the purposes of section 243A or (as the case may be) section 244.

(7) Where this subsection applies—

  (a) if P is released under this section before that date, P's licence must include a curfew condition complying with section 253, and

  (b) P is not to be so released (despite subsections (1)(b) and (5)) unless the Secretary of State is satisfied that arrangements are in place to enable that condition to be complied with.

(8) Subsection (9) applies if, after P has been informed that he or she will be released under this section, the Secretary of State receives further information about P (whether or not relating to any time before P was recalled).

(9) If the Secretary of State determines, having regard to that and any other relevant information, that P is not suitable for automatic release—

  (a) the Secretary of State must inform P that he or she will not be released under this section, and

  (b) section 255C applies to P as if the Secretary of State had determined, on P's recall, that P was not suitable for automatic release.

255C Specified offence prisoners and those not suitable for automatic release

(1) This section applies to a prisoner ('P') who—

  (a) is an extended sentence prisoner, or

  (b) is not considered to be suitable for automatic release.

(2) The Secretary of State may, at any time after P is returned to prison, release P again on licence under this Chapter.

(3) The Secretary of State must not release P under subsection (2) unless the Secretary of State is satisfied that it is not necessary for the protection of the public that P should remain in prison.

(4) The Secretary of State must refer P's case to the Board—

  (a) if P makes representations under section 254(2) before the end of the period of 28 days beginning with the date on which P returns to custody, on the making of those representations, or

  (b) if, at the end of that period, P has not been released under subsection (2) and has not made such representations, at that time.

(5) Where on a reference under subsection (4) the Board directs P's immediate release on licence under this Chapter, the Secretary of State must give effect to the direction.

(6) Subsection (7) applies if P is recalled before the date on which P would (but for the earlier release) have served the requisite custodial period for the purposes of section 243A or (as the case may be) section 244.

(7) Where this subsection applies—

  (a) if P is released under this section before that date, P's licence must include a curfew condition complying with section 253, and

  (b) P is not to be so released (despite subsection (5)) unless the Secretary of State is satisfied that arrangements are in place to enable that condition to be complied with.

(8) For the purposes of this section, P returns to custody when P, having been recalled, is detained (whether or not in prison) in pursuance of the sentence.

256 Review by the Board

(1) Where on a reference under section 255B(4) or 255C(4) in relation to any person, the Board does not direct his immediate release on licence under this Chapter, the Board must either—

  (a) fix a date for the person's release on licence, or

  (b) determine the reference by making no direction as to his release.

(2) Any date fixed under subsection (1)(a) must not be later than the first anniversary of the date on which the decision is taken.

(4) Where the Board has fixed a date under subsection (1)(a), it is the duty of the Secretary of State to release him on licence on that date.

256A   Further review

(1) The Secretary of State must, not later than the first anniversary of a determination by the Board under section 256(1) or subsection (4) below, refer the person's case to the Board.

(2) The Secretary of State may, at any time before that anniversary, refer the person's case to the Board.

(3) The Board may at any time recommend to the Secretary of State that a person's case be referred under subsection (2).

(4) On a reference under subsection (1) or (2), the Board must determine the reference by—
>   (a) directing the person's immediate release on licence under this Chapter,
>   (b) fixing a date for his release on licence, or
>   (c) making no direction as to his release.

(5) The Secretary of State—
>   (a) where the Board makes a direction under subsection (4)(a) for the person's immediate release on licence, must give effect to the direction; and
>   (b) where the Board fixes a release date under subsection (4)(b), must release the person on licence on that date.

256AA   Supervision after end of sentence of prisoners serving less than 2 years

(1) This section applies where a person ('the offender') has served a fixed-term sentence which was for a term of more than 1 day but less than 2 years, except where—
>   (a) the offender was aged under 18 on the last day of the requisite custodial period (as defined in section 243A(3)),
>   (b) the sentence was an extended sentence imposed under section 226A or 226B ,
>   (ba) the sentence was imposed under section 236A, or
>   (c) the sentence was imposed in respect of an offence committed before the day on which section 2(2) of the Offender Rehabilitation Act 2014 came into force.

(2) The offender must comply with the supervision requirements during the supervision period, except at any time when the offender is—
>   (a) in legal custody,
>   (b) subject to a licence under this Chapter or Chapter 2 of Part 2 of the 1997 Act, or
>   (c) subject to DTO supervision.

(3) The supervision requirements are the requirements for the time being specified in a notice given to the offender by the Secretary of State (but see the restrictions in section 256AB).

(4) 'The supervision period' is the period which—
>   (a) begins on the expiry of the sentence, and
>   (b) ends on the expiry of the period of 12 months beginning immediately after the offender has served the requisite custodial period (as defined in section 244(3)).

(5) The purpose of the supervision period is the rehabilitation of the offender.

(6) The Secretary of State must have regard to that purpose when specifying requirements under this section.

(7) The supervisor must have regard to that purpose when carrying out functions in relation to the requirements.

(8) In this Chapter, 'the supervisor', in relation to a person subject to supervision requirements under this section, means a person who is for the time being responsible for discharging the functions conferred by this Chapter on the supervisor in accordance with arrangements made by the Secretary of State.

(9) In relation to a person subject to supervision requirements under this section following a sentence of detention under section 91 of the Sentencing Act, the supervisor must be—

    (a) an officer of a provider of probation services, or

    (b) a member of the youth offending team established by the local authority in whose area the offender resides for the time being.

(10) In relation to any other person, the supervisor must be an officer of a provider of probation services.

(11) In this section 'DTO supervision' means supervision under—

    (a) a detention and training order (including an order under section 211 of the Armed Forces Act 2006), or

    (b) an order under section 104(3)(aa) of the Powers of Criminal Courts (Sentencing) Act 2002 (breach of supervision requirements of detention and training order).

(12) This section has effect subject to section 264(3C)(b) and (3D).

256AB   Supervision requirements under section 256AA

(1) The only requirements that the Secretary of State may specify in a notice under section 256AA are—

    (a) a requirement to be of good behaviour and not to behave in a way which undermines the purpose of the supervision period;

    (b) a requirement not to commit any offence;

    (c) a requirement to keep in touch with the supervisor in accordance with instructions given by the supervisor;

    (d) a requirement to receive visits from the supervisor in accordance with instructions given by the supervisor;

    (e) a requirement to reside permanently at an address approved by the supervisor and to obtain the prior permission of the supervisor for any stay of one or more nights at a different address;

    (f) a requirement not to undertake work, or a particular type of work, unless it is approved by the supervisor and to notify the supervisor in advance of any proposal to undertake work or a particular type of work;

    (g) a requirement not to travel outside the British Islands, except with the prior permission of the supervisor or in order to comply with a legal obligation (whether or not arising under the law of any part of the British Islands);

    (h) a requirement to participate in activities in accordance with any instructions given by the supervisor;

    (i) a drug testing requirement (see section 256D);

    (j) a drug appointment requirement (see section 256E).

(2) Where a requirement is imposed under subsection (1)(h), section 200A(5) to (10) apply in relation to the requirement (reading references to the responsible officer as references to the supervisor).

(3) Paragraphs (i) and (j) of subsection (1) have effect subject to the restrictions in sections 256D(2) and 256E(2).

(4) The Secretary of State may by order—

    (a) add requirements that may be specified in a notice under section 256AA,

    (b) remove or amend such requirements,

    (c) make provision about such requirements, including about the circumstances in which they may be imposed, and

    (d) make provision about instructions given for the purposes of such requirements.

(5) An order under subsection (4) may amend this Act.

(6) In this section 'work' includes paid and unpaid work.

256AC   Breach of supervision requirements imposed under section 256AA

(1) Where it appears on information to a justice of the peace that a person has failed to comply with a supervision requirement imposed under section 256AA, the justice may—

(a) issue a summons requiring the offender to appear at the place and time specified in the summons, or

(b) if the information is in writing and on oath, issue a warrant for the offender's arrest.

(2) Any summons or warrant issued under this section must direct the person to appear or be brought—

(a) before a magistrates' court acting for the local justice area in which the offender resides, or

(b) if it is not known where the person resides, before a magistrates' court acting for the same local justice area as the justice who issued the summons or warrant.

(3) Where the person does not appear in answer to a summons issued under subsection (1)(a), the court may issue a warrant for the person's arrest.

(4) If it is proved to the satisfaction of the court that the person has failed without reasonable excuse to comply with a supervision requirement imposed under section 256AA, the court may—

(a) order the person to be committed to prison for a period not exceeding 14 days (subject to subsection (7)),

(b) order the person to pay a fine not exceeding level 3 on the standard scale, or

(c) make an order (a 'supervision default order') imposing on the person—

(i) an unpaid work requirement (as defined by section 199), or

(ii) a curfew requirement (as defined by section 204).

(5) Section 177(3) (obligation to impose electronic monitoring requirement) applies in relation to a supervision default order that imposes a curfew requirement as it applies in relation to a community order that imposes such a requirement.

(6) If the court deals with the person under subsection (4), it must revoke any supervision default order which is in force at that time in respect of that person.

(7) Where the person is under the age of 21—

(a) an order under subsection (4)(a) in respect of the person must be for committal to a young offender institution instead of to prison, but

(b) the Secretary of State may from time to time direct that a person committed to a young offender institution by such an order is to be detained in a prison or remand centre instead.

(8) A person committed to prison or a young offender institution by an order under subsection (4)(a) is to be regarded as being in legal custody.

(9) A fine imposed under subsection (4)(b) is to be treated, for the purposes of any enactment, as being a sum adjudged to be paid by a conviction.

(10) In Schedule 19A (supervision default orders)—

(a) Part 1 makes provision about requirements of supervision default orders, and

(b) Part 2 makes provision about the breach, revocation and amendment of supervision default orders.

(11) A person dealt with under this section may appeal to the Crown Court against—

(a) the order made by the court under this section, and

(b) an order made by the court under section 21A of the Prosecution of Offences Act 1985 (criminal courts charge) when dealing with the person under this section.

256B   Supervision after release of certain young offenders serving less than 12 months

(1) This section applies where a person ('the offender') is released under this Chapter if—

(a) the person is, at the time of the release, serving a sentence of detention under section 91 of the Sentencing Act which is for a term of less than 12 months, and

(b) the person is aged under 18 on the last day of the requisite custodial period (as defined in section 243A(3)).

(1A) This section also applies where a person ('the offender') is released under this Chapter if—

(a) the person is, at the time of the release, serving a sentence of detention under section 91 or 96 of the Sentencing Act which is for a term of less than 12 months, and

(b) the sentence was imposed in respect of an offence committed before the day on which section 1 of the Offender Rehabilitation Act 2014 came into force.

(2) The offender is to be under the supervision of—

(a) an officer of a provider of probation services,

(b) a social worker of a local authority, or

(c) a member of the youth offending team.

(3) Where the supervision is to be provided by an officer of a provider of probation services, the officer must be an officer acting in the local justice area in which the offender resides for the time being.

(4) Where the supervision is to be provided by—

(a) a social worker of a local authority, or

(b) a member of a youth offending team,

the social worker or member must be a social worker of, or a member of a youth offending team established by, the local authority within whose area the offender resides for the time being.

(5) The supervision period begins on the offender's release and ends three months later (whether or not the offender is detained under section 256C or otherwise during that period).

(6) During the supervision period, the offender must comply with such requirements, if any, as may for the time being be specified in a notice from the Secretary of State.

(7) The requirements that may be specified in a notice under subsection (6) include—

(a) requirements to submit to electronic monitoring of the offender's compliance with any other requirements specified in the notice;

(b) requirements to submit to electronic monitoring of the offender's whereabouts (otherwise than for the purpose of securing compliance with requirements specified in the notice);

(c) where the offender is aged 18 or over—

(i) drug testing requirements (see section 256D);

(ii) drug appointment requirements (see section 256E).

(7A) Paragraph (c)(i) and (ii) of subsection (7) have effect subject to the restrictions in sections 256D(2) and 256E(2).

(9) The Secretary of State may make rules about the requirements that may be imposed by virtue of subsection (7)(a) or (b).

256C Breach of supervision requirements imposed under section 256B

(1) Where an offender is under supervision under section 256B and it appears on information to a justice of the peace that the offender has failed to comply with requirements under section 256B(6), the justice may—

(a) issue a summons requiring the offender to appear at the place and time specified in the summons, or

(b) if the information is in writing and on oath, issue a warrant for the offender's arrest.

(2) Any summons or warrant issued under this section must direct the offender to appear or be brought—

(a) before a court acting for the local justice area in which the offender resides, or

(b) if it is not known where the offender resides, before a court acting for same local justice area as the justice who issued the summons or warrant.

(3) Where the offender does not appear in answer to a summons issued under subsection (1)(a), the court may issue a warrant for the offender's arrest.

(4) If it is proved to the satisfaction of the court that the offender has failed to comply with requirements under section 256B(6), the court may—

(a) order the offender to be detained, in prison or such youth detention accommodation as the Secretary of State may determine, for such period, not exceeding 30 days, as the court may specify, or

(b) order the offender to pay a fine not exceeding level 3 on the standard scale.

(5) An offender detained in pursuance of an order under subsection (4)(a) is to be regarded as being in legal custody.

(6) A fine imposed under subsection (4)(b) is to be treated, for the purposes of any enactment, as being a sum adjudged to be paid by a conviction.

(7) An offender may appeal to the Crown Court against any order made under subsection (4)(a) or (b).

(8) In this section 'court' means—

(a) if the offender has attained the age of 18 years at the date of release, a magistrates' court other than a youth court;

(b) if the offender is under the age of 18 years at the date of release, a youth court.

256D   Drug testing requirements

(1) 'Drug testing requirement', in relation to an offender subject to supervision under this Chapter, means a requirement that, when instructed to do so by the supervisor, the offender provide a sample mentioned in the instruction for the purpose of ascertaining whether the offender has a specified Class A drug or a specified Class B drug in his or her body.

(2) A drug testing requirement may be imposed on an offender subject to supervision under this Chapter only if—

(a) the Secretary of State is satisfied of the matters in subsection (3), and

(b) the requirement is being imposed for the purpose of determining whether the offender is complying with any other supervision requirement.

(3) Those matters are—

(a) that the misuse by the offender of a specified class A drug or a specified class B drug caused or contributed to an offence of which the offender has been convicted or is likely to cause or contribute to the commission of further offences by the offender, and

(b) that the offender is dependent on, or has a propensity to misuse, a specified class A drug or a specified class B drug.

(4) An instruction given for the purpose of a drug testing requirement must be given in accordance with guidance given from time to time by the Secretary of State.

(5) The Secretary of State may make rules regulating the provision of samples in accordance with such an instruction.

(6) In this section, 'specified Class A drug' and 'specified Class B drug' have the same meaning as in Part 3 of the Criminal Justice and Court Services Act 2000.

256E   Drug appointment requirements

(1) 'Drug appointment requirement', in relation to an offender subject to supervision under this Chapter, means a requirement that the offender, in accordance with instructions given by the supervisor, attend appointments with a view to addressing the offender's dependency on, or propensity to misuse, a controlled drug.

(2) A drug appointment requirement may be imposed on an offender subject to supervision under this Chapter only if—

(a) the supervisor has recommended to the Secretary of State that such a requirement be imposed on the offender, and

(b) the Secretary of State is satisfied of the matters in subsection (3).

(3) Those matters are—

    (a) that the misuse by the offender of a controlled drug caused or contributed to an offence of which the offender has been convicted or is likely to cause or contribute to the commission of further offences by the offender,

    (b) that the offender is dependent on, or has a propensity to misuse, a controlled drug,

    (c) that the dependency or propensity requires, and may be susceptible to, treatment, and

    (d) that arrangements have been made, or can be made, for the offender to have treatment.

(4) The requirement must specify—

    (a) the person with whom the offender is to meet or under whose direction the appointments are to take place, and

    (b) where the appointments are to take place.

(5) The person specified under subsection (4)(a) must be a person who has the necessary qualifications or experience.

(6) The only instructions that the supervisor may give for the purposes of the requirement are instructions as to—

    (a) the duration of each appointment, and

    (b) when each appointment is to take place.

(7) For the purposes of this section, references to a requirement to attend an appointment do not include a requirement to submit to treatment.

(8) In this section, 'controlled drug' has the same meaning as in the Misuse of Drugs Act 1971.

257   Additional days for disciplinary offences

(1) Prison rules, that is to say, rules made under section 47 of the Prison Act 1952 (c. 52), may include provision for the award of additional days—

    (a) to fixed-term prisoners, or

    (b) conditionally on their subsequently becoming such prisoners, to persons on remand,

who (in either case) are guilty of disciplinary offences.

(2) Where additional days are awarded to a fixed—term prisoner, or to a person on remand who subsequently becomes such a prisoner, and are not remitted in accordance with prison rules—

    (a) any period which he must serve before becoming entitled to or eligible for release under this Chapter,

    (b) any period which he must serve before he can be removed from prison under section 260, and

    (c) any period for which a licence granted to him under this Chapter remains in force,

is extended by the aggregate of those additional days.

258   Early release of fine defaulters and contemnors

(1) This section applies in relation to a person committed to prison—

    (a) in default of payment of a sum adjudged to be paid by a conviction, or

    (b) for contempt of court or any kindred offence.

(2) As soon as a person to whom this section applies has served one-half of the term for which he was committed, it is the duty of the Secretary of State to release him unconditionally.

(2A) Subsection (2) is subject to paragraph 35 of Schedule 20B (transitional cases).

(2B) Subsection (2) does not apply to a person within subsection (1)(a) if the sum in question is a sum of more than £10 million ordered to be paid under a confiscation order made under Part 2 of the Proceeds of Crime Act 2002.

(2C) The Secretary of State may by order amend the amount for the time being specified in subsection (2B).

(3) Where a person to whom this section applies is also serving one or more sentences of imprisonment or detention in a young offender institution, nothing in this section or in paragraph 35 of Schedule 20B requires the Secretary of State to release him until he is also required to release him in respect of that sentence or each of those sentences.

(3A) The reference in subsection (3) to sentences of imprisonment includes sentences of detention under section 91 or 96 of the Sentencing Act or under section 226A, 226B, 227, 228 or 236A of this Act.

(4) The Secretary of State may at any time release unconditionally a person to whom this section applies if he is satisfied that exceptional circumstances exist which justify the person's release on compassionate grounds.

259 Persons liable to removal from the United Kingdom

For the purposes of this Chapter a person is liable to removal from the United Kingdom if—
- (a) he is liable to deportation under section 3(5) of the Immigration Act 1971 (c. 77) and has been notified of a decision to make a deportation order against him,
- (b) he is liable to deportation under section 3(6) of that Act,
- (c) he has been notified of a decision to refuse him leave to enter the United Kingdom,
- (d) he is an illegal entrant within the meaning of section 33(1) of that Act, or
- (e) he is liable to removal under section 10 of the Immigration and Asylum Act 1999 (c. 33).

260 Early removals of prisoners liable to removal from United Kingdom

(1) Subject to subsection (2), where a fixed-term prisoner is liable to removal from the United Kingdom, the Secretary of State may remove him from prison under this section at any time during the period of 270 days ending with the day on which the prisoner will have served the requisite custodial period.

(2) Subsection (1) does not apply in relation to a prisoner unless he has served at least one-half of the requisite custodial period.

(2A) If a fixed-term prisoner serving an extended sentence imposed under section 226A or 226B or a sentence under section 236A—
- (a) is liable to removal from the United Kingdom, and
- (b) has not been removed from prison under this section during the period mentioned in subsection (1),

the Secretary of State may remove the prisoner from prison under this section at any time after the end of that period.

(2B) Subsection (2A) applies whether or not the Board has directed the prisoner's release under this Chapter.

(4) A prisoner removed from prison under this section—
- (a) is so removed only for the purpose of enabling the Secretary of State to remove him from the United Kingdom under powers conferred by—
  - (i) Schedule 2 or 3 to the Immigration Act 1971, or
  - (ii) section 10 of the Immigration and Asylum Act 1999 (c. 33), and
- (b) so long as remaining in the United Kingdom, remains liable to be detained in pursuance of his sentence until he has served the requisite custodial period.

(5) So long as a prisoner removed from prison under this section remains in the United Kingdom but has not been returned to prison, any duty or power of the Secretary of State under section 243A, 244, 244A, 246A, 247 or 248 is exercisable in relation to him as if he were in prison.

(6) The Secretary of State may by order—
- (a) amend the number of days for the time being specified in subsection (1)
- (c) amend the fraction for the time being specified in subsection (2)

(8) Paragraphs 36 and 37 of Schedule 20B (transitional cases) make further provision about early removal of certain prisoners.

261 Re-entry into United Kingdom of offender removed from prison early

(1) This section applies in relation to a person who, after being removed from prison under section 260, has been removed from the United Kingdom before he has served the requisite custodial period.

(2) If a person to whom this section applies enters the United Kingdom at any time before his sentence expiry date, he is liable to be detained in pursuance of his sentence from the time of his entry into the United Kingdom until whichever is the earlier of the following—

  (a) the end of a period ('the further custodial period') beginning with that time and equal in length to the outstanding custodial period, and

  (b) his sentence expiry date.

(3) A person who is liable to be detained by virtue of subsection (2) is, if at large, to be taken for the purposes of section 49 of the Prison Act 1952 (c. 52) (persons unlawfully at large) to be unlawfully at large.

(4) Subsection (2) does not prevent the further removal from the United Kingdom of a person falling within that subsection.

(5) Where, in the case of a person returned to prison by virtue of subsection (2), the further custodial period ends before the sentence expiry date—

  (b) section 243A, 244, 244A, 246A or 247 (as the case may be) has effect in relation to him as if the reference to the requisite custodial period were a reference to the further custodial period.

(6) In this section—

'further custodial period' has the meaning given by subsection (2)(a);

'outstanding custodial period', in relation to a person to whom this section applies, means the period beginning with the date of his removal from the United Kingdom and ending with the date on which he would, but for his removal, have served the requisite custodial period;

'sentence expiry date', in relation to a person to whom this section applies, means the date on which, but for his release from prison and removal from the United Kingdom, he would have served the whole of the sentence.

263 Concurrent terms

(1) This section applies where—

  (a) a person ('the offender') has been sentenced to two or more terms of imprisonment which are wholly or partly concurrent, and

  (b) the sentences were passed on the same occasion or, where they were passed on different occasions, the person has not been released under this Chapter at any time during the period beginning with the first and ending with the last of those occasions.

(2) Where this section applies—

  (a)   nothing in this Chapter requires the Secretary of State to release the offender in respect of any of the terms unless and until he is required to release him in respect of each of the others,

  (aa) the offender's release is to be unconditional if section 243A so requires in respect of each of the sentences (and in any other case is to be on licence),

  (b)   section 246 does not authorise the Secretary of State to release him on licence under that section in respect of any of the terms unless and until that section authorises the Secretary of State to do so in respect of each of the others to which that section applies,

  (c)   on and after his release under this Chapter (unless that release is unconditional) the offender is to be on licence

      (i)   until the last date on which the offender is required to be on licence in respect of any of the terms, and

      (ii) subject to such conditions as are required by this Chapter in respect of any of the sentences.

(4) In this section 'term of imprisonment' includes a determinate sentence of detention under section 91 or 96 of the Sentencing Act or under section 227, 228 or 236A of this Act or a sentence of detention in a young offender institution under section 96 of the Sentencing Act or section 226A, 226B, or 227 of this Act.

(5) This section is subject to paragraphs 21, 31 and 32 of Schedule 20B (transitional cases).

264 Consecutive terms

(1) This section applies where—

(a) a person ('the offender') has been sentenced to two or more terms of imprisonment which are to be served consecutively on each other, and

(b) the sentences were passed on the same occasion or, where they were passed on different occasions, the person has not been released under this Chapter at any time during the period beginning with the first and ending with the last of those occasions

(2) Nothing in this Chapter requires the Secretary of State to release the offender until he has served a period equal in length to the aggregate of the length of the custodial periods in relation to each of the terms of imprisonment.

(3B) The offender's release under this Chapter is to be unconditional if—

(a) the aggregate length of the terms of imprisonment is less than 12 months, and

(b) section 243A so requires in respect of each of the sentences,

but in any other case is to be on licence.

(3C) If the offender is released on licence under this Chapter—

(a) the offender is to be on licence, on and after the release, until the offender would, but for the release, have served a term equal in length to the aggregate length of the terms of imprisonment (but see section 264B);

(b) the offender is to be subject to supervision requirements under section 256AA if (and only if)—

(i) section 256AA so requires in respect of one or more of the sentences, and

(ii) the aggregate length of the terms of imprisonment is less than 2 years.

(3D) If the offender is subject to supervision requirements under section 256AA, the supervision period for the purposes of that section begins on the expiry of the period during which the offender is on licence by virtue of subsection (3C)(a).

(3E) When the offender is released under this Chapter (whether unconditionally or on licence), the offender is to be subject to supervision requirements under section 256B if that section so requires in respect of one or more of the sentences.

(6) In this section 'custodial period' means—

(a) in relation to an extended sentence imposed under section 226A or 226B, two-thirds of the appropriate custodial term determined by the court under that section,

(b) in relation to an extended sentence imposed under section 227 or 228, one-half of the appropriate custodial term determined by the court under that section,

(c) in relation to a sentence imposed under section 236A, one-half of the appropriate custodial term determined by the court under that section, and

(d) in relation to any other sentence, one-half of the sentence.

(7) This section applies to a determinate sentence of detention under section 91 or 96 of the Sentencing Act or under section 227, 228 or 236A of this Act or a sentence of detention in a young offender institution under section 96 of the Sentencing Act or section 226A, 226B or 227 of this Act as it applies to a term of imprisonment.

(8) This section is subject to paragraphs 21, 22, 31, 32 and 33 of Schedule 20B (transitional cases).

264B Consecutive terms: supplementary

(1) This section applies in a case in which section 264 applies where—

(a) the offender is released on licence under this Chapter,

(b) the aggregate length of the terms of imprisonment mentioned in section 264(1)(a) is less than 12 months, and

(c) those terms include one or more terms of imprisonment ('short transitional terms') which were imposed in respect of an offence committed before the day on which section 1 of the Offender Rehabilitation Act 2014 came into force, as well as one or more terms imposed in respect of an offence committed on or after that day.

(2) The offender is to be on licence until the offender would, but for the release, have served a term equal in length to the aggregate of—

(a) the custodial period in relation to each of the short transitional terms, and

(b) the full length of each of the other terms.

(3) In this section 'custodial period' has the same meaning as in section 264.

265 Restriction on consecutive sentences for released prisoners

(1) A court sentencing a person to a term of imprisonment may not order or direct that the term is to commence on the expiry of any other sentence of imprisonment from which he has been released —

(a) under this Chapter; or

(b) under Part 2 of the Criminal Justice Act 1991.

(2) In this section 'sentence of imprisonment' includes a sentence of detention under section 91 or 96 of the Sentencing Act or section 227, 228 or 236A of this Act or a sentence of detention in a young offender institution under section 96 of the Sentencing Act or under section 226A, 226B, 227 of this Act, and 'term of imprisonment' is to be read accordingly.

267 Alteration by order of relevant proportion of sentence

The Secretary of State may by order provide that any reference in section 243A(3)(a), section 244(3)(a), section 247(2) or section 264(6)(a)(ii) to a particular proportion of a prisoner's sentence is to be read as a reference to such other proportion of a prisoner's sentence as may be specified in the order.

. . .

268 Interpretation of Chapter 6

In this Chapter—

'the 1997 Act' means the Crime (Sentences) Act 1997 (c. 43);

'the Board' means the Parole Board;

'fixed-term prisoner' and 'fixed-term sentence' have the meaning given by section 237(1) (as extended by section 237(1B));

'prison' and 'prisoner' are to be read in accordance with section 237(2)

'supervision default order' means an order described in section 256AC(4)(c), whether made under that provision or under paragraph 9 of Schedule 19A;

'the supervision period', in relation to an offender subject to supervision under this Chapter, has the meaning given in section 256AA or 256B (as appropriate);

'the supervisor'—

(a) in relation to an offender subject to supervision requirements under section 256AA, has the meaning given in that section, and

(b) in relation to an offender subject to supervision requirements under section 256B, means the person who provides supervision under that section.

(1A) In this Chapter, 'the requisite custodial period' means—

(a) in relation to a person serving an extended sentence imposed under section 226A or 226B, the requisite custodial period for the purposes of section 246A;

(b) in relation to a person serving an extended sentence imposed under section 227 or 228, the requisite custodial period for the purposes of section 247;

(c) in relation to a person serving a sentence imposed under section 236A, the requisite custodial period for the purposes of section 244A;

(d) in relation to any other fixed-term prisoner, the requisite custodial period for the purposes of section 243A or section 244 (as appropriate).

(2) For the purposes of sections 243A(1A), 256AA(1), 256B(1A) and 264B(1), where an offence is found to have been committed over a period of 2 or more days, or at some time during a period of 2 or more days, it must be taken to have been committed on the last of those days.

269 Determination of minimum term in relation to mandatory life sentence

(1) This section applies where after the commencement of this section a court passes a life sentence in circumstances where the sentence is fixed by law.

(2) The court must, unless it makes an order under subsection (4), order that the provisions of section 28(5) to (8) of the Crime (Sentences) Act 1997 (referred to in this Chapter as 'the early release provisions') are to apply to the offender as soon as he has served the part of his sentence which is specified in the order.

(3) The part of his sentence is to be such as the court considers appropriate taking into account—

> (a) the seriousness of the offence, or of the combination of the offence and any one or more offences associated with it, and
> (b) the effect of section 240ZA (crediting periods of remand in custody) or of any direction which it would have given under section 240A (crediting periods of remand on certain types of bail) if it had sentenced him to a term of imprisonment.

(3A) The reference in subsection (3)(b) to section 240ZA includes section 246 of the Armed Forces Act 2006 (crediting periods in service custody).

(4) If the offender was 21 or over when he committed the offence and the court is of the opinion that, because of the seriousness of the offence, or of the combination of the offence and one or more offences associated with it, no order should be made under subsection (2), the court must order that the early release provisions are not to apply to the offender.

(5) In considering under subsection (3) or (4) the seriousness of an offence (or of the combination of an offence and one or more offences associated with it), the court must have regard to—

> (a) the general principles set out in Schedule 21, and
> (b) any guidelines relating to offences in general which are relevant to the case and are not incompatible with the provisions of Schedule 21.

(6) The Lord Chancellor may by order amend Schedule 21.

(7) Before making an order under subsection (6), the Lord Chancellor must consult the Sentencing Council for England and Wales

270 Duty to give reasons

(1) Subsection (2) applies where a court makes an order under section 269(2) or (4).

(2) In complying with the duty under section 174(2) to state its reasons for deciding on the order made, the court must, in particular—

> (a) state which of the starting points in Schedule 21 it has chosen and its reasons for doing so, and
> (b) state its reasons for any departure from that starting point.

271 Appeals

(1) In section 9 of the Criminal Appeal Act 1968 (c. 19) (appeal against sentence following conviction on indictment), after subsection (1) there is inserted—

'(1A) In subsection (1) of this section, the reference to a sentence fixed by law does not include a reference to an order made under subsection (2) or (4) of section 269 of the Criminal Justice Act 2003 in relation to a life sentence (as defined in section 277 of that Act) that is fixed by law.'

(2) In section 8 of the Courts-Martial (Appeals) Act 1968 (c. 20) (right of appeal from court-martial to Courts-Martial Appeal Court) after subsection (1) there is inserted—

'(1ZA) In subsection (1) above, the reference to a sentence fixed by law does not include a reference to an order made under subsection (2) or (4) of section 269 of the Criminal Justice Act 2003 in relation to a life sentence (as defined in section 277 of that Act) that is fixed by law.'

272 Review of minimum term on a reference by Attorney General

(1) In section 36 of the Criminal Justice Act 1988 (c. 33) (reviews of sentencing) after subsection (3) there is inserted—

'(3A) Where a reference under this section relates to an order under subsection (2) of section 269 of the Criminal Justice Act 2003 (determination of minimum term in relation to mandatory life sentence), the Court of Appeal shall not, in deciding what order under that section is appropriate for the case, make any allowance for the fact that the person to whom it relates is being sentenced for a second time.'

273   Life prisoners transferred to England and Wales

(1)   The Secretary of State must refer the case of any transferred life prisoner to the High Court for the making of one or more relevant orders.

(2)   In subsection (1) 'transferred life prisoner' means a person—

(a)   on whom a court in a country or territory outside the British Islands has imposed one or more sentences of imprisonment or detention for an indeterminate period, and

(b)   who has been transferred to England and Wales after the commencement of this section in pursuance of—

(i)   an order made by the Secretary of State under section 2 of the Colonial Prisoners Removal Act 1884 (c. 31), or

(ii)   a warrant issued by the Secretary of State under the Repatriation of Prisoners Act 1984 (c. 47),

there to serve his sentence or sentences or the remainder of his sentence or sentences.

(3)   In subsection (1) 'a relevant order' means—

(a)   in the case of an offence which appears to the court to be an offence for which, if it had been committed in England and Wales, the sentence would have been fixed by law, an order under subsection (2) or (4) of section 269, and

(b)   in any other case, an order under subsection (2) or (4) of section 82A of the Sentencing Act.

(4)   In section 34(1) of the Crime (Sentences) Act 1997 (c. 43) (meaning of 'life prisoner' in Chapter 2 of Part 2 of that Act) at the end there is inserted 'and includes a transferred life prisoner as defined by section 273 of the Criminal Justice Act 2003'.

(5)   The reference in subsection (2)(b) above to a person who has been transferred to England and Wales in pursuance of a warrant issued under the Repatriation of Prisoners Act 1984 includes a reference to a person who is detained in England and Wales in pursuance of a warrant under section 4A of that Act (warrant transferring responsibility for detention and release of offender).

...

275   Duty to release certain life prisoners

(1)   Section 28 of the Crime (Sentences) Act 1997 (c. 43) (duty to release certain life prisoners) is amended as follows.

(2)   For subsection (1A) there is substituted—

'(1A) This section applies to a life prisoner in respect of whom a minimum term order has been made; and any reference in this section to the relevant part of such a prisoner's sentence is a reference to the part of the sentence specified in the order.'

(3)   In subsection (1B)(a)—

(a)   for the words from the beginning to 'applies' there is substituted 'this section does not apply to him', and

(b)   for the words from 'such an order' to 'appropriate stage' there is substituted 'a minimum term order has been made in respect of each of those sentences'.

(4)   After subsection (8) there is inserted—

'(8A) In this section "minimum term order" means an order under—

(a)   subsection (2) of section 82A of the Powers of Criminal Courts (Sentencing) Act 2000 (determination of minimum term in respect of life sentence that is not fixed by law), or

(b)   subsection (2) of section 269 of the Criminal Justice Act 2003 (determination of minimum term in respect of mandatory life sentence).'.

276   Mandatory life sentences: transitional cases

Schedule 22 (which relates to the effect in transitional cases of mandatory life sentences) shall have effect.

277   Interpretation of Chapter 7

In this Chapter—

'court' includes the Court Martial;

'guidelines' means sentencing guidelines issued by the Sentencing Council for England and Wales as definitive guidelines under section 120 of the Coroners and Justice Act 2009, as revised by any subsequent guidelines so issued;

'life sentence' means—

(a) a sentence of imprisonment for life,

(b) a sentence of detention during Her Majesty's pleasure, or

(c) a sentence of custody for life passed before the commencement of section 61(1) of the Criminal Justice and Court Services Act 2000 (c. 43) (which abolishes that sentence).

284   Increase in penalties for drug-related offences

(1) Schedule 28 (increase in penalties for certain drug-related offences) shall have effect.

(2) That Schedule does not affect the penalty for any offence committed before the commencement of that Schedule.

285   Increase in penalties for certain driving-related offences

(1) In section 12A of the Theft Act 1968 (c. 60) (aggravated vehicle-taking), in subsection (4), for 'five years' there is substituted 'fourteen years'.

(2) Part 1 of Schedule 2 to the Road Traffic Offenders Act 1988 (c. 53) (prosecution and punishment of offences) is amended in accordance with subsections (3) and (4).

(3) In the entry relating to section 1 of the Road Traffic Act 1988 (c. 52) (causing death by dangerous driving), in column 4, for '10 years' there is substituted '14 years'.

(4) In the entry relating to section 3A of that Act (causing death by careless driving when under influence of drink or drugs), in column 4, for '10 years' there is substituted '14 years'.

(5) Part I of Schedule 1 to the Road Traffic Offenders (Northern Ireland) Order 1996 (S.I. 1996/1320 (N.I. 10)) (prosecution and punishment of offences) is amended in accordance with subsections (6) and (7).

(6) In the entry relating to Article 9 of the Road Traffic (Northern Ireland) Order 1995 (S.I. 1995/2994 (N.I. 18)) (causing death or grievous bodily injury by dangerous driving), in column 4, for '10 years' there is substituted '14 years'.

(7) In the entry relating to Article 14 of that Order (causing death or grievous bodily injury by careless driving when under the influence of drink or drugs), in column 4, for '10 years' there is substituted '14 years'.

(8) This section does not affect the penalty for any offence committed before the commencement of this section.

286   Increase in penalties for offences under section 174 of Road Traffic Act 1988

(1) In Part 1 of Schedule 2 to the Road Traffic Offenders Act 1988 (c. 53) (prosecution and punishment of offences), in the entry relating to section 174 of the Road Traffic Act 1988 (c. 52) (false statements and withholding material information), for columns (3) and (4) there is substituted—

'(a) Summarily	(a) 6 months or the statutory maximum or both
(b) On indictment	(b) 2 years or a fine or both.'

(2) Section 282(3) (increase in maximum term that may be imposed on summary conviction of offence triable either way) has effect in relation to the entry amended by subsection (1) as it has effect in relation to any other enactment contained in an Act passed before this Act.

(3) This section does not apply in relation to any offence committed before the commencement of this section.

287   Minimum sentence for certain firearms offences

After section 51 of the Firearms Act 1968 (c. 27) there is inserted the following section—

'51A   Minimum sentence for certain offences under s. 5

(1) This section applies where—

    (a) an individual is convicted of—

        (i)   an offence under section 5(1)(a), (ab), (aba), (ac), (ad), (ae), (af) or (c) of this Act, or

        (ii) an offence under section 5(1A)(a) of this Act, and

    (b) the offence was committed after the commencement of this section and at a time when he was aged 16 or over.

(2) The court shall impose an appropriate custodial sentence (or order for detention) for a term of at least the required minimum term (with or without a fine) unless the court is of the opinion that there are exceptional circumstances relating to the offence or to the offender which justify its not doing so.

(3) Where an offence is found to have been committed over a period of two or more days, or at some time during a period of two or more days, it shall be taken for the purposes of this section to have been committed on the last of those days.

(4) In this section "appropriate custodial sentence (or order for detention)" means—

    (a) in relation to England and Wales—

        (i)   in the case of an offender who is aged 18 or over when convicted, a sentence of imprisonment, and

        (ii) in the case of an offender who is aged under 18 at that time, a sentence of detention under section 91 of the Powers of Criminal Courts (Sentencing) Act 2000;

    (b) in relation to Scotland—

        (i)   in the case of an offender who is aged 21 or over when convicted, a sentence of imprisonment,

        (ii) in the case of an offender who is aged under 21 at that time (not being an offender mentioned in sub-paragraph (iii)), a sentence of detention under section 207 of the Criminal Procedure (Scotland) Act 1995, and

        (iii) in the case of an offender who is aged under 18 at that time and is subject to a supervision requirement, an order for detention under section 44, or sentence of detention under section 208, of that Act.

(5) In this section "the required minimum term" means—

    (a) in relation to England and Wales—

        (i)   in the case of an offender who was aged 18 or over when he committed the offence, five years, and

        (ii) in the case of an offender who was under 18 at that time, three years, and

    (b) in relation to Scotland—

        (i)   in the case of an offender who was aged 21 or over when he committed the offence, five years, and

        (ii) in the case of an offender who was aged under 21 at that time, three years.'

288   Certain firearms offences to be triable only on indictment

In Part 1 of Schedule 6 to the Firearms Act 1968 (c. 27) (prosecution and punishment of offences) for the entries relating to offences under section 5(1) (possessing or distributing prohibited weapons or ammunition) and section 5(1A) (possessing or distributing other prohibited weapons) there is substituted—

'Section 5(1)(a), (ab), (aba), (ac), (ad), (ae), (af) or (c)	Possessing or distributing prohibited weapons or ammunition.	On indictment	10 years or a fine, or both.
Section 5(1)(b)	Possessing or distributing prohibited weapon designed for discharge of noxious liquid etc.	(a) Summary	6 months or a fine of the statutory maximum, or both.
		(b) On indictment	10 years or a fine or both.
Section 5(1A)(a)	Possessing or distributing firearm disguised as other object.	On indictment	10 years or a fine, or both.
Section 5(1A)(b), (c), (d), (e), (f) or (g)	Possessing or distributing other prohibited weapons.	(a) Summary	6 months or a fine of the statutory maximum, or both.
		(b) On indictment	10 years or a fine, or both.'

289   Power to sentence young offender to detention in respect of certain firearms offences: England and Wales

(1) Section 91 of the Sentencing Act (offenders under 18 convicted of certain serious offences: power to detain for specified period) is amended as follows.

(2) After subsection (1) there is inserted—

'(1A) Subsection (3) below also applies where—

  (a) a person aged under 18 is convicted on indictment of an offence—

    (i)   under subsection (1)(a), (ab), (aba), (ac), (ad), (ae), (af) or (c) of section 5 of the Firearms Act 1968 (prohibited weapons), or

    (ii) under subsection (1A)(a) of that section,

  (b) the offence was committed after the commencement of section 51A of that Act and at a time when he was aged 16 or over, and

  (c) the court is of the opinion mentioned in section 51A(2) of that Act (exceptional circumstances which justify its not imposing required custodial sentence).'

(3) After subsection (4) there is inserted—

'(5) Where subsection (2) of section 51A of the Firearms Act 1968 requires the imposition of a sentence of detention under this section for a term of at least the required minimum term (within the meaning of that section), the court shall sentence the offender to be detained for such period, of at least that term but not exceeding the maximum term of imprisonment with which the offence is punishable in the case of a person aged 18 or over, as may be specified in the sentence.'.

. . .

291   Power by order to exclude application of minimum sentence to those under 18

(1) The Secretary of State may by order—

  (a) amend section 51A(1)(b) of the Firearms Act 1968 (c. 27) by substituting for the word '16' the word '18',

  (aa) amend section 29(3)(a) of the Violent Crime Reduction Act 2006 by substituting for the word '16' the word '18',

  (b) repeal section 91(1A)(c) and (5) of the Sentencing Act,

  (c) amend subsection (3) of section 49 of the Criminal Procedure (Scotland) Act 1995 by repealing the exception to that subsection,

  (d) repeal section 208(2) of that Act, and

(e) make such other provision as he considers necessary or expedient in consequence of, or in connection with, the provision made by virtue of paragraphs (a) to (d).

(2) The provision that may be made by virtue of subsection (1)(e) includes, in particular, provision amending or repealing any provision of an Act (whenever passed), including any provision of this Act.

293 Increase in penalty for offences relating to importation or exportation of certain firearms

(1) The Customs and Excise Management Act 1979 (c. 2) is amended as follows.

(2) In section 50 (penalty for improper importation of goods), for subsection (5A) there is substituted—

'(5A) In the case of—

    (a) an offence under subsection (2) or (3) above committed in Great Britain in connection with a prohibition or restriction on the importation of any weapon or ammunition that is of a kind mentioned in section 5(1)(a), (ab), (aba), (ac), (ad), (ae), (af) or (c) or (1A)(a) of the Firearms Act 1968,

    (b) any such offence committed in Northern Ireland in connection with a prohibition or restriction on the importation of any weapon or ammunition that is of a kind mentioned in Article 6(1)(a), (ab), (ac), (ad), (ae) or (c) or (1A)(a) of the Firearms (Northern Ireland) Order 1981, or

    (c) any such offence committed in connection with the prohibition contained in section 20 of the Forgery and Counterfeiting Act 1981,

subsection (4)(b) above shall have effect as if for the words "7 years" there were substituted the words "10 years".'

(3) In section 68 (offences in relation to exportation of prohibited or restricted goods) for subsection (4A) there is substituted—

'(4A) In the case of—

    (a) an offence under subsection (2) or (3) above committed in Great Britain in connection with a prohibition or restriction on the exportation of any weapon or ammunition that is of a kind mentioned in section 5(1)(a), (ab), (aba), (ac), (ad), (ae), (af) or (c) or (1A)(a) of the Firearms Act 1968,

    (b) any such offence committed in Northern Ireland in connection with a prohibition or restriction on the exportation of any weapon or ammunition that is of a kind mentioned in Article 6(1)(a), (ab), (ac), (ad), (ae) or (c) or (1A)(a) of the Firearms (Northern Ireland) Order 1981, or

    (c) any such offence committed in connection with the prohibition contained in section 21 of the Forgery and Counterfeiting Act 1981,

subsection (3)(b) above shall have effect as if for the words "7 years" there were substituted the words "10 years".'

(4) In section 170 (penalty for fraudulent evasion of duty, etc), for subsection (4A) there is substituted—

'(4A) In the case of—

    (a) an offence under subsection (2) or (3) above committed in Great Britain in connection with a prohibition or restriction on the importation or exportation of any weapon or ammunition that is of a kind mentioned in section 5(1)(a), (ab), (aba), (ac), (ad), (ae), (af) or (c) or (1A)(a) of the Firearms Act 1968,

    (b) any such offence committed in Northern Ireland in connection with a prohibition or restriction on the importation or exportation of any weapon or ammunition that is of a kind mentioned in Article 6(1)(a), (ab), (ac), (ad), (ae) or (c) or (1A)(a) of the Firearms (Northern Ireland) Order 1981, or

    (c) any such offence committed in connection with the prohibitions contained in sections 20 and 21 of the Forgery and Counterfeiting Act 1981, subsection (3)(b) above shall have effect as if for the words "7 years" there were substituted the words "10 years".'

(5) This section does not affect the penalty for any offence committed before the commencement of this section.

294   Duration of directions under Mental Health Act 1983 in relation to offenders

(1) Section 50 of the Mental Health Act 1983 (c. 20) (further provisions as to prisoners under sentence) is amended as follows.

(2) In subsection (1), for 'the expiration of that person's sentence' there is substituted 'his release date'.

(3) For subsections (2) and (3) there is substituted—

'(2) A restriction direction in the case of a person serving a sentence of imprisonment shall cease to have effect, if it has not previously done so, on his release date.

(3) In this section, references to a person's release date are to the day (if any) on which he would be entitled to be released (whether unconditionally or on licence) from any prison or other institution in which he might have been detained if the transfer direction had not been given; and in determining that day there shall be disregarded—

(a) any powers that would be exercisable by the Parole Board if he were detained in such a prison or other institution, and

(b) any practice of the Secretary of State in relation to the early release under discretionary powers of persons detained in such a prison or other institution.'.

295   Access to Parole Board for certain patients serving prison sentences

In section 74 of the Mental Health Act 1983 (restricted patients subject to restriction directions) after subsection (5) there is inserted—

'(5A) Where the tribunal have made a recommendation under subsection (1)(b) above in the case of a patient who is subject to a restriction direction or a limitation direction—

(a) the fact that the restriction direction or limitation direction remains in force does not prevent the making of any application or reference to the Parole Board by or in respect of him or the exercise by him of any power to require the Secretary of State to refer his case to the Parole Board, and

(b) if the Parole Board make a direction or recommendation by virtue of which the patient would become entitled to be released (whether unconditionally or on licence) from any prison or other institution in which he might have been detained if he had not been removed to hospital, the restriction direction or limitation direction shall cease to have effect at the time when he would become entitled to be so released.'

300   Power to impose unpaid work requirement curfew requirement or attendance centre requirement on fine defaulter

(1) Subsection (2) applies in any case where, in respect of a person aged 16 or over, a magistrates' court—

(a) has power under Part 3 of the Magistrates' Courts Act 1980 (c. 43) to issue a warrant of commitment for default in paying a sum adjudged to be paid by a conviction (other than a sum ordered to be paid under section 6 of the Proceeds of Crime Act 2002 (c. 29)), or

(b) would, but for section 89 of the Sentencing Act (restrictions on custodial sentences for persons under 18), have power to issue such a warrant for such default.

(2) The magistrates' court may, instead of issuing a warrant of commitment or, as the case may be, proceeding under section 81 of the Magistrates' Courts Act 1980 (enforcement of fines imposed on young offender), order the person in default to comply with—

(a) an unpaid work requirement (as defined by section 199), or

(b) a curfew requirement (as defined by section 204), or

(c) in a case where the person is aged under 25, an attendance centre requirement (as defined by section 214).

(3) In this Part 'default order' means an order under subsection (2).

(4) Subsections (3) and (4) of section 177 (which relate to electronic monitoring) have effect in relation to a default order as they have effect in relation to a community order.

(5) Where a magistrates' court has power to make a default order, it may, if it thinks it expedient to do so, postpone the making of the order until such time and on such conditions (if any) as it thinks just.

(6) Schedule 8 (breach, revocation or amendment of community order), Schedule 9 (transfer of community orders to Scotland or Northern Ireland) and Chapter 4 (further provisions about orders under Chapters 2 and 3) have effect in relation to default orders as they have effect in relation to community orders, but subject to the modifications contained in Schedule 31.

(7) Where a default order has been made for default in paying any sum—

(a) on payment of the whole sum to any person authorised to receive it, the order shall cease to have effect, and

(b) on payment of a part of the sum to any such person, the total number of hours or days to which the order relates is to be taken to be reduced by a proportion corresponding to that which the part paid bears to the whole sum.

(8) In calculating any reduction required by subsection (7)(b), any fraction of a day or hour is to be disregarded.

301   Fine defaulters: driving disqualification

(1) Subsection (2) applies in any case where a magistrates' court—

(a) has power under Part 3 of the Magistrates' Courts Act 1980 (c. 43) to issue a warrant of commitment for default in paying a sum adjudged to be paid by a conviction (other than a sum ordered to be paid under section 6 of the Proceeds of Crime Act 2002 (c. 29)), or

(b) would, but for section 89 of the Sentencing Act (restrictions on custodial sentences for persons under 18), have power to issue such a warrant for such default.

(2) The magistrates' court may, instead of issuing a warrant of commitment or, as the case may be, proceeding under section 81 of the Magistrates' Courts Act 1980 (enforcement of fines imposed on young offenders), order the person in default to be disqualified, for such period not exceeding twelve months as it thinks fit, for holding or obtaining a driving licence.

(3) Where an order has been made under subsection (2) for default in paying any sum—

(a) on payment of the whole sum to any person authorised to receive it, the order shall cease to have effect, and

(b) on payment of part of the sum to any such person, the total number of weeks or months to which the order relates is to be taken to be reduced by a proportion corresponding to that which the part paid bears to the whole sum.

(4) In calculating any reduction required by subsection (3)(b) any fraction of a week or month is to be disregarded.

(5) The Secretary of State may by order amend subsection (2) by substituting, for the period there specified, such other period as may be specified in the order.

(6) A court which makes an order under this section disqualifying a person for holding or obtaining a driving licence shall require him to produce—

(a) any such licence held by him; or

(b) in the case where he holds a Community licence (within the meaning of Part 3 of the Road Traffic Act 1988 (c. 52)), his Community licence.

(7) In this section—

'driving licence' means a licence to drive a motor vehicle granted under Part 3 of that Act.

SCHEDULE 15 SPECIFIED OFFENCES FOR PURPOSES OF CHAPTER 5 OF PART 12

PART 1 SPECIFIED VIOLENT OFFENCES

1 Manslaughter.

2 Kidnapping.

3 False imprisonment.

4 An offence under section 4 of the Offences against the Person Act 1861 (c. 100) (soliciting murder).

5 An offence under section 16 of that Act (threats to kill).

6 An offence under section 18 of that Act (wounding with intent to cause grievous bodily harm).

7 An offence under section 20 of that Act (malicious wounding).

8 An offence under section 21 of that Act (attempting to choke, suffocate or strangle in order to commit or assist in committing an indictable offence).

9 An offence under section 22 of that Act (using chloroform etc. to commit or assist in the committing of any indictable offence).

10 An offence under section 23 of that Act (maliciously administering poison etc. so as to endanger life or inflict grievous bodily harm).

11 An offence under section 27 of that Act (abandoning children).

12 An offence under section 28 of that Act (causing bodily injury by explosives).

13 An offence under section 29 of that Act (using explosives etc. with intent to do grievous bodily harm).

14 An offence under section 30 of that Act (placing explosives with intent to do bodily injury).

15 An offence under section 31 of that Act (setting spring guns etc. with intent to do grievous bodily harm).

16 An offence under section 32 of that Act (endangering the safety of railway passengers).

17 An offence under section 35 of that Act (injuring persons by furious driving).

18 An offence under section 37 of that Act (assaulting officer preserving wreck).

19 An offence under section 38 of that Act (assault with intent to resist arrest).

20 An offence under section 47 of that Act (assault occasioning actual bodily harm).

21 An offence under section 2 of the Explosive Substances Act 1883 (c. 3) (causing explosion likely to endanger life or property).

22 An offence under section 3 of that Act (attempt to cause explosion, or making or keeping explosive with intent to endanger life or property).

22A An offence under section 4 of that Act (making or possession of explosive under suspicious circumstances).

23 An offence under section 1 of the Infant Life (Preservation) Act 1929 (c. 34) (child destruction).

24 An offence under section 1 of the Children and Young Persons Act 1933 (c. 12) (cruelty to children).

25 An offence under section 1 of the Infanticide Act 1938 (c. 36) (infanticide).

26 An offence under section 16 of the Firearms Act 1968 (c. 27) (possession of firearm with intent to endanger life).

27 An offence under section 16A of that Act (possession of firearm with intent to cause fear of violence).

28 An offence under section 17(1) of that Act (use of firearm to resist arrest).

29 An offence under section 17(2) of that Act (possession of firearm at time of committing or being arrested for offence specified in Schedule 1 to that Act).

30 An offence under section 18 of that Act (carrying a firearm with criminal intent).

31 An offence under section 8 of the Theft Act 1968 (c. 60) (robbery or assault with intent to rob).

32 An offence under section 9 of that Act of burglary with intent to—
  (a) inflict grievous bodily harm on a person, or
  (b) do unlawful damage to a building or anything in it.

33 An offence under section 10 of that Act (aggravated burglary).

34 An offence under section 12A of that Act (aggravated vehicle-taking) involving an accident which caused the death of any person.

35 An offence of arson under section 1 of the Criminal Damage Act 1971 (c. 48).

36 An offence under section 1(2) of that Act (destroying or damaging property) other than an offence of arson.

37 An offence under section 1 of the Taking of Hostages Act 1982 (c. 28) (hostage-taking).

38 An offence under section 1 of the Aviation Security Act 1982 (c. 36) (hijacking).

39 An offence under section 2 of that Act (destroying, damaging or endangering safety of aircraft).

40 An offence under section 3 of that Act (other acts endangering or likely to endanger safety of aircraft).

41 An offence under section 4 of that Act (offences in relation to certain dangerous articles).

42 An offence under section 127 of the Mental Health Act 1983 (c. 20) (ill-treatment of patients).

43 An offence under section 1 of the Prohibition of Female Circumcision Act 1985 (c. 38) (prohibition of female circumcision).

44 An offence under section 1 of the Public Order Act 1986 (c. 64) (riot).

45 An offence under section 2 of that Act (violent disorder).

46 An offence under section 3 of that Act (affray).

47 An offence under section 134 of the Criminal Justice Act 1988 (c. 33) (torture).

48 An offence under section 1 of the Road Traffic Act 1988 (c. 52) (causing death by dangerous driving).

48A An offence under section 3ZC of that Act (causing death by driving: disqualified drivers).

49 An offence under section 3A of that Act (causing death by careless driving when under influence of drink or drugs).

50 An offence under section 1 of the Aviation and Maritime Security Act 1990 (c. 31) (endangering safety at aerodromes).

51 An offence under section 9 of that Act (hijacking of ships).

52 An offence under section 10 of that Act (seizing or exercising control of fixed platforms).

53 An offence under section 11 of that Act (destroying fixed platforms or endangering their safety).

54 An offence under section 12 of that Act (other acts endangering or likely to endanger safe navigation).

55 An offence under section 13 of that Act (offences involving threats).

56 An offence under Part II of the Channel Tunnel (Security) Order 1994 (S.I. 1994/570) (offences relating to Channel Tunnel trains and the tunnel system).

57 An offence under section 4 or 4A of the Protection from Harassment Act 1997 (c. 40) (putting people in fear of violence and stalking involving fear of violence or serious alarm or distress).

58 An offence under section 29 of the Crime and Disorder Act 1998 (c. 37) (racially or religiously aggravated assaults).

59 An offence falling within section 31(1)(a) or (b) of that Act (racially or religiously aggravated offences under section 4 or 4A of the Public Order Act 1986 (c. 64)).

59A An offence under section 54 of the Terrorism Act 2000 (weapons training).

59B An offence under section 56 of that Act (directing terrorist organisation).

59C An offence under section 57 of that Act (possession of article for terrorist purposes).

59D An offence under section 59 of that Act (inciting terrorism overseas).

60 An offence under section 51 or 52 of the International Criminal Court Act 2001 (c. 17) (genocide, crimes against humanity, war crimes and related offences), other than one involving murder.

60A An offence under section 47 of the Anti-terrorism, Crime and Security Act 2001 (use etc of nuclear weapons).

60B An offence under section 50 of that Act (assisting or inducing certain weapons-related acts overseas).

60C An offence under section 113 of that Act (use of noxious substance or thing to cause harm or intimidate).

61 An offence under section 1 of the Female Genital Mutilation Act 2003 (c. 31) (female genital mutilation).

62 An offence under section 2 of that Act (assisting a girl to mutilate her own genitalia).

63 An offence under section 3 of that Act (assisting a non-UK person to mutilate overseas a girl's genitalia).

63A An offence under section 5 of the Domestic Violence, Crime and Victims Act 2004 (causing or allowing a child or vulnerable adult to die or suffer serious physical harm).

63B An offence under section 5 of the Terrorism Act 2006 (preparation of terrorist acts).

63C An offence under section 6 of that Act (training for terrorism).

63D An offence under section 9 of that Act (making or possession of radioactive device or material).

63E An offence under section 10 of that Act (use of radioactive device or material for terrorist purposes etc).

63F An offence under section 11 of that Act (terrorist threats relating to radioactive devices etc).

63G An offence under section 1 of the Modern Slavery Act 2015 (slavery, servitude and forced or compulsory labour).

63H An offence under section 2 of that Act (human trafficking) which is not within Part 2 of this Schedule.

64 (1) Aiding, abetting, counselling or procuring the commission of an offence specified in the preceding paragraphs of this Part of this Schedule.

(2) An attempt to commit such an offence.

(3) Conspiracy to commit such an offence.

(4) Incitement to commit such an offence.

(5) An offence under Part 2 of the Serious Crime Act 2007 in relation to which an offence specified in the preceding paragraphs of this Part of this Schedule is the offence (or one of the offences) which the person intended or believed would be committed.

65 (1) An attempt to commit murder.

(2) Conspiracy to commit murder.

(3) Incitement to commit murder.

(4) An offence under Part 2 of the Serious Crime Act 2007 in relation to which murder is the offence (or one of the offences) which the person intended or believed would be committed.

PART 2 SPECIFIED SEXUAL OFFENCES

66 An offence under section 1 of the Sexual Offences Act 1956 (c. 69) (rape).

67 An offence under section 2 of that Act (procurement of woman by threats).

68 An offence under section 3 of that Act (procurement of woman by false pretences).

69 An offence under section 4 of that Act (administering drugs to obtain or facilitate intercourse).

70 An offence under section 5 of that Act (intercourse with girl under thirteen).

71 An offence under section 6 of that Act (intercourse with girl under 16).

72 An offence under section 7 of that Act (intercourse with a defective).

73 An offence under section 9 of that Act (procurement of a defective).

74 An offence under section 10 of that Act (incest by a man).

75 An offence under section 11 of that Act (incest by a woman).

76 An offence under section 14 of that Act (indecent assault on a woman).

77 An offence under section 15 of that Act (indecent assault on a man).

78 An offence under section 16 of that Act (assault with intent to commit buggery).

79 An offence under section 17 of that Act (abduction of woman by force or for the sake of her property).

80 An offence under section 19 of that Act (abduction of unmarried girl under eighteen from parent or guardian).

81 An offence under section 20 of that Act (abduction of unmarried girl under sixteen from parent or guardian).

82 An offence under section 21 of that Act (abduction of defective from parent or guardian).

83 An offence under section 22 of that Act (causing prostitution of women).

84 An offence under section 23 of that Act (procuration of girl under twenty-one).

85 An offence under section 24 of that Act (detention of woman in brothel).

86 An offence under section 25 of that Act (permitting girl under thirteen to use premises for intercourse).

87 An offence under section 26 of that Act (permitting girl under sixteen to use premises for intercourse).

88 An offence under section 27 of that Act (permitting defective to use premises for intercourse).

89 An offence under section 28 of that Act (causing or encouraging the prostitution of, intercourse with or indecent assault on girl under sixteen).

90 An offence under section 29 of that Act (causing or encouraging prostitution of defective).

91 An offence under section 32 of that Act (soliciting by men).

92A An offence under section 33A of that Act (keeping a brothel used for prostitution).

93 An offence under section 128 of the Mental Health Act 1959 (c. 72) (sexual intercourse with patients).

94 An offence under section 1 of the Indecency with Children Act 1960 (c. 33) (indecent conduct towards young child).

95 An offence under section 4 of the Sexual Offences Act 1967 (c. 60) (procuring others to commit homosexual acts).

96 An offence under section 5 of that Act (living on earnings of male prostitution).

97 An offence under section 9 of the Theft Act 1968 (c. 60) of burglary with intent to commit rape.

98 An offence under section 54 of the Criminal Law Act 1977 (c. 45) (inciting girl under sixteen to have incestuous sexual intercourse).

99 An offence under section 1 of the Protection of Children Act 1978 (c. 37) (indecent photographs of children).

100 An offence under section 170 of the Customs and Excise Management Act 1979 (c. 2) (penalty for fraudulent evasion of duty etc.) in relation to goods prohibited to be imported under section 42 of the Customs Consolidation Act 1876 (c. 36) (indecent or obscene articles).

101 An offence under section 160 of the Criminal Justice Act 1988 (c. 33) (possession of indecent photograph of a child).

102 An offence under section 1 of the Sexual Offences Act 2003 (c. 42) (rape).

103 An offence under section 2 of that Act (assault by penetration).

104 An offence under section 3 of that Act (sexual assault).

105 An offence under section 4 of that Act (causing a person to engage in sexual activity without consent).

106 An offence under section 5 of that Act (rape of a child under 13).

107 An offence under section 6 of that Act (assault of a child under 13 by penetration).

108 An offence under section 7 of that Act (sexual assault of a child under 13).

109 An offence under section 8 of that Act (causing or inciting a child under 13 to engage in sexual activity).

110 An offence under section 9 of that Act (sexual activity with a child).

111 An offence under section 10 of that Act (causing or inciting a child to engage in sexual activity).

112 An offence under section 11 of that Act (engaging in sexual activity in the presence of a child).

113 An offence under section 12 of that Act (causing a child to watch a sexual act).

114 An offence under section 13 of that Act (child sex offences committed by children or young persons).

115 An offence under section 14 of that Act (arranging or facilitating commission of a child sex offence).

116 An offence under section 15 of that Act (meeting a child following sexual grooming etc.).

117 An offence under section 16 of that Act (abuse of position of trust: sexual activity with a child).

118 An offence under section 17 of that Act (abuse of position of trust: causing or inciting a child to engage in sexual activity).

119 An offence under section 18 of that Act (abuse of position of trust: sexual activity in the presence of a child).

120 An offence under section 19 of that Act (abuse of position of trust: causing a child to watch a sexual act).

121 An offence under section 25 of that Act (sexual activity with a child family member).

122 An offence under section 26 of that Act (inciting a child family member to engage in sexual activity).

123 An offence under section 30 of that Act (sexual activity with a person with a mental disorder impeding choice).

124 An offence under section 31 of that Act (causing or inciting a person with a mental disorder impeding choice to engage in sexual activity).

125 An offence under section 32 of that Act (engaging in sexual activity in the presence of a person with a mental disorder impeding choice).

126 An offence under section 33 of that Act (causing a person with a mental disorder impeding choice to watch a sexual act).

127 An offence under section 34 of that Act (inducement, threat or deception to procure sexual activity with a person with a mental disorder).

128 An offence under section 35 of that Act (causing a person with a mental disorder to engage in or agree to engage in sexual activity by inducement, threat or deception).

129 An offence under section 36 of that Act (engaging in sexual activity in the presence, procured by inducement, threat or deception, of a person with a mental disorder).

130 An offence under section 37 of that Act (causing a person with a mental disorder to watch a sexual act by inducement, threat or deception).

131 An offence under section 38 of that Act (care workers: sexual activity with a person with a mental disorder).

132 An offence under section 39 of that Act (care workers: causing or inciting sexual activity).

133 An offence under section 40 of that Act (care workers: sexual activity in the presence of a person with a mental disorder).

134 An offence under section 41 of that Act (care workers: causing a person with a mental disorder to watch a sexual act).

135 An offence under section 47 of that Act (paying for sexual services of a child).

136 An offence under section 48 of that Act (causing or inciting sexual exploitation of a child or pornography).

137 An offence under section 49 of that Act (controlling a child in relation to sexual exploitation).

138 An offence under section 50 of that Act (arranging or facilitating sexual exploitation of a child).

139 An offence under section 52 of that Act (causing or inciting prostitution for gain).

140 An offence under section 53 of that Act (controlling prostitution for gain).

141 An offence under section 57 of that Act (trafficking into the UK for sexual exploitation).

142 An offence under section 58 of that Act (trafficking within the UK for sexual exploitation).

143 An offence under section 59 of that Act (trafficking out of the UK for sexual exploitation).

143A An offence under section 59A of that Act (trafficking for sexual exploitation).

144 An offence under section 61 of that Act (administering a substance with intent).

145 An offence under section 62 of that Act (committing an offence with intent to commit a sexual offence).

146 An offence under section 63 of that Act (trespass with intent to commit a sexual offence).

147 An offence under section 64 of that Act (sex with an adult relative: penetration).

148 An offence under section 65 of that Act (sex with an adult relative: consenting to penetration).

149 An offence under section 66 of that Act (exposure).

150 An offence under section 67 of that Act (voyeurism).

151 An offence under section 69 of that Act (intercourse with an animal).

152 An offence under section 70 of that Act (sexual penetration of a corpse).

152A An offence under section 2 of the Modern Slavery Act 2015 (human trafficking) committed with a view to exploitation that consists of or includes behaviour within section 3(3) of that Act (sexual exploitation).

153 (1) Aiding, abetting, counselling or procuring the commission of an offence specified in this Part of this Schedule.

(2) An attempt to commit such an offence.

(3) Conspiracy to commit such an offence.

(4) Incitement to commit such an offence.

(5) An offence under Part 2 of the Serious Crime Act 2007 in relation to which an offence specified in this Part of this Schedule is the offence (or one of the offences) which the person intended or believed would be committed.

SCHEDULE 15B OFFENCES LISTED FOR THE PURPOSES OF SECTIONS 224A, 226A AND 246A

PART 1 OFFENCES UNDER THE LAW OF ENGLAND AND WALES LISTED FOR THE PURPOSES OF SECTIONS 224A(1), 224A(4), 226A AND 246A

1 Manslaughter.

2 An offence under section 4 of the Offences against the Person Act 1861 (soliciting murder).

3 An offence under section 18 of that Act (wounding with intent to cause grievous bodily harm).

3A An offence under section 28 of that Act (causing bodily injury by explosives).

3B An offence under section 29 of that Act (using explosives etc with intent to do grievous bodily harm).

3C An offence under section 2 of the Explosive Substances Act 1883 (causing explosion likely to endanger life or property).

3D An offence under section 3 of that Act (attempt to cause explosion, or making or keeping explosive with intent to endanger life or property).

3E An offence under section 4 of that Act (making or possession of explosive under suspicious circumstances).

4 An offence under section 16 of the Firearms Act 1968 (possession of a firearm with intent to endanger life).

5 An offence under section 17(1) of that Act (use of a firearm to resist arrest).

6 An offence under section 18 of that Act (carrying a firearm with criminal intent).

7 An offence of robbery under section 8 of the Theft Act 1968 where, at some time during the commission of the offence, the offender had in his possession a firearm or an imitation firearm within the meaning of the Firearms Act 1968.

8 An offence under section 1 of the Protection of Children Act 1978 (indecent images of children).

8A An offence under section 54 of the Terrorism Act 2000 (weapons training).

9 An offence under section 56 of that Act (directing terrorist organisation).

10 An offence under section 57 of that Act (possession of article for terrorist purposes).

11 An offence under section 59 of that Act (inciting terrorism overseas) if the offender is liable on conviction on indictment to imprisonment for life.

12 An offence under section 47 of the Anti-terrorism, Crime and Security Act 2001 (use etc of nuclear weapons).

13 An offence under section 50 of that Act (assisting or inducing certain weapons-related acts overseas).

14 An offence under section 113 of that Act (use of noxious substance or thing to cause harm or intimidate).

15 An offence under section 1 of the Sexual Offences Act 2003 (rape).

16 An offence under section 2 of that Act (assault by penetration).

17 An offence under section 4 of that Act (causing a person to engage in sexual activity without consent) if the offender is liable on conviction on indictment to imprisonment for life.

18 An offence under section 5 of that Act (rape of a child under 13).

19 An offence under section 6 of that Act (assault of a child under 13 by penetration).

20 An offence under section 7 of that Act (sexual assault of a child under 13).

21 An offence under section 8 of that Act (causing or inciting a child under 13 to engage in sexual activity).

22 An offence under section 9 of that Act (sexual activity with a child).

23 An offence under section 10 of that Act (causing or inciting a child to engage in sexual activity).

24 An offence under section 11 of that Act (engaging in sexual activity in the presence of a child).

25 An offence under section 12 of that Act (causing a child to watch a sexual act).

26 An offence under section 14 of that Act (arranging or facilitating commission of a child sex offence).

27 An offence under section 15 of that Act (meeting a child following sexual grooming etc).

28 An offence under section 25 of that Act (sexual activity with a child family member) if the offender is aged 18 or over at the time of the offence.

29 An offence under section 26 of that Act (inciting a child family member to engage in sexual activity) if the offender is aged 18 or over at the time of the offence.

30 An offence under section 30 of that Act (sexual activity with a person with a mental disorder impeding choice) if the offender is liable on conviction on indictment to imprisonment for life.

31 An offence under section 31 of that Act (causing or inciting a person with a mental disorder to engage in sexual activity) if the offender is liable on conviction on indictment to imprisonment for life.

32 An offence under section 34 of that Act (inducement, threat or deception to procure sexual activity with a person with a mental disorder) if the offender is liable on conviction on indictment to imprisonment for life.

33 An offence under section 35 of that Act (causing a person with a mental disorder to engage in or agree to engage in sexual activity by inducement etc) if the offender is liable on conviction on indictment to imprisonment for life.

34 An offence under section 47 of that Act (paying for sexual services of a child) against a person aged under 16.

35 An offence under section 48 of that Act (causing or inciting sexual exploitation of a child).

36 An offence under section 49 of that Act (controlling a child in relation to sexual exploitation).

37 An offence under section 50 of that Act (arranging or facilitating sexual exploitation of a child).

38 An offence under section 62 of that Act (committing an offence with intent to commit a sexual offence) if the offender is liable on conviction on indictment to imprisonment for life.

39 An offence under section 5 of the Domestic Violence, Crime and Victims Act 2004 (causing or allowing the death of a child or vulnerable adult).

40 An offence under section 5 of the Terrorism Act 2006 (preparation of terrorist acts).

40A An offence under section 6 of that Act (training for terrorism).

41 An offence under section 9 of that Act (making or possession of radioactive device or materials).

42 An offence under section 10 of that Act (misuse of radioactive devices or material and misuse and damage of facilities).

43 An offence under section 11 of that Act (terrorist threats relating to radioactive devices, materials or facilities).

43A An offence under section 1 of the Modern Slavery Act 2015 (slavery, servitude and forced or compulsory labour).

43B An offence under section 2 of that Act (human trafficking).

44 (1) An attempt to commit an offence specified in the preceding paragraphs of this Part of this Schedule ('a listed offence') or murder.

(2) Conspiracy to commit a listed offence or murder.

(3) Incitement to commit a listed offence or murder.

(4) An offence under Part 2 of the Serious Crime Act 2007 in relation to which a listed offence or murder is the offence (or one of the offences) which the person intended or believed would be committed.

(5) Aiding, abetting, counselling or procuring the commission of a listed offence.

PART 2 FURTHER OFFENCES UNDER THE LAW OF ENGLAND AND WALES LISTED FOR THE PURPOSES OF SECTIONS 224A(4), 226A AND 246A

45 Murder.

46 (1) Any offence that—

(a) was abolished (with or without savings) before the coming into force of this Schedule, and

(b) would, if committed on the relevant day, have constituted an offence specified in Part 1 of this Schedule.

(2) 'Relevant day', in relation to an offence, means—

(a) for the purposes of this paragraph as it applies for the purposes of section 246A(2), the day on which the offender was convicted of that offence, and

(b) for the purposes of this paragraph as it applies for the purposes of sections 224A(4) and 226A(2), the day on which the offender was convicted of the offence referred to in section 224A(1)(a) or 226A(1)(a) (as appropriate).

PART 3 OFFENCES UNDER SERVICE LAW LISTED FOR THE PURPOSES OF SECTIONS 224A(4), 226A AND 246A

47 An offence under section 70 of the Army Act 1955, section 70 of the Air Force Act 1955 or section 42 of the Naval Discipline Act 1957 as respects which the corresponding civil offence (within the meaning of the Act in question) is an offence specified in Part 1 or 2 of this Schedule.

48 (1) An offence under section 42 of the Armed Forces Act 2006 as respects which the corresponding offence under the law of England and Wales (within the meaning given by that section) is an offence specified in Part 1 or 2 of this Schedule.

(2) Section 48 of the Armed Forces Act 2006 (attempts, conspiracy etc) applies for the purposes of this paragraph as if the reference in subsection (3)(b) of that section to any of the following provisions of that Act were a reference to this paragraph.

...

PART 5 INTERPRETATION

50 In this Schedule 'imprisonment for life' includes custody for life and detention for life.

SCHEDULE 21 DETERMINATION OF MINIMUM TERM IN RELATION TO MANDATORY LIFE SENTENCE

Interpretation

1 In this Schedule—

'child' means a person under 18 years;

'mandatory life sentence' means a life sentence passed in circumstances where the sentence is fixed by law;

'minimum term', in relation to a mandatory life sentence, means the part of the sentence to be specified in an order under section 269(2);

'whole life order' means an order under subsection (4) of section 269.

2 Section 28 of the Crime and Disorder Act 1998 (c. 37) (meaning of 'racially or religiously aggravated') applies for the purposes of this Schedule as it applies for the purposes of sections 29 to 32 of that Act.

3 For the purposes of this Schedule—

    (a) an offence is aggravated by sexual orientation if it is committed in circumstances mentioned in section 146(2)(a)(i) or (b)(i);

    (b) an offence is aggravated by disability if it is committed in circumstances mentioned in section 146(2)(a)(ii) or (b)(ii);

    (c) an offence is aggravated by transgender identity if it is committed in circumstances mentioned in section 146(2)(a)(iii) or (b)(iii).

4 (1) If—

    (a) the court considers that the seriousness of the offence (or the combination of the offence and one or more offences associated with it) is exceptionally high, and

    (b) the offender was aged 21 or over when he committed the offence,

the appropriate starting point is a whole life order.

(2) Cases that would normally fall within sub-paragraph (1)(a) include—

    (a) the murder of two or more persons, where each murder involves any of the following—

        (i) a substantial degree of premeditation or planning,

        (ii) the abduction of the victim, or

        (iii) sexual or sadistic conduct,

    (b) the murder of a child if involving the abduction of the child or sexual or sadistic motivation,

    (ba) the murder of a police officer or prison officer in the course of his or her duty,

    (c) a murder done for the purpose of advancing a political, religious, racial or ideological cause, or

    (d) a murder by an offender previously convicted of murder.

5 (1) If—

    (a) the case does not fall within paragraph 4(1) but the court considers that the seriousness of the offence (or the combination of the offence and one or more offences associated with it) is particularly high, and

    (b) the offender was aged 18 or over when he committed the offence,

the appropriate starting point, in determining the minimum term, is 30 years.

(2) Cases that (if not falling within paragraph 4(1)) would normally fall within sub-paragraph (1)(a) include—

(b) a murder involving the use of a firearm or explosive,

(c) a murder done for gain (such as a murder done in the course or furtherance of robbery or burglary, done for payment or done in the expectation of gain as a result of the death),

(d) a murder intended to obstruct or interfere with the course of justice,

(e) a murder involving sexual or sadistic conduct,

(f) the murder of two or more persons,

(g) a murder that is racially or religiously aggravated or aggravated by sexual orientation, disability or transgender identity, or

(h) a murder falling within paragraph 4(2) committed by an offender who was aged under 21 when he committed the offence.

5A. (1) If—

(a) the case does not fall within paragraph 4(1) or 5(1),

(b) the offence falls within sub-paragraph (2), and

(c) the offender was aged 18 or over when the offender committed the offence,

the offence is normally to be regarded as sufficiently serious for the appropriate starting point, in determining the minimum term, to be 25 years.

(2) The offence falls within this sub-paragraph if the offender took a knife or other weapon to the scene intending to—

(a) commit any offence, or

(b) have it available to use as a weapon,

and used that knife or other weapon in committing the murder.

6 If the offender was aged 18 or over when he committed the offence and the case does not fall within paragraph 4(1), 5(1) or 5A(1), the appropriate starting point, in determining the minimum term, is 15 years.

7 If the offender was aged under 18 when he committed the offence, the appropriate starting point, in determining the minimum term, is 12 years.

8 Having chosen a starting point, the court should take into account any aggravating or mitigating factors, to the extent that it has not allowed for them in its choice of starting point.

9 Detailed consideration of aggravating or mitigating factors may result in a minimum term of any length (whatever the starting point), or in the making of a whole life order.

10 Aggravating factors (additional to those mentioned in paragraph 4(2), 5(2) and 5A(2)) that may be relevant to the offence of murder include—

(a) a significant degree of planning or premeditation,

(b) the fact that the victim was particularly vulnerable because of age or disability,

(c) mental or physical suffering inflicted on the victim before death,

(d) the abuse of a position of trust,

(e) the use of duress or threats against another person to facilitate the commission of the offence,

(f) the fact that the victim was providing a public service or performing a public duty, and

(g) concealment, destruction or dismemberment of the body.

11 Mitigating factors that may be relevant to the offence of murder include—

(a) an intention to cause serious bodily harm rather than to kill,

(b) lack of premeditation,

(c) the fact that the offender suffered from any mental disorder or mental disability which (although not falling within section 2(1) of the Homicide Act 1957 (c. 11)), lowered his degree of culpability,

(d) the fact that the offender was provoked (for example, by prolonged stress),

(e) the fact that the offender acted to any extent in self-defence or in fear of violence,

(f) a belief by the offender that the murder was an act of mercy, and

(g) the age of the offender.

12   Nothing in this Schedule restricts the application of—

(a) section 143(2) (previous convictions),

(b) section 143(3) (bail), or

(c) section 144 (guilty plea),

or of section 238(1)(b) or (c) or 239 of the Armed Forces Act 2006.

Sexual Offences Act 2003

80   Persons becoming subject to notification requirements

(1) A person is subject to the notification requirements of this Part for the period set out in section 82 ('the notification period') if—

(a) he is convicted of an offence listed in Schedule 3;

(b) he is found not guilty of such an offence by reason of insanity;

(c) he is found to be under a disability and to have done the act charged against him in respect of such an offence; or

(d) in England and Wales or Northern Ireland, he is cautioned in respect of such an offence.

(2) A person for the time being subject to the notification requirements of this Part is referred to in this Part as a 'relevant offender'.

81   Persons formerly subject to Part 1 of the Sex Offenders Act 1997

(1) A person is, from the commencement of this Part until the end of the notification period, subject to the notification requirements of this Part if, before the commencement of this Part—

(a) he was convicted of an offence listed in Schedule 3;

(b) he was found not guilty of such an offence by reason of insanity;

(c) he was found to be under a disability and to have done the act charged against him in respect of such an offence; or

(d) in England and Wales or Northern Ireland, he was cautioned in respect of such an offence.

(2) Subsection (1) does not apply if the notification period ended before the commencement of this Part.

(3) Subsection (1)(a) does not apply to a conviction before 1st September 1997 unless, at the beginning of that day, the person—

(a) had not been dealt with in respect of the offence;

(b) was serving a sentence of imprisonment or was subject to a community order, in respect of the offence;

(c) was subject to supervision, having been released from prison after serving the whole or part of a sentence of imprisonment in respect of the offence; or

(d) was detained in a hospital or was subject to a guardianship order, following the conviction.

(4) Paragraphs (b) and (c) of subsection (1) do not apply to a finding made before 1st September 1997 unless, at the beginning of that day, the person—

(a) had not been dealt with in respect of the finding; or

(b) was detained in a hospital, following the finding.

(5) Subsection (1)(d) does not apply to a caution given before 1st September 1997.

(6) A person who would have been within subsection (3)(b) or (d) or (4)(b) but for the fact that at the beginning of 1st September 1997 he was unlawfully at large or absent without leave, on temporary release or leave of absence, or on bail pending an appeal, is to be treated as being within that provision.

(7) Where, immediately before the commencement of this Part, an order under a provision within subsection (8) was in force in respect of a person, the person is subject to the notification requirements of this Part from that commencement until the order is discharged or otherwise ceases to have effect.

(8) The provisions are—

    (a) section 5A of the Sex Offenders Act 1997 (c. 51) (restraining orders);

    (b) section 2 of the Crime and Disorder Act 1998 (c. 37) (sex offender orders made in England and Wales);

    (c) section 2A of the Crime and Disorder Act 1998 (interim orders made in England and Wales);

    (d) section 20 of the Crime and Disorder Act 1998 (sex offender orders and interim orders made in Scotland);

    (e) Article 6 of the Criminal Justice (Northern Ireland) Order 1998 (S.I. 1998/2839 (N.I. 20)) (sex offender orders made in Northern Ireland);

    (f) Article 6A of the Criminal Justice (Northern Ireland) Order 1998 (interim orders made in Northern Ireland).

82 The notification period

(1) The notification period for a person within section 80(1) or 81(1) is the period in the second column of the following Table opposite the description that applies to him.

Table

Description of relevant offender	Notification period
A person who, in respect of the offence, is or has been sentenced to imprisonment for life, to imprisonment for public protection under section 225 of the Criminal Justice Act 2003, to an indeterminate custodial sentence under Article 13(4)(a) of the Criminal Justice (Northern Ireland) Order 2008 or to imprisonment for a term of 30 months or more	An indefinite period beginning with the relevant date
A person who, in respect of the offence, has been made the subject of an order under section 210F(1) of the Criminal Procedure (Scotland) Act 1995 (order for lifelong restriction)	An indefinite period beginning with that date
A person who, in respect of the offence or finding, is or has been admitted to a hospital subject to a restriction order	An indefinite period beginning with that date
A person who, in respect of the offence, is or has been sentenced to imprisonment for a term of more than 6 months but less than 30 months	10 years beginning with that date
A person who, in respect of the offence, is or has been sentenced to imprisonment for a term of 6 months or less	7 years beginning with that date
A person who, in respect of the offence or finding, is or has been admitted to a hospital without being subject to a restriction order	7 years beginning with that date
A person within section 80(1)(d)	2 years beginning with that date
A person in whose case an order for conditional discharge or, in Scotland, a community payback order imposing an offender supervision requirement, is made in respect of the offence	The period of conditional discharge or, in Scotland, the specified period for the offender supervision requirement
A person of any other description	5 years beginning with the relevant date

(2) Where a person is under 18 on the relevant date, subsection (1) has effect as if for any reference to a period of 10 years, 7 years, 5 years or 2 years there were substituted a reference to one-half of that period.

(3) Subsection (4) applies where a relevant offender within section 80(1)(a) or 81(1)(a) is or has been sentenced, in respect of two or more offences listed in Schedule 3—

    (a) to consecutive terms of imprisonment; or

    (b) to terms of imprisonment which are partly concurrent.

(4) Where this subsection applies, subsection (1) has effect as if the relevant offender were or had been sentenced, in respect of each of the offences, to a term of imprisonment which—

    (a) in the case of consecutive terms, is equal to the aggregate of those terms;

    (b) in the case of partly concurrent terms (X and Y, which overlap for a period Z), is equal to X plus Y minus Z.

(5) Where a relevant offender the subject of a finding within section 80(1)(c) or 81(1)(c) is subsequently tried for the offence, the notification period relating to the finding ends at the conclusion of the trial.

(6) In this Part, 'relevant date' means—

    (a) in the case of a person within section 80(1)(a) or 81(1)(a), the date of the conviction;

    (b) in the case of a person within section 80(1)(b) or (c) or 81(1)(b) or (c), the date of the finding;

    (c) in the case of a person within section 80(1)(d) or 81(1)(d), the date of the caution;

    (d) in the case of a person within section 81(7), the date which, for the purposes of Part 1 of the Sex Offenders Act 1997 (c. 51), was the relevant date in relation to that person.

(7) Schedule 3A (which provides for the review and discharge of indefinite notification requirements) has effect.

83   Notification requirements: initial notification

(1) A relevant offender must, within the period of 3 days beginning with the relevant date (or, if later, the commencement of this Part), notify to the police the information set out in subsection (5).

(2) Subsection (1) does not apply to a relevant offender in respect of a conviction, finding or caution within section 80(1) if—

    (a) immediately before the conviction, finding or caution, he was subject to the notification requirements of this Part as a result of another conviction, finding or caution or an order of a court ('the earlier event'),

    (b) at that time, he had made a notification under subsection (1) in respect of the earlier event, and

    (c) throughout the period referred to in subsection (1), he remains subject to the notification requirements as a result of the earlier event.

(3) Subsection (1) does not apply to a relevant offender in respect of a conviction, finding or caution within section 81(1) or an order within section 81(7) if the offender complied with section 2(1) of the Sex Offenders Act 1997 in respect of the conviction, finding, caution or order.

(4) Where a notification order is made in respect of a conviction, finding or caution, subsection (1) does not apply to the relevant offender in respect of the conviction, finding or caution if—

    (a) immediately before the order was made, he was subject to the notification requirements of this Part as a result of another conviction, finding or caution or an order of a court ('the earlier event'),

    (b) at that time, he had made a notification under subsection (1) in respect of the earlier event, and

    (c) throughout the period referred to in subsection (1), he remains subject to the notification requirements as a result of the earlier event.

(5) The information is—

    (a) the relevant offender's date of birth;

    (b) his national insurance number;

    (c) his name on the relevant date and, where he used one or more other names on that date, each of those names;

    (d) his home address on the relevant date;

    (e) his name on the date on which notification is given and, where he uses one or more other names on that date, each of those names;

    (f) his home address on the date on which notification is given;

    (g) the address of any other premises in the United Kingdom at which, at the time the notification is given, he regularly resides or stays;

    (h) any prescribed information.

(5A) In subsection (5)(h) 'prescribed' means prescribed by regulations made by the Secretary of State.

(6) When determining the period for the purpose of subsection (1), there is to be disregarded any time when the relevant offender is—

    (a) remanded in or committed to custody by an order of a court or kept in service custody;

    (b) serving a sentence of imprisonment or a term of service detention;

    (c) detained in a hospital; or

    (d) outside the United Kingdom.

(7) In this Part, 'home address' means, in relation to any person—

    (a) the address of his sole or main residence in the United Kingdom, or

    (b) where he has no such residence, the address or location of a place in the United Kingdom where he can regularly be found and, if there is more than one such place, such one of those places as the person may select.

84 Notification requirements: changes

(1) A relevant offender must, within the period of 3 days beginning with—

    (a) his using a name which has not been notified to the police under section 83(1), this subsection, or section 2 of the Sex Offenders Act 1997 (c. 51),

    (b) any change of his home address,

    (c) his having resided or stayed, for a qualifying period, at any premises in the United Kingdom the address of which has not been notified to the police under section 83(1), this subsection, or section 2 of the Sex Offenders Act 1997,

    (ca) any prescribed change of circumstances, or

    (d) his release from custody pursuant to an order of a court or from imprisonment, service detention or detention in a hospital,

notify to the police that name, the new home address, the address of those premises, the prescribed details or (as the case may be) the fact that he has been released, and (in addition) the information set out in section 83(5).

(2) A notification under subsection (1) may be given before the name is used, the change of home address or the prescribed change of circumstances occurs or the qualifying period ends, but in that case the relevant offender must also specify the date when the event is expected to occur.

(3) If a notification is given in accordance with subsection (2) and the event to which it relates occurs more than 2 days before the date specified, the notification does not affect the duty imposed by subsection (1).

(4) If a notification is given in accordance with subsection (2) and the event to which it relates has not occurred by the end of the period of 3 days beginning with the date specified—

    (a) the notification does not affect the duty imposed by subsection (1), and

    (b) the relevant offender must, within the period of 6 days beginning with the date specified, notify to the police the fact that the event did not occur within the period of 3 days beginning with the date specified.

(5) Section 83(6) applies to the determination of the period of 3 days mentioned in subsection (1) and the period of 6 days mentioned in subsection (4)(b), as it applies to the determination of the period mentioned in section 83(1).

(5A) In this section—

    (a) 'prescribed change of circumstances' means any change—

        (i)   occurring in relation to any matter in respect of which information is required to be notified by virtue of section 83(5)(h), and

        (ii) of a description prescribed by regulations made by the Secretary of State;

    (b) 'the prescribed details', in relation to a prescribed change of circumstances, means such details of the change as may be so prescribed.

(6) In this section, 'qualifying period' means—

    (a) a period of 7 days, or

    (b) two or more periods, in any period of 12 months, which taken together amount to 7 days.

85　Notification requirements: periodic notification

(1) A relevant offender must, within the applicable period after each event within subsection (2), notify to the police the information set out in section 83(5), unless within that period he has given a notification under section 84(1).

(2) The events are—

    (a) the commencement of this Part (but only in the case of a person who is a relevant offender from that commencement);

    (b) any notification given by the relevant offender under section 83(1) or 84(1); and

    (c) any notification given by him under subsection (1).

(3) Where the applicable period would (apart from this subsection) end whilst subsection (4) applies to the relevant offender, that period is to be treated as continuing until the end of the period of 3 days beginning when subsection (4) first ceases to apply to him.

(4) This subsection applies to the relevant offender if he is—

    (a) remanded in or committed to custody by an order of a court or kept in service custody,

    (b) serving a sentence of imprisonment or a term of service detention,

    (c) detained in a hospital, or

    (d) outside the United Kingdom.

(5) In this section, 'the applicable period' means—

    (a) in any case where subsection (6) applies to the relevant offender, such period as may be prescribed by regulations made by the Secretary of State, and

    (b) in any other case, the period of one year.

(6) This subsection applies to the relevant offender if the last home address notified by him under section 83(1) or 84(1) or subsection (1) was the address or location of such a place as is mentioned in section 83(7)(b).

86　Notification requirements: travel outside the United Kingdom

(1) The Secretary of State may by regulations make provision requiring relevant offenders who leave the United Kingdom, or any description of such offenders—

    (a) to give in accordance with the regulations, before they leave, a notification under subsection (2);

    (b) if they subsequently return to the United Kingdom, to give in accordance with the regulations a notification under subsection (3).

(2) A notification under this subsection must disclose—

    (a) the date on which the offender will leave the United Kingdom;

    (b) the country (or, if there is more than one, the first country) to which he will travel and his point of arrival (determined in accordance with the regulations) in that country;

    (c) any other information prescribed by the regulations which the offender holds about his departure from or return to the United Kingdom or his movements while outside the United Kingdom.

(3) A notification under this subsection must disclose any information prescribed by the regulations about the offender's return to the United Kingdom.

87 Method of notification and related matters

(1) A person gives a notification under section 83(1), 84(1) or 85(1) by—

    (a) attending at such police station in his local police area as the Secretary of State may by regulations prescribe or, if there is more than one, at any of them, and

    (b) giving an oral notification to any police officer, or to any person authorised for the purpose by the officer in charge of the station.

(2) A person giving a notification under section 84(1)—

    (a) in relation to a prospective change of home address, or

    (b) in relation to premises referred to in subsection (1)(c) of that section,

may give the notification at a police station that would fall within subsection (1) above if the change in home address had already occurred or (as the case may be) if the address of those premises were his home address.

(3) Any notification under this section must be acknowledged; and an acknowledgment under this subsection must be in writing, and in such form as the Secretary of State may direct.

(4) Where a notification is given under section 83(1), 84(1) or 85(1), the relevant offender must, if requested to do so by the police officer or person referred to in subsection (1)(b), allow the officer or person to—

    (a) take his fingerprints,

    (b) photograph any part of him, or

    (c) do both these things.

(5) The power in subsection (4) is exercisable for the purpose of verifying the identity of the relevant offender.

88 Section 87: interpretation

(1) Subsections (2) to (4) apply for the purposes of section 87.

(2) 'Photograph' includes any process by means of which an image may be produced.

(3) 'Local police area' means, in relation to a person—

    (a) the police area in which his home address is situated;

    (b) in the absence of a home address, the police area in which the home address last notified is situated;

    (c) in the absence of a home address and of any such notification, the police area in which the court which last dealt with the person in a way mentioned in subsection (4) is situated.

(4) The ways are—

    (a) dealing with a person in respect of an offence listed in Schedule 3 or a finding in relation to such an offence;

    (b) dealing with a person in respect of an offence under section 128 or a finding in relation to such an offence;

    (c) making, in respect of a person, a notification order, interim notification order, sexual offences prevention order or interim sexual offences prevention order;

    (d) making, in respect of a person, an order under section 2, 2A or 20 of the Crime and Disorder Act 1998 (c. 37) (sex offender orders and interim orders made in England and Wales or Scotland) or Article 6 or 6A of the Criminal Justice (Northern Ireland) Order 1998 (S.I. 1998/2839 (N.I. 20)) (sex offender orders and interim orders made in Northern Ireland);

and in paragraphs (a) and (b), 'finding' in relation to an offence means a finding of not guilty of the offence by reason of insanity or a finding that the person was under a disability and did the act or omission charged against him in respect of the offence.

(5) Subsection (3) applies as if Northern Ireland were a police area.

88A Review of indefinite notification requirements: applicable persons

(1) Sections 88B to 88H apply to—

    (a) a person who, on or after 28th January 2011, becomes subject to the notification requirements of this Part for an indefinite period by virtue of section 80(1) or a notification order made under section 97(5); and

(b) a person who immediately before that date was subject to the notification requirements of this Part for an indefinite period by virtue of—

    (i) section 80(1);

    (ii) section 81(1); or

    (iii) a notification order made under section 97(5).

(2) A person who falls within subsection (1)(a) or (b) is referred to in sections 88B to 88G as a 'relevant sex offender'.

88B Review of indefinite notification requirements: date of discharge and further date of discharge

(1) For the purposes of this Part, the date of discharge is—

    (a) where the relevant sex offender was aged 18 or over on the relevant date, the date falling 15 years after that date;

    (b) where the relevant sex offender was aged under 18 on the relevant date, the date falling 8 years after that date.

(2) In determining the date of discharge under subsection (1), there is to be disregarded any time when the relevant sex offender was—

    (a) remanded in or committed to custody by order of a court;

    (b) serving a sentence of imprisonment or a term of service detention;

    (c) detained in hospital; or

    (d) outside the United Kingdom,

before the relevant sex offender first notified information to the police under section 2(1) of the Sex Offenders Act 1997 or section 83(1) of this Part.

(3) Subsection (4) applies where—

    (a) the relevant sex offender is subject to the notification requirements of this Part;

    (b) after the relevant sex offender first notified information to the police under section 2(1) of the Sex Offenders Act 1997 or section 83(1) of this Part, the relevant sex offender was sentenced to a period of imprisonment or a term of service detention in respect of the offence (or offences) to which the notification requirements relate; and

    (c) the date of discharge would, apart from subsection (4), fall on or after 28th January 2011.

(4) In determining the date of discharge under subsection (1), there is also to be disregarded any time when the relevant sex offender was serving a sentence of imprisonment or a term of service detention in respect of that offence (or those offences).

(5) Where a notification continuation order made under this Part has effect in respect of the relevant sex offender, for the purposes of this Part the further date of discharge is the date of expiry of the fixed period specified in that order.

(6) In this section and section 88D 'relevant date'—

    (a) in relation to a relevant sex offender who is subject to the notification requirements of this Part for an indefinite period by virtue of section 80(1) or 81(1), has the meaning applicable to that offender specified in section 82(6)(a) to (c);

    (b) in relation to a relevant sex offender who is subject to the notification requirements of this Part for an indefinite period by virtue of a notification order made under section 97(5), has the meaning applicable to that offender specified in section 98(2).

88C Review of the indefinite notification requirements: procedure and grounds

(1) The relevant chief constable must no later than the date of discharge—

    (a) make a notification continuation order in respect of the relevant sex offender; or

    (b) notify the relevant sex offender that the offender ceases to be subject to the notification requirements of this Part on the date of discharge.

(2) A notification continuation order is an order making the relevant sex offender subject to the notification requirements of this Part for a fixed period of not more than 15 years from the date which would, but for the order, have been the date of discharge.

(3) The relevant chief constable may make a notification continuation order only if satisfied, on the balance of probabilities, that the relevant sex offender poses a risk of sexual harm to the public, or any particular members of the public, in the United Kingdom.

(4) In deciding whether to make a notification continuation order, the relevant chief constable must take into account—

(a) the seriousness of the offence (or offences)—
   (i) of which the relevant sex offender was convicted;
   (ii) of which the relevant sex offender was found not guilty by reason of insanity;
   (iii) in respect of which the relevant sex offender was found to be under a disability and to have done the act charged; or
   (iv) in respect of which the relevant sex offender was cautioned in England and Wales or Northern Ireland,

   which made the relevant sex offender subject to the notification requirements of this Part for an indefinite period;

(b) the period of time which has elapsed since the relevant sex offender committed the offence (or offences);

(c) where the relevant sex offender falls within section 88A(1)(b)(ii), whether the relevant sex offender committed any offence under section 3 of the Sex Offenders Act 1997;

(d) whether the relevant sex offender has committed any offence under section 91 of this Act;

(e) the age of the relevant sex offender at the time of the decision;

(f) the age of the relevant sex offender at the time the offence (or offences) referred to in paragraph (a) was (or were) committed;

(g) the age of any person who was a victim of any such offence (where applicable) and the difference in age between the victim and the relevant sex offender at the time the offence was committed;

(h) any convictions or findings made by a court in respect of the relevant sex offender for any other offence listed in Schedule 3;

(i) any caution which the relevant sex offender has received for an offence in England and Wales or Northern Ireland which is listed in Schedule 3;

(j) whether any criminal proceedings for any offences listed in Schedule 3 have been instituted against the relevant sex offender but have not concluded;

(k) any assessment of the risk posed by the relevant sex offender which has been made by the responsible authorities under the joint arrangements for managing and assessing risk established under section 10 of the Management of Offenders etc. (Scotland) Act 2005;

(l) any other submission or evidence of the risk of sexual harm posed by the relevant sex offender to the public, or any particular members of the public, in the United Kingdom;

(m) any submission or evidence presented by or on behalf of the relevant sex offender which demonstrates that the relevant sex offender does not pose a risk of sexual harm to the public, or any particular members of the public, in the United Kingdom; and

(n) any other matter which the relevant chief constable considers to be appropriate.

(5) A notification continuation order must state—

(a) the reasons why the order was made; and
(b) the reasons for the determination of the fixed period in the order.

(6) A notification continuation order must be notified to the relevant sex offender by—

(a) the relevant chief constable sending a copy of the order to the relevant sex offender by registered post or by the recorded delivery service (an acknowledgement or certificate of delivery of a copy so sent, issued by the Post Office, being sufficient evidence of the delivery of the copy on the day specified in the acknowledgement or certificate); or

(b) a constable serving a copy of the order on the relevant sex offender.

(7) In this section—

'sexual harm' means physical or psychological harm caused by the relevant sex offender doing anything which would constitute an offence listed in Schedule 3 if done in any part of the United Kingdom; and

'responsible authorities' has the meaning given by section 10(7) of the Management of Offenders etc. (Scotland) Act 2005.

(8) In this section and sections 88D to 88G, 'relevant chief constable' means the chief constable of the Police Service of Scotland.

. . .

88H　Review of indefinite notification requirements: power to amend periods

The Secretary of State may by order amend—

    (a) the periods specified in sections 88B(1)(a) and (b); and

    (b) the fixed period specified in section 88C(2).

88I　Discharge from indefinite notification requirements: England, Wales and Northern Ireland

(1) A relevant offender who is, under the relevant legislation, discharged from the notification requirements of this Part by a court, person or body in England and Wales or Northern Ireland is, by virtue of the discharge, also discharged from the notification requirements of this Part as it applies to Scotland.

(2) In subsection (1) 'relevant legislation' means legislation which makes provision equivalent to that made by sections 88A to 88H and this section for a relevant offender who is subject to the notification requirements of this Part as it applies to England and Wales or, as the case may be, Northern Ireland for an indefinite period to be discharged from those notification requirements.

89　Young offenders: parental directions

(1) Where a person within the first column of the following Table ('the young offender') is under 18 (or, in Scotland, 16) when he is before the court referred to in the second column of the Table opposite the description that applies to him, that court may direct that subsection (2) applies in respect of an individual ('the parent') having parental responsibility for (or, in Scotland, parental responsibilities in relation to) the young offender.

Table

Description of person	Court which may make the direction
A relevant offender within section 80(1)(a) to (c) or 81(1)(a) to (c)	The court which deals with the offender in respect of the offence or finding
A relevant offender within section 129(1)(a) to (c)	The court which deals with the offender in respect of the offence or finding
A person who is the subject of a notification order, interim notification order, sexual harm prevention order, interim sexual harm prevention order, sexual offences prevention order or interim sexual offences prevention order	The court which makes the order
A relevant offender who is the defendant to an application under subsection (4) (or, in Scotland, the subject of an application under subsection (5))	The court which hears the application

(2) Where this subsection applies—

    (a) the obligations that would (apart from this subsection) be imposed by or under sections 83 to 86 on the young offender are to be treated instead as obligations on the parent, and

(b) the parent must ensure that the young offender attends at the police station with him, when a notification is being given.

(3) A direction under subsection (1) takes immediate effect and applies—

(a) until the young offender attains the age of 18 (or, where a court in Scotland gives the direction, 16); or

(b) for such shorter period as the court may, at the time the direction is given, direct.

(4) A chief officer of police may, by complaint to any magistrates' court whose commission area includes any part of his police area, apply for a direction under subsection (1) in respect of a relevant offender ('the defendant')—

(a) who resides in his police area, or who the chief officer believes is in or is intending to come to his police area, and

(b) who the chief officer believes is under 18.

(5) In Scotland, the chief constable of the Police Service of Scotland may, by summary application to any sheriff, apply for a direction under subsection (1) in respect of a relevant offender ('the subject')—

(a) who resides in that area, or who the chief constable believes is in or is intending to come to that area, and

(b) who the chief constable believes is under 16.

90 Parental directions: variations, renewals and discharges

(1) A person within subsection (2) may apply to the appropriate court for an order varying, renewing or discharging a direction under section 89(1).

(2) The persons are—

(a) the young offender;

(b) the parent;

(c) the chief officer of police for the area in which the young offender resides;

(d) a chief officer of police who believes that the young offender is in, or is intending to come to, his police area;

(e) in Scotland, where the appropriate court is a civil court—

(i) the chief constable of the police force within the area of which the young offender resides;

(ii) a chief constable who believes that the young offender is in, or is intending to come to, the area of his police force,

and in any other case, the prosecutor;

(f) where the direction was made on an application under section 89(4), the chief officer of police who made the application;

(g) where the direction was made on an application under section 89(5), the chief constable who made the application.

(3) An application under subsection (1) may be made—

(a) where the appropriate court is the Crown Court (or in Scotland a criminal court), in accordance with rules of court;

(b) in any other case, by complaint (or, in Scotland, by summary application).

(4) On the application the court, after hearing the person making the application and (if they wish to be heard) the other persons mentioned in subsection (2), may make any order, varying, renewing or discharging the direction, that the court considers appropriate.

(5) In this section, the 'appropriate court' means—

(a) where the Court of Appeal made the order, the Crown Court;

(b) in any other case, the court that made the direction under section 89(1).

91 Offences relating to notification

(1) A person commits an offence if he—

(a) fails, without reasonable excuse, to comply with section 83(1), 84(1), 84(4)(b), 85(1), 87(4) or 89(2)(b) or any requirement imposed by regulations made under section 86(1); or

(b) notifies to the police, in purported compliance with section 83(1), 84(1) or 85(1) or any requirement imposed by regulations made under section 86(1), any information which he knows to be false.

(2) A person guilty of an offence under this section is liable—

(a) on summary conviction, to imprisonment for a term not exceeding 6 months or a fine not exceeding the statutory maximum or both;

(b) on conviction on indictment, to imprisonment for a term not exceeding 5 years.

(3) A person commits an offence under paragraph (a) of subsection (1) on the day on which he first fails, without reasonable excuse, to comply with section 83(1), 84(1) or 85(1) or a requirement imposed by regulations made under section 86(1), and continues to commit it throughout any period during which the failure continues; but a person must not be prosecuted under subsection (1) more than once in respect of the same failure.

(4) Proceedings for an offence under this section may be commenced in any court having jurisdiction in any place where the person charged with the offence resides or is found.

92   Certificates for purposes of Part 2

(1) Subsection (2) applies where on any date a person is—

(a) convicted of an offence listed in Schedule 3;

(b) found not guilty of such an offence by reason of insanity; or

(c) found to be under a disability and to have done the act charged against him in respect of such an offence.

(2) If the court by or before which the person is so convicted or found—

(a) states in open court—

(i) that on that date he has been convicted, found not guilty by reason of insanity or found to be under a disability and to have done the act charged against him, and

(ii) that the offence in question is an offence listed in Schedule 3, and

(b) certifies those facts, whether at the time or subsequently,

the certificate is, for the purposes of this Part, evidence (or, in Scotland, sufficient evidence) of those facts.

(3) Subsection (4) applies where on any date a person is, in England and Wales or Northern Ireland, cautioned in respect of an offence listed in Schedule 3.

(4) If the constable—

(a) informs the person that he has been cautioned on that date and that the offence in question is an offence listed in Schedule 3, and

(b) certifies those facts, whether at the time or subsequently, in such form as the Secretary of State may by order prescribe,

the certificate is, for the purposes of this Part, evidence (or, in Scotland, sufficient evidence) of those facts.

103A   Sexual harm prevention orders: applications and grounds

(1) A court may make an order under this section (a 'sexual harm prevention order') in respect of a person ('the defendant') where subsection (2) or (3) applies to the defendant.

(2) This subsection applies to the defendant where—

(a) the court deals with the defendant in respect of—

(i) an offence listed in Schedule 3 or 5, or

(ii) a finding that the defendant is not guilty of an offence listed in Schedule 3 or 5 by reason of insanity, or

(iii) a finding that the defendant is under a disability and has done the act charged against the defendant in respect of an offence listed in Schedule 3 or 5, and

(b) the court is satisfied that it is necessary to make a sexual harm prevention order, for the purpose of—

(i) protecting the public or any particular members of the public from sexual harm from the defendant, or

      (ii) protecting children or vulnerable adults generally, or any particular children or vulnerable adults, from sexual harm from the defendant outside the United Kingdom.

   (3) This subsection applies to the defendant where—

     (a) an application under subsection (4) has been made in respect of the defendant and it is proved on the application that the defendant is a qualifying offender, and

     (b) the court is satisfied that the defendant's behaviour since the appropriate date makes it necessary to make a sexual harm prevention order, for the purpose of—

        (i) protecting the public or any particular members of the public from sexual harm from the defendant, or

       (ii) protecting children or vulnerable adults generally, or any particular children or vulnerable adults, from sexual harm from the defendant outside the United Kingdom.

   (4) A chief officer of police or the Director General of the National Crime Agency ('the Director General') may by complaint to a magistrates' court apply for a sexual harm prevention order in respect of a person if it appears to the chief officer or the Director General that—

     (a) the person is a qualifying offender, and

     (b) the person has since the appropriate date acted in such a way as to give reasonable cause to believe that it is necessary for such an order to be made.

   (5) A chief officer of police may make an application under subsection (4) only in respect of a person—

     (a) who resides in the chief officer's police area, or

     (b) who the chief officer believes is in that area or is intending to come to it.

   (6) An application under subsection (4) may be made to any magistrates' court acting for a local justice area that includes—

     (a) any part of a relevant police area, or

     (b) any place where it is alleged that the person acted in a way mentioned in subsection (4)(b).

   (7) The Director General must as soon as practicable notify the chief officer of police for a relevant police area of any application that the Director has made under subsection (4).

   (8) Where the defendant is a child, a reference in this section to a magistrates' court is to be taken as referring to a youth court (subject to any rules of court made under section 103K(1)).

   (9) In this section 'relevant police area' means—

     (a) where the applicant is a chief officer of police, the officer's police area;

     (b) where the applicant is the Director General—

        (i) the police area where the person in question resides, or

       (ii) a police area which the Director General believes the person is in or is intending to come to.

122A   Sexual risk orders: applications, grounds and effect

   (1) A chief officer of police or the Director General of the National Crime Agency ('the Director General') may by complaint to a magistrates' court apply for an order under this section (a 'sexual risk order') in respect of a person ('the defendant') if it appears to the chief officer or the Director General that the following condition is met.

   (2) The condition is that the defendant has, whether before or after the commencement of this Part, done an act of a sexual nature as a result of which there is reasonable cause to believe that it is necessary for a sexual risk order to be made.

   (3) A chief officer of police may make an application under subsection (1) only in respect of a person—

     (a) who resides in the chief officer's police area, or

     (b) who the chief officer believes is in that area or is intending to come to it.

   (4) An application under subsection (1) may be made to any magistrates' court acting for a local justice area that includes—

     (a) any part of a relevant police area, or

     (b) any place where it is alleged that the person acted in a way mentioned in subsection (2).

(5) The Director General must as soon as practicable notify the chief officer of police for a relevant police area of any application that the Director has made under subsection (1).

(6) On an application under subsection (1), the court may make a sexual risk order if it is satisfied that the defendant has, whether before or after the commencement of this Part, done an act of a sexual nature as a result of which it is necessary to make such an order for the purpose of—

> (a) protecting the public or any particular members of the public from harm from the defendant, or
>
> (b) protecting children or vulnerable adults generally, or any particular children or vulnerable adults, from harm from the defendant outside the United Kingdom.

(7) Such an order—

> (a) prohibits the defendant from doing anything described in the order;
>
> (b) has effect for a fixed period (not less than 2 years) specified in the order or until further order.

(8) A sexual risk order may specify different periods for different prohibitions.

(9) The only prohibitions that may be imposed are those necessary for the purpose of—

> (a) protecting the public or any particular members of the public from harm from the defendant, or
>
> (b) protecting children or vulnerable adults generally, or any particular children or vulnerable adults, from harm from the defendant outside the United Kingdom.

(10) Where a court makes a sexual risk order in relation to a person who is already subject to such an order (whether made by that court or another), the earlier order ceases to have effect.

Violent Crime Reduction Act 2006

29 Penalties etc. for offence under s. 28

(1) This section applies where a person ('the offender') is guilty of an offence under section 28.

(2) Where the dangerous weapon in respect of which the offence was committed is a weapon to which section 141 or 141A of the Criminal Justice Act 1988 (specified offensive weapons, knives and bladed weapons) applies, the offender shall be liable, on conviction on indictment, to imprisonment for a term not exceeding 4 years or to a fine, or to both.

(3) Where—

> (a) at the time of the offence, the offender was aged 16 or over, and
>
> (b) the dangerous weapon in respect of which the offence was committed was a firearm mentioned in section 5(1)(a) to (af) or (c) or section 5(1A)(a) of the 1968 Act (firearms possession of which attracts a minimum sentence),

the offender shall be liable, on conviction on indictment, to imprisonment for a term not exceeding 10 years or to a fine, or to both.

(4) On a conviction in England and Wales, where—

> (a) subsection (3) applies, and
>
> (b) the offender is aged 18 or over at the time of conviction,

the court must impose (with or without a fine) a term of imprisonment of not less than 5 years, unless it is of the opinion that there are exceptional circumstances relating to the offence or to the offender which justify its not doing so.

(5) In relation to times before the commencement of paragraph 180 of Schedule 7 to the Criminal Justice and Court Services Act 2000 (c. 43), the reference in subsection (4) to a sentence of imprisonment, in relation to an offender aged under 21 at the time of conviction, is to be read as a reference to a sentence of detention in a young offender institution.

(6) On a conviction in England and Wales, where—

> (a) subsection (3) applies, and
>
> (b) the offender is aged under 18 at the time of conviction,

the court must impose (with or without a fine) a term of detention under section 91 of the Powers of Criminal Courts (Sentencing) Act 2000 (c. 6) of not less than 3 years, unless it is of the opinion that there are exceptional circumstances relating to the offence or to the offender which justify its not doing so.

(7) On a conviction in Scotland, where—

(a) subsection (3) applies, and

(b) the offender is aged 21 or over at the time of conviction,

the court must impose (with or without a fine) a sentence of imprisonment of not less than 5 years, unless it is of the opinion that there are exceptional circumstances relating to the offence or to the offender which justify its not doing so.

(8) On a conviction in Scotland, where—

(a) subsection (3) applies, and

(b) the offender is aged under 21 at the time of conviction and is not a person in whose case subsection (9) applies,

the court must impose (with or without a fine) a sentence of detention under section 207 of the Criminal Procedure (Scotland) Act 1995 (c. 46) of not less than 3 years, unless it is of the opinion that there are exceptional circumstances relating to the offence or to the offender which justify its not doing so.

(9) On a conviction in Scotland, where—

(a) subsection (3) applies, and

(b) the offender is, at the time of conviction, both aged under 18 and subject to a supervision requirement,

the court must impose (with or without a fine) a sentence of detention under section 208 of the Criminal Procedure (Scotland) Act 1995 of not less than 3 years, unless it is of the opinion that there are exceptional circumstances relating to the offence or to the offender which justify its not doing so.

(10) In any case not mentioned in subsection (2) or (3), the offender shall be liable, on conviction on indictment, to imprisonment for a term not exceeding 5 years or to a fine, or to both.

(11) Where—

(a) a court is considering for the purposes of sentencing the seriousness of an offence under section 28, and

(b) at the time of the offence the offender was aged 18 or over and the person used to look after, hide or transport the weapon was not,

the court must treat the fact that that person was under the age of 18 at that time as an aggravating factor (that is to say, a factor increasing the seriousness of the offence).

(12) Where a court treats a person's age as an aggravating factor in accordance with subsection (11), it must state in open court that the offence was aggravated as mentioned in that subsection.

(13) Where—

(a) an offence under section 28 of using another person for a particular purpose is found to have involved that other person's having possession of a weapon, or being able to make it available, over a period of two or more days, or at some time during a period of two or more days, and

(b) on any day in that period, an age requirement was satisfied,

the question whether subsection (3) applies or (as the case may be) the question whether the offence was aggravated under this section is to be determined as if the offence had been committed on that day.

(14) In subsection (13) the reference to an age requirement is a reference to either of the following—

(a) the requirement of subsection (3) that the offender was aged 16 or over at the time of the offence;

(b) the requirement of subsection (11) that the offender was aged 18 or over at that time and that the other person was not.

(15) In its application to Scotland, this section has effect with the omission of subsection (2), and of the reference to it in subsection (10).

Serious Crime Act 2007

1   Serious crime prevention orders

(1) The High Court in England and Wales may make an order if—

(a) it is satisfied that a person has been involved in serious crime (whether in England and Wales or elsewhere); and

(b) it has reasonable grounds to believe that the order would protect the public by preventing, restricting or disrupting involvement by the person in serious crime in England and Wales.

(1A) The appropriate court in Scotland may make an order if—

(a) it is satisfied that a person has been involved in serious crime (whether in Scotland or elsewhere); and

(b) it has reasonable grounds to believe that the order would protect the public by preventing, restricting or disrupting involvement by the person in serious crime in Scotland.

(2) The High Court in Northern Ireland may make an order if—

(a) it is satisfied that a person has been involved in serious crime (whether in Northern Ireland or elsewhere); and

(b) it has reasonable grounds to believe that the order would protect the public by preventing, restricting or disrupting involvement by the person in serious crime in Northern Ireland.

(3) An order under this section may contain—

(a) such prohibitions, restrictions or requirements; and

(b) such other terms;

as the court considers appropriate for the purpose of protecting the public by preventing, restricting or disrupting involvement by the person concerned in serious crime in England and Wales, Scotland or (as the case may be) Northern Ireland.

(4) The powers of the court in respect of an order under this section are subject to sections 6 to 15 (safeguards).

(5) In this Part—

'appropriate court' means the Court of Session or sheriff;

'serious crime prevention order' means—

(a) an order under this section;

(b) an order under section 19 (corresponding order of the Crown Court on conviction); or

(c) an order under section 22A (corresponding order of the High Court of Justiciary or sheriff on conviction).

(6) For the purposes of this Part references to the person who is the subject of a serious crime prevention order are references to the person against whom the public are to be protected.

2   Involvement in serious crime: England and Wales orders

(1) For the purposes of this Part, a person has been involved in serious crime in England and Wales if he—

(a) has committed a serious offence in England and Wales;

(b) has facilitated the commission by another person of a serious offence in England and Wales; or

(c) has conducted himself in a way that was likely to facilitate the commission by himself or another person of a serious offence in England and Wales (whether or not such an offence was committed).

(2) In this Part 'a serious offence in England and Wales' means an offence under the law of England and Wales which, at the time when the court is considering the application or matter in question—

(a) is specified, or falls within a description specified, in Part 1 of Schedule 1; or

(b) is one which, in the particular circumstances of the case, the court considers to be suf-ficiently serious to be treated for the purposes of the application or matter as if it were so specified.

(3) For the purposes of this Part, involvement in serious crime in England and Wales is any one or more of the following—

(a) the commission of a serious offence in England and Wales;

(b) conduct which facilitates the commission by another person of a serious offence in England and Wales;

(c) conduct which is likely to facilitate the commission, by the person whose conduct it is or another person, of a serious offence in England and Wales (whether or not such an offence is committed).

(4) For the purposes of section 1(1)(a), a person has been involved in serious crime elsewhere than in England and Wales if he—

(a) has committed a serious offence in a country outside England and Wales;

(b) has facilitated the commission by another person of a serious offence in a country outside England and Wales; or

(c) has conducted himself in a way that was likely to facilitate the commission by himself or another person of a serious offence in a country outside England and Wales (whether or not such an offence was committed).

(5) In subsection (4) 'a serious offence in a country outside England and Wales' means an offence under the law of a country outside England and Wales which, at the time when the court is consider-ing the application or matter in question—

(a) would be an offence under the law of England and Wales if committed in or as regards England and Wales; and

(b) either—

(i) would be an offence which is specified, or falls within a description specified, in Part 1 of Schedule 1 if committed in or as regards England and Wales; or

(ii) is conduct which, in the particular circumstances of the case, the court considers to be sufficiently serious to be treated for the purposes of the application or matter as if it meets the test in sub-paragraph (i).

(6) The test in subsection (4) is to be used instead of the tests in sections 2A(1) and 3(1) in deciding for the purposes of section 1(1)(a) whether a person has been involved in serious crime in Scotland or (as the case may be) Northern Ireland.

(7) An act punishable under the law of a country outside the United Kingdom constitutes an offence under that law for the purposes of subsection (5), however it is described in that law.

5   Type of provision that may be made by orders

(1) This section contains examples of the type of provision that may be made by a serious crime prevention order but it does not limit the type of provision that may be made by such an order.

(2) Examples of prohibitions, restrictions or requirements that may be imposed by serious crime prevention orders in England and Wales, Scotland or Northern Ireland include prohibitions, restric-tions or requirements in relation to places other than England and Wales, Scotland or (as the case may be) Northern Ireland.

(3) Examples of prohibitions, restrictions or requirements that may be imposed on individu-als (including partners in a partnership) by serious crime prevention orders include prohibitions or restrictions on, or requirements in relation to—

(a) an individual's financial, property or business dealings or holdings;

(b) an individual's working arrangements;

(c) the means by which an individual communicates or associates with others, or the persons with whom he communicates or associates;

(d) the premises to which an individual has access;

(e) the use of any premises or item by an individual;

(f) an individual's travel (whether within the United Kingdom, between the United Kingdom and other places or otherwise).

(4) Examples of prohibitions, restrictions or requirements that may be imposed on bodies corporate, partnerships and unincorporated associations by serious crime prevention orders include prohibitions or restrictions on, or requirements in relation to—

(a) financial, property or business dealings or holdings of such persons;

(b) the types of agreements to which such persons may be a party;

(c) the provision of goods or services by such persons;

(d) the premises to which such persons have access;

(e) the use of any premises or item by such persons;

(f) the employment of staff by such persons.

(5) Examples of requirements that may be imposed on any persons by serious crime prevention orders include—

(a) a requirement on a person to answer questions, or provide information, specified or described in an order—

(i) at a time, within a period or at a frequency;

(ii) at a place;

(iii) in a form and manner; and

(iv) to a law enforcement officer or description of law enforcement officer;

notified to the person by a law enforcement officer specified or described in the order;

(b) a requirement on a person to produce documents specified or described in an order—

(i) at a time, within a period or at a frequency;

(ii) at a place;

(iii) in a manner; and

(iv) to a law enforcement officer or description of law enforcement officer;

notified to the person by a law enforcement officer specified or described in the order.

(6) The prohibitions, restrictions or requirements that may be imposed on individuals by serious crime prevention orders include prohibitions, restrictions or requirements in relation to an individual's private dwelling (including, for example, prohibitions or restrictions on, or requirements in relation to, where an individual may reside).

(7) In this Part—

'document' means anything in which information of any description is recorded (whether or not in legible form);

'a law enforcement officer' means—

(a) a constable;

(b) a National Crime Agency officer who is for the time being designated under section 9 or 10 of the Crime and Courts Act 2013;

(c) an officer of Revenue and Customs; or

(d) a member of the Serious Fraud Office; and

'premises' includes any land, vehicle, vessel, aircraft or hovercraft.

(8) Any reference in this Part to the production of documents is, in the case of a document which contains information recorded otherwise than in legible form, a reference to the production of a copy of the information in legible form.

5A Verification and disclosure of information

(1) This section applies where information is provided to a law enforcement officer in response to an information requirement imposed by a serious crime prevention order.

'Information requirement' means a requirement of the kind referred to in section 5(5)(a) or (b).

(2) The law enforcement officer may, for the purpose of—

(a) checking the accuracy of the information, or

(b) discovering the true position,

disclose the information to any person who the officer reasonably believes may be able to contribute to doing either of those things.

(3) Any other person may disclose information to—

    (a) the law enforcement officer, or

    (b) a person to whom the law enforcement officer has disclosed information under subsection (2),

for the purpose of contributing to doing either of the things mentioned in subsection (2)(a) and (b).

(4) The law enforcement officer may also disclose the information referred to in subsection (1) for the purposes of—

    (a) the prevention, detection, investigation or prosecution of criminal offences, whether in the United Kingdom or elsewhere, or

    (b) the prevention, detection or investigation of conduct for which penalties other than criminal penalties are provided under the law of any part of the United Kingdom or of any country or territory outside the United Kingdom.

(5) A disclosure under this section does not breach—

    (a) any obligation of confidence owed by the person making the disclosure, or

    (b) any other restriction on the disclosure of information (however imposed).

(6) But nothing in this section authorises a disclosure, in contravention of any provisions of the Data Protection Act 1998, of personal data which are not exempt from those provisions.

6   Any individual must be 18 or over

An individual under the age of 18 may not be the subject of a serious crime prevention order

7   Other exceptions

(1) A person may not be made the subject of a serious crime prevention order in England and Wales if the person falls within a description specified by order of the Secretary of State.

(1A) A person may not be made the subject of a serious crime prevention order in Scotland if the person falls within a description specified by order of the Scottish Ministers.

(2) A person may not be made the subject of a serious crime prevention order in Northern Ireland if the person falls within a description specified by order of the Department of Justice in Northern Ireland.

8   Limited class of applicants for making of orders

A serious crime prevention order may be made only on an application by—

    (a) in the case of an order in England and Wales—

        (i)   the Director of Public Prosecutions;

        (ii) the Director of Revenue and Customs Prosecutions; or

        (iii) the Director of the Serious Fraud Office; and

    (aa) in the case of an order in Scotland, the Lord Advocate;

    (b) in the case of an order in Northern Ireland, the Director of Public Prosecutions for Northern Ireland.

16   Duration of orders

(1) A serious crime prevention order must specify when it is to come into force and when it is to cease to be in force.

(2) An order is not to be in force for more than 5 years beginning with the coming into force of the order.

(3) An order can specify different times for the coming into force, or ceasing to be in force, of different provisions of the order.

(4) Where it specifies different times in accordance with subsection (3), the order—

    (a) must specify when each provision is to come into force and cease to be in force; and

    (b) is not to be in force for more than 5 years beginning with the coming into force of the first provision of the order to come into force.

(5) The fact that an order, or any provision of an order, ceases to be in force does not prevent the court from making a new order to the same or similar effect.

(6) A new order may be made in anticipation of an earlier order or provision ceasing to be in force.

(7) Subsections (2) and (4)(b) have effect subject to section 22E.

Criminal Justice and Immigration Act 2008

1   Youth rehabilitation orders

(1) Where a person aged under 18 is convicted of an offence, the court by or before which the person is convicted may in accordance with Schedule 1 make an order (in this Part referred to as a 'youth rehabilitation order') imposing on the person any one or more of the following requirements—

    (a) an activity requirement (see paragraphs 6 to 8 of Schedule 1),

    (b) a supervision requirement (see paragraph 9 of that Schedule),

    (c) in a case where the offender is aged 16 or 17 at the time of the conviction, an unpaid work requirement (see paragraph 10 of that Schedule),

    (d) a programme requirement (see paragraph 11 of that Schedule),

    (e) an attendance centre requirement (see paragraph 12 of that Schedule),

    (f) a prohibited activity requirement (see paragraph 13 of that Schedule),

    (g) a curfew requirement (see paragraph 14 of that Schedule),

    (h) an exclusion requirement (see paragraph 15 of that Schedule),

    (i) a residence requirement (see paragraph 16 of that Schedule),

    (j) a local authority residence requirement (see paragraph 17 of that Schedule),

    (k) a mental health treatment requirement (see paragraph 20 of that Schedule),

    (l) a drug treatment requirement (see paragraph 22 of that Schedule),

    (m) a drug testing requirement (see paragraph 23 of that Schedule),

    (n) an intoxicating substance treatment requirement (see paragraph 24 of that Schedule), and

    (o) an education requirement (see paragraph 25 of that Schedule).

(2) A youth rehabilitation order—

    (a) may also impose an electronic monitoring requirement (see paragraph 26 of Schedule 1), and

    (b) must do so if paragraph 2 of that Schedule so requires.

(3) A youth rehabilitation order may be—

    (a) a youth rehabilitation order with intensive supervision and surveillance (see paragraph 3 of Schedule 1), or

    (b) a youth rehabilitation order with fostering (see paragraph 4 of that Schedule).

(4) But a court may only make an order mentioned in subsection (3)(a) or (b) if—

    (a) the court is dealing with the offender for an offence which is punishable with imprisonment,

    (b) the court is of the opinion that the offence, or the combination of the offence and one or more offences associated with it, was so serious that, but for paragraph 3 or 4 of Schedule 1, a custodial sentence would be appropriate (or, if the offender was aged under 12 at the time of conviction, would be appropriate if the offender had been aged 12), and

    (c) if the offender was aged under 15 at the time of conviction, the court is of the opinion that the offender is a persistent offender.

(5) Schedule 1 makes further provision about youth rehabilitation orders.

(6) This section is subject to—

    (a) sections 148 and 150 of the Criminal Justice Act 2003 (c. 44) (restrictions on community sentences etc.), and

    (b) the provisions of Parts 1 and 3 of Schedule 1.

2   Breach, revocation or amendment of youth rehabilitation orders

Schedule 2 makes provision about failures to comply with the requirements of youth rehabilitation orders and about the revocation or amendment of such orders.

. . .

4   Meaning of 'the responsible officer'

(1) For the purposes of this Part, 'the responsible officer', in relation to an offender to whom a youth rehabilitation order relates, means—

(a) in a case where the order—

   (i) imposes a curfew requirement or an exclusion requirement but no other require- ment mentioned in section 1(1), and

   (ii) imposes an electronic monitoring requirement,

   the person who under paragraph 26(4) of Schedule 1 is responsible for the electronic monitoring required by the order;

(b) in a case where the only requirement imposed by the order is an attendance centre re- quirement, the officer in charge of the attendance centre in question;

(c) in any other case, the qualifying officer who, as respects the offender, is for the time being responsible for discharging the functions conferred by this Part on the responsible officer.

(2) In this section 'qualifying officer', in relation to a youth rehabilitation order, means—

(a) a member of a youth offending team established by a local authority for the time being specified in the order for the purposes of this section, or

(b) an officer of a local probation board appointed for or assigned to the local justice area for the time being so specified or (as the case may be) an officer of a provider of probation services acting in the local justice area for the time being so specified.

(3) The Secretary of State may by order—

(a) amend subsections (1) and (2), and

(b) make any other amendments of—

   (i) this Part, or

   (ii) Chapter 1 of Part 12 of the Criminal Justice Act 2003 (c. 44) (general provisions about sentencing),

   that appear to be necessary or expedient in consequence of any amendment made by virtue of paragraph (a).

(4) An order under subsection (3) may, in particular, provide for the court to determine which of two or more descriptions of responsible officer is to apply in relation to any youth rehabilitation order.

5   Responsible officer and offender: duties in relation to the other

(1) Where a youth rehabilitation order has effect, it is the duty of the responsible officer—

(a) to make any arrangements that are necessary in connection with the requirements imposed by the order,

(b) to promote the offender's compliance with those requirements, and

(c) where appropriate, to take steps to enforce those requirements.

(2) In subsection (1) 'responsible officer' does not include a person falling within section 4(1)(a).

(3) In giving instructions in pursuance of a youth rehabilitation order relating to an offender, the responsible officer must ensure, as far as practicable, that any instruction is such as to avoid—

(a) any conflict with the offender's religious beliefs,

(b) any interference with the times, if any, at which the offender normally works or attends school or any other educational establishment, and

(c) any conflict with the requirements of any other youth rehabilitation order to which the offender may be subject.

(4) The Secretary of State may by order provide that subsection (3) is to have effect with such additional restrictions as may be specified in the order.

(5) An offender in respect of whom a youth rehabilitation order is in force—

(a) must keep in touch with the responsible officer in accordance with such instructions as the offender may from time to time be given by that officer, and

(b) must notify the responsible officer of any change of address.

(6) The obligation imposed by subsection (5) is enforceable as if it were a requirement imposed by the order.

6   Abolition of certain youth orders and related amendments

(1) Chapters 1, 2, 4 and 5 of Part 4 of (and Schedules 3 and 5 to 7 to) the Powers of Criminal Courts (Sentencing) Act 2000 (c. 6) (curfew orders, exclusion orders, attendance centre orders, supervision orders and action plan orders) cease to have effect.

(2) Part 1 of Schedule 4 makes amendments consequential on provisions of this Part.

(3) Part 2 of Schedule 4 makes minor amendments regarding other community orders which are related to the consequential amendments in Part 1 of that Schedule.

7   Youth rehabilitation orders: interpretation

(1) In this Part, except where the contrary intention appears—

'accommodation provided by or on behalf of a local authority' has the same meaning as it has in the Children Act 1989 (c. 41) by virtue of section 105 of that Act;

'activity requirement', in relation to a youth rehabilitation order, has the meaning given by paragraph 6 of Schedule 1;

'associated', in relation to offences, is to be read in accordance with section 161(1) of the Powers of Criminal Courts (Sentencing) Act 2000 (c. 6);

'attendance centre' has the meaning given by section 221(2) of the Criminal Justice Act 2003 (c. 44);

'attendance centre requirement', in relation to a youth rehabilitation order, has the meaning given by paragraph 12 of Schedule 1;

'curfew requirement', in relation to a youth rehabilitation order, has the meaning given by paragraph 14 of Schedule 1;

'custodial sentence' has the meaning given by section 76 of the Powers of Criminal Courts (Sentencing) Act 2000;

'detention and training order' has the same meaning as it has in that Act by virtue of section 163 of that Act;

'drug treatment requirement', in relation to a youth rehabilitation order, has the meaning given by paragraph 22 of Schedule 1;

'drug testing requirement', in relation to a youth rehabilitation order, has the meaning given by paragraph 23 of Schedule 1;

'education requirement', in relation to a youth rehabilitation order, has the meaning given by paragraph 25 of Schedule 1;

'electronic monitoring requirement', in relation to a youth rehabilitation order, has the meaning given by paragraph 26 of Schedule 1;

'exclusion requirement', in relation to a youth rehabilitation order, has the meaning given by paragraph 15 of Schedule 1;

'extended activity requirement', in relation to a youth rehabilitation order, has the meaning given by paragraph 3 of Schedule 1;

'fostering requirement', in relation to a youth rehabilitation order with fostering, has the meaning given by paragraph 18 of Schedule 1;

'guardian' has the same meaning as in the Children and Young Persons Act 1933 (c. 12);

'intoxicating substance treatment requirement', in relation to a youth rehabilitation order, has the meaning given by paragraph 24 of Schedule 1;

'local authority' means—

    (a) in relation to England—
        (i)   a county council,
        (ii) a district council whose district does not form part of an area that has a county council,
        (iii) a London borough council, or
        (iv) the Common Council of the City of London in its capacity as a local authority, and
    (b) in relation to Wales—
        (i)   a county council, or
        (ii) a county borough council;

'local authority residence requirement', in relation to a youth rehabilitation order, has the meaning given by paragraph 17 of Schedule 1;

'local probation board' means a local probation board established under section 4 of the Criminal Justice and Court Services Act 2000 (c. 43);

'mental health treatment requirement', in relation to a youth rehabilitation order, has the meaning given by paragraph 20 of Schedule 1;

'programme requirement', in relation to a youth rehabilitation order, has the meaning given by paragraph 11 of Schedule 1;

'prohibited activity requirement', in relation to a youth rehabilitation order, has the meaning given by paragraph 13 of Schedule 1;

'residence requirement', in relation to a youth rehabilitation order, has the meaning given by paragraph 16 of Schedule 1;

'the responsible officer', in relation to an offender to whom a youth rehabilitation order relates, has the meaning given by section 4;

'supervision requirement', in relation to a youth rehabilitation order, has the meaning given by paragraph 9 of Schedule 1;

'unpaid work requirement', in relation to a youth rehabilitation order, has the meaning given by paragraph 10 of Schedule 1;

'youth offending team' means a team established under section 39 of the Crime and Disorder Act 1998 (c. 37);

'youth rehabilitation order' has the meaning given by section 1;

'youth rehabilitation order with fostering' has the meaning given by paragraph 4 of Schedule 1;

'youth rehabilitation order with intensive supervision and surveillance' has the meaning given by paragraph 3 of Schedule 1.

    (2) For the purposes of any provision of this Part which requires the determination of the age of a person by the court, the Secretary of State or a local authority, the person's age is to be taken to be that which it appears to the court or (as the case may be) the Secretary of State or a local authority to be after considering any available evidence.

    (3) Any reference in this Part to an offence punishable with imprisonment is to be read without regard to any prohibition or restriction imposed by or under any Act on the imprisonment of young offenders.

    (4) If a local authority has parental responsibility for an offender who is in its care or provided with accommodation by it in the exercise of any social services functions, any reference in this Part (except in paragraphs 4 and 25 of Schedule 1) to the offender's parent or guardian is to be read as a reference to that authority.

    (5) In subsection (4)—

'parental responsibility' has the same meaning as it has in the Children Act 1989 (c. 41) by virtue of section 3 of that Act, and

'social services functions' has the same meaning as it has in the Local Authority Social Services Act 1970 (c. 42) by virtue of section 1A of that Act.

10   Effect of restriction on imposing community sentences

In section 148 of the Criminal Justice Act 2003 (c. 44) (restrictions on imposing community sentences), after subsection (4) insert—

'(5) The fact that by virtue of any provision of this section—

(a) a community sentence may be passed in relation to an offence; or

(b) particular restrictions on liberty may be imposed by a community order or youth rehabilitation order,

does not require a court to pass such a sentence or to impose those restrictions.'

Coroners and Justice Act 2009

118   Sentencing Council for England and Wales

(1) There is to be a Sentencing Council for England and Wales.

(2) Schedule 15 makes provision about the Council.

119   Annual report

(1) The Council must, as soon as practicable after the end of each financial year, make to the Lord Chancellor a report on the exercise of the Council's functions during the year.

(2) The Lord Chancellor must lay a copy of the report before Parliament.

(3) The Council must publish the report once a copy has been so laid.

(4) Sections 128(3), 130 and 131 make further provision about the content of reports under this section.

(5) If section 118 comes into force after the beginning of a financial year, the first report may relate to a period beginning with the day on which that section comes into force and ending with the end of the next financial year.

120   Sentencing guidelines

(1) In this Chapter 'sentencing guidelines' means guidelines relating to the sentencing of offenders.

(2) A sentencing guideline may be general in nature or limited to a particular offence, particular category of offence or particular category of offender.

(3) The Council must prepare—

(a) sentencing guidelines about the discharge of a court's duty under section 144 of the Criminal Justice Act 2003 (c. 44) (reduction in sentences for guilty pleas), and

(b) sentencing guidelines about the application of any rule of law as to the totality of sentences.

(4) The Council may prepare sentencing guidelines about any other matter.

(5) Where the Council has prepared guidelines under subsection (3) or (4), it must publish them as draft guidelines.

(6) The Council must consult the following persons about the draft guidelines—

(a) the Lord Chancellor;

(b) such persons as the Lord Chancellor may direct;

(c) the Justice Select Committee of the House of Commons (or, if there ceases to be a committee of that name, such committee of the House of Commons as the Lord Chancellor directs);

(d) such other persons as the Council considers appropriate.

(7) In the case of guidelines within subsection (3), the Council must, after making any amendments of the guidelines which it considers appropriate, issue them as definitive guidelines.

(8) In any other case, the Council may, after making such amendments, issue them as definitive guidelines.

(9) The Council may, from time to time, review the sentencing guidelines issued under this section, and may revise them.

(10) Subsections (5), (6) and (8) apply to a revision of the guidelines as they apply to their preparation (and subsection (8) applies even if the guidelines being revised are within subsection (3)).

(11) When exercising functions under this section, the Council must have regard to the following matters—

(a) the sentences imposed by courts in England and Wales for offences;

(b) the need to promote consistency in sentencing;

(c) the impact of sentencing decisions on victims of offences;

(d) the need to promote public confidence in the criminal justice system;

(e) the cost of different sentences and their relative effectiveness in preventing re-offending;

(f) the results of the monitoring carried out under section 128.

121   Sentencing ranges

(1) When exercising functions under section 120, the Council is to have regard to the desirability of sentencing guidelines which relate to a particular offence being structured in the way described in subsections (2) to (9).

(2) The guidelines should, if reasonably practicable given the nature of the offence, describe, by reference to one or more of the factors mentioned in subsection (3), different categories of case involving the commission of the offence which illustrate in general terms the varying degrees of seriousness with which the offence may be committed.

(3) Those factors are—

(a) the offender's culpability in committing the offence;

(b) the harm caused, or intended to be caused or which might foreseeably have been caused, by the offence;

(c) such other factors as the Council considers to be particularly relevant to the seriousness of the offence in question.

(4) The guidelines should—

(a) specify the range of sentences ('the offence range') which, in the opinion of the Council, it may be appropriate for a court to impose on an offender convicted of that offence, and

(b) if the guidelines describe different categories of case in accordance with subsection (2), specify for each category the range of sentences ('the category range') within the offence range which, in the opinion of the Council, it may be appropriate for a court to impose on an offender in a case which falls within the category.

(5) The guidelines should also—

(a) specify the sentencing starting point in the offence range, or

(b) if the guidelines describe different categories of case in accordance with subsection (2), specify the sentencing starting point in the offence range for each of those categories.

(6) The guidelines should—

(a) (to the extent not already taken into account by categories of case described in accordance with subsection (2)) list any aggravating or mitigating factors which, by virtue of any enactment or other rule of law, the court is required to take into account when considering the seriousness of the offence and any other aggravating or mitigating factors which the Council considers are relevant to such a consideration,

(b) list any other mitigating factors which the Council considers are relevant in mitigation of sentence for the offence, and

(c) include criteria, and provide guidance, for determining the weight to be given to previous convictions of the offender and such of the other factors within paragraph (a) or (b) as the Council considers to be of particular significance in relation to the offence or the offender.

(7) For the purposes of subsection (6)(b) the following are to be disregarded—

(a) the requirements of section 144 of the Criminal Justice Act 2003 (c. 44) (reduction in sentences for guilty pleas);

(b) sections 73 and 74 of the Serious Organised Crime and Police Act 2005 (assistance by defendants: reduction or review of sentence) and any other rule of law by virtue of which an offender may receive a discounted sentence in consequence of assistance given (or offered to be given) by the offender to the prosecutor or investigator of an offence;

(c) any rule of law as to the totality of sentences.

(8) The provision made in accordance with subsection (6)(c) should be framed in such manner as the Council considers most appropriate for the purpose of assisting the court, when sentencing an offender for the offence, to determine the appropriate sentence within the offence range.

(9) The provision made in accordance with subsections (2) to (8) may be different for different circumstances or cases involving the offence.

(10) The sentencing starting point in the offence range—

(a) for a category of case described in the guidelines in accordance with subsection (2), is the sentence within that range which the Council considers to be the appropriate starting point for cases within that category—

(i) before taking account of the factors mentioned in subsection (6), and

(ii) assuming the offender has pleaded not guilty, and

(b) where the guidelines do not describe categories of case in accordance with subsection (2), is the sentence within that range which the Council considers to be the appropriate starting point for the offence—

(i) before taking account of the factors mentioned in subsection (6), and

(ii) assuming the offender has pleaded not guilty.

122 Allocation guidelines

(1) In this Chapter 'allocation guidelines' means guidelines relating to decisions by a magistrates' court under section 19 of the Magistrates' Courts Act 1980 (c. 43), or the Crown Court under paragraph 7(7) or 8(2)(d) of Schedule 3 to the Crime and Disorder Act 1998 (c. 37), as to whether an offence is more suitable for summary trial or trial on indictment.

(2) The Council may prepare allocation guidelines.

(3) Where the Council has prepared guidelines under subsection (2), it must publish them as draft guidelines.

(4) The Council must consult the following persons about the draft guidelines—

(a) the Lord Chancellor;

(b) such persons as the Lord Chancellor may direct;

(c) the Justice Select Committee of the House of Commons (or, if there ceases to be a committee of that name, such committee of the House of Commons as the Lord Chancellor directs);

(d) such other persons as the Council considers appropriate.

(5) The Council may, after making any amendment of the draft guidelines which it considers appropriate, issue the guidelines as definitive guidelines.

(6) The Council may, from time to time, review the allocation guidelines issued under this section, and may revise them.

(7) Subsections (3) to (5) apply to a revision of the guidelines as they apply to their preparation.

(8) When exercising functions under this section, the Council must have regard to—

(a) the need to promote consistency in decisions of the kind mentioned in subsection (1), and

(b) the results of the monitoring carried out under section 128.

123 Preparation or revision of guidelines in urgent cases

(1) This section applies where the Council—

(a) decides to prepare or revise sentencing guidelines or allocation guidelines, and

(b) is of the opinion that the urgency of the case makes it impractical to comply with the procedural requirements of section 120 or (as the case may be) section 122.

(2) The Council may prepare or revise the guidelines without complying with—

(a) in the case of sentencing guidelines, section 120(5), and

(b) in the case of allocation guidelines, section 122(3).

(3) The Council may—

    (a) in the case of sentencing guidelines, amend and issue the guidelines under section 120(7) or (8) without having complied with the requirements of section 120(6)(b) to (d), and

    (b) in the case of allocation guidelines, amend and issue the guidelines under section 122(5) without having complied with the requirements of section 122(4)(b) to (d).

(4) The guidelines or revised guidelines must—

    (a) state that the Council was of the opinion mentioned in subsection (1)(b), and

    (b) give the Council's reasons for that opinion.

124 Proposals by Lord Chancellor or Court of Appeal

(1) The Lord Chancellor may propose to the Council—

    (a) that sentencing guidelines be prepared or revised by the Council under section 120—

        (i) in relation to a particular offence, particular category of offence or particular category of offenders, or

        (ii) in relation to a particular matter affecting sentencing;

    (b) that allocation guidelines be prepared or revised by the Council under section 122.

(2) Subsection (3) applies where the criminal division of the Court of Appeal ('the appeal court') is seised of an appeal against, or a reference under section 36 of the Criminal Justice Act 1988 (c. 33) (reviews of sentencing) with respect to, the sentence passed for an offence ('the relevant offence').

(3) The appeal court may propose to the Council that sentencing guidelines be prepared or revised by the Council under section 120—

    (a) in relation to the relevant offence, or

    (b) in relation to a category of offences within which the relevant offence falls.

(4) A proposal under subsection (3) may be included in the appeal court's judgment in the appeal.

(5) If the Council receives a proposal under subsection (1) or (3) to prepare or revise any guidelines, it must consider whether to do so.

(6) For the purposes of this section, the appeal court is seised of an appeal against a sentence if—

    (a) the court or a single judge has granted leave to appeal against the sentence under section 9 or 10 of the Criminal Appeal Act 1968 (c. 19) (appeals against sentence), or

    (b) in a case where the judge who passed the sentence granted a certificate of fitness for appeal under section 9 or 10 of that Act, notice of appeal has been given,

and the appeal has not been abandoned or disposed of.

(7) For the purposes of this section, the appeal court is seised of a reference under section 36 of the Criminal Justice Act 1988 (reviews of sentencing) if it has given leave under subsection (1) of that section and the reference has not been disposed of.

(8) This section is without prejudice to any power of the appeal court to provide guidance relating to the sentencing of offenders in a judgment of the court.

125 Sentencing guidelines: duty of court

(1) Every court—

    (a) must, in sentencing an offender, follow any sentencing guidelines which are relevant to the offender's case, and

    (b) must, in exercising any other function relating to the sentencing of offenders, follow any sentencing guidelines which are relevant to the exercise of the function,

unless the court is satisfied that it would be contrary to the interests of justice to do so.

(2) Subsections (3) and (4) apply where—

    (a) a court is deciding what sentence to impose on a person ('P') who is guilty of an offence, and

(b) sentencing guidelines have been issued in relation to that offence which are structured in the way described in section 121(2) to (5) ('the offence specific guidelines').

(3) The duty imposed on a court by subsection (1)(a) to follow any sentencing guidelines which are relevant to the offender's case includes—

(a) in all cases, a duty to impose on P, in accordance with the offence specific guidelines, a sentence which is within the offence range, and

(b) where the offence-specific guidelines describe categories of case in accordance with section 121(2), a duty to decide which of the categories most resembles P's case in order to identify the sentencing starting point in the offence range;

but nothing in this section imposes on the court a separate duty, in a case within paragraph (b), to impose a sentence which is within the category range.

(4) Subsection (3)(b) does not apply if the court is of the opinion that, for the purpose of identifying the sentence within the offence range which is the appropriate starting point, none of the categories sufficiently resembles P's case.

(5) Subsection (3)(a) is subject to—

(a) section 144 of the Criminal Justice Act 2003 (c. 44) (reduction in sentences for guilty pleas),

(b) sections 73 and 74 of the Serious Organised Crime and Police Act 2005 (c. 15) (assistance by defendants: reduction or review of sentence) and any other rule of law by virtue of which an offender may receive a discounted sentence in consequence of assistance given (or offered to be given) by the offender to the prosecutor or investigator of an offence, and

(c) any rule of law as to the totality of sentences.

(6) The duty imposed by subsection (1) is subject to the following provisions—

(a) section 148(1) and (2) of the Criminal Justice Act 2003 (restrictions on imposing community sentences);

(b) section 152 of that Act (restrictions on imposing discretionary custodial sentences);

(c) section 153 of that Act (custodial sentence must be for shortest term commensurate with seriousness of offence);

(d) section 164(2) of that Act (fine must reflect seriousness of offence);

(da) section 224A of that Act (life sentence for second listed offence for certain dangerous offenders);

(e) section 269 of and Schedule 21 to that Act (determination of minimum term in relation to mandatory life sentence);

(ea) sections 1(2B) and 1A(5) of the Prevention of Crime Act 1953 (minimum sentence for certain offences involving offensive weapons);

(f) section 51A of the Firearms Act 1968 (c. 27) (minimum sentence for certain offences under section 5 etc);

(fa) sections 139(6B), 139A(5B) and 139AA(7) of the Criminal Justice Act 1988 (minimum sentence certain offences involving article with blade or point or offensive weapon);

(g) sections 110(2) and 111(2) of the Powers of Criminal Courts (Sentencing) Act 2000 (c. 6) (minimum sentences for certain drug trafficking and burglary offences);

(h) section 29(4) and (6) of the Violent Crime Reduction Act 2006 (c. 38) (minimum sentences for certain offences involving firearms).

(7) Nothing in this section or section 126 is to be taken as restricting any power (whether under the Mental Health Act 1983 (c. 20) or otherwise) which enables a court to deal with a mentally disordered offender in the manner it considers to be most appropriate in all the circumstances.

(8) In this section—

'mentally disordered', in relation to a person, means suffering from a mental disorder within the meaning of the Mental Health Act 1983;

'sentencing guidelines' means definitive sentencing guidelines.

126 Determination of tariffs etc

(1) Section 125(3) (except as applied by virtue of subsection (3) below) is subject to any power a court has to impose—

(c) an extended sentence of imprisonment by virtue of section 226A of the Criminal Justice Act 2003;

(d) an extended sentence of detention by virtue of section 226B of that Act.

(2) Subsection (3) applies where a court determines the notional determinate term for the purpose of determining in any case—

(a) the order to be made under section 82A of the Powers of Criminal Courts (Sentencing) Act 2000 (life sentence: determination of tariffs),

(c) the appropriate custodial term for the purposes of 226A(6) of the Criminal Justice Act 2003 (extended sentence for certain violent or sexual offences: persons 18 or over), or

(d) the appropriate term for the purposes of section 226B(4) of that Act (extended sentence for certain violent or sexual offences: persons under 18).

(3) Subsections (2) to (5) of section 125 apply for the purposes of determining the notional determinate term in relation to an offence as they apply for the purposes of determining the sentence for an offence.

(4) In this section references to the notional determinate term are to the determinate sentence that would have been passed in the case if the need to protect the public and the potential danger of the offender had not required the court to impose a life sentence (in circumstances where the sentence is not fixed by law) or, as the case may be, an extended sentence of imprisonment or detention.

(5) In subsection (4) 'life sentence' means a sentence mentioned in subsection (2) of section 34 of the Crime (Sentences) Act 1997 other than a sentence mentioned in paragraph (d) or (e) of that subsection.

127 Resource implications of guidelines

(1) This section applies where the Council—

(a) publishes draft guidelines under section 120 or 122, or

(b) issues guidelines as definitive guidelines under either of those sections.

(2) The Council must publish a resource assessment in respect of the guidelines.

(3) A resource assessment in respect of any guidelines is an assessment by the Council of the likely effect of the guidelines on—

(a) the resources required for the provision of prison places,

(b) the resources required for probation provision, and

(c) the resources required for the provision of youth justice services.

(4) The resources assessment must be published—

(a) in a case within subsection (1)(a), at the time of publication of the draft guidelines;

(b) in a case within subsection (1)(b), at the time the guidelines are issued or, where the guidelines are issued by virtue of section 123, as soon as reasonably practicable after the guidelines are issued.

(5) The Council must keep under review any resource assessment published under this section, and, if the assessment is found to be inaccurate in a material respect, publish a revised resource assessment.

128 Monitoring

(1) The Council must—

(a) monitor the operation and effect of its sentencing guidelines, and

(b) consider what conclusions can be drawn from the information obtained by virtue of paragraph (a).

(2) The Council must, in particular, discharge its duty under subsection (1)(a) with a view to drawing conclusions about—

(a) the frequency with which, and extent to which, courts depart from sentencing guidelines;

(b) the factors which influence the sentences imposed by courts;

(c) the effect of the guidelines on the promotion of consistency in sentencing;

(d) the effect of the guidelines on the promotion of public confidence in the criminal justice system.

(3) When reporting on the exercise of its functions under this section in its annual report for a financial year, the Council must include—

(a) a summary of the information obtained under subsection (1)(a), and

(b) a report of any conclusions drawn by the Council under subsection (1)(b).

129   Promoting awareness

(1) The Council must publish, at such intervals as it considers appropriate—

(a) in relation to each local justice area, information regarding the sentencing practice of the magistrates' courts acting in that area, and

(b) in relation to each location at which the Crown Court sits, information regarding the sentencing practice of the Crown Court when it sits at that location.

(2) The Council may promote awareness of matters relating to the sentencing of offenders by courts in England and Wales, including, in particular—

(a) the sentences imposed by courts in England and Wales;

(b) the cost of different sentences and their relative effectiveness in preventing re-offending;

(c) the operation and effect of guidelines under this Chapter.

(3) For the purposes of subsection (2), the Council may, in particular, publish any information obtained or produced by it in connection with its functions under section 128(1).

130   Resources: effect of sentencing practice

(1) The annual report for a financial year must contain a sentencing factors report.

(2) A sentencing factors report is an assessment made by the Council, using the information available to it, of the effect which any changes in the sentencing practice of courts are having or are likely to have on each of the following—

(a) the resources required for the provision of prison places;

(b) the resources required for probation provision;

(c) the resources required for the provision of youth justice services.

131   Resources: effect of factors not related to sentencing

(1) The annual report for a financial year must contain a non-sentencing factors report.

(2) The Council may, at any other time, provide the Lord Chancellor with a non-sentencing factors report, and may publish that report.

(3) A non-sentencing factors report is a report by the Council of any significant quantitative effect (or any significant change in quantitative effect) which non-sentencing factors are having or are likely to have on the resources needed or available for giving effect to sentences imposed by courts in England and Wales.

(4) Non-sentencing factors are factors which do not relate to the sentencing practice of the courts, and include—

(a) the recalling of persons to prison;

(b) breaches of orders within subsection (5);

(c) patterns of re-offending;

(d) decisions or recommendations for release made by the Parole Board;

(e) the early release under discretionary powers of persons detained in prison;

(f) the remanding of persons in custody.

(5) The orders within this subsection are—

(a) community orders (within the meaning of section 177 of the Criminal Justice Act 2003 (c. 44)),

(b) suspended sentence orders (within the meaning of section 189(7) of that Act), and

(c) youth rehabilitation orders (within the meaning of Part 1 of the Criminal Justice and Immigration Act 2008 (c. 4)).

132   Duty to assess impact of policy and legislative proposals

(1) This section applies where the Lord Chancellor refers to the Council any government policy proposal, or government proposal for legislation, which the Lord Chancellor considers may have a significant effect on one or more of the following—

  (a) the resources required for the provision of prison places;

  (b) the resources required for probation provision;

  (c) the resources required for the provision of youth justice services.

(2) For the purposes of subsection (1)—

'government policy proposal' includes a policy proposal of the Welsh Ministers;

'government proposal for legislation' includes a proposal of the Welsh Ministers for legislation.

(3) The Council must assess the likely effect of the proposal on the matters mentioned in paragraphs (a) to (c) of subsection (1).

(4) The Council must prepare a report of the assessment and send the report—

  (a) to the Lord Chancellor, and

  (b) if the report relates to a proposal of the Welsh Ministers, to the Welsh Ministers.

(5) A single report may be prepared of the assessments relating to 2 or more proposals.

(6) If the Lord Chancellor receives a report under subsection (4) the Lord Chancellor must, unless it relates only to a proposal of the Welsh Ministers, lay a copy of it before each House of Parliament.

(7) If the Welsh Ministers receive a report under subsection (4) they must lay a copy of it before the National Assembly for Wales.

(8) The Council must publish a report which has been laid in accordance with subsections (6) and (7).

(9) In this section 'legislation' means—

  (a) an Act of Parliament if, or to the extent that, it extends to England and Wales;

  (b) subordinate legislation made under an Act of Parliament if, or to the extent that, the subordinate legislation extends to England and Wales;

  (c) a Measure or Act of the National Assembly for Wales or subordinate legislation made under such a Measure or Act.

133   Assistance by the Lord Chancellor

The Lord Chancellor may provide the Council with such assistance as it requests in connection with the performance of its functions.

135   Abolition of existing sentencing bodies

The following are abolished—

  (a) the Sentencing Guidelines Council;

  (b) the Sentencing Advisory Panel.

Index